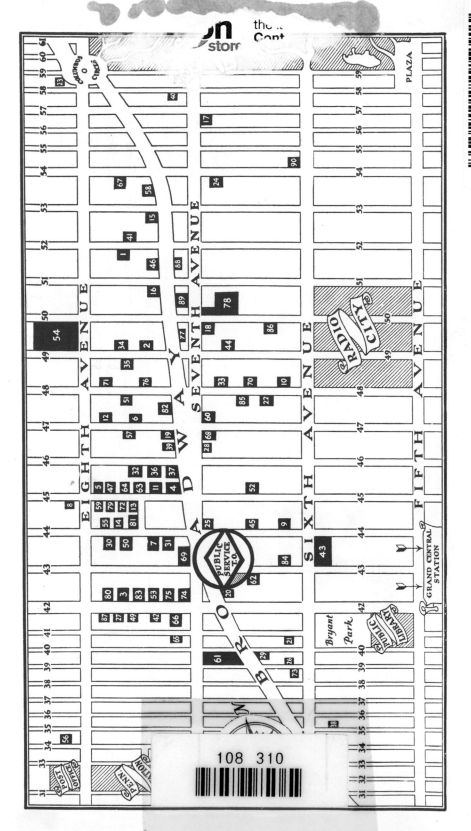

OPENING NIGHT ON BROADWAY

OPENING NIGHT ON BROADWAY

A Critical Quotebook of the Golden Era

of the Musical Theatre,

Oklahoma! *(1943)* to Fiddler on the Roof *(1964)*

STEVEN SUSKIN

Foreword by Carol Channing

SCHIRMER BOOKS

A Division of Macmillan, Inc.

NEW YORK

Collier Macmillan Canada

TORONTO

Maxwell Macmillan International

NEW YORK   OXFORD   SINGAPORE   SYDNEY

Schirmer Books
A Division of Macmillan, Inc.
866 Third Avenue, New York, N.Y. 10022

Collier Macmillan Canada, Inc.
1200 Eglinton Avenue East, Suite 200
Don Mills, Ontario M3C 3N1

Library of Congress Catalog Card Number: 90-8689

Printed in the United States of America

printing number
1   2   3   4   5   6   7   8   9   10

Library of Congress Cataloging-in-Publication Data

Suskin, Steven.
    Opening night on Broadway : a critical quotebook of the golden era
of the musical theatre, Oklahoma! (1943) to Fiddler on the roof
(1964) / Steven Suskin ; foreword by Carol Channing.
        p.   cm.
    Includes index.
    ISBN 0-02-872625-1
    1. Musicals—New York (N.Y.)—History and criticism.   2. Reviews—
New York (N.Y.)—History and criticism.   I. Title.
ML1711.8.N3S9   1990
792.6'09747'109045—dc20   90-8689
                                                              CIP

for
Andrea Rosenthal

Contents

Foreword by Carol Channing   xv
Acknowledgments   xxi

OVERTURE   1

THE MUSICALS OF THE GOLDEN ERA

Alive and Kicking	33
All American	36
All for Love	38
Allah Be Praised!	40
Allegro	42
Along Fifth Avenue	47
Angel in the Wings	48
Ankles Aweigh	50
Annie Get Your Gun	53
Anyone Can Whistle	58
Arms and the Girl	61
Around the World (in Eighty Days)	62
As the Girls Go	65
At the Drop of a Hat	66
Ballet Ballads	67
Barefoot Boy with Cheek	71
The Barrier	72
Beg, Borrow or Steal	73
Beggar's Holiday	74
Bells Are Ringing	78
Ben Franklin in Paris	82
Billion Dollar Baby	84
The Billy Barnes People	86
Bless You All	88
Bloomer Girl	89
Blossom Time (1943 revival)	93

Blue Holiday	94
The Body Beautiful	95
The Boy Friend	98
Bravo Giovanni	100
Brigadoon	103
Bright Lights of 1944	107
Buttrio Square	109
By the Beautiful Sea	111
Bye Bye Birdie	113
Cafe Crown	115
Call Me Madam	117
Call Me Mister	120
Camelot	122
Can-Can	126
Candide	130
Caribbean Carnival	132
Carmen Jones	133
Carnival	137
Carnival in Flanders	140
Carousel	144
Catch a Star!	148
Chauve-Souris 1943	150
Christine	151
Concert Varieties	153
A Connecticut Yankee (1943 revival)	154
The Conquering Hero	157
The Consul	160
Copper and Brass	164
The Cradle Will Rock (1947 revival)	166
Cranks	168
Damn Yankees	169
Dance Me a Song	174
The Day Before Spring	175
Destry Rides Again	179
Do Re Mi	181
Donnybrook!	185
Dream with Music	186
The Duchess Misbehaves	189
Early to Bed	191
Eddie Fisher at the Winter Garden	193
An Evening with Beatrice Lillie	195

Fade Out—Fade In	197
A Family Affair	201
Fanny	203
Fiddler on the Roof	207
Finian's Rainbow	210
Fiorello!	215
The Firebrand of Florence	218
First Impressions	221
Flahooley	222
Flower Drum Song	226
Follow the Girls	228
Four Saints in Three Acts (1952 revival)	231
Foxy	231
From A to Z	234
Funny Girl	236
A Funny Thing Happened on the Way to the Forum	239
The Gay Life	243
Gentlemen Prefer Blondes	246
The Girl from Nantucket	249
The Girl in Pink Tights	253
The Girl Who Came to Supper	256
The Girls Against the Boys	258
The Golden Apple	259
Golden Boy	262
Goldilocks	266
Greenwillow	269
Guys and Dolls	272
Gypsy	276
Gypsy Lady	279
Hairpin Harmony	281
The Happiest Girl in the World	283
Happy as Larry	285
Happy Hunting	287
Happy Town	289
Hayride	291
Hazel Flagg	292
Heaven on Earth	295
Hello, Dolly!	297
Here's Love	301
High Button Shoes	303
High Spirits	307

Hit the Trail	310
Hold It!	311
Hollywood Pinafore; or, The Lad Who Loved a Salary	313
Hot Spot	316
House of Flowers	319
How to Succeed in Business Without Really Trying	323
I Can Get It for You Wholesale	327
I Had a Ball	331
If the Shoe Fits	332
Inside U.S.A.	334
Iolanthe (1955 revival)	337
Irma La Douce	338
Jackpot	341
Jamaica	343
Jennie	347
John Murray Anderson's Almanac	352
Juno	353
Kean	356
The King and I	358
The King and I (1960 revival)	362
Kismet	364
Kiss Me, Kate	367
Kwamina	371
La Plume de Ma Tante	373
A Lady Says Yes	376
Laffing Room Only	378
Laugh Time	380
Lend an Ear	380
Let It Ride!	383
Let's Make an Opera	386
The Liar	387
Li'l Abner	388
Little Me	391
The Littlest Revue	394
Livin' the Life	395
Look, Ma, I'm Dancin'!	396
Lost in the Stars	400
Louisiana Lady	403
Love Life	405
Lute Song	408
Magdalena	411

Maggie	414
Make a Wish	415
Make Mine Manhattan	418
Man in the Moon	421
Maria Golovin	422
Marinka	424
Mask and Gown	425
Me and Juliet	426
The Medium and The Telephone (L'Amour à Trois)	429
Memphis Bound	431
The Merry Widow (1943 revival)	433
Mexican Hayride	435
Michael Todd's Peep Show	438
Milk and Honey	441
Miss Liberty	443
Mr. President	446
Mr. Strauss Goes to Boston	448
Mr. Wonderful	450
The Most Happy Fella	453
Music in My Heart	456
Music in the Air (1951 revival)	458
The Music Man	460
My Darlin' Aida	464
My Dear Public	466
My Fair Lady	468
My Romance	472
Nellie Bly	473
The Nervous Set	475
New Faces of 1952	478
New Faces of 1956	480
New Faces of 1962	483
New Girl in Town	484
No Strings	488
Nowhere to Go but Up	492
Of Thee I Sing (1952 revival)	495
Oh Captain!	496
Oklahoma!	499
Oklahoma! (1951 return engagement)	503
Oklahoma! (1953 return engagement)	505
Oliver!	508
On the Town	511

On Your Toes (1954 revival)   516
Once Upon a Mattress   518
110 in the Shade   520
One Touch of Venus   523
Out of This World   527
Paint Your Wagon   529
The Pajama Game   533
Pal Joey (1952 revival)   537
Pal Joey (1961 revival)   540
Park Avenue   543
A Party with Betty Comden and Adolph Green   546
Peter Pan   548
Phoenix '55   552
Pipe Dream   554
The Pirates of Penzance (1948 revival)   556
Plain and Fancy   557
Polonaise   559
Porgy and Bess (1953 revival)   561
Portofino   565
Razzle Dazzle   566
The Red Mill (1945 revival)   567
Redhead   568
Regina   571
Rhapsody   575
Rugantino   576
Rumple   577
Sadie Thompson   579
Sail Away   583
St. Louis Woman   584
The Saint of Bleecker Street   590
Sally (1948 revival)   591
Saratoga   592
Say, Darling   595
The Seven Lively Arts   597
Seventeen   600
Seventh Heaven   601
Shangri-La   603
She Loves Me   605
Shinbone Alley   609
Show Boat (1946 revival)   612
Show Girl   615

Silk Stockings	618
Sing Out, Sweet Land!	621
Sleepy Hollow	623
Small Wonder	624
Something for the Boys	625
Something More!	628
Song of Norway	631
Sophie	633
The Sound of Music	635
South Pacific	639
Stop the World—I Want to Get Off	643
Street Scene	645
Subways Are for Sleeping	649
Sweethearts (1947 revival)	652
Take a Bow	655
Take Me Along	656
Tenderloin	658
13 Daughters	659
Three for Tonight	660
Three to Make Ready	664
Three Wishes for Jamie	665
Top Banana	666
Touch and Go	670
Tovarich	671
A Tree Grows in Brooklyn	674
Two on the Aisle	678
Two's Company	681
The Unsinkable Molly Brown	684
Up in Central Park	686
The Vagabond King (1943 revival)	688
The Vamp	689
Vintage '60	692
West Side Story	693
What Makes Sammy Run?	698
What's Up	701
Where's Charley?	702
Whoop-Up	706
Wiener Blut (Vienna Life)	709
Wildcat	710
Wish You Were Here	713
Wonderful Town	715

Ziegfeld Follies of 1943   720
Ziegfeld Follies of 1957   722

Broadway Scorecard Summary   725
*Chronological List of the Broadway Musicals
   of the Golden Era*   731
Notable Careers in the Musical Theatre   741
The Critics   773

Index   785

Foreword

———————◆———————

*T*HERE comes a time in everyone's career, in almost every occupation, when it's make or break, sink or swim and all that. Which is to say that I am aware of the fact that the do-or-die pressure of an opening night on Broadway is not exclusive to theatre people.

For instance, I knew Jack Dempsey. I realize that's dropping a name, but I did know Jack Dempsey. One night he said, "You know what a champion is? A champion is a person who's ready when the gong rings—not just before, not just after, but right when it rings." That's it. That's an opening night on Broadway.

Like the opening of *Gentlemen Prefer Blondes*, my first starring part. I don't remember applause, I don't remember laughter. I only remember a reflex action that enabled me to time the applause and the laughter. I was clinging with all my being to this Anita Loos character of Lorelei Lee. I was in love with Lorelei Lee and that must have had something to do with sustaining me. Being in love has to be stronger than any other human emotion, I have just decided. Stronger than panic or fear or the possibility of certain death. This was my first time up at bat, with the responsibility of the entire production resting on me. Prior to this, I had not had star billing and it very well *could* have been certain death.

After the show, I could not leave my dressing room until Anita Loos (the original creator), Jule Styne (the composer), Oliver Smith (coproducer and set designer), Miles White (costume designer), Agnes de Mille (choreographer), Herman Levin (producer), and all the powers that be, had advance notice from the newspapers that we were a hit. They came running back to tell me, and I could hear them through the intercom in my dressing room as they rushed across the stage calling, "Carol, we're a hit!" When they finally got

Carol Channing, as Lorelei Lee, extols the virtues of diamonds. "The most fabulous comic creation of this dreary period in history," per Brooks Atkinson. (set by Oliver Smith, costume by Miles White, photo by Fred Fehl)

up the stairs to me I was halfway down yelling, "You don't mean unanimous notices?" Anita explained, "Carol, you will never get unanimous notices. The fact that it thrilled most people has to mean that it irritated some. If it stirred up the air at all, it has to run smack against somebody."

And sure enough, the next morning the leading columnist for the Hearst Syndicate wrote for her headline, "Gentlemen Must Prefer Amazons." Well, she was right. In Lorelei's spike heels I was over six feet tall and built strong, and it *was* a funny headline.

Anita always said that there are two ways of casting Lorelei. One is to find a girl who is the cutest, the prettiest, the most adorable to play her, and the other is to get a comedienne who will satirize the cutest, prettiest, most adorable. Wasn't I lucky? *Blondes'* creators were loyal to the idea of its being a comedy comment on Lorelei. On the other hand, 20th Century Fox, in the motion picture of *Gentlemen Prefer Blondes,* starred Marilyn Monroe. Need I say more? And I do think it was one of her best movies. But I digress. Opening nights on Broadway is our subject. Forgive.

I came out of my hiding place—my dressing room—and went with the creators to the opening night party at the St. Regis. I read later in *Time* magazine that it was the biggest opening night celebration in a decade: "The guests were towering eminences whose very names are magical incantations along Broadway." But I was still feeling the responsibility of the evening. After all, Alfred Lunt and Lynn Fontanne were investors, along with Rodgers and Hammerstein, Joshua Logan, Leland Hayward, and Billy Rose. Mainly because I didn't want to slight anyone in my gratitude, I naturally never relaxed or enjoyed the party for a second.

Many people have asked me if one knows a show is going to be a hit before it opens. I always say, "No," but, just between us, there *is* a strange phenomenon that comes just before the opening night of shows like *Gentlemen Prefer Blondes*. As you know, there are weeks of rehearsal, with each section of the show centered in a different place. You go to this room to learn your dances, to that room to put them with the chorus, to this room to learn the songs, to the stage for the dialogue. There is a full company run-through every week. And then—it happened, at one of the dress rehearsals! There, standing in the middle of all this, I suddenly felt and saw the aura of our show for the first time, and it was a beautiful, laughing aura. I felt I knew the level of it. I knew where my character fit in. I do not know how the rest of the company felt, but

I suspect that at that moment we all knew. It was a vision—"the holy city of new Jerusalem descending out of heaven like unto a cloud." It was a pat on all our heads and a blessing. I almost cried.

The same thing happened in every hit show that I played. But I learned more from my flop, *The Vamp*, than I did from any hits. I couldn't hear a peep out of the audience, but I remember instinct telling me not to force. *Don't press. You can't make them like this show. Just let it slide through your fingers into failure, like a muddy rainstorm on your prom dress. There's nothing you can do to stop it, so just let it die. If it won't hold up without your forcing, it won't hold up anyway.* It was difficult to do, of course, but at least I didn't insult anyone's intelligence.

The main thing I learned was this: if there is no "benevolent despot" at the head, then the book writer thinks the show is about *this*, the choreographer thinks it's about *that*, the composer has another idea, the costumer and set man another, the lyricist, the lighting man, yet another. And I'm sure *I* thought it was about something nobody else thought of. No "holy city" ever descended on that show, and by the time it didn't, it was too late.

There was an opening that I well remember because the audience was not vocal. We weren't getting our usual laughs and the applause didn't build. My friend, Jack Benny, was in the audience. He came backstage where I was inconsolable about the reaction and said, "But Carol, remember, you can't hear a smile. It's going to be a hit," and Jack was right.

This book is entitled *Opening Night on Broadway*. Since 1966 there have been no more opening nights in the traditional sense. Newspaper and magazine critics all come to cover the show when it is convenient for them, on different nights during the previews. That was why it used to be necessary to have tryout openings out of town, to perfect the show. Instead, now, in most cases, we have extended New York previews.

By the time *Hello, Dolly!* opened in 1964, I had had many long nation-wide tours beginning with *Gentlemen Prefer Blondes* and they were invaluable experiences for me. We faced a battery of critics in each new and important city and there is something indelible about a critic's opinion because it is in print. To me, an opinion in print makes it a fact—forever! Anyone can look it up at any time. And, of course, we all know that ticket sales, too, go up or down according to the reviews in each city.

For me, every opening night is sheer, agonizing panic. The

problem is that, in the theatre, we are all dealing with intangibles and ephemerals—moods, auras, emotions. Anything can blow them away.

The question is not how to keep a show as alive as it is on Opening Night. The question for me is how to get the opening to be as good as all the following shows. There is no true emotion unless it flows through relaxation. Even if you're playing nervous tension, it doesn't come out as nervous tension if you are really nervous and tense.

I learned on these tours to embrace fright. I found that with fright a wonderful thing called adrenaline shoots through your body and enables you to be brighter, clearer, more lithe than at any other time. An actor must tell the story with his body, face, and voice, and that's all at top pitch with adrenaline. At least, it was getting to be for me. I was learning that stress is God-given.

So, by the time the New York *Hello, Dolly!* opening came, I was able to sense, at the times I was alone on stage with the audience, that there was a solid block of people in the center section from about the third row to nearly one-third of the way back: the first-night critics. There was absolutely no honeying up to this block. There was no enjoying life together with—no falling in love with—no laughter or tears with this block. Beyond this solid block everyone seemed to be having a fine time. But I realized that this block of people was in exactly the same fix we actors were in. They had to call the cards right. They were as stage-frightened as we were. This was their opening night too, and I couldn't stop feeling like Florence Nightingale. *These people need help! Just like I do!* Way in the back of my mind, I couldn't keep from nursing them all through opening night—kindred souls.

Sometimes I like to think that our job, fundamentally, is to nurse humanity, to uplift lives—like a veritable Florence Nightingale. That's our banner and mission, the creed we live by. All of us do. (And please don't tell us we're not nursing humanity. It probably isn't true, but we have to go on believing it.)

Mr. Merrick produced another show a few years later, at the time when critics first began to review preview performances. The night before the official opening, he saw a very important critic in the audience. Feeling that this particular show (Brian Friel's *Philadelphia, Here I Come*) was not yet ready to be reviewed, Merrick instructed his staff to turn off the lights and cancel the performance. When asked why, he answered that there was an electrical failure. "How did that happen?" he was asked. "There's a rat in the generator," Merrick replied.

Abe Burrows once told me that the worst thing about an opening night is to be the playwright or the director. If the actors are going too fast or too slowly, there is not a thing in the world he can do about it. He has to just sit there in misery. I am sure that's true for every creative member of a show except, of course, the actors.

We are all asked what it feels like to read good reviews about one's self. My overwhelming feeling is, "Thank you, Now all the wonderful dreams we dreamed about this show, the dreams I had about this monumental character—now, I will have the time to perfect her. You have given us the chance to bring the performance all the way up to all of our highest visions. What a privilege you have given me!"

This is exactly how I feel about every good review in any show. "Thank you for letting us run. That's all we ever wanted or needed."

And the bad reviews that Anita Loos warned me about—wasn't that good advice? Certainly. But it still doesn't help at all when you read a bad one. As George Burns once asked me, with his sly smile, "Why do we only remember the bad reviews? Every word of them? The good ones fade into a warm feeling, but the bad ones stay with us forever." I was so relieved to hear such a thing from a man who spreads so much joy. I thought there was something melancholy about my nature. Not at all!

The important thing, George says, is to "thank God the people only remember your hits." That speaks well for human nature, doesn't it? Go ahead and do it. Stumble and fall. "They only remember your hits," and when you have a hit on Broadway, it's always a Golden Era!

Carol Channing

Acknowledgments

———————◆———————

OPENING Night on Broadway couldn't exist, needless to say, without the critics (or the producers and writers and directors and actors, for that matter). I hereby offer them—the critics—my deepest appreciation. Most of them are no longer with us, but it is my hope that they'd be delighted to find that their thoughts of thirty or forty years ago—which until now could be found only in research libraries—are suddenly back in the hands of the theatre-loving public. Their comments are instructive, constructive, and often entertaining in their own right, which is more than you can say for some of the shows!

Most (though not all) of the newspaper reviews excerpted in this book are reprinted in full in the *New York Theatre Critics' Reviews* series, available in many libraries. A sizable amount of information was gathered from articles, interviews, releases, and column items that appeared in various New York and tryout town newspapers, as well as from the infinitely helpful *Variety*. (Everything you read in papers is not necessarily accurate: part of the job of the hapless press agent is to get certain things *into* print and keep other things *out*!) Information has also been gathered from souvenir programs, record album notes, private letters, and contracts.

This book was researched mostly at the Billy Rose Theatre Collection of The Performing Arts Research Center at Lincoln Center. Their collection of newspaper clippings solved any number of mysteries (and raised as many new questions). Various divisions of the Library of Congress in Washington, D.C., were also helpful, and it was extremely thoughtful of them to open a convenient new branch on the roof of the Kennedy Center. Much of the writing of this book, actually, was done backstage at various theatres in Washington, Boston, New Haven, and New York—which is rather fitting, isn't it?

The *Theatre World* and *Best Plays* series have been of great help in compiling the data sections, as has the invaluable *Biographical Encyclopedia and Who's Who of the American Theatre*. I have also consulted books by George Abbott, Ken Bloom, Gerald Bordman, Abe Burrows, Cheryl Crawford, Agnes de Mille, Howard Dietz, Vernon Duke, Hugh Fordin, William Goldman, Leslie Halliwell, Theresa Helburn, Elinor Hughes, Ed Jablonski, Lawrence Langner, Alan Jay Lerner, Mary Martin, George Jean Nathan, Hal Prince, Richard Rodgers, Charles Schwartz, Jerry Stagg, and Stanley Green.

I would like to thank a handful of friends who provided clarifications and anecdotes about shows they worked on: Charles Blackwell, Morty Halpern, Leo Herbert, Samuel "Biff" Liff, Leonard Soloway, and Gene Wolsk. I received background information on critical and other matters from veteran press agents Dick Weaver, Merle Debuskey, and Harvey Sabinson. Max Woodward and Paul Newman offered helpful suggestions and graciously allowed access to their extensive collections of theatrical artwork, for which I'm greatly indebted. I would also like to express my appreciation for the guidance and support of Robert J. Axelrod, my editor. Finally, I'd like to thank the following for general assistance, encouragement, and other accommodations: William C. Appleton, Tiki Davies, Mitchell Erickson, Kate Glasner, Kathleen Griffin, Janice Herbert, Richard Kidwell, Carol Patella, Skipp Porteous, Kim Sellon, Mark Sendroff, Barbara Simon, Mary Jo Slater, and Jane Tamlyn.

OVERTURE

*C*ONSIDER the following Broad-
way musicals: *Oklahoma!, On the Town, Carousel, Annie Get Your
Gun, Finian's Rainbow, Brigadoon, Kiss Me, Kate, South Pacific,
Gentlemen Prefer Blondes, Guys and Dolls, The King and I, Wonderful Town, The Pajama Game, My Fair Lady, The Most Happy
Fella, West Side Story, The Music Man, Gypsy, Fiorello!, How to
Succeed in Business Without Really Trying, A Funny Thing Happened on the Way to the Forum, Hello, Dolly!, Fiddler on the
Roof.* Titles that—to a lover of musical theatre—immediately con-
jure up a world of enchanted evenings. A Broadway where on any
opening night you might, like as not, stumble onto another magical
new musical. These shows were all produced between 1943 and
1964, an incredibly innovative period considered to be the "Golden
Era" of the Broadway musical. So golden is this era, in fact, that
these hit musicals came along at a rate of *more than one a year!*
(How many shows of the last twenty-five years belong in such
illustrious company?)

Books about the Broadway musical usually provide the same old
generalized information: who wrote it, who was in it, what it was
about, and were there any hit songs. These questions can easily be
answered by reading liner notes of a cast album—and in the case of
some existing reference books, it seems to be what the authors
have done. But so much of the magic of Broadway is contributed by
directors, choreographers, designers, and sometimes even
producers—magic that doesn't necessarily show up in the script,
on the record, or in production photos. Many long-running hits, in
fact, have succeeded *despite* weak material. What were the shows
really like for the audiences sitting in the theatres? What was it
about the classic musicals that set them apart? Were ground-

3

breaking innovations immediately recognized as such? Were now-legendary performers and performances instantly hailed? It's easy enough to find out what the musicals were *about*; but how can we learn what they were actually *like*?

We may do so by going back to reviews written when the shows were fresh, the songs new, and the surprises delightfully unexpected. With the opening night critics as our guide, we can share that exhilarating moment when Eliza Doolittle clearly enunciated "The Rain in Spain" and the first-nighters—no less astonished than Professor Higgins—exploded in delirium! We can join the audience in nearly tearing up the seats as that animated kewpie doll Dolly Gallagher Levi trotted onto the runway surrounding the orchestra pit and danced rings around the conductor! Cling to the electric thrill of Robert Preston's jim-dandy salesman fidgeting, flitting, and setting the scenery swaying with zest, gusto, and slam-bang trombones! Experience the electrifying explosion as two spitting groups of Robbins's street dancers advanced with bared teeth and clawed fists, mixing together until their bodies flew wildly through space under buttermilk clouds! These and many other fabled moments are relived in these reviews, enabling us to share the immediate excitement of those long-ago opening nights.

All musicals of the Golden Era weren't golden, of course; but Broadway's true collaborators had created an atmosphere in which truly wondrous shows kept coming along. Almost 300 productions—the best, as well as some of the worst—have been selected for discussion, featuring excerpts culled from more than 2,500 opening night reviews. Offsetting the acknowledged classics are good shows that the public rejected, poor shows that the public loved, and flawed-but-worthy attempts that just missed. Then, too, there are the amateurishly hopeless ones that left critics and theatregoers shaking their heads in wonderment, yet offer profitable lessons on what makes a show work (or not). By extracting concise, informed opinions from as many as seven different reviews, a representative view of each show has been assembled. Accompanying the excerpts are detailed production data; clarification of hidden credits and other "inside" information; pertinent—and sometimes impertinent—commentary on the production and people; and summaries of the overall critical and commercial consensus. Original artwork and photographers have been included from many of the shows, helping to recapture their original flavor and excitement.

THE GOLDEN ERA

The Golden Era of the Musical Theatre began on the evening of March 31, 1943, when *Oklahoma!* came sweepin' down the plain. But the Broadway musical had long been in development. It all started back in 1866, when a visiting ballet company (from Paris) was burned out of their New York booking. With no other stage available, the *danseuses* were incorporated into a melodrama, and the combined result, dubbed *The Black Crook*, ran forever. (At a time when a hit lasted 150 nights, 474 performances *seemed* like forever.) The prime lure, in a day when a leg was a limb and a naked ankle was racy, was the presence of girls in pink (flesh-colored) tights. *The Black Crook* played Niblo's Garden, on the northeast corner of Broadway and Prince Street: thus the first "Broadway" musical. Scratching their whiskers and surveying the immense success of this hastily thrown-together hybrid, the Shuberts and Nederlanders of the day were heard to say, "Hmmmm." Had *The Black Crook* closed that Saturday night, where would we all be today?

Things remained relatively quiet until the late 1880s, when the commercial Broadway world as we know it began to develop. Speaking in general terms, operetta occupied the classy side of the musical theatre street, led by (and patterned after) British and Continental imports. The Dublin-born, Berlin-trained Victor Herbert settled here and established his own American brand of "light opera" in the 1890s. For the masses there were native songshows, filled with low-brow jokes and randomly interpolated Tin Pan Alley ditties. These entertainments usually had a strong ethnic slant— leading comedy teams were the Irish Harrigan & Hart, and the "Dutch" (actually German) Weber & Fields. At the turn of the century composer/lyricist/librettist/producer/hoofer George M. Cohan appeared on the scene. By concentrating on specific (if stereotyped) characters in definitely plotted (if lightweight) stories, Cohan developed a primitive musical comedy form. He also brought a much-needed calibre of professionalism to the field, along with the brash American cockiness of the Yankee Doodle Boy.

America's 1914 neutrality saw a sudden halt to the imports that the carriage trade so favored. Composer Jerome Kern, who had spent a decade sprucing up these imports for local consumption, suddenly had an audience for his own, "American"-style music.

The result: the legendary Princess Theatre shows from Kern, Guy Bolton, and P.G. Wodehouse. Here were intelligent, comic musicals in the style of Gilbert and Sullivan (although several paces behind, as Sir William and Sir Arthur were without Peers). The Princess triumvirate molded a formula combining contemporary rhythms, intelligently witty words, and relatively realistic characters. This noble experiment lasted only sixteen months—ego triumphed over compatibility of talent, as usual—but it laid the groundwork for what was to follow. Perhaps most importantly, it directly influenced five local teenagers: George Gershwin, Ira Gershwin, Lorenz Hart, Richard Rodgers, and Vincent Youmans. The styles of these youngsters were to be rooted in the dance rhythm's of the post-war "Jazz Age," as opposed to the more politely anglicized tone of the Princess gents. Meanwhile, a Columbia University colleague of Hart's named Hammerstein was apprenticing in a tamer tradition: his Uncle Arthur was the Ziegfeld of the operetta kingdom, riding high with Victor Herbert's successor, Rudolf Friml. (Oscar 2nd's theatrical background was incredibly well-rounded: grandfather Oscar 1st established his own grand opera company, in opposition to the Metropolitan, while father Willie operated New York's premier vaudeville house.)

By the mid-1920s, Broadway—and America— was dancing to the new rhythms. Youmans was the first to hit it big; his initial lyricists, oddly enough, were Ira Gershwin (writing as Arthur Francis) and Oscar Hammerstein. Then came George, who revolutionized American popular music in 1924 with *Rhapsody in Blue* and the Astaire show *Lady, Be Good*. Kern, whose peppy but colorless tunes had been overshadowed by the syncopated rhythms of Youmans, Gershwin, and the upcoming Rodgers, wandered into a collaboration with Hammerstein. (Hammerstein had already written hit musicals with Youmans, Friml, Romberg, and Gershwin, but nothing with Rodgers except a few songs for amateur shows.) Kern and Hammerstein developed a new-style operetta, which Florenz Ziegfeld moored at his theatre during the last week of 1927. *Show Boat* was, indeed, a major breakthrough: a dramatic musical with a dramatic—and bountiful—score. The book had its lapses, but audiences were so enthralled with the music and the Ziegfeldian production that the muddled dramaturgy went unnoticed. (It's ironic that our first mature musical was saddled with second act trouble.) While Broadway has heard some great scores in the sixty-odd years since, *Show Boat* still ranks among the best.

Musical theatre innovations continued at a somewhat sluggish pace throughout the Depression. *Of Thee I Sing* (1931), from the Gershwins and librettists George S. Kaufman and Morrie Ryskind, was not so much a forward step as a sideways leap. The writers combined a razor-sharp libretto with a dazzlingly playful score, resulting in perfect political satire in the Gilbert and Sullivan tradition—except *this* brilliant lyricist was dedicated to supporting (rather than competing with) his composer. *Of Thee I Sing* went so far as to win the Pulitzer Prize, which raised many eyebrows in a day when mere songshows belonged several rungs below the Olympian heights of the Drama. *Of Thee I Sing's* brilliance was impossible to duplicate, though, as the authors themselves discovered when they attempted to write a sequel.

Kern and Hammerstein's *Music in the Air* (1932) was another forward step. By devising a story about singers, musicians, and songwriters, the authors were able to make the songs grow more-or-less naturally out of the action, rather than just being shoe-horned in via handy song cues. It was quite an innovation at the time; but the operetta-like plot was more of a functional skeleton than a dramatic story, as was clearly evident when *Music in the Air* was remounted twenty years later. (All of these landmark musicals were revived during the Golden Era, with varying results, as we shall see.)

Porgy and Bess (1935), from the Gershwins and DuBose Heyward, was a self-proclaimed "folk opera" in which score and story were integrated, although the music was more Broadway than opera. George built the score in his usual manner, assembling songs, choral ensembles, and rhythmic dance specialties. But here the music was all of a piece thematically! Even more crucially, the various theatrical elements—scenery, lighting, movement, acting performances—were meticulously assembled (or "integrated") to support the mood of the score and text. This had never really happened before, and wouldn't occur all too frequently in the future. Director Rouben Mamoulian was a crucial force here, and would play a crucial role in the development of musical drama. (Look at group photos of Mamoulian musicals like *Porgy and Bess*, *Carousel* [1945], or *Lost in the Stars* [1949]. Every actor—even the chorus—is dramatically involved; some are carefully half-hidden in shadows, their arms and hands framing the principals.) Because the original *Porgy and Bess* was a commercial failure, Mamoulian didn't return to Broadway until 1943. But the Golden

Era of the Broadway musical was to begin the night Mamoulian came back to town.

On Your Toes (1936) came from Rodgers, Hart, and George Abbott, another trio who set about revolutionizing musical comedy. *Toes* told of a ballet company, which quite naturally allowed the inclusion of a couple of ballets. As these master showmen were also interested in entertainment, they saw to it that the ballets were (a) relevant to the action, and (b) so lively and amusing that the audience wouldn't sleep through them. They also saw fit to bring in a real choreographer, George Balanchine of the Ballets Russe, instead of one of the time-step dance directors that Broadway had favored since the Spanish-American War.

The *Toes* trio returned (with novelist John O'Hara) for *Pal Joey* (1940). This time they told an "adult" story, with a hero who wasn't a nice guy. We've become used to anti-heroes (are there any other kind?), but back in 1940 the bad guy was supposed to be punished, killed, or reformed by the Love of a Good Woman. Joey Evans wasn't, and controversy was stirred. "If it is possible to make an entertaining musical comedy out of an odious story, *Pal Joey* is it," commented Brooks Atkinson of the all-important *Times*, concluding that "although *Pal Joey* is expertly done, can you draw sweet water from a foul well?" When the show was triumphantly revived in 1952, Atkinson was somewhat relieved at the opportunity to revise his opinion.

In the months following Pearl Harbor, business on Broadway finally recovered from the Depression-long slump: New York was suddenly packed with war workers hungering for entertainment, but the quality and quantity of musical offerings was still at Depression levels. As 1943 crept in, only two musical comedies were running, both star vehicles from star songwriters (and neither particularly good). *Let's Face It* (1941) was a service farce built around Danny Kaye as a hapless enlistee pursued by man-hungry war widows. Cole Porter's score included such all-time great hits as— well, there weren't any. *By Jupiter* (1942), the final Rodgers and Hart show, also had a wartime theme; the soldiers, though, were leggy Amazons, and the chief warrior's husband was poor little Ray Bolger. The score was much better than Porter's; Rodgers and Hart didn't know how to be boring! But their book was barely serviceable, dusting off all the old male–female reversal jokes. Five other musical offerings were held over. The operetta *Rosalinda* (1942), a revision of Johann Strauss's *Die Fledermaus* (1873), proved a sizable hit and spawned a string of revivals of already-ancient operettas. *Star and Garter* (1942) was Mike Todd's burlesque revue, starring his gal Gypsy Rose Lee. City License Commissioner Moss had just banned the striptease in order to close down the 42nd St. grind houses, so Mike brought the girls on "nekkid" to begin with— at a $4.40 top rather than Minsky's 40¢! *Show Time* (1942) was a half-baked vaudeville program starring George Jessel. A lacklustre edition of Leonard Sillman's *New Faces* (1942) series was also briefly on hand, the most notable face being that of pucker-pussed Alice Pearce. Biggest hit of all was the musical whatnot *Sons o' Fun* (1941), Olsen & Johnson's long-running sequel to their even longer running *Hellzapoppin'* (1938).

This was the stage upon which *Oklahoma!* burst into town. Rodgers, Hammerstein, and Mamoulian were, perhaps, the perfect collaborators at this moment in their careers: they shared a history of past musical theatre innovations and a desire to continue to explore the form. The foundation was set by *Show Boat*, which demonstrated that a musical could be more than just a bunch of songs tied together by a plot; rather, it could be a dramatic story expressed and embellished by music and lyrics. The collaborators set out with several key goals: to make the songs grow naturally out of the situation, as in *Music in the Air*; to meticulously "paint"—Mamoulian treated the stage as a canvas— the entire production around the material, as in *Porgy and Bess*; and to use dance—rather than dialogue or lyrics—to express crucial plot and character information, as in *On Your Toes*. This last objective was placed in the charge of choreographer Agnes de Mille, who was as determined as her strong-willed collaborators to make *Oklahoma!* unparalled and truly wondrous.

The Golden Era arrived, heralded by *Oklahoma!* and quickly followed by three cracklingly fresh musicals: *Carmen Jones* (1943), *On the Town* (1944), and *Carousel* (1945). Each expanded, advanced, and exploded the parameters of the musical theatre, as will be seen in the review excerpts. (It's rather remarkable that three of the four came from Hammerstein, as did *Show Boat* and *Music in the Air*.) By the time *Carousel* opened, critics and audiences alike *knew* that a new age had begun.

This is not to say that all musicals of the Golden Era were golden. Old-fashioned formula musicals would continue to be churned out, some of them pretty good (like *Annie Get Your Gun* [1946], coproduced by—yes—Hammerstein), but most of them were pretty old-fashioned. There were also the usual assortment of second- and third-rate offerings from second- and third-rate talents.

But the public—still fighting to get tickets for the new-style hits—was ready, eager, and hungry to embrace new musical theatre innovations. When two unlikely, unconventional, and unheralded smash hits turned up early in 1947, everyone was delighted and overjoyed—but nobody was surprised. Great new musicals were suddenly something to be expected. *Finian's Rainbow* and *Brigadoon* joined *Oklahoma!*, *Carousel*, and *Annie Get Your Gun*. What a week of theatre-going!

Broadway's Depression-long slump had suddenly lifted, and a talented corps of musical theatre craftsmen were ready to seize the opportunity. Two of the Golden Era's most important songwriting teams made their debuts in 1943: Rodgers and Hammerstein (who were well-established individually) and Alan Jay Lerner and Frederick Loewe (who were virtually unknown). Lerner and Loewe's maiden effort, *What's Up*, was just another quickly forgotten flop; but their sophomore try was the distinctly promising *The Day Before Spring* (1945), and then came *Brigadoon*. Both teams moved in the direction of lyrical musical drama, often abetted by choreographer de Mille. Another group soon appeared who would explore the fast-paced, comic musical comedy pioneered by Rodgers and Abbott in *On Your Toes* and *Pal Joey*. Composer Leonard Bernstein, lyricist/librettists Betty Comden and Adolph Green, and choreographer Jerome Robbins—under the guidance of George Abbott—literally burst upon the scene in 1944 with *On the Town*. Working in various combinations with various composers, Abbott, Robbins, and Comden and Green developed the well-made American musical comedy. By 1948 four more major talents had also appeared: songwriters Jule Styne and Frank Loesser (both shepherded by Abbott) and choreographers Michael Kidd and Gower Champion. Is it any wonder that miracle musicals—shows in which everything seemed to work perfectly—kept occurring?

That's how things were to continue for twenty years. In 1951 you could catch the original productions of *Kiss Me, Kate, South Pacific, Call Me Madam, Guys and Dolls*, and *The King and I*—if you could get tickets, that is. In the spring of 1960, choices included *My Fair Lady, The Music Man, Gypsy, The Sound of Music, Fiorello!*, and *Bye Bye Birdie*. It would be cruel and heartless to list the choices of showgoers in the spring of 1970, 1980, or—so help us—1990.

The change came abruptly, just after *Fiddler on the Roof* opened in the fall of 1964. Not that the balance of the decade didn't see some notable shows: *Man of La Mancha* (1965), *Mame* (1966), *Cabaret* (1966), *Hair* (1968), *Promises, Promises* (1968), and *1776* (1969) were all entertaining and certainly effective. But each was somewhat uneven in its attributes; and while several hit songs emanated from the bunch, there isn't a score among them that belongs with the Golden Era greats. The 1970s and 1980s were remarkably lean, with virtually nothing worthwhile except *A Chorus Line* (1975) and a few exceptional Sondheim scores tied to flawed shows.

What happened? To begin with, most of the great songwriters were gone. Arlen, Berlin, Bernstein, Hammerstein, Loesser, Loewe, Porter, and Weill were all dead, retired or otherwise occupied. Only Richard Rodgers and Alan Jay Lerner kept plugging away, with repeatedly discouraging results. The new generation of composers proved incapable of repeating the achievements of their mentors. Jerry Herman, Cy Coleman, Harvey Schmidt, John Kander, and Charles Strouse all displayed talent and met with occasional—sometimes phenomenal—success; but is there a single great score among their works? Jerry Bock *did* come up with a first-rate score or two, but unfortunately he chose to retire after a couple of post-*Fiddler* failures; and there seems to be little point in bringing Andrew Lloyd Webber's imports into the discussion. That leaves only Sondheim, who composed two Golden Era scores which received such stony receptions that he couldn't get another Broadway hearing until *Company* (1970). Sondheim *has* written some brilliant scores, but one man alone cannot revive a tarnished Golden Era.

Perhaps some of the blame belongs, strangely enough, with *Hello, Dolly!* and *Fiddler* (and Champion and Robbins). These two 1964 super-hits proved that a musical could be a landmark, record-breaking, classic, all-time hit *without* a remarkable score. Broadway's previous hats-in-the-air smashes were sturdily built on foundations of great songs, like *South Pacific, Guys and Dolls, My Fair Lady,* and *West Side Story* (1957). The *Fiddler* score, on the other hand, is certainly a couple of notches below great, and *Dolly!*—with contributions from a handful of other hands—is

merely better-than-average. The uncontested magic of these last
two shows wasn't in the material, as the critics clearly pointed out
the morning after opening night; it was in the staging, the star
performances, and the overall productions.

There were other reasons for the end of the Golden Age, some
of which had more to do with what was going on outside, than
inside the theatre. America was changing, pop music was changing, and the commercial realities of Broadway were changing.
While World War II and the Korean War were both popular pa-
triotic causes (and good for business along the Rialto), the unde-
clared Vietnam War created a mood of social unrest. Meanwhile, a
revolution in popular music was pushing rock into the foreground.
Broadway songs had held an especially high place in the pop music
world since the 1920s; this ended abruptly.

And as the Broadway musical moved into a period of desperation, shows became bigger and bigger, costs began to climb, and
ticket prices leaped disproportionately. Let's consider the cost of
an orchestra seat for the newest musical in town:

Oklahoma!	1943	$4.40
Bloomer Girl	1944	$5.40
Carousel	1945	$6.00
Annie Get Your Gun	1946	$6.60
As the Girls Go	1948	$7.20
South Pacific	1949	$6.00
Call Me Madam	1950	$7.20
Guys and Dolls	1950	$6.00
Wonderful Town	1953	$6.60
Damn Yankees	1955	$8.05
Seventh Heaven	1955	$8.30
My Fair Lady	1956	$7.50
New Girl in Town	1957	$9.20
West Side Story	1957	$7.50
The Music Man	1957	$8.05
Goldilocks	1958	$9.90
Gypsy	1959	$9.40
The Sound of Music	1959	$9.90
Carnival	1961	$8.60
Hello, Dolly!	1964	$9.40
Funny Girl	1964	$9.60
Fiddler on the Roof	1964	$9.40

On a Clear Day You Can See Forever	1965	$11.90
Zorba	1968	$15.00
Annie	1977	$20.00
Sweeney Todd	1978	$25.00
Evita	1979	$30.00
42nd Street	1980	$40.00
La Cage aux Folles	1983	$47.50
Les Miserables	1987	$50.00
Jerome Robbins' Broadway	1989	$55.00

In November 1989 *Robbins* went to a $60-top. By January 1990 it was on twofers, by Labor Day it was gone—but the $60 ducat remains.

Yes, costs keep going up and inflation keeps inflating, but you don't have to be an economist to realize that there is something seriously wrong with these ticket prices. Broadway broke the $10 barrier in 1965, just as the Golden Era ended and the decline began; by 1977 the price had doubled. The increases since then have been ludicrous, especially if you consider the quality of the shows! (It should also be added that long-running musicals gradually raise their prices to cover increased costs and keep up with the competition. A perhaps unparalleled example: *A Chorus Line*, which opened in 1975 at $15, closed in 1990 at $50!)

By contrast, let us compare the price of a seat at the movies. In 1943 the charge for a first-run film in New York City was $1.10. (The New Year's attraction at the Paramount was the all-star film musical *Star Spangled Rhythm*, along with a live stage show featuring Benny Goodman *and* Frank Sinatra.) The 1989 movie top has climbed to $7.50. It should also be reported that a Rialto dog now goes for four bits, which for those of youse whose Runyonese is rusty means you can buy a frankfurter at the corner of 42nd Street and Seventh Avenue for 50¢. (I'm not saying you can *eat* it.)

The Broadway musical has become a luxury item, no longer within the reach of the common man. (Remember the "I Love Lucy" episode when Lucy and Ricky and Fred and Ethel went to see *The Most Happy Fella*?) Even the "cheap" seats in the last rows of the balcony cost as much as $45. Speaking as a Broadway manager, I can tell you this: there are many excellent reasons why ticket prices *won't* go down, most of them beginning with a dollar sign.

So where is one to look for a new beginning in the musical theater? That is a puzzlement, as they used to say in Siam-on-the-

Hudson. Is it possible that we'll see a new Golden Era? Highly unlikely: there's no practical training ground for new writers, and knowledgeable directors and creative producers—so very crucial to the shaping and editing process—are virtually nonexistent. Is it possible for new musicals to arrive which belong on the list of classics heading this introduction? *Absolutely!* And a careful examination of the musicals of the Golden Era—the ones that worked (and why), and the ones that didn't work (and why)—will provide helpful and valuable guidance.

THE PRESS AND THE CRITICS

Since we shall be relying on the so-called gentlemen of the press for eyewitness reports, it is instructive first to take a brief look at the journalists and their journals. Who were these critics? Which ones were respected, influential, important? What is this "power" the press holds over Broadway?

In 1948, New York City had nine major daily newspapers. By 1964 this number had diminished to six, and since 1967 there have been only three. While good reviews have always been of primary importance to the survival of a show, the impact of individual critics has changed with the times (or should we say the *Times*?). Not only has the number of papers diminished; so has the proportional number of readers. Into the mid-1950s, many people read both a morning and an evening paper. Today, those theatre-ticket buyers who read *any* paper at all—rather than getting their view of the world solely from television and radio—usually read only one newspaper. In most cases the paper is the *Times*.

This situation is not, of course, the fault of the *Times*. It has long been the "best" of the New York dailies. The only major nontabloid competitor since the Depression was the *Herald Tribune*, which ceased publication in 1966. The *Trib*'s readership—and *Trib* critic Walter Kerr—switched to the *Times*, and the blessing of the *Times* critic has been critical to theatrical success ever since. This is not to say that you can't fight a bad review in the *Times*; life in the theatre is a whole lot easier, though, if the *Times* smiles beneficently.

The reduced number of newspapers drastically increased the influence of the individual critic. A press agent putting together a quote ad in the 1940s had eight or nine dailies—plus numerous other local area papers—to choose from. The *Times* and the *Trib* didn't like it? Okay, you could still come up with an impressive-looking, jam-packed assemblage of quotes from the others. This could be followed up with additional ammunition from the big weekly magazines, which have also dwindled.

The other weapon of press agents on the defensive (with a "soft" or hard-to-sell attraction) was publicity. Nine papers, each with several pages of amusement news, had a continuous need for stories, photos, and column items. Many shows combatted mixed notices with high-powered press coverage; and once a show runs long enough, the public seems to forget negative reviews.

Today there are only three major New York City dailies. This makes specialized papers like *The Wall Street Journal, Women's Wear Daily* and the suburban-based *New York Newsday* more noticeable, but they remain of secondary importance in reaching theatregoers. Several of the major magazines—*Time, Newsweek, New York* (which includes vestiges of *Cue*) and *The New Yorker*—retain their theatre-oriented audience; but their reviews can appear a week or more after the opening (and sometimes the closing). The one magazine which regularly devoted enormous space to Broadway—with reviews, full-color photo layouts, and occasional cover stories—was the weekly *Life*, which should not be confused with the present-day monthly of the same name. Broadway lost one of its most important publicity outlets when *Life* died.

The diminishing number of newspapers has been offset by the increasingly important television critics, who reach an immense audience. But their reviews are subject to severe time constrictions: how much depth can you expect to get in 250 words? Some of these critics are quite perceptive, actually, but viewers of the evening news are not interested in close analysis; a successful TV critic is one who makes his or her reviews entertaining, regardless of the show under discussion. Oral reviews present an additional problem: the listener gets only what can be absorbed in a quick hearing. Not only is a printed review more complete in detail and richer (hopefully) in analysis, but you can read it at your own speed, go back to that paragraph you skimmed over, or save it to read later. A TV critic offers more of an impression than a critique, and radio reviews have even less impact.

The power of the three dailies (in general) and the *Times* (in particular) has become monstrous; unless, of course, they like your show. For all the griping that exists within the theatrical community, you'll note that complaints are heard *only* when the reviews are bad. This brings us to a fundamental question: why do we need reviews? Why does the whole wide world—Broadway, that is— quake and totter in terror, in anticipation of a few columns of newsprint? Why do theatregoers read them, and why do publishers publish them?

To quote visionary critic John Anderson: "Every time the critic keeps the playgoer from spending $3.00 for a bad play, he is helping the theatre."

Ticket prices have risen somewhat since this remark was made in 1941, but the point still holds. Nobody in the theatre is helped by bad shows; they do immense harm to us all. Anyone who gambles $3 or $60 on an evening's entertainment and enjoys him- or herself is likely to come back again. Give them theatrical trash—shows which Broadway insiders wouldn't dream of paying to see—and you drive them away for good. Partisans of a couple of recent "big" musicals, *Rags* (1986) and *Legs Diamond* (1988), complained vociferously about their handling by the press. Turning back to Richard Watts Jr., regarding the 1949 attraction (?) which opened the very same theatre that housed the above-named flops: "If any critic ever, through misplaced kindness of heart, led a prospective playgoer to pay money to see *All for Love,* he would be committing a sin against the entire theatre." (The Mark Hellinger Theatre, as fate and real estate men would have it, recently got religion and became a church, which would presumably amuse gangster-land columnist Hellinger.)

Bad shows help nobody and the critic does the theatre a service by shooing hapless playgoers away from shows that they're sure not to like. At last count, we seem to have more bad shows than bad critics. I must add, parenthetically, that it seemed to this theatregoer that *Rags* was worth every bit of $3.

In discussing the overall validity of critical opinion, there is a further complicating factor: negative (or shall we say awful?) reviews often meet with a gleeful reception along 45th Street so long as it's someone else's show. Although few theatrefolk would admit it, a set of raves usually meets with intramural grumbling—except on the rare occasion when the show is actually *that* good.

Let's turn to the critics themselves, and their relative influence. During the multinewspaper years, four papers were of primary importance: the morning *Times, Herald Tribune,* and *Daily News,* and the afternoon *Post* (although unanimous morning pans could kill a show before the afternoon papers hit the streets!).

Leading the list was always the *Times*, which for most of the Golden Era meant Brooks Atkinson. Atkinson became drama critic in 1925, at a time when the *Times* was particularly theatre-conscious. (His supervising editor was none other than George S. Kaufman; already a highly successful playwright, Kaufman continued to hold the job "just in case.") The American theatre made incredible advances through the late 1920s and 1930s, aided and encouraged by Atkinson's supportive helping hand. Following a Pulitzer Prize–winning stint as war correspondent, Atkinson refused a promotion to the editorial page and returned to the aisle in 1946—he loved the theatre and that's where he wanted to be. Upon his reaching the *Times*'s mandatory retirement age in 1960, Broadway's Mansfield Theatre was renamed in his honor. Atkinson's reviews are straightforward, precise, and professional. He was somewhat more proficient at analysing plays than musicals; while his comments were always apt, several of his colleagues had a better understanding of music and the inner workings of the form. But as an overall drama critic, Brooks Atkinson was peerless.

Walter Kerr, unlike his colleagues, was not a newspaperman: he was, first and foremost, a man of the theatre. Before joining the *Herald Tribune* in 1951, he wrote three musicals which transferred from Catholic University in Washington, D.C. (where he was a professor) to Broadway, under the sponsorship of the Shuberts, the Theatre Guild, and George Abbott. Kerr's reviews display an uncanny understanding of the musical form; were it not for his journalistic career, he very possibly could have become a top musical comedy director in the Abbott tradition. His descriptions of performers at work, especially comedians, are remarkable; the magic of Beatrice Lillie or Bert Lahr is suddenly made clear to readers who know them only through recorded or filmed performances. Many of his reviews are highly entertaining—again, he is primarily a theatrical writer, not a newspaperman. The commentary is usually precise, trenchant, and immensely constructive. Had Kerr been writing in one of the tryout towns, a lot of bad musicals could surely have been improved before reaching New York. That is, if the producers and writers and directors had bothered to listen. Kerr won a Pulitzer Prize in 1978 for his drama criticism, and in 1990 Broadway's Ritz Theatre was renamed the Walter Kerr.

John Chapman replaced veteran critic Burns Mantle at the *Daily News* shortly after *Oklahoma!* opened in 1943. By the late 1960s, Chapman seemed old-fashioned and inconclusive; it's a pleasant surprise to discover that his earlier reviews are well-informed, to-the-point, and highly impressive. Pick a musical with an interesting score: he is almost always on target, not only telling us that the songs were good but *why* he liked them. When he loved a show—especially a hard-sell—he went out of his way to provide enthusiastic "quote" lines. He could also be lethal, when necessary, with a few well-chosen words. A true lover of Broadway, Chapman played an inside role in keeping the Tony Awards alive through the beleaguered period before the League of New York Theatres took over their administration (and funding) in 1965. Highly respected within the profession, he was eulogized upon his death in 1972 by the unlikely trio of Richard Rodgers, Walter Kerr, and David Merrick.

Richard Watts Jr. reviewed Broadway for almost fifty years, at the *Herald Tribune* and—during the Golden Era—the *Post.* Like John Chapman, he was a backup critic in the 1920s. Remarkably, Watts covered the openings of both *The Desert Song* (1926) and *Follies* (1971)! Unlike most of his colleagues, he was rarely vicious or destructive. A perceptive critic, his reviews are somewhat marred by an imprecise writing style; he did not have the power of expression of Atkinson, Kerr, Chapman, and others. Nevertheless, Watts provided his readers with dependable, consistent criticism— and his opinions carried weight.

Many other first-string critics are well-represented in the pages that follow. John Anderson, of the *Journal-American*, was both popular and influential. He defended his colleagues in public debate as "the sanitary department which stands between the public and some unpleasant evenings." His sudden death in 1943 (of meningitis) received extensive press coverage, with mourning from critics and theatrefolk alike. Howard Barnes, of the *Herald Tribune*, wrote workmanlike, adequate reviews. The *Trib* didn't move into undisputed "second place" in importance until 1951, when Barnes was replaced by Walter Kerr. Robert Coleman was the voice of the *Daily Mirror* (later called the *Mirror*), joining the paper in 1924 and remaining until it ceased publication in 1963. A courtly Southern gentleman, Coleman was a highly visible opening night fixture—he sported a set of side-whiskers (choppers)! William Hawkins, of the *World-Telegram*, was a surprise replacement for

Burton Rascoe, coming to the job with virtually no qualifications except a recommendation from his father (who was chairman of the board of the newspaper chain). Strangely enough, he turned out to be an intelligent, informed critic. Robert Garland, of the *Journal-American*, was at various times a playwright, press agent, and actor (with little success on any count). During the 1930s, when he was critic for the *World-Telegram*, he was married to musical comedy star Queenie Smith. I am told by a veteran press agent that Garland was highly susceptible to inside tips. ("Keep your eye on so-and-so . . . future star . . . movie studio. . . .") Louis Kronenberger, of *PM*, was also drama critic for *Time* magazine. He gained notoriety in the Time–Life Empire and around the Drama Critics' Circle by retaining his job despite a pan for the 1938 comedy *Kiss the Boys Goodbye*, by editor in chief Henry Luce's wife Claire Boothe. Kronenberger also wrote the Broadway translation of Jean Anouilh's *Mademoiselle Colombe* (1954). John Lardner was critic for the short-lived *Star*. A sports columnist by trade, Lardner's musical theatre criticism is amazingly perceptive. His father, Ring, was one of the great satirists of our century; his occasional Broadway activity included the classic pop-music satire *June Moon* (1929, with George S. Kaufman) and lyrics for about a dozen show tunes (to music by Vincent Youmans, Jerome Kern, and others). Burns Mantle, of the *Daily News*, was the grand old man on the aisle as the Golden Era began. A Broadway critic since 1911, he retired in 1943. From 1920 until his death in 1948, Mantle was official chronicler of Broadway with his *Best Plays* series. John McClain, of Hearst's *Journal-American*, was a fairly good reviewer but strongly right wing (he complained that *Li'l Abner* [1956] was subversive!). McClain was the only "high-society" critic of his time: he arrived on opening nights in a chauffered Bentley. Ward Morehouse, of the *Sun*, was a stage-struck reporter, playwright, and screenwriter. Two of his books, *Matinee Tomorrow* (1949) and the semi-autobiographical *Forty-Five Minutes Past Eight* (1939), are entertaining chronicles of early Broadway. Norman Nadel, of the *World-Telegram & Sun*, was a former symphonic trombonist. He was one of the only critics with any musical training—not an unimportant consideration when reviewing musical theatre. Lewis Nichols, wartime replacement for Brooks Atkinson on the *Times*, was one of the better critics of the day. A consistent leader in *Variety*'s Annual Critics' Poll (which rated the critics' reviews against the shows' ultimate commercial fate), it's somewhat surprising that Nichols wasn't quickly snapped up by the competition. Burton Rascoe of the *World-Telegram*, on the other hand, was the perennial holder of the last place in the Critics' Poll. A rave from Rascoe, I am told, was "the kiss of death": all the other reviews were sure to be awful. After a string of especially outlandish reviews (including a rave for the otherwise ravaged *Nellie Bly* [1946]), his editor refused to run a pan of *Henry IV, Part One* in which the critic castigated Laurence Olivier, Ralph Richardson, and the Old Vic Company at length because he couldn't understand their accents. Rascoe (who as editor in chief of the Literary Guild had advised his readers that John Steinbeck's 1939 novel *The Grapes of Wrath* was "absolutely not worth reading") resigned from the *World-Telegram* in a huff— which was exactly what his editor had in mind. Howard Taubman, music critic of the *Times*, was moved over as replacement for the retiring Brooks Atkinson in 1960. The Broadway establishment railed against Taubman, whom they considered unintelligible. (David Merrick took Taubman's pan of *Stop the World* [1962] and reran it in the *Times* as an ad—translated into Greek!) Taubman was finally removed from the aisle in 1965; his replacement, Stanley Kauffman, was even more objectionable and his tenure, more short-lived. (Kauffmann was axed when Merrick found a stack of copies of his 1952 novel *The Philanderer*—which had been prosecuted on obscenity charges in England—and sent them to 89 important editors and columnists. "If I'm lucky," commented the Abominable Showman, "I'll get arrested for sending unseemly matter through the mails." Producer Alexander H. Cohen, who continually and hopelessly tried to out-Merrick Merrick, attempted a similar coup by sending out Christmas gifts of toilet paper picturing *New York Magazine* critic John Simon—which only made *Cohen* look like an ass. But I digress.) Wilella Waldorf took over at the *Post* in 1941. A highly capable critic, she had been on the movie desk since the presound days of 1926. As we enter the 1990s, Waldorf remains the only female to have ever served as first-string drama critic on a major New York paper. Biographical data on these critics can be found at the end of the book.

A number of other critics—interim first-stringers, second-stringers, and occasional subs from other departments—are also represented. They include Jim Aronson, Frank Aston, Robert Bagar, Herrick Brown, Alton Cook, Judith Crist, Tom Donnelly, Lewis Funke, Otis L. Guernsey Jr., Leonard Harris, Frances Herridge, Bert McCord, Jim O'Connor, Frank Quinn, Vernon

Rice, Alan Rich, Bill Slocum, Robert Sylvester, Walter Terry, and Doug Watt.

NOTES ON THE EXCERPTS

The excerpts have been selected from over 2,500 reviews of musicals which opened on Broadway during the Golden Era, from 1943 through 1964. Calendar years have been used rather than "seasons," as the latter can be confusing. (Some say the season begins on Labor Day, others pick the first Monday in June. Award deadline dates, meanwhile, have fluctuated widely through the years.) No effort has been made to include every show produced during this period: productions of minimal interest have been ignored unless the critics told us something worth noting. British, French, and other foreign imports have been included. Off-Broadway shows are not, except for attractions of the Phoenix Theatre and City Center (which were regularly covered by the first-string critics).

Critical comments have been edited for clarity and consciousness. Redundant reportorial information—"the new musical comedy, which opened last night at the Shubert Theatre"—has been deleted, except where it adversely affects the writing style. Other unnecessarily repeated phrases have been condensed: "Rodgers and Hammerstein," for example, is used in place of references to "composer Richard Rodgers and lyricist/librettist Oscar Hammerstein 2nd." Contemporary references which might be obscure to today's reader have been clarified in brackets. "Theatre" has been used over "theater" throughout, except where "Theater" was part of a title or producing organization.

I've taken the liberty of condensing and juxtaposing critical thoughts, always careful to preserve the critics's personal style. Errors in identification, spelling, and song titles have been corrected. The critics were, after all, writing on a tight deadline—in some cases forced to rush out into the night before the final curtain. Brooks Atkinson, for example, worked in longhand, submitting his review paragraph-by-paragraph. Within forty-five minutes of arriving back at the *Times*, his notice was typeset, proofed, and on the presses! (The current habit of attending preview performances and taking a day or two to write the notice dates back to 1966, and the brief reign of Stanley Kauffmann at the *Times*.) The aim has been to make the excerpts readable, concise, and informative while still reflecting the general tone of the entire original review.

The Credits

Discussion of each show is preceded by credits for the production. Headings have been standardized: people with "production staged by" and "dance and ensembles by" billing are listed as, respectively, director and choreographer. Sometimes multiple and/or conflicting credits were billed, such as "entire production staged by" and "book directed by." These cases have been clarified, as necessary. Similarly, the phrase "in association with" has been used for all associate and "by arrangement with" producers. Leading performers have been listed, as well as certain featured and nonbilled players of interest. Names have been given more or less in the order of prominence of original billing. Some people changed or altered their names over the years, so the reader may notice seeming inconsistencies. (With his first directing credit in 1962, producer Harold S. Prince officially became Harold Prince; his initial Broadway job had been as stage manager H. Smith Prince. And producer Arnold Saint Subber added a hyphen after the Saint, then dropped the Arnold and the hyphen, and eventually settled on Saint-Subber.) Married couples working the same show have been so indicated. In the movies this usually meant some important guy got his nontalented wife the job; in the theatre, though, it was often the other way around! The date of the official Broadway opening is given, as well as the name of the theatre. Many long-running shows moved from theatre to theatre; this information is included only when a nonprofit limited engagement transferred to a commercial run.

The official billing, though, does not always tell the full story. Musical theatre, as we've been told on innumerable occasions, is a collaboration. The success of a musical is not determined solely by the quality of the material the writers wrote, but by what it all looked like from orchestra center, many months later, on Opening Night. On any number of occasions, people whose names don't appear in the "official" billing were actually instrumental in a show's failure or success. Blame for a poorly assembled musical often goes to the director, but does a director called in at the last minute to try to salvage a disaster deserve all the abuse? How about the guy who guided the writers, chose the designers, approved the designs, cast the cast, rehearsed the actors, and remained in charge through two or three tryout towns? Sudden cast changes can also make an enormous difference: it goes without saying that a show written-to-order around a specific star can be severely weakened when said star is suddenly fired or quits (or dies).

If the reader gets the idea that proceedings didn't always proceed as planned, the reader will be getting the right idea. One of the things we discover is that some of our best musicals actually *benefited* from unplanned detours. Inside squabbles, ghosts, and skeletons—sometimes alluded to by the critics, though the names were rarely named—can be crucial to an explanation of what made these musicals work (or not work). Hidden knowledge can also provide the key to an understanding of the growth and development of specific talents.

For example, take the case of Bob Fosse. After three consecutive hits as a choreographer, he made his directorial debut with *Redhead* (1959)—which Brooks Atkinson greeted by suggesting that "perhaps in the future all musical comedies should be written by choreographers." (Little did we know!) *Redhead* was an award-winning smash, but the record books imply that Fosse wasn't given another Broadway show to direct until 1966! Something, clearly, must have happened in the interim, and the answer lies behind the "official" billing of *The Conquering Hero* (1961). Fired during the tryout, Fosse went to arbitration to protect the integrity of his work. This sort of thing can get you the reputation of being difficult, especially when you're tangling with two of Broadway's most respected producers. The reviews gave high praise to the anonymously credited ballets: "Suggests a whole new profitable vein for musical comedy choreography," said Walter Kerr. Doesn't Fosse deserve credit for what he considered his best work, work which clearly led to his future style? And isn't this episode crucial to an understanding of Fosse's artistic development and overall career?

The book of another musical was written by play doctor Abe Burrows, although the men he replaced retained their official billing (by contract). While the trio shared a Tony Award, the Pulitzer Committee knew enough to present their Prize to Burrows only. This same show, *How to Succeed in Business Without Really Try-*

ing (1961), also billed a choreographer who was fired; the replacement—Bob Fosse, coincidentally enough—received billing under the heading "musical staging by."

In other cases, the departed presumably deserve some of the credit. One comparatively recent musical saw the departure of director, choreographer, librettist, and star during the tryout. (The guys they should have fired, needless to say, were the producers.) Unable to find a new librettist, the book was "improved" by assorted bystanders. Since facing the critics without naming an author is an open admission of disaster, the new director/choreographer—a supremely talented man, but not a writer—put his name on the book. And ended up with a Tony nomination! Who, if anyone, deserved that nomination? Michael Stewart, who did most of the actual writing, or Michael Bennett? (It would make a better story if the book had won a Tony and the show—*Seesaw* [1973]—had been a hit; but it didn't, and it wasn't. Because, as that impeccable wordsmith Sheldon Harnick once said, "You can't wash garbage.")

The Awards

Information has been given on Tony, New York Drama Critics' Circle, Pulitzer, and Donaldson Awards won by the shows and their participants. Awards categories and rules changed over the years. Seasonal cut-off dates varied, which can cause confusion. For example: *Carnival* won the 1961 Critics' Circle Award but lost the 1962 Best Musical Tony to *How to Succeed*—which won the 1962 Critics' Circle Award. *The Consul* won eight 1950 Donaldson Awards, the 1950 Critics' Circle Award, and a Pulitzer Prize—but no Tonys, as the shifting cut-off date pitted it against the 1949 Donaldson, Critics' Circle, and Pulitzer winner *South Pacific.*

The Tony Awards were first given in 1947, although there was no category for Best Musical or Best Composer until 1949. Categories varied through the years, resulting in what might seem unexplainable omissions. Lyricists Hammerstein, Porter, Loesser, and Lerner did not receive awards for *South Pacific* (1949), *Kiss Me, Kate* (1948), *Guys and Dolls* (1950), and *My Fair Lady* (1956). The reason: the Best Lyricist Award wasn't established until 1965. (They gave Tonys in those days to stagehands, though.) You will also notice relatively few Best Director winners; while choreographers were honored from the start, directors of musicals and plays were competing for the same award until 1960.

The Drama Critics' Circle created a separate category for musicals following their controversial selection of *Carousel* (1945) over Lindsay and Crouse's *State of the Union*. (The latter won the Pulitzer, *Carousel* being ineligible because it was an adaptation of a play.) The Pulitzer Prize for Drama was awarded to only three Golden Era musicals: two others received the Prize for Music.

The long-forgotten Donaldson Awards were established in 1944 by the trade magazine *Billboard*, in memory of founder W. H. Donaldson. Although administered by *Billboard*, they were democratically voted upon by the theatrical profession at large—unlike the Tonys, which were chosen for many years by the board of the American Theatre Wing, a closed group of as few as fifteen of the Broadway elite. So Donaldson Awardees might in some cases have been more deserving than the "inner-sanctum" selections of the Tony committee. There was no question of predetermined eligibility; you could vote for whomever you thought deserved the award. In fact, on three occasions nonstarred actors won both the star *and* supporting awards for the same performance! In addition to the Tony categories, Donaldsons were given to lyricists, directors of musicals, dancers, and performers making their debut. The Donaldsons were discontinued in 1955, being unable to compete with the officially sanctioned Tonys.

The Illustrations

Almost half of the entries are accompanied by illustrations—usually the original artwork, or "logo," created to attract ticket buyers. Artwork has been reproduced from heralds (program inserts used to encourage advance sales), window cards, souvenir programs, sheet music, record album covers, and ad slicks. Especially illuminating production photographs have also been included, although we have tried to avoid the overly familiar shots used elsewhere again and again. Some material includes people who departed before the Broadway opening, others name replacement and/or touring casts (as indicated). Logos were sometimes changed along the way to stimulate sales; at least, that's what the producers must have thought. Where alternate artwork for the same show was available, we've been guided by condition, completeness of credits, and general interest. Artists frequently represented include Don Freeman, Al Hirschfeld, Tom Morrow, and Marcel Vertès. Other contributors include Peter Arno, Cecil

Beaton, Jack Davis, Jules Feiffer, William Steig, Alberto Vargas, and Miles White. The majority of the photographs come from the studios of Friedman-Abeles (Leo Friedman and Joseph Abeles) and Florence Vandamm, with others by George Karger, Fred Fehl, Eileen Darby, and Richard Avedon. The illustrations we have used—many of them exceedingly rare and unseen for decades— are dedicated to those of us who on Sunday mornings do *not* first grab for the sports pages or comics, but eagerly turn to the amusement section for that first glance at the announcement ads for the new shows. (Sometimes the ads prove more amusing than the show, alas.) It's my hope that these illustrations include many exciting "new" musicals for you to muse over!

The Broadway Scorecard

The quoted excerpts usually reflect the individual critic's overall opinion of the show in question. But what was the consensus of the six-to-nine opening night reviews? Were they in agreement, or sharply divided as to a show's merits (or flaws)? And how did their opinion ultimately affect the box office? The Broadway Scorecard offers a capsulized summary of each show's critical and commercial reception. The reviews fall into five categories:

RAVE: A rave is a rave is a rave, no question about it. The critic is saying, simply and strongly, *go!* Sometimes there's a little incidental carping, but the critic's overall enthusiasm is clear—and sometimes hysterical.

FAVORABLE: The very fact that a good review is not a rave is a qualification. Favorable reviews usually indicate one of two things. The show might be good, pleasant, entertaining, well-crafted, intelligent—but it's simply not earthshaking. Other favorable reviews tell us that the show is not so good but more than redeemed by a performance or two, or the dances, or even the sets. The critic is clearly recommending that you attend, you should like it. Probably.

MIXED: Some elements of the show work, others don't. The critic doesn't exactly tell you to buy a ticket, but he refrains from advising against it. Constructive critics sometimes rewarded adventurous failures with mixed reviews, suggesting you'll want to see it if you're really interested in musical theatre (but go quickly). Mixed reviews also occur when the critic likes a show he thinks his readers won't. Other mixed reviews are simply inconclusive or poorly written; you can't tell whether the critic liked it or not.

UNFAVORABLE: The polite category for shows that aren't good enough or just don't work. The review might be matter-of-fact or regretful, but the conclusion is always the same: don't bother to go. A favorable review might say that the brilliant so-and-so makes mediocre material shine; an unfavorable review says that even the brilliant so-and-so can't make up for the mediocre material.

PAN: There are shows that don't work, and then there are shows that can't—and shouldn't—work. It's not merely that the critic didn't enjoy the show; there's a distinct tone of annoyance. Pans are the most entertaining reviews to read and the easiest to write: since the perpetrators are unquestionably guilty, no holds are barred. Respectable failures usually get unfavorable reviews, as the critics tend to give the creators the benefit of a doubt—unless they *really* don't deserve it.

This scoring system is not perfect, as two people reading the same review will not necessarily agree on the critic's opinion, but it gives us an idea. There can be little question about a show which received unanimous reviews, good, bad, or indifferent. If the ratings range across the scoreboard, though, things, are not so clear-cut.

The show's financial success or failure is indicated by the "$" entry which tells whether it ultimately made money (" + ") or lost money (" − "). As these records are not always available, I have in some cases made well-educated guesses. Financial ratings are not applicable ("NA") to limited engagements of touring shows, subscription offerings, and other special attractions.

The Theatres

The particular theatre in which a show played sometimes had a definite (if subtle) influence on the results. This had to do not only with the physical layout and condition of the house, but with past experiences there.

Tenants of the Ziegfeld, for example, were often compared to the Great Glorifier's own shows; an extra air of excitement was reflected in reviews of *Gentlemen Prefer Blondes* (1949), with the critics opining that Ziegfeld himself would have been proud. The St. James was a house of hits from 1943 to 1970, with three blockbusters—*Oklahoma!* (1943) *The King and I* (1951), and *Hello,*

Dolly! (1964)—accounting for more than fifteen years. Certain the-atres had a special aura: the Alvin, home of great Gershwin and Porter musicals from its opening attraction *Funny Face* (1927) through *Red, Hot, and Blue!* (1936); the Imperial, with Merman's *Annie Get Your Gun* (1946), *Call Me Madam* (1950), and the trans-fer of *Gypsy* (1959); and the Winter Garden, home of Al Jolson, J.J. Shubert's annual *Passing Shows*, and—as we were reminded on extremely dismal occasions—the former site of the American Horse Exchange. The lowly Adelphi, meanwhile, was a "dump of dumps" (per leading man Billy Gaxton). Home to no-chance offerings which couldn't get better bookings—usually with good reason—the crit-ics went prepared for turkey. When crossed up with a *good* Adel-phi show like *On the Town* (1944), the sheer surprise added an extra exhilaration to their raves. *On the Town*, not surprisingly, transferred to 44th Street as quickly as possible.

Several theatres which housed shows discussed in this book have been demolished, while others have undergone name changes. In order to avoid confusion, departed and/or renamed theatres are identified below. An immensely helpful map of Broadway theatres, circa 1932, can be found on the endpapers of this volume.

The **Adelphi** was located at 152 West 54th St., between 6th and 7th Avenues on the south side of the street. Originally the **Craig**, it was also called the **54th Street** and the **George Abbott**. It was demol-ished in 1970.

The **Alvin**, built by the Gershwins' producers Al(ex) Aarons and Vin(ton) Freedley, is the present **Neil Simon**.

The **ANTA** (American National Theatre & Academy), originally the **Guild** (built by the Theatre Guild), is the present **Virginia**.

The **Bijou** was located at 209 West 45th Street, sandwiched be-tween the (Oliver) **Morosco** (across from Shubert Alley) and the **Astor** (on the corner of Broadway). These three theatres—along with their back-to-back neighbors the **Fulton/Helen Hayes** and the **Gaiety/Victoria**—were demolished in 1982 despite vehement pro-tests from members of the theatrical community.

The **Century** was located at 932 7th Avenue, between 58th and 59th Streets on the west side of the street. Originally **Jolson's 59th**

Street Theatre (built by the Shuberts for their number one star), it was also called the **Venice** and the **New Century**. It was demolished in 1962.

The **Coronet**, originally the (Edwin) **Forrest**, is the present **Eugene O'Neill**.

The **44th Street** was located at 216 West 44th Street, between Broadway and 8th Avenues on the south side of the street (next to the Sardi Building). Originally **Weber & Fields' New Music Hall**, it was demolished in 1945.

The **46th Street** is the present **Richard Rodgers**.

Henry Miller's Theatre (at 124 West 43rd Street) is presently a disco.

The **International** was located at 5 Columbus Circle, a site which presently serves as a plaza immediately in front of the New York Coliseum. Originally the old **Majestic**, it was also called the **Cosmopolitan**. It was demolished in 1954.

The (Richard) **Mansfield** is the present **Brooks Atkinson**. (Poor Richard Mansfield! The **Lyric**, which the Shuberts built in 1903 as a showplace for their first "legit" star, has been a 42nd Street grind house for sixty years, and the theatre built to honor his memory was renamed for a drama critic!)

The **National**, which was also called the **Billy Rose**, is the present **Nederlander**.

The **Phoenix**, originally the **Yiddish Art Theatre** and most recently called the **Second Avenue Theatre,** is at this writing being converted into a movie house.

The (Florenz) **Ziegfeld** was on the northwest corner of 6th Avenue and 54th Street. It was demolished in 1967.

THE MUSICALS
OF THE
GOLDEN ERA

ALIVE AND KICKING

a musical revue, with music by Hal Bourne, Sammy Fain, Hoagy Carmichael, and others; lyrics mostly by Paul Francis Webster and Ray Golden; "special" music and lyrics by Harold Rome; sketches by Ray Golden, I.A.L. Diamond, Henry Morgan, Jerome Chodorov, Joseph Stein and Will Glickman, Michael Stuart [Stewart], and others; sketches edited by William R. Katzell

directed by Robert H. Gordon; choreographed by Jack Cole
produced by William R. Katzell and Ray Golden
with "Jack Cole and his dancers" (Marie Groscup and Gwen Verdon), David Burns, Lenore Lonergan, Jack Gilford, and Carl Reiner

opened January 17, 1950   Winter Garden Theatre

BROOKS ATKINSON, *Times*

Not only are Jack Cole and his dancers fascinating people, but he is an authentic artist. Fortunately for him and for us, Raoul Pène du Bois has designed the settings and the costumes, and he is an artist, too. He is economical with wood and canvas, but he is rich in color and painting; and the decor of *Alive and Kicking* is the most distinguished of this season. Mr. Cole has happily designed the choreography with no relation to anything else in the show. Every step and number in it is bizarre and graphic. Ever since he first turned up in Broadway showshops, Mr. Cole has never strayed very far from the primitive. It is either Harlem or Africa that is always beating the strange rhythms for his ballets. There are four numbers in his smoldering portfolio, and Gwen Verdon and Marie

"This musical revue has something for everybody ... Side-splitting sketches ... Impressive dancing ... Good music."
—Philadelphia Evening Bulletin

WILLIAM R. KATZELL
and RAY GOLDEN

present

The
New
Musical

Alive and Kicking

"Critics hailed
Lenore Lonergan
as new star"
—WALTER WINCHELL

with

DAVID BURNS · LENORE LONERGAN
JACK GILFORD · CARL REINER
JACK COLE and his dancers
AND A COMPANY OF 40

Songs and Sketches by
PAUL FRANCIS WEBSTER RAY GOLDEN HAL BORNE IRMA JURIST SAMMY FAIN
HAROLD ROME HENRY MORGAN JOSEPH STEIN JEROME CHODOROV
WILL GLICKMAN SONNY BURKE LEONARD GERSHE I. A. L. DIAMOND
Choreography by JACK COLE
Settings & Costumes by RAOUL PENE DU BOIS   Musical Director LEHMAN ENGEL
Production Edited by MR. KATZELL
Production Directed by ROBERT H. GORDON

HERSHEY COMMUNITY THEATRE
5 DAYS ONLY, BEG. TUESDAY EVENING, JANUARY 10
MATINEE SATURDAY

One of Jack Cole's dancers is Alive and Kicking *so high that she loses her shoe. The model seems to be Gwen Verdon; the back of the herald, in fact has Broadway's earliest photo of the star-to-be—captioned "Jack Cole and Dancer." Pre-Broadway credits.* (drawing by Stahlhut)

34

Groscup appear in them with him. Mr. Cole is a superb dancer. He is like a macabre manikin out of a decadent show-window, with sharp features, spectral eyes and a bullet head. When he dances he is all unearthly fire and flickering motion—his fingers dancing as wildly as his feet. Anyone who wants to become invisible is advised to appear on the stage with Jack Cole. For it is difficult to notice anyone else when he is dancing. There could hardly be a more unlikely setting for his magnificent ballets than this stale and un-talented revue.

JOHN CHAPMAN, *Daily News*

In the company are Jack Cole and Gwen Verdon, very interest-ing dancers; David Burns, a comedian who can make practically anything seem funny; Lenore Lonergan, who sounds as though she studied singing under Bill Klem, the baseball umpire; and a young fellow named Bobby Van who behaves like an upcoming Ray Bolger.

ROBERT COLEMAN, *Daily Mirror*

It isn't sufficiently alive nor original nor clever to be kicking around for long. It is amazing that Raoul Pène du Bois, who has done some of the smartest settings and costumes of our time, should have designed such a cheap and shoddy production as this. The choreography by Jack Cole also leaves something to be de-sired.

ROBERT GARLAND, *Journal-American*

When *Alive and Kicking* gets rough to follow, you can pass the time by counting the names that have gone into its making. Unless programs are mistaken, these add up to twenty-three. Take the songs, of which there are fourteen. These are credited to five "lyric and music" writers, four "additional lyric and music" writers, and one "special lyric and music" writer. Then there are seven sketch concocters, exclusive of those group-listed as "and others."

RICHARD WATTS JR., *Post*

There is an almost constant waste of talent. Jack Gilford, a good comedian, has no chance whatever. Carl Reiner, a newcomer to me, gave indications of comic skill but he, too, had no opportunity.

☆

Alive and Kicking contained an impressive array of undiscovered talent—including Jack Cole's "invisible" dance partner and assistant choreographer, Gwen Verdon. Strangely enough, a remarkably similar and similarly negligible revue (*Dance Me a Song*) opened just three days later. Hidden away in that one was a small-time husband and wife dance team, Fosse & Niles.

A Donaldson Award was won by Jack Cole (choreographer).

```
○○○○○○○○○○○○○○○○○○○○○○○○○○○○○○○○○○○○○○○○○○○○
○                                                              ○
○        BROADWAY SCORECARD / perfs: 46 / $: −                ○
○                                                              ○
○     rave    favorable    mixed    unfavorable    pan        ○
○                                                              ○
○              1           2            2           2         ○
○                                                              ○
○○○○○○○○○○○○○○○○○○○○○○○○○○○○○○○○○○○○○○○○○○○○○○
```

ALL AMERICAN

a musical satire, with music by Charles Strouse; lyrics by Lee Adams; book by Mel Brooks, from the 1950 novel *Professor Fodorski* by Robert Lewis Taylor

directed by Joshua Logan; choreographed by Danny Daniels
produced by Edward Padula in association with L. Slade Brown
with Ray Bolger, Eileen Herlie, Ron Husmann, Anita Gillette, and Fritz Weaver

opened March 19, 1962   Winter Garden Theatre

JOHN CHAPMAN, *Daily News*

There are many impish and surprising moments in this jolly story—as when the ad genius is shooting pictures of Whistler's mother holding a giant bottle of whisky. . . . One of the dances depicting a football game, staged by a newcomer, Danny Daniels, is an incredibly expert roughhouse. The male chorus must be unique in Broadway history, for it consists of roughnecks, acrobats, and strong men, most of them ugly.

WALTER KERR, *Herald Tribune*

The last time Ray Bolger was on Broadway he took a charming little song called "Once in Love with Amy" [in *Where's Charley?* (1948)] and he danced around it, and he sang around it, and he clowned around it until they had to chase the customers out of the theatre in order to get it ready for the next day's matinee. Lord, you thought he'd never stop. And he shouldn't have. For the new show they've given him is the kind in which Mr. Bolger is never fascinating until he stands right up and tells you he is. The announcement comes very late in "I'm Fascinating," and its very first bars give this animated question-mark of a performer his very first opportunity to lift his lofty eyebrows, tilt his nose in high hauteur, and do a tap dance that is full of disdain. Now he is on top of things, prim, imperious, and ready to stamp out the plebeian world that barely exists beneath his feet. In great double-spins he gallops about the stage, one leg flying to the right while the other wonders whether or not to follow it (and decides no). The floor itself hesitates, and begins to go in the opposite direction, just as he touches it in unexpected descent. His whole improbable frame staggers, threatens to wilt, and then, in the near-nick of time, a graceful second leg comes up from under—easy as satin and thoroughly proud of itself—to rescue everything.

HOWARD TAUBMAN, *Times*

With a stageful of choice targets in sight, *All American* has managed the amazing feat of hitting none. The principal trouble with the marksmanship of the new musical is that it can't make up its mind what it's shooting at. It is not sure whether it means to be sentimental, satirical or simply rowdy, and it ends by being dreary. What a lot of ideas and talent are involved in *All American*. Consider the topics it deals with: America as the land of opportunity, immigrants, football, education, Madison Avenue techniques, self-adulation, a man on the make, love, and sin. By seeking to touch on all, the new musical fails to deal satisfyingly with any.

With the success of the refreshing *Bye Bye Birdie* (1960), David Merrick swooped in and hired away half the creative team—Gower Champion and Michael Stewart—for *Carnival* (1961). The remainder of the *Birdie* boys attempted a second satirical musical, with Joshua Logan and Mel Brooks trying to fill in the gaps. But the unfocused and frenetic *All American* quickly fizzled. Musing on his musical comedy misadventures, Mel Brooks wondered what would happen if someone actually tried to produce an *intentionally* awful musical. The result: the movie *The Producers* (1968), with its mini-musical *Springtime for Hitler*.

```
○○○○○○○○○○○○○○○○○○○○○○○○○○○○○○○○○○○○○○○○○○○○○
○                                                   ○
○        BROADWAY SCORECARD / perfs: 80 / $: −       ○
○                                                   ○
○     rave    favorable    mixed    unfavorable    pan    ○
○                                                   ○
○       1         1          2          1          2      ○
○                                                   ○
○○○○○○○○○○○○○○○○○○○○○○○○○○○○○○○○○○○○○○○○○○○○○○
```

ALL FOR LOVE

a musical revue, with music and lyrics by Allan Roberts and Lester Lee; sketches edited by Max Shulman

directed by Edward Reveaux; choreographed by Eric Victor
produced by Sammy Lambert and Anthony B. Farrell
with Grace and Paul Hartman, and Bert Wheeler

opened January 22, 1949   Mark Hellinger Theatre

JOHN CHAPMAN, *Daily News*

The hero of *All for Love* is Anthony B. Farrell, a showstruck gent from the State Capitol who made his debut as producer of *Hold It!* last May and since then has had more publicity than Olivia De Havilland. He has spent generously and cheerfully. He bought the Warners' Broadway movie theatre, which is a comfortable big place, redecorated it at great cost, and renamed it in memory of Mark Hellinger, who was everybody's great friend. Like everybody else, I have welcomed Mr. Farrell to the producing ranks, for anybody with money and enthusiasm should be coddled in any business. But, after witnessing *All for Love*, I have a feeling that we have been taking Mr. Farrell for a ride. A showman can make money—but money cannot make a showman. The making of a showman requires taste in judgment based on experience; so let's put *All for Love* down as experience for Mr. Farrell—and hope that his enthusiasm and his money hold out.

ROBERT GARLAND, *Journal-American*

After last season's hapless *Hold It!*, Angel-in-the-Open Anthony Farrell should have called his new one "Drop It" and followed the advice of its rightful title. *All for Love*, "Drop It," "Farrell's Folly," or whatever you choose to call the handsome mishap at the Mark Hellinger, proves that an ardent amateur is no better for the theatre than a slack professional. . . . Max Shulman has telegraphed to deny [his billing].

JOHN LARDNER, *Star*

The producer, and owner of the theatre, Anthony B. Farrell, is described by Broadway handicappers as a man looking for ways and means to lose two-and-a-half million bucks. Perhaps *All for Love* is not the quickest short cut, the northwest passage to that goal, but it does offer certain valuable hints for the next free spender who comes along. If I wanted to liquidate my millions, God forbid, I would borrow Mr. Farrell's general principle, and his sketchwriters and song-writers, too. Possibly Mr. Farrell got what he was after in *All for Love*, but personally I would just as soon see a patrol of the Boy Scouts of America in a good, brisk exhibition of building a fire without matches.

WARD MOREHOUSE, *Sun*

Anthony B. Farrell, that amiable man of inexhaustible and unresisting millions, has beautified a big Broadway theatre [the Hollywood, a movie palace] and has given it a new name, and on Saturday evening he opened it with a revue as tasteless and witless as anything the New York stage has had during the past half-century. *All for Love* is a production of unlimited expenditure, overpowering ineptitude, and unfathomable dullness. Tony Farrell could have given us a season of Shaw, plus a bit of Wilde and a dash of Pinero, for probably half of what *All for Love* has cost. Another Albany fortune has been spent on nothing at all.

RICHARD WATTS JR., *Post*

All for Love is, indeed, a calamity of epic proportions. Under the blight of dullness, tastelessness, and overpowering lack of good sense, reason totters as one contemplates the waste of money, the wreck of talent, the absence of humor and imagination, and the tedious vulgarity involved in the proceedings. It was suggested to me after the opening that we reviewers would be less widely regarded as ogres if we were kind to pathetic offerings like the monstrosity at the Mark Hellinger and tried to let them down easily. All

I can say is that if any critic ever, through misplaced kindness of heart, led a prospective playgoer to pay money to see *All for Love* he would be committing a sin against the entire theatre.

The comment by Richard Watts on vicious reviews for vicious revues is particularly apt. While on rare occasions a critic might perhaps seem just a wee tiny bit vindictive, certain professionally mounted entertainments demand protection for the unwary ticket buyer, even today. Meanwhile, the lavishly appointed *All for Love* was the first Broadway show to lose more than half a million dollars. Which in those days was a lot of money.

BROADWAY SCORECARD / perfs: 121 / $: —

rave	favorable	mixed	unfavorable	pan
			2	7

ALLAH BE PRAISED!

a musical comedy, with music by Don Walker and Baldwin Bergersen; book and lyrics by George Marion, Jr.

directed by Robert H. Gordon and Jack Small; choreographed by Jack Cole
produced by Alfred Bloomingdale
with Patricia Morison, John Hoysradt, Mary Jane Walsh, Joey Faye, and Milada Mladova

opened April 20, 1944   Adelphi Theatre

JOHN CHAPMAN, *Daily News*

The plot can be completely outlined in four words—"Let's go to Persia." Somebody says that in the prologue, so—whoosh, with the speed of a stagehand we go to Persia, and, of course, we land in a harem, where all the girls have bare bellies and bouncing bottoms. Little Joey Faye, a good burlesque comedian, works manfully with too little to do. Working with him is Jayne Manners, who is prob-

Allah Be Praised!, *but for what?* (drawing by Vertès)

ably the most beautiful tall girl in the world or the tallest beautiful girl, I forget which. Every time she swishes a bare thigh at Mr. Faye I bet Alexander Calder's mobiles quiver over at the Museum of Modern Art [a block away].

LOUIS KRONENBERGER, *PM*

Allah be praised, if you like, but just what for it would not be easy to say.

WARD MOREHOUSE, *Sun*

If you're interested in the so-called story the numbers are strung to, it's something about a land-lease harem in Persia after the war, all optimistically taking place in 1948. The plot seems to center around a lady United States Senator, two brothers, one of them also a Senator, and the latters' sister, who is bent on becoming a member of the harem. There are also a couple of stooges named Sludge and McSlump. Now you go on from there.

Producer Bloomingdale asked play doctor Cy Howard what he should do with the show. "Throw it away," came the response, "and keep the store open nights." This is the same Bloomingdale who later became a prominent Reaganite (with a front-page palimony scandal following his death).

```
BROADWAY SCORECARD / perfs: 20 / $ —

rave    favorable    mixed    unfavorable    pan

                                              8
```

ALLEGRO

a musical play, with music by Richard Rodgers; book and lyrics by Oscar Hammerstein 2nd

directed and choreographed by Agnes de Mille
produced by the Theatre Guild

with John Battles, Roberta Jonay, Annamary Dickey, John Conte, and Lisa Kirk

opened October 10, 1947   Majestic Theatre

BROOKS ATKINSON, *Times*

Having carried song-writing to its logical conclusion, Richard Rodgers and Oscar Hammerstein 2nd have gone one step further. They have composed a musical play without any of the conventions of form. For at least half its length it is a work of great beauty and purity, as if *Our Town* [1938] could be written with music. Abandoning the routine of musical comedy choruses, *Allegro* returns the chorus to its original function as comment and interpretation. All the elements of theatre are so perfectly blended that the music and the ballet are interwoven into one singing pattern of narrative; and here *Allegro* is torn out of the folk life of America. . . . *Allegro* has made history on Broadway. Before the mood breaks after the first act it is full of a kind of unexploited glory. If this review sounds ungratefully reluctant it is because Mr. Rodgers and Mr. Hammerstein have just missed the final splendor of a perfect work of art.

ROBERT COLEMAN, *Daily Mirror*

Perfection is a thrilling thing, be it a Sid Luckman forward pass, a Ken Strong place kick, a Joe DiMaggio catch of an outfield drive, a Cushing brain operation, a Rembrandt painting, a Whistler etching, a Markova–Dolin *Giselle*, or *Allegro*, the great new musical by Richard Rodgers and Oscar Hammerstein. Perfection and great are not words to be lightly used. They have become commonplace through misuse. But *Allegro* is perfection, great. It is a stunning blend of beauty, integrity, intelligence, imagination, taste, and skill. It races the pulses and puts lumps in the throat. But for its utmost enjoyment, the patron out front must respond with mind and heart.

ROBERT GARLAND, *Journal-American*

To the Messrs. Funk and Wagnalls, publishers of *The Standard Dictionary*, "allegro" means "brisk," "lively," and even downright "gay." But to the Messrs. Rodgers and Hammerstein the word means nothing of the kind. They seem to have confused "allegro" with, say, "lento." Last night, their *Allegro* went its slow, unhur-

"Direct from 1 Year on Broadway" something of an exaggeration, as **Allegro** *barely made it through nine months. The national tour closed after only four. The artwork is symptomatic of the show itself: everyone dances, but what's the point?* (drawing by Don Freeman)

ried way, telling, with the aid of moving platforms, traveling curtains, lantern slides, Greek choruses, loud speakers, a huge
company of actors, singers and dancers, and a symphony orchestra,
a simple run-of-the-U.S.A. biography. Too little has been spared to
make *Allegro* a production milestone in the American showshop.
The could-be heartening narrative of a small town medico who goes
to the big town and sees the error of his ways is all but lost in the
contrivance of its projection. Don't get me wrong. *Allegro* is bigger
and better than anything the Messrs. Rodgers and Hammerstein
have written. But I do wish it had more consistently lived up to its
title.

WILLIAM HAWKINS, *World-Telegram*

A vast disappointment. The early conception of the work has a
worthy beauty, but its realization crosses the stage like an impoverished sophomore class production. It lacks consistency of mood,
visual excitement, and theatrical stimulation. The progress of the
show sees the original conception blotted out by unimaginative
tricks. In the end it seems like the creation of a pretentious passé
costumer who has nothing but cambric to work with.

LOUIS KRONENBERGER, *PM*

Allegro, I'm afraid I must say right off, is a very grave disappointment. I'm afraid, in fact, that it can be called an out-right
failure. It's not rough edges, or bold strokes that don't come off,
which damage *Allegro*. On the contrary, the one thing this Rodgers
and Hammerstein experiment clearly has is completely professional smoothness. What it hasn't got is any real quality; what it
hasn't got is any real lure. *Allegro* doesn't know the difference
between the simple and the over-weighted; it doesn't know the
difference between the simple and the obvious. Sometimes rouged
with satire, sometimes rosy with song, a hundred clichés of American thinking and emotion marched by in procession, on a very
vast, very unhomey, very trick-lighted stage [sets and lighting by
Jo Mielziner]. Had the cliches merely sauntered by, no bigger than
life, you might have forgotten their age and focussed on their
truthfulness. As it was, they left you quite unmoved; they left you
downright bored. And that's the really strange thing about
Allegro—not that it lacks depth, but that it lacks showmanship; not
that it's bad but that it's boring.

RICHARD WATTS JR., *Post*

Allegro has been the cause of so much speculation and prediction, with everything about it discussed, from the expensiveness of its production to the ambitiousness of its intentions, that the skeptical doubted if it could live up to it all. Now that it has opened with fanfare and flourishes, it can be reported that it has overcome the handicap of its premature fame and is revealed as a distinguished musical play, beautiful, imaginative, original, and honestly moving. I have certain reservations about it, but there is no disputing the fact that it is a notable achievement in its field and another landmark in pushing back the frontier of the American music drama. . . . It sticks to what it has to say with straightforwardness and integrity. Although Mr. Rodgers's music, Mr. Hammerstein's lyrics, and Miss de Mille's ballets are splendid, they are always more concerned with keeping to the mood of the narrative rather than with being flashy or sensational on their own account.

The innovative new musical was from the authors of *Oklahoma!* (1943) and *Carousel* (1945) and the choreographer of those hits as well as *Bloomer Girl* (1944) and *Brigadoon* (1947). Not unnaturally, *Allegro* generated more advance excitement than any show of the decade. Not unnaturally, it was a serious disappointment. Hammerstein tried to come up with a provocative statement on the corruptions of society; what came across was stodgy and bordering on the pretentious. (Hammerstein's 17-year-old protégé, Stephen Sondheim, later tried his own treatment of the theme, running into more pretension and less success with *Merrily We Roll Along* [1981].) Certainly, a Mamoulian or Logan at the helm would have helped clarify matters. De Mille never made it as a director. Her two future attempts, *Out of this World* (1950) and *Come Summer* (1969), were even more muddled. De Mille had already peaked with *Brigadoon*; only two of her future shows—*Gentlemen Prefer Blondes* (1949) and *110 in the Shade* (1963)—were successful, and in these her work was relatively incidental. Post-War audiences clearly favored the more contemporary style of newcomers Robbins and Kidd. As for *Allegro*, the insurmountable problem was quite simple: the songs weren't good enough.

Donaldson Awards were won by Richard Rodgers (composer) and
Oscar Hammerstein 2nd (lyricist; librettist).

```
BROADWAY SCORECARD / perfs: 315 / $: −

 rave     favorable    mixed    unfavorable    pan

   4          1                      2            2
```

ALONG FIFTH AVENUE

a musical revue, with music mostly by Gordon Jenkins; lyrics
mostly by Tom Adair; sketches by Charles Sherman and Nat Hiken

director unbilled (Charles Friedman, replaced by Robert H. Gordon); choreographed by Robert Sidney
produced by Arthur Lesser
with Nancy Walker, Jackie Gleason (replacing Willie Howard),
Hank Ladd, and Carol Bruce

opened January 13, 1949   Broadhurst Theatre

BROOKS ATKINSON, *Times*

Jackie Gleason, serving as second buffoon, will starve to death if
his diet ever gets much leaner [down to 175 pounds, from 266].
Mr. Gleason is a cheerful wag with laughing eyes and a droll map.
He knows how to inhabit burlesque costumes. He can also move—
which is a priceless accomplishment in a man who wants to be
funny on the stage. But there seems to be no place *Along Fifth
Avenue* where he can let go with the slapstick properly and entertain the customers royally.

HOWARD BARNES, *Herald Tribune*

There may have been a director of the production, but he has
failed to claim credit. That is understandable.

JOHN LARDNER, *Star*

Along Fifth Avenue possesses one asset. which has grown in
value, to my way of thinking, with each succeeding year, namely
the services of Nancy Walker. The lady may not be ready yet for

the mantle of Fanny Brice but she is closing in on it. In the new revue she is better than she was in *Best Foot Forward* (1941), *On the Town* (1944), and *Look, Ma, I'm Dancin'* (1948), and she was pretty good in all of those. Her comedy is easier and more natural now than it used to be. Her control is improving. She no longer depends as much as she did on noise, mannerisms, and a high, wide fast ball. . . . The great Willie Howard, who died last week [January 12, 1949], was to have headed the male side of the cast. He would have been of immense value to the production, as Jackie Gleason and Hank Ladd, struggling with mediocre prose and rhyme, prove clearly in a roundabout kind of way.

A Donaldson Award was won by Viola Essen (female dancer).

BROADWAY SCORECARD / perfs: 180 / $: −				
rave	favorable	mixed	unfavorable	pan
1	4		3	1

ANGEL IN THE WINGS

an intimate revue, with music and lyrics by Carl Sigman and Bob Hilliard; sketches by Hank Ladd, Ted Luce, and Paul and Grace Hartman

directed by John Kennedy; choreographed by Edward Noll
produced by Marjorie and Sherman Ewing
with Paul and Grace Hartman, Hank Ladd, Eileen Barton, and Elaine Stritch

opened December 11, 1947   Coronet Theatre

BROOKS ATKINSON, *Times*

For years the Hartmans have been making serious dancing totally unnecessary in this town with their inspired parodies. They offer two in *Angel in the Wings*, one of which presents them as dauntless explorers interpreting a native dance to a ladies' garden club. It is a devastatingly humorous satire on lecture platform explorers, native dancing, garden clubs and just about anything else you can think of. For the whole world looks pretty giddy when the Hartmans start performing. Paul has one of the most peculiar faces in show business. No one can look quite so dazed; no one can be so desperately puzzled. In his fleeting rhapsodic moods, he does not look much better, to tell the truth. Somehow his teeth seem to be dropping through, for there is a kind of hang-dog quality to his rapture. Grace is the wholesome and intelligent member of the team, with a pleasant smile, a spirit of decision and a giggle. Teamed up with an ambling dope, she is the one who makes things work. Those are the characters they play. But there is an instinctive modesty about the Hartmans that make their humor not only hilarious but disarming and captivating. They are a royal pair of entertainers, and *Angel in the Wings* is a capital show.

JOHN CHAPMAN, *Daily News*

In the case of most revues which are called intimate, the word intimate means no dough. Often it means no fun, either. In the case of *Angel in the Wings*, the word means just what it says. The show is a cozy affair, and because it has Paul and Grace Hartman and Hank Ladd in it it is funny, too. Very funny, in fact. . . . Mr. Ladd, pretending that he is the angel of the show, introduces the numbers. He describes a typical Tennessee Williams heroine as a girl who is disappointed because she has two ears.

RICHARD WATTS JR., *Post*

Elaine Stritch, an energetic girl, tries a parody of Hildegarde, and I submit that it is not possible to do a parody of Hildegarde. No matter how malicious the intended impersonation may be, it cannot be as incredible as the original, and, fiercely as Miss Stritch worked, she couldn't be expected to be up to it. Among the features of the show is a song called "Civilization," which is already among the big hits of the day. Strenuously sung by the aforementioned Miss Stritch, it is a lively and enjoyable number, but my favorite musical item of the evening is one in which Mr. Ladd tells about losing his girl in the Thousand Islands and not remembering which island ["The Thousand Island Song"].

☆

A summer-stock package (formerly titled *Heaven Help the Angels*), *Angel in the Wings* came as a surprise hit—and the Hartmans walked off with the first Tony Awards for Best Actress and Best Actor in a musical. They are the only husband-and-wife performers to win for a joint appearance, and—under present-day conditions— likely to remain so.

Tony Awards were won by Grace Hartman (actress) and Paul Hartman (actor). A Donaldson Award was won by Paul Hartman (actor).

BROADWAY SCORECARD / perfs: 308 / $: +

rave	favorable	mixed	unfavorable	pan
3	5	1		

ANKLES AWEIGH

a musical comedy, with music by Sammy Fain; lyrics by Dan Shapiro; book by Guy Bolton and Eddie Davis

directed by Fred F. Finklehoffe; choreographed by Tony Charmoli
produced by Howard Hoyt, Reginald Hammerstein, and Fred F. Finklehoffe (replaced by Anthony B. Farrell)
with Betty Kean, Jane Kean, Lew Parker (replacing Myron Mc-Cormick), Mark Dawson (replacing Sonny Tufts), Gabriel Dell, and Mike Kellin

opened April 18, 1955   Mark Hellinger Theatre

BROOKS ATKINSON, *Times*

Imagine that nothing interesting has developed in the field of musical comedy for the last ten or fifteen years. There you have *Ankles Aweigh*. It leaves off where modern musical comedy began, before the cold war started chilling the world. To many playgoers that appears to be a good thing. But these comments are written by one of the silent travelers who could see nothing in *Ankles Aweigh* except the wornout staples of show business that presumably were laid away in the storehouse a long time ago. Sammy Fain has

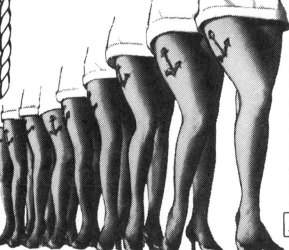

ANTHONY B. FARRELL
presents

THE NEW MUSICAL COMEDY

ANKLES AWEIGH

STARRING

BETTY AND JANE KEAN

with

**LEW   MARK
PARKER   DAWSON**

and

GABRIEL DELL   THELMA CARPENTER
MIKE KELLIN   MARILYNN BRADLEY

Book by GUY BOLTON and EDDIE DAVIS

Music by SAMMY FAIN

Lyrics by DAN SHAPIRO

Choreography by TONY CHARMOLI

Scenery & Lighting by GEORGE JENKINS

Costumes by MILES WHITE

Vocal & Orchestral Arrangements by DON WALKER

Musical Director, ROBERT STANLEY

Dance Music Devised by ROGER ADAMS

Staged by FRED F. FINKLEHOFFE

MARK HELLINGER THEATRE

51st STREET WEST OF BROADWAY

MATINEES WEDNESDAYS and SATURDAYS

Ankles Aweigh, *to say nothing of thighs.*

written a score destitute of originality, and Don Walker has scored it by feeding the melodies into a Univac machine. Dan Shapiro's lyrics are equally mechanical. Everyone sings every line in full voice with deafening bravado. Foolish jokes come hurtling across the footlights like dum-dum bullets. As things go on Broadway, it is difficult to find a show that contains no talent. But *Ankles Aweigh* has a certain fascination in that respect. Betty and Jane Kean, described in the program as "the funniest women in show business," are hackneyed performers with the mannerisms of small-time vaudeville. . . . It is merely a succession of show-shop cliches. It is *Kismet* (1953) without music borrowed from Borodin.

WILLIAM HAWKINS, *World-Telegram & Sun*

Miles White has dressed the show so it looks as if every girl in it had the choice of her lifetime dress to wear.

WALTER KERR, *Herald Tribune*

Some of us have been campaigning lately for a return to the old-fashioned, slam-bang, gags-and-girls musical comedy. Some of us ought to be shot. . . . A line of absolutely dazzling show girls stalks out, hesitates for inspection, and stalks off. You pick a couple out to notice again, the next time around. You remember that this once was fun. The dancers on stage begin to grab their toes and spin meaninglessly—the boys at this moment are dressed in pink, purple, and chartreuse trousers, white jackets, and polka-dot scarves—and you guess it might be amusing to have the dances non-integrated for a change. The singers in the front line drop to their knees at the footlights, wave their arms wildly, and roar so vociferously that you can't tell what the lyrics are—let alone whether they are good or bad. A pony parade in sailor caps and baggy blouses prances from the wings, precision-style. Everything brings back memories of an irresponsible, irrepressible, gay-as-all-get-out time. But before you can say "Lollobrigida"—someone does say "Lollobrigida" and some one else says "Lollobrigida is falling down"—a chill wind begins to blow through the Piazza.

RICHARD WATTS JR., *Post*

Anyone who goes to a show with a name like that has been sufficiently warned.

☆

Third-rate musical comedy, 1950s style. Theatre-owner Anthony B. Farrell—he of *All for Love* (1949)—bought the show after the opening and kept it limping along through the summer. Comedy leads Betty Kean and Lew Parker incidentally, got married and lived happily ever after.

```
○○○○○○○○○○○○○○○○○○○○○○○○○○○○○○○○○○○○○○○○○○○○○○
○                                                      ○
○       BROADWAY SCORECARD / perfs: 176 / $: −        ○
○                                                      ○
○     rave    favorable    mixed    unfavorable    pan ○
○                                                      ○
○                            1        2            4   ○
○                                                      ○
○○○○○○○○○○○○○○○○○○○○○○○○○○○○○○○○○○○○○○○○○○○○○○○○
```

ANNIE GET YOUR GUN

a musical biography of Annie Oakley Butler (1860–1926), with music and lyrics by Irving Berlin (replacing Jerome Kern and Dorothy Fields); book by Herbert and Dorothy Fields

directed by Joshua Logan; choreographed by Helen Tamiris
produced by Richard Rodgers and Oscar Hammerstein 2nd
with Ethel Merman, Ray Middleton, Harry Bellaver, and Marty May

opened May 16, 1946   Imperial Theatre

JOHN CHAPMAN, *Daily News*

In competition with some good lyrics and tunes by Irving Berlin, with a lot of Jo Mielziner's best scenery and with the razzle-dazzle atmosphere of a big-time show, she is the champ. Ever since *Girl Crazy* (1930) it has been known that Miss Merman can wrap up a song and put it away—and it has been a long time since *Girl Crazy*. It also has been known that she can wear smart clothes with an air that makes them look smarter. Now, in *Annie Get Your Gun*, she is looking to the future. She is a better comedienne than she ever was before, with some of the earthy humor of Fanny Brice, and that is why I predict a great future for her. Singers can't last forever, but comediennes can. There is no immediate reason for worrying about her singing, either. Miss Merman can wrap 'em up and put 'em away with the zing, the punch, and the instinct for showmanship she first revealed when she came out upon the Alvin stage

Ethel, alone on the steps of the circus wagon, confesses "I Got Lost in His Arms." (costume by Lucinda Ballard, photo by Fred Fehl)

and hurled "I Got Rhythm" at all us delighted discoverers. . . . *Annie* is a good, standard, lavish, big musical and I'm sure it will be a huge success—but it isn't the greatest show in the world.

WILLIAM HAWKINS, *World-Telegram*

Ethel Merman shot a bull's eye last night with *Annie Get Your Gun*. For verve and buoyancy, unslackening, there has seldom if ever been a show like it. It would not be a bad idea to declare an annual Merman Day of all May 16ths in the future. Merman is bright as a whip, sure as her shooting, and generously the foremost lady clown of her time. . . . The girls in *Annie* have the beauty and character of looks one associates with a Rodgers and Hammerstein show. And the production has in every way the distinction that has become their hallmark.

LOUIS KRONENBERGER, *PM*

The news is cheerful, but very far from overpowering. It's a big Broadway show, in all ways professional, in many ways routine. But it has, for which its producers and patrons can alike be intensely grateful, Ethel Merman. Miss Merman is in fine form. She is in fine form as a contralto, giving to ditty after Irving Berlin ditty her celebrated sand-blast treatment. She is in fine form as a comedienne, pining (mouth ajar and eyes a-goggle) with amorousness; making her body talk and her stride talk back; raising an oak of a laugh out of an acorn of a joke. She is in fine form as a personality—tough, rowdy, gusty, outstaring, and outsnooting anybody who gets in her way. For me, *Annie* is mainly Miss Merman's show, though the rest of it is competent enough of its kind. It knows its formula, and sticks to it like a well-raised baby. If the show hasn't a trace of style, at least it hasn't a trace of artiness. It has size, a primary-colors picturesqueness, the kind of organized activity which can pass for pep. . . . Irving Berlin's score is musically not exciting—of the real songs, only one or two are tuneful. But Mr. Berlin has contrived a number of pleasant ditties and has laced them with lyrics that, if seldom witty, are almost always brisk.

WARD MOREHOUSE, *Sun*

The big news about *Annie Get Your Gun* is that it reveals Ethel Merman in her best form since *Anything Goes* (1934), and that wasn't just the other afternoon. Miss Merman, now wearing buckskin as the redoubtable sharpshooter from the Kentucky hills, is her own hearty, brassy, noisy self. She shouts the Berlin music with good effect. She often comes stridently to the aid of a sagging book. She has a great time all evening. Irving Berlin's score is not a notable one, but his tunes are singable and pleasant and his lyrics are particularly good. The book? It's on the flimsy side, definitely. And rather witless, too. But in the case of *Annie Get Your Gun* a listless story won't matter a great deal. Somehow in shows as big as this, such a fault is sometimes blithely overlooked.

LEWIS NICHOLS, *Times*

It has a pleasant score by Irving Berlin (his first since *This Is the Army* [1942]) and it has Ethel Merman to roll her eyes and to shout down the rafters. The colors are pretty, the dancing is amiable and unaffected, and Broadway by this time is well used to a book which doesn't get anywhere in particular. *Annie*, in short, is an agreeable evening on the town, and it takes little gift for prophecy to add that it, and she, will chant their saga of sharp-shooting for many months to come. If there are abrupt pauses with some frequency—well, Miss Merman must change costumes.

VERNON RICE, *Post*

Irving Berlin has outdone himself this time. No use trying to pick a hit tune, for all the tunes are hits. One is just as hummable and singable as the next. Ethel Merman is at her lusty, free and easy best. Some time ago Miss Merman jumped from a singing star to a singing comedy star, but last evening she came through as the supreme artist in the musical comedy field. No longer is she just Ethel Merman cutting capers upon the stage. She is now able to develop a consistent characterization and stay with it to the show's end. And when she opens her mouth to sing, she sings! Nice, loud, clear tones with not a word of the lyrics kept a secret for just her and those on stage to share. As if this weren't enough, Richard Rodgers and Oscar Hammerstein 2nd, who produced the musical, continued merrily on their way stuffing the production to overflowing with eye-filling and ear-filling goodness. Jo Mielziner's sets were colorful and opulent, Lucinda Ballard's costumes were as bright as morning's sun in spring, Helen Tamiris's choreography was breathtaking, and Joshua Logan directed the whole thing with the idea that a show moves some place besides out of the theatre at the end of its first week.

Rodgers and Hammerstein *and* Berlin (and Merman)? Not your typical lineup. The Fieldses, in search of an idea for their fifth Merman musical—following *Something for the Boys* (1943)—came upon the life and times of sharpshooter Annie Oakley. Their producer, Mike Todd, passed on it; he hadn't liked *Oklahoma!* (1943) either. (Todd walked out during the first act of the New Haven opening, issuing the famous pronouncement "No legs, no jokes, no chance.") The brother and sister librettists went to Rodgers and Hammerstein, who in 1944 had started producing hit shows when they weren't busy writing hit shows. Papa Lew Fields, of the turn-of-the-century comedy team Weber and Fields, had launched Rodgers and Hart on Broadway in 1919. Herb had been partnered with Rodgers and Hart for their 1920s triumphs, while sister Dorothy appeared as a teen-aged leading lady in some of their early amateur shows. Realizing that Merman as "Annie" was a sure-as-shootin' hit, the producers brought in Hammerstein's former (and Dorothy's recent) collaborator Jerome Kern—who died before starting work. Berlin was the obvious replacement choice; but egos being what they are, this was not too likely. Irving surprised everybody and agreed to do it, with Dorothy relinquishing the lyric assignment. Everything when according to plan and *Annie* was an immense hit, the second musical comedy to go over the 1,000-performance plateau. (Until *My Fair Lady* came along in 1956, the four longest-running musicals were *Oklahoma!*, *South Pacific* [1949], *The King and I* [1951], and *Annie*. All from Rodgers and Hammerstein!) While *Annie* isn't one of the greats—it's basically a not-too-well-made, old-fashioned star-vehicle—the sturdy score is certainly full of well-crafted, highly entertaining songs.

Donaldson Awards were won by Irving Berlin (composer; lyricist); Joshua Logan (director); and Ethel Merman (actress).

BROADWAY SCORECARD / perfs: 1,147 / $: +

rave	favorable	mixed	unfavorable	pan
4	4			

ANYONE CAN WHISTLE

an allegorical musical comedy, with music and lyrics by Stephen
Sondheim; book by Arthur Laurents; previously announced as *Side
Show*

directed by Arthur Laurents; choreographed by Herbert Ross
produced by Kermit Bloomgarden and Diana Krasny
with Lee Remick, Angela Lansbury, Harry Guardino, and Gabriel
Dell (replacing Henry Lascoe)

opened April 4, 1964   Majestic Theatre

JOHN CHAPMAN, *Daily News*

An unusual, far-out musical with a briskly syncopated score,
educated lyrics, original and frisky dances, waltzing scenery, and
an imaginative story which the cast and I had to cope with rather
strenuously. This book and the lack of a melody *I* could whistle
impeded my enjoyment of the last two acts, which didn't quite
fulfill the high promise of the joyously daffy first act.

WALTER KERR, *Herald Tribune*

Anyone Can Whistle is an exasperating musical comedy. It is
exasperating because it isn't very musical. Anyone can whistle, but
nobody can sing. It is exasperating because it isn't very comical. It
has trouble on its mind—the trouble the world is in, the trouble we
all are in, the trouble that comes when a librettist has nothing on
his mind. . . . Angela Lansbury [is] a creature who can toss her
head, her arms, and her shapely legs until the sparkle from her
bracelets and the sparkle from her earrings seem one and the same
sparkle. . . . Miss Remick, come back [in another musical]. *Anyone Can Whistle*, forget it.

JOHN McCLAIN, *Journal-American*

Lee Remick is utterly adorable. Angela Lansbury is incredibly
agile and engaging, and Harry Guardino is masculine and melodic
in this new musical. The William and Jean Eckart sets are inventive enough to become at times almost part of the plot, and the
choreography by Herbert Ross caused the opening night audience
frequently to cheer numbers in the midst of their execution. The
show would seem to be a sure-pop success. The score may not be

Lee Remick Angela Lansbury
Harry Guardino

IN

ARTHUR LAURENTS - STEPHEN SONDHEIM'S

Anyone can Whistle
A WILD MUSICAL

with

HENRY LASCOE

ARNOLD SOBOLOFF   JAMES FRAWLEY

Scenery designed by **WILLIAM** and **JEAN ECKART**

Costumes designed by **THEONI V. ALDREDGE**

Lighting designed by **JULES FISHER**

Vocal Arrangements and
Musical Direction by **HERBERT GREENE**

Orchestrations by **DON WALKER**

Dances and Musical
Numbers Staged by **HERBERT ROSS**

Entire Production
Staged by **ARTHUR LAURENTS**

FORREST THEATRE
PHILADELPHIA
3 Weeks Only! Mon., March 2 thru Sat., March 21
MATINEES THURSDAYS & SATURDAYS
A Theatre Guild-American Theatre Society Subscription Play under the auspices of the Council of the Living Theatre

The little bird with fedora and stogie was replaced in the final version of the artwork by a whistling redhead with a bunch of crumbling "cookies" (asylum inmates). It didn't make much difference. Pre-Broadway credits.

immediately ingratiating, but I thought the lyrics were bright and original, and there is no question about the brilliance of the choreography. *Anyone Can Whistle* should enjoy a happy life: it is fey and fantastic and I believe it will give you a happy escapist evening.

NORMAN NADEL, *World-Telegram & Sun*

Were I a less inhibited creature, I'd spend the next month hurling roses at the Majestic Theatre and at the beautiful people of *Anyone Can Whistle*. You have no idea how many breath-taking surprises are in store for you in the Arthur Laurents-Stephen Sondheim musical. At a time when even the good musicals look a little or a lot like something out of a recent season, it is exciting to encounter one so spectacularly original. . . . "The Cookie Chase" is the ballet that will be remembered most ecstatically. A set of waltz variations, it becomes the funniest and most ingenious parody on classical ballet you're likely to see. No musical can touch *Anyone Can Whistle* either in choreographic design or dance performance. Sondheim's music and lyrics deserve an entire review in themselves, and maybe when the season lets up a bit, they'll get it in this corner. His overture is shaped of intriguing, mild dissonances, with scant, pleasantly tantalizing fragments of theme started in short, irregular phrases. Then it moves quickly into the action; it's only a couple of minutes. The blending of lyrics, melody, dance rhythms and orchestral texture is remarkable; the lyrics are more clever than the spoken dialogue.

"A wild new musical" is what they called it in the ads, and it certainly was. Sondheim's score for the hit *A Funny Thing Happened on the Way to the Forum* (1962) had been severely underappreciated; *Whistle* received an even stonier reception, resulting in his absence from Broadway—as composer—for the rest of the decade. Of the critical corps, only Norman Nadel (a former symphonic trombonist) seems to have realized that here was a composer who could *write*. (Nadel had slammed *Forum*'s music.) Of all the *Whistle* people, only Angela Lansbury came out looking good. An M-G-M villainess of the 1940s, Lansbury had impressed Broadway in the farce *Hotel Paradiso* (1957) and the serious drama *A Taste of Honey* (1961). Her *Whistle* success led directly to *Mame* (1966) and more.

BROADWAY SCORECARD / perfs: 9 / $: −

rave	favorable	mixed	unfavorable	pan
2		1	3	

ARMS AND THE GIRL

a musical comedy, with music by Morton Gould; lyrics by Dorothy Fields; book by Herbert and Dorothy Fields and Rouben Mamoulian, from the 1933 comedy *The Pursuit of Happiness* by Alan Child (Lawrence Langner) and Isabelle Louden (Armina Marshall Langner)

directed by Rouben Mamoulian; choreographed by Michael Kidd produced by the Theatre Guild (Lawrence Langner and Theresa Helburn) in association with Anthony B. Farrell
with Nanette Fabray, Georges Guétary, John Conte, and Pearl Bailey
opened February 2, 1950   46th Street Theatre

JOHN CHAPMAN, *Daily News*

Nanette Fabray plays a zealous young patriot of the American Revolution in the britches, boots, and tricorn of a soldier. Miss Fabray is by all odds the liveliest of our musical comedy heroines. She is pretty, she is coquettish, and she can sing. She also can be a splendid knockabout clown, and the scene in which she captures a lover and attempts to catch a spy by luring him to her "bundling" bed is so fast and funny in its movement that it reminds me of an old Mack Sennett comedy. There is Pearl Bailey, portraying an escaped slave. Miss Bailey used to be called Virginia because that was where she was; now that she is in Ridgefield, Fairfield County, she calls herself Connecticut. At one point, under questioning, she claims she is from Pennsylvania. When asked whereabouts, she shrugs, "I dunno. Some little town up there." Every time Miss Bailey puts foot on the stage for a comedy scene or a song she takes charge of the show and picks it right up.

ROBERT COLEMAN, *Daily Mirror*

Michael Kidd, a graduate of the *Mirror*'s city room, has contrived sprightly dances.

WILLIAM HAWKINS, *World-Telegram & Sun*

You can stash *Arms and the Girl* somewhere between the bottom of the top drawer and the top of the second. It misses being real class of the ever-memorable kind because of the corrugated aspect of its fun. When it is good, it is rip-roaring musical comedy. Such as when Nanette Fabray does a Colonial strip, or Georges Guétary holds a high note like nothing heard since Friml used to get such sounds out of tenors, or when Pearl Bailey just opens her mouth. Between stuff like this and the pretty wonderful dances there are moments that just plain thud.

```
BROADWAY SCORECARD / perfs: 134 / $: —

  rave      favorable      mixed      unfavorable      pan

    1            2            2             2
```

AROUND THE WORLD (IN EIGHTY DAYS)

a musical extravaganza, with music and lyrics by Cole Porter; book by Orson Welles, from the 1873 novel by Jules Verne

directed by Orson Welles; choreographed by Nelson Barclift
produced by the Mercury Theatre (Orson Welles), presented by Orson Welles
with Arthur Margetson, Mary Healy, Julie Warren, Larry Laurence (Enzo Stuarti), and Orson Welles

opened May 31, 1946   Adelphi Theatre

JOHN CHAPMAN, *Daily News*

It is wonderful, exciting, and funny, and the most thorough and individual example of showmanship of the season—or of any season since Billy Rose put on *Jumbo* [1935] at the Hippodrome. It is not the custom to treat Mr. Welles very seriously, because he is noisy, naughty, paunchy, and opinionated—and this is a pity. He has a sense of theatre, a love of theatre, which is exciting—and he has the doggedness to fight through to whatever effect he wants to achieve. He is, in addition to being a publicity-gathering screwball, a thoroughgoing perfectionist, and the technical details of his staging of *Around the World* are fabulous.

ROBERT GARLAND, *Journal-American*

Around the World, or "Wellesapoppin' " as Abel Green [of *Variety*] was calling it last night, must have looked like fun on paper. On stage, in the self-styled Mercury Production written, sponsored, and performed by Orson for his own amazement, it is something else again. With countless interludes, and twice that many characters, with magic, movies, and music thrown in for no good reason, it is a show shown by a show-off, full of sets and costumes, signifying nothing in particular. At the Adelphi, Orson is poppin' out all over. It is fun for him, but not too easy on the outsider. . . . Half-way through his journey, Phileas stops off in Yokohama for a circus. There, jugglers juggle, contortionists contortion, roustabouts roustabout, and clowns clown while Orson, disguised as a magician, makes ducks, geese, and chickens disappear. He is good at this disappearing stuff, is Mr. Welles. So good is he that, by the time *Around the World* is half-way over, he has made the plot disappear as well. No plot, no show!

WILLIAM HAWKINS, *World-Telegram*

One gets the feeling that Mr. Welles, the author, got his characters to a certain spot, then said to himself in desperation, "What must I do now?" Then he answered, "Let's have a circus," or "Let's run another reel of movie," or more frequently, "Let's shoot some more guns off." . . . The costumes Alvin Colt has designed are sometimes awkward to the point of being ugly, and the colors have a way of disliking each other's company.

LOUIS KRONENBERGER, *PM*

Orson Welles is not just a man of many bold ideas; he's a man who does something about them. Now he has taken Jules Verne's famous yarn and tried to dynamite it into a super-burlesque of the old-time thriller, and a super-extravaganza for

Broadway. There are 34 scenes [designed by Robert Davison] in *Around the World*; there are movies, there are commotions in the aisles and feathers in the air. There must be a hundred people in the cast, and there are probably 600 scene-shifters backstage. It would be one hell of an entertainment if only it were more entertaining. I have no quarrel with Mr. Welles's love of noise and size. I enjoy his ingenuity even when it smacks more of an amusement park than of the stage. I thoroughly admire his showmanship—but it is not quite a substitute for a show. His sawdust elephants and eagles, his exploding firearms and collapsing bridges provide very lively moments; but *Around the World* is an affair of some two and a half hours, and as such it doesn't make the grade.

VERNON RICE, *Post*

Seldom has Welles been accused of understatement, but this time he can be charged with making one when he calls his work an "extravaganza." There is hardly a word descriptive enough to fit this musical fare. It is mammoth, it is gigantic, it is lavish. It is also dull.

The "Boy Wonder" of a few years earlier retreated to Broadway after getting into hot Hollywood water. He didn't do so hot here either, breaking new Broadway ground with a record $300,000 loss. In trying to fill the bottomless money pit, Welles was forced to barter away his movie rights to the Verne novel—to Mike Todd, who made out extremely well on the deal. (Todd, who had produced Cole Porter's two most recent hit musicals, did not use any of the stage material in the film.)

BROADWAY SCORECARD / perfs: 75 / $: −

rave	favorable	mixed	unfavorable	pan
1	1		6	

AS THE GIRLS GO

a musical comedy, with music by Jimmy McHugh; lyrics by Harold Adamson; book by William Roos

directed by Howard Bay; choreographed by Hermes Pan
produced by Michael Todd
with Bobby Clark, Irene Rich, Bill Callahan, and Kathryn Lee

opened November 13, 1948   Winter Garden Theatre

BROOKS ATKINSON, *Times*

Bobby goes skylarking through a whole wardrobe of jack-in-the-box costumes, masquerades as a rather loosely assembled manicurist, drills a bugle corps ("Forward—halt!" he orders in his crispest command), puffs feverishly on his familiar heater, cuts hair lyrically, pours high tea from a considerable altitude, and sings low ballads against the distracting background of tall show girls who are ungirded for battle. No one plunges more ferociously into the business of stirring up laughter than Bobby, the running king of the comic spirit. Most of his skullduggery we have seen before in one form or another. But his supernatural exuberance keeps it fresh and incomparably funny.

JOHN LARDNER, *Star*

The comic talent of Bobby Clark is a wide and elastic thing, but I guess there are limits to its stretching power, and I guess those limits were approached right up to the snapping point Saturday night when this gifted clown assumed the task of covering up for Michael Todd's new and threadbare musical comedy. The mental and spiritual nudity of the show is almost too much for him. There is no reason, of course, why he should try to conceal its physical nudity, and he doesn't. In fact, he pushes it along. Mr. Clark is a sound judge of values, and he obviously knows that apart from himself, the enterprise has no assets whatever but the architecture of a dozen or so tall, gorgeous tomatoes of early Gothic design. Mr. Clark will wind up with spine trouble yet from carrying vehicles like this on his back.

RICHARD WATTS JR., *Post*

The great, magnificent, and incomparable Bobby Clark met in head-on collision with a musical-comedy book at the Winter Garden Saturday night, and I am happy to report that it was the First Comic who emerged victorious. . . . Michael Todd has picked chorus girls who look as exciting and implausible as chorus girls should and seldom do, and Oleg Cassini has designed sensational and correctly revealing clothes for them.

One of the last of the old-style musicals built around star comics (like Bobby Clark, Ed Wynn, Joe Cook, or even the Marx Brothers). They'd go through all the time-honored routines while a flimsy story unraveled, with ingénue and juvenile singing syrupy ballads in the background. This time, Bobby played the First Husband (i.e., spouse of our first lady President). But time seems to have passed *As the Girls Go* by, and Bobby Clark's final Broadway musical became the first show to lose money despite a full-year's run. Clark's final legit appearance was as the devilish "Applegate" in the National Company of *Damn Yankees*; his star turn threw the show somewhat off balance. Clark died on February 12, 1960.

A Tony Award was won by Max Meth (musical director).

BROADWAY SCORECARD / perfs: 414 / $: −

rave	favorable	mixed	unfavorable	pan
5	1	1	1	1

AT THE DROP OF A HAT

a British two-character revue, with music by Donald Swann; lyrics and sketches by Michael Flanders

produced by Alexander H. Cohen in association with Joseph I. Levine

with Michael Flanders and Donald Swann

opened October 8, 1959   John Golden Theatre

WALTER KERR, *Herald Tribune*

At the Drop of a Hat has no scenery, no costumes, no orchestra—just two men alone on the stage completely surrounded by talent. I didn't know what to make of Donald Swann early-on in the evening. He's serious, I thought—only the other man is hilariously funny. Let him be. Then little tell-tale mannerisms began to crop up. Sometimes his head would fly higher than his hands while he was attacking the piano. In one number ("The Wompom," I think) he began to cackle noticeably. After a while, he stopped everything to do a song entirely in Greek, very enthusiastically. And by the time he was pretending to be a stubborn cannibal child who wouldn't listen to reason and just wouldn't eat people, beating the piano-top with his bare fists and then sullenly clasping and unclasping his hands in distraught defiance, the secret was out. This may be the man James Thurber has had in mind all the time.

BROADWAY SCORECARD / perfs: 216 / $: +

rave	favorable	mixed	unfavorable	pan
4	2		1	

BALLET BALLADS

three "dance plays," with music by Jerome Moross; words by John Latouche

directed by Mary Hunter; "Susannah and the Elders" choreographed by Katherine Litz, "Willie the Weeper" choreographed by Paul Godkin, and "The Eccentricities of Davey Crockett" choreographed by Hanya Holm
produced by Nat Karson for The Experimental Theatre, Inc.; presented by the American National Theatre and Academy
with Sono Osato, Paul Godkin, Katherine Litz, Robert Lenn, Ted Lawrie, and Barbara Ashley

opened May 9, 1948   Maxine Elliot's Theatre
transferred May 18, 1948   Music Box Theatre

ROBERT GARLAND, *Journal-American*

Something new has been added to ANTA's Experimental Theatre. Something fresh and exciting, as American as a hot dog spiked with mustard. Something chancey and unordinary, right and experimental. In two words, *Ballet Ballads*. When I pause to consider the Ballet Theatre wasting your time on "Fall River Legend" and other over-de-Mille-to-the-Storehouse ballets, and the Experimental Theatre enriching your time with *Ballet Ballads*. . . .

ROBERT SYLVESTER, *Daily News*

The Experimental Theatre's *Ballet Ballads* is not only the best song-and-dance show ever attempted by a little theatre group but is also—in this opinion, at least—the best song-and-dance show to reach Broadway this season. Watching what producer [and designer] Nat Karson did with last night's premiere—using buttons for money—makes you bleed for those commercial managers who "can't find a script." And it makes you bleed twice as hard for the two or three producers who held *Ballet Ballads* and then dropped them in fear or ignorance. My personal favorite was Paul Godkin's "Willie the Weeper." Willie is a marijuana weed-head who is getting nowhere, as the musicians say, until he gets on that "gage." Then things really happen to him—physically and vocally. Sung by Robert Lenn and danced by Godkin, this is one of the most exciting pieces of theatre of the season. In it is utilized an angle of wooden bleachers. Up and down these steps, in the treacherous dim light, Godkin races with frightening confidence. Also used is a section of rope ladder. Godkin's dancers bounce and dangle off this ladder like mad acrobats. In "Willie," Moross and Latouche come closest to modernism. The music simplifies boogie back to what Jack the Bear used to call a "walking bass" and it has lyrics like "I crave a little affection in a not too simple form." It also brings back to us Sono Osato. This writer has always contended that Sono can do more real dancing with her hands than most dancers do with their feet.

WALTER TERRY, *Herald Tribune*

Ballet Ballads has been a long time coming. Ever since Agnes de Mille created the now-historical dances for "Oakland!" [*sic*] our theatre has been reaching toward a form which might be described as choreographed folk opera. It has even achieved something of the

sort in two or three musical comedies, but the Experimental Theatre's new production has come closest to arriving at the desired
integration of drama, song, and dance. In "The Eccentricities of
Davey Crockett" one was rarely aware of the switches from one
medium of theatre expression to another. Transitions were smooth,
for a phrase of acting, a gesture, expanded logically into dance or
the lift of a dance movement extended itself into song. "Davey
Crockett" had integrity of form, a new form in which three major
arts united to create compelling theatre. Mr. Latouche has written
wonderful lyrics, which lend themselves to melody and to the
potential imageries of dance. He has done equal justice to the hero
and to the legend and Jerome Moross has matched the text with a
score which has wit, bravado, and nostalgia. The final credit, and
an equal share of it, goes to Hanya Holm for her superb choreography which gives this ballet ballad substance and entity. She has
not only created lively and humorous visions of Davey's adventures
with a comet, with marauding Indians, and with a bear, but she has
given pattern and rhythmic punch to those scenes which place the
accent on song.

RICHARD WATTS JR., *Post*

Nothing I have seen all season in the vital field of the American
musical show had the imagination, creative freshness, and theatrical intelligence revealed in the program of *Ballet Ballads* with
which the embattled Experimental Theatre richly justified its existence at Maxine Elliott's Sunday night. There may be some question as to whether the proceedings belong technically under the
head of ballet or musical comedy, but there is none at all that they
are theatrically enchanting. John Latouche and Jerome Moross
have created a trio of works which will be described here as folk
dance-plays. Representing a happy amalgamation of the gayest features of ballet, music, and folk drama, they are, above all else,
bright, humorous, and completely lacking in any suggestion of
cultural pedantry. Without ever seeming to strive self-consciously
for popularity, artistry, or originality they succeeded in being successful in all three endeavors. All the talents involved in the enterprise have combined their achievements so cooperatively that
the result is a winning amalgamation of three arts of the theatre
into a finely integrated whole. The most important feature is that
it is not only a successful experiment in mixing words, music, and

dance but also in such good fun. Any expensive Broadway show would be proud to offer such superior comic creations. Indeed, the mermaid [in "Davey Crockett"] is so much more hilarious than the one impersonated by the great Bea Lillie in *Inside U.S.A.* [1948] that it is almost a sacrilege to say so.

The American National Theatre and Academy was chartered (without Federal funding) by Franklin D. Roosevelt in 1935. It first became active in the late 1940s with limited-run experimental productions, several of which transferred for commercial runs. *Ballet Ballads* was probably the most exciting ANTA project, although the promising premise of the "dance play" has never been taken up and developed by Broadway. Unfortunately, *Ballet Ballads* was poorly timed (opening in May), and the major newspapers covered it as a dance rather than theatre event. One of the many exciting elements of the piece was that none of the choreographers or performers had previously appeared on Broadway except for Sono Osato, lead dancer of de Mille's *One Touch of Venus* (1943) and Robbins's *On the Town* (1944), and Paul Godkin of *High Button Shoes* (October 9, 1947). Hanya Holm received immediate recognition and was quickly signed for her first musical, *Kiss Me, Kate* (1948). She replaced de Mille as Broadway's favored "classical" choreographer, with credits including *My Fair Lady* (1956) and *Camelot* (1960). Paul Godkin also quickly got a spot as choreographer to first-time director Jerome Robbins on *That's the Ticket!* (1948), a Harold Rome musical which lasted all of a week on the road. *Ballet Ballads* eventually paid a direct dividend in the innovative *The Golden Apple* (1954) from Moross, Latouche, Holm, and producer T. Edward Hambleton, who transferred *Ballet Ballads* to the Music Box for a seven-week run.

BROADWAY SCORECARD / perfs: 69 / $: NA

rave	favorable	mixed	unfavorable	pan
4	2	2		

BAREFOOT BOY WITH CHEEK

a satirical musical comedy, with music by Sidney Lippman; lyrics by Sylvia Dee; book by Max Shulman, from his 1943 novel

directed by George Abbott; choreographed by Richard Barstow
produced by George Abbott
with Nancy Walker, Billy (William) Redfield, Red Buttons, and Ellen Hanley

opened April 3, 1947   Martin Beck Theatre

WILLIAM HAWKINS, *World-Telegram*

Like time, the river, death, and taxes, there is a certain type of undergraduate musical comedy that goes on forever. *Barefoot Boy with Cheek* is right in the traditional groove. George Abbott has no peer at collecting a lot of leather-lunged young Indians to put whooping and stomping through a couple of hours of frantic paces. He has had better material in the past for his kids to work with. But if there is nothing unfamiliar here, nothing familiar is left out. Like ice cream, it may not be a novelty but an awful lot of people still order it. . . . Nancy Walker [as Yetta Samovar, a coed communistic campus cut-up] continues to grow in the finest traditions of clowns. With less standing on her ear than in the past, she is much funnier. Her timing and pantomime are expert. She has always been able to put over a song, but now she can act 40 or 50 people off the stage with a shrug of her shoulder.

LOUIS KRONENBERGER, *PM*

As a producer, George Abbott has long looked rather askance at any stage character who is old enough to vote; and in *Barefoot Boy with Cheek* he has whipped up another musical comedy spoofing college life. It has some of the familiar Abbott virtues—pace, youthfulness, cheerful nonsense—but the trouble with them is that they have become a little *too* familiar. Moreover, Mr. Abbott has counted on them too much. They make excellent baking powder, but they are selling here as pretty much the whole cake. Mr. Abbott has assembled some nice people, and something better than that in Nancy Walker and Philip Coolidge; but the music of *Barefoot Boy* is glaringly mediocre, the dances are never more than conventionally lively, and the book, though at times rather bright, is many other times merely cheesy. *Barefoot Boy* has its merits; but it is so much the Abbott mixture as before, only weaker, that I found it a pretty unrewarding evening.

RICHARD WATTS JR., *Post*

I never did quite get over the shock of noting that its young men belong to a fraternity hilariously known as Alpha Cholera. I wasn't too happy, either, to find that some of the characters are named Asa Hearthrug, Shyster Fiscal, Noblese Oblige, Clothilde Pfefferkorn, and Boris Fiveyearplan. I hope I can persuade the composing room that the football player is called Eino Fflliikkiinnenn. . . . There is something disconcerting in the thought that, while the rest of us are getting older, George Abbott keeps getting younger. At least, his musical shows, which were never exactly middle-aged in their manner, appear to be rapidly becoming so callow that they are almost ostentatious about it.

○○
○   ○
○   BROADWAY SCORECARD / perfs: 108 / $: —   ○
○   ○
○   *rave   favorable   mixed   unfavorable   pan*   ○
○   ○
○   4   5   ○
○○○

THE BARRIER

an opera, with music by Jan Meyerowitz; book and lyrics by Langston Hughes, from Hughes's 1935 melodrama *Mulatto*

directed by Doris Humphrey; choreographed by Charles Weidman and Doris Humphrey
produced by Michael Myerberg and Joel Spector
with Lawrence Tibbett, Muriel Rahn, and Wilton Clary

November 2, 1950   Broadhurst Theatre

JOHN CHAPMAN, *Daily News*

Meyerowitz's score, a taut, busy, and even nervous affair is strictly modernist and dissonant. The music belongs with the theatrical work of Menotti and Blitzstein, and probably is as well made as Menotti's setting for *The Consul* [1950]—and that is what's wrong. George Gershwin took a strong Negro tragedy, *Porgy* [1927], and made it into a fine folk opera [*Porgy and Bess*, 1935], because he had a profound feeling for the music of the Negro. Mr. Meyerowitz has no such feeling; he avoids the simple and shuns the melodic, and only in one scene does he get down to plain emotion. Mr. Hughes' libretto, like his play, is a work of poignancy; as Mr. Tibbett sings it, it is the tragedy of "a terrible puzzle without any answer." But there is little poignancy, little heartbreak, in the music. It belongs in a different world. . . . Herbert Zipper conducts an excellent orchestra—and the composer has taken care to keep every man in the pit as busy as a cat on a Quonset hut.

A virtually forgotten music drama. Production was no doubt encouraged by the (artistic) success of Hughes's collaboration with Kurt Weill on *Street Scene* (1947).

BROADWAY SCORECARD / perfs: 4 / $: −

rave	favorable	mixed	unfavorable	pan
	1	1	5	

BEG, BORROW OR STEAL

a musical satire, with music by Leon Pober; book and lyrics by Bud Freeman, from a story by Marvin Seiger and Bud Freeman

staged by Billy Matthews (replaced by David Doyle); directed by David Doyle; choreographed by Peter Hamilton
produced by Eddie Bracken in association with Carroll and Harris Masterson
with Larry Parks, Betty Garrett (Parks), Eddie Bracken, Biff McGuire, and David Doyle

opened February 10, 1960   Martin Beck Theatre

FRANK ASTON, *World-Telegram & Sun*

This observer wanted to whimper all the way home. Man, any square who ventures to this one is going to get beat, real beat. Be warned.

BROOKS ATKINSON, *Times*

Having chosen a humorless subject the authors have one thing to their credit. They are consistent. They never tamper with the dullness.

JOHN CHAPMAN, *Daily News*

Beg, Borrow or Steal concerns itself with beards, Buddhism, and beatniks and it has one beautnik in it, Betty Garrett. Its plot is a plotnik. One low moment, a Zen Buddhist ballet, lasted so long that it threw me into a deep state of contemplation in which I wondered if I'd ever get outdoors again.

Larry Parks—star of the 1946 movie *The Jolson Story*—was the only actor among the House Un-American Activities Committee's "Unfriendly Nineteen," and therefore their most visible victim. His wife, musical comedienne Betty Garrett of *Call Me Mister* (1946), was also blacklisted out of circulation. Curiously enough, the pair had a couple of weeks of Broadway employment in 1957, when they were vacation replacements for Judy Holliday and Sydney Chaplin in "friendly witness" Jerome Robbins's *Bells Are Ringing*.

BROADWAY SCORECARD / perfs: 5 / $: −

rave	favorable	mixed	unfavorable	pan
			2	5

BEGGAR'S HOLIDAY

a musical comedy, with music by Edward "Duke" Ellington; book and lyrics by John Latouche, from the 1728 British musical *The Beggar's Opera* by John Gay

directed by Nicholas Ray (replacing John Houseman and George Abbott); choreographed by Valerie Bettis
produced by Perry Watkins and John R. Sheppard, Jr.
with Alfred Drake, Zero Mostel, Bernice Parks (replacing Libby Holman), Jet McDonald, and Avon Long

opened December 26, 1946   Broadway Theatre

BROOKS ATKINSON, *Times*

Mr. Ellington, the hot drum-major, and Mr. Latouche, the metronomic word man, have constructed a musical play from the ground up with an eloquent score, brisk ballets, and a cast of dancers and singers who are up to snuff. Mr. Ellington has been dashing off songs with remarkable virtuosity. Without alerting the basic style, he has written them in several moods—wry romances, a sardonic lullaby, a good hurdy-gurdy number, a rollicking melody that lets go expansively. An angular ballet comes off his music rack as neatly as a waterfront ballad. No conventional composer, he has not written a pattern of song hits to be lifted out of context, but rather an integral musical composition that carries the old Gay picaresque yarn through its dark modern setting. There are obvious limitations to this style of composing. As a musical show, *Beggar's Holiday* never quite breaks through the restraints of a sophisticated attitude towards music and showmanship. And Zero Mostel's grotesque and sweaty posturing as Hamilton Peachum is no substitute for comic skylarking.

ROBERT BAGAR, *World-Telegram*

Mr. Ellington's score is a generous outpouring of his individual talent, filled with the spirit and warmth of his music, the pulsing beat of his rhythms, the strength and the refreshing colors of his modern harmonies. Mr. Latouche has struck gold occasionally in his adaptation and always in his lyrics. Together, the music and text ,combine in as felicitous a wedding as the Broadway stage has offered in months. So you will hear in the rather tightly knit score a varied expression of the Ellington–Latouche genius, songs of humor, others of gayety and rhythmic charm, and still others of deepest blue. All in all, a remarkable fusion of talents, creative and performing, culled from among superior white and Negro artists.

Macheath (Alfred Drake) pulls a gun on poppa Peachum (Zero Mostel), while daughter Polly (Jet McDonald) and Chief Lockit (Rollin Smith) look on. Note the 1939 New York World's Fair de-sign over the piano in this modernized version of the 1728 Beggar's Opera. (set by Oliver Smith, costumes by Walter Florell, photo by Vandamm)

John Chapman, *Daily News*

Beggar's Holiday is the most interesting musical since *Porgy and Bess* [1935]. It is so far away from the music-show formula that it often loses track of itself and becomes confusing, but for its score, its cast, its wonderful sets [designed by Oliver Smith] and the imagination with which it has been staged it rates extraordinary consideration. It is easy to make a smash hit musical. All one needs is a tunesmith like Irving Berlin, a lyric writer like Irving Berlin, some kind of a plot and about $300,000—and the thing is in. Any season there is something just as good as *Annie Get Your Gun* [1946]. Making *Beggar's Holiday* is more difficult, because the formula of hit tunes and a simple boy–girl story has been ignored and a striving for originality has taken its place. . . . In this mixing of Negro and white performers there seems to be no scheme, except that the whites are useful and the Negroes are necessary for Mr. Ellington's music. Zero Mostel is there for laughs, and surprisingly gets some.

Robert Garland, *Journal-American*

Between the first act and the second, the conscience which makes cowards of most of us sets in. Satire turns to slapstick. Bitterness disappears. Storytelling falls back on cops and robbers. Zero Mostel takes over. And it is time that the Voice of Experience told Broadway producers and directors that a nightclub is one thing, a theatre is another. Mr. Mostel, who gives Mr. Peachum the floor-show works in *Beggar's Holiday*, may be a funny fellow in the small closed spaces of Café Society [a nightclub], but he is nothing of the kind in the great open spaces of the Broadway Theatre. As Polly Peachum's pernicious paternal parent, Zero Mostel is an impressive example of under-casting. On the other hand, the Macheath of Alfred Drake belongs wholeheartedly. I have never seen a better singing-dancing-acting bad man than his.

Louis Kronenberger, *PM*

Beggar's Holiday, as the program says, is based on *The Beggar's Opera*. But it is so far from a mere jazzed-up "revival" that it can best be described as a very laudable attempt to do something really different in the musical field. Exactly what, however, you never find out—for the crushing reason that its fashioners seem not to have known themselves. The praise-worthy thing about their show is that it travels its own road; the highly unsatisfactory thing is that it never fetches up at any destination. Despite energetic and excellent things en route, *Beggar's Holiday* leaves you, and itself, stranded.

WARD MOREHOUSE, *Sun*

In the up-to-date retelling Latouche has made Macheath the leader of a gang of whites and Negroes in the slums of New York, and has portrayed the women who are enamored of him as a bordel keeper and the daughter of a crooked politician.

A trouble-ridden, ill-fated attempt which certainly seems to have excited the critics. It should be pointed out that *The Threepenny Opera* (1928), Kurt Weill and Bertolt Brecht's adaptation of *The Beggar's Opera*, was virtually unknown here at the time. Broadway had briefly seen an indifferent production in 1933; it wasn't until 1954 that Marc Blitzstein's translation began its 2,706-performance, off-Broadway run.

BROADWAY SCORECARD / perfs: 111 / $: −

rave	favorable	mixed	unfavorable	pan
1	2		5	

BELLS ARE RINGING

a musical comedy, with music by Jule Styne; book and lyrics by Betty Comden and Adolph Green

directed by Jerome Robbins; choreographed by Jerome Robbins and Bob Fosse
produced by the Theatre Guild
with Judy Holliday, Sydney Chaplin, Jean Stapleton, and Eddie Lawrence

opened November 29, 1956   Shubert Theatre

Bells Are Ringing *but that's all right: Judy Holliday is at the switch-*
board. (costume by Raoul Pène du Bois, photo by Friedman-Abeles)

BROOKS ATKINSON, *Times*

Judy Holliday is even more talented than you may have suspected. In *Bells Are Ringing* she sings, dances, clowns, and also carries on her shoulders one of the most antiquated plots of the season. She has gusto enough to triumph in every kind of music hall antic. She needs the gusto. And Sydney Chaplin needs the warmth, taste, skill, and grace that make him an admirable leading man. For this is the season when writers seem to be breaking down all over town. There have not been so many surprised hellos, inept song cues and dance signals since *Oklahoma!* [1943] drove hackneyed musical comedy out of business.

JOHN CHAPMAN, *Daily News*

The Comden-Green plot makes some happy side-trips off the path of standard musical comedy romance—such as presenting us with a dentist who is a would-be songwriter. This character is played by Bernie West almost as amusingly as the original of the character—the late Dr. Nathaniel Lief, who was my dentist and who used to practice his lyrics on me instead of using novocaine.

ROBERT COLEMAN, *Daily Mirror*

Bells Are Ringing really bongs the golden gong. It strikes a happy, Holliday note.

TOM DONNELLY, *World-Telegram & Sun*

Somehow or other they have gotten hold of the solemn end of the stick in *Bells Are Ringing*. Every now and then the show perks up and goes crazy, in the best musical comedy tradition, or, to narrow it down, in the best tradition of Betty Comden and Adolph Green, who have turned out some notably bright and bouncy librettos in the last few years. But by and large *Bells Are Ringing* is constructed of the stuff that women's magazine romances are made of. Jerome Robbins, who supervised the show, hasn't done much to get the dynamos whirring. The over-all pace is slow, the dances are few and far between, and not terribly stimulating.

WALTER KERR, *Herald Tribune*

I know it's getting on for Christmas in New York City, but it's already spring at the Shubert. You can tell by the slightly balmy breeze that seems to waft Judy Holliday this way and that, with a glazed look in her dark eyes and a surprised smile on her face. Watch her whip on a smudge of lipstick before she takes a curtain call. It's an old gag, but Miss Holliday means it. Listen to her trickle out a sneaky little laugh as she plans a double-cross that will bring fame and fortune to a couple of her customers. It's Machiavelli with a heart of gold. And attend carefully as her knees grow rhythmic, her fingers start waving, and her high nasal soprano quavers to a "Swanee" beat while she explains that if she'd been on the switchboard when Romeo and Juliet were dating "those two kids would be alive today." Friar Laurence could take lessons. . . . The quality that most distinguishes *Bells Are Ringing* is its homey, comfortable, old-shoe belief in its attractive people and its wide-eyed love story.

JOHN MCCLAIN, *Journal-American*

A big brilliant success, the best original book show in recent memory. The whole thing seems to be a happy union of Miss Holliday's unique talents with the intelligent scripting of Betty Comden and Adolph Green, the engaging music of Jule Styne, and the swift and sure direction of Jerome Robbins. Add to this a delightful break-in performance by Sydney Chaplin, son of Charlie, playing opposite the star. Miss Holliday is only sensational. The same wistful, zany qualities are there, but now she unwinds a new and brilliant talent in selling a song. It will be many a day before we are treated to anything equalling her socko delivery of "I'm Goin' Back."

RICHARD WATTS JR., *Post*

It hasn't been exactly a secret in recent years that Judy Holliday is a comedienne of rare deftness, warmth, and charm. But you hardly know the extent of her powers if you haven't seen her in *Bells Are Ringing*. To sum up the situation as succinctly as possible, the show is a good one and Miss Holliday is immense. The outstanding virtue of both *Bells Are Ringing* and its star is a warm-hearted friendliness that is wonderfully endearing.

Something of a class project by the graduating seniors at George Abbott U. Strangely enough, *Bells Are Ringing* was at its weakest on its toes. Mr. A. had always known enough to spot his dance department prominently (George Balanchine, Robert Alton, Robbins, Fosse); *Bells*, though, was constructed around four nondancing principals. The only real opportunity was a speciality in the style of Fosse's "Steam Heat" and "Who's Got the Pain?" respectively from *The Pajama Game* (1954) and *Damn Yankees* (1955); but the inferior "Mu-cha-cha" might just as well have been staged by dancer Peter Gennaro (of "Steam Heat," who was to cochoreograph Robbins's upcoming *West Side Story* [1957]).

Tony Awards were won by Judy Holliday (actress) and Sydney Chaplin (supporting actor).

BROADWAY SCORECARD / perfs: 924 / $: +

rave	favorable	mixed	unfavorable	pan
3	3		1	

BEN FRANKLIN IN PARIS

a musical comedy, with music by Mark Sandrich, Jr.; book and lyrics by Sidney Michaels (additional music and lyrics by Jerry Herman)

directed by Michael Kidd (replacing Noel Willman); and choreographed by Michael Kidd
produced by George W. George and Frank Granat
with Robert Preston, Ulla Sallert, Susan Watson (replacing Jacqueline Mayro), and Franklin Kiser

opened October 27, 1964   Lunt-Fontanne Theatre

WALTER KERR, *Herald Tribune*

I detect that operetta, that sneak, is back with us. Once upon a time there was a form called operetta, and people like Victor Herbert and Sigmund Romberg and Franz Lehár wrote tunes for the ladies in Maypole dresses. Then operetta was ruled old-fashioned and gave way to the peppy, boyish-bobbed musicals of the twenties, and then those in turn gave way to the deeper, richer, more integrated shows not all of which were called *Oklahoma!* [1943]. But do you know what is happening? All of the while operetta was just biding its time, waiting for the dresses to get long enough again, waiting for someone to put on a wig and pick up a flag and go stomping off to Paris to say *"chocolat, m'sieur?"* As of last evening at the Lunt-Fontanne, the integrated musical turned back into operetta again, and I do hope the town's costumers are happy. If you don't believe me, you can go to see *Ben Franklin in Paris* yourself, though I suggest you believe me. . . . I've got to believe that Mr. Franklin had more fun in Paris than Mr. Preston is permitted to.

JOHN McCLAIN, *Journal-American*

The story was going around that poor Bob Preston had shaved his head to uncover the noble brow and receding hairline of Benjamin Franklin for the musical *Ben Franklin in Paris* and that it was such a shame because the show was a bomb and would probably close right away and leave him looking pretty silly, a sort of poor man's Yul Brynner. . . . The big ballad "To Be Alone with You" is sung by Preston and Ulla Sallert in a balloon floating over Paris and it is a good tune with an intelligent lyric and the effect, with the back drop rolling up and down to give the impression of the balloon's rise and fall and drift, is gay and inventive. [Scenic design by Oliver Smith.]

HOWARD TAUBMAN, *Times*

Neither the wig nor the fine 18th-century coat, waistcoat, breeches, and boots can fool us. That genial, lightfooted, resourceful salesman who answers to the name of Ben Franklin is really our old friend selling band instruments in Iowa. . . . Airborne in the balloon's basketlike gondola, Mr. Preston and Miss Sallert sing Mark Sandrich, Jr.'s best tune, "To Be Alone with You." While the mood of Mr. Michael's lyric and Mr. Sandrich's melody is hardly in a classical French vein, it is an attractive Broadway number.

Mr. Sandrich's "big ballad," "To Be Alone With You," was one of the interpolations from the atelier of J. Herman. And why not? *Dolly!* had been transfused by a trio of Broadway tunesmiths, with favorable results. Sons of Fathers Dept.: composer Sandrich was the Jr. of the director of four of the Astaire–Rogers films, while producer George George was the former George Goldberg, son of cartoonist Rube.

BROADWAY SCORECARD / perfs: 215 / $: −

rave	favorable	mixed	unfavorable	pan
	3	2	1	

BILLION DOLLAR BABY

a musical satire, with music by Morton Gould; book and lyrics by Betty Comden and Adolph Green

directed by George Abbott; choreographed by Jerome Robbins
produced by Paul Feigay and Oliver Smith
with Mitzi Green, Joan McCracken, William Tabbert, and David Burns

opened December 21, 1945   Alvin Theatre

JOHN CHAPMAN, *Daily News*

Oliver Smith and Paul Feigay, who produced *On the Town* [1944], have come up with a musical called *Billion Dollar Baby* which is even better. Its success does not lie with its principals or, possibly, with its authors, good as they are. Oliver Smith, who designed the sets; Jerome Robbins, who devised the dances and staged the musical numbers; and George Abbott, who directed the whole show, are the real stars. Together they have assembled and routined an evening of song and dance which is swift and smart and which never tries to bowl you over with 10 tons of scenery or two tons of Powers models. The costumes, by Irene Sharaff, are superb. They look like caricatures of the flapper dress of the Tasteless Twenties, but I have a sickening feeling that they aren't caricatures at all, but very accurate examples of what the well-clad female wore in the days when I was young and had no judgment whatever.

ROBERT GARLAND, *Journal-American*

Yes, sir, that's my *Billion Dollar Baby* that talked, sang, and danced its oft-times tough, sometimes tender, and constantly dis-illusioned way last night across the stage of the Alvin Theatre. It's my *Billion Dollar Baby* until, shortly before the finale, it runs headlong into a pedestrian ballet from which it never quite recov-ers. From then on, I wouldn't give much more than a million dollars for it. Subtitled *A Musical Play of the Terrific Twenties*, *Billion Dollar Baby* is a fine, fresh feather in the producing cap of the Paul Feigay and Oliver Smith whose *On the Town* still runs successfully. Here, again, the youthful impresari have called on Betty Comden and Adolph Green for book and lyrics; Jerome Rob-bins for choreography, and George Abbott for over-all direction. Only Leonard Bernstein is missing as composer. In his stead is Morton Gould, which may—or may not be an asset! For Mr. Gould's brilliantly self-orchestrated score calls for quite a bit of hearing. It's certainly not up anybody's Tin Pan Alley. . . . *Billion Dollar Baby* is not entirely unrelated to the *Pal Joey* [1940] which, also under George Abbott's directional jurisdiction, flourished some time back. With more than a dancing touch of "Slaughter on Tenth Avenue" thrown in.

LOUIS KRONENBERGER, *PM*

Perhaps, after *On the Town*, one was a little too greedy in what one asked of Santa Claus. In any case: though it is a musical that contains some delightful things, though it is a musical you are always rooting for and always respect, *Billion Dollar Baby* falls just a trifle short. The people who have put it together have courage as well as talent. They will have no truck with the hackneyed formulas and hammy notions of run-of-the-mine Broadway musicals. They want to do something original and alive, and they climb out on a limb without the slightest trepidations about the critical ax that may chop them down. As a result, *Billion Dollar Baby* is no more commonplace than *On the Town* was. In fact, it is far more ambi-tious. That is at least one reason, and a very honorable one, why it is far less successful.

BURTON RASCOE, *World-Telegram*

The multiple begettors of the very successful ballet-musical, *On the Town*, decided (perhaps in too great a hurry) to give us more of the same, on a more ornate and expensive scale. Again, the musical is largely dependent upon the choreography of Jerome Robbins, who follows and embellishes a thin book, which is weak in comedy and sparse in lyrics, by Betty Comden and Adolph Green. There is a very satisfactory first act, fast moving, clever, rhythmical, broadly satirical, and diverting. But the second act shows signs that the authors were fatigued; satiric inspiration lags; there is no surprise; and the comedy, anemic in the first place, gives up the ghost entirely. . . . The music by Morton Gould is stunty without being melodic.

On the Town had been a new-style, fast-paced musical—with good, old-fashioned entertainment carefully mixed in. *Billion Dollar Baby* was perhaps too experimental, especially in the music department. Along with his "modern" ballets, Leonard Bernstein had provided a handful of sturdy show tunes—which Morton Gould was incapable of doing. The *Billion Dollar* score is highly musical, but not especially tuneful. The show had its champions, though, and played an important part in the formulation of the "Abbott" musical.

Donaldson Awards were won by George Abbott (director); Jerome Robbins (choreographer); and Joan McCracken (supporting actress; female dancer).

BROADWAY SCORECARD / perfs: 219 / $: +

rave	favorable	mixed	unfavorable	pan
2	2	2	2	

THE BILLY BARNES PEOPLE

a musical revue, with music and lyrics by Billy Barnes; sketches by Bob Rodgers

directed by Bob Rodgers
produced by John Pool

with Joyce Jameson, Ken Berry, Dave Ketchum, Jo Anne Worley, and Dick Patterson

opened June 13, 1961   Royale Theatre

WALTER KERR, *Herald Tribune*

It can be assumed that the people of *The Billy Barnes People* were brave to go on as scheduled Tuesday—right on the heels of a city-wide power failure, with the air-conditioning out, with the audience reduced to shirtsleeves, and with the curtain forty-five minutes late. But you don't know how brave. Consider the plight, say, of a kinky-haired comedian with a lantern jaw named Dave Ketchum. Mr. Ketchum had to bounce vigorously onto the stage as though fresh from the shower. He had to smile and wring his hands in a glossy show of welcome. He had to watch all of those customers fanning themselves with programs and mopping their brows, without even daring to reach for a handkerchief himself. And then he had to say a line like "I am a pimp with pimpsicles" and look as though he hoped to get a laugh with it. Well, the emergency was universal. Composer Billy Barnes and sketch-writer Bob Rodgers had simply neglected to write any lyrics or devise any blackouts capable of taking care of themselves, and there was nothing for the company to do but insist upon the sheer humor of their presence in a theatre. . . . The Billy Barnes People ought to speak to Billy Barnes, sharply.

JOHN McCLAIN, *Journal-American*

Billy Barnes cannot be blamed for the power failure that blanked the air conditioning system in the Royale Theatre last night. But he can be held largely accountable for the inept and embarrassing charade presented by the eight striving and sweltering youngsters who toiled under his banner. It wasn't the heat—it was the stupidity.

```
BROADWAY SCORECARD / perfs: 8 / $: —

 rave    favorable    mixed    unfavorable    pan

                1                      2          4
```

BLESS YOU ALL

a musical revue, with music and lyrics by Harold Rome; sketches by Arnold Auerbach

directed by John C. Wilson; choreographed by Helen Tamiris
produced by Herman Levin and Oliver Smith
with Jules Munshin, Mary McCarty, Pearl Bailey, and Valerie Bettis

opened December 14, 1950   Mark Hellinger Theatre

BROOKS ATKINSON, *Times*

Bless the scene and costume designers of *Bless You All*, which opened last night. They are [co-producer] Oliver Smith and Miles White. By putting their heads together, they have made the new revue the most stunning show in town. It looks both crisp and elegant, like a modern fashion magazine. But in the opinion of one willing theatregoer, the material seldom matches the decor or acquires the gusto and scope of a first-rate revue.

JOHN CHAPMAN, *Daily News*

The best two sketches involve Mr. Munshin, whose resourcefulness as a good, low comedian is increasing. In one elaborate number, he is running for the Presidency in 1960 and is conducting his campaign entirely by television—and here the writer, Mr. Auerbach, is at his funniest as he flails heartily away at TV revues and national politics. Mr. Munshin is even more amusing than Mr. Truman has been lately. Miss McCarty, always ready with bounce and good will, has a fine, humorous song, giving reasonable reasons why she has just walled her husband up in the cellar ["Little Things (Meant So Much to Me)"], and she next hits a peak of fun by playing Jean Arthur in a sequel to *Peter Pan* [1950] [having trouble with the flying equipment]. A couple of times during the evening Miss Bailey saunters out on the stage and takes over with typical Bailey numbers. She should be made an honorary member of the stage hands' union, for when she is out there "in one" the men behind the curtain know they can take all the time they need to set the next scene. . . . The director, John C. Wilson, might have fared better had he held a long, sharp needle in one hand and a long, sharp pair of cutting shears in the other.

JOHN MCCLAIN, *Journal-American*

There are so many high spots in *Bless You All* that it seems almost a matter of criminal incompetence when parts of it fall below the level which it originally promises. I think the ballet "The Desert Flame," as performed by Valerie Bettis and others, is one of the most exciting things I've seen in the theatre since "Slaughter on Tenth Avenue" [from *On Your Toes* (1936)], from which it both borrowed and added much. Pearl Bailey can do no wrong in my manifesto, and so I was transfixed with her two big numbers. You will also be delighted to see what the management calls "a swarm of sultry sylphs." In fact, I think you will have a good time. It's just too bad you won't have an exceedingly good time.

Bless You All couldn't win: it was up against everybody's jubilant memories of *Call Me Mister* (1946). The earlier Rome/Auerbach/Levin revue not only had better material; it had irrepressible enthusiasm while *Bless You All* was merely professional.

A Tony Award was won by Miles White (costume designer).

```
○○○○○○○○○○○○○○○○○○○○○○○○○○○○○○○○○○○○○○○○○○○○○
○                                                       ○
○        BROADWAY SCORECARD / perfs: 84 / $: —          ○
○                                                       ○
○     rave    favorable    mixed    unfavorable    pan  ○
○                                                       ○
○                 5           2                         ○
○                                                       ○
○○○○○○○○○○○○○○○○○○○○○○○○○○○○○○○○○○○○○○○○○○○○○○○
```

BLOOMER GIRL

a period musical comedy, with music by Harold Arlen; lyrics by E. Y. Harburg; book by Sig Herzig and Fred Saidy, from an unproduced play by Lilith and Dan James

directed by E. Y. Harburg; book directed by William Schorr; choreographed by Agnes de Mille
produced by John C. Wilson in association with Nat Goldstone
with Celeste Holm, Margaret Douglass, Joan McCracken, David Brooks, and Dooley Wilson

opened October 5, 1944   Shubert Theatre

Evelina in hoopskirt and bloomers, with beau. Post-Broadway credits. (costume design by Miles White)

90

HOWARD BARNES, *Herald Tribune*

The theatre exercised its prerogative in magnificent fashion last evening. *Bloomer Girl* is a show of magical delight. In the loose framework of a musical, it blends songs, dancing, drama, and spectacle in an enchanting and prodigal entertainment. Not since the happy advent of *Oklahoma!* [1943] has there been such cause for rejoicing. With a jubilant gesture, it wipes away the disappointments of the early season and restores the stage to its proud estate. The Harold Arlen score, the choreography of Agnes de Mille, the costumes of Miles White and the infinitely modulated performing of the company headed by Celeste Holm and Joan McCracken make for what might well be termed an event. An entertainment to remember for a long, long time.

JOHN CHAPMAN, *Daily News*

"Sunday in Cicero Falls" is the finest combination of spectacle, movement and music I have seen since Irving Berlin's and Hassard Short's "Rotogravure Page," better known as the "Easter Parade" number [from *As Thousands Cheer* (1933)]. Miles White's costumes should make women jump right into the biggest hoopskirts they can get made. . . . When Miss de Mille's otherwise delightful dancers chose to fight the whole darn Civil War in ten minutes I got downright restless.

LEWIS NICHOLS, *Times*

Preceded by approximately as much fanfare as the elections, *Bloomer Girl* moved into the Shubert last evening. Let the elections be as satisfactory. Beautiful to look upon, with a good score and bright lyrics and an engaging cast to sing them, the town's newest musical show is what the town has been awaiting for some time. Nothing has been spared to make *Bloomer Girl* one of the better evenings in the Broadway theatre and, since care calls forth its own reward, the new show is just that. It probably will be resident on Forty-fourth Street until the hoop skirts, in the usual cycle of women's fashions, come back again. That won't be tomorrow.

JIM O'CONNOR, *Journal-American*

Bloomer Girl, which blossomed in its pre-Broadway tryout in Philadelphia burst into full bloom last night. Seldom has a play received such an enthusiastic welcome. They could be taking curtain calls yet. *Oklahoma!* will now have to move over and make room for *Bloomer Girl*, but *Oklahoma!* can take credit for producing the stars who have made *Bloomer Girl* the latest sensation on Broadway. They are Joan McCracken, Agnes de Mille, and Celeste Holm. The newcomer is fresh, vigorous, radiant, enchanting, and thoroughly American. It is superior entertainment, and lives up to expectations—quite an accomplishment in itself.

BURTON RASCOE, *World-Telegram*

Miss McCracken is cute, but she was so damned busy being cute last night that (to me) she was irritating. On the credit side there is, first of all, Celeste Holm. She is lovelier to look at than ever, but her charm is something greater than mere beauty; she is one of the few natural comediennes we have and a consummate artist, with intelligence as well as grace and spirit. As everyone knows, of course, she has no singing voice to speak of (last night she put David Brooks, who can sing, to a stiff test in a duet by apparently singing a different tune than the one he was singing), but she doesn't need to sing—she can recite a song better than most good singers can sing it.

WILELLA WALDORF, *Post*

The fabulous success of *Oklahoma!* was bound to have its effect on the Broadway musical market. Let's face it. We are in for several seasons of intensely old-fashioned quaintness, most of it with choreography by Agnes de Mille. *Bloomer Girl*, the first of what is sure to be a long series of elaborately cute period pieces, arrived last night. It was a box-office success before it moved in, ecstatic tidings of its greatness having drifted in from the out-of-town tryout. Tickets are already being booked for the Christmas matinee of 1946, according to report, and although it just reached Broadway last night, an old gentleman who lives in Rittenhouse Square has already seen it fourteen times and is convinced we're still fighting the Civil War. The "book" is based on a play (probably a very poor play) which may possibly be the reason so many "dramatic" actors and actresses are in it. Unfortunately, they are called upon not only to act but to sing Harold Arlen's songs. If we had composed *Bloomer Girl* and had to listen to it "sung" as it was "sung" last night, we'd be discovered out in Shubert Alley this morning riddled by machine-gun bullets fired by our own hand. Just because Celeste Holm shouted something at the top of her lungs in *Oklahoma!* (there's that thing cropping up again) is no reason for anybody to assume that she can carry a score like Arlen's, and it's a pity, for she's a lovely person and a nice actress. For Heaven's sake, Miss Holm, go back to the drama where you belong. You're killing us.

Oklahoma! without Rodgers, Hammerstein, and Mamoulian, *Bloomer Girl* did fairly well at the time—due mostly to its nostalgic appeal to wartime audiences—but it has had virtually no afterlife. The material is better than average, but it's not terribly exciting. The major critical complaint was alleviated when Nanette Fabray— a survivor of the grisly twosome *My Dear Public* (1943) and *Jackpot* (1944)—stepped into Celeste Holm's hoopskirts, becoming third to Merman and Martin on the musical comedy leading lady list until the advent of Gwen Verdon.

Donaldson Awards were won by Joan McCracken (supporting actress) and Miles White (costume designer).

```
BROADWAY SCORECARD / perfs: 657 / $: +

 rave      favorable     mixed     unfavorable     pan

  4            2                        1            1
```

BLOSSOM TIME

a touring revival of the 1921 operetta, with music by Sigmund Romberg (from melodies by Franz Schubert and H. Berté); book and lyrics by Dorothy Donnelly

directed by J. J. Shubert; choreographed by Carthay
produced by the Messrs. Shubert
with Alexander Gray, Barbara Scully, and Roy Cropper

opened September 4, 1943   Ambassador Theatre

BURTON RASCOE, *World-Telegram*

The finest male voice in the cast is that of Roy Barnes, as Vogel, a voice truly extraordinary and beautiful in tone. It is too bad that Mr. Barnes has ears like Clark Gable and there the resemblance ends—precipitously; for if he were more romantic looking, what an operetta star he would make! (Mr. Barnes, by the way, wears the same brown coat he wore in *The Student Prince* [a 1943 Shubert revival], and it apparently hasn't been pressed since *The Student Prince* opened three months ago.)

WILELLA WALDORF, *Post*

Ever since *White Lilacs* [1928] we have been a trifle wary of operettas based on the lives, loves, and music of great composers. *White Lilacs* concerned Chopin and in it Mme. George Sand swept down a long staircase smoking a cigar and singing "Oh, To Be Kissed by Chopin or Liszt." . . . The scenic investiture may be described as early Shubert (no "c" there, printer).

A return engagement of a typical Shubert touring company of the time. A standing joke well into the 1950s was that there was a lost company of *Blossom Time* still out on the road. Somewhere.

```
BROADWAY SCORECARD / perfs: 47 / $: NA

  rave     favorable    mixed    unfavorable    pan

                          2            2          4
```

BLUE HOLIDAY

a vaudeville revue

directed by Monroe B. Hack (replaced by Jed Harris, unbilled)
produced by Irvin Shapiro and Doris Cole (Abraham)
with Ethel Waters, Josh White, Mary Lou Williams, and the Katherine Dunham Dancers

opened May 21, 1945   Belasco Theatre

HERRICK BROWN, *Sun*

After the sponsors of *Blue Holiday* decided at the last minute on Friday that their show wasn't ready for unveiling that evening, they called in Jed Harris to help with the revamping. According to reports, he cut out enough material to reduce the running time a good thirty minutes. Despite this pruning, *Blue Holiday* is still too long, and the tendency of some of the performers to rush back for encores at the first encouraging hand-clap, didn't help matters any.

ROBERT GARLAND, *Journal-American*

There's no telling to whom Ethel Waters has been listening. Not to her better judgment, I'm sure. For *Blue Holiday* is well off her familiar, her fascinating, her friendly beam. Somebody has been messing with her material. That somebody should be ashamed. Confidentially, I think I know the meddler's name. Words and music have been streamlined, brought unbecomingly down-to-date. Miss Waters has been streamlined, too. Her heart-warming simplicity has been unsimplified, made fussy, foolish, and unfamiliar. I've no idea how good, bad, or indifferent *Blue Holiday* was before Jed Harris came rushing to its rescue. But, at the same time, I'm only too well aware that it misses its mark.

BURTON RASCOE, *World-Telegram*

Vaudeville raised its feeble head at the Belasco last night and sank right back into a coma.

BROADWAY SCORECARD / perfs: 8 / $: −

rave	favorable	mixed	unfavorable	pan
			3	5

THE BODY BEAUTIFUL

a musical comedy, with music by Jerry Bock; lyrics by Sheldon Harnick; book by Joseph Stein and Will Glickman

directed by George Schaefer; choreographed by Herbert Ross produced by Richard Kollmar and Albert Selden with Mindy Carson, Jack Warden, Steve Forrest, Lonnie Sattin, and Barbara McNair

opened January 23, 1958   *Broadway Theatre*

BROOKS ATKINSON, *Times*

If an author is not lucky enough to be Damon Runyon, a musical comedy like *The Body Beautiful* is about as much as we can expect. As put on last evening it is a second-rate show with intermittent improvements. Joseph Stein and Will Glickman are the authors who do not have Damon Runyon's flair, and Jerry Bock is the song-writer who is not so talented as Frank Loesser. Using a book and a score that are generally mediocre, a typical mob of Broadway actors goes through the motions of providing a good time. Lack of originality is the most conspicuous thing that the authors, composer, and lyric writer have brought to their cauliflower comedy. [Excepting Jack Warden, Mindy Carson, and the settings by William and Jean Eckart], *The Body Beautiful* is heavy-footed, hackneyed, and mediocre. It takes first-rate writers like Damon Runyon and Ring Lardner to make comedy out of seedy rackets like the fight game. It takes perspective. The standards of writing have to be higher than the material.

ROBERT COLEMAN, *Daily Mirror*

In ring parlance, it's an agressive but not-too clever lightweight, overmatched against the Rialto's heavyweight song-and-dance champs. The trouble with this newcomer is that it's willing, but not very skillful. It relies on brawn rather than brain to conquer the customers. It has a spindly-legged book by Joseph Stein and Will Glickman that wobbles along for much of the evening, erupting into fast-stepping humor all too seldom. *The Body Beautiful* is loaded with talent, muscles, and curves. At its best, it's swell entertainment. Unfortunately, like some padded-glove donners, it punches for only half a minute out of the three in every round. . . . Lyricist Sheldon Harnick and composer Jerry Bock have teamed to equip the new entry with several songs that should delight the juke-box aficionados. The wordage is often amusing, and the tunes zingy.

WALTER KERR, *Herald Tribune*

The problem of the prize-fighting hero of *The Body Beautiful* is that he has a good build, a good college record in the ring, an intelligent grasp of what the champs are doing, only he can't win a fight. It seems to be that the new musical at the Broadway faces just about the same problem. Why doesn't the show do better than its mild-mannered hero? Perhaps its own manners are too mild; no one ever gets up the energy to blast through a kind of curtain of sleepiness that hovers over the pit. There's no point in picking on the particular indiscretions of a show that is on the one hand inoffensive and on the other indifferent. It just doesn't know how to land a haymaker, that's all.

RICHARD WATTS JR., *Post*

A pall of the ordinary and familiar hangs sullenly over *The Body Beautiful*, and the chief offender in this respect is the book. Since it is the work of Joseph Stein and Will Glickman, who wrote the charming *Plain and Fancy* [1955], the weakness is particularly disappointing, but there is no getting around the melancholy impression that their story of the mild young man who wants to be a prize fighter is a veritable anthology of the clichés of musical comedy. The score by Jerry Bock contains a couple of pleasant songs but, on the whole, it is considerably less than exhilarating. Sheldon Harnick's lyrics try gallantly for witty sophistication, even going in for a few cultural references, but it doesn't make them very stimulating. . . . The first act was so commonplace and clumsy that it almost appeared done on purpose to make the second act seem at least fairly passable by contrast.

An uninspired formula musical, this was the initial collaboration of Jerry [*Mr. Wonderful* (1956)] Bock and Sheldon ["Boston Beguine"] Harnick. Their somewhat encouraging debut was immediately followed by a Pulitzer Prize–winning musical knockout, *Fiorello!* (1959).

```
BROADWAY SCORECARD / perfs: 60 / $: —

rave     favorable     mixed     unfavorable     pan

              3           1            3
```

THE BOY FRIEND

a British musical comedy satire, with book, music, and lyrics by Sandy Wilson

directed by Vida Hope (replaced by Cy Feuer); choreographed by John Heawood
produced by Cy Feuer and Ernest H. Martin
with Julie Andrews, John Hewer, Eric Berry, Ruth Altman, and Bob Scheerer

opened September 30, 1954   Royale Theatre

BROOKS ATKINSON, *Times*

Dressed in the flapper, knee-length gowns of the Twenties, with cloche hats, and made up in the garish stage style of the period, the girls are grotesquely funny to look at before the show properly begins. But there is a lot more to the caricature than the costumes. For the director has revived all the coy stage routines of the day, and they are hilarious. The toothy charm, the girlish shrugs, the screeching laughter, the fraudulently innocent glee—they are all present and accounted for, the more horrible, the more uproarious. Was the musical stage as silly as this in the Twenties? Well, it was. According to the program, Vida Hope, who directed the London production, has directed the American facsimile. Since this department does not know all the details of the intramural rumpus during the rehearsal period, it will take the program at face value and give Miss Hope credit for a brisk, witty performance. . . . It is probably Julie Andrews who gives *The Boy Friend* its special quality. She burlesques the insipidity of the part. She keeps the romance very sad. Her hesitating gestures and her wistful, shy mannerisms are very comic. But, by golly, there is more than irony in her performance. There is something genuine in it, too. I was happier than she was when she found Prince Charming in the last buttery scene.

WILLIAM HAWKINS, *World-Telegram & Sun*

The music has beat and banjos. The hero and heroine look like Mary Eaton and Oscar Shaw. You won't believe this, but once he lifts her coyly to a footstool, and she whistles a chorus while he does his softshoe specialty ["I Could Be Happy with You"]!

WALTER KERR, *Herald Tribune*

It isn't really a parody at all. It's a romantic adolescent's love-letter to a girl in a cloche hat. . . . *The Boy Friend* has a treasure in that heroine. Her name is Polly, and she is played by Julie Andrews, and any one who stopped dreaming with Mary Eaton can start dreaming again. Miss Andrews is perfect. With trembling upper lip, a blonde marcel, the largest amount of blue eye-shadow I have ever seen anywhere, and hands clasped winsomely just above her nice right knee, she breathes lunatic sincerity into [the romance]. She is also sincere about song-cues. Her own singing voice has the piercing charm of an old family photograph, and she has an attractive habit of pursing her teeth on the key consonant in each line of lyric.

JOHN McCLAIN, *Journal-American*

From the first note of the overture, rendered by a band replete with banjo and wood block, you are transplanted to the hilarious days of John Held, Jr., the Charleston, and flat-front dresses. You are aware that your leg is being pulled, at the same time you feel a tug at your heart strings. What keeps it better than just an enlarged sketch is that you really get carried away by the romance of the boy and the girl. Julie Andrews, The Girl, looks like all the musical comedy heroines you've ever seen, only more so. . . . I don't know who wound up as director, as I hear Cy Feuer finally got the duke, but in any case it was a job well done.

RICHARD WATTS JR., *Post*

When I saw *The Boy Friend* in London last summer, I was in considerable doubt about its chances for a New York success. Fortunately, I gave myself an out. I said that the gift for showmanship possessed by Feuer and Martin, who were importing it, might provide the added touch that was required for local audiences. This is just what happened. By giving the American production an added skill and vitality and gathering together a rather more attractive cast than was playing it in the West End, they have made the show brighter and better than it seemed abroad. It is possibly true that *The Boy Friend* is played more straight in London than in New York. But the local production has just the right combination of parody, nostalgia, and candid paraphrase of a period, and it's a constant pleasure.

Producers Feuer and Martin barred author Sandy Wilson and director Vida Hope from rehearsals, hiring private detectives to keep them out of the theatre. Meanwhile, *The Boy Friend* was Broadway's first full-scale British musical import since *The Two Bouquets* (1938) and the first successful transfer since Cole Porter's West End revue *Wake Up and Dream* (1929). Times, it seems, have changed. . . .

A Donaldson Award was won by Julie Andrews (female debut).

```
ooooooooooooooooooooooooooooooooooooooooo
o                                        o
o      BROADWAY SCORECARD / perfs: 485 / $: +    o
o                                        o
o    rave    favorable    mixed    unfavorable    pan    o
o                                        o
o      6           1                              o
o                                        o
ooooooooooooooooooooooooooooooooooooooooo
```

BRAVO GIOVANNI

a musical comedy with music by Milton Shafer; lyrics by Ronny Graham; book by A. J. Russell, from the 1959 novel *The Crime of Giovanni Venturi* by Howard Shaw

directed by Stanley Prager; choreographed by Carol Haney
produced by Philip Rose
with Cesare Siepi, David Opatoshu, Michèle Lee, Maria Karnilova (Irving), and George S. Irving

opened May 19, 1962   Broadhurst Theatre

WALTER KERR, *Herald Tribune*

For the purposes of the Broadway musical *Bravo Giovanni*, basso Cesare Siepi has been brought over from the Metropolitan Opera. Mr. Siepi comes equipped with a great big booming voice which, by the way, surely does not have to be amplified. The plot, however, does. The new entertainment at the Broadhurst, which would be wistful if it were not so witless, hangs itself—in several senses of the word—on one of those story-lines that not even the actors could possibly believe in. . . . Michèle Lee is most competent in every conceivable way; but her competence has come out of a deep-freeze. Holding her lips exactly so far apart in a smile, holding her eyes exactly so far open, she makes you wish that somebody backstage would lose the key which is now being used to wind her up. Left to herself, and with all that styling thawed out of her, she might turn out to be somebody, and maybe nice. Perhaps we should speak of director Stanley Prager next, for it must be he who has driven, or at least encouraged, ex-ballerina Maria Karnilova to leer, grimace, and mug to a point where a high-school auditorium would shudder on its very foundations. It is certainly pleasant to watch Miss Karnilova move, even when she is moving to a tune called "The Kangaroo," which is like nothing I've seen since Balaban and Katz were boys.

NORMAN NADEL, *World-Telegram & Sun*

Declare a Roman holiday. *Bravo Giovanni* is *magnifico!* This exuberant new musical swept over Broadway Saturday night like Vesuvian lava over Pompeii, but with happier consequences for all concerned. *Bravo Giovanni* would be a blessing just with Siepi's singing. He can set the spine tingling with pedal tones of mahogany timbre, then on the same breath trot up an arpeggio and into a shimmering upper register. He is an artist. But this is more than a very good vocal recital. When Maria Karnilova takes over the stage, in her role as the aged widow, the show becomes triumphant all over again and on brand new terms. She tangos, she kangaroos, black bottoms, and twists. She leers, she leaps. Compared to her, a satyr would seem lead-footed. This frolicsome senior-citizen faun is altogether amazing. Someone should do a statue of her, if she could hold still long enough. Michèle Lee, 19, a newcomer from the West Coast, captures the audience with her first song, belted out energetically, phrased meaningfully, and sung accurately but she looks about as Italian as apple pie; also, the posture and hand-clenching give away that good old American show biz background, but she still rings bells.

HOWARD TAUBMAN, *Times*

Michèle Lee, 19 years old and pretty enough to stir up the wolves in New York or Rome, has a big, earthy voice, which she uses in the popular manner; her energy will remind you of a young Ethel Merman. . . . Stanley Prager, the director, and Carol Haney, the choreographer, have arranged a marvelously demented scene in the kitchen of the restaurant, to a pounding rhythmic number. This interlude has the sharp, comic comment of moments in René Clair's *À Nous La Liberté* (1931) and Charlie Chaplin's *Modern Times* (1936).

If Broadway was good enough for Metropolitan Opera stars Ezio Pinza (*South Pacific* [1949]) and Robert Weede (*The Most Happy Fella* [1956]), why not Cesare Siepi? The material, that's why! *Giovanni* was fun in parts, with especially amusing lyrics by Ronny Graham of *New Faces of 1952*. The villain's *turisti* restaurant had a decor featuring a Norman Rockwell Roman scene, a bust of Dante which—with a tug of the earlobe—provided *café expresso*, served homogenized *tortoni* in 29 flavors, and in the lavatories, "each booth . . . [was] a replica of the Arch of Constantine." Musically, though, this was not some enchanted evening. *Giovanni* did serve to launch a new ingénue, billed here somewhat continentally as Michèle Lee. She soon moved into the femme lead of the season's reigning hit *How to Succeed in Business Without Really Trying* (without the accent).

BROADWAY SCORECARD / perfs: 76 / $: −

rave	favorable	mixed	unfavorable	pan
2	1	3		1

BRIGADOON

a romantic musical fantasy, with music by Frederick Loewe; book and lyrics by Alan Jay Lerner

directed by Robert Lewis; choreographed by Agnes de Mille
produced by Cheryl Crawford
with David Brooks, Marion Bell, Pamela Britton, Lee Sullivan, George Keane, and James Mitchell

opened March 13, 1947   Ziegfeld Theatre

BROOKS ATKINSON, *Times*

To the growing list of major achievements of the musical stage add one more—*Brigadoon*. For once, the modest label "musical play" has a precise meaning. For it is impossible to say where the music and dancing leave off and the story begins in this beautifully orchestrated Scotch idyll. Under Bob Lewis's direction all the arts of the theatre have been woven into a singing pattern of enchantment. A kind of idyllic rhythm flows through the whole pattern of the production, and Miss de Mille has dipped again into the Pandora's box where she keeps her dance designs. Some of the dances are merely illustrations for the music. One or two of them are conventional, if lovely, maiden round dances. But some of them, like the desperate chase in the forest, are fiercely dramatic. The funeral dance to the dour tune of bag-pipes brings the footstep of doom into the forest. And the sword dance, done magnificently by James Mitchell, is tremendously exciting with its stylization of primitive ideas.

HOWARD BARNES, *Herald Tribune*

A bonny thing for Broadway, a scintillating song and dance fantasy that has given theatregoers reason to toss tamoshanters in air.

JOHN CHAPMAN, *Daily News*

Some of the highlights of this new offering are the dances by Agnes de Mille, but, if I am going to be a hard-boiled editor, I must opine that there may be one too many of them and that another runs too long. Just when I get pleasantly steamed up about the love of Mr. Brooks and Miss Bell, I don't want to be cooled off by

A kilted Highland-flinger, clad in Scotch plaid, beckons us to his
enchanted village in the heather-covered hills. (drawing by David Klein)

watching a herd of gazelles from Chorus Equity running around as
though Agnes herself were after them. . . . William Hansen [as
Mr. Lundie, the schoomaster] is so irresistibly able to persuade
you that if there isn't a village named *Brigadoon*, there ought to be.

ROBERT COLEMAN, *Daily Mirror*

It took courage to produce *Brigadoon*, an unconventional musical show of marked originality. But in this instance, courage will be
richly rewarded. Compromising less than *Finian's Rainbow* [1947]
with Broadway and Tin Pan Alley, born of the imagination that
went into *Dark of the Moon* [1945], as artistic as a modern dance
recital, it still manages to pack a tartan full of popular appeal.

ROBERT GARLAND, *Journal-American*

Pamela Britton escaped from both M.G.M. and Frank Sinatra in
time to be tough as a Scottish temptress, and rough as a singer of
raffish songs. . . . I wish George Balanchine would come on over
from the Century [a 1947 revival of Oscar Straus's *The Chocolate
Soldier* (1909)] and learn how to create choreography for a Broadway song-and-dance show.

LOUIS KRONENBERGER, *PM*

A title so attractive as *Brigadoon* is something to live up to; but
Brigadoon lives up to it. And the musical fantasy not only has
charm; it shows a good deal of independence. It calls its own tune;
in the very act of making Broadway seem brighter, it makes it seem
a touch less Broadwayish. It is so successful because it has hit on a
very pleasant fantasy for a musical, and then known what to do with
it. *Brigadoon* has realized, moreover, that its charm must lie less
in any story it tells than in the general mood it creates; and it has
created that mood by fusing a number of theatre elements as
densely as possible. *Brigadoon* shows so much desire (as *Finian's
Rainbow* didn't) to make Broadway keep its distance, to avoid
shoddiness, to hold to a superior and stylish level—and so generally succeeds—that one feels a little cranky even mentioning its
weak points. The second act does, however, let the mood partly
dissolve and the charm rather peter out; and the last two scenes are
an outright blunder. Whether *Brigadoon* was to have a bittersweet
ending or a happy one was of very little moment, but it should not

have one ending slapped on top of the other—and in the corniest Broadway fashion. As for the final ending, even in fantasy one good miracle doesn't deserve another. Even worse, shows like *Brigadoon* should run like hell from those gauze-curtain visions of one's lost love standing forlornly on a hill top.

WARD MOREHOUSE, *Sun*

A stunning show, a beautiful and enticing show, *Brigadoon* has color and charm, enough for a dozen productions. It has whimsy, beguiling music, exciting dancing—and it has a book. That is news! *Brigadoon* is by far the best musical play the season has produced, and it is certainly one of the best within my entire play-going experience. And that's considerable. Aye, mon, *Brigadoon* is a grand show.

RICHARD WATTS JR., *Post*

I have seen other musical comedies that I enjoyed more, but few for which I have a deeper admiration. In *The Day Before Spring* [1945] last season the Messrs. Lerner and Loewe demonstrated that they had ideas and the ability to write engaging scores. My impression on first hearing is that the songs for *Brigadoon* are attractive but slightly less immediately winning than those in the previous work. If my first emotion last night was admiration rather than sheer enjoyment, it was because the proceedings seemed to me more marked by taste and style than by emotional warmth in book and music, but there is no denying that the authors have matured as theatrical craftsmen.

A Scottish Highlands fantasy with bagpipers a-pipin', lassies a-leapin', and kilts a-kiltin' certainly couldn't have sounded all too promising to the post-War, modern-times crowd. But *Brigadoon*'s setting was incidental to its message and the writing—from the previously nonsuccessful team of Lerner and Loewe—was not only unhackneyed but completely enchanting. The theme of life and eternal love after death was not only universal, but almost painfully timely. (*Brigadoon*'s costume designer David Ffolkes—winner of the first set-design Tony for *Henry VIII* [1946]—was recently out of a Japanese prison camp, where he had been forced to design a

Shinto temple!) A controversy started when George Jean Nathan pointed out that the plot—with its modern-day adventurer stumbling upon a quaint village which appears out of the mist every hundred years, and falling in love with the local ingénue—was lifted intact from *"Germelshausen,"* an 1862 German story by Friedrich Wilhelm Gerstäcker. Lerner continually and vociferously denied this assertion, claiming—after the critic's death—that Nathan was simply jealous of his relationship with soprano Marion Bell. (Lerner eventually married his leading lady, and not for the only time.) Why Lerner felt the need to defend *Brigadoon* as his own is unclear; certainly he didn't begrudge George Bernard Shaw's contribution to *My Fair Lady.* "*Germelshausen*" was not an unknown obscurity; Marc Connelly also used it for his "fantasy of escapism," *The Land of the Living* (1938), in which a modern-day flier crash-lands in the mountains of Serenity, New Hampshire, circa 1740. When Connelly's play was finally produced—in London in 1958, retitled *Hunter's Moon*—critics complained that it was simply *Brigadoon* without the songs!

Winner of the New York Drama Critics' Circle Award. A Tony Award was won by Agnes de Mille (choreographer, tied with Michael Kidd for *Finian's Rainbow*). Donaldson Awards were won by Agnes de Mille (choreographer); Marion Bell (female debut); James Mitchell (male dancer); Oliver Smith (scenic designer); and David Ffolkes (costume designer).

BROADWAY SCORECARD / perfs: 581 / $: +

rave	favorable	mixed	unfavorable	pan
9				

BRIGHT LIGHTS OF 1944

an intimate revue, with music by Jerry Livingston; lyrics by Mack David; book by Norman Anthony and Charles Sherman (with Joseph Erens)

directed by Dan Eckley (replacing Anthony Brown)
produced by Alexander H. Cohen in association with Martin Poll and Joseph Kipness

with James Barton, Joe Smith & Charles Dale, Frances Williams, and Buddy Clark

opened September 16, 1943   Forrest Theatre

LOUIS KRONENBERGER, *PM*

As a tottering survivor of last week's *My Dear Public* and now of *Bright Lights of 1944*, I should like to make a modest suggestion. I think a great deal of suffering could be avoided if for a limited time—say 150 years—no one produced a musical show about people producing a musical show. These little efforts seem to have something the matter with them. They bring on some alarming ailment in the dialogue writers which spreads to the cast and is even transmitted to the audience. *Bright Lights,* for example, is about a bunch of people who congregate in Sardi's—a blameless institution where I have spent many pleasant hours—and work up a revue. Their plans involve a good deal of humorous conversation that is spectacularly ghastly. It would not be tolerated in even the most abandoned home, which is doubtless why it is foisted on Sardi's.

BURTON RASCOE, *World-Telegram*

It is, as a whole, vastly inferior in quality to a standard revue in the better night clubs and is more likely a badly arranged tryout for the benefit of talent scouts, with one or two good numbers thrown in for sucker bait.

WILELLA WALDORF, *Post*

Bright Lights of 1944 is about as bright as lower Fifth Avenue in the dimout. How anybody connected with the production could ever have imagined for an instant that it would last until 1944 is impossible to say. If it is still here next week, we shall be amazed. . . . Renee Carroll, Sardi's familiar hat check girl, made a couple of brief appearances as herself, remarking at one point that she had money in the show. We hope for Renee's sake it was just a gag.

☆

An early tuner from producer Alexander H. Cohen, whose big-scale song-and-dancers were to include such memorable evenings as *Rugantino* (1964); *Baker Street* (1965); *A Time for Singing* (1966); the Soupy Sales *Hellzapoppin'* (1967), which closed out of town; *Dear World* (1969); *Prettybelle* (1971), which closed out of town; the Jerry Lewis *Hellzapoppin'* (1976), which closed out of town; and *I Remember Mama* (1979).

BROADWAY SCORECARD / perfs: 4 / $: −

rave	favorable	mixed	unfavorable	pan
		1	3	4

BUTTRIO SQUARE

a musical comedy, with music by Arthur Jones and Fred Stamer; lyrics by Gen Genovese; book by Billy Gilbert and Gen Genovese, from a play by Hal Cranton based on a story by Gen Genovese

directed by Eugene Loring (replacing Dale Wasserman); choreographed by Eugene Loring
produced by Gen Genovese and Edward Woods
with Billy Gilbert, Lawrence Brooks, Lois Hunt, and Susan Johnson

opened October 14, 1952   New Century Theatre

BROOKS ATKINSON, *Times*

A certain malicious logic runs through the whole production. For want of an idea, the book is muddled. For want of a book, the direction is muddled. Once *Buttrio Square* gets off to a hackneyed start, nothing can change the race toward oblivion. Eugene Loring's stage direction is like rush-hour on the subway. Since Billy Gilbert is down as one of the co-authors, he cannot blame the writers for the part he is playing. He is starred, it says in small print on the program, but his part seems to have no connection with the play. Mr. Gilbert stammers coyly, seldom finishes a sentence, raises his eyes to heaven in sentimental anguish, and fumbles everything in an old-fashioned comic way. As a writer Mr. Gilbert has made his job as an actor impossible.

WILLIAM HAWKINS, *World-Telegram & Sun*

If the energy and spirit of the ensemble, and the fresh comic presence of Susan Johnson, were the sole gauges for *Buttrio Square,* the new musical would be a raging hit. Miss Johnson has the touch and timing of a veteran. She suggests some of the best features of June Allyson and Eve Arden, a mighty combine in one little girl, and managed to be very funny in overalls without a moment ceasing to be feminine.

WALTER KERR, *Herald Tribune*

All kinds of things have been happening to *Buttrio Square.* Half of its financing disappeared during rehearsal. Directors were switched in midstream. It had to postpone. The acting company had to dig into their own pockets to see that the curtain went up. And the worst thing of all happened to it Tuesday night: it did. Knowing the vicissitudes that had beset a gallant crew, no one could go to the Century last night without crossing his fingers and wishing everybody well. During the overture you hoped it would be good. During the first number you hoped it would be good. After that you just hoped it would be over. . . . The best thing that can be said for the score as a whole is that it isn't derivative. At least I never heard anything like it before.

RICHARD WATTS JR., *Post*

Billy Gilbert, who used to be a movie specialist in sneezing, has written himself a sentimental characterization as a poor old fellow with delusions of fatherhood, and I think I even prefer him sneezing.

Due to underfinancing and heavy tryout losses, an additional $20,000 was needed to get to opening night. Marti Stevens, a singer in a small role (and daughter of Hollywood exec Nicholas Schenck), agreed to put up $10,000 if Actors' Equity would make $10,000 worth of concessions. Actors' Equity, not surprisingly, would not. Choreographer Eugene Loring came up with a plan to raise the matching funds: fifty members of the cast and company put up $200 each, and the show went on. And under.

BROADWAY SCORECARD / perfs: 7 / $: −

rave	favorable	mixed	unfavorable	pan
				7

BY THE BEAUTIFUL SEA

a musical comedy, with music by Arthur Schwartz; lyrics by Dorothy Fields; book by Herbert and Dorothy Fields

directed by Marshall Jamison (replacing Charles Walters); choreographed by Helen Tamiris (replacing Donald Saddler)
produced by Robert Fryer and Lawrence Carr
with Shirley Booth, Wilbur Evans, Cameron Prud'homme, Mae Barnes, and Richard France (replacing Ray Malone)

opened April 8, 1954   Majestic Theatre

WILLIAM HAWKINS, *World-Telegram & Sun*

The honors won by Miss Booth never come from spotlights, gleaming entrances, or carefully protected routines. She is adored because of her warm, personal quality, her contagious gaiety, and the great good taste that keeps her from putting pressure on the audience. The well-meaning experts who built *By the Beautiful Sea* rarely protect the star. Conspicuous songs go to supporting players. Miss Booth is asked to follow thunderous numbers with subdued pathos. Yet she finishes the evening undisputedly stellar. It is a triumph of mime over clatter. This is a remarkable performance, maybe a unique one. If you want to know what really being a star is, see Shirley Booth in *By the Beautiful Sea*. She is a million-dollar value in show business. This musical often tucks that gold into a sock under a mattress, instead of investing it. Despite all that, she blithely pays off. Shirley Booth has already been named the World's Best Actress. *By the Beautiful Sea* adds the title of the Theatre's Best Sport.

WALTER KERR, *Herald Tribune*

In *By the Beautiful Sea* there is a splendid balloon, designed by Jo Mielziner, that sails right up off the ground. There is also a book by Herbert and Dorothy Fields that never does. Between the airborne scenery and the earthbound book stands Shirley Booth, foursquare against the world. After last night's exhibition, I think there can no longer be any reasonable doubt: Miss Booth is the champ. It doesn't matter to her that the things she is asked to do are always pedestrian and sometimes even incoherent. It doesn't matter to her that the show's lyrics never get a lot better than "I'd make your lips fit mine just like a glove." It doesn't worry her that the jokes run to "He's only broke from not having money." She has come in for the evening to entertain, she has a very clear idea of how she's going to do it, and she does it with the least fuss imaginable. There is nothing pushy about this easygoing Duse's comic method. She strides cooly across the stage, flicks a finger at her feather boa, and coos out an epithet like "You're somewhat of a little stinker, aren't you?" with all the gentleness in the world. There is such kindness in this nasal voice that no gag ever comes down hard. There is so much warmth behind the blowzy facade that the most routine musical-comedy love scene takes on a sudden defiant shine.

A Tree Grows in Brooklyn (1951) was a first-rate (if slightly flawed) Shirley Booth starrer from Schwartz, Fields, Abbott, and Fryer. *By the Beautiful Sea* was a second turn-of-the-century Shirley Booth Brooklyn tuner—set in Coney Island rather than Williamsburg—from Schwartz, Fields, and Fryer. Guess which name is missing.

A Donaldson Award was won by Shirley Booth (actress).

BROADWAY SCORECARD / perfs: 270 / $: −

rave	favorable	mixed	unfavorable	pan
4	1	2		

BYE BYE BIRDIE

a musical satire, with music by Charles Strouse; lyrics by Lee Adams; book by Michael Stewart, from the unproduced libretto "Let's Go Steady" by Warren Miller and Raphael Millian

directed and choreographed by Gower Champion
produced by Edward Padula in association with L. Slade Brown
with Chita Rivera, Dick Van Dyke, Kay Medford, Paul Lynde, and Dick Gautier

opened April 14, 1960   Martin Beck Theatre

FRANK ASTON, *World-Telegram & Sun*

The curtain at the Martin Beck has been down 22 minutes. To give some idea of what has been happening, this reviewer's wife became so enthusiastic over the new show she lost her hat in the dark and hasn't found it yet. In terms of Broadway musicals, *Bye Bye Birdie* is the peak of the season. Chita Rivera, a canasta of streamlines [*sic*], is triumphant as dancer, comic, and warbler. . . . Where do you suppose that hat got to? What a show!

BROOKS ATKINSON, *Times*

The audience was beside itself with pleasure. This department was able to contain itself. *Bye Bye Birdie* is neither fish, fowl, nor good musical comedy. It needs work.

JOHN CHAPMAN, *Daily News*

Bye Bye Birdie is the funniest, most captivating, and most expert musical comedy one could hope to see in several seasons of show-going. And one of the best things about it is that practically nobody is connected with it. Who ever heard of Edward Padula, the producer? Who except their fans has heard of the composer and lyric writer, Charles Strouse and Lee Adams, who have dabbled in revues and night club shows? Who ever heard of Gower Champion except a few million TV watchers? The show is pure, plain musical comedy, with jokes, dancing, oddball costumes [designed by Miles White], exceptionally catchy orchestrations by Robert Ginzler, and a completely enthusiastic cast. The sooner you go to the box office, the sooner you will be able to enjoy a happy, zestful, clean, smart musical.

ROBERT COLEMAN, *Daily Mirror*

Edward Padula put over a sleeper in the Broadway sweepstakes and it's going to pay off in big figures to its backers. First-nighters had been waiting for something to cheer, and they found it last evening. They made the Beck's walls rock 'n' roll like a town hall hit by a tornado. Chita Rivera explodes like a bomb over West 45th Street. Michael Stewart has penned a sassy and fresh book, while Lee Adams and Charles Strouse have matched it with tongue-in-cheek lyrics and music. This trio should have local impresarios beating a path to their doors this morning. And by the time *Birdie* has ended its run, they should be penthouse doors. *Bye Bye Birdie* is a howling hit, as invigorating as the Spring breezes we're enjoying. Maestro George Abbott, a wizard with such frolics, will probably be doffing his chapeau in admiration of Gower Champion by the time you read this rave.

WALTER KERR, *Herald Tribune*

I do mean to suggest that Mr. Champion has been very much responsible for the gayety, the winsomeness, and the exuberant zing of the occasion. As nearly as one can see through the jolly production to the paper on which it was written, he has not always been given the very best to work with. Mr. Van Dyke's jokes, when you aren't whizzing past them, tend to run to denunciations of traitors "who stabbed me in the heart while my back was turned." Every once in a while Michael Stewart's book starts to break down and cry: a plot twist involving an imported blonde, and a first act finale that must mug awfully hard to keep going, are briefly disturbing. Lee Adams's lyrics lean rather heavily on the new "talk-out-the-plot" technique, and Charles Strouse's tunes, though jaunty, are whisper-thin.

One of the biggest "sleepers" in Broadway history, from a bunch of novices. First-time producer Edward Padula, a stage manager for Maurice Evans, optioned the property when Evans dropped it. Mike Stewart came in late, adding the "Conrad Birdie" storyline to what had been "a teen-age musical in the mood of *Good News!*" (1927). Gower Champion's prior efforts—*Lend an Ear* (1948), *Make a Wish* (1951), and *Three for Tonight* (1955)—made his "overnight" rise to eminence seem inevitable. A new type of musical was emerging, far from the Rodgers and Hammerstein tradition; more like an Abbott show—fast, funny, almost farcical—but with winged feet. Everybody seemed to love *Birdie* except Brooks Atkinson, who ended his four decades at the *Times* a month later.

In addition to winning the Tony Award for Best Musical, Tonys were won by Michael Stewart (librettist); Gower Champion (director); Gower Champion (choreographer); Edward Padula (producer); and Dick Van Dyke (supporting actor). For the only time since the Best Composer category was established in 1949, no award was given (other also-rans included *Camelot*, *Irma La Douce*, and *The Unsinkable Molly Brown.*) The only time until the 1988–89 season, that is, when no awards were given for score *or* book.

BROADWAY SCORECARD / perfs: 607 / $: +

rave	favorable	mixed	unfavorable	pan
6		1		

CAFE CROWN

a musical comedy, with music by Albert Hague; lyrics by Marty Brill; book by Hy Kraft, from his 1942 comedy

directed by Jerome Eskow; choreographed by Ronald (Ron) Field
produced by Philip Rose and Swanlee
with Sam Levene, Theodore Bikel (replacing Joseph Schildkraut), Brenda Lewis, Tommy Rall, and Alan Alda

opened April 15, 1964   Martin Beck Theatre

LEONARD HARRIS, *World-Telegram & Sun*

Cafe Crown could use a bowl of chicken soup.

WALTER KERR, *Herald Tribune*

A memorial service for *Cafe Crown* was held at the Martin Beck Theatre last night. A few friends and well-wishers of Sam Levene gathered to console him for the loss of his show. Mr. Levene has been cast as a waiter in a Second Avenue restaurant, and he has nothing to do but wait—wait on tables, wait for the author to give someone else a funny line (it's clear, after a time, that none are coming his way), wait for the choreographer to get through doing a grisly ballet based on *King Lear*, wait, perhaps, for the show to close. The performers are deeply embarrassed, and there isn't a thing they can do about it. Theodore Bikel is pallid and palpitating as a Second Avenue theatrical partriarch, looking rather like Ludwig van Beethoven without the spectacles but sounding, courtesy of the musical arrangements [by Hershy Kay], as though no key in the world would suit him. For the second time this season, and for the second time in a disaster, special mention must be made of Alan Alda. He plays a dentist from Buffalo who learns that there is no difference between chopped liver and chopped herring if you chop it fine enough (that's about as good a line as Mr. Levene ever gets). Alda remains alert enough to land a genuine laugh of his own as late as Act Two, Scene Four. Mr. Alda should be noted by people who have better shows in mind.

RICHARD WATTS JR., *Post*

The atmosphere of the early '30s is suggested chiefly by a passing reference to Lon Chaney.

Perhaps Joseph Schildkraut could have pulled this one off; when he died on January 21, 1964, they replaced him as best (?) they could, and the show went on. But not very far. Theodore Bikel, whose Broadway musical debut had been as the guitar-strumming Baron in *The Sound of Music* (1959), soon got to do a second "Cafe" musical: *Pousse-Café* (1966), Jerome Weidman, Duke Ellington, and José Quintero's version of the 1930 German movie *The Blue Angel*. Set in New Orleans, Lilo of *Can-Can* (1953) played the Dietrich role. Sounds good, no? Every bit as good as *Cafe Crown*, *Pousse-Café* enjoyed three performances and out. Alan Alda fared somewhat better: producer Philip Rose, who introduced the son of Robert (*Guys and Dolls* [1950]) Alda to Broadway in *Purlie Victorious* (1961), soon starred him opposite Diana Sands in *The Owl and the Pussycat* (1964).

BROADWAY SCORECARD / perfs: 3 / $: —

rave	favorable	mixed	unfavorable	pan
			1	5

CALL ME MADAM

a musical comedy, with music and lyrics by Irving Berlin; book by Howard Lindsay and Russel Crouse, suggested by the 1949 appointment of Washington hostess Perle Mesta as Ambassadress to Luxembourg

directed by George Abbott; choreographed by Jerome Robbins
produced by Leland Hayward
with Ethel Merman, Paul Lukas, Alan Hewitt, Russell Nype, and Galina Talva

opened October 12, 1950   Imperial Theatre

BROOKS ATKINSON, *Times*

A good-hearted show with a very happy manner. And Ethel Merman is in it. Russell Nype made a lot of friends last evening by acting with modesty and sincerity. As a timid grind fresh out of college he does not look very promising in the early scenes. But eventually it turns out that Mr. Nype can also sing. When Miss Merman and he sing "You're Just in Love," which is Mr. Berlin's top achievement for the evening, *Call Me Madam* throws a little stardust around the theatre and sets the audience roaring. Quite an evening on the whole.

JOHN CHAPMAN, *Daily News*

A curious combination of *State of the Union* (1945), *A Texas Steer* (1890), and *The Red Mill* (1906). The authors of the bright, sharp *State of the Union* have fallen down pretty badly in the humor department. Their jokes about Senators and foreign loans are not uproarious, and last evening I got a little tired of Miss Merman answering the phone, saying "Hello, Harry" and asking

The initial announcement ad states that no threatre parties would be accepted: why pay commissions to party agents when you have a sure-fire hit? The ban on brokers and 6-ticket limit were a response to highly public Shubert box office scandals on Annie Get Your Gun and South Pacific. (drawing by Peter Arno)

how Margaret did in her last concert. Chic Johnson [of Olsen and Johnson] takes care of Margaret quicker in *Pardon our French* (1950) by shooting her right off the bat. . . . Miss Merman is her old great self, singing like a boat whistle, and leering like a female Valentino except when that confounded Graustarkian plot slows her down.

ROBERT COLEMAN, *Daily Mirror*

Thanks to the incomparable Ethel Merman, they'll be calling *Call Me Madam* a smash hit. What Joe DiMaggio is in the clutch for the Yankees, so La Merman is when the chips are down for the new arrival at the Imperial. It is the terrific Ethel who has to hit the homers after her associates have walked or singled. And she never lets the team down. *Call Me Madam* opened to an historic advance sale of close to a $1,000,000 at a $7.20 top. By curtain time, would-be first-nighters were offering as high as $400 a pair for any seats in the house, with no sellers reported. The ermine wrap and white-tie set embraced *Call Me Madam* affectionately, and gave Miss Merman a richly deserved ovation. What a trouper! As Walter Winchell put it: "They ought to call it 'Call Me Merman'!" . . . There is a snappy campaign song called "They Like Ike." Among those who enjoyed Pat Harrington's rollicking rendition of it was none other than General Eisenhower himself.

WILLIAM HAWKINS, *World-Telegram & Sun*

With the nervous excitement and glitter in the Imperial last night, you could have sent a rocket to the moon. It just had to be tops. The curtain went up, some gentlemen parted company, and there was Ethel Merman. She opened her mouth, and the reassurance in the house was as tangible as the joy of a kid getting a promised pony. . . . Irving Berlin has officially nominated Eisenhower for the Presidency in a song called "They Like Ike" which draws so much applause you can hardly hear the lyric.

A mildly satirical, old-fashioned musical which got by on the power of its star (at the height of her popularity) and Berlin's final hit show tune, "You're Just in Love." As the program noted, "Neither the character of Mrs. Sally Adams, nor Miss Ethel Merman, resembles any other person alive or dead." Within a decade *Call Me Madam* was hopelessly dated, as Berlin himself discovered in 1967 when he wrote additional songs for a television version which never got produced.

Tony Awards were won by Ethel Merman (actress); Russell Nype (supporting actor); and Pete Feller (stage technician). A Donaldson Award was won by Russell Nype (supporting actor).

BROADWAY SCORECARD / perfs: 644 / $: +

rave	favorable	mixed	unfavorable	pan
5	1		1	

CALL ME MISTER

a musical revue, with music and lyrics by Harold J. Rome; sketches mostly by Arnold Auerbach

directed by Robert H. Gordon; choreographed by John Wray
produced by Melvyn Douglas and Herman Levin
with Betty Garrett, Jules Munshin, Bill Callahan, and Lawrence Winters

opened April 18, 1946   National Theatre

HOWARD BARNES, *Herald Tribune*

Vitality and finesse are blended happily in *Call Me Mister*. This G.I. show about G.I. Joes is something of a boisterous romp as it takes satirical cognizance of military life, problems of reconversion, Park Avenue, the deep South, and even South American dances. But there is no dearth of artful showmanship in the new revue. The ex-G.I.s and erstwhile U.S.O. entertainers have had a major break in their material. The Rome music and lyrics are as excellent as they are varied, ranging from simple songs to splendidly integrated choral numbers. *Call Me Mister* is a captivating show. It is fresh, vigorous, and, what was least to have been expected, it has great style. It brightens the waning season no end.

ROBERT GARLAND, *Journal-American*

Call Me Mister has everything it takes to make a grand night of theatregoing. I can't remember when I've had a better time on Broadway. Song-and-dance shows such as this ex-servicemen's and ex-servicewomen's revue are a rarity. *Call Me Mister* is youthful without being juvenile, funny without being forced, satiric without being bitter. Best are the words and music of Harold Rome. Having dropped the "S.S." which used to stand for "social significance" in the middle of his name, Mr. Rome combines lyrics that are brilliant without being strained with tunes that are memorable without being derivative.

WILLIAM HAWKINS, *World-Telegram*

If the future of America is in the hands of G.I. Joes and Janes like those involved in *Call Me Mister* nobody need worry. They are conscious of their country's problems and can be good humored about them. They throw all they have into the job, but never oversell you. They quit when work is well done while you still want more. *Call Me Mister* is welcome—and it's a hit.

VERNON RICE, *Post*

Whatever it is that is in an ex-G.I.'s heart when he first hears the word "Mister," that quality has been transposed upon the stage of the National. The sheer joy of hearing the word pronounced warms the soul, and so does the show. It is probably no news to anyone that the lastest addition to the roster of Broadway musicals is composed entirely of men who were in some branch of the Armed Forces during World War II, and that goes for Melvyn Douglas, co-producer with Herman Levin; Harold J. Rome, who wrote the music and lyrics; and Arnold Auerbach, the person responsible for the sketches. If a girl performer weren't a Wac or a Wave or some such, she was either a U.S.O. trouper, a hospital performer, or a canteen entertainer. From the rise of the curtain on the opening number to the final curtain, buoyant energy is all over the place. And it flows from the stage to you. Much of the musical has a specialized appeal for those just out of uniform, or for those who have someone in that state or about to be. With the war having been so all-inclusive, that doesn't exclude very many people. In *Call Me Mister* are a touch of pathos, a good portion of laughter mixed with pleasant sights and sounds, timely appeal, and youthful high spirits.

A sleeper, seemingly thrown together by a bunch of guys and gobs. The refreshingly unpretentious *Call Me Mister* perfectly captured the mood of the day and held its own against flashier entertainments—including the season's four-star monster smash *Annie Get Your Gun* (1946). *Mister* was shepherded by two novice producers: Hollywood star Melvyn Douglas (who went back to acting) and Harold Rome's lawyer Herman Levin (who went on to *Gentlemen Prefer Blondes* [1949] and *My Fair Lady* [1956]).

Donaldson Awards were won by Betty Garrett (actress) and Jules Munshin (male debut).

BROADWAY SCORECARD / perfs: 734 / $: +

rave	favorable	mixed	unfavorable	pan
6	2			

CAMELOT

a musical play, with music by Frederick Loewe; book and lyrics by Alan Jay Lerner, from the 1958 book *The Once and Future King* by T. H. White.

directed by Moss Hart (with Alan Jay Lerner); choreographed by Hanya Holm
produced by Alan Jay Lerner, Frederick Loewe, and Moss Hart
with Richard Burton, Julie Andrews, Roddy McDowell, Robert Coote, and Robert Goulet

opened December 3, 1960   Majestic Theatre

JOHN CHAPMAN, *Daily News*

Camelot is magnificent. Its songs are lovely and unfailingly right. Its cast is superb. The sets and costumes of its 20 scenes have far more than splendor; together they make a single, thrilling work of art. Good taste—the instinctive knowledge of what is right and proper—is paramount. . . . Why should *Camelot* have given Moss Hart a heart attack and Alan Jay Lerner serious ulcer trouble when it made me feel so well?

ROBERT COLEMAN, *Daily Mirror*

Lerner, Loewe, and Hart spent so much to mount *Camelot* that the wisecrackers have been calling it "Costallot." Rialto rumor has it that the new musical represents an investment of more than $500,000. And it looks it, too. If it's pageantry and spectacle you're willing to settle for, *Camelot* offers a lot. But, in our book, it's no *My Fair Lady* [1956]. We suspect that Lerner set out to pen a serious satire on knighthood in flower, and missed the boat. His philosophy lacks true depth, and there's too little wit about the premises. There's all too little of the tongue-in-cheek that marked Rodgers and Hart's delightful *A Connecticut Yankee* [1927], a spoof on the same theme.

WALTER KERR, *Herald Tribune*

Our myth-crossed romancers are all on hand now [after Lancelot's entrance song, *"C'est Moi"*], beautifully dressed, beautifully spoken, ever so promising. Then, incredibly there is a slip of the pen. Two slips. Librettist Lerner fails to define the flowering relationship between Arthur and Guenevere; we don't know what we are to feel, to hope, to fear for them. And the moment in which Guenevere's unwilling passion leaps toward Lancelot is missing; it is indicated in the staging, during a very long silence, but it is not there emotionally. Now, instead of being tugged two ways and to a fare-thee-well we are tugged not at all. Beneath the unfailing splendor, the pulse stops. With no truly affecting legend of love to go on, the balance of the evening is filled with wayward gestures. "Once there was a fleeting wisp of glory!" cries Richard Burton as he awaits the last curtain alone. And there was. But for *Camelot* as well as for Arthur's court, it is the glory of a steadily setting sun. . . . It is impossible to assess Moss Hart's direction at this juncture, because the secure, precise hand that guided *My Fair Lady* was so early and so unluckily withdrawn.

Lancelot (Robert Goulet), Guenevere (Julie Andrews), and King Arthur (Richard Burton) furrow their brows over book trouble. (set by Oliver Smith, Costumes by Adrian and Tony Duquette, photo by Friedman-Abeles)

JOHN McCLAIN, *Journal-American*

It would seem to be impossible to top *My Fair Lady* and indeed it is. . . . Great Holy Grail!, it is the most beautiful and resplendent show in the world. It is as though the boys realized they hadn't come up with much of a book, certainly no tunes to equal "On the Street Where You Live" or "Gigi," had hence turned to Oliver Smith, the scenic designer, handed him the ball and told him to run with it—and a fig for cost. Some similar instructions must have been relayed to Adrian [the M.G.M. designer, who died in 1959] and Tony Duquette, the costume creators, for the combination of these two elements has produced a series of living tableaux which for color and conception could chase many an old master off the walls of our museums. The result, of course, is that the splendor of the surroundings overpowers everything else. *Camelot* is by no means the most notable effort of the Messrs. Lerner, Loewe, and Hart. But, thanks to Mr. Smith, it shore is purty!

HOWARD TAUBMAN, *Times*

Although its people are handsome and its vistas beautiful, *Camelot* is a partly enchanted city. At the outset, the new musical glows with magic. The impossible seems to have happened. The inspired creators of *My Fair Lady* appear to have passed another miracle. In "Camelot" [the end of the opening scene], they sing of the wonders of enchantment, and we, too, are enchanted. Almost two hours of playing time elapse before we arrive at a similarly enchanted scene. Unfortunately, *Camelot* is weighed down by the burden of its book. The style of the story-telling is inconsistent. It shifts uneasily between light-hearted fancy and uninflected reality. Graceful and sumptuous though it is, *Camelot* leans dangerously in the direction of old-hat operetta. It has intervals of enchantment, as it must with talented men like Lerner, Loewe, and Hart in charge. It would be unjust to tax them with not attaining the heights of *My Fair Lady*, but it cannot be denied that they badly miss their late collaborator—Bernard Shaw. . . . Lancelot, sung and played splendidly though he is by Robert Goulet, is a pompous bore. Were it not for the personal communication of Miss Andrews and Mr. Burton, Guenevere and Arthur would not be very engaging.

☆

The *My Fair Lady* men decided they didn't even need a producer, they could do it all themselves. They couldn't. The *Camelot* experience sent them all to the hospital. Moss Hart never quite recovered, dying on December 20, 1961, while Frederick Loewe simply walked away from Alan Lerner and retired altogether. Lerner hung around for the rest of his life, offering Broadway a handful of additional musicals (that Broadway rejected out-of-hand).

Tony Awards were won by Richard Burton (actor); Oliver Smith (scenic designer, for *Camelot* and *Becket*); Tony Duquette and Adrian (costume designers); and Franz Allers (musical director).

BROADWAY SCORECARD / perfs: 873 / $: +

rave	favorable	mixed	unfavorable	pan
1	1	2	3	

CAN-CAN

a musical comedy, with music and lyrics by Cole Porter; book by Abe Burrows

directed by Abe Burrows; choreographed by Michael Kidd
produced by Cy Feuer and Ernest H. Martin
with Lilo, Peter Cookson, Hans Conried, Gwen Verdon, and Erik Rhodes

opened May 7, 1953   Shubert Theatre

JOHN CHAPMAN, *Daily News*

The greatest joy of last evening was a lissome lass with reddish hair and a docked pony-tail coiffure, Miss Gwen Verdon. Miss Verdon, a dancer and a comedienne, stole the show from Burrows, Porter, Cookson, Lilo, costumer Motley, and scenic designer Jo Mielziner. In this happy theft Miss Verdon was aided by Michael Kidd, who has devised three splendid ballets. One is a history of what happened in the "Garden of Eden" in one easy lesson, and the sight of Miss Verdon taking a chunk out of the old apple and

An Impressionistic logo somewhat more exciting than Can-Can itself. (*drawing by F. Canore*)

immediately discovering the usefulness of a fig leaf is one of the funniest moments of the stage season.

WILLIAM HAWKINS, *World-Telegram & Sun*

Last night the audience did some elevation on the billing. The little French import, Lilo, went into the show a star. And Gwen Verdon came out of it a star. The crowd's increasing delight with Miss Verdon was exciting to feel. She spellbound the house with the quadrille and the can-can, and after the *"Apache"* uproar they had to send her out for a last bow with her costume already off and clutched in front of her.

WALTER KERR, *Herald Tribune*

The text sounds as though Burrows had been called in to do one of his famous rewrite jobs and had only got around to yocking up a couple of scenes. And Cole Porter's score is by no means his most distinguished. No Porter score is hard to listen to; neither is this one. But it couldn't have been hard to write, either. *Can-Can* is far and away at its most dynamic when Mr. Kidd is in charge. The first act finale is a splendidly idiotic miming of certain historic events in the "Garden of Eden," studded with enchantingly animated sea-horses, leopards, caterpillars, and kangaroos. Kidd has done us the further service of introducing a red-headed extrovert named Gwen Verdon. From the time she starts playing footsie with a tempting apple in that first act finish, she is the dance discovery of the season. Miss Verdon comes upon sex with a magnificent astonishment, rueful, dismayed, interested, and deeply pleased all at once. And the abandon with which she takes over the later *"Apache"* business—sending chairs and males spinning with a flick of her ankle—is devastating. The audience held up the show for some minutes in Miss Verdon's honor last evening, causing the actress to take a breathless bow in even greater *déshabillé* than the producers of *Can-Can* probably intended.

A not-so-good show which nevertheless managed an impressive run (it was a not-so-good season). Gwen Verdon, choreographer Jack Cole's dance assistant, had previously appeared in the brief *Alive and Kicking* (1950). After summarily eclipsing *Can-Can* lead-

Eve discovers the forbidden fruit in the "Garden of Eden" and Broadway discovers its newest star: Gwen Verdon, flanked by inch-worms Ina Hahn and Socrates Birsky. (set by Jo Mielziner, costumes by Motley, photo by Carl S. Perutz)

ing lady Lilo, Verdon moved on to full stardom with *Damn Yankees* (1955) and Bob Fosse. Michael Kidd's ensemble included *four* future Broadway choreographers: Ralph Beaumont (*Saratoga* [1959]), Dania Krupska (*The Most Happy Fella* [1956]), Tom Panko (*Golden Rainbow* [1968]), and Deedee Wood (*Do Re Mi* [1960]). Also on hand was specialty dancer Eddie Phillips, who went with Verdon into *Damn Yankees* ("Who's Got the Pain?") and the 1957 *New Girl in Town* ("Sunshine Girl"). The singers included Arthur Rubin, whose glorious high tenor was prominent in *Silk Stockings* (1955), *The Most Happy Fella*, *Juno* (1959), *Kean* (1961), and *Here's Love* (1963). Rubin eventually became general manager of the Nederlander Theatres, in which capacity he coproduced the 1980 Broadway revival of *Can-Can*—no Michael Kidd or Gwen Verdon, just that mediocre score and book. Five performances and out.

Tony Awards were won by Michael Kidd (choreographer) and Gwen Verdon (supporting actress). Donaldson Awards were won by Michael Kidd (choreographer) and Gwen Verdon (supporting actress; female dancer).

BROADWAY SCORECARD / perfs: 892 / $: +

rave	favorable	mixed	unfavorable	pan
2	3	2		

CANDIDE

a satirical operetta, with music by Leonard Bernstein; lyrics by Richard Wilbur, additional lyrics by John Latouche, Dorothy Parker, and Leonard Bernstein; book by Lillian Hellman, from the 1758 satire by Voltaire

directed by Tyrone Guthrie; "choreographic assistance" by Anna Sokolow
produced by Ethel Linder Reiner in association with Lester Osterman, Jr.
with Max Adrian, Robert Rounseville, Barbara Cook, and Irra Petina

opened December 1, 1956   Martin Beck Theatre

BROOKS ATKINSON, *Times*

Since Voltaire was a brilliant writer, it is only right that his *Candide* should turn out to be a brilliant musical satire. Voltaire's cynical acceptance of war, greed, treachery, venery, snobbishness, and mendacity as staples of civilization provokes no disbelief in the middle of the twentieth century. . . . Barbara Cook is a lustrous singer, particularly in Mr. Bernstein's own version of how a jewel song should be written ["Glitter and Be Gay"]. And her acting portrayal of a lyrical maiden who quickly learns how to connive with the world is sketched with skill, spirit, and humor.

JOHN CHAPMAN, *Daily News*

Sixty seconds after conductor Samuel Krachmalnick brought down his baton for the overture, one sensed that here was going to be an evening of uncommon quality. It developed into an artistic triumph—the best light opera, I think, since Richard Strauss wrote *Der Rosenkavalier* in 1911. It is a great contribution to the richness of the American musical comedy stage. Many artists of many skills have had a hand in fashioning *Candide*, but it is Bernstein's profoundly sophisticated and witty score which puts it in a class by itself on Broadway. Bernstein has put an enormous amount of music, and a great variety of it, into his score. The comic highlight is his witty burlesque of a coloratura aria in which Miss Cook exults, "Glitter and Be Gay." There are trios, quarters, waltzes, ballads, a wonderful tango, hornpipes, and many other exciting offerings. Generally speaking, the music achieves an 18th-Century effect with remarkably modern methods. It is a work of genius. Now all I can hope is that Broadway, which is unpredictable and which does not always like to be jogged out of its routine, will cherish it as it should be cherished.

TOM DONNELLY, *World-Telegram & Sun*

To get the big news out in a hurry, Leonard Bernstein's music is lush, lovely, and electric. When it isn't voluptuous as velvet, it is as frostily pretty as a diamond bell. It is easily the best score Mr. Bernstein has written for the theatre. To go a step further, it is one of the most attractive scores anyone has written for the theatre. . . . Miss Cook tears down the house with a coloratura attack on a song called "Glitter and Be Gay," lustily achieving the trill beyond the trill beyond the trill [ref. Kern and Hammerstein's "There's a Hill Beyond a Hill" from *Music in the Air* (1932)].

WALTER KERR, *Herald Tribune*

Three of the most talented people our theatre possesses—Lillian Hellman, Leonard Bernstein, Tyrone Guthrie—have joined hands to transform Voltaire's *Candide* into a really spectacular disaster. Who is mostly responsible for the great ghostly wreck that sails like a Flying Dutchman across the fogbound stage of the Martin Beck? That would be hard to say, the honors are so evenly distributed. . . . Satire, as I understand it, is a matter of humor—partly of good humor, partly of snappish wit. Miss Hellman's attack on it is academic, blunt, and barefaced. Pessimism is the order of the evening.

Contrary to legend, the original production of *Candide* created great (if not unanimous) excitement, and Bernstein's score received instant (and in some cases rapturous) acclaim. But tart satire and costume operetta were not smoothly combined, and the times were not conducive to the message. *Candide* was revised and revived by director Harold Prince in 1974 with considerably greater success. The grandeur of Bernstein's musical satire was lost in the scaling-down process, though, as were some of the deliciously dazzling lyrics (replaced by lesser ones from the pen of Stephen Sondheim). But the 1974 version moved *Candide* from the cult failure class to a world classic, which is all to the good.

BROADWAY SCORECARD / perfs: 73 / $: −				
rave	favorable	mixed	unfavorable	pan
2	2	2		1

CARIBBEAN CARNIVAL

"the first Calypso musical ever presented," with music and lyrics by Samuel L. Manning and Adolph Thenstead; book uncredited

directed by Samuel L. Manning and Col. John J. Hirshman; choreographed by Claude Marchant (with Pearl Primus)
produced by Adolph Thenstead
with Pearl Primus, Josephine Premice, and Claude Marchant
opened December 5, 1947   International Theatre

JOHN CHAPMAN, *Daily News*

Caribbean Carnival was effective enough to drive me out into Columbus Circle with a throbbing head, a feeling of unrest, and a resolve not to look at anybody's big toes, including mine, for a long time. . . . The beat beat beat of the tom-toms as the jungle shadows fell made me feel like the Emperor Jones: I wanted to get out of there.

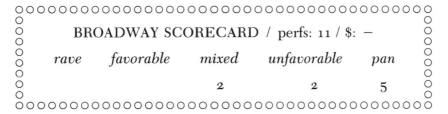

BROADWAY SCORECARD / perfs: 11 / $: —

rave	favorable	mixed	unfavorable	pan
		2	2	5

CARMEN JONES

an Americanization of the 1875 opera *Carmen*, with music by Georges Bizet; book and lyrics by Oscar Hammerstein 2nd, from Henri Meilhac and Ludovic Halévy's libretto adapted from the 1845 novel by Prosper Mérimée

"staging, lighting, and color schemes of the entire production" by Hassard Short; book directed by Charles Friedman; choreographed by Eugene Loring
produced by Billy Rose
with Muriel Smith, Luther Saxon, Glenn Bryant, and Carlotta Franzell
opened December 2, 1943   Broadway Theatre

HOWARD BARNES, *Herald Tribune*

The theatre and music have had a memorable wedding in *Carmen Jones*. This new Billy Rose production is as wonderful and

Parachute factory-worker Carmen Jones (Muriel Smith) entices heavyweight champ Husky Miller (Glenn Bryant), as Cozy Cole "Beats Out Dat Rhythm on a Drum."

exciting as it is audacious. It retains the score of the celebrated Bizet opera, but it clothes it with such miraculous showmanship that for once drama takes its right place in a music drama. The libretto has been brilliantly translated by Oscar Hammerstein 2nd into a contemporary Negro fable. It is magnificently performed and ably sung by an all-colored cast, and it has been staged with cunning and splendor. *Carmen Jones* is something more than a major theatrical event. It opens infinite and challenging horizons for the fusion of two art forms. *Carmen Jones* is not *Carmen*, but what *Carmen* might have been had it achieved a more perfect balance of theatre, spectacle, song, and dancing in the first place. A whole job of showmanship has rarely been more inspired and successful. Hassard Short has done a masterly job of over-all directing, giving color, variety, and significant action. For some of us skeptics it shows that the opera form is not as moribund as we suspected. In any case it is superlative entertainment.

JOHN CHAPMAN, *Daily News*

It rates all of the handsome adjectives that hurried fingers can find on a midnight keyboard. It is superb; it is enchantingly beautiful; it is musically exciting and visually stunning—and it still is *Carmen*, straight and pure. Last night's Carmen, Muriel Smith, is the best one I ever saw. She is believably sensuous and not just a strutter. She can sing and, believe me, she can act. She's a camera store clerk from Philadelphia and this is her first stage appearance. Last night's Joe was Luther Saxon, and he made of Joe an appealing guy. Saxon was a checker in the Philadelphia Navy Yard. And big, dominant, and quite wonderful as Husky Miller is Glenn Bryant, a New York cop on leave. Who says the theatre is falling apart, when it can find talent in navy yards, shops, and station houses? The choruses, as one might guess because they are Negro voices, are superb—better than any I ever heard at the Met. Billy Rose, my hat is off to you and I bow low.

ALTON COOK, *World-Telegram*

Billy Rose's gambling imagination has struck pay dirt in another unexplored region. The opening of his *Carmen Jones* last night poured out a rich flow of melody, humor, and color. It is opera, all right—opera with the addition of a wild, primitive charm. . . . The principal arias are all there. Surprisingly enough, the words that seemed to be so incongruous fit into the mood of the music thoroughly, frequently adding a new vitality. All of *Carmen Jones* is such a startling and unexpected departure from anything you ever saw before, the whole thing has the air of a dream production. A mighty nice dream, too.

ROBERT GARLAND, *Journal-American*

Billy Rose, the erstwhile bantam Barnum, has fetched something fresh, stalwart, and exciting onto the more or less stereotyped Broadway scene. *Carmen Jones* is, I am convinced, a memorable milestone in the upward and onward course of the great American showshop. In theatrical history it will go down as something fresh, imaginative, and, for the most part, hitherto unattempted in the theatre of today. With an all-colored cast, an intelligible American (God be praised!) libretto, and an expanded title, *Carmen Jones* is not only a great, but a stirring operetta. It is also a resounding hit!

LEWIS NICHOLS, *Times*

Billy Rose is a little man with gigantic ideas, which at suitable intervals explode over the city like a burst of fireworks. The display of last evening was one of the greatest of them all. *Carmen Jones* is beautifully done in every way, with gay colors and gay ballets, and singers who can sing as though they meant it and were on the stage for business. Since it is an opera under discussion, just call it wonderful, quite wonderful. . . . As Carmen and Joe sing "Dere's a Café on de Corner," which used to be the "*Sequidilla*"; or as Joe's "Flower Song" comes out as "Dis Flower," or the "Card Song" as "Dat Ol' Boy," going to the theatre seems again one of the necessities of life.

The phenomenal success of *Oklahoma!* (1943) made Hammerstein's adaptation of *Carmen* worth a shot. Billy Rose produced it at popular prices, to enormous success. While *Oklahoma!* is generally credited as *the* landmark in the development of the American musical, it was Hammerstein's mixture of drama, humor, and music in *Carmen Jones*—written just before *Oklahoma!*—that paved the way for *Carousel* (1945), *South Pacific* (1949), *West Side Story* (1957), *Sweeney Todd* (1979), et al.

In addition to winning the Donaldson Award for Best Musical, Donaldsons were won by Georges Bizet (composer); Oscar Hammerstein 2nd (lyricist; librettist); Hassard Short (director); Howard Bay (scenic designer); and Miles White (costume designer).

BROADWAY SCORECARD / perfs: 502 / $: +

rave	favorable	mixed	unfavorable	pan
7			1	

CARNIVAL

a musical, with music and lyrics by Bob Merrill; book by Michael Stewart, from the 1953 screenplay *Lili* by Helen Deutsch, adapted from the 1950 story "The Man Who Hated People" by Paul Gallico; previously announced as *Carrot Top*

directed and choreographed by Gower Champion
produced by David Merrick
with Anna Maria Alberghetti, James Mitchell, Kaye Ballard, Pierre Olaf, and Jerry Orbach
opened April 13, 1961   Imperial Theatre

JOHN CHAPMAN, *Daily News*

There are many kinds of magic in the musical *Carnival,* including the magic of the theatre itself, when so many different elements come miraculously together—the performances, the songs, the wonderfully imagined settings by Will Steven Armstrong and the costumes by Freddy Wittop. *And* the direction of story and dances by Gower Champion. The effect is one of enchantment from the moment the house lights go down. The curtain already is up on a bare stage when this happens, and now a carnival takes shape before one's eyes, setting up its tent and marquees and wagons. The mechanical complexities of the staging seem to vanish under the direction of Champion.

WALTER KERR, *Herald Tribune*

From the time that Pierre Olaf's accordion lets loose its first longing wheeze, while a straggle of tumblers and trumpeters make their way beneath two leafless trees, [Champion's] paint-brush is

*Horr'ble Henry (left), Carrot Top (center), and Anna Maria Al-
berghetti explain why "Loves Makes the World Go Round."* (set by
Will Steven Armstrong, *costume by Freddy Wittop, puppets by Tom Tichenor, photo by*
Friedman-Abeles)

unerringly in command. Over the misty pallet hover the wistful threads of dangling lights and the flapping, pastel, canvas flags Will Steven Armstrong has so moodily, and so successfully, designed. . . . *Carnival* is a world of shadows—wonderful to look at, as most shadows are, graceful and glancing and dancing lightly as smoke, and somewhat distant. Why is the pictorially perfect evening a little remote in its emotional effect? I have the feeling that such difficulty as exists comes from *Carnival's* inability to catch us unawares. Its sources of charm tend to announce themselves too plainly. The very magic of Mr. Champion's dreamlike opening insists that, as we come to know the people, the magic increases. But it stays more or less the same—a distillation of shade and supple movement that is itself more interesting than the folk who glide through it. *Carnival* is something more than sheer showmanship. It is painted on frosted glass, done with a hand that cares. But it is also something less than the impeccable style of its mounting: if the shadows are forever moving, the people are forever shadows.

JOHN McCLAIN, *Journal-American*

There was every prediction that David Merrick had a real big one in *Carnival*, and it is a delight to report that this musical is merely superb. It justifies all the preliminary ballyhoo, and goes on to establish itself as something quite unostentatious and very tasteful and enormously endearing. Plaudits must go principally to Bob Merrill, who here rises to eminence with an intelligent and exciting score; to Michael Stewart, for an inventive book, brought happily to date from the material from the Helen Deutsch screenplay; and predominantly to Gower Champion. A sense of style pervades the whole evening; it doesn't go like the usual musicals. They bring in all the gimmicks of a traveling carnival show, but they are never pushed. There are the jugglers, some animals, a grind girl or two, but they come along as though they belonged. The roustabouts put up the sets and take them down. But when Mr. Champion decides to give them a big number—hold onto your hat, Buster! It sails. In simple terms, *Carnival* is a monumental musical. Let Mr. K. [Khrushchev, a recent New York visitor] catch up with this one!

RICHARD WATTS JR., *Post*

The range indicated by Gower Champion's change of mood from the gay exuberance of *Bye Bye Birdie* [1960] to the romantic spell of *Carnival* suggests his remarkable creative talent for stagecraft, and his staging of the new show, the capturing and maintaining of a spirit compounded of sentiment and gayety, is a distinguished achievement. A hundred touches of high inventiveness brighten the narrative, and, without ever seeming to strain at it, he has never been at a loss for something to do that gives the evening style and avoids saccharinity.

While not as successful as *Birdie, Dolly!* (1964), or *42nd Street* (1980), *Carnival* might have been Champion's *best* musical. Built on movement and magic, the material was at all times in key with the overall mood. There were, indeed, show-stoppers; but they never distracted from the atmosphere created and enforced by Champion. Pure magic.

Winner of the New York Drama Critics' Circle Award. Tony Awards were won by Anna Maria Alberghetti (actress, tied with Diahann Carroll for *No Strings* [1962]) and Will Steven Armstrong (scenic designer).

BROADWAY SCORECARD / perfs: 719 / $: +

rave	favorable	mixed	unfavorable	pan
5	2			

CARNIVAL IN FLANDERS

a musical comedy, with music by James Van Heusen; lyrics by Johnny Burke; book by Preston Sturges (replacing George Oppenheimer and Herbert and Dorothy Fields), from the 1935 screenplay, *La Kermesse Héroïque* by Charles Spaak, Jacques Feyder, and Bernard Zimmer

directed by Preston Sturges (replacing Bretaigne Windust); choreographed by Helen Tamiris (replacing Jack Cole)
produced by Paula Stone (Sloane), Michael Sloane, and the Messrs. Burke and Van Heusen
with Dolores Gray, John Raitt, Roy Roberts (replacing William Gaxton and Walter Abel), and Pat Stanley
opened September 8, 1953   Century Theatre

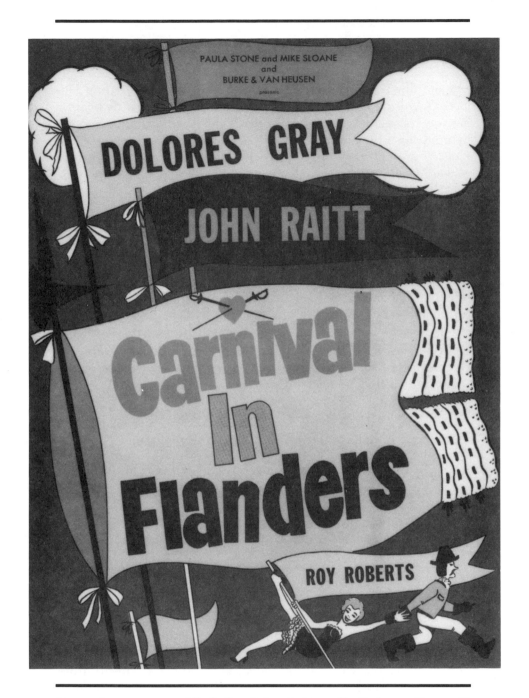

Beneath a pennant-filled sky, John Raitt pulls Dolores Gray off-stage kicking. She gets in one last bow, however. The title seems to be written on an oddly-shaped pair of ladies' bloomers.

BROOKS ATKINSON, *Times*

Some day something will have to be done about rescuing Dolores Gray from mediocrity. At the moment she is gallantly beating her way through *Carnival in Flanders*. She is authoritative enough to bring down the house with some of the maudlin songs James Van Heusen and Johnny Burke have flung together for the current ruckus. Having fought a gallant uphill tussle in *Two on the Aisle* (1951) and now having imparted some moments of glamor to *Carnival in Flanders*, Miss Gray is entitled to a part that can help her instead of the other way round. She should not be expected to supply first aid to patients that are gasping. If John Raitt had not had a good part in *Carousel* (1945) he, too, would be entitled to special consideration. He also brings the house down with a stupid song that becomes an excellent imitation of music by the time he is through with it. Although Mr. Raitt has had one good part in the last decade, he has also applied his talents to *Magdalena* (1948) and *Three Wishes for Jamie* (1952) and now to *Carnival in Flanders*. He is entitled to be in something that a theatregoer can enjoy. [Raitt starred in *The Pajama Game* (1954) later that season.]

WILLIAM HAWKINS, *World-Telegram & Sun*

There are periods in the evening when the whole thing begins to resemble a concert by Dolores Gray. As the mayor's wife, she is ever in evidence. Clearly whenever anyone was at a loss, the solution was to give Miss Gray another number. She does duets, production numbers, solos, and winds up with a one-woman cantata.

WALTER KERR, *Herald Tribune*

A lot of the intended comedy in *Carnival in Flanders* has to do with the problem of placing a floral wreath on a corpse. Let me place mine here now. It seems that a good many collaborators have come and gone during the production's tryout stands on the road, and it is impossible to say how much Mr. Sturges has had to do with draining the wit, the buoyance, and the droll asperity from the original [film]. But drained it has been. . . . The numbers sound agreeable enough, one by one. But they don't come one by one. They pile up on one another with a deadening similarity of structure and lyrical device, and even the infinitely resourceful Dolores Gray is hard put to keep you from thinking she's doing an endless series of reprises. Though the evening is clearly coming down about her ears, she strides through it all with aplomb. Nothing is going to deflect her own responsible performance, and she is still able, along about 10 o'clock, to build a lament called "Here's That Rainy Day" into a show-stopper.

RICHARD WATTS JR., *Post*

As for Miss Gray, I don't think anyone can doubt that she is a wonderful girl, with great skill and excitement about her. Few people in the modern theatre have been able to put over a number so thrillingly. You can understand every word of the lyrics she sings, which is more than some of her songs deserve. The romantic Spanish officer is played by John Raitt, who has a fine voice but is perhaps inclined to throw masculinity and the flash of teeth about a trifle self-consciously.

William Gaxton—leading man of *Of Thee I Sing* (1931) and *Anything Goes* (1934)—was the smartest of all: he left before the first rehearsal. When things didn't go too well in Philadelphia, colibrettist George Oppenheimer "withdrew" (as they say). Dorothy Fields came in, wrote a whole new first act, then withdrew, too, with brother Herb. Next, the brilliant Hollywood director/writer Preston Sturges—who was by this time washed up—was brought in to rewrite and redirect. Who makes these decisions, anyway? All the while, Dolores Gray's role got bigger and bigger and bigger. Stage mothers are, by reputation, an obnoxious lot; Oppenheimer reports that Mama Gray was particularly lethal, making Lady Macbeth look like a hoyden. (Did Oppenheimer share his woes with his TV collaborator at the time, young Sondheim, who was to write a musical about another famous stage mother?) Incidental note: Investors brought in by Hollywood songwriters Burke and Van Heusen (responsible for raising half of the $250,000 budget) included Bing Crosby, Dolores (Mrs. Bob) Hope, and Gower and Marge Champion.

A Tony Award was won, naturally enough, by Dolores Gray (actress). Quite a feat considering the show ran less than a week. It was a sleepy year, though.

BROADWAY SCORECARD / perfs: 6 / $: —

rave	favorable	mixed	unfavorable	pan
			3	4

CAROUSEL

a musical play, with music by Richard Rodgers; book and lyrics by Oscar Hammerstein 2nd, from the 1921 drama *Liliom* by Ferenc Molnár (as adapted by Benjamin F. Glazer)

directed by Rouben Mamoulian; choreographed by Agnes de Mille
produced by the Theatre Guild (with Richard Rodgers and Oscar Hammerstein 2nd)
with John Raitt, Jan Clayton, Eric Mattson, Jean Darling, and Murvyn Vye

opened April 19, 1945   Majestic Theatre

JOHN CHAPMAN, *Daily News*

One of the finest musical plays I have seen and I shall remember it always. It has everything the professional theatre can give it— and something besides; heart, integrity, an inner glow—I don't know just what to call it. Since those who have made *Carousel* are those who made *Oklahoma!* (1943) one might expect another *Oklahoma!*—but one shouldn't. The older work is bright, lean, and gay—a musical comedy. *Carousel* is tender, rueful, almost tragic, and does not fit the pattern of musical comedy, operetta, *opera bouffe,* or even opera. Those looking for a happy and foolish evening had better go elsewhere, for although *Carousel* has all the trappings of a big-time Broadway show—the sets, the songs, the production numbers, the ballets—it is essentially something else. It is a story of a wistful, touching love, and it takes time to tell it. The zip, the pace, the timing of the ordinary musical are not in it, but it offers stirring rewards for the listener who will adapt himself to the slower progression and let it tell and sing its story in its own way.

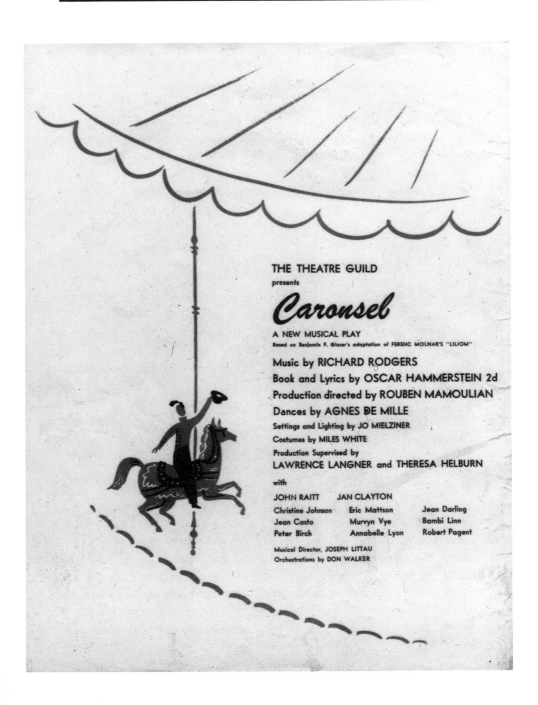

THE THEATRE GUILD

presents

Carousel

A NEW MUSICAL PLAY

Based on Benjamin F. Glazer's adaptation of FERENC MOLNAR'S "LILIOM"

Music by RICHARD RODGERS
Book and Lyrics by OSCAR HAMMERSTEIN 2d
Production directed by ROUBEN MAMOULIAN
Dances by AGNES DE MILLE
Settings and Lighting by JO MIELZINER
Costumes by MILES WHITE
Production Supervised by
LAWRENCE LANGNER and THERESA HELBURN

with

JOHN RAITT   JAN CLAYTON

Christine Johnson	Eric Mattson	Jean Darling
Jean Casto	Murvyn Vye	Bambi Linn
Peter Birch	Annabelle Lyon	Robert Pagent

Musical Director, JOSEPH LITTAU
Orchestrations by DON WALKER

Fanciful silhouette of Billy Bigelow (with forelock) on the Carousel.

ROBERT GARLAND, *Journal-American*

Yes, yes, a thousand times yes! When somebody writes a better musical-play than *Carousel*, Richard Rodgers and Oscar Hammerstein will have to write it. *Carousel*, for which I'm deliberately going off the deep end, is the song-and-dance translation of Ferenc Molnár's *Liliom*. A professional fault-finder by trade, I can't find anything to complain about where the Theatre Guild's latest musical play is concerned. As one who sees no good reason for comparing *Carousel* with *Oklahoma!*, as one who prefers to let each stand on its perfected own, let me assure you that the Theatre Guild's new play-with-music is romantic, melodramatic, fantastical, colorful, comic, tragic, melodic, and an evening of sheer theatrical enchantment.

OTIS L. GUERNSEY JR. *Herald Tribune*

The soaring gayety of other musicals never comes up through the heavy atmosphere of this one. But the combination of the *Oklahoma!* talents has found material to overcome the handicap. With a lovely musical score, a letter-perfect cast, a fine production, and a tale told with sincerity, *Carousel* is definitely something to see. The show has been assembled with the unmistakable Rodgers-Hammerstein touch. You will find few "breaks" in *Carousel*—it flows smoothly through the music and dialogue, and, as is the technique of the authors, the drama is unfolded in songs and lyrics as much as in conversation. Since there is very little time for comedy in *Carousel*, the score is a series of variations on the theme of love or sorrows; it avoids monotony only by its excellence. In it is set a brilliant diamond of a number entitled "If I Loved You," asking and deserving to be called the song of the Broadway musical year. The creators of *Carousel* posed for themselves a difficult problem in this serious musical play, and they have come up with an unusual piece of Broadway stagecraft. Rodgers, Hammerstein, and the rest have proved that music and real drama can be combined outside the opera with very good entertainment results.

LOUIS KRONENBERGER, *PM*

I suppose a comparison between the two shows is inevitable. It is hardly, however, profitable; the two shows are not enough alike. The high spirits of *Oklahoma!*, the meadow freshness of it at its best, its fetching qualities as a "show" have no counterpart in *Carousel;* nor does *Carousel* have the same succession of tunes that quickly sing themselves into your memory. But *Carousel* has for me more charm; its story (familiar though it was) held me as *Oklahoma's* did not; and though it may not run for years and years, it may yet seem more of a milestone in the years to come.

UNSIGNED REVIEW, *World-Telegram*

Another beautiful musical. Hammerstein and Rodgers appear to have combined the successful device of *Carmen Jones* [1943]—the adaptation of a classic to modern scene and tempo—with the outstanding quality of *Oklahoma!.* . . . Richard Rodgers, who has injured his back recently, watched the performance from behind curtains, propped up on a stretcher.

WILELLA WALDORF, *Post*

Carousel seemed to us a rather long evening. The *Oklahoma!* formula is becoming a bit monotonous, and so are Miss de Mille's ballets. All right, go ahead and shoot.

An extraspecial, perfect piece of theatre. Rodgers, Hammerstein, Mamoulian, and de Mille were each at the height of their talents when they joined to create *Carousel.* They knew exactly what they were doing—virtually every moment was just as it should be. With any luck, we'll one day see a carefully assembled, tasteful revival that remains true to the intentions of the creators.

Winner of the New York Drama Critics' Circle Award, the first musical to do so. (Beginning the following season, separate categories were established for American Play, Foreign Play, and Musical.) In addition to winning the Donaldson Award for Best Musical, Donaldsons were won by Richard Rodgers (composer); Oscar Hammerstein 2nd (lyricist; librettist); Rouben Mamoulian (director); Agnes de Mille (choreographer); John Raitt (actor); Bambi Linn (female dancer); and Peter Birch (male dancer).

CATCH A STAR!

an intimate musical revue, with music by Sammy Fain and Phil Charig; lyrics by Paul Francis Webster and Ray Golden; sketches by Danny and Neil Simon

conceived and supervised by Ray Golden; sketches directed by Danny Simon; choreographed by Lee Sherman
produced by Sy Kleinman
with Pat Carroll, David Burns, and Elaine Dunn

opened September 6, 1955   Plymouth Theatre

JOHN CHAPMAN, *Daily News*

Some of the songs are pretty awful. My advice is to pay no attention to several—including one which goes, "That moon is here again. . . . It's all too clear again"—and wait almost to the end of the show for one called "Fly Little Heart" [composer Jerry Bock's first song on Broadway, with lyric by Larry Holofcener]. This one, I think, is excellent.

ROBERT COLEMAN, *Daily Mirror*

The skits, mostly by Danny and Neil Simon, have first-rate satiric ideas which fluff out at the end because of weak punchlines. The Simon boys can come up with funny topical material.

WALTER KERR, *Herald Tribune*

It occurs to me that no one really wants to hear about a pleasant, lightweight, generally ingratiating show. The disastrously bad ones are fun to talk about, because the gags at their expense come fairly easy. The great ones are exciting to talk about because the season catches fire, Broadway shines brighter, and the race to the box office is an adventure in itself. But there are such things as truly passable entertainments—those that keep you happy enough without making you want to wire your mother. What do you call something that falls between a flop and a smash? . . . Pat Carroll has a shrewd, darting, to-the-point attack. After three or four sketches, you're convinced that the girl can do anything. And that, you suddenly realize, is her single problem. In the process of doing everything, and doing everything differently, she has never quite settled for a single personality of her own. Stardom may miss her by just that much, as things stand. But as things stand, she's still fun.

RICHARD WATTS JR., *Post*

One of its chief virtues is that Danny and Neil Simon have written for it several genuinely amusing items in the almost lost field of the topical sketch, many of them dealing with the theatre. There is, for example, an excellent number about a group of gossipy women playgoers and a long-suffering male at a matinee performance of *Damn Yankees*. There is fun, too, in a sketch wherein the technique of the theatre is introduced into the restaurant business. Naturally, there is also some satirical comment on the prevalence of the Marlon Brando school of acting. While the majority of the revue's sketches do concern themselves, and quite entertainingly, with the idiosyncrasies of show business, the happiest among the contributions of the Simons is one that forgets about such topical concerns and goes in for the loftier matter of authentic character humor. It is called simply "Arty" [after Paddy Chayefsky's teleplay "Marty" (1955)], and deals with the determination of a stubborn mother to get her reluctant son a wife. Without losing its status as a revue number or neglecting the requisite blackout, it achieves humor and maintains real characterization, too.

Neil Simon went back to television, where he was writing not only comedy sketches but librettos for musical specials like "Heidi" (1955) and Alfred Drake's "Marco Polo" (1956). Simon's first Broadway play, *Come Blow Your Horn* (1961), did fairly well despite blistering reviews. Then came *Little Me* (1962), with "Heidi" lyricist Carolyn Leigh; and *then* came *Barefoot in the Park* (1963), *The Odd Couple* (1965) and the rest.

BROADWAY SCORECARD / perfs: 23 / $: −

rave	favorable	mixed	unfavorable	pan
	2	3	2	

CHAUVE-SOURIS 1943

the fifth edition of the late Nikita Balieff's Russian revue

directed by Michel Michon; choreographed by Vecheslav Swoboda and Boris Romanoff
produced by Leon Greanin by arrangement with Mme. Nakita Balieff
with Leon Greanin

opened August 12, 1943   Royale Theatre

JOHN CHAPMAN, *Daily News*

Russians in Russia last night continued heroically to push back the German line; push it back upon Kharkov, ever back toward the Dnieper. Russians in New York last night quite gallantly tried a more difficult feat—to push back time. Time wouldn't budge much. . . . The first *Chauve-Souris* was too good.

BURTON RASCOE, *World-Telegram*

I strongly suspect that Leon Greanin had some Petrillo trouble [James C. Petrillo, president of the American Federation of Musicians] at the last minute before the curtain arose. Indeed, the circumstantial evidence seemed to be that the poor chap had practically a paralytic stroke of Petrillo trouble between one number and the next; for, standing in front of the curtain as master of ceremonies, he announced a number in rather specific detail only to discover, when he got behind the curtain, that the number had been cancelled while he was out front. If my guess is correct, Mr. Greanin is so naive as not to have known that if you are going to put on a show which has as much as one note blown on a harmonica in it, you had better consult Mr. Petrillo because Mr. Petrillo may rule that you have to hire 10 harmonica players not to play in order to have one union harmonica play that note. From the program, it would seem that Mr. Greanin intended to have some guitars, accordions, and a bunch of balalaikas up on the stage playing music by Shostakovich, Douaevsky, and Zakharoff, and that he was still under the delusion that this music could be part of his show until about 9:17 last evening. Five parts of the next number and three whole numbers scheduled for Act II were dropped out. . . . Dania Krupska in "Katinka's Birthday" found considerable favor with the audience.

The first Broadway edition of *Chauve-Souris* (1922)—a high society, "White Russian" vaudeville—was an enormous hit with 1920s sophisticates. Three new editions were offered before the Stock Market Crash. Dania Krupska, who danced Katinka, went on to choreograph *The Most Happy Fella* (1956) and other musicals.

BROADWAY SCORECARD / perfs: 12 / $: −

rave	favorable	mixed	unfavorable	pan
			5	3

CHRISTINE

a musical comedy, with music by Sammy Fain; lyrics by Paul Francis Webster; book by Pearl S. Buck and Charles K. Peck, Jr., from the 1945 novel *My Indian Family* by Hilda Wernher

director unbilled (Jerome Chodorov); choreographed by Hanya Holm
produced by Oscar S. Lerman and Martin B. Cohen in association with Walter Cohen
with Maureen O'Hara, Morley Meredith, Nancy Andrews, and Phil Leeds

opened April 28, 1960   46th Street Theatre

FRANK ASTON, *World-Telegram & Sun*

Maureen O'Hara is so spring-gardenly beautiful with that red hair and everything that someone should call the fire department, not to mention a director to help her take the wood out of her speech. Maybe it isn't the wood, but the writing of Pearl Buck and Charles K. Peck, Jr. It comes out like *Little Women*, only the speakers press their palms together as in the Orient.

WALTER KERR, *Herald Tribune*

Miss O'Hara has a difficulty, which is that she has been unable to repulse the authors and the management who persuaded her to appear in this bargain-basement version of *East is West* [the 1918 melodrama] out of *The King and I* [1951]. But she is also utterly unable to shake loose her leading man. She tries, dear thing, she tries. The first act contains no fewer than three scenes in which she tilts her chin, raises her voice an octave in a manner favored by young leading ladies in summer camps, turns unsteadily on one high heel and tries to get out of there. . . . In spite of a sizable score from composer Sammy Fain (it is Hollywood Viennesse, but sometimes quite pleasant), and all those dancers stripped where Akbaradadians strip, *Christine* is not really a musical. It is a sandwich. There is a layer of international goodwill (including "The UNICEF Song"), a layer of Oriental passivity ("It was fate, it was Karma"), a layer of straight caramel ("We will climb as high as the pine trees or beyond them to the junipers"), and a layer of vulgarity (dignified native girls slipping into a Charleston). Paul Francis Webster's lyrics add to the rummage-sale effect upon occasion by being sufficiently unlyrical to fit into the plot ("I have been taught that science is the alpha and omega and the key" or "I walk alone in a mood of defiance, with all my science").

BROADWAY SCORECARD / perfs: 12 / $: —

rave	favorable	mixed	unfavorable	pan
1			4	2

CONCERT VARIETIES

a vaudeville revue

assembled and produced by Billy Rose
with Deems Taylor, Zero Mostel, Eddie Mayehoff, Imogene Coca,
Katherine Dunham and Company, Jerome Robbins and Company
(including Michael Kidd)

opened June 1, 1945   Ziegfeld Theatre

HOWARD BARNES, *Herald Tribune*

"Interplay" is a remarkably fluent and eloquent ballet, with Robbins and his assistants keeping a stage instinct with explicit movement. The music by Morton Gould ["American Concertette"] is on the prosaic and derivative side, but it is an adequate accompaniment for a delightful dance pantomime.

ROBERT GARLAND, *Journal-American*

Zero lives up to his given name.

WILELLA WALDORF, *Post*

Katherine Dunham and her company, with the fascinating Miss Dunham herself on hand to streak around the stage in a series of outlandish costumes, sometimes smoking a large cigar, perform three numbers from their repertory with the customary theatrical dash and color. Lest anything in the dance line be overlooked, Imogene Coca and William Archibald perform a burlesque of "Afternoon of a Faun" that is one of the funniest interludes of an evening that is not precisely overwhelmed by laughs. . . . Zero Mostel, with Deems Taylor as straight man, does a fairly amusing take-off on an explosive Italian tenor, then repeats his inevitable Senatorial harangue, and winds up by bubbling like a percolator. Of the rest, Eddie Mayehoff turns out to be a sort of Zero Mostel without quite so much talent or perspiration.

Jerome Robbins's ballet "Interplay," to music by Morton Gould, led to the pair's collaboration on *Billion Dollar Baby* (1945). Robbins and Mostel, who had similar political views at the time, did not get along too well after the former's 1953 appearance before the House Un-American Activities Committee. They would meet again later, on *Forum* (1962) and *Fiddler* (1964).

BROADWAY SCORECARD / perfs: 36 / $: —

rave	favorable	mixed	unfavorable	pan
	2	2	4	

A CONNECTICUT YANKEE

a revised version of the 1927 musical comedy, with music by Richard Rodgers; lyrics by Lorenz Hart; book by Herbert Fields, from the 1889 novel *A Connecticut Yankee in King Arthur's Court* by Mark Twain

directed by John C. Wilson; choreographed by William Holbrooke and Al White, Jr.
produced by Richard Rodgers
with Vivienne Segal, Dick Foran, Julie Warren, Vera-Ellen, and Chester Stratton

opened November 17, 1943   Martin Beck Theatre

LOUIS KRONENBERGER, *PM*

Another flower has managed to jut up among the cactus. Decked out in partly new armor, our old friend the *Connecticut Yankee*, if a little slow in getting around, proves an entertaining, likeable, and warm-voiced fellow. . . . "To Keep My Love Alive" gives Lorenz Hart the chance to go to town with his wittiest and funniest lyric in years, and Vivienne Segal puts the song across with real showmanship. It's the high point of the show.

LEWIS NICHOLS, *Times*

Any musical which has Richard Rodgers tunes has won about half its battle by the time the orchestra has finished the overture, but this one does not stop dead at that point. For in offering his first gesture as a manager, the same Mr. Rodgers has bedecked his

The Connecticut Yankee *takes the Demoiselle Alisande la Courteloise—Sandy to you—slumming through Camelot, circa 528 A.D. Updating the 1927 adaptation of the 1889 novel to 1943 (note the jeep) proved at least one anachronism too many.*

show with colorful costumes and good settings [designed by Nat Karson] and his filled his stage with people who obviously are cheerful about taking the Mark Twain trip from Hartford, Conn. to the Court of King Arthur. Rodgers and Hart have added a number of new songs: "To Keep My Love Alive," which is a pretty wonderful tale told by a lady who has been killing her husbands; "Can't You Do a Friend a Favor?," and some more. They are in Mr. Rodgers's amiable style, and in Mr. Hart's best mood—the one which rhymes "cantalope" and "antelope" and thinks nothing of it. . . . The young lady who put the most life into the musical was Vera-Ellen, not the greatest singer in the world but certainly one of the world's most engaging performers as a dancer or minor comedienne.

BURTON RASCOE, *World-Telegram*

Mr. Foran was agreeable enough as Martin; but I wish his two youngsters had been there last night to tell pop to wipe that red stuff off his lips, which made him look like a sissy.

WILELLA WALDORF, *Post*

Vivienne Segal has one new number, "To Keep My Love Alive," which she delivers in the inimitable Segal manner and which is worth the price of a seat all by itself. In case we seem to be dwelling unduly on Miss Segal, it is because *A Connecticut Yankee* leans on her so persistently that it often seems in danger of falling into a light slumber when she isn't on hand to give it a sly poke in the ribs to wake things up.

The Rodgers and Hart collaboration had ended with *By Jupiter* (1942), when the lyricist chose not to work on the project that became *Oklahoma!* (1943). In an attempt to pull Hart out of a severe alcoholic slump, Rodgers and the pair's long-time collaborator Herbert Fields encouraged Hart to participate in this partially successful revision of their early hit. Classic songs like "My Heart Stood Still" and "Thou Swell" were supplemented with five new numbers (and some great lyrics). On opening night, the unruly Hart was ejected from the theatre for disrupting the performance. On his final binge, he contracted pneumonia and died on November 22, 1943.

THE CONQUERING HERO

a musical comedy, with music by Moose Charlap; lyrics by Norman Gimbel; book by Larry Gelbart, from the 1944 screenplay *Hail, the Conquering Hero* by Preston Sturges

director uncredited (Bob Fosse replaced by Albert Marre); choreographer uncredited (Bob Fosse replaced by Todd Bolender) produced by Robert Whitehead and Roger L. Stevens (with ANTA) with Tom Poston, Lionel Stander, Kay Brown (replacing Cherry Davis), and Jane Mason

opened January 16, 1961   ANTA Theatre

WALTER KERR, *Herald Tribune*

There's a dance quite early on that has its tongue in its toes and that suggests a whole new profitable vein for musical comedy choreography. Our hero's mother is prattling away on the small-town telephone, telling the neighbors how dense those Guadalcanal jungles were ("You know how things get when you let them go") and lovingly recounting her boy's fabulous exploits. The dance, as we fade through some transparent underbrush, is as fabulous as it ought to be. The Japanese are not only tricky foes to be tangling with: they are so confident that they have time to spin plates—the way they always used to spin plates at the Palace—on the tips of their bayonets. And the Americans, as we learn, are really "different"—so different that they are free to soar, in blithe ballet grace, almost above the treetops. Nothing is labored here. The uncredited choreography is all very deadpan and very funny.

"The Conquering Hero"

A New Musical Comedy

ROBERT WHITEHEAD & ROGER L. STEVENS present
A New Musical Comedy

"The Conquering
Hero"

starring
TOM POSTON

with
Cherry DAVIS   Jane MASON   Fred STEWART
and LIONEL STANDER

Book by   Music by   Lyrics by
LARRY GELBART   MOOSE CHARLAP   NORMAN GIMBEL

Production Staged and
Choreographed by BOB FOSSE

Settings Designed by JEAN ROSENTHAL & WILLIAM PITKIN
Lighting by JEAN ROSENTHAL
Costumes Designed by PATTON CAMPBELL

Arrangements and Orchestrations by SID RAMIN & ROBERT GINZLER
Dance Music Arranged by FRED WERNER
Musical Director SHERMAN FRANK

Associate Choreographer ROBERT TUCKER
Production Associate ROBERT LINDEN
AN AMERICAN NATIONAL THEATRE AND ACADEMY PRODUCTION

Original Cast Album by RCA Victor

ANTA THEATRE
52nd Street West of Broadway
Matinees Wednesday and Saturday

Our Conquering Hero *eyes the hometown crowd uncertainly (with good reason). Pre-Broadway credits.* (drawing by William Steig)

JOHN MCCLAIN, *Journal-American*

An utterly charming, fast-moving, and unpretentious musical—happily in the old tradition, and offering the rarity of a good, workable little book. The score is amiable and haunting, and Larry Gelbart has done a creditable job of adapting the story. I believe it should persevere. . . . The Playbill made no note of either direction or choreography, although it is understood Albert Marre had something to do with the staging and Robert Fosse, the dances. In any case, there is a Fosse-type number recounting the heroism of Pvt. Poston at Guadalcanal that shook the house up, as did a later one involving his campaign speech.

HOWARD TAUBMAN, *Times*

A musical cannot be assembled; it must be created. *The Conquering Hero* has been put together, as the trade knows, with immense travail. An indication of the troubles it has known is that the program lists neither stage director nor choreographer. Whoever mixed the ingredients failed to produce freshness or excitement.

RICHARD WATTS JR., *Post*

Astonishingly stale, flat, and unprofitable. It is symbolic that no director was willing to bear public responsibility for the poor waif. What is particularly unfortunate is its waste of the talents of Tom Poston, an expert farceur, a skillful leading man, and an attractive all-around performer.

Bob Fosse—4-for-4 as a choreographer, including a successful directorial debut with *Redhead* (1959)—set out to create his own musical. Choosing Preston Sturges's brilliant cinemasatire *Hail, the Conquering Hero*, Fosse brought the package to distinguished producer Robert Whitehead. (Note in passing: it is virtually impossible to musicalize brilliant satire—particularly if your songwriters aren't brilliant satirists.) Flash forward to the National Theatre, Washington, D.C., where Fosse found himself in the embarrassing position of being fired from his own show. "It needed a fresh approach," explained Whitehead, whose musical past included *Goldilocks* (1958) and whose musical future included *Foxy*

(1964) and *1600 Pennsylvania Avenue* (1976). Knowing it would be fatal to withdraw the dances just weeks before the Broadway opening, Fosse agreed to their continued use—on the condition that his two major ballets be used intact or not at all. Whitehead responded by hiring a new choreographer to "supervise" Fosse's work, so Fosse went to arbitration. In a 500-word telegram of explanation to the *New York Times*, he called the ballets "the best work I've ever done" and quoted the out-of-town raves (for the ballets, not the show) at great length. Fosse was vindicated, winning the arbitration—eight months after *The Conquering Hero* conked out. (He asked for token damages, and was awarded 6¢.) The non-profit organization ANTA had taken a second mortgage on their theatre and invested $100,000 in the show, for reasons known only to the ANTA board (Robert Whitehead, vice-president; Roger L. Stevens, treasurer). As a grim reminder of the episode, a weather-beaten rooftop *Conquering Hero* billboard continued to haunt the ANTA in the 1980s. The last word belongs to librettist Larry Gelbart: "If Hitler's alive, I hope he's out-of-town with a musical."

BROADWAY SCORECARD / perfs: 8 / $: −

rave	favorable	mixed	unfavorable	pan
	2	1	3	1

THE CONSUL

a Cold War opera, with music and words by Gian-Carlo Menotti

directed by Gian-Carlo Menotti; choreographed by John Butler
produced by Chandler Cowles and Efrem Zimbalist, Jr.
with Marie Powers and Patricia Neway

opened March 15, 1950   Ethel Barrymore Theatre

HOWARD BARNES, *Herald Tribune*

A musical drama of lurid and sombre fascination. *The Consul* is a threnody about the dispossessed, living in a police state somewhere in Europe and having no way of escape. The dramatist-composer-director has achieved scenes of high theatrical

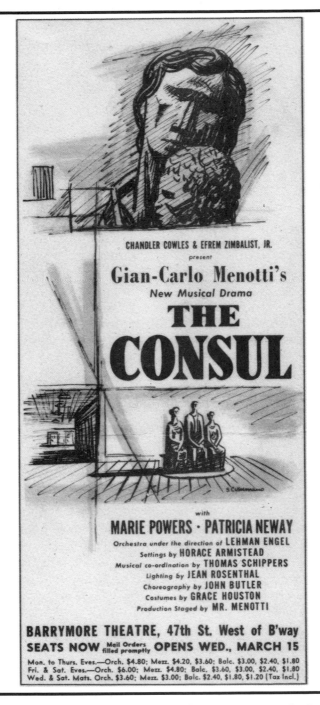

Gian-Carlo Menotti's stunning Cold War opera, which won the writer/director four *Donaldson Awards and a Pulitzer Prize.* (drawing by S. Cusumano)

excitement and moments of genuine poignance. The melodrama, in the true and original sense of the word, rings with passion and meaning. The climax, in which a woman asks her pardon of God after having lost everyone who is dear to her and turns on the gas, is grim. It is also something not to miss.

JOHN CHAPMAN, *Daily News*

The story is vividly theatrical—the kind of story that Carol Reed and Graham Greene might have whipped into one of those quiet, intense movie dramas. It is about a young couple who are trying to get out of some unnamed country into some other happier country. They are hounded by secret police and baffled by the red tape of getting a visa from the consulate of the happier country. As a piece of theatre alone, *The Consul* is skillfully plotted. As a piece of music, it bears the Menotti stamp which was evident in *The Medium* [1947]—a peculiar dissonant singsong in the narrative passages and a bold and imaginative orchestration in the dramatic moments. Menotti is working for himself and by himself; he is not trying to be excessively modern and he is not particularly respectful toward old operatic conventions. He is an individual, and he manages to be an individual without resorting to phony musical stunts. I don't think *The Consul* is grand opera. It is more clever than heroic. But it most certainly is top-grade musical theatre.

ROBERT COLEMAN, *Daily Mirror*

The versatile Gian-Carlo Menotti delivers a slashing operatic blow at totalitarianism—Nazism, Black Fascism and Red Fascism, or Communism, if you prefer. We hope all the local comrades who think life behind the Iron Curtain is just dandy will see *The Consul*. It might help to open the eyes of these dim-witted dupes, and it will certainly make good Americans proud of their democratic Republic. Though the Menotti work is in operatic form, it is terrific theatre. It had the Barrymore's sturdy walls vibrating from salvos of cheers. It is something that must be seen.

ROBERT GARLAND, *Journal-American*

Knowing little about music, not even knowing what I'm not supposed to like, I like Gian-Carlo Menotti's *The Consul*. They, meaning an ardently appreciative first audience, were giving it the hand-clap, cat-call, bravo routine as I left the Ethel Barrymore last evening. I wish I could have hung around to help them. But, alas, I had to go and put this plaudit in the paper. *The Consul* is grand opera, so make the most of it. I did, and had myself a grand opera time.

WILLIAM HAWKINS, *World-Telegram & Sun*

Last night Gian-Carlo Menotti put a hefty unanswerable veto on the gloomy argument that the theatre is dead or even very sick. Here is lyric drama of freshness and freedom, carved to the bone in every element, so it repeatedly jolts you till your teeth jar. More importantly, here is theatre talking intimately about the world of today and tomorrow. This is the story of the Twentieth Century's oppressed, told vividly enough to strike home in a Park Avenue penthouse. Suspense and dramatic shock are Menotti's principal tools. It is his immense fertility for dramatic effect that makes *The Consul* so vivid. Constantly there are peaks of action that electrify you and leave you worn out. Repeatedly the composer tops them. His joining of dialogue and music is so simple and natural that it is like picking up with both hands a weight that might be too much for either one. But Menotti uses music to relax the drama. Consequently his medium can stand big punches when he needs them. . . . Patricia Neway as Magda became a star over Gotham by 10 o'clock last night.

The Consul's immediate impact was stunning, both artistically and politically. Menotti's timely Cold War opera came just as the Berlin airlift ended and the Korean War began, a few weeks after the conviction of Alger Hiss for selling State Department secrets to the Russians. Its very topicality, alas, made it date very quickly.

Winner of the Pulitzer Prize for Music. Winner of the New York Drama Critics' Circle Award. A Tony Award was won by Lehman Engel (musical director). In addition to winning the Donaldson Award for Best Musical, Donaldsons were won by Gian-Carlo Menotti (*four!*, as composer, lyricist, librettist, and director); Patricia Neway (actress); and Gloria Lane (supporting actress; female debut).

COPPER AND BRASS

a musical comedy, with music by David Baker; lyrics by David Craig; book by Ellen Violett and David Craig

directed by Marc Daniels; choreographed by Anna Sokolow (with Bob Fosse)
produced by Lyn Austin and Thomas Noyes in association with Anderson Lawler
with Nancy Walker (Craig), Benay Venuta (replacing Joan Blondell), Dick Williams, Alice Pearce, and Alan Bunce

opened October 17, 1957   Martin Beck Theatre

BROOKS ATKINSON, *Times*

Members of the Nancy Walker Association will now have to adopt a new constitution and elect a new set of officers. *Copper and Brass* proves that the present policy is not working at all. *Copper and Brass* is a standard, old-fashioned show with a breathlessly unfunny book, uninteresting music, unlovely ballets, and a general look of banality and routine. You would think that nothing in the field of musical comedy has changed since the theatre went bankrupt in the Nineteen Thirties. There is no use pretending that *Copper and Brass* is of any use to Miss Walker or to the members of the Association. Something will have to be done.

WALTER KERR, *Herald Tribune*

Every time Nancy Walker can get her busy colleagues to agree to a few seconds' silence—no lyrics, no dialogue, just a brief, precious vacuum to be inventively filled—the results are lovely. Watch her slow things down to a magnificent standstill during a session in the Holland Tunnel. Everything stops cold while Miss Walker [as a policewoman] simply climbs a ladder, perspiring hand over per-

Lyn Austin and Thomas Noyes
present

NANCY WALKER

in the new musical comedy

"COPPER and BRASS"

also starring

JOAN BLONDELL

with

DICK WILLIAMS   ALICE PEARCE   ALAN BUNCE

Norma Douglas   Peter Conlow

Book by **ELLEN VIOLETT** and **DAVID CRAIG**

Music by **DAVID BAKER**

Lyrics by **DAVID CRAIG**

Directed by **MARC DANIELS**

Dances and Musical Numbers by **ANNA SOKOLOW**

Settings and Lighting by **WILLIAM** and **JEAN ECKART**

Costumes by **ALVIN COLT**

Orchestrations by
Ralph Burns

Musical Direction and Vocal Arrangements by
Maurice Levine

Dance Arrangements by
John Morris

SHUBERT THEATRE

NEW HAVEN

Fri. Eve., Sept. 13 thru Sat. Eve., Sept. 21

MATINEES WEDNESDAY AND SATURDAY

Nancy Walker was the "copper," built not unlike an inverted sax-ophone. Pre-Broadway credits. (drawing by Al Hirschfeld)

165

spiring hand, her beleaguered countenance contorted into a dazzling array of unspoken epithets. The oncoming traffic, invariable but noisy, hurls our unsteady heroine flat and flailing against vast cement walls. She teeters over the road bed, descends into the maelstrom, blows a hasty whistle, and watches in innocent, gratified awe as screeching trucks pile up in the distance. At one point in the proceedings Miss Walker gets herself throttled by a mile-long fox fur. The fur she can handle; it's the script that's stifling. An appalling waste of one of our richer, more lunatic talents. . . . The trouble with *Copper and Brass* is that the librettists were hired to write a book, the team of David Baker and David Craig were asked to provide a score, and the lot of them are now naturally anxious that their work be heard. Hearing it interferes seriously with one's pleasure in the solemn, private humours of the star. The silences that are filled with our girl's grimaces are rewarding; the silences that greet the jokes are simply eerie.

JOHN McCLAIN, *Journal-American*

The rock and roll episode, "My Baby's Baby," was a suitable tribute to Bob Fosse, who came in late in the show's preparation—unhappily, too late.

○○
BROADWAY SCORECARD / perfs: 36 / $: —

rave   favorable   mixed   unfavorable   pan

1   6
○○

THE CRADLE WILL ROCK

Leonard Bernstein's City Center production of the 1937 "play in music" by Marc Blitzstein

directed by Howard Da Silva
produced by Michael Myerberg
with Alfred Drake, Vivian Vance, Muriel Smith, Will Geer, and Leonard Bernstein

opened December 26, 1947   Mansfield Theatre

BROOKS ATKINSON, *Times*

A blistering revival of the most vivid proletarian drama ever written in this country. Although it has now acquired such tokens of respectability as Leonard Bernstein in a boiled shirt, bull fiddles, greased horns, and other cultured instruments, it is no less militant and exciting than it was a decade ago when Mr Blitzstein wore a soft shirt and played the whole score on a one-man piano. The extraordinary vitality of *The Cradle Will Rock* derives from the vigorous eloquence of the score, the sharp bite of the lyrics, and the graphic simplicity of the production. As in any genuine work of art, form and content are identical. Having something passionate to say, Mr. Blitzstein has said it with startling directness, making no concession to dramatic conventions. At the moment it is impossible to recall another musical drama so candid, so original, and so fresh in stage conception.

ROBERT GARLAND, *Journal-American*

Stupid and shortsighted, venal and vindictive, like all Americans with a balance in the bank, I had to see Marc Blitzstein's *The Cradle Will Rock* at least four times before I discovered how to go about enjoying this 10-year-old propaganda piece with music. Last night, at the Mansfield, it dawned on me suddenly. All you've got to do is make up your mind that everybody with their balance in the bank is, as I've said, stupid and shortsighted, venal and vindictive, while everybody without a balance in the bank is bright and farsighted, honest and forgiving. So white are the moneyless, so bright are the monied that you're sorry you're faring as well as you are. This, however, can be remedied by joining almost any nearby union.

RICHARD WATTS JR., *Post*

When Marc Blitzstein's labor opera was presented in 1937, I described it as "an exciting and savagely humorous social cartoon with music." As revived last night, it continued to be stirring and amusing, even though time has deprived it of its topical bite. This, it should be quickly added, is not because its ideas about industrial conflict are no longer important, but merely because details are changed. . . . Leonard Bernstein directed the orchestra, and did a slight bit of acting.

☆

Marc Blitzstein's powerful proletarian propaganda remained highly controversial even in the new, post-war world, stirring up both sides with its strong message and high theatricality. Blitzstein was a role model for Bernstein, who made his first public splash when he mounted a 1939 Boston edition of *Cradle* as a Harvard undergrad. Blitzstein's life/work was similarly enkindled when, as a student in Berlin, he first heard Kurt Weill's *Die Dreigroschenoper* (1933). Bernstein remained a champion of his mentor, instigating this revival and sponsoring the first hearing of Blitzstein's version of the Weill musical, eventually staged off-Broadway in 1954 as *The Threepenny Opera*.

BROADWAY SCORECARD / perfs: 34 / $: —

rave	favorable	mixed	unfavorable	pan
2	2	2	1	2

CRANKS

a British revue, with music by John Addison; written and directed by John Cranko
produced by Richard Carlton and John Krimsky
with Hugh Bryant, Annie Ross, Anthony Newley, and Gilbert Vernon

opened November 26, 1956   Bijou Theatre

ROBERT COLEMAN, *Daily Mirror*

Crazy, man, crazy. If you're hovering on the brink of a nervous breakdown, this little import will push you right over the edge. *Cranks* ran for some nine months in London. We suspect it will be running toward a Britain-bound boat before you can say Piccadilly.

TOM DONNELLY, *World-Telegram & Sun*

Anthony Newley shines with a macabre intensity. He suggests an evil child who has discovered all the dreadful secrets of the universe, and is rolling them around in his mouth like a nickel's worth of jawbreakers.

JOHN MCCLAIN, *Journal-American*

Emerging from the Bijou Theatre last night, I wouldn't have been surprised if some men in white coats had ushered me into a wagon and taken me off to the laughing academy. Such is the mood in which one is left after viewing *Cranks*, a small British revue. I haven't the shadiest idea of what it's about, but I think it's swell. Other people in England, where it played for some time, have described it as the union of Salvador Dali and the man who wrote *Waiting For Godot*. *Cranks* will not be everybody's ticket to dementia, but it certainly sent me.

BROADWAY SCORECARD / perfs: 40 / $: −

rave	favorable	mixed	unfavorable	pan
	2	3	1	1

DAMN YANKEES

a musical comedy with music and lyrics by Richard Adler and Jerry Ross, book by George Abbott and Douglas Wallop (with Richard Bissell, unbilled), from Wallop's 1954 novel *The Year the Yankees Lost the Pennant*

directed by George Abbott; choreographed by Bob Fosse
produced by Frederick Brisson, Robert E. Griffith, and Harold S. Prince in association with Albert B. Taylor
with Gwen Verdon, Stephen Douglass, Ray Walston, Russ Brown, and Shannon Bolin

opened May 5, 1955   46th Street Theatre

JOHN CHAPMAN, *Daily News*

That cagey old manager, George Abbott, and a team of actors, dancers, songwriters, and scene designers in championship form, played an all-hitter under the lights last evening. Their show is *Damn Yankees*. Their battery was—and will be, I hope, for a cou-

Gwen Verdon explains why Lola always gets "Whatever Lola Wants." (costume by William and Jean Eckart, photo by Fred Fehl)

ple or three years—Gwen Verdon and Ray Walston, and Stephen Douglass was a very good man in a pinch. Bob Fosse has staged some admirable dances, including a ballplayers' ballet that is a miracle of humorous invention. I didn't think any dance director could ever equal Fosse's "Steam Heat" dance in *The Pajama Game* [1954] as a novelty number, but he—with Miss Verdon's collaboration—has come up with another gem in "Who's Got the Pain?," which is danced by the glamorous Gwen and Eddie Phillips [choreographed by Fosse and Verdon]. . . . Nathaniel Frey [as Smokey, the catcher] acts more like Yogi Berra than Yogi Berra.

ROBERT COLEMAN, *Daily Mirror*

The new song-and-dance sockeroo. Baseball is the great national pastime, and we predict that *Damn Yankees* will become a great national entertainment. It's packed with power all down the line, from lead-off man to the pitcher. There isn't a weak spot in the lineup. Here's a pennant winner if we ever saw one. A real champ! . . . Remember Gwen Verdon? The sexy siren in *Can-Can*'s [1953] "Garden of Eden"? She was terrific in that one. Now she's titanic as the devilish Delilah bent on luring weak-willed wallopers to their destruction. The town's newest dynamic darling! In the good old days, they'd have been sipping champagne out of her slippers in the cabarets.

LEWIS FUNKE, *Times*

As shiny as a new baseball and almost as smooth. As far as this umpire is concerned you can count it among the healthy clouts of the campaign. Even the most ardent supporters of Casey Stengel's minions should have a good time. And, as for the Dodgers crowd, well, you can imagine. Looks like Mr. Abbott has another pennant winner. . . . "Shoeless Joe From Hannibal, Mo." sets the stage for a splendid hoedown for Robert Fosse, who attended to the choreography. Mr. Fosse, with Miss Verdon's aid, is one of the evening's heroes. His dance numbers are full of fun and vitality. In "Whatever Lola Wants," there is a first-class gem in which music, lyrics, and dance combine to make a memorable episode of the femme fatale operating on the hapless male. "Who's Got the Pain?" involves Miss Verdon and Eddie Phillips in a mambo and "Two Lost Souls" puts on a torrid and rowdy bacchanal just to prove everyone's versatility.

WILLIAM HAWKINS, *World-Telegram & Sun*

Gwen Verdon sprinkled a sauce of pink starlight over all *Damn Yankees*. The girl everyone was discovering in *Can-Can* proves she can be a winner in any musical derby she cares to enter. She is seductive, impertinent, subtle, luscious, and talented. The red hair, the big eyes, and the fabulous figure are magical. She may well restore female hips to their rightful position of importance, thus ending the Monroe-Russell era. . . . The dancing of Bob Fosse's design is first-rate. Miss Verdon's treatment of "Whatever Lola Wants," the impish mambo "Who's Got the Pain?," are both masterpieces of understatement and wicked humor. Go see the most glamorous woman on the local stage make wild and expert fun of everything she appears to be.

WALTER KERR, *Herald Tribune*

Miss Verdon is, I believe, some sort of a mobile designed by a man without a conscience. As she prances mockingly through a seduction scene ["Whatever Lola Wants"], flipping a black glove over her shoulder as her hips go into mysterious but extremely interesting action, beating the floor idiotically with whatever clothing she has removed, coiling all over a locker-room bench while batting absurd eyelashes at her terrified victim, she is simply and insanely inspired. Elsewhere—in a leftfield rat-race called "Who's Got the Pain?," in a baby-talk bit about her brains and her talent, in a rueful little duet labeled "Two Lost Souls"—she is everything undesirable made absolutely and forever desirable. *Damn Yankees* gets past second base on some other counts. Every time the male chorus turns front and hurls a Richard Adler-Jerry Ross showtune at the customers, the back walls bend a little. "Heart," "Shoeless Joe," and "The Game" are blockbusters in the best George Abbott tradition. But apart from the roistering hymns handed the chorus, [the score] is never much more than serviceable. In short, *Damn Yankees* has an appealing idea, a couple of first-rate performers, and an intermittent flair for raising the roof. What it hasn't got is staying power, a knack for hanging onto its gains and snowballing them into hilarity.

JOHN McCLAIN, *Journal-American*

Well, this is it—a truly tremendous musical, a brilliant song-and-dancer which should last as long as Gwen Verdon. And judging from the shape she was in last night that should be forever. *Damn*

Yankees is a jubilant combination of the town's best talents. Dr. Abbott has provided the punch, pace, and polish for which he's famous; Gwen Verdon has never been given more magnificent material or complimentary costumes and she takes full advantage of both; Stephen Douglass and Ray Walston give her generous support; the score by Richard Adler and Jerry Ross is certainly ingenious if not inspired; the scenery and costumes by William and Jean Eckart are exceptional and original, and Bob Fosse has had a complete field day in building his choreography around a baseball background.

The skillfully assembled *Pajama Game* was a first-rate triumph, with all departments combining to make pretty good material look brilliant. *Damn Yankees* was not quite so good; the score was uneven, with very good specialty material offset by mediocre ballads, and the book lacked *The Pajama Game*'s droll flavor. Richard Bissell came in from the bull pen with some very funny, very folksy jokes; but Frank Loesser was understandably not on the bench to pinch-hit, and it shows in the love songs. Where *Damn Yankees* surpassed the earlier show was in the star performance and—since the star was a dancer—in the choreography. Gwen Verdon became leading lady of the decade, with Bob Fosse showing her the steps. Some Broadwayites had assumed that Jerome Robbins deserved credit for *Pajama Game*'s "Steam Heat" and "Hernando's Hideaway"; Fosse's *Damn Yankees*, with a quartet of dazzling dances, cleared that up quick. Six months after the opening, 29-year-old songwriter Jerry Ross—an ex-child star of the Yiddish Theatre—died of a bronchial ailment. Richard Adler went on alone, but not very auspiciously, to *Kwamina* (1961), the out-of-town failure *A Mother's Kisses* (1968), and the in-town failure *Music Is* (1976).

In addition to winning the Tony Award for Best Musical, Tonys were won by Richard Adler and Jerry Ross (composers); George Abbott and Douglass Wallop (librettists); Frederick Brisson, Robert E. Griffith, and Harold S. Prince in association with Albert B. Taylor (producers); Bob Fosse (choreographer); Gwen Verdon (actress); Ray Walston (actor); Russ Brown (supporting actor); and Harold Hastings (musical director).

○○○
BROADWAY SCORECARD / perfs: 1,019 / $: +

rave	favorable	mixed	unfavorable	pan
5	2			

○○○

DANCE ME A SONG

a musical revue, with music and lyrics mostly by James Shelton; sketches by Jimmy (James) Kirkwood and Lee Goodman, George Oppenheimer and Vincente Minnelli, Marya Mannes, Robert Anderson, James Shelton, and Wally Cox

directed by James Shelton; choreographed by Robert Sidney produced by Dwight Deere Wiman in association with Robert Ross with Joan McCracken, Bob Scheerer, Erik Rhodes, Wally Cox, Jimmy Kirkwood and Lee Goodman, and Fosse and Niles

opened January 20, 1950   Royale Theatre

BROOKS ATKINSON, *Times*

The producer has rounded up a number of attractive young people who could dance a song if a song had been written for them. Joan McCracken is still a refreshing dancer—better when she sticks to the innocent style than when she tries mimicry or sophistication. There are any number of swift and likeable dancers—Mary-Ann Niles [Fosse], Bob Scheerer, Cliff Ferre, and Bob Fosse, to mention a few who do steps that are clearly impossible.

ROBERT COLEMAN, *Daily Mirror*

The hit of the evening was a runty little fellow with an ingratiating kid smile named Wally Cox. Wally was smart. He brought his own material. Runner-ups for comedy were Lee Goodman and Jimmy Kirkwood with a skit called "Buck and the Bobbie," a satire on radio kid horror programs. They also brought along their own material which has stood the test in numerous niteries.

RICHARD WATTS JR., *Post*

It provides a showcase for the possessor of the freshest and most original new comic talent the theatre has had to offer in a shockingly long time. He is a young man named Wally Cox, and to say that he does quiet little homespun monologues is to provide a most inadequate explanation. It doesn't help much, either, to add that he has a modest, deceptively shy manner. I suppose there is a trace of Charles Butterworth, the sainted Will Rogers, and the other eminent monologists of the past about the young man, but he is so completely individual in manner and method that it is pedantic to say so. Just put him down as the humorous find of the year. . . . Some weeks ago I suggested that it might be an interesting idea if the Lunts tried out the popular notion that they would be good even if reciting the telephone book. The new revue has a number showing them [Joan McCracken and Alan Ross] in the act of trying that very thing, but here it doesn't work out too well.

Fosse, of Fosse & Niles, divorced partner Niles to marry star Joan McCracken, whose first husband, Jack Dunphy, left her for Truman Capote. Kirkwood, of Kirkwood and Goodman, went on to coauthor *A Chorus Line* (1976).

A Donaldson Award was won by Wally Cox (supporting actor).

BROADWAY SCORECARD / perfs: 35 / $: −

rave	favorable	mixed	unfavorable	pan
	2	1	2	2

THE DAY BEFORE SPRING

a musical comedy, with music by Frederick Loewe; book and lyrics by Alan Jay Lerner

directed by John C. Wilson; book directed by Edward Padula; choreographed by Anthony Tudor
produced by John C. Wilson
with Irene Manning, Bill Johnson, John Archer, Patricia Marshall, and Tom Helmore

opened November 22, 1945   National Theatre

Irene Manning confers with Cupid as she clutches the novel-within-the-play that stirs up all the trouble. Looking on are novelist/former suitor Bill Johnson (right) and husband John Archer (left).
(*drawing by Dove*)

JOHN CHAPMAN, *Daily News*

The Day Before Spring is refreshing as a June breeze—and urbane, humorous, tuneful, and performed by a set of principals who have not only the will to entertain but also the know-how. Alan Jay Lerner has contrived several song lyrics much better than average and a plot involving a tenth-year college reunion which is interesting, integrated, and full of pleasant surprises. Frederick Loewe has composed a generous and beguiling score. . . . Patricia Marshall, who has the luck to get the "Jug of Wine" song, is a hot little darling who has been cooling off in ice shows for a couple of years, and I'm glad Mr. Wilson found her.

ROBERT GARLAND, *Journal-American*

There's something fresh, delightfully disarming about this show. Suppose the lyrics are better than the book and the music is better than the lyrics; suppose the settings [designed by Robert Davison] are better than the ballets and the costumes [designed by Miles White] are better than the settings. Comparisons are still odorous. So suffice it to report that Thanksgiving night's arrival is a welcome addition to the town's top musicals, an adult and affable, slick and showy, gay and gracious, literate and sometimes laughable song-and-dance show to take its place among Broadway's brighter extravaganzas.

LOUIS KRONENBERGER, *PM*

The Day Before Spring tries hard to be a lot of very nice things, but only succeeds in being a few of them. It strove for good taste and achieved it; it put a proper stress on music, and the music, if not original, is buoyant and bright and very well orchestrated [by Harold Byrns]. But *The Day Before Spring* never really achieved the freshness prinked with sophistication that it very palpably goes after. Such a combination (which worked last season, on very different lines, in *On the Town* [1944]) is obviously the very devil to come by. Here the combination fails because, too often, what's meant to seem fresh only seems forced; and because what's meant to be a trifle sophisticated winds up more than a trifle pretentious. To its credit, *The Day Before Spring* didn't want the usual breezy tone of a Broadway musical, or the usual comedy. But instead of a gay informality of tone it has a muddled air; and instead of something like real wit, it has only an immature cleverness. It is Mr. Loewe's music that gives the show most of its lift.

BURTON RASCOE, *World-Telegram*

A sweet and charming musical that has everything an operetta, American style, should possess. It has a book by Alan Jay Lerner that has substance, wit, and point. The lyrics, also by Mr. Lerner, are an integral part of the story, not just songs stuck with no relation to the text; and these lyrics are as clean as fresh snow on a hillside and almost as brilliantly textured as snow crystals. The music by Frederick Loewe gives evidence that the author and composer have worked with that harmony in creative collaboration that has distinguished the work of Richard Rodgers and Oscar Hammerstein 2nd.

WILELLA WALDORF, *Post*

The book by Alan Jay Lerner is a curious mixture of pseudo-sophisticated marital philosophy and the sort of collegiate comedy that might grace a Junior Show. . . . If Miles White, the costume designer, really knows what the co-eds are wearing this season, American campuses must look more peculiar than ever.

While too unconventional in form and subject matter for popular success, *The Day Before Spring* clearly created excitement: several critics immediately recognized that Lerner and Loewe—with only a negligible flop behind them, *What's Up* (1943)—were potential successors to Rodgers and Hammerstein.

A Donaldson Award was won by Tom Helmore (supporting actor).

	BROADWAY SCORECARD / perfs: 167 / $: −			
rave	favorable	mixed	unfavorable	pan
2	2		3	1

DESTRY RIDES AGAIN

a musical Western, with music and lyrics by Harold Rome; book by Leonard Gershe, from the 1930 novel by Frederick Faust (Max Brand)

directed and choreographed by Michael Kidd
produced by David Merrick in association with Max Brown
with Andy Griffith, Dolores Gray, Scott Brady (replacing John Ireland), Jack Prince, and Libi Staiger

opened April 23, 1959   Imperial Theatre

FRANK ASTON, *World-Telegram & Sun*

The dances, brain children of Mr. Kidd, were so successful in several instances that the show had to wait until people out front finished clapping. First-nighters are not in the habit of hollering approval, not even for cowboys. The sensation of the affair is "Kent's Gang," Marc Breaux, Swen Swenson, and George Reeder. Their names should be set a foot high for their whip cracking, furniture smashing, and acrobatic dancing which looks dangerous enough to kill three ordinary gymnasts.

JOHN CHAPMAN, *Daily News*

One-word review of *Destry Rides Again:* Yipee!!!! This musical comedy of the wild and impossible West swept into the Imperial Theatre last evening like a prairie wind and bowled over the first-nighters like a bunch of tumbleweed. Give your television set a swift kick in the chaparejos and go see a *real* Western, *Destry Rides Again.*

ROBERT COLEMAN, *Daily Mirror*

Destry Rides Again is a rip-roaring rouser, a triumphant preem for an exciting landmark in horse operas. An extra-added attraction that even non-ticket holders could enjoy was a line of mounted cowpokes prancing over a tanbark-strewn section of 45th St.

WALTER KERR, *Herald Tribune*

Everything that happens at the Imperial is wild enough. Why isn't it more winning? I wonder if this is the ultimate triumph of efficiency. Nothing could be sleeker, slicker, more swiftly and more

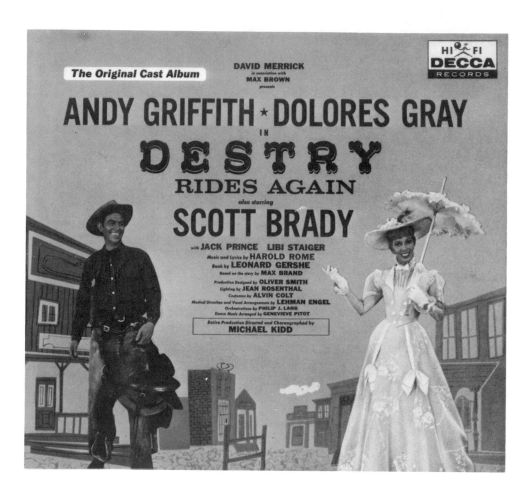

Andy Griffith as Tom Destry, sheriff without a gun, grins while dance-hall gal Dolores Gray steals the spotlight. (costumes by Alvin Colt, photos by Friedman-Abeles)

sharply defined than the rattle-snake coil director Michael Kidd has lashed and snapped across the brilliantly painted barroom of the Last Chance Saloon. But in the end there is little genuine exuberance beneath the frenzies that have kept the front curtain whipping back and forth: there is simply skill. *Destry* does everything well except make you care. For some odd reason, fondness has been finessed right out of it. . . . Nor are all of the better effects deafening in their drive (though most of them are). There is one spectacularly quiet, stunningly etched image in which four immobile outlaws stand in breath-taking dimension before an Oliver Smith backdrop that sends a small, lonely cluster of store-fronts drifting into infinity. A very deep nod here to Jean Rosenthal's lighting.

With shows like *Finian's Rainbow* (1947) and *Guys and Dolls* (1950), Michael Kidd proved he was one of Broadway's finest choreographers. *Destry Rides Again* proved that he just couldn't direct. He got by with the high-spirited *Li'l Abner* (1956), but even crackling dances couldn't save *Destry*. After which Kidd seems to have lost his choreographic touch, too.

A Tony Award was won by Michael Kidd (choreographer).

BROADWAY SCORECARD / perfs: 472 / $: —

rave	favorable	mixed	unfavorable	pan
2	3	2		

DO RE MI

a musical satire, with music by Jule Styne; lyrics by Betty Comden and Adolph Green; book by Garson Kanin, from his 1955 novella

directed by Garson Kanin; choreographed by Marc Breaux and Deedee Wood (Breaux)
produced by David Merrick
with Phil Silvers, Nancy Walker, John Reardon, David Burns, and Nancy Dussault

opened December 26, 1960   St. James Theatre

Phil Silvers doffs his hat to a bunch of Casa Cabana girls. (drawing by Al Hirschfeld)

JOHN CHAPMAN, *Daily News*

A great big razzle-dazzle of a musical.

ROBERT COLEMAN, *Daily Mirror*

Do Re Mi, thanks to Phil Silvers and Nancy Walker, spells lots of the same at the box-office. These very funny folk have a field day in the wacky song-and-dance that Garson Kanin, Jule Styne, Betty Comden, and Adolph Green have tailored to their order. The first-nighters taxed their ribs laughing and blistered their palms applauding. Silvers and Walker have riotously funny scenes, and, for contrast, a couple of sock sentimental songs. They belt both across the footlights like the champs they are. It's a pleasure to watch clever *farceurs* at work, particularly when they've got good material. It is co-author Kanin, doubling as director, who has really paced the wonderful zanies to triumphant success. Kanin, who learned the tricks of the trade from Maestro George Abbott, has pulled out all the stops on this one. The result is a laugh frolic that will have the St. James's treasurer, Hugh McGauley, bending his back toting the loot to the bank. This one is "in." It's a smasheroo. A red-hot ticket.

WALTER KERR, *Herald Tribune*

Do Re Mi is a musical for people who haven't been going to musicals lately. You know what it is? It's fun. Silly fun, loud fun, fast fun, old-fashioned fun, inconsequential fun, grand fun. . . . Mr. Silvers, with his one toe eternally posed as though he were about to step into a sunken bathtub, does try to pose as Torquemade every now and then, setting his teeth in the meanest smirk he can manage as he bitterly says "I love kids." But the poor man has the soul of a kindergarten teacher, and a kindergarten teacher who used to take all of his tots to a vaudeville show on Saturday afternoons. Jule Styne has pulled out a whole anthology of bent-knee ballads and buck-and-wing exits, and to watch Mr. Silvers make for the portals like a drum-majorette who has lately taken to marihuana is—quite simply—to live again. There's a bit of Ed Wynn in him, and a bit of Harold Lloyd, and a bit of Leon Errol, and a bit of Bugs Bunny (his cheeks chock full of the most flavorsome nuts), plus a whole lot of the Mr. Silvers who is the only man left alive who can do all this, and, if you don't mind my saying so, hooray. . . . It has been an especially felicitous idea to have Boris

Aronson do the settings for a musical, what with all those indigestible marvels of glass-and-plastic jukebox colors virtually dribbling down the front drops.

JOHN McCLAIN, *Journal-American*

David Merrick last night continued his drive to monopolize the Broadway theatrical scene with a brassy and bountiful blockbuster. This big musical is mounted and paced in the old tradition; there are the delightful dollies, the blazing dance numbers, the haunting ballads, and the ample portion of cornball humor. This is a sure hit; it could better be called "Dough Re Mi."

RICHARD WATTS JR., *Post*

Fast, professional, tuneful, funny, and delightful. The new musical comedy is loaded with talent in the acting, writing, and production departments, and all its skills are functioning in unison and at their best. Does anyone suspect that the modern American musical show has tended to lose its sense of fun? If by any chance *Bye Bye Birdie* [1960] didn't destroy that false impression, *Do Re Mi* should.

A rough-house, "star comic" musical with a wonderfully clever *pastiche* score. But the show was apparently too brash to please 1961 audiences, and *Do Re Mi* failed despite unanimously favorable reviews. The satire was carried over to the physical production, with excitingly expressionistic sets by Boris Aronson. Aronson hadn't had a musical outing since the days of *Sadie Thompson* (1946) and *Love Life* (1948); he became a major force in the musical theatre with his next effort, *Fiddler on the Roof* (1964).

BROADWAY SCORECARD / perfs: 400 / $: −

rave	favorable	mixed	unfavorable	pan
5	2			

DONNYBROOK!

a musical comedy, with music and lyrics by Johnny Burke; book by Robert E. McEnroe, from the novel *The Quiet Man* by Maurice Walsh

directed and choreographed by Jack Cole
produced by Fred Hebert and David Kapp
with Eddie Foy (Jr.), Art Lund, Joan Fagan (replacing Kipp Hamilton), Susan Johnson, and Philip Bosco

opened May 18, 1961   46th Street Theatre

ROBERT COLEMAN, *Mirror*

Donnybrook! roared into the 46th St. Theatre last night like a gale coming off the Irish Sea. This, despite the fact it is a musical version of a film called *The Quiet Man*. Believe us, there's nothing quiet about this one, and in our book, there's the rub.

WALTER KERR, *Herald Tribune*

Susan Johnson is so much in control of the song about her husband's demise ["Sad Was the Day"] that she is able to make an audience say uncle, or encore, with both hands tied—not behind her back, as it happens, but genteely clasped at her breast. Eddie Foy is essentially a truant, escaped long ago from the Keith–Albee school and never brought back, which is lucky for the rest of us. Ask him to do a couple of numbers with Miss Johnson—numbers that are presumably related to what is going on—and he floats off all by himself, doing experimental and highly illicit things with his feet. "What's he doing?" you ask yourself as he seems to be teaching his spats to stammer, or to shiver like visualized growing pains. But you don't really care what he's doing, it's so lovely the way he's doing it. Yes, Mr. Foy does, as always, try to break up the partner he's playing ring-a-round-a-rosy with, and he does break Miss Johnson up, and the show stops for a while right there so that even the stagehands can catch their breath (they apparently need to, since the backdrops were constantly two inches too high or too low all evening). How the company can turn wide-eyed innocent and genuinely straight-faced again after Mr. Foy has walked on his ankles, danced on his knees, and wiped a spinet with his elbows I don't know, but it does.

RICHARD WATTS JR., *Post*

It was accurately reported of *Donnybrook!* before it reached town that, although its action took place in Ireland, none of the characters said either "begorrah" or "bejabers." I wonder why they went to the trouble of leaving them out. All of the other stereotypes of the roistering, madcap, battling, hard-drinking, hard-loving, lovable Irish of stage and screen are certainly presented in abundance. One of the songs is entitled "I Could Hate the Lovable Irish," and it is, I believe, intended to be ironic. But it does seem that *Donnybrook!* is curiously bent on making a good case for the viewpoint suggested by the number.

An attempt at another *Brigadoon* (1947) or *Finian's Rainbow* (1947), only without the material or the imagination. Coproducer David Kapp—formerly of Decca Records—was the man responsible for pioneering the original broadway cast recording with three 1943 musicals, *Oklahoma!*, *One Touch of Venus*, and *Carmen Jones*. *Donnybrook!* didn't do too well for Kapp Records, but he picked a real sleeper in *Man of La Mancha* (1965).

BROADWAY SCORECARD / perfs: 68 / $: −

rave	favorable	mixed	unfavorable	pan
1	4		2	

DREAM WITH MUSIC

a musical fantasy, with music by Clay Warnick; lyrics by Edward Eager; book by Sidney Sheldon, Dorothy Kilgallen (Kollmar), and Ben Roberts

directed by Richard Kollmar; choreographed by George Balanchine
produced by Richard Kollmar
with Vera Zorina (Balanchine), Ronald Graham, and Joy Hodges (replacing June Knight)

opened May 18, 1944   Majestic Theatre

The lavish dream of a soap opera writer who sees herself as Scheherazade, with music and plenty of scenery. It only seemed longer than 1,001 nights.

JOHN CHAPMAN, *Daily News*

There were 1,001 installments in the original Arabian Nights. At the Majestic it only seems longer. The only way to improve *Dream with Music* would be to put it in two or three sections, so a customer could take two or three nights for sleeping through it and perhaps gain more refreshment. Even this, I'm afraid, would not save the show. Not since Earl Carroll tapped a cash-happy angel, looted several dry goods emporiums and put on *Fioretta* [a 1929 Fanny Brice costume operetta] has so elaborate a load been dumped on a stage. By now producer Richard Kollmar must realize that money isn't everything and good intentions are not enough in show business. He gave his musical comedy everything—everything but spirit. As it unfolded, unrolled, and even slid upon the stage of the Majestic last night, its splendors were vast. But its torpor was vaster. Stewart Chaney, a master designer, has dreamed with a sketchbook and paint brush and come up with ten or a dozen sets which range from palaces to enchanted forests, from Bagdad bazaars to the Magic Carpet itself. . . . The cast is large enough to staff the Pentagon Building with pretty usherettes. Joy Hodges looks more like Myrna Loy than Miss Loy does.

ROBERT GARLAND, *Journal-American*

So fancy are its fixings—settings by Stewart Chaney; costumes by Miles White; choreography by George Balanchine; caryatids by Mother Nature—that house electricians at the Majestic blew out the theatre's master fuse.

WILELLA WALDORF, *Post*

Dream with Music advances the sensational idea that a young woman who writes "soap operas" for the radio day in and day out is not unlike Scheherazade of Arabian Nights fame. Having evolved this striking parallel, the authors of *Dream with Music* were apparently so exhausted by the mental effort that they were unable to contribute much of anything else. After arranging that the heroine should fall asleep and dream she was actually Scheherazade, they likewise dozed off and called in a brigade of designers and technicians. The designers and technicians have had themselves a time to the tune of something approaching $175,000. It's a trifle difficult to imagine Vera Zorina as a composer of radio serials for the washing powder trade, but she makes a fetching Scheherazade, riding with

Aladdin on his Magic Carpet, bailing out to dance on a cloud and hunt for the moon, visiting the animals in an enchanted forest, and generally behaving like the heroine of a children's fairy story. Every now and then the authors, sleeping but fitfully, awoke from their slumbers and contributed immensely dull driblets of routine musical comedy chatter interspersed with songs which sounded so much alike, and were equipped with such uninspired lyrics, that they quickly removed any charm generated by the efforts of the designers.

Producer Richard Kollmar had better luck with his previous production, "Fats" Waller's *Early to Bed* (1943). Dorothy Kilgallen (Kollmar) was a powerful newspaper columnist of the day; the couple hosted a long-running radio talk show, "Breakfast with Dorothy and Dick" (1945–63). Star Vera Zorina played the lead in the 1937 London edition of *On Your Toes* (1936), after which Balanchine divorced his wife (Tamara Geva, who created the *Toes* role) to marry his new ballerina. Zorina—a Norwegian sprite given a properly Russian name when she joined the Ballets Russe—came to Broadway in the custom-tailored title role of the Rodgers-Hart-Logan-Balanchine hit *I Married an Angel* (1938). After retirement she remained in the musical theatre world as the wife of Goddard Lieberson, dean of original cast recording producers.

```
OOOOOOOOOOOOOOOOOOOOOOOOOOOOOOOOOOOOOOOOOO
O                                                          O
O        BROADWAY SCORECARD / perfs: 28 / $: −            O
O                                                          O
O     rave    favorable    mixed    unfavorable    pan    O
O                                                          O
O                                          2        6     O
O                                                          O
OOOOOOOOOOOOOOOOOOOOOOOOOOOOOOOOOOOOOOOOOO
```

THE DUCHESS MISBEHAVES

a farce musical, with music by Dr. Frank Black; book and lyrics by Gladys Shelley; additional dialogue by Joe Bigelow

"production supervised" by Chet O'Brien; directed by Martin Manulis; choreographed by George Tapps (replacing John Wray) produced by A. P. Waxman with Audrey Christie, George Tapps, Paula Laurence (replacing Luella Gear), and Joey Faye (replacing Jackie Gleason)

opened February 13, 1946   Adelphi Theatre

HOWARD BARNES, *Herald Tribune*

Frolicsome is the word the sponsors use to describe *The Duchess Misbehaves*. The adjective might be applied to a three-legged elephant, but it would be quite as inept. The new musical comedy is so lacking in wit, charm, and musical eloquence that it is a crashing bore, both tasteless and turgid. The lyrics rhyme souse with louse; the libretto is as disconnected as a cross-word puzzle, and the music is only worthy of attention when a piece of Manuel De Falla is being played. Unfortunately, De Falla did not write the score. If *The Duchess Misbehaves* is frolicsome, I'll take a steam-shovel. . . . George Tapps contributes pretentious terpsichorean interludes to an entertainment which has no more bounce than a croquet ball.

JOHN CHAPMAN, *Daily News*

The Duchess Misbehaves is more a misdemeanor than a misbehaviour and should be let off with a two-dollar fine on complaint from the Department of Sanitation. . . . A sample lyric rhymes "anguish" with "language"—and I just languish.

ROBERT GARLAND, *Journal-American*

Come back, *Nellie Bly*. You are forgiven. [*Nellie* preceded *The Duchess* at the hapless Adelphi].

LOUIS KRONENBERGER, *PM*

Kicking its 18th-century heels on West 54th Street is one of the most maddening musicals of the decade. I can't conceive what *The Duchess Misbehaves* was even trying to do. It is all a noisy and witless mess—abysmal book, anemic tunes, schoolboy lyrics, absurdly pretentious dancing—and a shocking waste of several competent performers' time. The leaden jokes pile up on the Adelphi stage until it would take ten husky stevedores to lug them away. Joey Faye, leaping into the part at the very last minute, and not looking before he leaped, performs as Goya. He was letter-perfect in his lines on opening night, which was possibly a mistake. Mr. Faye can be funny given a chance, but he is never given half a one, and so marches to his doom.

VERNON RICE, *Post*

Misfortune has befallen *The Duchess Misbehaves* almost since its inception. Last night, however, it had its greatest misfortune. It opened. Just for the records let it be said that it is a musical comedy in which a timid little sign painter in a department store is knocked out by some thieves who are stealing the valuable Goya painting of the Duchess of Alba. The one in which she is nude, of course. He has a dream that he is Goya and that Crystal Shalimar [Audrey Christie], his dream girl in life, is his dream girl in the dream and the Duchess as well. . . . In the spirit of the show's bum jokes, I say it will Goya way soon.

News From The Front. Jan. 21—Jackie Gleason rewriting the show. Jan. 31—Jackie Gleason sprains ankle on stage. Feb. 1— Jackie Gleason returns after missing two performances. Feb. 11— Jackie Gleason suddenly quits. Feb. 13—*The Duchess Misbehaves* on Broadway, with Joey Faye. B'way crack: This show was so bad that the star deliberately broke his leg to get out of it.

BROADWAY SCORECARD / perfs: 5 / $: —

rave	favorable	mixed	unfavorable	pan
				8

EARLY TO BED

a musical farce, with music by Thomas "Fats" Waller; book and lyrics by George Marion, Jr.

production supervised by Alfred Bloomingdale; directed and choreographed by Robert Alton
produced by Richard Kollmar

with Muriel Angelus, Richard Kollmar, Mary Small, and Jane Kean

opened June 17, 1943   Broadhurst Theatre

HERRICK BROWN, *Sun*

The program describes it as "a fairy tale for grown-ups." It's not one for juveniles, certainly, nor for the squeamish, either. Its difficulties in Boston [with the censor] arose because its plot complications hinge on the fact that a Martinique house of ill repute is mistaken for a girls' seminary by the members of a college track team from California. . . . Lyricist George Marion, Jr., isn't above rhyming "Delilah" with "miler."

BURNS MANTLE, *Daily News*

It is noisy, gorgeous, leggy, and without wit. It is faster than fast, rhythmical and harsh and carries loads of dirt to the dirty. It is a bordello's night dream and is happiest when it goes into its exceptionally good dances. Anyone within reach of the box office is privileged to take it or leave it. The responsibility of this reporter ends with a fair warning that it is staged deliberately to catch the trade that a year ago went to *Star and Garter* [Mike Todd's racy 1942 burlesque revue starring Gypsy Rose Lee]. A large audience welcomed *Early to Bed* and smirked with satisfaction.

BURTON RASCOE, *World-Telegram*

The show has spice and spizzerinktum and is a joy to the eye and ear.

WILELLA WALDORF, *Post*

Strangely enough, the loudest bursts of applause came when Mr. [George] Jenkins's scenery started moving around as if Tallulah Bankhead were after it with her feather duster [as in *The Skin of Our Teeth* (1942)]. The first time it moved the audience was in such a state of ecstasy that we were surprised they didn't do the routine over again by way of encore. If songs can be reprised, why can't scenery be moved twice when it gets a great big hand?

☆

A wartime hit, with producer Richard Kollmar—juvenile of Kurt Weill's *Knickerbocker Holiday* (1938) and Rodgers and Hart's *Too Many Girls* (1939)—playing El Magnifico, an on-the-skids bull-fighter. Real classy stuff. George Jenkins's early mechanized scenery is worth noting; this sort of thing would become standard, but not until the mid-1950s.

BROADWAY SCORECARD / perfs: 382 / $: +

rave	favorable	mixed	unfavorable	pan
2		1	4	1

EDDIE FISHER AT THE WINTER GARDEN

three night-club acts, with special material for Juliet Prowse by Sammy Cahn and Jimmy Van Heusen

directed by John Fearnley; Juliet Prowse's act directed and choreographed by Tony Charmoli
produced by Monte Proser and Milton Blackstone
with Eddie Fisher, Juliet Prowse, and Dick Gregory

opened October 2, 1962   Winter Garden Theatre

JOHN CHAPMAN, *Daily News*

In interviews Fisher has said it has long been his dream to sing in the house that once was Al Jolson's. As a tribute he did a pot-pourri of Jolson favorites and they sounded fine as long as Eddie had a microphone in his hands and a cord on it long enough to run a vacuum cleaner from my basement to my attic. . . . After Dick Gregory came Prowse, who is billed in the ads and the program as Miss Juliet Prowse. I personally don't care a hoot in a rain barrel if she is Miss or Mrs. She is a combination cooch dancer and shouter and she is very, very vulgar. One of her numbers is a "musical version" of the story of Joan of Arc, and it is the most tasteless exhibition I have seen on a stage since the Phoenix Theatre reviewed *Lysistrata* [1959].

ROBERT COLEMAN, *Mirror*

The curvaceous and vivacious Juliet Prowse, assisted by a male sextet, offered some of the most tasteless songs and dances heard and seen hereabouts of late. It is difficult to believe that Oscar-winners Sammy Cahn and Jimmy Van Heusen could have been guilty of such inept words and music, or Tony Charmoli such suggestive and embarrassing choreography. Particularly offensive was a take-off on Joan of Arc, replete with wiggles and bumps. And her salutes to Camille and Cleopatra—the latter featuring a Gilda Gray-ish shimmy—were strictly for the Las Vegas trade. All right, so *Eddie Fisher at the Winter Garden* failed to make our pulses race. But you can't laugh off the $10,000-a-day advance sale he's been piling up. If this entertainment isn't exactly our dish of tea, it appeared to be choice Oolong or Ceylon for a majority of our neighbors.

NORMAN NADEL, *World-Telegram & Sun*

There is a temptation to describe *Eddie Fisher at the Winter Garden* as the most appalling modern catastrophe north of the Mason-Dixon Line. . . . A pit orchestra about the size of the Berlin Philharmonic was blasting the ears off the audience—good playing, though. Fisher used electronic amplification, and probably sounded better in the last row, or on Tenth Ave. than he did in the front of the house. Well, Eddie's voice has developed more body, and richer timbre in the lower register, but he still hasn't much range. He smiled nicely, sang the familiar songs—almost all in an unvarying slam-bang style—and was grievously flat half the time. His Al Jolson group not only was poor Jolson, it was poor Eddie Fisher.

HOWARD TAUBMAN, *Times*

Dick Gregory's relaxed delivery and his slashing brand of humor cuts and probes in any forum. One of the strengths of his approach is that as a Negro he pokes fun at Negro and white alike. His material remains at its best, not when he goes chasing after gags about the Kennedys and the other targets favored by most stand-up comics, but when he deals with themes he feels strongly about. In closing he pays an edged compliment to America as a land in which "I have the worst housing, eat the worst food, get the worst schools, and am paid $5,000 a week to talk about it."

BROADWAY SCORECARD / perfs: 48 / $: NA

rave	favorable	mixed	unfavorable	pan
1			5	1

AN EVENING WITH BEATRICE LILLIE

an intimate revue, with songs and sketches by various writers

directed and produced by Edward Duryea Dowling
with Beatrice Lillie and Reginald Gardiner
opened October 2, 1952   Booth Theatre

BROOKS ATKINSON, *Times*

Beatrice Lillie is the funniest woman in the world. Geniuses on the stage are always highly individual, no matter what part they happen to be playing. So it is with Miss Lillie in this show. The slender, sharp-featured lady with the polite, embarrassed smile and the dainty manner dominates the material, the stage, and the theatre. She radiates satiric comedy even when she is standing still. She sits at a table and looks blank: it is funny. She pauses for a beat in a song: it is funny. It almost seems as though her thoughts were funny. For she is one of the most eloquent actresses in the theatre, and she can set the audience to laughing without saying a word, singing a note, or making a gesture. Although she has the presence of a lady—of a very jaunty lady—she is an enormously funny low comedienne. There is plenty of vulgarity in the stuff she does. She is as anatomical as Willie Howard used to be, and one of the songs she sings is bluer than the scarf she wears in her opening number. But her ribaldries somehow seem to be immaculate. For her style is always demure on the surface; the manner is dry, the gestures sharp and spare, the pace is like quicksilver, and the whole thing adds up to the most brilliant comic spirit of our time.

ROBERT COLEMAN, *Daily Mirror*

Miss Lillie is the last of the great femme clowns. We say that affectionately, for clowning is a great art and she is a great artist. There are three "greats" in a row for you, and we put them there knowingly. That's the right word for Lillie. She defies analysis. She has a small, piping voice. She isn't afraid to use a good old-fashioned slapstick. It really isn't so much what she does. It's how she does it. She can transmute the rowdiest hokum into gorgeous, subtle hilarity. Perhaps the secret of it all is that beneath the heart, that behind the broadest gesture is sensitivity. She is Fratellini, Ariel, and Tinker Bell all in one. She's a sprite, a pixie. Boy, will she hate this! But it's so true. She mugs, she twitches her body into awkward positions, she even flexes her tiny muscles like Sandow. But she does it all with amazing grace. There's careful thought behind everything she does. But it comes across the footlights as spontaneity. She has the art that conceals art.

WALTER KERR, *Herald Tribune*

With a pianist named Rack to help her keep joyously off pitch, Miss Lillie runs through all the numbers you'd have requested if you'd been asked to assemble your dream program. She squares her jaw over a helpful brandy, stares her invisible companion cooly in the eye, and proceeds to bare both their souls in "Maude, You're Rotten to the Core." She postures prettily through "There Are Fairies at the Bottom of My Garden." She murders the conventional medley of tried and very tired tunes in that old favorite called "Rhythm" [by Rodgers and Hart], forcing her pianist to rise while she does a few bars of Francis Scott Key. And the passion with which she pursues a rising note to infinity in a sad little song labeled "Not Wanted on the Voyage" produces as delectable a lunatic moment as any honest man can ask for in an entire season. The fact that practically everything is familiar to Miss Lillie's indefatigable fans does nothing to diminish either the gayety or the spontaneity of the performance. Whether the star is inadvertently throttling herself with a scarf, swinging a necklace at improbable angles, or destroying the institution of the stage microphone with a few judicious yawps, she is as fresh, as poised, and as slyly poisonous as though she were doing it for the first time. And the impact out front seemed to me headier than ever.

RICHARD WATTS JR., *Post*

Miss Lillie is one of the performers whose fans take on all the proportions of a cult. This means, among other things, that she has merely to assume an expression, make a movement, or open her mouth to have her enthusiasts convulsed with ecstatic mirth. In the case of most stars, this is enough to cause cooler heads among the customers to grow a little wary, and it is one of the highest tributes to the art of Beatrice Lillie to say that she justifies even the hysterics of her worshippers. I think it should also be said for Miss Lillie, in case there is anyone about who has forgotten it, that it isn't paying her enough of a compliment to say that she is the foremost lady clown. She is much better than this would imply. There is a cool, deft, wonderfully winning style about everything she does, a strange quality of grace and charm in even her wildest hilarity, and an ability to remain an attractive woman while indulging in her most riotous foolery that would indicate to even a visitor from Mars that she is a personage.

Love letters for Bea Lillie. And this time she had good material, handpicked from her all-time "bests." Sounds like quite *An Evening*, doesn't it?

Beatrice Lillie received a special Tony Award.

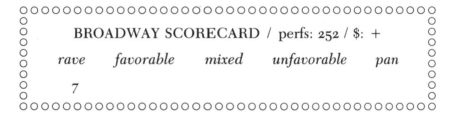

BROADWAY SCORECARD / perfs: 252 / $: +

rave	favorable	mixed	unfavorable	pan
7				

FADE OUT—FADE IN

a musical satire, with music by Jule Styne; book and lyrics by Betty Comden and Adolph Green; previously announced as *A Girl to Remember*

directed by George Abbott; choreographed by Ernest Flatt
produced by Lester Osterman and Jule Styne (with ABC-Paramount)
with Carol Burnett, Jack Cassidy, Lou Jacobi, Tina Louise, and Dick Patterson

opened May 26, 1964   Mark Hellinger Theatre

JOHN CHAPMAN, *Daily News*

A real World's Fair musical, with something in it for everybody and everything in it for somebody. Count me among the somebodies, for I never stopped enjoying it while it was on. *Fade Out—Fade In* is a summer festival all by itself. . . . Amidst all this and that and these, one finds Carol Burnett, a girl of extraordinary resource. She can whoop up a song in Merman style, she can dance—or hoof, anyhow—and she is a wonderful clown. Miss Burnett is teamed with the handsomest, most masculine, and vainest baritone in filmdom. Jack Cassidy is thoroughly delightful and skillful in this role, even though he looks disturbingly like Tessie O'Shea when he flashes his teeth.

WALTER KERR, *Herald Tribune*

I sat there last night watching *Fade Out—Fade In* and I plain didn't see why I couldn't like it. There was Carol Burnett, a friendly girl with a blissful bleat of a voice and a marvelous trick of making her arms go limp as a gorilla's, especially when not playing the violin. There were Jule Styne sounds coming constantly from the pit, all of them familiar and some of them fun, there was George Abbott to see that nothing ever happened without something happening next, and—flexing his smile like a fox with an appetite—there was silver-haired, urbane, predatory Jack Cassidy. Why do Mr. Cassidy's teeth look like whiskers? Everything workable, everything swift, and I never could persuade myself that any of it was necessary. The question is simply "*Now* what do we do?" and what we do now is what we did last. Everybody is so game that I feel like a game warden, but the affair is pure improvisation around a workable personality and this time the improvisation isn't impish enough.

NORMAN NADEL, *World-Telegram & Sun*

Look no further than *Fade Out—Fade In*, which rode into town on a wave of laughter last night, to learn the ABC's of comedy. They are Abbott (George), Burnett (Carol) and Cassidy (Jack). . . . It occurred to me that others might have written this same musical, for better or worse—in fact, others have written quite a few like it. And most of the cast, competent as it is, could be replaced without tragic loss. I envisioned jacking up Abbott, Burnett, and Cassidy, and sliding another (almost any other) musical under them. Then

Hollywood hopeful Carol Burnett beats the pavement in a sandwich-board, while back at the studio they film the title song of "The Fiddler and the Fighter." (drawing by Al Hirschfeld)

it would become a hit, too. George Abbott is endowed with that elusive and fragile talent known in academic circles as the old razz-ma-tazz. As a director, he can so overwhelm an audience with showmanship that any weaknesses in dialogue, situations, or music go almost unnoticed. In his hands, *Fade Out—Fade In* maintains a wild pace. He has exploited every potential laugh, and probably invented a few of his own along the way.

RICHARD WATTS JR., *Post*

The new musical comedy is pretty commonplace in its ingredients, but it has enough enthusiastic relish and sheer gusto to make it entertaining. . . . Tina Louise is very beautiful as the shallow girl the boss meant to hire, and a seal called Smaxie [a cousin to M-G-M's Leo the Lion] indicates strength of character by pretending to hold her in contempt.

Another zany Hollywood satire, but not as strong as Comden and Green's prior attempts. And hadn't there been enough Hollywood satire already? *Fade Out* was initially postponed from its original November 1963 date by Burnett's pregnancy. Then, seven weeks after the show finally opened, the star was injured in a taxicab accident. Suffering from whiplash, Burnett missed over two dozen performances as the box office gross plummeted from $64,000 (more than competitors *Dolly!* or *Funny Girl*) to $18,000. Meanwhile "The Entertainers," Burnett's first TV series, went on the air. Osterman tried to enjoin her from appearing while she was too "ill" for Broadway; Burnett countered by accusing him of attempting to destroy her career by attacking her "personal and professional integrity." She also offered $500,000 to buy out her contract. In mid-October Burnett moved into the hospital and left *Fade Out* altogether, forcing the show to fade out altogether. Actors' Equity supported the producers' claim in arbitration, and Burnett returned after her recovery to play out her contract. *Fade Out—Fade In* reopened on February 15, 1965, with Dick Shawn replacing Jack Cassidy, but the show was unable to regain momentum and closed permanently two months later. Just a happy little musical comedy, that's all.

BROADWAY SCORECARD / perfs: 271 / $: —

rave	favorable	mixed	unfavorable	pan
	5		1	

A FAMILY AFFAIR

an intimate musical comedy by James Goldman, John Kander, and William Goldman

directed by Harold Prince (replacing Word Baker); choreographed by John Butler (replaced by Bob Herget); "musical staging" by Bob Herget
produced by Andrew Siff
with Shelley Berman, Eileen Heckart, Morris Carnovsky, Larry Kert, and Rita Gardner

opened January 27, 1962   Billy Rose Theatre

WALTER KERR, *Herald Tribune*

Part of the grinning goodness is due to the fact that the stage is full of actors who not only have hearts of gold but can also act, and part of it is due to what the authors have decided to do with the shape of musical comedy. They have decided to housebreak it, for one thing, closing the outside door that leads to all those big production numbers and insisting that the folk settle down by a reasonably cozy hearth, and fight there. . . . *A Family Affair* has genuine charm, and if it would only get up off its charm and [do] something a little more definite a little more often, it might easily land in the big-time. Everything in view is intimate, innocent, easygoing, and hopefully fresh. What keeps the entertainment from becoming a memorable innovation is the fact that it goes around and around instead of up. It's like one of those spinning discs at an amusement park: the feeling is pleasant, but you keep falling off. *A Family Affair* falls off in the vacuousness of some of its blackouts, falls off in the repetitiousness of quarrels that don't progress, falls off most notoriously in its second-act reaching for incidental numbrs (such as a bachelor party) that are far enough afield to be arrested for vagrancy.

JOHN MCCLAIN, *Journal-American*

There are more than enough personable and gifted people on hand, but the story never gets beyond the level of an endless squabble; the few tunes with distinction are feebly presented; the laughs are force-fed and far between; the choreography is nearly non-existent, and even the scenery and costumes fail to add any charm of their own to the proceedings. Harold Prince has been credited with the direction, a rather minor distinction under the circumstances.

NORMAN NADEL, *World-Telegram & Sun*

Even the supporting players perform like stars. To name one— Linda Lavin—as a crying girl in a dress shop, a playgirl at a bachelor party, and a dress designer. She builds her own bright fire whenever she steps on stage.

HOWARD TAUBMAN, *Times*

Although *A Family Affair* is a musical of normal length, it seems to go on forever. Its single fragile idea splashes endlessly in a sticky sea of sentimentality and vulgarity. James Goldman, John Kander, and William Goldman have attempted to rear their musical comedy on a notion so thin it might be good for one fast joke. They stretch it with slight variations of the essential jest and with noisy repetitions of the basic bickering until it all but snaps. The writing of *A Family Affair* is not strong on taste; it resorts to the clichés of Jewish domestic attitudes. Nor is it fresh in style; it often has the air of a busy, good-humored borrower from various musical comedy sources. Since some of these sources are first-rate, some numbers are lively.

RICHARD WATTS JR., *Post*

The program doesn't say which of the authors, James Goldman, John Kander, and William Goldman, wrote the music [Kander, dance music arranger of Merrick's *Gypsy* (1959) and *Irma La Douce* (1960)], but he has rather the better of it.

☆

First-time director Harold Prince came in after the Philadelphia opening, replacing Word Baker (whose *The Fantasticks* [1960], meanwhile, is *still* running!!). Not much could be done, but Prince did hook up with future authors of *Flora, the Red Menace* (1965), *Cabaret* (1966), *Zorba* (1968) and *Follies* (1971). He also dropped his middle initial. The *Family Affair* music, meanwhile, is actually quite interesting.

BROADWAY SCORECARD / perfs: 65 / $: −

rave	favorable	mixed	unfavorable	pan
1	2	1		3

FANNY

a musical drama, with music and lyrics by Harold Rome; book by S. N. Behrman and Joshua Logan, from the French screenplays *Marius* (1931), *Fanny* (1932), and *Cesar* (1936) by Marcel Pagnol

directed by Joshua Logan; choreographed by Helen Tamiris (replacing James Starbuck)
produced by David Merrick and Joshua Logan
with Ezio Pinza, Walter Slezak, Florence Henderson, and William Tabbert

opened November 4, 1954   Majestic Theatre

BROOKS ATKINSON, *Times*

All the bounty of showmanship that Mr. Logan has brought to it is of first rank. But for once this theatregoer finds himself impatient with Mr. Logan's passion for the supercolossal. For the dramatic content of *Fanny* is fine enough to stand on its own feet. The story is a simple one that involves appealing characters and the style is sentimental with a tart, worldly flavor. And Harold Rome has written an idiomatic score that conveys the simple emotions of the story. There is nothing in the showmanship half so affecting as Mr. Pinza's artless singing of an idyll called "Love Is a Very Light Thing," or his exultant "Why Be Afraid to Dance?" or his domestic rhapsody called "Welcome Home." Luxurious and imposing as the

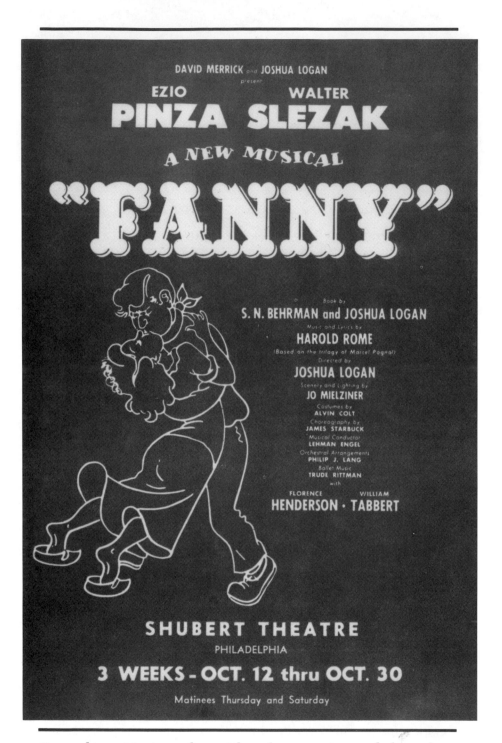

Fanny kisses Marius, a boy with no heart to give, and almost loses her shoes. Pre-Broadway credits.

salesmanship may be, it cheapens the theme, as though Mr. Logan had been frightened by *Kismet* [1953]. As the writers of a raffish and romantic story, Mr. Behrman and Mr. Logan need nothing but a composer and some actors. The composer has caught the mood beautifully. The actors have a bold style, a sense of humor, and a lot of color. *Fanny* is a fine folk tale because the writers and actors are sound.

WILLIAM HAWKINS, *World-Telegram & Sun*

The Mielziner production outdoes anything that even he has conceived before. The transitions are like mirages, so subtly and quickly do they occur, as curtains and lights appear and disappear by magic.

WALTER KERR, *Herald Tribune*

The Messrs. Pinza and Slezak give *Fanny* its funniest moments and its most moving moments. They also give it what virtually no one else in the company can force out—flavor. *Fanny* is adapted from Marcel Pagnol's trilogy of screenplays detailing the mismatched loves of a couple of port-town families. In co-producing, co-authoring, and directing the musical amalgam, Joshua Logan has done everything within reason to preserve the earthy tartness, the shrewd realism, the robust honesty. But the racy, pungent, cantankerous accent of the original is subdued and attenuated. In part this is due to the simple fact of its musicalization for Broadway: spread a simple, fairly folksy comedy out to the dimensions of a vast and glittering proscenium and something of its simplicity is bound to vanish. A batch of chorus boys and chorus girls offering gifts to a baby on its first birthday is more a curious than an affecting picture. Nor do the young lovers of the piece, pleasantly played and sung by William Tabbert and Florence Henderson, seem to be in Marseilles; they seem to be downstage. Ezio Pinza has an appealing episode during which he tries to teach his errant son how to make vermouth cassis without too much seltzer. *Fanny*, I think, has too much seltzer. It is often difficult to taste the wine.

JOHN McCLAIN, *Journal-American*

Sad to report, *Fanny* is a serious disappointment. Perhaps we all expected too much from Joshua Logan, S. N. Behrman, and Harold Rome, but the fact remains that it lacks anything very distinguished in the way of pace, humor, music, or excitement. Sure, it is big and beautiful, but it is also hollow. It is difficult to understand how so much talent could go so far astray.

RICHARD WATTS JR., *Post*

Fanny is so frequently bogged down in its story that it rarely moves along with the proper emotional or musical effectiveness. Book and score, instead of being mutually helpful, appear to get in each other's way. There are attractive songs, which are always admirably sung, and the performances never fail to be striking and alive, but an air of heavy-handedness settles down over the proceedings. It may be said of *Fanny*, then, that it is colorful, human, tuneful, and both richly and handsomely decked out. But it substitutes color and size for inspiration.

David Merrick's first musical was somewhat overproduced, suffering from Josh Logan's attempt to outdo Rodgers and Hammerstein. (Logan's long, successful association with Rodgers was ruptured by the success of *South Pacific* [1949]. The director/coauthor/coproducer felt undercredited and underpaid; turned down *The King and I* [1951]; had a nervous breakdown; and then tried to get Rodgers and Hammerstein to write *Fanny*.) In any event, Merrick turned the show's flaw into an asset, successfully hawking *Fanny* as an extravaganza. High-class stuff like placing a nude statue of the show's belly dancer in Central Park and affixing stickers in the men's rooms of the town bearing (baring) the burning question, "Have you seen *Fanny?*" Incidental note: when *Fanny* was forced to vacate Broadway's biggest theater by the Mielziner-produced *Happy Hunting* (1956), they crammed it into the tiny Belasco!

A Tony Award was won by Walter Slezak (actor).

BROADWAY SCORECARD / perfs: 888 / $: +				
rave	favorable	mixed	unfavorable	pan
1	2	2	2	

FIDDLER ON THE ROOF

a musical, with music by Jerry Bock; lyrics by Sheldon Harnick; book by Joseph Stein, from stories by Sholom Aleichem; previously announced as *Tevye and His Daughters*

directed and choreographed by Jerome Robbins
produced by Harold Prince (replacing Fred Coe)
with Zero Mostel, Maria Karnilova, and Beatrice Arthur

opened September 22, 1964   Imperial Theatre

JOHN CHAPMAN, *Daily News*

One of the great works of the American musical theatre. It is darling, touching, beautiful, warm, funny, and inspiring. It is a work of art. The lyrics, as important as narrative as they are entertaining, are by Sheldon Harnick. The score, by Jerry Bock, is a jubilant celebration. Boris Aronson, an Artist with a capital A, has contributed settings of great beauty.

WALTER KERR, *Herald Tribune*

I do not speak of Mr. Mostel as a dolphin because he is light on his feet, a fact known to everyone, but because in at least one exceedingly liquid melody he contrives to sound like a dolphin, a Jewish dolphin. [In "If I Were a Rich Man"] he dreams in vocalized snuggles, not in words. For every other line of the lyric he simply substitutes gratified gargles and cascading coos until he has arrived, mystically, at a kind of cabalistic coloratura. The effect is what we all had in mind when we last thought of satisfaction in depth. He is less Mother Courage than Father Complaint. . . . I think it might be an altogether charming musical if only the people of Anatevka did not pause every now and then to give their regards to Broadway, with remembrances to Herald Square. [The result] is a very-near-miss, and I very much miss what it might have been.

JOHN MCCLAIN, *Journal-American*

The show has a fine folksy style, with exceptional direction and choreography by Jerome Robbins, and the plaintive and generally appealing music by Jerry Bock and Sheldon Harnick. There are arid areas in the book by Joseph Stein, and it seemed to me there was an overabundance of self-pity displayed. But there seems little

HAROLD PRINCE and FRED COE
present

Zero Mostel
in
Fiddler on the Roof

a new musical

Book by JOSEPH STEIN
(based on Sholem Aleichem's stories by special permission of Arnold Perl)

Music by JERRY BOCK

Lyrics by SHELDON HARNICK

with

MARIA KARNILOVA   BEATRICE ARTHUR

JOANNA   AUSTIN   BERT   JULIA
MERLIN   PENDLETON   CONVY   MAGENES

MICHAEL   JOSEPH   TANYA   ROBERT
GRANGER SULLIVAN EVERETT BERDEEN

Entire Production Directed & Choreographed by
JEROME ROBBINS

Settings by   Costumes by
BORIS ARONSON   PATRICIA ZIPPRODT

Orchestrations by   Lighting by   Musical Direction & Vocal Arrangements by
DON WALKER   JEAN ROSENTHAL   MILTON GREENE

Opens Tuesday Evening, September 22
AIR
CONDITIONED   IMPERIAL THEATRE
45th St. West of Broadway   -:-   Matinees Wednesday and Saturday

A fiddler dances on the roof, a daughter waves her kerchief, and a rooster crows over the moon in this Chagall-inspired logo. The daughter was displaced after the opening by an overstuffed Zero-with-fiddle. Pre-Broadway credits, including co-producer Fred Coe. (drawing by Tom Morrow)

question that *Fiddler* will be up on that roof for many a moon. The show has taste and humor and style.

NORMAN NADEL, *World-Telegram & Sun*

You don't have to be Jewish to love Tevye. Some of the dance numbers—especially "To Life"—make it almost impossible to keep from dancing in the aisles.

HOWARD TAUBMAN, *Times*

Compounded of the familiar materials of the musical theatre—popular song, vivid dance movement, comedy, and emotion—it combines and transcends them to arrive at an integrated achievement of uncommon quality. Mr. Mostel's Tevye is one of the most glowing creations in the history of the musical theatre. He does not keep his acting and singing or his walking and dancing in separate compartments. His Tevye is a unified, lyrical conception. With the exception of a grimace or a gesture several times that score easy laughs, Tevye stays in character. . . . Criticism of a work of this calibre is relative. If I cavil, it is because *Fiddler on the Roof* is so fine that it deserves counsels toward perfection.

RICHARD WATTS JR., *Post*

Although *Fiddler on the Roof* has its unfortunate weaknesses to stand in the way, it is a musical play that has originality and a feeling of truth. That it works out as effectively as it does is due partly to the taste and imagination of the production. But chiefly it is the result of the brilliantly resourceful and intelligent performance that Zero Mostel offers in the central role.

Oddly enough, *Fiddler* marked a less-than-happy turning point in the history of the musical theatre. For here was a classic made brilliant by an imaginative production, rather than by the material itself. *Carousel* (1945), *Kiss Me, Kate* (1948), *South Pacific* (1949), *Guys and Dolls* (1950), *My Fair Lady* (1956), *West Side Story* (1957), and *Gypsy* (1959) all have *great* scores. *Fiddler's* is certainly quite good, but just as certainly less than great. Fortunately, the several flaws were more than compensated for by the

Messrs. Robbins, Aronson, et al. Although the general consensus of the *Fiddler* folk was that Mostel was a hindrance rather than a help, he sure carried the show past the less-than-overwhelmed critics.

Winner of the New York Drama Critics' Circle Award. In addition to winning the Tony Award for Best Musical, Tonys were won by Jerry Bock and Sheldon Harnick (composer and lyricist); Joseph Stein (librettist); Jerome Robbins (director); Jerome Robbins (choreographer); Harold Prince (producer); Zero Mostel (actor); Maria Karnilova (supporting actress); and Patricia Zipprodt (costume designer). Scenic designer Boris Aronson lost to Oliver Smith for *Baker Street* (1965).

BROADWAY SCORECARD / perfs: 3,242 / $: +

rave	favorable	mixed	unfavorable	pan
2	4			

FINIAN'S RAINBOW

a musical satire, with music by Burton Lane; lyrics by E. Y. Harburg; book by E. Y. Harburg and Fred Saidy

directed by Bretaigne Windust; choreographed by Michael Kidd
produced by Lee Sabinson and William R. Katzell
with Ella Logan, Albert Sharpe, Donald Richards, David Wayne, and Anita Alvarez

opened January 10, 1947   46th Street Theatre

BROOKS ATKINSON, *Times*

Jettisoning most of the buncombe of the traditional musical show, E. Y. Harburg and Fred Saidy have written an original and humorous fantasy. Do not be terrified by the news that it whirls around a leprechaun and a magic pot of gold. For Mr. Harburg and Mr. Saidy wrote *Bloomer Girl* [1944] two seasons ago, and that was no sissy show. With some clarion music by Burton Lane and some joyous dancing by a company of inspired sprites, the authors have conjured

LEE SABINSON and WILLIAM R. KATZELL

present

FINIAN'S RAINBOW

A Completely Captivating Musical

Book by
E. Y. HARBURG and FRED SAIDY

Lyrics by
E. Y. HARBURG

Music by
BURTON LANE

Directed by
BRETAIGNE WINDUST

Scenery and Lighting by
JO MIELZINER

Dances and Musical Numbers by
MICHAEL KIDD

Costumes by
ELEANOR GOLDSMITH

Orchestrations by
ROBERT RUSSELL BENNET and DON WALKER

Vocal arrangements by LYN MURRAY

SHUBERT THEATRE
BOSTON

Opens Monday Evening, October 18

MATINEES WEDNESDAY and SATURDAY

491

Og the Leprechaun gazes in wonderment at Susan the Silent, confessing "When I'm Not Near the Girl I Love (I love the girl I'm near)." In the immortal words of Mr. Harburg: "Long as they've got a boo-som, I woos 'em." (drawing by Don Freeman)

up a raree-show of enchantment, humor, and beauty, to say nothing of enough social significance to hold the franchise. It puts the American musical stage several steps forward for the imagination with which it is written and for the stunning virtuousity of the performance. . . . If the American musical stage continues to improve, it will no longer be necessary for anyone to speak dialogue on the stage. Everything essential can be said in song and dancing. Against a wide rhapsodic setting by Jo Mielziner, the ballet dancers of *Finian's Rainbow* begin the evening with some lyrical springtime rites of real glory. If notes of music could leap across the stage, they would be no lighter or lovelier than this joyous ballet of a young and free people. Mr. Kidd has designed it with skill and enthusiasm. He and his band of dancers have interpreted the theme of *Finian's Rainbow* like thoroughbreds and artists.

JOHN CHAPMAN, *Daily News*

Finian's Rainbow has more charms than a young girl's bracelet. It is the box of circus candy with the special prize inside—the Good Humor on the lucky stick. . . . In pursuit of the stolen pot of gold comes a leprechaun [David Wayne], and never was a man-size sprite more spritely. Next to the atom-bomb, whimsey is the most dangerous stuff to fool with. In the wrong hands it will blow up in one's face—but Mr. Wayne's are the right hands. He can cast a spell in a manner that is quite magical.

ROBERT GARLAND, *Journal-American*

Excuse my rave review, but—this is it. The brand new musical has everything a grand new musical should have. Not since Annie got her gun and settled down at the Imperial have I felt so rave-reviewish about a song-and-dance show. But *Finian's Rainbow* is something about which to rave, an answer to a theatre-goer's prayers. It has the genius which is the result of the taking of infinite plans. The story has fact and fancy. The lyrics are racy and romantic. The music is melodious and modern. And the production—direction, scenery, costumes, choreography—is fresh and effective. Especially the choreography.

WILLIAM HAWKINS, *World-Telegram*

The dances are of the kick up your heels, let your hair fly, and bounce off the floor variety. They fill the stage with flashing energy, then seem to blow away.

Louis Kronenberger, *PM*

Finian has the kind of novelty and surface freshness that Broadway is always the better for. It combines fairly batty fantasy with fairly purposeful satire; it is, in fact, a musical with a social conscience, with message in its madness. Moreover, the people concerned in turning it out have a good deal to offer. They know how to be gay; they know how to be funny; they know how to be tuneful; they even know, here and there, how to be surprising. The whole show has about it a sense of trying for something different and original. It's just because this is so that there is disappointment in the midst of pleasure, and a frequent sudden sense that what had seemed to be rolling out of a horn of plenty is only tumbling out of the ragbag. *Finian* hasn't enough taste or sensibility or integrity; and at the level it professes to work on, these deficiencies stick out like sore thumbs. There is, for my money, a harrowing cuteness in some of the goings-on, and even the lyrics, of the show; and I'm afraid Ella Logan, proficient as she is with a song, rather contributes to it. There is a needlessly bad gag for every good one. Worst of all, *Finian* descends at times to cheap and even outhouse humor. All this gives you a sense of people who are running away from the standard Broadway scene but continually sneaking back for another glimpse of it. *Finian* has plenty of popular appeal; but what sets it a little apart has the kind of value that ought not and need not have been cheapened.

Richard Watts Jr., *Post*

Among other things, *Finian's Rainbow* is equipped with what may well be the most elaborate plot since *War and Peace*. Taking in its stride handsomely diversified elements from pseudo-Irish mythology, complete with an oversized leprechaun and a mystic pot of gold, to left-wing social criticism, embracing sharecroppers, the poll tax, anti-Negro senators, atomic energy, the gold at Fort Knox, the Tennessee Valley Authority, and the economic future of mankind, the book mingles its authors' imagination with their politics amid much abandon. I suspect that the narrative is neither as rich in its imaginative flights nor as biting in its editorial comments as E. Y. Harburg and Fred Saidy anticipated, but it is considerably above average. I hope it does not seem too ungracious of me to add that it might have been not just a good show, but a brilliant one. What I found missing was a certain quality of taste and judgement. If only some of the political comment were just a little less blatant, the plot just a bit more inventive in its manipulation and, above all, if the occasional propensity for bathroom humor—which certainly doesn't fit in with the quality of imagination the show frequently achieves—had been dropped altogether.

Oklahoma! (1943), *On the Town* (1944), and *Carousel* (1945) had exploded on Broadway in quick succession, shattering conventions and breaking new ground, after which nothing adventurous happened for almost two years. (Sure, *Annie Get Your Gun* [1946] was a hit, but an old-hat hit.) Hence, the unheralded *Finian's Rainbow* broke through like a thunderbolt. It was quickly followed by another, even less conventional fantasy: *Brigadoon.* Notice that these were all strong dance shows; this is not merely coincidental. *Finian's* book was sharply satirical—including a bigoted Southern Senator transformed into a Negro Gospeller by a magic crock of gold!—and the standout score combined refreshingly bright music with amazingly playful lyrics. The satire has slightly aged with time, but the work of the Messrs. Lane and Harburg remains goldenly grandish.

Tony Awards were won by Michael Kidd (choreographer, tied with Agnes de Mille for *Brigadoon*) and David Wayne (supporting actor). In addition to winning the Donaldson Award for Best Musical, Donaldsons were won by E. Y. Harburg and Fred Saidy (librettists); David Wayne (actor; supporting actor—he must have been *really* good); Albert Sharpe (male debut); and Anita Alvarez (female dancer).

BROADWAY SCORECARD / perfs: 725 / $: +

rave	favorable	mixed	unfavorable	pan
6	1		1	

FIORELLO!

a musical biography of Fiorello H. La Guardia (1882–1947), with music by Jerry Bock; lyrics by Sheldon Harnick; book by Jerome Weidman and George Abbott

directed by George Abbott (replacing Arthur Penn); choreographed by Peter Gennaro
produced by Robert E. Griffith and Harold S. Prince
with Tom Bosley, Patricia Wilson, Ellen Hanley, Howard Da Silva, Pat Stanley, Mark Dawson, and Nathaniel Frey

opened November 23, 1959   Broadhurst Theatre

FRANK ASTON, *World-Telegram & Sun*

There are at least two songs that will be worth hearing over and over again. Both issue from a male septet, led by that fine, braying comedian, Howard Da Silva. One is "Politics and Poker" with the beat of a little German band—and there is a hearty tuba umpahing along in Hal Hastings' pit. The other is a lament for grafters, "Little Tin Box." If you know about the standards of high-gutter statesman, this number will throw you into tizzies of delight, as it did the opening audience.

BROOKS ATKINSON, *Times*

Jerry Bock has set it to a bouncy score that has a satiric line as well as a wonderful waltz of the period, and a good deal of the ingenuity of Frank Loesser's music. As the writer of lyrics, Sheldon Harnick is in an unfailingly humorous frame of mind. Under Mr. Abbott's invincible stage direction, the whole show comes to life with gusto. It is extraordinary how right the period is for a comic carnival. Against raffish city backgrounds, well designed by the Eckarts, the sidewalk ballets that Peter Gennaro has composed are spontaneous and exhilarating.

JOHN CHAPMAN, *Daily News*

Not since *Guys and Dolls* (1950) has there been a musical as down-to-the-sidewalks New York as *Fiorello!* is. Not since *Of Thee I Sing* (1931) has there been a musical which achieves the sophisticated but cheerful attitude towards politics that *Fiorello!* does. La

ROBERT E. GRIFFITH and HAROLD S. PRINCE
present

Fiorello!
A New Musical

Book by JEROME WEIDMAN and GEORGE ABBOTT
Music by JERRY BOCK
Lyrics by SHELDON HARNICK
with

TOM BOSLEY   PATRICIA WILSON   ELLEN HANLEY   HOWARD DA SILVA
MARK DAWSON   NATHANIEL FREY
and PAT STANLEY
Directed by GEORGE ABBOTT
Choreography by PETER GENNARO
Scenery & Costumes Designed by WILLIAM and JEAN ECKART
Musical Direction HAL HASTINGS   Orchestrations by IRWIN KOSTAL   Dance Music Arranged by JACK ELLIOTT

BROADHURST THEATRE
44th STREET WEST OF BROADWAY
Opens Monday, November 23
Matinees Wednesday and Saturday

A perfect logo: the La Guardia ink-blot is instantly recognizable, and forever unforgettable. (drawing by Fay Gage)

216

Guardia is being played with almost incredible realism by Tom Bosley, a man who has managed to learn about the theatre without ever having been on Broadway before. Bosley looks like La Guardia, sounds like him, waggles his head like him, scurries like him, and explodes like him. After the reception he got at the theatre last evening, I think he could be elected mayor even on a Confusion ticket. Yet he is no mere impersonator; he is a good actor who remains top man of a show which has been built around him. If we can't vote for La Guardia anymore, let's vote for Tom Bosley. And let Bosley give George Abbott any commissionership he wants.

ROBERT COLEMAN, *Daily Mirror*

Robert Griffith and Harold Prince are still batting 1.000. They put their hit streak on the line last night with *Fiorello!* and whacked out another four-bagger. As usual, they are managing a team of talented newcomers, with old pro George Abbott in the clean-up spot. *Fiorello!* scored a smashing victory at the polls with humor, heart, and zest. It's a box-office landslide. Wavering ducat purchasers will be climbing aboard the bandwagon by the time you read this. Griffith and Prince have another champ under their wing. A top ticket for the amusement vote.

WALTER KERR, *Herald Tribune*

Who is younger than springtime? George Abbott is younger than springtime. He has been around long enough to have patented all the formulas. And the one thing Mr. Abbott isn't interested in is the formula. Here he goes again. He forgets all those rules about how the dancing girls and boys had better hop out there every three or four minutes, how all the scenery had better be big and plush and picturesque, and how half of the ballads had better be tunes that are sufficiently unrelated to what is going on to make them sure-fire stuff with the disk jockeys, payola or no payola. Just as he did with the frolicsome and unfamiliar factory atmosphere of *The Pajama Game* [1954], Mr. Abbott seems to squint at a project, size it up, and then plant it on the stage on its own feet. What the old master is up to at the moment is a song-and-dance jamboree with a curious streak of honest journalism and a strong strain of rugged sobriety.

Fiorello! was not just a very good musical: it was *refreshingly* good. Opening just a week after the creakily old-fashioned *Sound of Music, Fiorello!* was an especially exciting sign that the horizons of the modern-day musical were still expanding. Just as entertaining as the best of the Abbott musicals—*Pal Joey* (1940), *On the Town* (1944), *Wonderful Town* (1953), *The Pajama Game* (1954)— *Fiorello!* brought something new: significant, thoughtful commentary on *our* life and times. *Fiorello!* was as topical in 1959 as a musical about Kennedy would be today. (Please! This is not a hint!) And unlike the delinquents of *West Side Story* (1957), *Fiorello!* was talking about "ordinary" people, especially in the dazzling work of emerging lyricist Sheldon Harnick. His character lyrics weren't any better than Hammerstein's or Lerner's; but his middle-class characters expressed emotion and thought in the vernacular of the common man.

Winner of the Pulitzer Prize for Drama, the third musical to be so honored following *Of Thee I Sing* (1931) and *South Pacific* (1949). Winner of the New York Drama Critics Circle Award. In addition to winning the Tony Award for Best Musical (tied with *The Sound of Music*), Tonys were won by Jerry Bock (composer, tied with Richard Rodgers); Jerome Weidman and George Abbott (librettists, tied with Howard Lindsay and Russel Crouse); George Abbott (director); Robert E. Griffith and Harold S. Prince (producers, tied with Leland Hayward, Richard Halliday, Richard Rodgers, and Oscar Hammerstein 2nd); and Tom Bosley (supporting actor).

BROADWAY SCORECARD / perfs: 795 / $: +

rave	favorable	mixed	unfavorable	pan
5	2			

THE FIREBRAND OF FLORENCE

a musical play, with music by Kurt Weill; lyrics by Ira Gershwin; book by Edwin Justus Mayer and Ira Gershwin, from Mayer's 1924 comedy *The Firebrand;* tryout title: *Much Ado About Love*

directed by John Murray Anderson; book directed by John Haggott; choreographed by Catherine Littlefield
produced by Max Gordon
with Melville Cooper, Earl Wrightson, Beverly Tyler, and Lotte Lenya (Weill)

opened March 22, 1945   Alvin Theatre

HOWARD BARNES, *Herald Tribune*

A musical show of rare delight. *The Firebrand of Florence* has melodic eloquence, lyrical felicity, and a company that can sing and still be understood. Ira Gershwin deserves a very large nod for the success of the enterprise. His lines are singularly singable and vastly entertaining, sustaining the mood of a swash-buckling sixteenth-century story with pertinent and comic exuberance. Kurt Weill's music does the rest. For this is certainly one of the finest scores that the gifted composer has written for the theatre.

JOHN CHAPMAN, *Daily News*

For *The Firebrand of Florence*
I have no abhorrence.
The Ira Gershwin lyrics
Induced in me hysteerics,
    Being tricky
    And seldom icky.
The music by Kurt Weill would beguile
The dullest ear; but I wish I could forget about the plot—
For *The Firebrand* is old-style operetta. Hot-cha!

Lotte Lenya, as the Duchess, is most unhappily cast. To her goes the best song of many excellent songs, "Sing Me Not a Ballad," and she fails to sell it because she and the number are not the same type. "Sing Me Not" would be a wow for Ethel Merman.

LOUIS KRONENBERGER, *PM*

Musically, *The Firebrand*—Edwin Justus Mayer's amusing historical comedy of the '20s—seems jinked. Fifteen years ago Horace Liveright [the publisher, and producer of the original play] sponsored a musical version of it, called *The Dagger and the Rose*, that died a-borning in Atlantic City. Now a good many highly gifted people have collaborated on an entirely new version; but their collaboration of talents seems half a conspiracy of dullness. *The Firebrand of Florence* is very unjust—as *The Firebrand* was not— to the gay impudence, the stylish gallantry, the dashing villainy, the inborn *désinvolture* of Benvenuto Cellini. It plays only a dull child's game of Cellini-meeny-miny-mo with him.

WILELLA WALDORF, *Post*

Much of Mr. Weill's music is uncommonly fine and he has arranged some skillful and beguiling orchestrations that often sound very lovely as Maurice Abravenel and his musicians interpret them. It is a pity that poor casting in some of the leading roles puts a strain on both book and music that neither are quite able to bear. Earl Wrightson is the only one of the principals who has a voice of quality and who sings with any sort of style. He is an attractive baritone, and it is a pleasure to listen to him. Unfortunately he is no actor, and possesses about as much Florentine fire as any nice young American in a church choir. As Benvenuto Cellini, he strikes very few sparks. Beverly Tyler as the model Angela is a pretty ingénue whose stage deportment is deplorably amateur and whose vocalizing is nearly always painful. As for Lotte Lenya as the Duchess, let us say simply that she fails to meet the demands of the part either as singer or comedienne.

This *Firebrand* suffered from fatal production and casting errors. Besides, there wasn't much of a market for an intelligently satirical costume operetta. Unfortunate, since the score is of the same calibre as Weill and Gershwin's *Lady in the Dark* (1941). Gershwin's playfully literate lyrics are especially worth savoring.

BROADWAY SCORECARD / perfs: 43 / $: −

rave	favorable	mixed	unfavorable	pan
1		1	1	5

FIRST IMPRESSIONS

a musical comedy with music and lyrics by Robert Goldman, Glen Paxton, and George Weiss; book by Abe Burrows, from Helen Jerome's 1935 dramatization of the 1813 novel *Pride and Prejudice* by Jane Austen; previously announced as *A Perfect Evening*

directed by Abe Burrows; choreographed by Jonathan Lucas
produced by George Gilbert, Edward Specter Productions, Inc., and the Jule Styne Organization
with Polly Bergen (replacing Giselle MacKenzie), Farley Granger, Hermione Gingold, James Mitchell, Phyllis Newman, Donald Madden, and Christopher Hewett (replacing Hiram Sherman)

opened March 19, 1959   Alvin Theatre

JOHN CHAPMAN, *Daily News*

If Alan Jay Lerner and Frederick Loewe had only written the lyrics and melodies, *First Impressions* would be the new *My Fair Lady* (1956)—which I am sure everybody involved in this lovely production hopes it will be. Among all the attractive, talented, or devoted people·involved in this musical, the only ones who have fallen just short of the mark are the songwriters. It is so easy to sing a song and so easy and wonderfully pleasant to listen to a song—so why should it be so hard to write one? . . . Anybody who says Miss Bergen isn't a lovely heroine is an idiot. Anybody who says Farley Granger isn't a lovely hero is likewise. Anybody who says Miss Gingold isn't a grand comedienne is in the minority, which includes me.

WALTER KERR, *Herald Tribune*

Jane Austen, like all masters and mistresses of the English tongue, is perfectly able to take care of herself, and no feeble, wretched, or otherwise undistinguished version of her work—on film, stage, or television screen—is ever going to matter a hoot to her reputation. What matters at this particularly unhappy moment in time is simply the independent quality of the work being done at the Alvin. The work being done at the Alvin is, independently, quite dreary.

RICHARD WATTS JR., *Post*

In a recent interview, Hermione Gingold said she was no admirer of Jane Austen, and it saddens me to report that I thought she proved it last night. As a series of vaudeville turns, Miss Gingold's playing would no doubt have been satisfactory. But the broad farcical strokes and her raucous humor, combined with the disturbing suggestion that she was acting the wicked stepmother in a British Christmas pantomime, seemed at best a savage caricature. Even when she was funny, which I felt happened only intermittently, she threw the period musical play out of focus, and the shock was too great for it.

BROADWAY SCORECARD / perfs: 84 / $: −

rave	favorable	mixed	unfavorable	pan
	2	1	3	1

FLAHOOLEY

a musical satire, with music by Sammy Fain; lyrics by E. Y. Harburg; special material by Moises Vivanco; book by E. Y. Harburg and Fred Saidy

directed by E. Y. Harburg and Fred Saidy; choreographed by Helen Tamiris
produced by Cheryl Crawford in association with E. Y. Harburg and Fred Saidy
with Ernest Truex, Yma Sumac, Jerome Courtland, Edith Atwater, Irwin Corey, Barbara Cook, and the Bil Baird Marionettes

opened May 14, 1951   Broadhurst Theatre

BROOKS ATKINSON, *Times*

The plot with which E. Y. Harburg and Fred Saidy have endowed their new production is one of the most complicated, verbose, and humorless of the season; and it weighs heavily against beautiful scenery and costumes, enchanting performers, and two or three gay puppet shows. More plot crosses the stage than Macy's

Broadway's Georgia Peach, 23-year-old Barbara Cook, discovers that the world is a toy balloon. "Come out of the woodwork, brother," suggest the Harburgian marionettes, "and join the Brotherwood of Man." (set by Howard Bay, costume by David Ffolkes, marionettes by Bil and Cora Baird, photo by George Karger)

Thanksgiving Day parade. But it seems to this column to be a colossal *non sequitur*. Mr. Harburg and Mr. Saidy have given themselves plot enough to hang a lovely looking show.

JOHN CHAPMAN, *Daily News*

Flahooley is a tuneful, extraordinarily beautiful, and delightfully imaginative musical. It also may be the most elaborately coated propaganda pill ever to be put on a stage, for along with the fabulous Bil and Cora Baird puppets, the magnificent Howard Bay sets and David Ffolkes costumes, the weird vocal nip-ups of Yma Sumac and the gay songs of Sammy Fain and E. Y. Harburg there is delivered a message. The message is an earnest plea for political liberalism, for an end to "witch hunts" and for an end to deliberate destruction of goods. *Flahooley* is at its best when it is being whimsical and nonsensical.

ROBERT COLEMAN, *Daily Mirror*

It could easily have been just the type of show for the entire family. But, unfortunately, the librettists have sacrificed laughs to the soap-box. The materials are there for a delightful, captivating fantasy, but, alas, they have been subordinated to lengthy passages critical of our politics, economics, and ethics. One first-nighter was overheard to say: "With the United States at war [in Korea], this is hardly the time to condemn a production system that has given us an amazingly high standard of living and, at the same time, managed to arm us and our allies." With employment at a record peak, with this country facing its greatest crisis, we echo these sentiments. *Flahooley* could have been a beguiling musical, a gala fiesta for young and old, had producer Crawford excised the hooey from the script.

ROBERT GARLAND, *Journal-American*

No matter how you spell it, *Flahooley* spells imagination. It has nearly everything. With a touch of *Babes in Toyland* [1903], a smattering of *The Wizard of Oz* [1939], and a suggestion of *Finian's Rainbow* [1947], it is all of these and none. It is as old as Aladdin's lamp and as young as the atom bomb, both of which are in it. And it laughs, even at the villainous saltpeter. So do we ageless children. Almost everyone. We haven't had a *Flahooley* since I don't know when. Maybe never! It is sweet and simple. It is wry and complex. It is a child's show, but it is never childish. It is a grown-up's show, but it is never grown up. It is also magic. It is as sophisticated as it is not, dealing with Aladdin's lamp and atom bomb at the same time, making fun of business and taking love seriously, singing, dancing, and cutting up, furnishing song and dance and beauty, almost concurrently. I like it. Especially before it gets so complicated.

WILLIAM HAWKINS, *World-Telegram & Sun*

Yma Sumac is a handsome woman who resembles Nita Naldi and comes from the same acting school. She is vastly publicized as having a vocal range of four octaves. She sings in all of them, a trick which has nothing to do with anything else about her character or the show. One lady in the audience remarked, "She's doing it beautifully, but what is she doing?" Barbara Cook and Jerome Courtland are comely enough juveniles who sing pleasantly.

VERNON RICE, *Post*

Lost anything lately? You might take a look at *Flahooley*. No doubt, it's all wrapped up in that plot. Everything else is. *Flahooley* has satire, fantasy, social comment, the State Dept., Arabians, a magic lamp, a genie, marionettes, the spirit of Christmas, a boy-girl love story, Sammy Fain's music, a doll who laughs instead of cries, and Ernest Truex. It also has Yma Sumac (how did she get here?), Helen Tamiris dances, valiant Edith Atwater, and a story so complicated that it makes a Republican's interpretation of the Truman–MacArthur difficulty seem simple. Don't expect me to explain it to you. I got lost early in the first act, soon after Miss Sumac, who is Peruvian, tried to explain to Mr. Truex, who couldn't be more American, the plot in a song which I guessed to be Arabian. It is hard to tell about Yma Sumac. She is truly remarkable. The program claims she can sing in four octaves. My bet is that the press department boys underestimated those octaves. I'd give her at least seven. She sounds, at times, like a lady frog who swallowed a siren. . . . It seems to me that the Messrs. Harburg and Saidy became so enamored with their *Finian's Rainbow* that they decided if they tripled the ingredients for *Flahooley*, the show would be three times as successful. Well, it didn't work out that way.

A controversial satire with plenty of everything, especially soapbox polemics. There was certainly good reason to be angry, but bitterness overwhelmed fantasy. E. Y. Harburg temporarily misplaced his sprightly playfulness with well-crafted but less-than-effective results. The exotic Yma Sumac, meanwhile, was rumored to have been one Amy Camus from Brooklyn.

BROADWAY SCORECARD / perfs: 40 / $: −

rave	favorable	mixed	unfavorable	pan
	2	1	4	1

FLOWER DRUM SONG

a musical comedy, with music by Richard Rodgers; lyrics by Oscar Hammerstein 2nd; book by Oscar Hammerstein 2nd and Joseph Fields, from the 1957 novel by C. Y. Lee

directed by Gene Kelly; choreographed by Carol Haney (Blyden) produced by Richard Rodgers and Oscar Hammerstein 2nd in association with Joseph Fields
with Miyoshi Umeki, Pat Suzuki, Larry Blyden (replacing Larry Storch), Juanita Hall, and Keye Luke
opened December 1, 1958   St. James Theatre

FRANK ASTON, *World-Telegram & Sun*

It was as if some genius of an engineer had arranged a tried-and-true assembly line and was showing, right before our very eyes, exactly how a perfect show is built. The parts fit together precisely, shiningly elegant, guaranteed to give satisfaction, resoundingly true to the mechanical ideal. There is a formalized air about *Flower Drum Song.* But there can be no doubt about it—here is a walloping hit.

BROOKS ATKINSON, *Times*

Being in an amiable frame of mind, Rodgers and Hammerstein have written a plesant musical play. Since they are the masters of the medium, it is customary to discuss them in more legendary language. But this is an occasion when their good feeling for the human race, their warmth, and their professionalism are the factors that make something pleasant out of something that does not have the distinction of their greatest work.

JOHN McCLAIN, *Journal-American*

Flower Drum Song is a big, fat Rodgers and Hammerstein hit, and nothing written here will have the slightest effect on the proceeds. The rich will get richer; many deserving actors will have long employment; there will be "national" companies and road companies, the dramatic society at Tenafly High may attempt it in a couple of years, and it will be translated and played in Swedish, German, French, and even Chinese. Actually it is a remarkably good but not stupendous musical. Everything is fine, nothing is sensational.

RICHARD WATTS JR., *Post*

Rodgers and Hammerstein's latest work is colorful, tuneful, and lively, and its cast contains some pleasant and talented performers, but with all its Oriental exoticism, it is astonishingly lacking in distinction. The distinguished authors must inevitably be judged by the high standards they have established, and this, it seems to me, is far from one of their classics. The spirit of the strip-tease girl and the finagling nightclub man appears to have descended on the authors, and an air of Broadway brashness dominates the delicacy of the touchingly romantic tale, giving *Flower Drum Song* the quality of a good, routine musical comedy of the conventional school, instead of the imaginative freshness we have come to expect. What bothered me through most of the evening was that, despite the charming people in the cast, there seemed an odd minimum of charm, a quality rarely missing from the works of Rodgers and Hammerstein.

After the highly disappointing *Me and Juliet* (1953) and the flop *Pipe Dream* (1955), Rodgers and Hammerstein concentrated on writing a commercial hit—nothing fancy, just successful. And the critics, it seems, decided to give the boys a break. *Flower Drum*

Song was slightly tired and rather old-fashioned, but it made money.

A Tony Award was won by Salvatore Dell 'Isola (conductor).

BROADWAY SCORECARD / perfs: 602 / $: +

rave	favorable	mixed	unfavorable	pan
2	4	1		

FOLLOW THE GIRLS

a burlesque musical, with music and lyrics by Dan Shapiro, Milton Pascal, and Phil Charig; book by Guy Bolton and Eddie Davis; additional dialogue by Fred Thompson

directed by Harry Delmar; choreographed by Catherine Littlefield
produced by Dave Wolper
with Gertrude Niesen, Frank Parker, Irina Baronova, and Jackie Gleason

opened April 8, 1944   New Century Theatre

JOHN CHAPMAN, *Daily News*

Out of the old Al Jolson Theatre next door to Central Park the Shuberts have made a gay and gaudy auditorium called the Century. You can tell it has been modernized because there aren't any racks for gents' hats under the seats. . . . The lady who gets top billing is Gertrude Niesen, who can sing a smokehouse song in a smoky voice. She has a dirty ditty called "I Wanna Get Married" which had Saturday's first-nighters asking for more after she had run through umpteen verses. She also has one of these slow songs for chest tones, titled "Twelve O'Clock and All is Well," which struck me as being quite good. Miss Niesen makes a great deal of use of her chest, but only sometimes for tones. And she flips her thighs with the cute abandon of a seal flapping his flippers. Which is as it should be, I suppose, because Miss Niesen's role is that of Bubbles, a strip tease queen. Which brings up the business of plot. Now that it has been duly brought up, let's drop it.

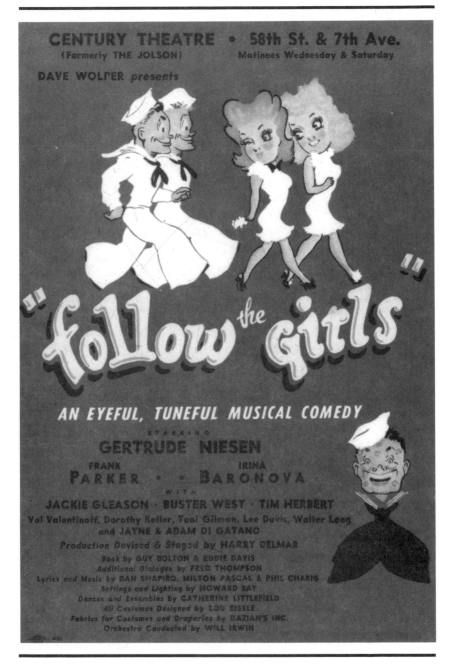

The gobs Follow the Girls, *for transparent reasons. Jackie Gleason—who was quickly moved up to second billing—is described in his bio as "a 4-F redwood that grew in Brooklyn, who has never walked away from a third helping of roast beef or lost a chance to convulse a customer."*

BURTON RASCOE, *World-Telegram*

Jackie Gleason, Miss Niesen's fat and comical vis-a-vis in the vague romance which trickles through *Follow the Girls*, is a good-natured and likable pantaloon with some of that engagingly honest naiveté which made Sonny Tufts such a pleasant addition to the ranks of movie players. Gleason does his stuff in an off-hand, apparently effortless manner, with none of that frantic, scenery-biting horseplay which some comedians indulge in. He has one stock gag, which, surprisingly enough, is always surprising and funny. [Per critic George Jean Nathan: The fat comic curves his right hand over his head and ejaculates, "What the hell!"]

WILELLA WALDORF, *Post*

Two-ton Jackie Gleason injects some roistering comedy into the proceedings. Jackie is funnier than we have ever seen him. Perhaps his high point of the evening was a terrific struggle getting into various garments officially worn by the WAVES. He made a very large WAVE indeed, almost a tidal WAVE.

The one about the striptease artiste who entertains the boys at the Stage Door Canteen. Frighteningly enough, *Follow the Girls* followed *Oklahoma!* (1943) as Broadway's second longest-running book musical! (*Carousel* [1945] displaced it by eight performances.) There was one flavorsome song, though, a risqué ditty entitled "I Wanna Get Married." ("I wanna order twin beds," sings our heroine, "then only use one"). The *Follow the Girls* boys, basking in their wartime glories, returned a decade later with an even creakier burlesque-flavored vehicle, *Ankles Aweigh* (1955). This time teacher rapped their knuckles with a ruler.

BROADWAY SCORECARD / perfs: 882 / $: +

rave	favorable	mixed	unfavorable	pan
3	3			2

FOUR SAINTS IN THREE ACTS

a revival of the 1934 opera, with music by Virgil Thomson; libretto by Gertrude Stein

"artistic direction" by Virgil Thomson; book directed by Maurice Grosser; choreographed by William Dollar
produced by the American National Theatre and Academy (Robert Whitehead) in association with Ethel Linder Reiner
with Inez Matthews, Edward Matthews, and Rawn Spearman

opened April 16, 1952   Broadway Theatre

ROBERT SYLVESTER, *Daily News*

Well, maybe I am just a dead pigeon on . . . uh . . . on the grass, alas, or even a magpie in the sky, the sky, but I liked that thing back in 1934 and I liked it even better last night. . . . There was a bit of extra dialogue last night which the late Miss Stein might have fully approved. In the first act Thomson and some of his musicians had a fairly loud discussion. Seems some of the boys were playing from page 43 instead of page 41. Nobody else noticed.

```
BROADWAY SCORECARD / perfs: 15 / $: −

   rave    favorable    mixed    unfavorable    pan

                  4          3
```

FOXY

a musical comedy, with music by Robert Emmett Dolan; lyrics by Johnny Mercer; book by Ian McLellan Hunter and Ring Lardner, Jr., from the 1606 satire *Volpone* by Ben Jonson

directed by Robert Lewis; choreographed by Jack Cole
produced by David Merrick (replacing Robert Whitehead)
with Bert Lahr, Larry Blyden, Julienne Marie, Cathryn Damon, and John Davidson

opened February 16, 1964   Ziegfeld Theatre

A trio of Yukon dance-hall girls "Rollin' in Gold." The tattooed heart of the dancer on the bottom left belongs to "DM." (The show's producer was known to have a penchant for chorus girls. *(drawing by Renning)*

WALTER KERR, *Herald Tribune*

Bert Lahr should be preserved like a fine old wine, or in one, it doesn't matter which. As the years go along his tang gets headier, his lifted pinky gets daintier, his moose call to the great beyond gets mellower and mellower, and, furthermore, he is beginning to carbonate. Watch him flinch, for instance. In the old days he would only whip one shoulder away and stand there panting, hurt to the quick but ready for anything that wasn't a fight. In *Foxy*, when he gets the challenge, he flinches all the way to the proscenium arch and then right on up until he reaches the top, where he maintains his ravaged dignity in spite of the fact that he is wrapped mainly in a plaid shawl and shod only with wool socks.

JOHN MCCLAIN, *Journal-American*

If you are not a Bert Lahr fan you should first have your head examined and then you should not pay any attention to anything I say about *Foxy*. For the evening is largely Lahr's, and while he's around everything is delicious; otherwise it is something less than a top-drawer attraction.

HOWARD TAUBMAN, *Times*

If you admire Bert Lahr—and it's un-American not to, you know—*Foxy* is for you. Given an injection with a hypodermic of brandy and asked solicitously, "How do you feel?" Mr. Lahr can do wonders with the reply, "Like a little soda." Masquerading as an English lord, he wears a mauve suit, deerstalker hat, and yellow gaiters and sings the clever *"Bon Vivant"* with droll preciosity. Attacked by the young man who adores Miss Marie, he dashes away like a terrified old tomcat and shinnies up the wall. The stage machines deserve an assist for this touch of madness, but no one can be so frightened, gallant, and funny as Mr. Lahr, hanging from the side of the proscenium wall. . . . Like its hearty ancestors of decades ago, *Foxy* is neither fancy nor arty. It does not fret over refinements of plot and characterization, but it wears its crudities with a grin and has delightful professional gusto. And can more be asked for in this vale of crises than to have Bert Lahr back on stage, mugging shamelessly or being as delicate as a viscount at an unexpectedly rowdy lawn party?

Foxy was an intimate, roughhouse musical initially produced at the 1962 Canadian Gold Rush Festival in Dawson City, Yukon Territory. When producer Robert Whitehead withdrew to concentrate on the formation of the Repertory Theater of Lincoln Center, David Merrick took over and turned *Foxy* into a big Broadway musical à la *Destry Rides Again* (1959). With dance hall girls, blaring orchestrations, garish sets, the works. When the time came to take out the improvements, Merrick was off concentrating on his other winter musical—the one about that foxy Yonkers matchmaker—and Bert Lahr's final Broadway show was deserted in childbirth. On opening night, Merrick sold his 30 percent share of *Foxy* to Billy Rose (owner of the Ziegfeld) for $10,000.

A Tony Award was won by Bert Lahr (actor).

BROADWAY SCORECARD / perfs: 72 / $: −

rave	favorable	mixed	unfavorable	pan
1	4	1		

FROM A TO Z

a musical revue, with material by various writers

directed by Christopher Hewett; choreographed by Ray Harrison
produced by Carroll and Harris Masterson
with Hermione Gingold, Elliott Reid, and Alvin Epstein

opened April 20, 1960   Plymouth Theatre

FRANK ASTON, *World-Telegram & Sun*

In a spoof of Mary Martin ["The Sound of Schmaltz," with music by William Dyer; words by Don Parks], Hermione Gingold is absolutely wonderful. At the start of the number, Miss Gingold is found under a mountain tree with one leg in the air and with cuteness oozing from all pores. Her roguishness is overwhelming as she sings her way into the hearts of seven young monsters to whom she becomes Nanny. The dialog, with its moonbeams and reverent larks, is above and beyond the drip of fudge. Here's to steel-tipped Hermione; long may she pierce.

JOHN CHAPMAN, *Daily News*

Hermione Gingold, the comedienne, has a great number of admirers, and a small fraction of them were enough to fill the Plymouth Theatre last evening—except for one seat. That seat was mine.

ROBERT COLEMAN, *Daily Mirror*

A couple of screwball numbers garnered lusty chuckles, [including] Woody Allen's "Surprise Party." A couple of diversion seekers discover that the babes at the revel have all decided to make up like Groucho Marx. That is, all except one who's a real blonde—Harpo.

WALTER KERR, *Herald Tribune*

Miss Gingold has come on in marceled white wigs, messy black wigs, and towering silver wigs studded with daisies. She has squinted at the audience with one sour eye, she has protruded her tongue far enough to get it caught between her teeth, she has leered like a bulldog and listed as though she were on shore leave. She has done everything she can to intimate comedy without actually being able to deliver it. . . . The level of the revue rarely rises above the business of two boys at a party discovering that all the girls are made up to look like Groucho Marx, or, in a parody of *The Sound of Music* (1959), the something less than hilarious notion that the hero should be called Baron von Klaptrap. In short, girls' school stuff, with the single consolation that there is no tea on the lawn afterward.

RICHARD WATTS JR., *Post*

One sketch, something about two young men who go to a party where all the girls look like Groucho Marx, save one who resembles Harpo, struck me as downright repulsive.

This otherwise undistinguished revue marked the Broadway debuts of contributors Woody Allen, Fred Ebb, and Jerry Herman.

Texas oil-millionaires Carroll and Harris Masterson replaced Anthony B. Farrell as vanity bankrollers of the day, pouring big bucks into a string of bombs.

```
○○○○○○○○○○○○○○○○○○○○○○○○○○○○○○○○○○○○○○○○○
○                                                                   ○
○        BROADWAY SCORECARD / perfs: 21 / $: −                      ○
○                                                                   ○
○      rave      favorable      mixed      unfavorable      pan     ○
○                                                                   ○
○                                  1            2            4      ○
○                                                                   ○
○○○○○○○○○○○○○○○○○○○○○○○○○○○○○○○○○○○○○○○○○○
```

FUNNY GIRL

a musical biography of Fanny Brice (1891–1951), with music by Jule Styne; lyrics by Bob Merrill; book by Isobel Lennart, from Lennart's unproduced screenplay

"staged" by Garson Kanin (replaced by Jerome Robbins); choreographed by Carol Haney; "production supervised" by Jerome Robbins
produced by Ray Stark (Brice's son-in-law)
with Barbra Streisand, Sydney Chaplin, Kay Medford, and Danny Meehan

opened March 26, 1964   Winter Garden Theatre

WALTER KERR, *Herald Tribune*

One other reservation must be entered. Miss Streisand is pretty much alone now [after the intermission], which means that she carries five out of six second-act numbers. The returns have got to diminish. The star's passion has many colors, her phrasing has many colors, but her voice does not have *that* many. One feels that the management is trying to cram an entire career into one show. Everything remains utterly professional; but inspiration wanes, and craft must make due in its place.

NORMAN NADEL, *World-Telegram & Sun*

Hail to thee, Barbra Streisand; Fanny Brice thou never wert! But there you have the whole paradox of this show—one spectacular talent in the role of another spectacular talent, but never

A knockout quote ad, skillfully assembled from less-than-knockout reviews. They all loved Barbra, and that was enough to make the show a smash. The logo was inspired by a cut song, "I Did It on Roller Skates."

becoming, or perhaps even trying to become, the woman this play is about. Streisand prefers to create a 1918 Barbra Streisand, and the justification is that she does it superbly. This young woman is a joy on any stage. A spontaneous comedian, a big-voiced, belting singer, and a brass gong of personality, she sets an audience tingling, time and time again. . . . Thinking back over the score, it occurs to me that the best song in the show is "My Heart at Thy Sweet Voice" from *Samson and Delilah*, which Danny Meehan whistles through his teeth while he is standing on his head. I do not mean that composer Jule Styne should compete with Saint-Saëns, though that is what happens. But it would be nice if one of his melodies could grab you like "My Heart." Styne has written some good stuff in this, as he has in about every show he's done. It isn't his best, though.

HOWARD TAUBMAN, *Times*

Fortunately, Miss Streisand can make a virtue out of suffering if she is allowed to sing about it. But that's show-business sagas for you. They rarely can untrack themselves from the hokum and schmaltz that authors and, for all one knows, show people consider standard operating procedure.

RICHARD WATTS JR., *Post*

Funny Girl has met with so many adversities and postponements, while everyone labored valiantly to bring it to successful fruition, that only the most cruel-hearted could resist praying for the best. While the dedicated work of all concerned with it has had some pleasant results, I can't help feeling that it remains a disappointing entertainment.

Funny Girl made a star out of Barbra Streisand, or maybe Barbra Streisand made a hit out of *Funny Girl*. At any rate, the show emerged victorious after more than three years of creative haggling. Coproducer David Merrick initially reassembled his *Gypsy* (1959) creators. Sondheim quickly withdrew, replaced by Bob Merrill of Merrick's *Carnival* (1961). Robbins was replaced by Garson Kanin of Merrick's *Do Re Mi* (1960), who was himself replaced during the tryout by—Robbins!, who "saved" the show.

Star Mary Martin, meanwhile, opted for *Jennie* (1963), after which Anne Bancroft—first choice for the title role of *Gypsy*—was the frontrunner. Then in came Streisand, from Merrick's *I Can Get It for You Wholesale* (1962), and you know the rest. Ultimately, Merrick himself withdrew from the show rather than continue to work with Ray Stark. Streisand and "People" did their job, and the mediocre *Funny Girl* became a long-running hit. But don't look for a revival—without Streisand, there's not much there.

Barbra Streisand lost the Tony Award to Carol Channing for *Hello, Dolly!* For recreating her role in the 1968 motion picture version, though, Streisand received the Best Actress Oscar (tied with Katharine Hepburn for *The Lion in Winter*).

BROADWAY SCORECARD / perfs: 1,348 / $: +

rave	favorable	mixed	unfavorable	pan
1	3	2		

A FUNNY THING HAPPENED ON THE WAY TO THE FORUM

a farce musical, with music and lyrics by Stephen Sondheim; book by Burt Shevelove and Larry Gelbart, from plays by Plautus; previously announced as *The Roman Comedy*

directed by George Abbott; choreographed by Jack Cole (with additional staging and choreography by Jerome Robbins)
produced by Harold Prince
with Zero Mostel, Jack Gilford, David Burns, Ruth Kobart, Raymond Walburn, and John Carradine

opened May 8, 1962   Alvin Theatre

ROBERT COLEMAN, *Mirror*

You won't find anything more hilarious the length of Broadway than the zany opening of *A Funny Thing Happened on the Way to the Forum* ["Comedy Tonight," staged by Jerome Robbins]. It has

"Everybody Ought to Have a Maid" for puttering around the house, and other pleasures. John Carradine, Jack Gilford, David Burns, and a jiggling Zero Mostel. (set and costumes by Tony Walton)

Zero Mostel, Eddie Phillips, George Reeder, and David Evans getting mixed up in a whirlwind of arms and legs. It's about as crazy as anything you've ever seen in old-time vaudeville or films. . . . We suspect that *A Funny Thing* will prove the most controversial song-and-dancer of the season. You'll either love it or loathe it. In our book, it looms as a hot ticket. A riotous and rowdy hit.

WALTER KERR, *Herald Tribune*

Composer Stephen Sondheim begins by giving his lightfooted fools some rather odd recitative as substitute for melody and some vaguely Oriental wood-block effects as substitute for lively accompaniment. You wonder. Then, with a foursome in which Mr. Mostel, Mr. Burns, Mr. Gilford, and a borrowed scarecrow named John Carradine take off to a tune called "Everybody Ought to Have a Maid," the odd figurations Mr. Sondheim is attracted to begin to pay off. There's a faint edge of musical Sarcasm to be dealt with here, and it crops up again—most effectively—in "I'm Calm," "Impossible," "That Dirty Old Man" and in Mr. Mostel's swooning reprise of a number that was mocking in the first place, "Lovely." The score is in and out, but wins out. The lyrics are fine. How perfect is the clambake as a whole? Well, each act takes time warming you up, for there's nothing but the comedy going for it, and our clowns need to pile up twenty or thirty gags on top of one another before the pyramid topples and you break up as it does. But the nonsense is true nonsense as the zanies are true zanies, and I find it kindly of director George Abbott to have given us an admittedly lowbrow and unpretentiously merry good time once again.

JOHN McCLAIN, *Journal-American*

Zero Mostel, a very animated blimp, will personally defy you not to like *A Funny Thing Happened on the Way to the Forum*. The clients laughed and seemed to enjoy themselves, but there was always the suggestion that had they not done so Mr. Mostel would have passed among them and belabored them with a baseball bat. The book by Burt Shevelove and Larry Gelbart (claiming some debt to Plautus) is a wispy affair, and Stephen Sondheim's score is less than inspired, but under George Abbott's slick direction the show moves and the audience roars. I believe Mr. Sondheim has a fair ballad in "Lovely"; otherwise I thought his lyrics far surpassed his music.

Norman Nadel, *World-Telegram & Sun*

A boy entering the Alvin Theatre last night called loudly to his companion (three feet away): "If this isn't a hit, I'm going to lynch your brother." I just hope the lad had some second thoughts about his attitude today, while he is lynching his friend's brother. Maybe he will learn in time to be grateful for small favors. Small indeed are the favors afforded by this new musical, except perhaps for Zero Mostel. . . . Stephen Sondheim's music would have been a second-rate score even in 1940, but he has come up with some catchy lyrics.

Howard Taubman, *Times*

A plastic-faced, rolling-eyed, Falstaff-like character like Zero Mostel playing zany follow-the-leader with three centurions ordered to keep an eye on him? A rubber-faced, murmurous David Burns playing an enamored old goat and cooing like an antiquated turtle dove? A bewigged and fluttering Jack Gilford got up in a shimmering white gown and pretending to be a dead, yet agitated, virgin? A lank, deep-voiced Shakespearean like John Carradine pretending to be a timid though agile dealer in courtesans? If stuff like that—wonder what word they had in the Colosseum for corn?—doesn't joggle your funny bone, keep away from the Alvin. George Abbott, who has been around a long time but surely staged nothing for the forum mob, has forgotten nothing and remembered everything. He has engineered a gay funeral sequence to a relentlessly snappy march by Stephen Sondheim. He has used mixed identities, swinging doors, kicks in the posterior, double takes, and all the rest of the familiar paraphernalia with the merciless disingenuousness of a man who knows you will be defenseless.

A funny thing indeed. Strangely enough, Stephen Sondheim's intelligent score was roundly attacked: he wasn't even nominated for a Tony, while competitors like *Bravo Giovanni* were. (How embarrassing! The winner was *Oliver!*, which at least makes *some* sense.) *Forum*'s tryout troubles and last-minute rescue by Jerome

Robbins—who requisitioned that zany opening number at the last minute—are too oft repeated to be repeated here. But Robbins had been on the show when it belonged to David Merrick, producer of the Sondheim/Robbins *Gypsy* (1959). Robbins decided he didn't want to work with Merrick again and left the project; then, after the authors had withdrawn the rights, Robbins came back—on condition that the show went to Harold Prince. After which, Robbins quit again. ("I am embarrassed by the turn of events on *The Roman Comedy*," Sondheim abashedly wrote Merrick. "As you predicted, Jerry slithered away.") *Forum* was Sondheim's first score (as a composer) to reach Broadway. An earlier project, *Saturday Night*, was stillborn when producer Lemuel Ayers died in 1955. A second pre-*Forum* project announced by producer Robert Whitehead in 1960 never got past the talking stage, but sounds pretty fascinating: a musicalization of Giraudoux's *Madwoman of Chaillot* (1945) from Sondheim, Behrman, and Fosse—and starring the Lunts!

In addition to winning the Tony Award for Best Musical, Tonys were won by Burt Shevelove and Larry Gelbart (librettists); George Abbott (director); Harold Prince (producer); Zero Mostel (actor); and David Burns (supporting actor).

BROADWAY SCORECARD / perfs: 964 / $: +

rave	favorable	mixed	unfavorable	pan
4	1	1	1	

THE GAY LIFE

a musical comedy, with music by Arthur Schwartz; lyrics by Howard Dietz; book by Fay and Michael Kanin, from the 1893 comedy *Anatol* by Arthur Schnitzler

directed by Gerald Freedman; choreographed by Herbert Ross
produced by Kermit Bloomgarden
with Walter Chiari, Barbara Cook, Jules Munshin, and Loring Smith

opened November 18, 1961   Shubert Theatre

JOHN CHAPMAN, *Daily News*

A great, big, gorgeous confection of Viennese pastry, thanks to the absolute wizardry of scenic artist Oliver Smith and costumer Lucinda Ballard [Dietz]. But the production is not all beautiful frosting; good, solid entertainment is to be found inside. It is good to have a team of old pros, composer Arthur Schwartz and lyricist Howard Dietz, back at work again. The Dietz lyrics are deft and gay, and they rediscover the art of the internal rhyme. Schwartz's music is a full-bodied score, being waltzy when it feels like it and incisive when necessary. And he has given Miss Cook, who sings like a dove, a melody in "Magic Moment" which will haunt us for a sweet long time.

WALTER KERR, *Herald Tribune*

Visions in black-lace-on-yellow emerge from the wings. The company is dressed in a manner that does honor to Vienna, Schnitzler, and sanity. If only the principals could be persuaded to stop and look at them, and perhaps join them. It isn't really the principals' fault. Presumably they have been guided into their arch, perspiring, and mechanical toy-shop posturing by director Gerald Freedman, whose staging is almost everywhere uncertain. Surely they are at the mercy of their librettists, whose flair is approximately as continental as a box of Cracker-Jack. It is interesting to note, though, how in the midst of so much that is dissipating itself, a single performer can assume the stage and intimate all the glories that might have been. After an ineffectual first entrance with a croquet mallet in her hand and absolutely nothing to say, Barbara Cook returns to compose herself quietly at center stage and sing an attractive Schwartz tune called "Magic Moment." As she lifts her sweet, precise voice and opens her earnest child's eyes, all of the atmosphere that has been lying in wait, unused, now wraps itself around her. The powdered-sugar Christmas that Oliver Smith is going to paint so invitingly, a little later on, is already with us. Whatever those other people are in, Miss Cook is in a success; her head and our hearts are high.

NORMAN NADEL, *World-Telegram & Sun*

The swirling elegance of *The Gay Life* has transformed 44th Street. More than that: it has recreated turn-of-the-century Vienna not in terms of then and there but of here and now. No mere pageant of reminiscent opulence, the stunning musical exudes the very gaiety of its name, and rapturously includes us all. Once again, the settings by Oliver Smith eclipse everything except other settings by Oliver Smith, and a comparable comment applies to Lucinda Ballard's gowns and hats, which—to say the least—are memorable. She has not only re-evoked the flourish and elegance of an era, but she has recaptured the loftiest level of taste as well. To select one of many possible examples, there is a ballroom scene ["*Oh, Mein Liebchen*"] in which all the girls wear red; that is a minor but amusing element of the plot. It has several impacts—as the punch line of a comedy situation; as a musical comedy metamorphosis of waltz (with apologies to Ravel); as the sheer excitement of rhythmic motion; as a sharp comment on girls competing for attention. Beyond all that, Miss Ballard's ball dresses achieve a mass excitement in total red, yet each is an individual achievement. Then the story permits her to introduce one yellow gown, and one blue, for electrifying contrast.

HOWARD TAUBMAN, *Times*

The *schlagober*, whipped cream that floats deliciously on Viennese coffee, skims the surface of *The Gay Life*, conferring innocence on its wickedness and elegance on its old-fashioned ways. But nicest of all the *gemütlich* things in *The Gay Life* is Barbara Cook.

Arthur Schwartz's oh-so-glorious score was sabotaged by poor direction and a weak libretto. What a waste!

A Tony Award was won by Lucinda Ballard (costume designer).

BROADWAY SCORECARD / perfs: 113 / $: —

rave	favorable	mixed	unfavorable	pan
2	2		3	

GENTLEMEN PREFER BLONDES

a musical comedy, with music by Jule Styne; lyrics by Leo Robin; book by Joseph Fields and Anita Loos, from the 1926 novel by Anita Loos

directed by John C. Wilson; choreographed by Agnes de Mille
produced by Herman Levin and Oliver Smith
with Carol Channing, Yvonne Adair, Jack McCauley, Eric Brotherson, Alice Pearce, and George S. Irving

opened December 8, 1949   Ziegfeld Theatre

BROOKS ATKINSON, *Times*

Happy days are here again. *Gentlemen Prefer Blondes* is a vastly enjoyable song-and-dance antic put on with humorous perfection. It brings back a good many familiar delights to a street that has been adding art to the musical stage for quite a long time. But thanks to the clowning of Carol Channing, it also brings us something new and refreshing. Let's call her portrait of the aureate Lee the most fabulous comic creation of this dreary period in history. In Miss Channing's somewhat sturdier image, Lorelei's rapacious innocence is uproariously amusing. Made-up to resemble a John Held creature, she goes through the play like a dazed automaton—husky enough to kick in the teeth of any gentleman on the stage, but mincing coyly in high-heel shoes and looking out on a confused world through big, wide, starry eyes. There has never been anything like this before.

JOHN CHAPMAN, *Daily News*

In the role of Lorelei Lee is big, googly-eyed Carol Channing, who certainly is the funniest female to hit the boards since Fanny Brice and Beatrice Lillie began knocking entire audiences out of their seats. Just wait until you see Miss Channing walk across the stage. Wait until you hear her sing "Diamonds Are a Girl's Best Friend." Wait until you hear her explain how the lawyer in Little Rock happened to get taken shot by her revolver. If you hurry over to the Ziegfeld or mail a check you may not have to wait too long—but no matter how long it is, the evening you go will be the holiday of the year.

Wide-eyed innocents Lorelei Lee and Dorothy Shaw, entirely sur-rounded by "sugar-daddies." This artwork was presumably pre-pared prior to the casting; see the foreword for Lorelei Lee, Channing-style. (drawing by Al Hirschfeld)

ROBERT COLEMAN, *Daily Mirror*

Carol Channing, as the bumptious blonde from Little Rock, scored what our ears told us was a triumph. Boy did she take us back to those wonderful old nights and morns at Texas Guinan's, the Madrid, and the Silver Slipper. What a gold-digger! What magic memories she evoked with her artful pretense, gravelly voice, and mincing walk. . . . Judging by the lusty applause, Lorelei Lee, set a-singing and a-dancing, is going to coin scads of new greenbacks.

ROBERT GARLAND, *Journal-American*

Happy musical-comedy days are here again. Hurray! Hurray! Hurray! Don't tell me Flo Ziegfeld's happy spirit isn't somewhere in his playhouse, applauding—as aren't we all?—a song-and-dancer he'd be glad to put his name to. For here's a gilt-and-girly extravaganza that, calling itself a musical comedy, lives all the way up to that delectable designation. No musical drama! No musical play! No musical makeshift of any kind!

WILLIAM HAWKINS, *World-Telegram*

Carol Channing is one of the most extraordinary people in the entertainment world today. Even when playing a chorus girl in *Lend an Ear* [1948], Miss Channing had a mastodon piquancy that attracted the eye and titillated the sense of humor. Here one suspects that as her endurance and resourcefulness were increasingly revealed in the tryout period, more and more of the show was tossed her way. Nothing has fazed her. She is giving one of the most ingenious comic performances we have ever seen. It is a brutal assignment, because the Lorelei of Miss Loos's famed chronicle has only one attitude toward life, one facet to her philosophy, and one purpose in mind. Her aim is purely and simply: Diamonds via men. The acquisition of the two is a solemn project. With posture and stare and the bass bleat in her voice, Miss Channing makes Lorelei a creature of constant surprise and delight. In a wonderful spirit of parody she brightens up the stage with manic elation when the material is there, and when there is little to bite into she indulges in an expression of relaxed pushover honesty that endears her to the world. Just as a Great Dane insists it is a lap dog, the Channing Lorelei resembles a golden eagle who believes it is a downy and buttercup-colored duckling. Dainty to the death, she trips about as if her slippers were so tight they hurt her all over.

RICHARD WATTS JR., *Post*

[Selecting] two such hearty and towering girls as Miss Channing and Yvonne Adair and sending them gallumphing about the stage added, I thought, a rather eerie touch to the proceedings. The sight of a couple of demure and petite young ladies making idiots out of a succession of stalwart men is an amusing joke, but I suspect the cream of the joke was spoiled when the girls gave every indication of being able to out-box and out-wrestle any four males in the cast. . . . It seemed to me that virtually all the brilliant wit and satire [of the novel] is absent from the new show, and a kind of routine extravaganza is substituted.

"Happy Days" must have indeed seemed here again to Roaring '20s folk who had survived Depression and War intact. Here was an unashamedly old-fashioned musical in an age of *South Pacific* (1949) and *Lost in the Stars* (1949)—but it was a *good* old-fashioned musical, with that arch nemesis of the o.f.m., Miss de Mille, kicking away in a nonsymbolic mood. *Gentlemen Prefer Blondes* offered nostalgia, high spirits, a perkily tuneful score, and Carol Channing as a decidedly unlikely, gold-digging vamp.

Donaldson Awards were won by Anita Alvarez (female dancer); Oliver Smith (scenic designer) and Miles White (costume designer).

BROADWAY SCORECARD / perfs: 740 / $: +

rave	favorable	mixed	unfavorable	pan
7			1	

THE GIRL FROM NANTUCKET

a musical comedy, with music by Jacques Belasco; lyrics by Kay Twomey, with additional music and lyrics by Hughie Prince and Dick Rogers; book by Paul Stanford and Harold Sherman, from a story by Fred Thompson and Berne Giler, with additional dialogue by Hy Cooper

staged by Henry Adrian; book directed by Edward Clarke Lilley;
choreographed by Val Raset
produced by Henry Adrian
with Jack Durant, Billy Lynn (replacing James Barton), Jane Kean,
and Bob Kennedy

opened November 8, 1945   Adelphi Theatre

JOHN CHAPMAN, *Daily News*

In the orchestra pit is a good set of musicians directed by the
able Harry Levant, but they have no music to work with and
cannot, being good musicians, keep up with the flatting that goes
on upon the stage. The flats at the Adelphi would clear up New
York's housing shortage if they could be rented out. To a lover like
myself of the American musical comedy, this show is 90% torture.
Its lyrics, by Kay Twomey, are so desperately smart they hurt, and
Jacques Belasco's score would seem just as good if Mr. Levant's
men played it upside down.

ROBERT GARLAND, *Journal-American*

Last night turned out to be an endurance contest between *The
Girl from Nantucket* up on the stage of the Adelphi Theatre and
The Audience From Manhattan down in the auditorium. There
were moments when I feared the make-believe off-islanders were
going to win. For the contestants from Massachusetts kept going on
and on, while the contestants from New York kept going out and
out. But a couple of handfuls of local lads remained until the end,
one handful composed of backers who were exhausted from applauding and another handful composed of critics who were just
exhausted.

LOUIS KRONENBERGER, *PM*

Mr. Henry Adrian, who only a short season or so back produced
one of the worst of all straight plays, *Victory Belles* [1943], has now
with *The Girl from Nantucket* produced one of the sorriest of all
musical comedies. The least he could have done was to give the
thing a more suitable title, such as "The Girl from Death Valley."
When in the first ten minutes a man is asked, "Aren't you taking
along a bag?" and answers, "No, she's not coming with me," you
pretty well know what's in store for you. Pretty well; you can't, for

Why is this whale smiling? Star James Barton wisely jumped ship during the tryout. Pre-Broadway credits. (drawing by Lou Eisele)

example, know about the ballet. "A Page from Old Nantucket," they call it, and I won't say more than that it contains a woman who symbolizes the sea, a whale who gets fresh with her, and a fisherman who, all through the hot stuff, chants poetry. I shudder to think what may be next on Mr. Adrian's agenda.

BURTON RASCOE, *World-Telegram*

The story is that a house painter used binoculars to watch a girl across the street get dressed and undressed, and then was so attracted to her that he got a job painting the outside sills of her bathroom window. By error he was awarded a commission to paint murals for a museum at Nantucket. He couldn't paint anything except surfaces, so the gal whom he had been looking at through his binoculars—who was an art student—did the job for him.

WILELLA WALDORF, *Post*

If the producers wish to lift something from this review for advertising purposes, they may quote us as saying, "It lacks everything."

BROADWAY SCORECARD / perfs: 12 / $: −

rave	favorable	mixed	unfavorable	pan
				8

THE GIRL IN PINK TIGHTS

a musical extravaganza, with music by Sigmund Romberg, "developed" by Don Walker; lyrics by Leo Robin; book by Jerome Chodorov and Joseph Fields, suggested by events surrounding the opening of the "first" American musical, *The Black Crook* (1866)

directed by Shepard Traube; choreographed by Agnes de Mille produced by Shepard Traube in association with Anthony B. Farrell

Jeanmaire en pointe. *She couldn't save this creaky Romberg operetta despite ecstatic personal reviews. Pre-Broadway credits.*

with (Renée Zizi) Jeanmaire, Charles Goldner, Brenda Lewis, and David Atkinson (replacing David Brooks)

opened March 5, 1954   Mark Hellinger Theatre

BROOKS ATKINSON, *Times*

Jeanmaire is a slender girl with a charming grin, a mischievous manner, and a willingness to enjoy performing, for she acknowledges an audience's right to have a good time. To tell the truth, she is a Gallic edition of Mary Martin, which is meant to be handsomely complimentary all the way round. . . . *The Girl in Pink Tights* shares with *Kismet* (1953) a lust for mediocrity. The score from the studio of the late Sigmund Romberg overflows with mechanical melodies out of a departed era. Leo Robin has written lyrics that match the commonplaceness of those in *Kismet*. "Why do I have to wax poetic?" Mr. Robin's grandest lover sighs in one of his most transfixed moments. Well, why not? Why must the words of songs sound feeble-minded? One by one the Rodgers and Hammerstein shows depart [ending their long runs], leaving us with Piltdown man musical entertainment—the triumph of industry over talent.

JOHN CHAPMAN, *Daily News*

About all I can say concerning the Romberg score is that it didn't hurt.

ROBERT COLEMAN, *Daily Mirror*

A skyrocket called Renée Jeanmaire zoomed over the Mark Hellinger's footlights last evening, and set a smart first-night audience to cheering. With a figure that could take a beauty prize any day, a short black windblown hairdo, a piquant face, and a pixieish red mouth and huge eyes, she explodes with the effect of a cannon cracker.

WILLIAM HAWKINS, *World-Telegram & Sun*

Jeanmaire is a black diamond at white heat. She is tiny, dark, and dazzling. She is impudent and authoritative. Essentially, she has that indefinable thing that glues your eyes on her the instant she walks on the stage. Jeanmaire is one of those rare and remarkable personalities whose tangible talent is so unimportant that it might as well be illusory. She is assured and chic. Jeanmaire has the two greatest qualities an entertainer can claim. Generosity makes her share with you all she enjoys, and her vulnerability urges you to take care of her. Jeanmaire, dancing or grinning, pretending to be a whistle on an elevated train, or setting out to seduce a man-about-town. This is a *star!*

WALTER KERR, *Herald Tribune*

The Girl in Pink Tights has three tremendous assets—a dancer named Jeanmaire, a singer named Jeanmaire, and a comedienne named Jeanmaire. The entrancing urchin in question is a diminutive lass with a wicked eye, a shattering smile, a home-made haircut and the general expression of a not-quite-trustworthy kewpie doll. She is—if I may just let myself go—adorable. For her talents as a dancer, Agnes de Mille has devised a first-act *"Pas de Deux"* that moves miraculously above the floor. The moment is breath-taking, perhaps all the more so because of the superb disdain with which the dancer regards her lithe, expressive, self-animating legs. (That's a curious phrase, but the effect is even more curious.) For her talents as a singer, Don Walker has dipped into a fragmentary score by the late Sigmund Romberg, amplified the tunes he found there, and offered this petulant powerhouse several workable numbers. For her talents as a comedienne—alas—librettists Jerome Chodorov and Joseph Fields have supplied virtually nothing at all. *The Girl in Pink Tights* is not a show with too few jokes. It is a show with practically no jokes at all. The Messrs. Chodorov and Fields have told their tale very literally, very baldly, and very badly.

JOHN McCLAIN, *Journal-American*

If you're expecting *Tights* to be terrific, you'd better fall in love with the lass who wears them. . . . One thing you can say about David Atkinson, the young hero of the piece, is that he is big and has a good voice and is almost indistinguishable from several other big young men, with good voices, who always play this same part in similar shows. It isn't the fault of these big men; it's just the part.

☆

A creakily old-fashioned musical, featuring Sigmund Romberg's final score (he died July 10, 1951). But what a set of valentines for Jeanmaire!

BROADWAY SCORECARD / perfs: 115 / $: —

rave	favorable	mixed	unfavorable	pan
	1	2	4	

THE GIRL WHO CAME TO SUPPER

a musical comedy, with music and lyrics by Noël Coward; book by Harry Kurnitz, from the 1953 comedy *The Sleeping Prince* by Terence Rattigan

directed and choreographed by Joe Layton
produced by Herman Levin
with José Ferrer, Florence Henderson, Irene Browne, Tessie O'Shea, and Roderick Cook

opened December 8, 1963   Broadway Theatre

WALTER KERR, *Herald Tribune*

During the intermission I laid bets with myself. Would Tessie O'Shea have a song in the second act? I bet not. Going back to my seat I picked up my program and ran down the list of numbers to come. Nope. I was right, and so, in a way, was the management. If Tessie O'Shea had had just five more minutes with the customers there wouldn't have been room or need for the whole long plot that has been borrowed from Rattigan's *Sleeping Prince*. Which, incidentally, would have been more or less all right with me. Tessie O'Shea. A name to be conjured with, a face to be cherished, a form to be whistled at if that's all you can do. (It's what the customers finally did last night, whistling at the girl and whistling at her until I thought they'd blow her through the backdrop.) I'd better add that Miss O'Shea's form is substantial, and no backdrop could be repaired that she ever went through. Displacing about as much weight as the Albert Memorial, with her blouse all baggy and her rolled yellow hair crunched just short of the jaunty black straw that suggests she has the blood of a thousand sailors in her about-to-burst veins, Miss O'Shea looks up surprised from her cart in St. Martin's Lane. She is surprised to see London again, though she never has left it. She is surprised to see you again, whoever you are. You'll be mad for her, if you can take everything that goes with her.

JOHN McCLAIN, *Journal-American*

A big, wonderful, tasteful, stylish smash. Not since *My Fair Lady* (1956)—and there is a slight affinity between the two—have I been so moved by a musical; it is the embodiment of what we do best. The book has ample humor and fascination to hold the evening together; Noël Coward has provided a score which is merely enchanting; Joe Layton has produced a series of dances and a conception of movement that is simply dazzling, and the sets by Oliver Smith, which are elegant, roll and fly around the stage like a mechanical toy. Mr. Ferrer sounds more like Noël Coward than Mr. Coward, and so this is a splendid bit of casting which may not have escaped the notice of the authors. Florence Henderson is a very decorative young lady with a fine voice, and high time she is given the big opportunity she has sought. . . . Miss O'Shea almost got the Noise Abatement Commission after her on opening night.

HOWARD TAUBMAN, *Times*

Where are the innocence of heart and the faith in romance to make green again that oldest of sentimental tales about the prince and the girl of humble birth? Not, to be candid, in *The Girl Who Came to Supper*. Harry Kurnitz and Noël Coward bring a touch of modern cynicism to this new musical on an ancient theme. At bottom they would have us believe, but *The Girl Who Came to Supper* refuses to waft us back into the magic land where such fables can charm and even ring true. It brings shrewd skills to its earnest attempt to recover the gaiety and deviltry of a sentimental past. Somehow the heart of the old gallantry is missing; and the glamour and romance seem imposed, as if by an effort of will.

When Lerner, Loewe, and Moss Hart decided to produce their follow-up to *My Fair Lady* (1956) by themselves, *My Fair Lady*

producer Herman Levin decided to do his own follow-up—with Noël Coward, no less. *Camelot* (1960) and *The Girl Who Came to Supper* were both properly "British" period pieces, certainly; but the former was overproduced and the latter underwritten. Lerner, Loewe, and Hart's show made them some money, but Levin seems to have come out better. At least he didn't wind up in the hospital, as did the *Camelot* trio.

A Tony Award was won by Tessie O'Shea (supporting actress).

BROADWAY SCORECARD / perfs: 113 / $: –

rave	favorable	mixed	unfavorable	pan
3	1	1	1	

THE GIRLS AGAINST THE BOYS

a musical revue, with music mostly by Richard Lewine and Albert Hague; lyrics and sketches mostly by Arnold B. Horwitt

directed by Aaron Rubin; choreographed by Boris Runanin
produced by Albert Selden
with Bert Lahr, Nancy Walker, Shelley Berman, and Dick Van Dyke

opened November 2, 1959   Alvin Theatre

ROBERT COLEMAN, *Daily Mirror*

Nancy Walker and Bert Lahr are two of the funniest people in the world, but even they have to have something that's called material in the trade. It seemed incredible that any charade co-starring Walker and Lahr could be so dull.

WALTER KERR, *Herald Tribune*

In a way, I wish you weren't reading this review. The great clowns are rapidly vanishing from this world. Nancy Walker and Bert Lahr are two of the very greatest clowns this tired world possesses, and you should want to go see them no matter what kind of show they're in. But if the truth must be told, and I suppose it must, a whole program load of writers, composers, and supporting blithe spirits have not been able to keep the entertainment going while the two irreplaceable stars change costumes.

BROADWAY SCORECARD / perfs: 16 / $: −

rave	favorable	mixed	unfavorable	pan
		2	5	

THE GOLDEN APPLE

a musical, with music by Jerome Moross; book and lyrics by John Latouche, from *The Odyssey* by Homer

directed by Norman Lloyd; choreographed by Hanya Holm
produced by the Phoenix Theatre (T. Edward Hambleton and Norris Houghton)
with Priscilla Gillette, Stephen Douglass, Kaye Ballard, and Jack Whiting

opened March 11, 1954   Phoenix Theatre
transferred April 20, 1954   Alvin Theatre

JOHN CHAPMAN, *Daily News*

An off-beat, off-rhyme, off-harmony musical which lifts our Broadway song-and-dance theatre right off the comfortable seat of its pants and then gives it a kick in said pants. *The Golden Apple* is the best thing that has happened in and to the theatre in a very long time. Every part of it—music, lyrics, staging, scenery, costumes, and company—is refreshing, tangy, delightful, and intelligent.

ROBERT COLEMAN, *Daily Mirror*

It's a magnificent achievement. A sensational success. Quite the most original and imaginative work of its kind to blaze across the theatrical horizon in many a moon. It is art, without being arty. For an evening of sheer delight, we urge you to visit the Phoenix.

THIRD PRODUCTION
1953-54 SEASON

PHOENIX **THEATRE**
T. EDWARD HAMBLETON   NORRIS HOUGHTON

presents

"THE GOLDEN APPLE"

A New Musical

WRITTEN BY   MUSIC BY
JOHN LATOUCHE   **JEROME MOROSS**

with

PRISCILLA   STEPHEN   KAYE   JACK
GILLETTE DOUGLASS BALLARD WHITING

BIBI OSTERWALD   **JONATHAN LUCAS**   **PORTIA NELSON**

Directed by
NORMAN LLOYD

Choreography by   Musical Director
HANYA HOLM   HUGH ROSS

Settings by   Costumes by
WILLIAM & JEAN ECKART   ALVIN COLT

Lighting by KLAUS HOLM

LIMITED
ENGAGEMENT **PHOENIX THEATRE** 2nd AVENUE
at 12th STREET
BEGINNING THURSDAY EVENING, MARCH 11
EVENINGS INCLUDING SUNDAYS - MATINEES SATURDAYS & SUNDAYS - (No Perf. Mondays)
PRICES: Evenings Sunday thru Friday - Orch. $3.60; Mezz. $3.00; Balc. $2.40, $1.80, $1.20
Saturday Evenings - Orch. $4.80; Mezz. $3.60; Balc. $3.00, $2.40, $1.80
Matinees Saturday & Sunday - Orch. $3.00; Mezz. $2.70; Balc. $2.40, $1.80, $1.20
No Performance Mondays - Tax Included

"UPTOWN SHOWS AT DOWNTOWN PRICES"

Ulysses (Stephen Douglass), cast adrift in the Big City in his store-bought suit, is entwined by five Sirenettes at the Goona–Goona Lagoon. "Those hula-dancing mamas are really Yama-Yamas," we're told—and they sure look it! (drawing by Al Hirschfeld)

JOHN MCCLAIN, *Journal-American*

Register herewith an unqualified rave for *The Golden Apple*. Although singularly unheralded, this is easily the most satisfactory and original song and dance effort of the past several seasons and, in my opinion, can be classed as an American Gilbert and Sullivan. Here is one of those rare and gratifying experiences in the theatre— with fulfillment of an idea long nurtured and finally brought to bloom after years of struggle and disappointment. Mr. Moross has evolved a flow of continuous music embodying some of the best elements of Stephen Foster, a hunk of early hillbilly, snatches reminiscent of the "You're Only a Girl That Men Forget" school, with interpolated bits from the Bunny Hug jazz era. And, in case you may think he can't be modern, he drops a Calypso and a Hula number later on. To accompany all this Mr. Latouche has devised a libretto which tells the story and yet, miraculously, keeps pace with the period and emotional moods of the music. It is odd, and quite exciting, to realize that a show can thus be so capably sustained entirely through lyrics. Special merit badges should be awarded William and Jean Eckart for the sets, an ingenious series of drops and backgrounds which are always bright and imaginative. *The Golden Apple* is some sort of milestone in the American musical theatre. This is a great show.

RICHARD WATTS JR., *Post*

It is certainly no exaggeration to describe it as the best new musical comedy of the season. It is even an understatement. *The Golden Apple* is a thorough delight in its freshness, imagination, charm, and brightness. After the fashion of their excellent *Ballet Ballads* (1948), Mr. Latouche and Mr. Moross have told their story entirely in song and dance. It is a play in music, rather than a play with music. And, happily, both men have been equally successful in their contributions. The Latouche lyrics are not only gay, satirical, intelligent, and versatile, but also carry on the narrative with theatrical effectiveness. The Moross music has the same admirable virtues, and the result is a splendidly integrated show that possesses an authentic style.

A uniquely inventive show with one of the musical theatre's most exciting scores. *The Golden Apple* was the first musical to transfer from off-Broadway. It never quite caught on with the general public, though, and was unable to make it through the summer; but what a show! What a score!

Winner of the New York Drama Critics Circle Award. In addition to winning the Donaldson Award for Best Musical, Donaldsons were won by John Latouche (lyricist; librettist); Jonathan Lucas (male dancer); and William and Jean Eckart (scenic designers).

BROADWAY SCORECARD / perfs: 173 / $: —

rave	favorable	mixed	unfavorable	pan
5	1	1		

GOLDEN BOY

a musical play, with music by Charles Strouse; lyrics by Lee Adams; book by Clifford Odets and William Gibson, from Odets's 1937 drama

directed by Arthur Penn (replacing Peter Coe); choreographed by Donald McKayle (with Jaime Rogers)
produced by Hillard Elkins
with Sammy Davis (Jr.), Billy Daniels, and Paula Wayne

opened October 20, 1964   Majestic Theatre

WALTER KERR, *Herald Tribune*

There's something very curious about *Golden Boy,* good as most of it is. At the same time that Sammy Davis is winning one fight, the book is losing another. And not because the book is flabby. On the contrary. Except for its final few scenes, the book packs so much basic weight that even attractive music comes as thinning-out beside it. The chief difficulty lies in the fact that the scenes, crisply curtailed as they are, could go back into a straight play again. They are direct enough and believable enough for that. Thus it often comes as a letdown to hear someone slipping from a pungent bit of dialogue into the routine lyric measures of "Stick around and you'll see some action, who can tell what the kid can do?" Or,

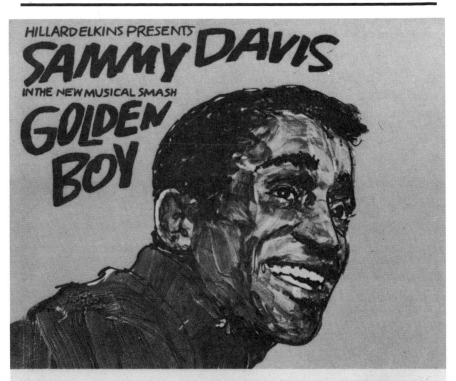

HILLARD ELKINS PRESENTS

SAMMY DAVIS

IN THE NEW MUSICAL SMASH

GOLDEN BOY

BOOK BY
CLIFFORD ODETS & WILLIAM GIBSON · MUSIC BY **CHARLES STROUSE** · LYRICS BY **LEE ADAMS**
BASED ON MR. ODETS' PLAY

WITH
BILLY DANIELS

PAULA WAYNE · KENNETH TOBEY

SCORE PUBLISHED BY **EDWIN H. MORRIS & CO.** · SETS, COSTUMES & PROJECTIONS DESIGNED BY **TONY WALTON** · LIGHTING BY **THARON MUSSER** · PROJECTIONS DEVISED BY **RICHARD PILBROW**

MUSICAL DIRECTION BY **ELLIOT LAWRENCE** · ORCHESTRATIONS BY **RALPH BURNS** · CHOREOGRAPHY BY **DONALD McKAYLE** · ASSOCIATE PRODUCER **GEORGE PLATT**

DIRECTED BY **ARTHUR PENN**

Original Cast Album by *Capitol*

MAJESTIC THEATRE
44th St. W. of B'way   Mats. Wed. & Sat.

"*Golden Boy is Broadway's new champ, and the dynamic and fabulous Sammy Davis wears the star's crown,*" says the back of the herald. "*A visit to New York is incomplete without seeing it*"— which is the same boast producer Elkins made about his Oh! Calcutta!

more seriously, to hear Miss Wayne drop from the abrasiveness of a real confrontation with Mr. Davis into the romantic musical conventionalities of "You make me wanna stay." The result is a bit like a first-act number in which we are distracted from what is being said and done by the vivid red and green of a stop-light that is blinking on and off overhead. When *Golden Boy* goes, it goes very well; it tends to stop to make time for a tune. But, overall, I'd be inclined to take a chance on it. Its visual design, its tart libretto, and its accomplished performing make it a more interesting musical than most.

John McClain, *Journal-American*

There is really no conceivable connection between the musical called *Golden Boy* and the original conception by Clifford Odets of a quarter century ago. There is no nonsense about his wanting to be a violin player, as of yore. But that is beside the point. When *Golden Boy* is good it is simply scrumptious, and I think there are enough such moments to make a go of it. I think they have gotten away with it; I think it is a fascinating show. . . . Mr. Davis is given a chance to do everything but play the tuba—he dances, sings, and acts brilliantly—but it seemed to me that either something happened to the amplifying system or else he had an unusual load of gravel in his throat.

Norman Nadel, *World-Telegram & Sun*

For the first five minutes, there is every reason to expect something triumphant. You find yourself thinking—and hoping: "If only they can sustain it at this level. . . ." They can't. *Golden Boy* emerges as a problem—regretfully, an unsolved problem—in engineering, like a bridge that is firmly secured at each end but slumps in the middle. In many respects it is generous with ingenuity and talent; there is much to enjoy and admire. Nevertheless, the show as a whole lacks cohesion, moves erratically, and never adequately defines the tragic conflict in the short, shrill life of a Negro boxer named Joe Wellington. Charles Strouse and lyricist Lee Adams have done their best work in the brighter, more zestful numbers. The soliloquies, laments, and ballads have some interesting musical phrases and well-worded lyrics, but they seem to lack form and climax. *Golden Boy* measures up visually through Tony

Walton's well-coordinated sets, projections [designed by Richard Pilbrow], and costumes. If everything about the musical were coordinated that well, it would gain significantly in theatrical effect.

HOWARD TAUBMAN, *Times*

The theatrical form of *Golden Boy* as a musical is as crisp as a left jab and as jolting as a right uppercut. One can have nothing but admiration for the snap, speed, and professionalism of the style of this musical. In two of its big production numbers ["Don't Forget 127th Street" and "While the City Sleeps"], *Golden Boy* is a knockout, not only for the whirling excitement of its action but also for the powerful pinch in its [lyrical] comment. But at the core of its story, *Golden Boy* hardly scores at all. Despite its constant reach for the heart, it does not land there convincingly. The blows have all the motion of the dazzling fight scene in savage pantomime, which comes at the end of the musical, and as little genuine impact. There is nothing wrong with the mood and atmosphere of *Golden Boy*. The trouble comes when Joe Wellington gets involved in romance. Intimations of soap opera were in the original play. But in the shorthand of storytelling incumbent on musicals, motives can only be suggested in quick broad strokes. Joe's abortive romance, in this version with a white girl, has no inner conviction. One feels detached about him and his Lorna. Mr. Davis is not to blame, nor is Paula Wayne, who plays the tough, tender Lorna with a blend of ardor and disillusion.

Elements of Clifford Odets's drama—the one about the prizefighting violinist—were so "borrowed" through the 1940s and 1950s that the original seems a mass of melodramatic cliches. Odets (and William Gibson, who took over after Odets's death on August 14, 1963) updated the play into a star vehicle for Sammy Davis, complete with an interracial romance. Unfortunately, a musically inexperienced production team (librettist, director, and producer) couldn't pull *Golden Boy* together, despite an impressive score by Strouse and Adams. The result: a long-running failure, by T.K.O.

```
BROADWAY SCORECARD / perfs: 569 / $: —

    rave      favorable      mixed      unfavorable      pan

                  1            5
```

GOLDILOCKS

a musical comedy, with music by Leroy Anderson; lyrics by Joan Ford, Walter and Jean Kerr; book by Walter and Jean Kerr

directed by Walter Kerr; choreographed by Agnes de Mille
produced by Robert Whitehead, presented by the Producers Theatre (Roger L. Stevens, Robert Whitehead, and Robert W. Dowling)
with Don Ameche (replacing Ben Gazzara and Barry Sullivan), Elaine Stritch, Russell Nype, and Pat Stanley

opened October 11, 1958   Lunt-Fontanne Theatre

FRANK ASTON, *World-Telegram & Sun*

Optically, with its ice-blues, yellows, grays, and golds, *Goldilocks* is magnificent [sets designed by Peter Larkin]. It has mass, glitter, glare, and blare, not to mention heavenly looking girls. But it is so lacking in a sense of direction that it never develops a personality of its own.

BROOKS ATKINSON, *Times*

A bountiful, handsome musical comedy with an uninteresting book. The book undoes what the actors and collaborating artists accomplish, which is a pity. For you could hardly ask for a more winning pair of actors than Don Ameche and Elaine Stritch, or more glorious costumes than the wardrobe Castillo has designed. Some of the Agnes de Mille ballets are tender and charming, and Leroy Anderson has written a melodic score in civilized style. Acting as his own director, Mr. Kerr has everything organized and has established a lively pace. But, like the book, the direction is not vigorous or versatile. Apart from the spectacle and the music, *Goldilocks* is an unexciting show.

The leading lady, ruefully musing "Who's been sleeping in my bed? (No one, that's who!)," is joined by a playfully dancing bear. Just like Goldilocks!

ROBERT COLEMAN, *Daily Mirror*

Goldilocks kids old-fashioned movies, musical comedies, and dance fads in a good old-fashioned way. After all, these things are so funny inherently as almost to defy satire. So the best thing to do is dish 'em up with sassy commentary, and let 'em speak for themselves. And that's just what Walter and Jean Kerr have done. In staging the frolic, Walter Kerr has been wise in pacing it with the speed of a hungry steed on the way to oats in his stable. That's all to the good, for this kind of show demands fast movement. With just enough time for the gags to get over. Joan Ford has helped the Kerrs with their lyrics, which ring the changes cleverly on the insult deadly. Some of them have the sting of a scorpion. They are set to a Leroy Anderson score that, though reminiscent, catches the spirit of the funfest. Frankly, *Goldilocks* is no gem of a show. It has faults, but the Kerrs have slickly glossed them over.

RICHARD WATTS JR., *Post*

Since drama critics and their wives are notoriously more brilliant than most people, a great deal is expected of them. And, when they are daring enough to challenge an envious world with a show of their own, nothing less than a masterpiece will satisfy the eager anticipation. Because *Goldilocks* seemed, to put it conservatively, rather short of that status in its debut, it was a disappointment. What made the dissatisfaction all the more upsetting was that the weaknesses of *Goldilocks* appeared to be chiefly in the writing contribution of the Kerrs.

Some things just don't work out. Too bad, as the individual elements of *Goldilocks* were better-than-average. The presence of an experienced producer (of musicals) might have helped: director/colibrettist/colyricist Kerr probably could have used some constructive guidance.

Tony Awards were won by Pat Stanley (supporting actress) and Russell Nype (supporting actor, tied with Leonard Stone for *Redhead* [1959]).

GREENWILLOW

a musical fantasy, with music and lyrics by Frank Loesser; book by Lesser Samuels and Frank Loesser, from the 1956 novel by B. J. Chute

directed by George Roy Hill; choreographed by Joe Layton
produced by Robert A. Willey in association with Frank (Loesser) Productions, Inc.
with Anthony Perkins, Cecil Kellaway, Pert Kelton, Ellen Mc-Cown (replacing Zeme North), and William Chapman
opened March 8, 1960   Alvin Theatre

FRANK ASTON, *World-Telegram & Sun*

At the start of *Greenwillow* a little boy [John Megna] dashed across stage. Your heart leaped as you wondered if there would be a *"Dites-Moi."* No. Moments later Pert Kelton was exercising the tin foil wrappings of her voice, and you thought maybe this would be another *Music Man* [1957]. It wasn't. Frank Loesser's musical can't make up its mind as to what it is. When William Chapman's baritone rolls out, the show sounds like a trick of a camp meeting. When Cecil Kellaway merrily chants "What a Blessing to Know There's a Devil," Mr. Loesser seems to kid the fundamentalists. There is a hint of opera in the air when a group lets go with Bruce McKay in "The Music of Home." And it is a dance show when Grover Dale leaps through recognizable joys of ballet. At these moments *Greenwillow* is a feast. Otherwise it skitters, no matter how stoutly George Roy Hill hauls on the controls. *Greenwillow* has flashes of excellence, some of the music is worth re-hearing, the cast is superb. But what happened to Frank Loesser's compass?

BROOKS ATKINSON, *Times*

Having selected an enchanted fable, Frank Loesser and his associates have had the taste to preserve its humors and sweetness. Out of his bountiful music box Mr. Loesser has provided a warm

NEVER WILL I MARRY

By
FRANK LOESSER

ROBERT A. WILLEY
in association with FRANK PRODUCTIONS, INC.
presents

Anthony Perkins

in

Greenwillow

the new musical

music and lyrics by **FRANK LOESSER**

book by LESSER SAMUELS and FRANK LOESSER
Based on the Best Selling Novel by B. J. Chute

directed by **GEORGE ROY HILL**

Choreography by **JOE LAYTON**

with

CECIL	PERT	ELLEN	WILLIAM
KELLAWAY	**KELTON**	**McCOWN**	**CHAPMAN**

Lee Bruce   Grover Elaine   Lynn Saralou   Bertha
CASS MacKAY   DALE SWANN   BRINKER COOPER   DUCKWORTH

Settings by **PETER LARKIN** costumes by **ALVIN COLT** Lighting by **FEDER**
Orchestrations by **DON WALKER**. Musical Direction by **ABBA BOGIN**

From The Score

THE MUSIC OF HOME
WALKING AWAY WHISTLING
SUMMERTIME LOVE
NEVER WILL I MARRY
FARAWAY BOY
GIDEON BRIGGS, I LOVE YOU

PRICE **.75** IN U.S.A.

000130 00
Printed in U. S. A.

Sole Selling Agents; **FRANK MUSIC CORP.** • 119 West 57th Street, New York, N. Y. 10019

Gideon Briggs and Dorrie nestle under the pastoral green willow tree, while brother Jabez plays and the Reverends Birdsong and Lapp look on. (drawing by I. W. Cohen)

270

and varied score that captures the simple moods of the story. Especially on the musical stage, taste is our scarcest commodity, and that is why the musical stage is so hackneyed. But the makers of *Greenwillow* have never faltered. If the taste of the production were not impeccable, the sentimentalities of *Greenwillow* could be cloying. But Mr. Loesser has taken care of that by writing music out of personal musical convictions. There isn't a Tin Pan Alley tune in the lot, nor is there a slovenly singer. In addition to being an impressive actor, Mr. Perkins turns out to be first-rate in his singing. "Summertime Love" and "Never Will I Marry" are full of lonely beauty when he sings them.

WALTER KERR, *Herald Tribune*

'Tis a fine day in Greenwillow 'til Gramma Briggs discovers riddle-weed growin' on the ground and everyone is quickly skeered because riddle-weed bodes trouble, and even if all the folks can still go on eating plum fritters and rowdy buns, it's likely that one boy and one girl will have to give up their walkin'-love promise and perhaps put off the marryin' day. If that paragraph sounds at all peculiar, it is because I am trying to give you a more or less precise idea of the single thing that is wrong with *Greenwillow*. The new musical is do-it-yourself folklore, which means that it is spun right out of somebody's head instead of out of somebody else's past, and folklore may just be the one dish in the world that can't be cooked to order. Greenwillow is nowhere—not in Brigadoon, not in Glocca Morra, not in the valley just below Old Smokey. Being neither Irish nor Dutch, Scotch nor good Broadway, it is forced to invent a language of its own that is a mélange of all four but with the special delights, rhythms, and authenticities of none. . . . Echoes from *Carousel* [1945] are not the ideal vehicle for Mr. Loesser's down-to-earth, and delectably down-to-earth, talents.

JOHN McCLAIN, *Journal-American*

Mr. Perkins seems to be able to do anything asked of him, short of playing goalie on the Olympic hockey team, and last night he unwound a small but extremely persuasive voice. He doesn't talk his songs, he sings—believe it or not. Combine this with his unquestioned appeal, and his gifts as an actor, and you have a rare hero in the theatre. Running him a close second, and giving away about 40 years, is Mr. Kellaway. His impish rendition of a great number, "What a Blessing" ("to know there's a Devil," it goes), will remain a small classic.

Frank Loesser couldn't quite pull off this attempt at a pastoral musical, although the failing was in conception and not in his admirable, atmospheric score. *Greenwillow* was obviously unworkable on stage, but it sure sounds wonderful.

BROADWAY SCORECARD / perfs: 95 / $: −

rave	favorable	mixed	unfavorable	pan
		2	1	4

GUYS AND DOLLS

a musical fable, with music and lyrics by Frank Loesser; book by Jo Swerling and Abe Burrows (actually by Burrows, replacing Swerling), from the story "The Idyll of Miss Sarah Brown" and other characters from the work of Damon Runyon

directed by George S. Kaufman; choreographed by Michael Kidd
produced by Cy Feuer and Ernest H. Martin
with Robert Alda, Vivian Blaine, Sam Levene, Isabel Bigley, Pat Rooney, Sr., and Stubby Kaye

opened November 24, 1950   46th Street Theatre

JOHN CHAPMAN, *Daily News*

The big trouble with *Guys and Dolls* is that a performance of it lasts only one evening, when it ought to last about a week. I did not want to leave the theatre after the premiere last night and come back here and write a piece about the show. I wanted to hang around, on the chance that they would raise the curtain again and put on a few numbers they'd forgotten—or, at least, start *Guys and Dolls* all over again. For here is New York's own musical comedy— as bright as a dime in a subway grating, as smart as a sidewalk

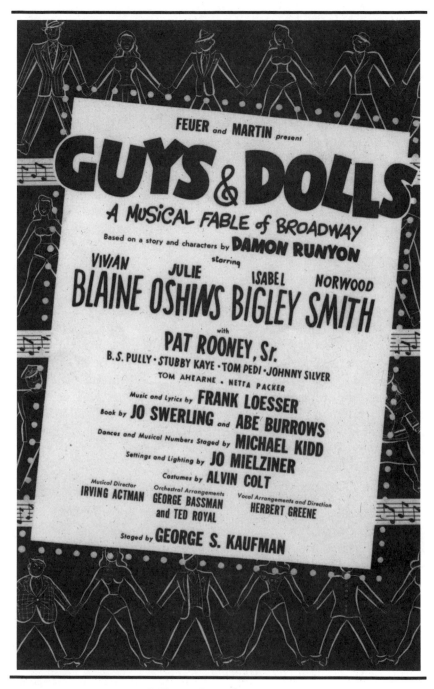

Runyonesque paper dolls and guys holding hands. The top row, from the left, shows Sky Masterson, Sarah Brown, Nathan Detroit and Adelaide, while Nicely-Nicely Johnson anchors the lower left corner. Broadway replacement cast.

pigeon, as professional as Joe DiMaggio, as enchanting as the sky-line, as new as the paper you're holding. In all departments *Guys and Dolls* is a perfect musical comedy. Under the masterful direction of George S. Kaufman, it is swift, crisp, and precise, with not a lagging instant. The book is a work of easy and delightful humor. Its music and lyrics, by Frank Loesser, are so right for the show and so completely lacking in banality, that they amount to an artistic triumph. Another just-right element is the staging of the dances and musical numbers by Michael Kidd; his ballet number about a crap game being played in a sewer is a dazzling bit of invention and execution. Jo Mielziner's sets are, like all Mielziner sets, just right, and so are Alvin Colt's costumes.

ROBERT COLEMAN, *Daily Mirror*

A smart first-night audience took off its gloves and blistered its palms applauding the new arrival. It has everything, as a top-flight stake runner should. Frank Loesser has written a score that will get a big play on the juke boxes, over the radio, and in bistros throughout the land. His lyrics are especially notable in that they help Burrows's topical gags to further the plot. *Guys and Dolls* is a heart-warming and hilarious re-creation of Runyon's kaliedoscopic cosmos of mugs and molls. We think Damon would have relished it as much as we did.

WILLIAM HAWKINS, *World-Telegram & Sun*

Love for the new musical spread faster last night than fire through dry grass in a high wind. *Guys and Dolls* brings Broadway in off the street so you can see and hear it sitting down. The show springs from Damon Runyon's stories. It recaptures what he knew about Broadway, that its wickedness is tinhorn, but its gallantry is as pure and young as Little Eva. It is all tender and rough at the same time, the way people who have never grown up very much can be tender and rough.

JOHN McCLAIN, *Journal-American*

This doesn't have to be a very long review because I can state the case of *Guys and Dolls* in one sentence: it is the best and most exciting thing of its kind since *Pal Joey* [1940]. It is a triumph and a delight, and I think it will run as long as the roof remains on the

Forty-Sixth Street Theatre. Run, don't walk, to the nearest ticket broker.

RICHARD WATTS JR., *Post*

Guys and Dolls is just what it should be to celebrate the Runyon spirit, vigorous, noisy, humorous, tough on the surface, and shamelessly sentimental underneath, filled with the salty characters and richly original language sacred to the memory of the late Master, and a pleasure to all beholders.

Guys and Dolls received what might be the most unanimously ecstatic set of reviews in Broadway history—tied with the other Loesser/Burrows collaboration, *How to Succeed in Business Without Really Trying* (1961). In both cases, curiously enough, Burrows was called in by producers Feuer and Martin to replace an existing libretto. Burrows made his theatrical debut here, under the tutelage of director George S. Kaufman of *Of Thee I Sing* (1931). This was a last moment of glory for the great satirist of the 1920s and 1930s. Kaufman was going through hard times: between 1941 and 1952 he wrote and/or directed 14 flops! But here everything was perfect, including Loesser's knockout score and clutch contributions from choreographer Michael Kidd and designer Jo Mielziner. When Pulitzer time came around, *Guys and Dolls* was apparently selected as winner—but Joseph Pulitzer's will gave the Trustees of Columbia University the right of veto, which they seem to have invoked due to Burrows's troubles with the House Un-American Activities Committee. No Pulitzer was awarded that year, though *Guys and Dolls* got (and deserved) everything else—including a record-breaking $1,000,000 motion picture sale!

Winner of the New York Drama Critics' Circle Award. In addition to winning the Tony Award for Best Musical, Tonys were won by Frank Loesser (composer); Jo Swerling and Abe Burrows (librettists); George S. Kaufman (director); Michael Kidd (choreographer); Cy Feuer and Ernest H. Martin (producers); Robert Alda (actor); and Isabel Bigley (supporting actress). In addition to winning the Donaldson Award for Best Musical, Donaldsons were won by Frank Loesser (composer; lyricist); Jo Swerling and Abe Burrows (librettists); George S. Kaufman (director); Vivian Blaine (female debut); and Robert Alda (male debut).

GYPSY

a musical fable, with music by Jule Styne; lyrics by Stephen Sondheim; book by Arthur Laurents, from the 1957 memoirs by Gypsy Rose Lee (Rose Louise Hovick, 1914–1970)

directed and choreographed by Jerome Robbins
produced by David Merrick and Leland Hayward
with Ethel Merman, Jack Klugman, and Sandra Church

opened May 21, 1959   Broadway Theatre

FRANK ASTON, *World-Telegram & Sun*

As experienced ladies of burlesque, Maria Karnilova wearing a mid-section butterfly, Faith Dane blowing a trumpet, and Chotzi Foley with advantageously placed light bulbs teach the hesitant Sandra Church the value of the gimmick in their trade ["You've Gotta Get a Gimmick"]. Loud, expert, and explicit, they threaten to sear the handsome new decor right off the Broadway's walls. This raucous turn might steal the show from anyone less formidable than the star. She tops it. To close the proceedings, Jerome Robbins puts her in a spot, with the whole stage open about her. Jo Mielziner's lamps paint changing letters against the background. And Miss Merman lets go in the best song Jule Styne and Stephen Sondheim have prepared for the evening, "Rose's Turn". . . . The ker-whalloping *Gypsy* is a sophisticate's dream.

JOHN CHAPMAN, *Daily News*

What this town has needed is Ethel Merman. What Miss Merman has needed is a good show. We got her and she got it last evening, when *Gypsy* opened at the Broadway Theatre. This mu-

The best damn critical quote ever! Compare this photo of Ethel (selling "Rose's Turn") with Peter Arno's uncanny Call Me Madam *(1950) caricature. (photo by Friedman-Abeles)*

sical is a great deal more than a flashy accommodation for Miss Merman's grand and well-known talent for playing and singing high, wide, and handsome. It is a story—a real story, and, funny though it seems to be, a touching story. It needs more than a musical comedy star to play it; it needs an actress—and Miss Merman turns out to be just the actress.

WALTER KERR, *Herald Tribune*

I'm not sure whether *Gypsy* is new fashioned, or old-fashioned, or integrated, or non-integrated. The only thing I'm sure of is that it's the best damn musical I've seen in years. Arthur Laurents's book is a clean knockout, to slip the most startling news in first. Jo Mielziner's vision of a lonely railway track that doesn't even meet infinity is breath-taking. The two-four rhythms that Jule Styne has composed to suggest all the tin and all the tang of tenth-rate vaudeville have the curious faculty of catching at your heart at the very moments when it is most deliberately steeped in corn. And better than all of them put together is Ethel Merman. . . . "If you've got a strong finish, they'll forgive you anything" says Miss Merman somewhere in the evening. *Gypsy* has one of the strongest musical comedy finishes I ever saw—and it doesn't even need it. Its generous authors have provided it with a great beginning, a great middle, and a great future.

RICHARD WATTS JR., *Post*

Two factors keep *Gypsy* from seeming almost too realistic a narrative of show business horror. One is that Miss Merman's quality of warm-heartedness causes the spectator to admire and cherish the mother for her spirit almost in spite of himself. The other is the brilliant showmanship that has gone into the presentation and into the remarkably candid narrative. Such phenomena of the theatre as the precocious child performers and the burlesque-show strippers are presented in all their appalling actuality but with delightfully entertaining humor.

One of Broadway's best musicals, *Gypsy*'s subject matter seems to have stood in the way of popular success. Despite laudatory critical reaction, its run was considerably shorter than Merrick's *Fanny*

(1954), half as long as *The Sound of Music* (1959) or the Styne/ Robbins *Funny Girl* (1964)—all considerably inferior musicals. There might have been other reasons: Robbins and Laurents both complained that Merman and (Styne's girlfriend) Church often walked through the show, resulting in disappointed audiences and adverse word-of-mouth. Nevertheless, *Gypsy* remains vibrant and alive.

The season's major awards were split between *Fiorello!* and *The Sound of Music*. Ethel Merman lost the Best Actress Tony Award to Mary Martin for *The Sound of Music*.

BROADWAY SCORECARD / perfs: 702 / $: +

rave	favorable	mixed	unfavorable	pan
5	2			

GYPSY LADY

a costume operetta incorporating music from Victor Herbert's *The Fortune Teller* (1898) and *The Serenade* (1897), with musical adaptation by Arthur Kay; lyrics by Robert Wright and George Forrest; book by Henry Myers

directed by Robert Wright and George Forrest; choreographed by Aida Broadbent
produced by Edwin Lester (and the Messrs. Shubert)
with Helena Bliss, Melville Cooper, John Tyers, George Britton, and Clarence Derwent

opened September 17, 1946   Century Theatre

BROOKS ATKINSON, *Times*

Folks, the main point is this: In order to listen to a few pleasant melodies by Victor Herbert, do we have to stand for all this nonsense? Some of the melodies are very pleasant, indeed, although there is no use pretending that everything Herbert wrote is immortal. To get the melodies behind footlights again, Henry Myers has written a new book, said on competent authority to be better than the two originals. But still a playgoer who is beginning to wonder what year is this anyway, can hardly help observing that the book depends upon snobberies that are no longer tolerable in this enlightened age; that the Duke of Roncevalle says, "Romance is piff-paff," with an air of discharging a witticism; and that the whole thing resounds in its mere impish moments to screams of girlish laughter.

JOHN CHAPMAN, *Daily News*

A new plot has been written by Henry Myers, now a novelist and screen writer who became famous years ago as a theatre press agent by sending out a bulletin to the press, "There is no news about 'Kibitzer' today." There isn't much news about the plot, either. Advance information supplied by the producer's office said that the story was to be a modern, tongue-in-cheek treatment of the stock period operetta, but I don't know whose cheek because the plot is just like any other operetta. The tunes are, of course, tuneful, being Herbert's and they all sound like old favorites even if you've never heard them before. Clarence Derwent [president of Actors' Equity] has the role of a French baron but I thought he was trying to imitate a pigeon. If he doesn't stop flapping his hands he's going to take off one of these nights and land in a tree in Central Park.

ROBERT GARLAND, *Journal-American*

Just why the old familiar books by Harry B. Smith had to be cast into the dust-bin and the new familiar book by Henry Myers had to be substituted is one of those things producer Edwin Lester alone can tell. To my way of listening, the new familiar book by Henry Myers belongs in the dust-bin, too.

LOUIS KRONENBERGER, *PM*

I guess even human nature will change before operetta-writing does. If that all-too-famous tune "Gypsy Love Song" was to grace the occasion, Mr. Myers obviously had to throw in a couple of gypsies; and if you throw in a couple of gypsies, Mr. Myers doubtless reasoned, you might as well throw in a carload. Then again, every operetta must plainly make a heavy raid on the peerage; and if you weave dukes and gypsies into the same plot—well, it just *is* the same plot, the one that grandpa saw on his twelfth birthday, and you sit through it with drooping spirits and drooping eyelids.

West Coast producer Edwin Lester's enormous success with the wartime *Song of Norway* (1944) encouraged him to assemble a string of "great composer" operettas, usually with Robert Wright and George Forrest at the helm. Initially mounted for Lester's Civic Light Opera series, a few made it to Broadway—although only *Kismet* (1953) matched *Norway's* success.

BROADWAY SCORECARD / perfs: 79 / $: −

rave	favorable	mixed	unfavorable	pan
1	1		1	5

HAIRPIN HARMONY

a musical farce, with book, music, and lyrics by Harold Orlob; additional dialogue by Don Witty

directed by Dora Maugham
produced by Harold Orlob
with Carlyle Blackwell, Lennie Kent, Maureen Cannon, and Gil Johnson

opened October 1, 1943   National Theatre

HOWARD BARNES, *Herald Tribune*

This Harold Orlob offering is all of a piece and it is all awful. It's about a fellow with a falsetto voice, who dresses up in diapers to fool a radio sponsor with breakfast foods to sell.

JOHN CHAPMAN, *Daily News*

There is no sense in embarrassing the singers, actors, and musicians involved in *Hairpin Harmony* by mentioning their names, because most of them acted ashamed of themselves on the stage.

ROBERT GARLAND, *Journal-American*

After postponements, cast-changings, and rewritings, Harold Orlob finally presented Harold Orlob's *Hairpin Harmony* last night at the National Theatre, with libretto by Harold Orlob, lyrics by Harold Orlob, and music by Harold Orlob. Harold Orlob wasn't in it, as far as programs say, unless Harold Orlob sang, danced, acted, or turned somersaults under another name. Man and boy, critic and playgoer, I've been going to the theatre for many a happy year. But, searching through my memory, I just can't seem to find the equal in ineptitude of last night's unfortunate performance.

LOUIS KRONENBERGER, *PM*

The ensuing dialogue convinced me that both my morals and my sanity would be best served if I said Aloha to the entertainment. As a matter of fact, most of my confreres had beat it much earlier.

WARD MOREHOUSE, *Sun*

The worst play I have seen since the high school in Guyton, Ga. put on *St. Elmo*.

WILELLA WALDORF, *Post*

One of the minor mysteries of the production was a note in the program saying the setting was by Donald Oenslager, one of Broadway's best-known designers until he entered the Air Force over a year ago. In an effort to keep from seeing and hearing what was going on in front of it, the thing began to look too familiar. We're not sure, but we rather think it's the Fifth Avenue mansion Mr. Oenslager designed for a turkey called *Pie in the Sky* [1941] nearly two years back.

BROADWAY SCORECARD / perfs: 3 / $: −

rave	favorable	mixed	unfavorable	pan
				8

THE HAPPIEST GIRL IN THE WORLD

a musical comedy, with music by Jacques Offenbach, adaptation by Jay Gorney; lyrics by E. Y. Harburg; book by Fred Saidy and Henry Myers, from an adaptation of *Lysistrata* by E. Y. Harburg "with a bow to Aristophanes and Bulfinch"

directed by Cyril Ritchard; choreographed by Dania Krupska
produced by Lee Guber
with Cyril Ritchard, Janice Rule, Dran Seitz, and Bruce Yarnell

opened April 13, 1961   Martin Beck Theatre

FRANK ASTON, *World-Telegram & Sun*

As for me, I'll stay in my chair at the Martin Beck for another half dozen performances of *The Happiest Girl in the World,* letting that score wash over me. The music is by Offenbach, lush stuff I first played on the Victrola while the kid next door duplicated it on his Edison. I've never got over it. It is an enormous splash of melody, talent, and production Lee Guber is presenting. Cyril Ritchard is director and star, appearing every few minutes as someone different but unfailingly "chic," as he would put it. . . . I expected to be bored. I was wrong.

WALTER KERR, *Herald Tribune*

I suppose Cyril Ritchard and Janice Rule could have danced all night, and it would have been dandy with me if they had. There are two or three times in *The Happiest Girl in the World* when this extremely unlikely combination—he tall and dimpled, she light and serious—begins to skip, goes on to scamper, and ends by shaking the chandeliers. Mr. Ritchard [bleats] like a noisy sheep that has been told *not* to come home. Hoisting his white-booted feet into the center ring just as the trainer taught him to, he is a sort of skyscraper Pan with slightly unstable foundations. Miss Rule is more like it. Here we have Diana, down from the heavens to see what she can do about all those warlike humans, and to her left we have Pluto, up from the smoky cellars of the Martin Beck to keep the ancient Greek world (and ours by implication, no doubt) steadily on the brink of disaster. Having met, do they disagree? Not at all. They link arms, lift their ears for a beat, and take off—to the lightest of Offenbach—as though they'd quite forgotten which

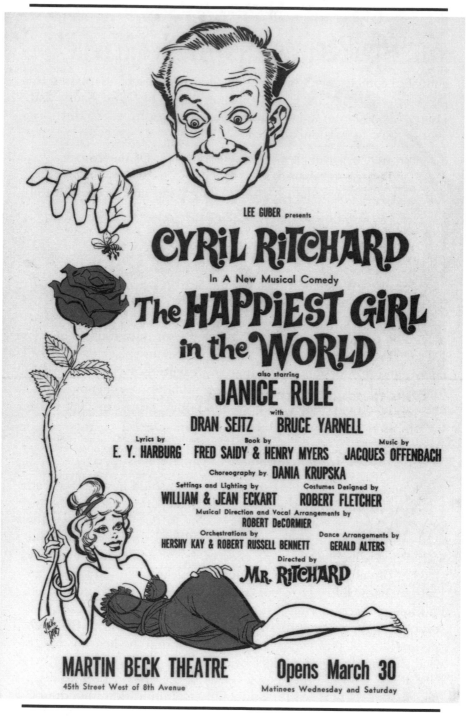

Pluto (Cyril Ritchard) arrives from the Underworld to stir up trouble for Lysistrata (Dran Seitz). (drawing by Jack Davis)

Palace they're supposed to have come from. Lovely work. . . . Is there a fly in the ambrosia, as they'd probably say in the half-borrowed book? Yes. When Offenbach stops and the comedy begins, you are pretty much given your choice of rather easy old jokes or rather less fetching new ones.

HOWARD TAUBMAN, *Times*

In seeking to combine Aristophanes and Offenbach, the writing team of E. Y. Harburg, Fred Saidy, and Henry Myers set itself a challenging, if not impossible, task. The essence of *Lysistrata* is the honest earthiness of its comedy aimed at a profound comment. The essence of Offenbach is the sparkle and airiness of its stylish high spirits. It is conceivable that Aristophanes's bawdry and Offenbach's elegance can be joined in graceful union, but *The Happiest Girl* has not achieved such a blessing.

RICHARD WATTS JR., *Post*

I think it should be reported that Harburg is the only lyricist I know of who ever put "ambivalent" in the words of a song, and it struck me as an agreeable achievement.

BROADWAY SCORECARD / perfs: 97 / $: −

rave	favorable	mixed	unfavorable	pan
2	2	1	2	

HAPPY AS LARRY

a musical fantasy, with music by Mischa and Wesley Portnoff; book and lyrics by Donagh MacDonagh, from MacDonagh's 1946 Irish verse play

directed by Burgess Meredith; choreographed by Anna Sokolow
produced by Leonard Sillman
with Burgess Meredith, Marguerite Piazza, Gene Barry, Barbara Perry, and Irwin Corey

opened January 6, 1950   Coronet Theatre

BROOKS ATKINSON, *Times*

As nearly as a theatregoer can tell without consulting a medium, it is the story of how a great lover is murdered by his rival, how his widow forgets him instantly, how he comes back to earth and renounces women for the rest of his life. It sounds as though it had been written by a village misogynist in love with his own archness and cleverness.

JOHN CHAPMAN, *Daily News*

Fantasy is a powerful drug. A little of it, properly administered, can put the patient in a state of extreme happiness—but an over-dose is dangerous. I grow dizzy with glee at one leprechaun in *Finian's Rainbow* [1947] or at one invisible rabbit named Harvey who is six feet, one-and-a-half inches tall. But I don't want a dozen leprechauns leaping all over me or a whole litter of tall rabbits leering at me from a cluster of lamp posts. They make me nervous.

ROBERT GARLAND, *Journal-American*

Having been led to believe that there's no business like it, show business took unfair advantage of the saying last Friday. Not even Leonard Sillman had any right to foster so phoney a festival on Broadway. Not with an unphony star such as Burgess Meredith! Frankly they do say it was Burgess Meredith's festival in the first place. Well, if *Happy As Larry* were a woman, I'd say Mr. Meredith was in love with her. Nobody but a man in love could become enamored of anything so second-rate and dress it up so fancy. In *Happy As Larry*—could "happy" be a misprint for "sappy"?— Donagh MacDonagh supplied the star with two acts of meretricious mumbo-jumbo. What was worse, it was whimsical-whamsical. What was even worse, it could have been verse in which the piece was written. But it wasn't! It was dubious doggerel.

WILLIAM HAWKINS, *World-Telegram & Sun*

The music is a strange combination of modern and trite. Sometimes the orchestrations [by Rudolph Goehr and Charles Cook] are provocative, and other times they sound like someone trying to remember Prokofieff, and playing on accordion, kazoo, and kitchen spoons.

RICHARD WATTS JR., *Post*

It is said that, when Mr. Meredith was giving *Happy As Larry* in local drawing rooms as a one-man show to interest potential backers in financing it, the result was a singularly winning theatrical tour-de-force. I can well believe it, because Burgess Meredith is one of the best and most thoroughly engaging actors on the American stage; but he is less fortunate as a director.

BROADWAY SCORECARD / perfs: 3 / $: −

rave	favorable	mixed	unfavorable	pan
			3	4

HAPPY HUNTING

a musical comedy, with music by Harold Karr; lyrics by Matt Dubey; book by Howard Lindsay and Russel Crouse, suggested by the 1956 wedding of Grace Kelly and Prince Rainier of Monaco

directed by Abe Burrows, choreographed by Alex Romero and Bob Herget
produced by Jo Mielziner
with Ethel Merman, Fernando Lamas, Virginia Gibson, and Gordon Polk

opened December 6, 1956   Majestic Theatre

BROOKS ATKINSON, *Times*

The explosion in Forty-fourth Street last evening was nothing to be alarmed by. It was merely Ethel Merman returning to the New York theatre. Howard Lindsay and Russel Crouse, who wrote her last show, *Call Me Madam* (1950), have put this one together with a minimum of originality and enterprise. Step by step the Broadway theatre is getting back to the mechanical mishmash of the old standard Shubert musical.

ROBERT COLEMAN, *Daily Mirror*

A Merman mirthquake. Tuneful, sassy, and satiric, it offers happy hilarity hunting for the holidays. It's a smasher, old bean, a smasher!

WALTER KERR, *Herald Tribune*

How can you resist an unladylike Kewpie-doll with sunrise eyes, tadpole eyebrows, and rhinestones all over her toes? What's left but rapt admiration for a kid who can teeter around on heels high enough to dwarf a pair of stilts, who can suddenly drop her head in such noisy shame that the plunk can be heard in the balcony, who can announce that she's got forty million and it ain't asparagus tips and double you up on the spot? But we still have a problem to consider. What kind of a Merman show is a show that never gives Merman the chance to stop it—not once? The score is a kind of musical plain-talk made up of liberal lyrics ("When the game of love begins, and the wheel of romance spins") and notes that keep jumping up and down on beat but don't seem to speak pleasantly to one another as they pass. Merman is Merman. But the roof is still on at the Majestic, and that's not right.

JOHN McCLAIN, *Journal-American*

The indifferent material doesn't matter. "Big Merm" just simply gets out there and take charge, she swaggers and struts, her numbers can be heard comfortably in Hohokus, N.J., and when she delivers a joke line she will come down in the audience and hit you with a juvenile if you don't laugh. She is plainly the greatest.

The plot of the competing *Bells Are Ringing* featured a songwriting dentist who wrote tunes on his air hose. *Happy Hunting* actually *was* composed by a dentist, without novocaine. When untried composer Stephen Sondheim was pushed on Merman for *Gypsy* (1959), "Big Merm"—who had personally "discovered" Dubey and Karr—insisted on veteran Jule Styne. No more amateurs for her!

HAPPY TOWN

a musical comedy, with music by Gordon Duffy; lyrics by Harry M. Haldane; additional music and lyrics by Paul Nassau; book uncredited (Harry M. Haldane), "adapted" by Max Hampton

directed by Allan A. Buckhantz; choreographed by Lee Scott
produced by B and M Productions (Allan A. Buckhantz and Mitchell May)
with Biff McGuire, Lee Venora, and Cindy Robbins

opened October 7, 1959   54th Street Theatre

JOHN CHAPMAN, *Daily News*

The show is about Texas, and if there can be one about Oklahoma it stands to reason—or so last night's backers must have thought—that a bigger and better one could be made about Oklahoma's rich neighbor. It is too late now to remind anyone that the most remarkable characteristic of Texas is that it is the flattest state in the union.

WALTER KERR, *Herald Tribune*

Choreographer Lee Scott has staged, with some vigor, what seemed to me to be the same dance in three different places. (Clap hands horizontally, clap hands vertically, girls swish skirts to right and left, everybody do the gallop that began with "Rodeo," then do it backward on one foot.) Librettist Hampton has been careful not to let the jokes get out of hand, confining himself to a discreet four, if I counted correctly. Following his ascetic procedure, I will quote only one: cowhand Tom Williams, who has spent a lot of time at rodeos, explains that he is "rodeoactive."

b & m productions present

HappyTown
a new musical

starring

HENRY HULL
BIFF McGUIRE, CINDY ROBBINS

with

**WILL WRIGHT, RALPH DUNN
DICK ELLIOTT, FREDERIC TOZERE, EDWIN STEFFE
TOM WILLIAMS, KAREN THORSELL**

book & lyrics by
HARRY M. HALDANE
music by
GORDON DUFFY
choreography by
LEE SCOTT
settings and lighting by
CURT NATIONS
costumes by
J. MICHAEL TRAVIS
musical direction & vocal arrangements by
SAMUEL KRACHMALNICK
orchestrations by NICHOLAS CARRAS
additional material by PAUL MASSAU

production directed by
ALLAN A. BUCKHANTZ

HappyTown

COLONIAL THEATRE
BOSTON

2½ Weeks Beginning Wednesday, September 9
MATS. 1st WEEK THURS. & SAT. THEREAFTER WED. & SAT.

Eves.: Orch. $6.25; 1st Balc. $5.50, $4.95, $4.40; 2nd Balc. $3.30
Mats.: Orch. $4.40; 1st Balc. $3.85, $3.30; 2nd Balc. $2.75 (Tax Included)

 491

*A not-so-happy vanity production, set in the only town in Texas
without a millionaire. Pre-Broadway credits.* (drawing by Luvak)

290

RICHARD WATTS JR., *Post*

The best I can say about it is that it was terrible. Not quite another *Portofino* (1958), but fairly close. Someone apparently remarked to someone that it would be a simply hilarious idea to write a musical comedy about a Texas town that didn't have a millionaire. Right there the inspiration, such as it was, came to a complete halt.

In a rare display of keen showmanship, the folks of *Happy Town* threw in the towel and closed in Boston. But hope—or should we say hopelessness?—springs eternal; the troupe was valiantly reassembled (*sans* star Henry Hull, who knew better); and *Happy Town* rose phoenixlike from the ashes to the ash-heap.

BROADWAY SCORECARD / perfs: 5 / $: —

rave	favorable	mixed	unfavorable	pan
				7

HAYRIDE

a hillbilly revue, with material by various writers

produced by Barron Howard and Jack Stone
with Sunshine Sue (Mary Arlene Higdon)

opened September 13, 1954   48th Street Theatre

JOHN CHAPMAN, *Daily News*

A natural for the burly fellows who drive tractors and trailers along the nation's highways and have to stop somewhere to pick up a toothpick. *Hayride* is a juke box with people. Maybe I could have stood it with a cup of coffee and a hamburger, but without these comforts I was in fairly desperate straits last night. *Hayride* comes from an eight-year run in Richmond, Va. It is made up of people who don't sing so good and don't play so good but are folksy as all hell in their hillbilly costumes. They pluck guitars, scratch fiddles, twang bass viols, plink banjos, strain accordions, and yowl their native songs. *Hayride* merely aroused the damyankee in me.

WALTER KERR, *Herald Tribune*

Aristotle once said that a certain kind of entertainment was supposed to fill the audience with pity and terror. Can he have been thinking of *Hayride?* At the 48th Street last evening a passel of young'uns was a-pickin' and a-singin', and a bunch of us old ones was a-settin' and a-shudderin'.

BROADWAY SCORECARD / perfs: 24 / $: —

rave	favorable	mixed	unfavorable	pan
	1	3	1	2

HAZEL FLAGG

a musical satire, with music by Jule Styne; lyrics by Bob Hilliard; book by Ben Hecht, from his 1937 screenplay *Nothing Sacred*, based on the story "Letter to the Editor" by James Street

book directed by David Alexander; production supervised and choreographed by Robert Alton
produced by Jule Styne in association with Anthony B. Farrell
with Helen Gallagher, Thomas Mitchell, Benay Venuta, John Howard, and Jack Whiting

opened February 11, 1953   Mark Hellinger Theatre

WILLIAM HAWKINS, *World-Telegram & Sun*

Billing never made a star, and Miss Gallagher is not one to push her luck. She gives the show the works, is sparing with bows, and never crams the spotlight. Her voice in a ballad has the old Garland ring, and she proves again, as she did in *Pal Joey* [the 1952 revival], that she can handle a comedy number with the best. Nobody in the theatre can define so clean a speedy comic dance as she can. When her lines want laughs she can zing them out into space like a shot-put champ. She sings her opening numbers like an early-

Small-town gal Hazel Flagg (Helen Gallagher)—mistakenly believed to be dying of radium poisoning—"becomes the sentimental toast of the most sentimental village (pop. 8,000,000) in the world."
(drawing by W. Hogarth)

morning bird, and ends up with a comic vocal tango ["Laura de Maupassant"] that combines all the things she does the best. She should be a proud baby today.

Walter Kerr, *Herald Tribune*

This irreverent fancy [*Nothing Sacred*] has been decked out in acres of Harry Horner scenery, hundreds of Miles White costumes, a whirlwind of Robert Alton dance steps, and a bagful of Jule Styne tunes. It has been staffed with attractive personalities and punched up to the tempo of 1953. But the caustic humors which were its principal distinction lie buried beneath the embellishments. The bite has gone out of a once brilliant antic. . . . In the middle of the first act Jack Whiting put in an appearance as the dapper Mayor of the big town, and he turns the stage upside down with an idiotic inspiration called "Ev'ry Street's a Boulevard in Old New York." As he ankles, struts, leers, and whispers through clenched teeth he becomes a magnificent parody of every nightclub or Palace entertainer you ever saw. Satire suddenly rears it head, and you get a fleeting image of what author Hecht and composer Styne may have had in mind for *Hazel Flagg*.

John McClain, *Journal-American*

Hazel Flagg represents some sort of triumph of noise and tempo over logic; it will stand (for some time, I believe) as a monument of how best to louse up a pretty good idea and still get away with an acceptable theatrical venture.

Jule Styne attempted to make a star out of Helen Gallagher, whose career had developed through Styne's *High Button Shoes* (1947), *Make a Wish* (1951), and *Pal Joey*. But lacklustre material did the talented dancer-singer-comedienne in. A few months later, Gwen Verdon came to town in *Can-Can*—and stole away the spotlight forever.

Tony Awards were won by Thomas Mitchell (actor); and Miles White (costume designer). Donaldson Awards were won by Thomas Mitchell (actor); Jack Whiting (supporting actor); and John Brascia (male dancer). Mitchell was popular choice for Best Actor in a Musical, even though he was appearing in a non-singing role! His award made him the second person (after Helen Hayes) to win an Oscar (*Stagecoach* [1939], against his own performance as Gerald "Land, Scarlet, land" O'Hara in *Gone With the Wind*); an Emmy (*Ah, Wilderness!* [1951]); and a Tony.

BROADWAY SCORECARD / perfs: 190 / $: −

rave	favorable	mixed	unfavorable	pan
	4	1	2	

HEAVEN ON EARTH

a musical fantasy, with music by Jay Gorney; book and lyrics by Barry Trivers

production supervised by Eddie Dowling; directed by John Murray Anderson; choreographed by Nick Castle
produced by Monte Proser in association with Ned C. Litwack
with Peter Lind Hayes, Dorothy Jarnac, Wynn Murray, David Burns, and Irwin Corey

opened September 16, 1948   Century Theatre

BROOKS ATKINSON, *Times*

Although our stricken nation has only just recovered from *Up in Central Park* [1945, which played the Century], a little something has come along to replace it. *Heaven on Earth*, which opened last evening, sets a very high standard for mediocrity and drives all our happy dreams away. Shaking the dust off some long-discarded formulas, Barry Trivers has written a yarn about an Irish Robin Hood who lives in Central Park, doing mawkish good to anyone who can bear it, and Jay ("Brother, Can You Spare a Dime?") Gorney has fitted it to a remarkably undistinguished score. There is one magical thing about dullness: it is infectious. Everybody gets into the act whole-heartedly. In performing the questionable service of escorting *Heaven on Earth* to a public stage, Eddie Dowling and John Murray Anderson have made the gaiety unbearable. And Raoul Pène du Bois, a genuine artist of recognized ability, has designed scenery and costumes that a honky-tonk might not willingly accept. If this is *Heaven on Earth*, where do the sinners go?

ROBERT GARLAND, *Journal-American*

The songs are lively, without being actually alive.

JOHN LARDNER, *Star*

If you like a bargain, friends, repair without delay to the Century Theatre, hard by the lazy glades of Central Park, where they are practically giving away the biggest sleeping pill in town. This giant, or economy size, barbiturate became available Thursday night, when a number of talented chemists took the wraps off their new formula, which goes by the name of *Heaven on Earth*, and is not dissimilar in effect to the bite of the adult tsetse fly. No expense has been spared in making the new musical comedy both a rich and a powerful narcotic. At the end of the first act, by way of ramming their point home, the manufacturers have arranged to have the characters on the stage curl up and go to sleep in front of one of Mr. du Bois's restful sets. The curtain is then lowered with surpassing gentleness, so as to make it unanimous onstage and off. . . . The music sounds as though it had been written on tracing paper.

WARD MOREHOUSE, *Sun*

The estimable Shubert attorney in the seat behind me had a good time, but I didn't.

Jackie Gleason, who left during the tryout, seems to have been replaced by Miss Wynn Murray, the belting butterball who rocked Broadway with Rodgers and Hart's "Johnny One Note" in *Babes in Arms* (1937) and "Sing for Your Supper" in *The Boys from Syracuse* (1938).

BROADWAY SCORECARD / perfs: 12 / $: −				
rave	*favorable*	*mixed*	*unfavorable*	*pan*
			4	5

HELLO, DOLLY!

a musical comedy, with music and lyrics by Jerry Herman (additional music and lyrics by Bob Merrill, Charles Strouse, and Lee Adams, unbilled); book by Michael Stewart, from the 1954 farce *The Matchmaker* by Thornton Wilder (an adaptation of Wilder's 1938 comedy *The Merchant of Yonkers*, from the 1835 English farce *A Day Well Spent* by John Oxenford, and the 1842 Austrian farce *Einen Jux Will er Sich Machen* by Johann Nestoy); previously announced as *Dolly: A Damned Exasperating Woman*

directed and choreographed by Gower Champion
produced by David Merrick (with [Gower] Champion Five, Inc.)
with Carol Channing, David Burns, Eileen Brennan, Sondra Lee, and Charles Nelson Reilly

opened January 16, 1964   St. James Theatre

JOHN CHAPMAN, *Daily News*

Miss Channing is the most outgoing woman on the musical stage today—big and warm, all eyes and smiles, in love with everybody in the theatre and possessing a unique voice ranging somewhat upward from a basso profundo. . . . I wouldn't say that Jerry Herman's music and lyrics are memorable and some aren't rememberable.

WALTER KERR, *Herald Tribune*

Don't bother holding onto your hats, because you won't be needing them. You'd only be throwing them into the air, anyway. *Hello, Dolly!* is a musical comedy dream, with Carol Channing the girl of it. Almost literally it's a dream, a drunken carnival, a happy nightmare, a wayward circus in which the mistress of ceremonies opens wide her big-as-millstone eyes, spreads her white-gloved arms in ecstatic abandon, trots out on a circular runway that surrounds the orchestra and proceeds to dance rings around the conductor. Miss Channing. Who *is* Miss Channing? Here, as she rocks her way in rhythm across that circular ramp, crossing and recrossing her leaping friends in the white spats, she is—she must be—everything from Fay Templeton to *The Black Crook* [1866] to Little Nellie Kelly [title character of a 1922 George M. Cohan musical] and back again. With hair like orange seafoam, a contralto like a horse's

DAVID MERRICK

presents

CAROL CHANNING in

The New Musical Comedy

HELLO, DOLLY!

Book by
MICHAEL STEWART

Music and Lyrics by
JERRY HERMAN

Based on "The Matchmaker" by Thornton Wilder

Also Starring
DAVID BURNS

with

EILEEN BRENNAN

SONDRA LEE

JAMES DYBAS   GORDON CONNELL   GLORIA LEROY
IGORS GAVON   ALICE PLAYTEN
and
CHARLES NELSON REILLY

Settings Designed by
OLIVER SMITH

Lighting by
JEAN ROSENTHAL

Costumes by
FREDDY WITTOP

Musical Direction and
Vocal Arrangements by
SHEPARD COLEMAN

Orchestrations
by
PHILIP J. LANG

Dance and Incidental Music
Arranged by
PETER HOWARD

Directed and Choreographed by

GOWER CHAMPION

A David Merrick and Champion-Five Inc. Production

NATIONAL THEATRE
WASHINGTON
4 Weeks Beg. Tues. Dec. 17
MATS. WED., DEC. 18, THURS., DEC. 26, WED., JAN. 1,
WED. JAN. 8 AT 2:00 AND SATS. AT 2:30

This Dolly looks somewhat more glamorous than the larger-than-life caricature created by Carol Channing (Ruth Gordon and Shirley Booth had played the non-musical Matchmaker). Along with other tryout changes, the lady on the logo was replaced by a heavily garbed Dolly sporting bow and arrow, à la Cupid. Pre-Broadway credits (drawing by Keretson)

neighing, and a confidential swagger that promises to baby-sit for the entire house, she fulfills for you a promise you made yourself as a boy: to see, someday, a musical comedy performer with all the blowzy glamor of the girls on the sheet music of 1916. Miss Channing has gone back for another look at that advertisement labeled "His master's voice," and she has swallowed the records, the Victrola, and quite possibly the dog. . . . Librettist Michael Stewart's lines are not always as funny as Miss Channing makes them, and sometimes Miss Channing simply drowns them out by eating dumplings.

JOHN MCCLAIN, *Journal-American*

A pot-walloping hit. Gower Champion deserves the big gong for performance beyond the call of duty. Seldom has a corps of dancers brought so much style and excitement to a production which could easily have been pedestrian, and he has certainly created a whole new career for Carol Channing, the star, who had been relegated for years to a fixation with diamonds as a girl's best friend. She dominates the proceedings like a hirsute Y. A. Tittle [the bald quarterback of the N. Y. Giants]. It is difficult to describe the emotion [the "Hello, Dolly!" number] produces. Last night the audience nearly tore up the seats as she led the parade of waiters in a series of encores over the semi-circular runway which extends around the orchestra pit out into the audience. It is a whale of a tribute to the personal appeal of Miss Channing and the magical inventiveness of Mr. Champion's staging. . . . The problem now is how to get tickets. At last report, the line starts in Yonkers.

HOWARD TAUBMAN, *Times*

The best musical of the season thus far. It could have been more than that. Were it not for lapses of taste, it could have been one of the notable ones. But Mr. Champion, whose staging and choreography abound in wit and invention, has tolerated certain cheapnesses. It is a pity because *Hello, Dolly!* does not need such crutches. Only musicals without ideas or talent must resort to desperate measures. . . . Resplendent in scarlet gown embroidered with jewels and a feathered headdress, and looking like a gorgeous, animated kewpie doll, Channing sings the rousing title song with earthy zest and leads a male chorus of waiters and chefs in a joyous promenade around the walk that circles the top of the pit.

RICHARD WATTS JR., *Post*

The new musical comedy is big, bouncing, handsome, rapidly-paced, and filled with the shrewdest ingredients of successful showmanship, and it provides Carol Channing with a cheerfully flamboyant role. The fact that it seems to me short on charm, warmth, and the intangible quality of distinction in no way alters my conviction that it will be an enormous popular success. Herman has composed a score that is always pleasant and agreeably tuneful, although the only number that comes to mind at the moment is the lively title song. His lyrics could be called serviceable.

Hello, Dolly! received a unique set of raves, with the critics waxing ecstatic *despite* a generally lukewarm reception for the score. (Herman's score was supplemented during the tryout with "Elegance" and "Motherhood March" by Bob Merrill, and "Before the Parade Passes By" by Charles Strouse, Lee Adams, and Jerry Herman. And the title song was kind of lifted from Mack David's "Sunflower" [1948], resulting in a six-figure settlement.) It was clearly Champion's vibrant magic and Channing's freshly minted performance which made *Dolly!* irresistible—two elements which aren't likely to be successfully recreated in revival, even those claiming to offer Champion's "original" staging. It should also be noted that despite the show's ecstatic reception, Champion responded to specific critical complaints by deleting a lackluster number ("Come and Be My Butterfly") after the Broadway opening.

Winner of the New York Drama Critics' Circle Award. In addition to winning the Tony Award for Best Musical, Tonys were won by Jerry Herman (composer); Michael Stewart (librettist); Gower Champion (director); Gower Champion (choreographer); David Merrick (producer); Carol Channing (actress); Oliver Smith (scenic designer); Freddy Wittop (costume designer); and Shepard Coleman (musical director).

BROADWAY SCORECARD / perfs: 2,844 / $: +

rave	favorable	mixed	unfavorable	pan
4	2			

HERE'S LOVE

a musical fantasy, with music, book, and lyrics by Meredith Willson, from a story by Valentine Davies and the 1947 screenplay *Miracle on 34th Street* by George Seaton

directed by Stuart Ostrow (replacing Norman Jewison); choreographed by Michael Kidd
produced by Stuart Ostrow
with Janis Paige, Craig Stevens, Laurence Naismith, Fred Gwynne, and Valerie Lee

opened October 3, 1963   Shubert Theatre

WALTER KERR, *Herald Tribune*

Drat. Half a dozen times during *Here's Love* last night I was ready to tear up all the captious little notes I was making on my yellow note-paper and come right out in favor of sentiment. I tell you, I was ready to give IN. Right off the bat, after only two or three minutes of stilted dialogue from chorus boys and children who were pretending to stare at Macy's Christmas parade, the parade itself started. In from the wings, two by two and large as life and waltzing and schmaltzing, came all the dancers choreographer Michael Kidd had hired to walk on their hands, point their noses, play violins as they haven't been played since *The Gold Diggers of 1932*, and dance on xylophones as they haven't been danced on since Will Mahoney was a lad. Ah, I thought, as I watched prancing prop-men tug at the giant toes of balloons big enough to take off the Shubert roof, Michael Kidd is back in form again, ready to give the theatre all of the sleek ragtime zip and the slide-trombone sweep that made him, not too long ago, one of the musical comedy's most engaging and impertinent inventors. . . . If *Here's Love* keeps having regular and distressing nervous breakdowns along the way (and for me it certainly does), it isn't because of the sentiment. What Mr. Willson must be rescued from is not his warm heart but his unfunny-bone. The evening's comedy is primitive. And it keeps coming up. A careless, coarse, slap-sticky tone in the book is what makes a now-and-then shambles of Mr. Willson's good deed.

JOHN McCLAIN, *Journal-American*

This is a bad day for the Meredith Willson Admiration Society, for it seems the boss has let us down. His *Here's Love* is very thin stuff indeed: it doesn't have much of a book, which can be forgiven, but it doesn't have a great tune, which can't. As the tale unfolds we keep waiting for the old Willson tunes to take over—and they just never do.

HOWARD TAUBMAN, *Times*

Here's *Here's Love*, right off the assembly line, shrewdly efficient, the model of an efficient musical. Meredith Willson's latest opus rarely rises above expediency. But it has ingredients that the great, uncomplicated public is supposed to want. The songs seem machine-tooled, guaranteed to do the job efficiently. Nearly everything about the package bears the mark of the right calculations. The product is wholesome, with a scattering of laughs, a hint of tremulous emotion, the triumph of true love, a touch of fantasy, all appearing just where you anticipate them. What is lacking most of the evening is that subtle, special gift that goes beyond dependable workmanship, that ignores the assembly line and that, out of sheer élan, magically equips a shining, smooth-running earthbound model with wings. The fantasy in the plot is not matched in the telling on the stage. *Here's Love* does not soar and does not enchant.

RICHARD WATTS JR., *Post*

The point made by *Here's Love* is that you can't fight Santa Claus, and it might serve as a warning to critics. Meredith Willson's new musical comedy is so filled with the benevolent and everloving spirit of Christmas and the happy smiles of little children that it would be virtually un-American to suggest that the sweetness and light tended to become a little oppressive. The danger of the cheery *Here's Love* is that its concentration on benevolence could bring out the beast in you.

A one-show *Music Man* (1957) can, apparently, get away with rah-rah bluster once—namely *The Unsinkable Molly Brown* (1960)—but only once. *Here's Love* was even weaker than *Molly*, and Willson's final musical—*1491* (1969), about guess who—foundered and sank along the golden California coast.

BROADWAY SCORECARD / perfs: 338 / $: -

rave	favorable	mixed	unfavorable	pan
4	1	1	3	

HIGH BUTTON SHOES

a musical comedy, with music by Jule Styne; lyrics by Sammy Cahn; book by Stephen Longstreet, from his 1946 novel *The Sisters Liked Them Handsome*

directed by George Abbott; choreographed by Jerome Robbins
produced by Monte Proser and Joseph Kipness
with Phil Silvers, Nanette Fabray, Jack McCauley, Mark Dawson, and Lois Lee

opened October 9, 1947   Century Theatre

HOWARD BARNES, *Herald Tribune*

The production has a lot of bounce. The trouble is that the ball is extremely elusive. It has definitely rewarding moments, but they are interrupted by devious vaudeville manipulations. The benisons of the show are more incidental than integral. Robbins has mounted an uproarious bit of dance miming in his take-off on early films. He has guided Helen Gallagher and Paul Godkin through a fetching "Tango" and Miss Fabray, McCauley, and what are known as the boys and girls through an enchanting number called "Papa, Won't You Dance with Me?" The Styne music is much better, though, than the Sammy Cahn lyrics with which it is coupled. Oliver Smith's settings and Miles White's costumes are worthy of a musical comedy triumph. *High Button Shoes* is scarcely that.

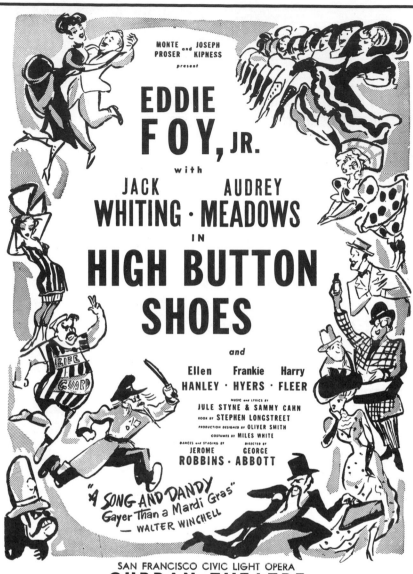

MONTE and JOSEPH
PROSER and KIPNESS

present

EDDIE FOY, JR.

with

JACK WHITING · AUDREY MEADOWS

IN

HIGH BUTTON SHOES

and

Ellen   Frankie   Harry
HANLEY · HYERS · FLEER

MUSIC and LYRICS BY
JULE STYNE & SAMMY CAHN
BOOK BY **STEPHEN LONGSTREET**
PRODUCTION DESIGNED BY **OLIVER SMITH**
COSTUMES BY **MILES WHITE**
DANCES and STAGING BY   DIRECTED BY
JEROME   **GEORGE**
ROBBINS · ABBOTT

*"A SONG AND DANDY
Gayer Than a Mardi Gras"
— WALTER WINCHELL*

SAN FRANCISCO CIVIC LIGHT OPERA
CURRAN THEATRE
Beginning Mon., Sept. 19—Evenings Including Sundays
MAIL ORDERS NOW! Prices: Evenings—Orchestra $4.80; Balcony $4.20, $3.60, $3.00; Gallery $2.40
WEDNESDAY MATINEE (SEPTEMBER 21 ONLY) AND SATURDAY MATINEES:
Orchestra $4.20; Balcony $3.60, $3.00, $2.40; Gallery $1.80 (All Prices Include Tax)
With mail order please send stamped, self-addressed envelope for return of tickets.
Make remittance payable to the S. F. Light Opera Association. Seats on sale September 13

*Con-man Phil Silvers (right, in the checked suit) and stooge Joey
Faye sell snake-oil, bathing beauties pose, and Keystone Kops chase
the villain while Mama Nanette Fabray gets Papa Jack McCauley to
dance with her (upper left). Post-Broadway credits, although artwork features original cast. (drawing by Don Freeman)*

304

JOHN CHAPMAN, *Daily News*

Even without the Mack Sennett ballet, *High Button Shoes* would be a very pleasant musical; with the ballet it becomes something special—a happy romp for people who just want to see a show without getting all cluttered up with art. The pursuit had the first-nighters almost paralyzed with delight, for Jerome Robbins, who can be a very tony choreographer when he wishes, has staged a hilarious melee involving the Keystone Komedy Kops, Gloria Swanson and the rest of the Sennett bathing beauties, life guards, a horrifying trio of crooks, an ape and, of course, Phil Silvers and his mournful stooge, Joey Faye. I don't know how Robbins ever managed to get so many people to do so many crazy things—all of them out of those wonderful Sennett one-reelers—without getting hurt or in each other's way. But he does it, and the ballet is a masterpiece. The rest of *High Button Shoes* is not so socko—fortunately, I guess, because nobody could stand the strain if it were.

ROBERT GARLAND, *Journal-American*

There's so much good in the best of it, and so much bad in the worst of it. *High Button Shoes* is like nothing so much as a straight play being rehearsed in a night club while the floor show's going on. Almost anything can happen. Practically everything does.

LOUIS KRONENBERGER, *PM*

For a musical that's not very good, *High Button Shoes* is a very good musical indeed. Some of it is wonderful, much of it is gay, and the rest has the merit of being bad without being boring. It's an upsy-downsy evening, but certainly as much sky as swamp; and if you'll frankly accept it for better or worse, I think you'll enjoy yourself. I've seen shows with twice as much class that weren't half as much fun. Jerome Robbins is the reason why the show at its best is wonderful. He has created a "Mack Sennett Ballet," a period fandango of bathing beauties and Atlantic City bath-houses, of Keystone Kops and robbers and all the rest, which as it keeps gaining in speed and growing in size and gyrating in all directions, becomes one of the comic glories of the age. Mr. Styne's score is pleasantly unsensational—or somewhat better than Mr. Cahn's lyrics, which are agreeably third-rate.

RICHARD WATTS JR., *Post*

As one who has never been particularly hospitable to the ballet in musical comedy, I hasten to report that the hero of the evening is Jerome Robbins. There is more humor and unconventional inventiveness and less stuffiness in Mr. Robbins than in most directors of the pirouette, and all of the dancing in *High Button Shoes* is agreeable. There is one number, however, that is a genuine masterpiece, a wild and hilarious affair in which everyone, including the principals of the cast, darts about frantically in the fashion of the treasured Keystone comedies of silent film days, meanwhile carrying on the plot furiously. With all appreciation of Mr. Robbins's distinguished work, there is another important contributor to the excellence of the new show's dancing. A young dancer, hitherto unknown to me, named Helen Gallagher, a slender and interesting girl, reveals an individuality and style which make her, in a small part, the most arresting player in the show.

While Jerome Robbins had done some impressive Broadway work before—*On the Town* (1944), *Billion Dollar Baby* (1945)— his "Mack Sennett Ballet" single-handedly carried an entire, uneven evening. The choreographer also made it clear that a show ballet could be hysterically funny. Otherwise, *High Button Shoes* was mediocre, with Hollywood tunesmith Jule Styne making a not-too-impressive Broadway debut. Two pop song hits ("Papa, Won't You Dance with Me?" and "I Still Get Jealous"), two star performances, and that phenomenal ballet more than made up for the lapses.

A Tony Award was won by Jerome Robbins (choreographer). In addition to winning the Donaldson Award for Best Musical, Donaldsons were won by George Abbott (director); Jerome Robbins (choreographer); Nanette Fabray (actress; supporting actress); Jack McCauley (supporting actor); Oliver Smith (scenic designer); and Miles White (costume designer).

HIGH SPIRITS

a musical comedy, with music, book, and lyrics by Hugh Martin and Timothy Gray, from the 1941 British farce *Blithe Spirit* by Noël Coward

directed by Noël Coward (replaced by Gower Champion);
choreography by Danny Daniels (replaced by Gower Champion)
produced by Lester Osterman (and Jule Styne), Robert Fletcher, and Richard Horner (with ABC-Paramount)
with Beatrice Lillie, Tammy Grimes, Edward Woodward, and Louise Troy

opened April 7, 1964   Alvin Theatre

WALTER KERR, *Herald Tribune*

She was back last night, the Killer as of yore, and in about two seconds I'd turned my critical faculties to someone who was sitting near me and surrendered. I was glad to go. Not everything was up to snuff. But Miss Lillie sniffs at what is not up to snuff and concentrates on other things: her feet, for instance. I don't know what it is that fascinates both of us about her feet. She looks down at them, and sort of twiddles them, particularly if she has nothing else to do and most particularly if she is being applauded. Then, after a time, she gets up and experiments with them, perhaps to see if they will walk. They do walk, in a flat-footed, floppy sort of way, and if she happens to be wearing bunny-slippers with long ears, the ears wave at her. She wonders about dancing. Give it a try? Off into a waltz-clog, as though she were determined to shake that flypaper from her soles and her soul. Then a fast-tap. Too fast. Cut it out. Toe-dancing. More spiritual. Backward she goes at a delicate and most majestic clip, pausing only to circumnavigate a nasty piece of floorboard she

Bea Lillie files through the air on her bicycle, while the ghostly Tammy Grimes seems to be walking on her co-star's head. (drawing by Joe Eula)

remembers—icily—from one or another rehearsal. Then a few harp-like plucks at the bars of her brass bedstead and she is ready to curl up for the night, sucking her thumb, while thunder sounds through the house.

NORMAN NADEL, *World-Telegram & Sun*

Not that there's ever been the slightest doubt, but Beatrice Lillie's performance as Madame Arcati, the happy medium in *High Spirits,* re-affirms her place in the recorded history of the 20th century, along with the Battle of Jutland and Salk vaccine. When she is on stage, the musical achieves both the sublime and the uproariously ridiculous. She has only to cock an ear toward the garden outside the French doors and observe, "That cuckoo is very angry," and the aloof facade of our sophisticated society collapses to the sound of laughter.

ABC-Paramount gave producers Lester Osterman and Jule Styne a million dollars to mount three 1964 musicals, all failures: *High Spirits, Fade-Out—Fade-In,* and *Something More.* (What an investment!) Gower Champion, fresh from *Hello Dolly!,* came in and tried to fix things. The Champion touch was evident in the show's ethereal physical movement (he replaced the old-fashioned blackouts—long pauses while everybody waited for the stagehands to finish—with visually choreographed set changes), and in the finely honed specifics of Bea Lillie's performance (built on less-than-adequate material, as usual). Forced into retirement by a stroke after filming *Thoroughly Modern Millie* (1967), the incomparable Lillie lingered on incapacitated for over two decades before dying at the age of 94 on January 20, 1989.

BROADWAY SCORECARD / perfs: 375 / $: —

rave	favorable	mixed	unfavorable	pan
	6			

HIT THE TRAIL

a musical comedy, with music by Frederico Valerio; lyrics by Elizabeth Miele; book by Frank O'Neill; tryout title: *On with the Show*

directed by Charles W. Christenberry, Jr., and Byrie Carr; choreographed by Gene Bayliss

produced by Elizabeth Miele
with Irra Petina, Robert Wright, and Paul Valentine

opened December 2, 1954   Mark Hellinger Theatre

ROBERT COLEMAN, *Daily Mirror*

Since turkey is usually served on Thanksgiving, Elizabeth Miele missed the boat by bringing her own juicy bird—*Hit the Trail*—to town a week later. It must have made a few cynics, who claimed *The Boy Friend* [1954] overshot the mark in satirizing vintage song-and-dancers, eat their words. For in every aspect, it smacks of the old-fashioned, outmoded musicals that seemed so ludicrous to the smart youngsters of today. The book is primitive, the lyrics June-moony, and the music mediocre. Frank O'Neill is blamed in the program for the limping libretto, and Frederico Valerio for the tinkly tunes. As for the lyrics, Miss Miele can blame only herself. . . . Early in the proceedings, a trouper sitting atop a stage coach remarked prophetically: "This is a disaster!" One we had to see to really believe it could happen in 1954.

WALTER KERR, *Herald Tribune*

Right in the middle of a long, languid song in the long, languid musical that opened Thursday, the baritone took out his watch and consulted it. This was the ultimate injury. There we were, sitting so politely—and *he* looks at his watch.

RICHARD WATTS JR., *Post*

Back in 1943, when this reviewer was briefly back in the United States between wartime assignments, he saw, as an innocent non-reviewing spectator, a musical comedy called *Hairpin Harmony*, and has always remembered it as one of the epoch-making disasters of his lifelong playgoing. Then a couple of years ago, there was a girl-and-music show known as *Buttrio Square* [1952], and it was memorably calamitous, too. There was something about both works that made them, in a singularly macabre sort of way, cling to my theatrical memory. I was thinking of them last night at the Mark Hellinger Theatre. . . . As for the lyrics, we all should conceivably have been warned when the opening number had the chorus rhyming "troupe" with "soup."

A vanity production, in vain.

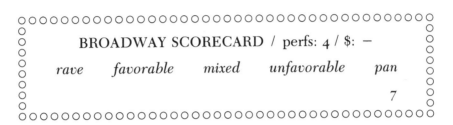

BROADWAY SCORECARD / perfs: 4 / $: —

rave	favorable	mixed	unfavorable	pan
				7

HOLD IT!

a musical comedy, with music by Gerald Marks; lyrics by Sam Lerner; book by Matt Brooks and Art Arthur

directed by Robert E. Perry; choreographed by Michael Kidd
produced by Sammy Lambert (and Anthony B. Farrell)
with Johnny Downs, "Red" Buttons, and Jet McDonald

opened May 5, 1948   National Theatre

BROOKS ATKINSON, *Times*

Quite a lot of young people are working quite hard to conceal a case of arrested musical comedy development at the National. The case is labeled *Hold It!*, which was put on at high speed last evening and ought to be removed without any appreciable slackening of pace.

HERRICK BROWN, *Sun*

Sammy Lambert, who has served as backstage manager for many a musical, and Anthony B. Farrell, who manufactures chains up in Albany, are the sponsors of *Hold It!*, and with the show they are making their debut as producer and "angel" respectively. It won't be hard for their next effort to be more worthy of their time and funds.

JOHN CHAPMAN, *Daily News*

Like all other modern college shows of stage or screen, it owes a great debt to World War II, for if the baritone happens be a chap you first saw in a show in 1935, his presence now at a seat of learning is explained by making him a GI who is absorbing belated knowledge under the Bill of Rights.

ROBERT GARLAND, *Journal-American*

For years there's been talk of setting *Charley's Aunt* [1892] to music. Well, nobody has made a song-and-dance show out of Brandon Thomas's comedy. But Matt Brooks and Art Arthur have taken a healthy hint from that good idea for the story of their *Hold It!* When I tell you that *Hold It!* is a George Abbott song-and-dance show without George Abbott, you know what I mean. [*Where's Charley?*, George Abbott and Frank Loesser's musicalization of *Charley's Aunt*, opened October 11, 1948] . . . Michael Kidd, following the fashion, is a choreographer who never heard of Agnes de Mille. But, with the Jerome Robbins of *High Button Shoes* [1947] he is obviously familiar. [Kidd danced with Robbins as one of the three leads in the premiere of the Bernstein/Robbins ballet "Fancy Free" (1944).] As director of the dances, he brings out the zest in them. And even if his big ballet—which, he says, isn't— does stem from Jerome Robbins's "Mack Sennett" number at the Shubert, which, in turn, stems from "Flickers" in Charles Weidman's repertoire, it's disarmingly un-Agnes-de-Mille-ian.

RICHARD WATTS JR., *Post*

The sort of show that you leave humming the hits of other musical comedies.

BROADWAY SCORECARD / perfs: 46 / $: −

rave	favorable	mixed	unfavorable	pan
	3		3	2

HOLLYWOOD PINAFORE; *or, The Lad Who Loved a Salary*

an Americanization of the 1878 comic opera *H.M.S. Pinafore*, with music by Sir Arthur Sullivan; book and lyrics revised by George S. Kaufman "with apologies to W.S. Gilbert"

production supervised by Arnold Saint Subber; directed by George S. Kaufman; choreographed by Douglas Coudy; ballet by Anthony Tudor
produced by Max Gordon in association with Meyer Davis
with William Gaxton, Victor Moore, Shirley Booth, and Mary Wickes

opened May 31, 1945   Alvin Theatre

JOHN CHAPMAN, *Daily News*

The Kaufman lyrics, which switch Gilbert into Hollywood and yet take no liberties with the Sullivan score, are frequently smart. Some times they also sound as though Mr. Kaufman has learned all he knows of Hollywood by reading *Variety* and *The Reporter* without ever having lived in the place. His most delightful conceit is the role of a columnist, Louhedda Hopsons, who sings "I'm Called Little Butter-Up." In this part Miss Booth is grand.

ROBERT GARLAND, *Journal-American*

Mr. Kaufman redoes it with his tongue in Mr. Gilbert's cheek. If hearing and seeing are believing, Mr. Gilbert doesn't care a whole lot for it. *Hollywood Pinafore* is better in theory than in performance. After all, a Kaufman is a Kaufman while a Gilbert is a genius. That nobody, not even Mr. Kaufman, will deny.

LOUIS KRONENBERGER, *PM*

Last week came *Memphis Bound*, or "Pinafore on the Mississippi"; last night came "Pinafore in Hollywood." I don't think it's simply because *Memphis Bound* got here first that *Hollywood Pinafore* comes in second. While *Memphis Bound* has an awful lot of faults, it adds up to an enjoyable evening; while *Hollywood Pinafore* has a number of virtues, it is really not much fun. One very big reason for the essential failure of the show is its Hollywood subject-matter. Not

Hollywood agent Dick Live-Eye (William Gaxton) and Pinafore Pictures exec Joseph W. Porter (Victor Moore) flank gossip columnist Louhedda Hopsons (Shirley Booth), who confesses that she's called "Little Butter-Up." (costumes by Kathryn Kuhn, photo by Vandamm)

even Mr. Kaufman can do a "Twice in a Lifetime." For one thing the time is long past; Hollywood—at least along the usual satiric lines—has been milked dry. And though Mr. Kaufman achieves some direct hits, he is plugging what is virtually a corpse. Moreover, he is writing in the broad terms of musical comedy, and is by so much the more forced to make his spoofing unsubtle.

BURTON RASCOE, *World-Telegram*

It looks to me as though Max Gordon and Meyer Davis had hit the jackpot with *Hollywood Pinafore.* It is a joyous thing—voluptuous and comical, sensuous and good-naturedly satirical, fast-paced, artistic, and melodious—an optical and auricular delight, with laughs for the diaphragm and for the cerebrum as well. And it brings back together that fine comedy team, William Gaxton and Victor Moore. Mr. Kaufman has Americanized and modernized a classic, and the apparent ease and cleverness with which he has done it make one wonder why it had never been done before. But it took someone as theatre-wise and as expert in the writing craft as Mr. Kaufman to do it.

WILELLA WALDORF, *Post*

Mr. Kaufman is the only modern playwright we can think of at the moment who would dare to tamper with Gilbert without getting shot for it; but it is our reluctant duty to report today that it almost never comes off. What, never? Well, hardly ever. Even as a spring frolic, it is none too frolicsome. The scene is the impressive entrance hall of Pinafore Pictures. Joseph Porter [Victor Moore] is no longer an admiral, but a big producer. Mike Corcoran isn't the captain of the ship. He's a director. Josephine, his daughter, is a movie star who loves a writer. Nothing could be further beneath her. Writers in Hollywood, according to Mr. Kaufman, are dressed in stripes like prisoners, and when allowed to attend story conferences they are gagged and bound. Dick Live-Eye [William Gaxton] is an agent who gets 10 per cent of everything. Miss Hebe is Mr. Porter's secretary, and his sisters and his cousins and his aunts—all very lovely—have nice, cushy jobs in the studio. This sounds very funny, but it isn't as funny as it sounds. . . . Mr. Moore is funniest when eating his graham crackers and milk at an interpolated story conference which has nothing to do with *Pinafore*, and Shirley Booth is comical as the syndicated columnist, Louhedda Hopsons.

☆

George S. Kaufman's two decades of comedic brilliance were over by World War II. The passage of time perhaps, or perhaps just the passing times. At any rate, his two 1940s musicals were weak, and he was to make only one more contribution to the general welfare of Broadway as director of the 1950 *Guys and Dolls*. This Holly-wooden satire couldn't begin to compare with Hart and Kaufman's razor-sharp *Once in a Lifetime* (1930). It did serve as a vehicle for William Gaxton and Victor Moore, who had first paired when Kaufman and associates cast them as President John P. (for Peppermint) Wintergreen and Alexander Throttlebottom, his Vice, in *Of Thee I Sing* (1931). But by now their formula, too, was tired; and the 51-year-old Gaxton—who was always more con-man than leading man, even in the original *Connecticut Yankee* (1927)—was now *really* too old to get the girl. Kaufman's producer was Max Gordon, whose early hits included Kaufman, Dietz, and Schwartz's *The Band Wagon* (1931), Jerome Kern's *The Cat and the Fiddle* (1931) and *Roberta* (1933), and others. Gordon called on Meyer Davis—society's "bandleader for millionaires"—for financing, and ex-stage manager Arnold Saint Subber to serve as production supervisor. Subber also supervised the next Kaufman/Gordon flop, *Park Avenue* (1946), after which he produced his first show, *Kiss Me, Kate* (1948) (after which he dropped the Arnold from his name).

BROADWAY SCORECARD / perfs: 52 / $: —

rave	favorable	mixed	unfavorable	pan
3			1	4

HOT SPOT

A musical comedy, with music by Mary Rodgers; lyrics by Martin Charnin (additional lyrics by Stephen Sondheim); book by Jack Weinstock and Willie Gilbert

director uncredited (Herbert Ross replacing Morton Da Costa, Richard Quine, and Robert Fryer); choreography uncredited (Herbert Ross replacing Onna White)

Judy's in a hot spot, all right, but not the kind they had in mind.
Pre-Broadway credits. (costume by Rouben Ter-Arutunian)

produced by Robert Fryer and Lawrence Carr in association with
John Herman
with Judy Holliday, Joseph Campanella, Joe Bova, Mary Louise
Wilson, and Carmen de Lavallade

opened April 19, 1963   Majestic Theatre

WALTER KERR, *Herald Tribune*

Judy Holliday is so sweetly proud of *Hot Spot* that you'd swear
she was its mother. She clucks over it, she coddles it, she fusses
and tidies and tucks everything into place. And then she looks up
at you with that wide abashed smile and those confidently implor-
ing eyes as if to say "Honestly, now, did you ever see anything
more adorable?" I don't see how a single one of us can bring
ourselves to tell her it isn't any good. Miss Holliday has got herself
into so much trouble in her Peace Corps assignments that she is
shuttled off to a country where nothing can happen, and just about
doesn't. The authors have decided to send their girl to a quiet
place, and the quiet place turns out to be the Majestic. Recogniz-
ing the fact that her voice always did sound like something sent in
from a ventriloquist, and making the most of its mere squeak, she
huffs, puffs, snuffles, snores, and does her best to go basso in what
is one of the clearest examples of mind over no matter in our time.
She is expected to take care of every thing; I'll bet they've got her
down in wardrobe between acts, sewing costumes. Again and again
she comes on to go it alone, standing in a spotlight and piping her
heart out to compensate for the fact that there aren't really any
dances (the dances, indeed, are motherless and fatherless, being
uncredited on the program) and although there is an ensemble
wandering around in grass skirts, it isn't put to much use. It's a
gesture here and a mild fling there, and then back to the star,
looking for help.

JOHN McCLAIN, *Journal-American*

It is difficult to conceive a property which can smother the prodigious and ebullient Miss Holliday, but I'm afraid *Hot Spot* gets
the job done.

NORMAN NADEL, *World-Telegram & Sun*

Hot Spot rewrote the book on pre-opening problems. It also
rewrote itself every rehearsal, and twice in between. Its troubles
became so widely known that the company frankly—even

cheerfully—admitted them. It inspired the local soothsayers to new depths of grim foreboding.

A perfect example of the big-time bonanza that's almost sure to bomb. The idea: Judy Holliday as a blundering Peace Corps volunteer. Holliday was everybody's favorite, and definitely a box-office name. But her last show, *Laurette* (1960), had closed in New Haven. (The stage bio of Laurette Taylor resurfaced as 1963's other big-time bonanza bomb, the Mary Martin-starrer *Jennie*.) The director came from the Broadway (1957) and Hollywood (1962) cornfields of *The Music Man*. Da Costa's deal called for a hefty 13.75 percent of the profits, as opposed to Jerome Robbins's 5 percent of *Gypsy* (1959). But Da Costa's last show had been the ill-conceived *Saratoga* (1959), which Da Costa wrote, directed, and ill-conceived. The librettists could boast of their current blockbuster *How to Succeed in Business Without Really Trying* (1961), but everyone knew that, billing notwithstanding, their *How to Succeed* work had been thrown out. Richard Rodgers's daughter Mary came from *Once Upon a Mattress* (1959), which was okay if not great. And wouldn't Dad come in and help out, if necessary? (No, he wouldn't—although Mary's pal Sondheim provided the drowning songwriters with a couple of bandaids.) Add it all together and what do you have? Another *Shangri-La* (1956) for producer Robert Fryer.

BROADWAY SCORECARD / perfs: 43 / $: −				
rave	*favorable*	*mixed*	*unfavorable*	*pan*
		1	3	3

HOUSE OF FLOWERS

a musical comedy, with music by Harold Arlen; lyrics by Truman Capote and Harold Arlen; book by Truman Capote, from his novella

directed by Peter Brook (replaced by Herbert Ross, unbilled); choreographed by Herbert Ross (replacing George Balanchine) produced by Saint Subber

SAINT SUBBER presents

TRUMAN CAPOTE and HAROLD ARLEN'S new musical

House of Flowers

starring PEARL BAILEY

direction
PETER BROOK

sets and costumes
OLIVER MESSEL

choreography
GEORGE BALANCHINE

with
| DIAHANN | JUANITA | JOSEPHINE | DINO | RAWN | JACQUES | GEOFFREY |
| CARROLL | HALL | PREMICE | DiLUCA | SPEARMAN | AUBUCHON | HOLDER |

and FREDERICK O'NEAL

musical director JERRY ARLEN   lighting JEAN ROSENTHAL   orchestrations TED ROYAL

•

WORLD PREMIERE
ERLANGER THEATRE
21st and Market Streets
3 ½ Weeks Beg. Wed. Nov. 24 thru Dec. 18
MATINEES THURSDAY (Thanksgiving Day), WEDNESDAYS & SATURDAYS

One of Madame Fleur's "flowers" lazily "waitin' for some sin to begin." Pre-Broadway credits. (photo by Richard Avedon)

320

with Pearl Bailey, Diahann Carroll, Juanita Hall, Ray Walston (replacing Jacques Aubuchon), and Dino DiLuca

opened December 30, 1954   Alvin Theatre

JOHN CHAPMAN, *Daily News*

It is too bad, and possibly disastrous, that Truman Capote conceived the first scene of *House of Flowers* out of a dirty little mind, for, once the plot and dialog have been shoved aside to make room for the scenery, the actors, and the music, the show is extraordinary, exotic, and jam full of grand new Harold Arlen music. Oliver Messel has devised some of the most beautiful pictures I have ever seen on a stage. An enormously imaginative stage artist and costume designer, his lovely trappings for *House of Flowers* make the works of Cecil Beaton look like something out of an old laundry bag. . . . I've never been to the West Indies. But if they look the way Messel makes them look, sound the way Arlen makes them sound, and if the people move the way Ross makes them dance, I want to go there. Without Capote.

ROBERT COLEMAN, *Daily Mirror*

A tropical hurricane called *House of Flowers* swept into the Alvin Theatre and devastated a distinguished first-night audience. . . . The book is short on humor and long on excitement and color. The jokes are rough and rowdy, but they fall between peaks of sensuous rhythm. For Arlen has composed a score that makes the pulses race. And, after all, wordage doesn't really matter while the musical storm is raging. . . . *House of Flowers*, for all its faults, is a fascinating fiesta. It moves with the speed of a rocket. It gives off sparks like a Roman candle. It's the town's newest sensation. But take our word for it, leave your Aunt Minnie at home, or you'll have a lot of explaining to do.

WILLIAM HAWKINS, *World-Telegram & Sun*

A gaudy, bawdy, tropical, horticultural show. *House of Flowers* is riotous, gay with tunes, awesome for its flippant humor, and lovely to look at. You have to catch "Mother" Bailey trailing a dozen yards of white feather boa around while she sings about her friends ["What Is a Friend For?"]. Nobody in the theatre has her deadly aim or deceptive relaxation. To that, add the haunting voice and the good looks of the dame, and you have a star.

WALTER KERR, *Herald Tribune*

House of Flowers starts off in a riot of promise. The sumptuous new musical takes wings with the overture itself, a magical medley that begins with the blast of a police whistle and ends in a cascade of drums. Looking back on things, I'd have been happy if they'd played it twice. It's an adventurous try, and all sorts of talent has gone into the effort to give musical comedy a fresh, saucy, strangely colorful shape. But Mr. Capote has run out of inspiration too soon, and the violence of drum beats cannot quite conceal the fact that a charming vision is slowly vanishing before our eyes. . . . If Miss Bailey has a rival in the show's musical department, it is a plaintive and extraordinarily appealing ingénue named Diahann Carroll. Several of Mr. Arlen's most evocative songs, "A Sleepin' Bee" and "House of Flowers" among them, fall to this engaging actress, and she delivers them with serious eyes and the enthusiasm of a newly hatched bird.

RICHARD WATTS JR., *Post*

Although Truman Capote's book for *House of Flowers* seems rather to have withered away during the process of production, the new musical play is so colorful, exotic, and generally enlivening an entertainment that its frailty as a story doesn't much matter. Aided particularly by enchanting sets and costumes and some excitingly dynamic dancing, this girl-and-music tour of a West Indies island gives every indication of being the town's newest hit.

A highly colorful musical with a first-rate Arlen score. But strange things happen when creative temperaments run rampant and no producer or director or author is in charge. By the time *Flowers* reached New York, the Messrs. Brook, Balanchine, and Capote were no longer around. Neither was third-featured Josephine Premice: the power that be decided she had too much good material, so her character was rewritten into two less-prominent roles. (Premice eventually returned to the *House,* playing the lead in Arlen, Capote, and Subber's 1968 off-Broadway revision.) For that matter, newcomer Diahann Carroll and Juanita Hall—Broadway's first black Tony Award Winner, for "Bloody Mary" in *South Pacific* (1949)—both lost songs during the tryout while Miss Bailey's role grew.

A Tony Award was won by Oliver Messel (scenic designer). Messel lost the costume award to Cecil Beaton (for *Quadrille*).

```
BROADWAY SCORECARD / perfs: 165 / $: −

 rave      favorable      mixed      unfavorable      pan

   2            2                         3
```

HOW TO SUCCEED IN BUSINESS WITHOUT REALLY TRYING

a musical satire, with music and lyrics by Frank Loesser; book by Abe Burrows, Jack Weinstock, and Willie Gilbert (actually by Burrows, replacing Weinstock and Gilbert), from the 1952 book by Shepherd Mead

directed by Abe Burrows; choreography by Hugh Lambert (replaced by Bob Fosse); "musical staging" by Bob Fosse
produced by Cy Feuer and Ernest H. Martin in association with Frank (Loesser) Productions, Inc.
with Robert Morse, Rudy Vallee, Bonnie Scott, Virginia Martin, and Charles Nelson Reilly

opened October 14, 1961   46th Street Theatre

JOHN CHAPMAN, *Daily News*

Eleven years ago next month *Guys and Dolls* opened at the 46th St. Theatre. It was the definitive musical about low life in New York. Last Saturday evening practically the same crew offered the definitive musical about high life in the city. This is not the high life of social doings and misdoings, but what goes on in the upper reaches of an office building. What goes on up here is murder— murder by stiletto, by poison, by decapitation. This splendidly

FEUER and MARTIN
in association with
FRANK PRODUCTIONS INC.
present
THE NEW

FRANK LOESSER and ABE BURROWS MUSICAL

"HOW TO SUCCEED IN BUSINESS WITHOUT REALLY TRYING"

Book by ABE BURROWS, JACK WEINSTOCK and WILLIE GILBERT
Based on "HOW TO SUCCEED IN BUSINESS WITHOUT REALLY TRYING" by SHEPHERD MEAD
Music and Lyrics by FRANK LOESSER

ROBERT MORSE   RUDY VALLEE

with BONNIE SCOTT · VIRGINIA MARTIN · CHARLES NELSON REILLY

Choreography by HUGH LAMBERT · Scenery & Lighting by ROBERT RANDOLPH
Costumes by ROBERT FLETCHER · Musical Direction by ELLIOT LAWRENCE
Orchestrations by ROBERT GINZLER

Musical Staging by BOB FOSSE
Directed by ABE BURROWS

Another great logo, instantly recognizable and perfectly capturing the flavor of the show. The physical production featured sets and props "drawn in" with black illustrator's ink, as in the base of the chair.

324

sardonic account of Big Business is an example of perfect musical comedy construction, swift, sharp, jam-packed with characters and incident and clear-headed as it moves unerringly through an interesting and funny story. Loesser is the perfect man for his end of the show—the songs; for he is a cynic without being tough. He has not put in a note of music or a syllable of lyric that doesn't carry the story along.

WALTER KERR, *Herald Tribune*

Not a sincere line is spoken in the new Abe Burrows–Frank Loesser musical, and what a relief that is. It is now clear that what has been killing musical comedy is sincerity. *How to Succeed* is crafty, conniving, sneaky, cynical, irreverent, impertinent, sly, malicious, and lovely, just lovely. What most distinguishes a sassy, gay, and exhilarating evening is—you'll never believe this—the book. Abe Burrows has done it, with acknowledged help from Jack Weinstock and Willie Gilbert. But what has happened is that, for the first time really, an entire musical comedy has been fashioned along the deadpan, and deadly, lines of Mr. Burrow's celebrated piano parodies. This is, and perhaps I should whisper it, a musical with a mind. A bland and caustic kidding of the American success story goes on all evening, without ever losing its frosty and lunatic attitude. Gags are subordinated to impish running commentary; Mr. Loesser's perky score is subordinated to the merry malice that is afoot; meaningful fantasy is given its head, and the point of view grins and glows with its own cocksure effrontery.

JOHN McCLAIN, *Journal-American*

The most inventive and stylized and altogether infectious new musical in recent recollection opened at the 46th St. Theatre Saturday night and should remain there until the building wears out. It is the sheerest farce, down to the last paper clip, there isn't a smidgin of "heart" on the horizon, and honesty is consistently the worst policy. It is gay, zingy, amoral, witty, and shot with style. It comes very close to being a new form in musicals. The score by Mr. Loesser is not great by "pop" standards; it is better than that. All the music has been integrated into the plot, to fit the mood as well as the momentum. His lyrics are generally superb; thoughtful, witty, and often hilarious. The numbers, under Bob Fosse's direction (with special credit to Hugh Lambert), are a whole new chapter in ingenuity. In most of these people jiggle on and off in little groups, the beats are small and fast, building to a story climax when the stage is filled for the finish, and the audience screams.

NORMAN NADEL, *World-Telegram & Sun*

Whichever white-winged angel watches over theatrical enterprises was sitting on top of the 46th St. Theatre Saturday night, joyously blasting away on a solid gold trumpet. And in the pouring rain. . . . Charles Reilly plays Frump, the nephew, like Mephistopheles on needles. His comedy is broad, his gestures are cosmic, his behavior, the ultimate in sheer panic, abysmal despair, or chortling, evil glee. It is a major achievement in hilarious exaggeration.

HOWARD TAUBMAN, *Times*

It's an open question whether big business in America should be warier of trust busters than of this new musical. The antitrust watchdogs can crack a mean whip, but *How to Succeed* applies a gigantic hotfoot. It stings mischievously and laughs uproariously. Big business is not likely to be the same again; it will be so busy chuckling at its reflection in this impish mirror of a musical that it won't have time to do big business. But you can bet this show will. It belongs to the blue chips among modern musicals. Let Wall Street and Madison Avenue tremble as the rest of us rejoice. . . . Imagine a combination of Horatio Alger and Machiavelli and you have Finch, the intrepid young hero of this sortie into the canyons of commerce. As played with unfaltering bravura and wit by Robert Morse, he is a rumpled, dimpled angel with a streak of Lucifer. Butter couldn't melt in his mouth because he is so occupied spreading it on anyone who can help him up a wrung of that ladder you've heard about.

A second perfect musical from the Messrs. Loesser, Burrows, Feuer and Martin—although it wasn't quite so effortless an undertaking as the breezy results indicate. The reviewers were beside themselves with praise, and no wonder. *How to Succeed*'s magic centered on its razor-sharp portrait of the modern-day American go-getter of the post-Eisenhower era. J. Pierpont Finch (a grandnephew of *Of Thee I Sing*'s J. P. Wintergreen?) was "a combination of Horatio Alger and Machiavelli," with a dimple. While for many the stodgy *Camelot* (1960) has come to symbolize the Kennedy years, *How to Succeed* gets my vote. This was to be the remarkable Loesser's final Broadway score, following *Where's Charley?* (1948), *Guys and Dolls* (1950), *The Most Happy Fella* (1956), and *Greenwillow* (1960). A sixth attempt, *Pleasures and Palaces* (1965), staggered through four weeks in Detroit before giving up. Under the stewardship of Bob Fosse, this one was a comic costume operetta about Catherine The Great (!) with a libretto from Sam (*Kiss Me, Kate* [1948]) Spewack. When asked why musicals are so difficult to put together, Loesser answered: "I don't know; maybe because people keep secrets from each other. Especially choreographers."

Winner of the Pulitzer Prize for Drama, the fourth musical so honored (awarded to Loesser and Burrows—but not to Weinstock and Gilbert, who were replaced by Burrows). Winner of the New York Drama Critics' Circle Award. In addition to winning the Tony for Best Musical, Tonys were won by Abe Burrows, Jack Weinstock, and Willie Gilbert (librettists); Abe Burrows (director); Cy Feuer and Ernest H. Martin in association with Frank (Loesser) Productions, Inc. (producers); Robert Morse (actor); Charles Nelson Reilly (supporting actor); and Elliot Lawrence (musical director). Loesser lost the Best Composer Award to Richard Rodgers, for *No Strings*.

BROADWAY SCORECARD / perfs: 1,417 / $: +

rave	favorable	mixed	unfavorable	pan
7				

I CAN GET IT FOR YOU WHOLESALE

a musical drama, with music and lyrics by Harold Rome; book by Jerome Weidman, from Weidman's 1937 novel

directed by Arthur Laurents; choreographed by Herbert Ross
produced by David Merrick
with Elliott Gould, Sheree North, Lillian Roth, Harold Lang, Marilyn Cooper, Barbra Streisand, and Bambi Linn

opened March 22, 1962   Shubert Theatre

"Why do they call me Miss Marmelstein?" complains 19-year-old *Barbra Streisand, who's being driven positively psychosomatic by the drab appellation with which she is persistently, perpetually, continually, inevitably addressed. ("Pardon the big words I apply," she apologizes, "but I was an English major at C.C.N.Y.")* (costume by Theoni V. Aldredge, photo by Freidman-Abeles)

328

WALTER KERR, *Herald Tribune*

Momma, momma, momma, what a good solid show (the phrase is courtesy of one of Harold Rome's lyrics, the show is *I Can Get It For You Wholesale*, which you can get retail at the Shubert). It is unbelievable how much that is touching can come from a show that is essentially tough. . . . The result of the compounded courage [of the creators]: a restless, pushy, meticulously honest story that can stand on its own two feet and is perfectly well able to dance on them, too. What counts is the economy, the speed, the straightforwardness, and the unblinking vigor with which a highly original project, with a great amount of stick-to-itiveness, keeps its vision clear, its head and toes high, and both its musical and dramatic intentions honor-bright.

JOHN McCLAIN, *Journal-American*

It has as its hero a young man with the same insatiable drive as the Machiavellian Mr. Morse of the big hit around the corner [*How to Succeed in Business Without Really Trying* (1961)], but the trouble is he doesn't have the same charm or ingenuity, and hence he doesn't really succeed. The same can be said for the entire new musical. We don't, finally, care too much about the fate of this young hustler in his relentless pursuit of the easy dollar. Maybe if he didn't try so hard he might succeed. . . . Barbra Streisand, who plays a secretary and resembles an amiable ant-eater, has her moment in the sun with "Miss Marmelstein."

NORMAN NADEL, *World-Telegram & Sun*

Spring begins, and 48 hours later it's Christmas. The princely gift, deposited last night at the Shubert Theatre, is *I Can Get It For You Wholesale*. If this doesn't charm the ever-loving daylights out of New York, I don't know what will. This new musical play hits the audience in the heart sooner, more deeply, and far more frequently than most of the comic or serious plays to have opened this year. More times than you can count, you are touched to the point of tears, dissolved in tenderness, or excited to a state of breathlessness. Actually, you do not watch *I Can Get It For You Wholesale*. You are in it. As Harry, the guy on the make, Elliott Gould's voice, his face, and his lean body have a Mephisthophelean twist. He is all grace and charm, but he can't keep the devil down. His eyes glaze with ambition fired by evil. He moves like a cross between Harpo

Marx and a Flamenco dancer. Brooklyn's Erasmus Hall High School should call a half-day holiday to celebrate the success of its spectacular alumna, Barbra Streisand. As a secretary, she sets the show in motion and hypos it all the way. Her song, "Miss Marmelstein," earns an ovation.

HOWARD TAUBMAN, *Times*

The evening's find is Barbra Streisand, a girl with an oafish expression, a loud irascible voice, and an arpeggiated laugh. Miss Streisand is a natural comedienne, and Mr. Rome has given her a brash amusing song, "Miss Marmelstein."

RICHARD WATTS JR., *Post*

It makes a point of being sardonic and unsentimental, and I thought it provided as uningratiating an evening as you could well find. *Pal Joey* [1940] proved that it is possible to base a delightful musical comedy on the adventures of a heel; the main trouble with *Wholesale* is not that its central figure's ethics are non-existent but that, in Elliott Gould's realistic performance, he is so uninteresting and unattractive.

A controversial musical with a heel of an anti-hero. *Wholesale* was received in the same manner as the original production of *Pal Joey*: while some people recognized its importance, most were scared away. When *Joey* was revived in 1952, it was universally hailed as a masterpiece; *Wholesale* has remained neglected, despite Harold Rome's first-rate score. Elliot Gould—from the chorus of *Say, Darling* (1958) and *Irma La Douce* (1960)—and Streisand were married shortly after *Wholesale* closed.

BROADWAY SCORECARD / perfs: 300 / $: −

rave	favorable	mixed	unfavorable	pan
2		1	2	2

I HAD A BALL

a Coney Island musical comedy, with music and lyrics by Jack
Lawrence and Stan Freeman; book by Jerome Chodorov

directed by Lloyd Richards; choreographed by Onna White
produced by Joseph Kipness
with Buddy Hackett, Richard Kiley, and Karen Morrow

opened December 15, 1964   Martin Beck Theatre

WALTER KERR, *Herald Tribune*

Hackett isn't human, exactly. He is more like a baked potato out
for a short stroll. Miss Morrow has what is called a "show voice,"
which means that you don't talk back to it, and she has a zany fire
in her eye. The score by Jack Lawrence and Stan Freeman is
beyond doubt the kind that sounds better louder. Softer, you might
hear it. It should be noted, too, that "Falling in Love with Love,"
even at an extremely agitated tempo, still sounds like "Falling in
Love with Love."

JOHN MCCLAIN, *Journal-American*

It seems there is this very handsome young man who has been
graduated summa cum laude and Phi Beta Kappa from Cornell
University and so naturally, after a few years, he winds up hawking
toy dogs on the Coney Island midway. . . . It is called *I Had a Ball*
but I'm afraid I didn't.

NORMAN NADEL, *World-Telegram & Sun*

With Buddy Hackett, Richard Kiley, and Karen Morrow on our
side, who needs to be first on the moon?

An old-fashioned "star comic" musical, done in by strong competition and weak material.

BROADWAY SCORECARD / perfs: 199 / $: −

rave	favorable	mixed	unfavorable	pan
1		2	3	

IF THE SHOE FITS

a musical comedy, with music by David Raskin; lyrics by June (Sillman) Carroll; book by June Carroll and Robert Duke, based on the fairy tale "Cinderella"

production supervised by Leonard Sillman; book directed by Eugene Bryden; choreographed by Charles Weidman
produced by Leonard Sillman
with Florence Desmond, Leila Ernst, and Joe Besser

opened December 5, 1946   New Century Theatre

BROOKS ATKINSON, *Times*

The score consists of one of the most continuous unpleasant sounds of our times, as if the music had been incorrectly transcribed by an organized gang of imps [orchestrations by Robert Russell Bennett].

JOHN CHAPMAN, *Daily News*

There is some very nice scenery at the New Century Theatre. There also is some very nice scenery in Central Park, nearby. Since the park is free and they are asking money at the Century, it is reasonable to expect something in addition to the view. This something in addition is a musical comedy titled *If the Shoe Fits*. I was there last night and I wished I were in the park, where the risk of mugging is not so great. Leonard Sillman's production is a witless and offensive affair which has the effrontery to dirty up the fairy story about Cinderella. . . . The fairy-tale backgrounds turn like the pages of a child's pop-up book, with the various scenes popping up as the pages swing. These settings are by Edward Gilbert, and besides being mechanically ingenious they are delightfully decorative. I won't go into the book by June Carroll and Robert Duke, and they shouldn't have, either. Mr. Sillman, an incurable amateur of the stage, should be spanked, made to wash his mouth with soap, put to bed, and cautioned not to go near the professional theatre again.

WILLIAM HAWKINS, *World-Telegram*

A flavorless Mother Goose-burger.

A rather fanciful Cinderella, Prince, and slipper adorn this music cover. The show itself, though, was tasteless in the extreme. (drawing by Vertès)

LOUIS KRONENBERGER, *PM*

Possibly on the theory that most musicals only end up re-telling the Cinderella story anyhow, *If the Shoe Fits* has gone straight back to Cinderella herself. This maneuver saved the librettists time, but a lot of time has been wasted for all that. The show is decidedly dull, and as lacking in taste as in liveliness. The librettists have not, to be sure, made the mistake of telling the simple old nursery tale straight. They have made the far worse mistake (in view of their talents) of spoofing it. The music, for the most part, consists of things that, far from being able to hum, I'd never in a million years be able to recognize.

The remarkable scenery created the illusion of a child's storybook, with painted scrims that bled through to reveal full, three-dimensional settings. The scrims would fly up, revealing the next scene as in a pop-up book, or travel off sideways giving the illusion of turning pages. If the sets were magical, the show was anything but.

A special Tony Award was won by T. A. MacDonald for constructing the scenery, the only set builder so honored.

BROADWAY SCORECARD / perfs: 20 / $: −

rave	favorable	mixed	unfavorable	pan
				8

INSIDE U.S.A.

a musical revue, with music by Arthur Schwartz; lyrics by Howard Dietz; sketches by Arnold Auerbach, Moss Hart, and Arnold B. Horwitt, "suggested by John Gunther's famous book"

directed by Robert H. Gordon; choreographed by Helen Tamiris
produced by Arthur Schwartz
with Beatrice Lillie, Jack Haley, and Valerie Bettis

opened April 30, 1948   Century Theatre

BROOKS ATKINSON, *Times*

If you want to be pedantic about it, most of the material inside *Inside U.S.A.* is not distinguished. But you will hardly notice that. All the way through the craftsmanship is keen and impeccable. As musical shows go, it is a thoroughbred that represents the best brains in our showshop. Since everyone knows that B. Lillie is a genius, there is no point in offering that as a discovery. She radiates wit whenever she comes popping on the stage with her jumpy walk, smiling in a sort of bogus embarrassment. Fantastically costumed and always underplaying with great eloquence, Miss Lillie turns every one of [her sketches] into hard-surfaced burlesque. With a sharp face, piercing eyes, a thin, almost shy grin, and only an occasional gesture, Miss Lillie translates everything into the most deliberate and intelligent wit that illuminates the musical stage of our day.

JOHN CHAPMAN, *Daily News*

What this country needs is more Beatrice Lillies—and the new revue, *Inside U.S.A.*, is mighty lucky to have the only one there is. Without her, it would be a pretty good show; with her, it is a whole lot better. Miss Lillie can make anything funny—absolutely anything, including *Medea*, I'll bet. It is the Lady Beatrice who makes the show. As a mermaid on Plymouth Rock, as a queen of the Mardi Gras, or as a maid in a stage star's dressing room, she is incomparable. She is funny, even as an Indian in Albuquerque who, with Mr. Haley as a fellow tribesman, declines the country people are always trying to give back to the Indians. She is a great clown and she is a great humorist. This country should make her the Forty-ninth State. . . . It is not as accurate as Mr. Gunther's book, for the lyrist, Howard Dietz, maintains that the Grand Canyon is in Colorado.

WILLIAM HAWKINS, *World-Telegram*

With Miss Lillie's exploitation of classical composers things begin to move like a toboggan. In this sketch she satirizes the moving picture conception of beautiful girls who inspire great music. It is uproarious, and the Lillie art of howling the house down with a faint smirk or twitch comes into full play. She later tells what it feels like to be a mermaid, pays a magnificent tribute to New Orleans's Mardi Gras, then tops everything else with her outra-

Beatrice Lillie as a Massachusetts Mermaid. Pilgrims beware! (set by
Lemuel Ayers, costume by Castillo, photo by Graphic House)

geous behavior as a theatre maid on a star's opening night. Miss Lillie wanders about in shoes that look more like leather bibs than anything else, and wraps the audience around her finger every time she shrugs. She is at her handsome best, and nothing more need be said.

A second "travelogue" revue for Bea Lillie, following up her earlier Dietz and Schwartz hit *At Home Abroad* (1935). *Inside U.S.A.* was less than impressive, but what did it matter with "Lady Beatrice"— who was, in fact, married to one Lord Peel—on hand?

Donaldson Awards were won by Valerie Bettis (female debut; female dancer).

BROADWAY SCORECARD / perfs: 339 / $: +

rave	favorable	mixed	unfavorable	pan
5	3			

IOLANTHE

the 1882 comic operetta, with music by Arthur Sullivan; book and lyrics by W. S. Gilbert

directed by Robert Gibson
produced by the D'Oyly Carte Opera Company
with Joyce Wright, Ann Drummond-Grant, and Peter Pratt

opened September 17, 1955   Sam S. Shubert Theatre

WALTER KERR, *Herald Tribune*

It must be distracting to play Gilbert and Sullivan. The singers are required, by the attractive conventions of this sort of spoof, to face directly front for a good part of the evening. And what they are looking at is a whole houseful of customers playing the show right back at them. At the Shubert Tuesday evening, I'd say that some four to five hundred happy playgoers were mouthing the lyrics with remarkable precision, virtually dictating—with a kind of mass nod of their heads—the proper emphases for the good folk on stage. Another four to five hundred were busy conducting the orchestra with such finesse and understanding that Isidore Godfrey might have dropped his baton, stepped into the alley for a cigarette, and been replaced in the pit at a moment's notice. The remaining onlookers were, I believe, taking pictures.

BROADWAY SCORECARD / perfs: 7 / $: NA

rave	favorable	mixed	unfavorable	pan
5	1			1

IRMA LA DOUCE

a French musical comedy, with music by Marguerite Monnot; book and lyrics by Alexandre Breffort, as adapted for the London stage by Julian More, David Heneker, and Monty Norman

directed by Peter Brook; choreographed by Onna White
produced by David Merrick in association with Donald Albery and H. M. Tennent, Ltd.
with Elizabeth Seal, Keith Michell, and Clive Revill

opened September 29, 1960   Plymouth Theatre

FRANK ASTON, *World-Telegram & Sun*

Elizabeth Seal's a honey. She is a dancer who does splits in midair at 90 miles an hour. She is 90 pounds of vivacity, blackclad legs, teeth, vigor and sex.

JOHN CHAPMAN, *Daily News*

There won't be a more captivating new musical on Broadway all this season than *Irma La Douce*. There will be bigger and grander shows, with stars and writers whose very names will spell Success, but I don't see how any of them can top this one for wit, charm,

"Irma la Douce, *the girl who helps all Paris to relax—for just a thousand francs, including tax.*" Producer Merrick placed these placards in taxicabs, enticing tourists toward the Plymouth Theatre.

impudence, and theatrical skill. . . . Miss Seal is the only girl present, and it would be silly to have any more.

WALTER KERR, *Herald Tribune*

Elizabeth Seal is playing and singing and dancing a Parisian *poule* (chicken, street-walker) who is lucky enough to be doing the work she loves, and when this will-o'-the-wisp wench is smartly rapping her ankle against a bar, or making impossibly melodic sounds with little more than her tongue, or sending the whole of Montmartre into a rhythmic itch during a spinning gala called "*Dis-Donc*" she convinces you that there is nothing left for you in life but to wrap her up and take her home, southern-fried. The music, too, has a curious late-riverboat or early music-hall magic about it. Marguerite Monnot, who has devised the tunes that sound so well on a xylophone and tissue-paper piano, seems just to have discovered the squarish beat that once set the world to wiggling in ragtime, and the strange jelly-roll sounds that come from the pit, and stir such jumping-jack animation in the principals on stage, are irresistibly jolly. If an original-cast album is made available in your neighborhood, get it.

JOHN McCLAIN, *Journal-American*

A socko success.

RICHARD WATTS JR., *Post*

It would deserve acclaim if only because it introduces to American audiences a wonderful girl named Elizabeth Seal, a young English actress, singer, and dancer who is a joy and a treasure and mustn't be allowed to leave us. There are, however, other reasons for enthusiasm over *Irma La Douce*. Since it has to do with the romance between a Paris prostitute and a young fellow who is, among other things, a procurer, and is filled with underworld characters and corrupt policemen, it may not represent the height of morality and will probably raise a few eyebrows. But its mixture of cynicism and romance is managed with such paradoxical charm, and Miss Seal gives it so enchanting an air of innocence, that it all seems delightfully warm-hearted.

☆

David Merrick's romance with "French" shows—*Fanny* (1954), *La Plume de Ma Tante* (1958), *Becket* (1960)—brought forth this giddily Parisian musical. Intimate, inventive (Peter Brook) and endearing, *Irma* was a jewel of a show. And that British *gamin* Elizabeth Seal (born in Genoa, Italy, actually) received the best set of notices since Gwen Verdon swept into town doing a *Can-Can* (1953).

A Tony Award was won by Elizabeth Seal (actress).

```
BROADWAY SCORECARD / perfs: 524 / $: +

rave    favorable    mixed    unfavorable    pan

 4          3
```

JACKPOT

a musical comedy, with music by Vernon Duke; lyrics by Howard Dietz; book by Guy Bolton, Sidney Sheldon, and Ben Roberts

directed by Roy Hargrave; choreographed by Loretta Jefferson; ballet choreographed by Charles Weidman
produced by Vinton Freedley
with Allan Jones, Jerry Lester, Benny Baker, Nanette Fabray, Mary Wickes, and Betty Garrett

opened January 13, 1944   Alvin Theatre

LOUIS KRONENBERGER, *PM*

There are few safe bets on Broadway, but a Vinton Freedley musical is usually one of them. Consequently *Jackpot* is something to sit through in amazement. It is a complete frost, an unmitigated bore, an ocean-crossing of tedium. The completeness of the disaster is hard to understand, seeing how many talented and experienced people are mixed up in it. One or two of them, you would think, might have taken a stand. But there is almost nothing in the music to make you forget the book, and less yet in the dancing to make you enjoy the music. The comics work their heads off, and are not funny. The chorus forms and reforms, and is not beguiling.

The costumes lack oomph. The lyrics lack cleverness. There isn't much you can do except look at Nanette Fabray—who is still a stunner—when she is on the stage, and snooze quietly when she is off.

Burton Rascoe, *World-Telegram*

With every number it sounds as though Mr. Duke had got a melody that was very good, but didn't know how to develop it melodically, with any rhythmic or tonal carry-through. After from four to eight bars the melody may break abruptly into a queer, unrelated theme in another key, often an octave lower and flatted so that the singer seems to be talking rather than singing. Or Mr. Duke will take a melody almost exactly like that of some recent very popular song, repeat it a couple of times and then go off into something that sounds like an eccentricity by Eric Satie or Darius Milhaud. With music like that to compose lyrics for, it is no wonder that Howard Dietz's verses are often banal and silly, with rhymes such as "triumph" with "my oomph."

Wilella Waldorf, *Post*

It is a very depressing sensation to charge into the Alvin Theatre ready to be rendered hysterical by the new Vinton Freedley musical show, *Jackpot*, and realize around the middle of the first act that you are slowly petrifying with boredom. As far as we know, there are no rules of etiquette to cover such an emergency. Is it better to go quietly off to sleep, hoping that things will pick up later on, or should one titter frantically and applaud with spurious warmth as the proceedings become more and more funereal? There were times last night when we decided it was all going on via a phonograph record, and the record was stuck. People kept cracking the same dull, sexy jokes, and nearly every time we happened to glance at the stage Marine Private Jerry Lester or Marine Private Benny Baker was being hugged by a female, or was trying not to be hugged by a female, or was hugging a female. Every now and then the hugging would be interrupted while Allan Jones sang a serious song about love, flanked by a sturdy quartet of fellow Marines. Nearly everybody seemed to be in the Marine Corps. Even Betty Garrett. . . . It is now apparently a rule that any Broadway musical comedy costing over $50,000 must feature (1) a ballet by Agnes de Mille, or (2) a take-off on a ballet by Agnes de Mille.

Jackpot has a take-off entitled "Grist for de Mille," staged by Charles Weidman. Like the rest of the show it is neither very good nor very bad, just mediocre.

Who was producer Vinton Freedley, who seems to have let everybody down so? A song-and-dance man in the first George and Ira Gershwin musical (the out-of-town flop *A Dangerous Maid* [1921]), Freedley joined with Alex A. Aarons to produce the second Gershwin Bros. musical, *Lady Be Good* (1924), starring Adele and Fred Astaire. There followed a string of Gershwin hits, including *Oh, Kay!* (1926), *Funny Face* (1927)—which opened the Al(ex)/Vin(ton) Theatre—and *Girl Crazy* (1930). But everything, including the Alvin, was lost in the Depression. Freedley bounced back without Aarons and Gershwin, producing several Porter hits including *Anything Goes* (1934) and *Red, Hot and Blue!* (1936). But after Vernon Duke's *Cabin in the Sky* (1940), Freedley lost his touch. *Jackpot* was preceded by Mary Martin's first bid at stardom, *Dancing in the Streets* (1943), a Duke/Dietz show which danced itself out on Tremont Street in Boston. Freedley's final musical, *Great to Be Alive!* (1950), was a haunted house mishap starring Vivienne Segal. It was so bland that the critics had nothing interesting to say about it, and neither to I.

BROADWAY SCORECARD / perfs: 69 / $: —

rave	favorable	mixed	unfavorable	pan
			2	6

JAMAICA

a musical comedy, with music by Harold Arlen; lyrics by E. Y. Harburg; book by E. Y. Harburg and Fred Saidy

directed by Robert Lewis; choreographed by Jack Cole
produced by David Merrick
with Lena Horne, Ricardo Montalban, Adelaide Hall, Josephine Premice, and Ossie Davis

opened October 31, 1957   Imperial Theatre

FRANK ASTON, *World-Telegram & Sun*

The production has glitter in depth, indicating no one worried much over expenses; but it seems that someone, with the best of intentions, ended up with a grand and glittering goof. The audience spends a couple of hours watching the natives bounding about in brown grace, hearing them sing, and listening to the humor of what is supposed to be their childlike concept of government, mushroom clouds, fine clothes, fidelity, infidelity, love, and John Foster Dulles. Thank goodness for that Horne girl.

BROOKS ATKINSON, *Times*

It gives Mr. Arlen an opportunity to add calypso to the blues, and it gives Lena Horne a number of opportunities to make songs strut, snarl, croon, laugh, and rhapsodize. As the lyric writer, Mr. Harburg has not tried to dazzle anyone in particular. His rhyming style is relaxed and genial. Everyone is in a pleasant mood because everyone is the master of his genre and does not feel under the necessity of proving it. Mr. Arlen seems to be writing tunes at leisure, and Miss Horne sings them without feeling that she must sell them. It is professional work in every department and most enjoyable, too.

JOHN CHAPMAN, *Daily News*

It becomes a series of musical numbers by Harold Arlen, all of which are in the calypso mood. They are, many of them, good numbers with bright lyrics, but there is a sameness to their form and beat which makes them wearisome to me. Before the evening ended I was longing to hear just one fragment of another kind of native music—the stuff turned out by the crazy tribe which inhabits Tin Pan Alley. . . . Miss Horne is a girl on the island and Montalban is a bare-chested boy. That is about all there is to the plot, except that a hurricane strikes the islet and the inhabitants discover that a fish to eat is worth more than a pearl to wear. Indeed, there is more social significance than sexual significance in *Jamaica*—and this is doing a musical plot the hard way.

ROBERT COLEMAN, *Daily Mirror*

A hurricane named Lena (Horne) blew into the Imperial Theatre Thursday night, and proceeded to provoke some of the

Tempestuous Hurricane Lena displays her teeth. "Probably the most beautiful woman in the world," reported Richard Watts Jr., "and it is sheer critical cowardice to stick in that weaseling word 'probably.'" (costume by Miles White, photo by Friedman-Abeles)

stormiest applause heard hereabouts in quite a spell. She brought in her wake a tempestuous musical titled *Jamaica*. To watch her on stage is like following the hypnotic movements of a brilliant flame. She is our idea of a definition for incandescent. She's alluring, sinuous, and magnetic. La Lena can make a mediocre line shimmer with meaning. She can take a song like "Take It Slow, Joe," and make it sizzle so that you wonder if the Fire Department isn't on its way. And that spells artistry, in our language. She's great—real great. . . . *Jamaica* bowed into the Imperial with an advance sale of close to $2,000,000. And no wonder. For, with Skipper Horne at the helm, it spells theatre—for that matter, box-office—magic. It's a grand gale of gala entertainment. In our book, another triumph for producer David Merrick.

WALTER KERR, *Herald Tribune*

Jamaica is the kind of musical that leads you to wonder whether it was produced simply because all concerned had such high, happy hopes for the original cast album. As she sings, she is going to make you forget that she has a very small voice for a very big theatre, and that she is being put to work every minute on the minute to keep the dialogue from intruding more than two lines at a time. Miss Horne is, at a most modest estimate, an enchantress. She stands lithe as a willow at the center of the stage, sucks in her breath as though she were inhaling a windstorm, and coos out the most improbable series of mating-pigeon sounds. I can't tell you why her "Take It Slow, Joe" arches over the auditorium like a long, taut faintly quivering suspension-bridge, but it does. There is a show of satire lurking behind the grass-roofed huts, with no fewer than four E. Y. Harburg lyrics dedicated to preserving the social significance that was so stimulating in the thirties and is so uncomfortable now. Mr. Harburg is, as every one knows, an absolutely dandy lyricist when he is being lyrical: the "crickets doin' nip-ups around the columbine" is in his vein. But there are an enormous number of rhymes involving barbituates, cyclotrons, *Anna Lucasta*, and the fact that we may all soon "be fissionable material," and I suspect that the title of one of these forays—"Leave the Atom Alone"—might well have been taken more seriously. . . . The question is: can you make a whole show out of sheet music?

RICHARD WATTS JR., *Post*

What difference does it make that *Jamaica* has an especially feeble book? The exotic new musical play has the stunning beauty and thrilling voice of Lena Horne. Miss Horne is probably the most beautiful woman in the world, and it is sheer critical cowardice to stick in that weascling word, "probably." But she happens to be considerably more than a great beauty. With her grace, her lithe dignity, her quiet humor, her curious combination of sullenness and sweetness, and her enormous and stirring skill at projecting a song for everything that is in it, if not a little more, she is one of the incomparable performers of our time.

David Merrick followed *Fanny* (1954) with *Jamaica*, another mediocre musical huckstered into a hit. Unlike its heavily ponderous predecessor, *Jamaica* was noticeably light on matter; E. Y. Harburg was so irate about the de-satirization of his libretto, in fact, that he refused to attend the opening! None of this mattered, though. Merrick had Lena Horne to sell, and sell he did.

BROADWAY SCORECARD / Perfs: 555 / $: +				
rave	favorable	mixed	unfavorable	pan
3	1	2	1	

JENNIE

a musical biography of Laurette Taylor (1884–1946), with music by Arthur Schwartz; lyrics by Howard Dietz; book by Arnold Schulman, from the 1955 biography *Laurette* by Marguerite Taylor Courtney

directed by Vincent J. Donehue; choreographed by Matt Mattox (replacing Carol Haney)
produced by Cheryl Crawford and Richard Halliday
with Mary Martin (Halliday), George Wallace (replacing Dennis O'Keefe), Robin Bailey, and Ethel Shutta

opened October 17, 1963   Majestic Theatre

Mary (upper right) reaches out to save baby from a plunge over the falls, while George Wallace of the Mounties stands by tied to a tree (lower left). The scenery was a whole lot more interesting than the show. (set by George Jenkins, costumes by Irene Sharaff, photo by Friedman-Abeles)

Mary Martin

AS

Jennie

A NEW MUSICAL

LYRICS BY

HOWARD DIETZ AND **ARTHUR SCHWARTZ**

MUSIC BY

BOOK BY

ARNOLD SCHULMAN

SUGGESTED BY "LAURETTE" BY MARGUERITE COURTNEY
BY ARRANGEMENT WITH ALAN J. PAKULA

ENTIRE PRODUCTION DIRECTED BY

VINCENT J. DONEHUE

CHOREOGRAPHY BY

MATT MATTOX

ALSO STARRING

George Wallace

WITH

ETHEL SHUTTA   JACK DE LON   IMELDA DE MARTIN   JEREMIAH MORRIS   CONNIE SCOTT

AND

Robin Bailey

SETTINGS DESIGNED BY
GEORGE JENKINS

COSTUMES DESIGNED BY
IRENE SHARAFF

LIGHTING BY
JEAN ROSENTHAL

MUSICAL DIRECTOR
JOHN LESKO

ORCHESTRATIONS BY
PHILIP J. LANG

ROBERT RUSSELL BENNETT

DANCE MUSIC AND
VOCAL ARRANGEMENTS BY
TRUDE RITTMAN

WALTER KERR, *Herald Tribune*

Imagine having Mary Martin play an entire show with the corners of her mouth down! It's like using the moon not to make love by. Poor brave Mary. She is brave in and out of character. In character, as a young mother roaming the tank-towns at the turn of the century in the claptrap melodramas dear to the period, she is to be seen suffering nightly, suffering from White Slavers, suffering from roaring waterfalls, suffering from great grisly bears. The last time we observed her being tied to the scenery she is a prisoner of The Sultan, who has strapped her fair form to a kind of revolving weenie-roast, with cobras streaking their tongues at her each time she goes by. And each time she goes by, she shakes her canary-blonde head to cry out, in that refined baritone we have come to know and love as her voice, "I won't tell, I won't tell, I won't tell!" She won't tell the sultan what he wants to know, and, steadfast girl that she is, she'll probably never tell the rest of us why she did *Jennie*, either. (For *Jennie* is a woeful tale of some woeful people told in a woeful way.) There is nothing you want for this musical comedy heroine except a moment's peace and some other musical comedy. The gestures are noble, the mood is fraught, and the songs can sing about the sun and the stars as much as they wish without really making a dent on the overcast. Miss Martin forever, but not as Jennie.

HOWARD TAUBMAN, *Times*

For more years than a gentleman should mention my heart has belonged to Mary Martin. But *Jennie* does not make it easy to remain faithful. Not that Miss Martin has lost her luster. She can still communicate good feeling with the radiance of an angel. She can still sing joyously and step lightly and gaily. She can still read a bright line with a flourish and a treacly one as if she believed in it. And she continues to make a game and resourceful trouper, willing to do an impossible backbend while being carried aloft, and game enough to let herself be whirled head over heels on a torture wrack and come up smiling and belting out a top note. The trouble is not with Miss Martin but with the saga she has given her heart to. . . . For the first melodrama George Jenkins has designed a set that's more amusing than any line in *Jennie*. A vast waterfall towers over us, and the real water that tumbles down its precipices only emphasizes the fact that it's made of can-

vas and lumber. Miss Martin as the heroic Melissa seeks to recover her baby from the evil Chang Lu, who puts the basket with
the infant into the roaring torrent. Miss Martin is delightful at
this sort of fooling. With a grand gesture she perches on the limb
of a tree, which obligingly lowers her. As the pit band throbs
silent movie music, she clutches the child. Then a bear threatens
her, but the Royal Mountie tears off the ropes that bind him and
shoots the beast, who brings his paws to his heart fatalistically
just as he falls.

RICHARD WATTS JR., *Post*

The indomitable Mary Martin can hurl a knife into the back of a
rascally Chinese, vanquish a bear, rescue a baby from a mountain
stream, defy a sultan and his eunuchs in his harem, scorn a den of
serpents, and remain imperturbable while being twisted about on
a spit. When *Jennie* confronts her with such minor ordeals, she is
unconquerable but the accompanying libretto presents difficulties
insurmountable for even her boldly adventurous spirit.

Cheryl Crawford and her pal Mary Martin had been looking for
a show to do together since their success with *One Touch of Venus* (1943). They found it (?), and Mary turned down *Dolly* and
Fanny (Brice) to do *Jennie*. (Judy Holliday's nonmusical stage bio
Laurette [1960] had closed on the road, so they changed the heroine's name. For luck?) Mary and husband/co-producer Richard
Halliday brought in Mary's pet director Vincent J. Donehue, battled viciously with songwriters Schwartz and Dietz, and the result was another one of those "can't miss" fiascos with huge
advance sales. To quote Miss Martin: "It all got very tacky." And
very ugly.

	rave	favorable	mixed	unfavorable	pan
		1	1	2	2

BROADWAY SCORECARD / perfs: 82 / $: −

JOHN MURRAY ANDERSON'S ALMANAC

a musical revue, with music and lyrics by Richard Adler and Jerry Ross and others; sketches by various writers

devised and staged by John Murray Anderson; sketches directed by Cyril Ritchard; choreographed by Donald Saddler
produced by Michael Grace, Stanley Gilkey, and Harry Rigby
with Hermione Gingold, Billy De Wolfe, Harry Belafonte, Polly Bergen, and Orson Bean

opened December 10, 1953   Imperial Theatre

BROOKS ATKINSON, *Times*

Let's give Anderson a vote of thanks for presenting Harry Belafonte with respect. Mr. Belafonte sings several numbers with an impassive sincerity that is stirring. One of them, a river ballad called "Mark Twain" [music and lyrics by Belafonte], is a masterpiece; and Mr. Belafonte's expository style as a singer and actor makes it the *Almanac*'s high point in theatrical artistry.

JOHN CHAPMAN, *Daily News*

Best of the sketches is one called "Don Brown's Body," by Jean Kerr, wife of Walter F. Kerr, drama critic of the Herald Tribune. Since Mr. Kerr might be a little bashful about praising his spouse in his own paper, I offer her some praise for her scrapbook in my own little publication. Mrs. Kerr's sketch is what a revue sketch should be—funny, ridiculous, and observant. It is a Mickey Spillane thriller told in the manner of *John Brown's Body* [director Charles Laughton's 1953 snob hit, a staged reading with Tyrone Power, Judith Anderson, and Raymond Massey], with all the folderol about the actors pretending to read and a chorus putting in side remarks. This number leads me to believe that Mrs. Kerr may be as good a drama critic as her old man is.

WILLIAM HAWKINS, *World-Telegram & Sun*

Miss Gingold as an intoxicating Victorian temptress is outrageously, uniquely funny. She is bitter but winning as a couple of ancient dames, and impertinently hilarious as a cellist. It is a wild, incisive, decapitating sense of humor, combined with a Miss America figure, and an elfin face like a lady jack-o-lantern. Her humor is served like droplets of hydrochloric acid, and her air is of villainous innocence.

WALTER KERR, *Herald Tribune*

Mr. Anderson has been pacing, pointing, and polishing other people's revues for a good many years. His trademark—except when he was drilling elephants for Barnum & Bailey—has always been a slick, smart simplicity. Now that he's been given his own show to ringmaster, he betrays a marked affection for limpid corn, and I didn't know he had it in him. . . . You will also find a couple of sketches by my wife.

JOHN McCLAIN, *Journal-American*

I was delighted by two sketches written by Jean Kerr, the wife of a fellow critic. (What does *my* wife do all afternoon?)

A Tony Award was won by Harry Belafonte (supporting actor). Donaldson Awards were won by Harry Belafonte (supporting actor); Hermione Gingold (female debut); and Billy De Wolfe (male debut).

BROADWAY SCORECARD / perfs: 227 / $: −

rave	favorable	mixed	unfavorable	pan
1	3	2	1	

JUNO

a musical drama, with music and lyrics by Marc Blitzstein; book by Joseph Stein, from the 1924 Irish play *Juno and the Paycock* by Sean O'Casey; previously announced as *Daarlin' Man*

directed by José Ferrer (replacing Tony Richardson and Vincent J. Donehue); choreographed by Agnes de Mille
produced by The Playwrights' Company, Oliver Smith, and Oliver Rea

Juno (Shirley Booth), Captain Boyle (Melvyn Douglas), and an unidentified tabby do a jig to "Music in the House." Pre-Broadway Credits. (drawing by David Klein)

with Shirley Booth, Melvyn Douglas, Jack MacGowran, Jean Stapleton (replacing Jane Rose), Monte Amundsen, Tommy Rall, and Sada Thompson

opened March 9, 1959   Winter Garden Theatre

BROOKS ATKINSON, *Times*

Juno begins with an overwhelming dance, song, and dramatic incident. Marc Blitzstein, Agnes de Mille, and Joseph Stein have managed to concentrate in one introductory scene the bitterness of O'Casey's *Juno and the Paycock*—the stealth, hatred, and tyranny, the uselessness of a political murder, the agony of the mother whose son has been slaughtered. "We're Alive" is the title of the bold song Mr. Blitzstein has written for the prologue. It epitomizes the terrible strength and fury of the O'Casey drama on which the musical has been based. Since *Juno* has a great theme, and since it is the season's first musical with a high purpose, it would be pleasant to report that the whole work has the distinction of that powerful prologue. But it seems to this theatregoer that *Juno* alternates between vigorous scenes and commonplaces. *Juno* is more earthbound than *Juno and the Paycock*. As a musical work, it does not have the drive, the scorn, and the fury of the play.

JOHN CHAPMAN, *Daily News*

A most impressive piece of modern musical theatre. *Juno* takes a bold and intelligent step away from Broadway formula to present an intense story which, for all its great incidental humor, is a tragic and bitter one. It is less impressive lyrically, for it fails to follow O'Casey, who is perhaps the only man alive who can write a song without ever needing music. The book and the lyrics are so busy with the details of a most touching story that they haven't the time or the art to make songs as O'Casey did, just by telling a tale with simple and beautiful words. All I wish is that O'Casey could have written the book, lyrics, and music of *Juno*.

WALTER KERR, *Herald Tribune*

Where is one to find an air for that peculiar and breathtaking combination of hilarious blarney and stabbing pathos that O'Casey once passed as a theatrical miracle? *Juno* comes to it at least twice. Early in the second act a gaudily-painted phonograph has set a whole Dublin tenement rocking on its heels and skipping under bridges to the tune of a "Liffey Waltz" only to have its abandon stopped cold by the entrance of a widow on the way to her son's funeral. Just a moment later, as a trail of keening women straggles toward church against an iron-gray sky, the lone and forlorn fellow who has been responsible for his buddy's death steps to the center of the stage. With fire in his eye and no real hope in his heart, he decides that he will still stomp the earth into some sound of gayety ["Johnny"]. Tommy Rall's frantic feet now flail and stammer at happier rhythms; choreographer Agnes de Mille gives him a bewildered girl or two to clutch at; and the simultaneous presence of tippling meter and mournful mood is achieved.

An ambitious attempt which probably would have failed even without the flaws. There's some remarkably powerful music from Mr. Blitzstein, though.

BROADWAY SCORECARD / perfs: 16 / $: −

rave	favorable	mixed	unfavorable	pan
	1	3	3	

KEAN

a musical biography of Edmund Kean (1787–1833), with music and lyrics by Robert Wright and George Forrest; book by Peter Stone, from Jean-Paul Sartre's 1953 adaptation of the 1836 drama by Alexandre Dumas

directed and choreographed by Jack Cole
produced by Robert Lantz (and Alfred Drake)
with Alfred Drake, Lee Venora, Oliver Gray, Joan Weldon, and Patricia Cutts

opened November 2, 1961   Broadway Theatre

WALTER KERR, *Herald Tribune*

Kean is an enormously ambitious entertainment filled with songs, philosophy, a search for identity, low comedy, swordplay, jugglers, Hamlet, Romeo, Othello, Hogarth, red plush, feathers, and stereophonic sound from the back of the house. In all of this, alas, the only thing that ever really begins to happen is Alfred Drake. Mr. Drake's natural equipment would stagger even the men who have been responsible for cramming the cauldron that gradually becomes a witches' brew at the Broadway. The star is perfectly capable of all the rococo posturing, and the dining upon cardboard scenery, that Alexandre Dumas [originally] cooked up. He is in possession, further, of the darkness of mien and the darkness of soul that Jean-Paul Sartre asked for when he turned Dumas's *Kean* into an existentialist *Kean* of his own. The additional burden of supporting an exceptional number of tunes—some of them exceedingly irrelevant, most of them prosaically phrased—adds fat, but not too much zest, to the proceedings. Mr. Drake can, of course, handle these with ease, too. No amount of singing, however, will bring any emotion to the licit and illicit love-knots that continued to ravel, unravel, and intertwine with so much coolness, so much indifference.

JOHN McCLAIN, *Journal-American*

Perhaps the expectations were too great, but the sad fact remains that *Kean* emerged last night with more pretention than promise. It is big, plush, sometimes amusing, often reminiscent, and constantly good to look at [scenic and costume design by Ed Wittstein]; but the team of Robert Wright and George Forrest has failed to produce a score of more than adequate dimensions, and Peter Stone's book gives us merely a troubled episode in the flamboyant career of the great Shakespearean actor. The story seems rarely to justify its resplendent mounting. In his closing speech Kean admits that he is merely a shadow, and in a sense he might have been talking about the show. It remains a diffuse image on a distant wall—decorative but dreary.

RICHARD WATTS JR., *Post*

Charles Lamb's famous line about Edmund Kean was that watching him play Shakespeare was like seeing the Bard through flashes of lightning. I thought there were few flashes of lightning in evidence at the Broadway Theatre last night. The new musical comedy is long, large, and elaborate, and Alfred Drake portrays the spectacular title role with all of his commanding vitality, but it seemed to me also heavy, ponderous, and strangely lacking excitement. A pall of heavy lethargy hangs over the elaborate production. Coming to New York after highly encouraging reports from out of town, *Kean* is a particular disappointment.

○○○
BROADWAY SCORECARD / perfs: 92 / $: −

rave	favorable	mixed	unfavorable	pan
1	1	2	3	

○○○

THE KING AND I

a musical drama, with music by Richard Rodgers; book and lyrics by Oscar Hammerstein 2nd, from the 1943 the biographical novel *Anna and the King of Siam* by Margaret Landon

directed by John van Druten (replaced by Oscar Hammerstein 2nd); choreographed by Jerome Robbins
produced by Richard Rodgers and Oscar Hammerstein 2nd
with Gertrude Lawrence, Yul Brynner, Dorothy Sarnoff, Doretta Morrow, and Larry Douglas

opened March 29, 1951   St. James Theatre

BROOKS ATKINSON, *Times*

It must be reported that *The King and I* is no match for *South Pacific* (1949), which was an inspired musical drama. But there is plenty of room for memorable music-making in the more familiar categories. Strictly on its own terms, *The King and I* is an original and beautiful excursion into the rich splendors of the Far East, done with impeccable taste by two artists and brought to life with a warm, romantic score, idiomatic lyrics, and some exquisite dancing. Don't expect another *South Pacific* nor an *Oklahoma!* [1943]. This time Mr. Rodgers and Mr. Hammerstein are not breaking any fresh trails. But they are accomplished artists of song and words in the theatre; and *The King and I* is a beautiful and lovable musical play.

RODGERS and HAMMERSTEIN
present
Gertrude
LAWRENCE
In A New Musical Play

The King and I

Music by
RICHARD RODGERS
Book and Lyrics by
OSCAR HAMMERSTEIN 2nd

Based on the Novel "Anna and the King of Siam" by
MARGARET LANDON
with
YUL · DOROTHY · MURVYN · DORETTA
BRYNNER · SARNOFF · VYE · MORROW

Directed by **JOHN van DRUTEN**
Choreography by **JEROME ROBBINS**
Settings and Lighting by **JO MIELZINER**
Costumes designed by **IRENE SHARAFF**

SHUBERT THEATRE BOSTON
Three Weeks Only!
BEGINNING TUESDAY, MARCH 6
Matinees: 1st Week Thursday and Saturday; Thereafter Wednesday and Saturday

No question about who's the star here; Yul Brynner is billed in smaller type than the choreographer! Murvyn Vye, who created Jigger in Carousel, *left during the tryout when his songs were cut and his role (The Kralahome) all but deleted. Pre-Broadway credits. (drawing by Stahlhut)*

JOHN CHAPMAN, *Daily News*

They have cut away from the usual music-show pattern once again and have achieved a very beautiful piece for the stage. It is beautifully set [by Jo Mielziner] and sumptuously, stunningly, excitingly costumed [by Irene Sharaff]. In it are some fine performances. In it is an enchanting ballet created by Jerome Robbins. In it is some interesting music. But the most important part of this big, long show is the work of Mr. Hammerstein as the librettist and lyrist. It is an intricate and expert piece of showmaking in which the story comes first—and the fine sets, the glorious costumes, the splendid cast, and the music are subordinate to this story. The visual highlight—and entertainment highlight—is a ballet representing the Siamese notion of how *Uncle Tom's Cabin* should be presented on a stage. It is a remarkable piece of work in which the dancers Yuriko and Michiko are outstanding, and in which the costuming by Irene Sharaff is notable. As a matter of truth, the costuming is notable from first to last.

OTIS L. GUERNSEY JR., *Herald Tribune*

This new show has everything that one has a right to expect of these talented collaborators, including a libretto that stands on its own merits, music that transposes emotion into melody, and a handsome production stylized according to a half-civilized, half-barbarous Eastern court. *The King and I* has not the masterpiece's brilliance, but it glows with its own softer lights of consistent entertainment. . . . Brynner manages to create a striking royal personality in an excellent performance. His impulsive yet pathetic monarch is the most vital element in the show, which almost always lets down a little when he is not on stage. Miss Lawrence sings her songs smoothly and maintains a stately, hoop-skirted demeanor in a role that is simply not as colorful as that of the prancing monarch.

JOHN McCLAIN, *Journal-American*

Miss Lawrence gave what I would regard as a thoroughly professional, though uninspired performance as Anna. It didn't quite seem that she was as carried away by the charm of the children and their prolific papa as she might have been. On the other hand, Mr. Brynner lent such strength and realism to his role that it became almost immediately acceptable that he should have a dozen wives,

scores of children, and still appear attractive in the eyes of a con-
servative lady of Western extraction.

RICHARD WATTS JR., *Post*

A show of rare quality. Unfairly but inevitably, everyone will
want to know if it is as good as *South Pacific,* and I will confess that
I don't suppose it is. But what is? The important thing is that *The
King and I* is a lovely and exciting achievement, of unusual taste
and imagination, and a great credit to its distinguished authors and
the American theatre. More than anything else, it is the perfect
taste, the wonderful atmospheric rightness, the high romantic
style, and the elusive air of sweetness that combine to make *The
King and I* an almost continuous joy. The score, I am forced to say,
didn't make the immediate impression on me that the songs in
South Pacific did, but it is none-the-less distinguished and impressive. There should be a special word for Mr. Brynner's notable
characterization of the King, with his brilliantly persuasive combination of ruthlessness and goodness, of the longing to be a pro-
gressive and modern monarch at war with the instinctive leaning
toward remaining a barbaric tyrant. Never does Mr. Brynner fall
into the facile way of being a dashing leading man putting on a
superficial Oriental masquerade. To an amazing extent, he gets
depth, honesty, and complete credibility into an authentic characterization of a man whose awakening mind and emotion are at
work.

The last of many ground-breaking musicals from Rodgers and/or
Hammerstein. An extra-lavish production made up for the general
sense of disappointment expressed in the reviews. *The King and I*
seems to have done all right, though. (Maybe critics were expecting a little too much?) The project had been brought to Rodgers
and Hammerstein by Gertrude Lawrence. A major Broadway star
since she stormed the town with Beatrice Lillie and Jack Buchanan
in the fabled *Charlot's Revue of 1924,* Lawrence hadn't appeared
in a musical since *Lady in the Dark* (1941). Part of the critical
disappointment stemmed from the feeling that Lawrence was
"holding back." As it turned out, she was ill: by the winter she was
missing shows with some frequency, and the quality of her perfor-

mance appears to have deteriorated. Rushed to the hospital after collapsing in her dressing room, Lawrence died of cancer on September 6, 1952. The role of the king, incidentally, was intended for Alfred Drake of *Oklahoma!* and *Kiss Me, Kate* (1948). Drake demanded $5,000 bucks a week, more than Broadway had ever paid anyone. He finally got his money from the producers of *Kismet* (1953), and proved well worth it. (Drake's only musical appearance between *Kate* and *Kismet*? A six-week stint subbing for vacationing King Brynner.)

In addition to winning the Tony Award for Best Musical, Tonys were won by Richard Rodgers (composer); Oscar Hammerstein 2nd (librettist); Rodgers and Hammerstein (producers); Gertrude Lawrence (actress); Yul Brynner (supporting actor); Jo Mielziner (scenic designer); and Irene Sharaff (costume designer). Donaldson Awards were won by Jerome Robbins (choreographer); Yul Brynner (actor); Doretta Morrow (supporting actress); Jo Mielziner (scenic designer); and Irene Sharaff (costume designer). For recreating his role in the 1956 motion picture version, Yul Brynner received an Oscar as Best Actor in a starring—as opposed to supporting—role.

BROADWAY SCORECARD / perfs: 1,246 / $: +

rave	favorable	mixed	unfavorable	pan
3	4			

THE KING AND I

a revival of the 1951 musical play

directed by John Fearnley; originally choreographed by Jerome Robbins, reproduced by Yuriko
produced by the New York City Center Light Opera Company (Jean Dalrymple)
with Farley Granger, Barbara Cook, and Anita Darian

opened May 11, 1960   City Center

FRANK ASTON, *World-Telegram & Sun*

These notes will attempt no comparisons. That would be looking back. As of last night's delightful opening there is only one way to look—straight at Barbara Cook with her pert septum and soothing larynx. When that youngster crosses she leaves the stage knee-deep in enchantment. Her charm overflows when she whistles down her fears, tells young lovers hello, bawls out an autocrat, gets to know the royal children, takes the autocrat's part, tries dictation prone, invites King Farley Granger to dance, and then whirls round and round Jo Mielziner's royal parlor with her skirts behaving like puffed pup tents.

BROOKS ATKINSON, *Times*

It may be no better than it was originally. But it sounds better. Musically, everything is as beautiful as Richard Rodgers's score deserves. With Pembroke Davenport conducting, the band gives the overture a clean and luminous performance that sets the standard for a remarkable evening. In the past, Barbara Cook has been playing provincial maidens—playing them especially well. As Anna, the English woman who flounces into nineteenth-century Siam, she is now playing a cultivated woman of maturity. It is the best performance of her career. Her voice has not only purity, it also has a weight that gives musical importance to "Hello, Young Lovers," "Getting to Know You" and "Shall I Tell You What I Think of You?"—all of them memorable songs. As an actress, Miss Cook's familiar candor also gives Anna a cool dignity that adds a little more stature to the part than it has had before. Until last evening, this department ranked the great Rodgers and Hammerstein works as follows: *Carousel* [1945], *South Pacific* [1949], *The King and I* [1951], and *Oklahoma!* [1943]. Let's advance *The King and I* one number.

RICHARD WATTS JR., *Post*

The two title roles are so youthfully portrayed that I was tempted to call it "The Son of The King and I."

BROADWAY SCORECARD / perfs: 23 / $: NA

rave	favorable	mixed	unfavorable	pan
1	6			

KISMET

a costume operetta, with music from Alexander Borodin, musical adaptation and lyrics by Robert Wright and George Forrest; book by Charles Lederer and Luther Davis, from the 1911 play by Edward Knoblock

directed by Albert Marre; choreographed by Jack Cole
produced by Edwin Lester; presented by Charles Lederer
with Alfred Drake, Doretta Morrow, Richard Kiley (replacing Glenn Burris), Joan Diener (Marre), and Henry Calvin

opened December 3, 1953   Ziegfeld Theatre

BROOKS ATKINSON, *Times*

Kismet has not been written. It has been assembled from a storehouse of spare parts. Many theatregoers are completely satisfied with ostentatious productions that are as full of carnival magnificence as a costume ball. But to one theatregoer the rich massiveness of *Kismet* is stupefying. It is a display of wealth, but it is not a work of art. For the good things that are in it are not artistically related. . . . In the course of *Kismet's* tour of the fleshpots and bazaars many lyrics are tossed across the footlights on the melody of Borodin's music. The lyrics comprise some of the most fearful poetry of our time. Robert Wright and George Forrest make the English language sound insensitive and pretentious. Fortunately, most of the lyrics are unintelligible in the singing, though one about "a nightingale singing at noon on a mulberry bud" does come through relentlessly. . . . As an abandoned hussy, brazenly made up and loosely clad, Joan Diener looks like a fine case of grand arson and warms up the whole show.

JOHN CHAPMAN, *Daily News*

The dances, staged by Jack Cole, are the best of all elements of a gorgeous show. The style is, of course, pure Jack Cole, which is a Broadway mixture of Balinese and Javenese—but nowadays who knows the diff between Bali and Baghdad. I do wish Alfred Drake could have one big song number with a lot of sock in it—for instance, something titled "My Heart Belongs to Baghdaddy." As for the girls in *Kismet*—well, they are the prettiest young ladies I have seen in the Ziegfeld since Ziegfeld.

Alfred Drake "Gesticulates" while the Barbaric Princesses of Ababu (Patricia Dunn, Bonnie Evans, and Reiko Sato) dance barbarically, Jack Cole style. (drawing by Al Hirschfeld)

ROBERT COLEMAN, *Daily Mirror*

Richard Kiley and Joan Diener, hitherto identified with straight plays, are outstanding as the likable Caliph and philandering wife of his police chief. For newcomers to the musical stage, they act and sing like veterans.

WILLIAM HAWKINS, *World-Telegram & Sun*

It has become smart to remark that *Kismet* is a hit because the newspapers could not publish notices of its opening. Well, a lot of people were haughty about *Can-Can*. It has been playing to stand-ees since the beginning of May. *Kismet* has a lot of the same vigorous, popular quality. It is noisy, spectacular, and vigorous. The biggest and brightest of magical carpets, it may not be subtle or original, but nobody intended it to be. It is melodic and gay. What's more, it has one great virtue in that it continually spoofs itself. . . . Lemuel Ayers never had a richer, fanciful scene to paint [scenic and costume design]. He has done it in terms of lovely, wildest dreams.

WALTER KERR, *Herald Tribune*

I guess about the only thing this song-and-dance *Kismet* hasn't got is any particular integrity—as satire, as Arabian Nights nonsense, as romantic moonshine, as honest operetta. It's the sort of show that would sell its soul for a joke, and the jokes should be better at the price. A rousing chorus of voices thunder out tunes rearranged from Borodin, and when Borodin straight isn't quite enough we get Borodin with a boogie-beat. It seems to me that Robert Wright and George Forrest have been fairly conscienceless about that Borodin score, too, respecting its quality whenever it suits them and chucking it for downbeat when things get desperate. The lyrics are passable in the more romantic moments. In the comic vein, a kind of collegiate wit keeps popping its head up—and ducking.

RICHARD WATTS JR., *Post*

Granted that Mr. Drake's musical-comedy heroes are pretty much alike, whether they are Oklahoma cowboys, Shakespearean rakes, or bearded Baghdad beggars, it is still true that he plays them with humor, vast skill, and authentic romantic style. He is easily the ablest man in the business at this sort of picturesque swagger, and he is at his best in *Kismet*, which is saying a lot. Joan

Diener is also one of the assets in *Kismet*, but I'm not sure it's in the way she intends to be. An interestingly but perhaps extravagantly constructed girl, she is supposed to be the epitome of sex excitement, and maybe she is. I think, though, that her important merit is that, whether she means to or not, she makes physical allure irresistibly absurd.

A colorful extravaganza—"A Musical Arabian Night," they called it—*Kismet* managed to overcome some rather condescending reviews, including nays from Atkinson and Kerr. Some of the reviews didn't get printed immediately, due to a newspaper strike; in the interim, strong word-of-mouth built *Kismet* into a hit. Musical novices Kiley and Diener would reunite with director Marre and choreographer Cole a dozen years later for *Man of La Mancha* (1965).

In addition to winning the Tony Award for Best Musical, Tonys were won by Alexander Borodin (composer, who must have been surprised—he died in 1887!); Charles Lederer and Luther Davis (librettists); Charles Lederer (producer); Alfred Drake (actor); and Louis Adrian (musical director). The competition was minimal: *Can-Can, Me and Juliet*, and *The Girl in Pink Tights*. Donaldson Awards were won by Alexander Borodin (composer); Albert Marre (director); Alfred Drake (actor); and Lemuel Ayers (costume designer).

BROADWAY SCORECARD / perfs: 583 / $: +

rave	favorable	mixed	unfavorable	pan
2	3		1	1

KISS ME, KATE

a musical comedy, with music and lyrics by Cole Porter; book by Bella and Samuel Spewack, incorporating *The Taming of the Shrew* by William Shakespeare

Saint Subber & Lemuel Ayers
present

ALFRED · PATRICIA
DRAKE · MORISON

in

KISS ME, KATE

Music & Lyrics by
COLE PORTER

Book by **SAMUEL & BELLA SPEWACK**
with
HAROLD LANG · LISA KIRK

Choreography by
HANYA HOLM

Settings & Costumes by
LEMUEL AYERS

Musical Director
Pembroke Davenport

Orchestrations by
Robert Russell Bennett

Production staged by
JOHN C. WILSON

A tamed shrew (Patricia Morison) after confessing to her tamer (Alfred Drake) that—to quote Shakespeare—"I Am Ashamed that Women Are So Simple." (costumes by Lemuel Ayers)

directed by John C. Wilson; choreographed by Hanya Holm
produced by Arnold Saint Subber and Lemuel Ayers
with Alfred Drake, Patricia Morison, Harold Lang, and Lisa Kirk

opened December 30, 1948   "New" Century Theatre

BROOKS ATKINSON, *Times*

Occasionally by some baffling miracle, everything seems to drop
gracefully into its appointed place in the composition of a song
show, and that is the case here. No one has had to break his neck
to dazzle the audience with his brilliance, and no one has had to
run at frantic speed to get across the rough spots. . . . The Italian
setting has another advantage. It gives Mr. Porter an opportunity
to poke beyond Tin Pan Alley into a romantic mood. Without
losing his sense of humor, he has written a remarkable melodious
score with an occasional suggestion of Puccini, who was a good
composer, too. Mr. Porter has always enjoyed the luxury of rowdy
tunes, and he has scribbled a few for the current festival. All his
lyrics are literate, and as usual some of them would shock the
editorial staff of *The Police Gazette.* But the interesting thing about
the new score is the enthusiasm Mr. Porter has for romantic melodies indigenous to the soft climate of the Mediterranean.

ROBERT COLEMAN, *Daily Mirror*

Lisa Kirk had the smart first-nighters blistering their distinguished palms over her delivery of Porter torch songs that should
be consoling and amusing heart-broken stay-up-lates for many a
bistro morn. The white-tied and be-ermined customers demanded
encore after encore of "Why Can't You Behave?" and "Always True
to You in My Fashion."

ROBERT GARLAND, *Journal-American*

If *Kiss Me, Kate* isn't the best musical-comedy I ever saw, I don't
remember what the best musical-comedy I ever saw was called. It
has everything. A show of shows that is literate without being
highbrow, sophisticated without being smarty, seasoned without
being soiled, and funny without being vulgar. When I left the
Century, the excited congregation was crying "Bravo" for Cole
Porter and Lee Shubert was in the box-office selling seats for next
year's Christmas holidays.

WILLIAM HAWKINS, *World-Telegram*

The show's most outstanding quality is its artful assurance, as everyone connected with it gives a superbly satisfactory contribution without suggesting that he has anywhere nearly exhausted his resources. As first class entertainment it is relaxing because it never strains. This temperance of delivery is only possible in a musical where there is a wealth of expert talent, and that is just what *Kiss Me, Kate* abounds in. Cole Porter has turned out one of his all-time best scores. It is studded with hits, has not a mediocre number in it, and offers line after line of those fabulously ticklish lyrics at which Porter at his best has no equal. John C. Wilson keeps a complicated show sliding hitchlessly along and has toned the performances with a smooth ease that makes the rambunctious plot all the more effective. Lemuel Ayers, coproducer and designer, ignites the stage with glowing heady Italian colors. Particularly memorable is the deep purple sky behind a street scene. Hanya Holm's dances are individual and effervescent, demanding great skill without ever suggesting a muscle-flexing contest. They have the rare gift of making each dancer look as if he had a purpose in what he does. Tops is the insinuating routine for "Were Thine That Special Face."

WARD MOREHOUSE, *Sun*

Kiss Me, Kate struck gold last night. This new and festive musical comedy is the best song-and-dance show of the season and one of the best Broadway has had in ten years. By the time these cheers get into print the box office queue will be reaching over into Central Park, and probably all the way to the reservoir. *Kiss Me, Kate* has everything. Captivating music, jaunty and witty lyrics, magical dancing, an amiable book—and also bits of Shakespeare.

RICHARD WATTS JR., *Post*

The electric excitement that comes to the theatre when everything goes right was present last night with the arrival of *Kiss Me, Kate*. From the opening number it was obvious to everybody that the first-nighters were seeing a smash hit of epic proportions, and nothing occurred throughout the evening to let them down. *Kiss Me, Kate* is beautiful, tuneful, witty, gay, high-spirited, and delightfully sung, acted, and danced. Again the American musical comedy proved itself the best in the world.

Cole Porter's finest show, and his first satisfying work since *DuBarry Was a Lady* (1939). The composer's four attempts of the early 1940s had been wartime hits, despite consistently mediocre scores. Then came two outright disasters, *Seven Lively Arts* (1944) and *Around the World* (1946). Porter seemed all washed up; raising money for *Kate* was a nightmare. But things worked out delectably, as the gentlemen of the press breathlessly attest.

In addition to winning the Tony Award for Best Musical, Tonys were won by Cole Porter (composer); Bella and Samuel Spewack (librettists); Saint Subber—who dropped the Arnold after the opening—and Lemuel Ayers (producers); and Lemuel Ayers (scenic designer). Donaldson Awards were won by Alfred Drake (actor); and Lemuel Ayers (scenic designer; costume designer).

```
BROADWAY SCORECARD / perfs: 1,077 / $: +

  rave     favorable     mixed     unfavorable     pan

   8           1
```

KWAMINA

a musical drama, with music and lyrics by Richard Adler; book by Robert Alan Aurthur

directed by Robert Lewis; choreographed by Agnes de Mille
produced by Alfred de Liagre, Jr.
with Sally Ann Howes (Adler), Terry Carter, and Brock Peters

opened October 23, 1961   54th Street Theatre

JOHN CHAPMAN, *Daily News*

Richard Adler has written his music and lyrics with bold originality and has avoided almost all the set-pieces of Tin Pan Alley. The orchestration, by Sid Ramin and Irwin Kostal, is similarly offbeat and highly colorful, and an exceptionally good orchestra and an exceptionally good conductor, Colin Romoff, do the music high justice. This has been a remarkable season for dancing in our musical theatre, and in *Kwamina* Miss de Mille reasserts her authority as the leader among Broadway's fine choreographers. Her dances, performed by a remarkable company of men and women, set the blood racing time and again.

WALTER KERR, *Herald Tribune*

Kwamina is its own worst advertisement. Early in the well-intentioned new musical a proposition is made clear. [The hero] wants to kill forever the prevalent white notion that Africans are better at dancing than at walking, at singing than at talking. Whereupon *Kwamina* goes on to show its lithe and lissome natives at their absolute best when they are dancing and singing, and at their feeblest when they are pausing to speak. Of course, this isn't Africa's fault. It's Robert Alan Aurthur's. Whatever has possessed librettist Aurthur to cast the dialogue for so contemporary an entertainment in the over-ripe idiom that used to be reserved for bad Biblical plays, I cannot imagine. Sentences are spooled from the tongue as though they had been translated from the Coptic and memorized by listening to Living Language records. The show in general is a thing of enormous good will and as much bad writing. . . . Sally Ann Howes, singing her heart out, is forced to tilt her pretty chin and recite her pretty lines until she seems not only white, but Pearl White. . . . "Seven Sheep, Four Red Shirts, and a Bottle of Gin" makes one wonder for a moment whether the show has its eye on the United Nations or United Artists.

NORMAN NADEL, *World-Telegram & Sun*

Forty-five minutes after the curtain rose there seemed every reason to believe glory held the show cupped in its hands. The stage surged with color. The dancing was almost too exciting to contain within the walls. If *Kwamina* had sustained that level, the very look of the season would have changed by now. But apparently the authors ran out—of ideas, of inspiration, of the creative force. Consider these assets: the overture—sometimes in the manner of Resphigi, sometimes Villa-Lobos—speaks in a stirring note for musical theatre. From the first phrases the promise is good. A work song, "The Cocoa Bean Song," is a crescendo of sound and action, bringing the Africans onto the stage to a compelling rhythm and a fetching melody. "Welcome Home" gloriously brings Kwamina back to his village. Disillusion starts to set in when Sally Ann Howes sings "Ordinary People." It might have some value as a go-home-humming song, but words and music are weak, Tin-Pan-Alleyish and out of the mood of the show. A bit late she tangles with "What Happened to Me Tonight?," and with that the singular spell of *Kwamina* is lost. The jingling banality of the words and music violate [*Kwamina*'s integrity]. The orchestra by now is playing blatant movie music, with the French horn anguishing like an elephant that backed into an open switch.

BILL SLOCUM, *Mirror*

Almost liked the play. Loved the loincloths.

Kind of "The King and I Go to Africa," as told by Eliza Doolittle (after graduating from med school). Too bad, as *Kwamina* attempted something different and potentially important; and half of the score—Adler's "native African" music—is impressive and exciting. But clichés take the day.

A Tony Award was won by Agnes de Mille (choreographer, tied with Joe Layton for *No Strings*).

```
BROADWAY SCORECARD / perfs: 32 / $: —

  rave    favorable    mixed    unfavorable    pan

                  1          2           4
```

LA PLUME DE MA TANTE

a French revue, with music by Gerald Calvi; devised and written by Robert Dhéry; English lyrics by Ross Parker

directed by Robert Dhéry; staged by Alec Shanks; choreographed by Colette Brosset (Dhéry)
produced by Jack Hylton, presented by David Merrick and Joseph Kipness
with Robert Dhéry, Colette Brosset, and Pierre Olaf
opened November 11, 1958   Royale Theatre

Robert Dhéry and Colette Brosset in a characteristic pose. La Plume *won the Critics' Circle Award for Best Musical and ran more than two years, out-legging competitors* West Side Story, Gypsy, Fiorello!, Bye Bye Birdie *and* Carnival.

FRANK ASTON, *World-Telegram & Sun*

The French are in charge of W. 54th St. Took over last night in the name of *La Plume de Ma Tante*. No opposition from the natives. Instead natives in attendance at the Royale cackled, yacked, giggled, and tossed in glee. People who hadn't used stomach muscles for laughing purposes in years suddenly learned how all over again.

ROBERT COLEMAN, *Daily Mirror*

Designed for the tired businessman, as well as the posh carriage trade. It's got scads of beauts, selected for personality and curves and legs, legs, legs. It has eye and ear appeal. It's a smart, satiric, sentimental tornado of merriment. David Merrick hasn't had much luck with art this season. But it looks as though he's drawn an ace from the deck with *La Plume de Ma Tante*, which had the Royale Theatre's walls quaking under barrages of laughter.

WALTER KERR, *Herald Tribune*

While everyone else has been moaning that the musical revue has—as a form—practically vanished from the earth, the French have discovered an absolutely perfect way of bringing it back to life. You just leave out the words. Oh, there are a few words spoken at the Royale as guitars catch fire, chickens hatch bald-headed men, and a tardy member of the orchestra tries desperately to get across the footlights and into the pit, but very little valuable time is wasted on them. A forlorn little straggler with a circumflex mouth (his name is Pierre Olaf, and remember it) does poke his head through the curtain while author Robert Dhéry is trying to identify the next unidentifiable number and try to get a thought in edgewise. He says "Maybe you will think I am stupid—", he is met with a very curt "Yes," and he disappears disconsolately, but immediately, to his dressing-room. . . . This is pantomime nonsense of the first order, bright, beguiling, and downright hilarious.

JOHN McCLAIN, *Journal-American*

A magnificently mad and miraculous revue and a sort of milestone in recent Broadway experience, especially with revues. It proves the point that there's nothing wrong with a revue that inspiration, ingenuity, insanity, and quite a lot of money can't cure. . . . Even the smallest joke is mounted with the greatest luxury: a man is waiting on the top of a portable stairway leading to a non-existent aircraft. A stewardess appears and announces that the plane to Paris will be delayed. He nods, spins his bow tie (to the roar of giant motors), and flies off.

La Plume de Ma Tante garnered a bouquet of stunning raves, the Critics' Circle Award and a two-year run. Sounds interesting, doesn't it—but a revival seems virtually impossible.

Winner of the New York Drama Critics' Circle Award (for Best Musical). The entire cast received a special Tony Award.

BROADWAY SCORECARD / perfs: 835 / $: +

rave	favorable	mixed	unfavorable	pan
5	2			

A LADY SAYS YES

a musical comedy, with music by Fred Spielman and Arthur Gershwin; lyrics by Stanley Adams; book by Clayton Ashley (Dr. Maxwell Maltz); tryout title: *A Lady of ?*

directed by J. J. Shubert (replacing Edgar MacGregor); choreographed by Boots McKenna and Natalie Kamarova
produced by J. J. Shubert in association with Clayton Ashley
with Carole Landis, Bobby Morris, Sue Ryan, and Jacqueline Susann

opened January 10, 1945   Broadhurst Theatre

HOWARD BARNES, *Herald Tribune*

The new musical show leaps ponderously from a local hospital to sixteenth-century Venice. It sandwiches a song about Brooklyn between a pseudo-operatic duet and a Chinese ballet; puts on a prizefight on the banks of the Grand Canal and mixes rough-and-tumble clowning with fancy-dress carnival scenes.

JOHN CHAPMAN, *Daily News*

As you know from the movies, Miss Landis is something of a national monument in human architecture. Even in repose she always looks as though she'd just taken a deep breath. Her dressmaker has spared no effort in draping her suitably from necklace to waistline. . . . Its book is the work of Dr. Maxwell Maltz, a plastic surgeon, and it needs cutting. Dr. Maltz, working under the writer's alias of Clayton Ashley, has thought it fitting to tell the story of an old Florentine superstition—the belief that if a man's nose has suffered damage and been repaired, his abilities as a bee are lessened to the point where people go around talking about him. I think Dr. Maltz invented this old Florentine superstition. The humor? Well, Mr. Morris asks Miss Ryan if she likes Kipling and she says, "I don't know—I've never been kippled." I liked it better when they used to ask Ed Wynn if he liked O. Henry and he said, "No, the peanuts stick in my teeth."

BURTON RASCOE, *World-Telegram*

Here are some of the comic lines:
Mr. Morris (to Miss Ryan): "I'm the greatest lover in the world. Did you ever hear of Don Juan? Well, I'm Don Two."
Mr. Morris: "Marco Polo is here."
Jacqueline Susann: "He? I thought Marco Polo was something you played on horses with sticks."
Christine Ayres wore some stunning gowns and danced a sort of "Dance of the Seven Veils" in a harem-like setting, with only one veil. This was very well received.

A vanity production from Park Avenue. *A Lady Says Yes*—Chapman's review was headed "A Critic Says No"—played its tryout under the title *A Lady of ?*, which gives you an idea. Yes, Arthur Gershwin was George and Ira's little brother, but you wouldn't have known it from his only professional effort. Featured player Jacqueline Susann appeared in a half-dozen musicals before moving into another line of work.

LAFFING ROOM ONLY

a vaudeville revue, with music and lyrics by Burton Lane; book by Ole Olsen, Chic Johnson, and Eugene Conrad

directed by John Murray Anderson; comedy directed by Edward Cline; choreographed by Robert Alton
produced by the Messrs. Shubert and Olsen and Johnson
with Ole Olsen, Chic Johnson, Frank Libuse, and Betty Garrett

opened December 23, 1944   Winter Garden Theatre

JOHN CHAPMAN, *Daily News*

They had shotguns, pretty girls, brassieres, seltzer siphons, a piano with boxing gloves, a man with rabbits, stooges in boxes, stooges in the audience, community singing, a couple of dirty gags, a midget who grabbed your legs as you went out for intermission, a race between a soldier and a sailor trying to put on women's underthings and then run around the house, some more siphons of seltzer and the general pretense of busting a gut in the hope that you might bust one of your own in appreciation. . . . The songs, by Burton Lane, are just corny enough to be catchy—and I prefer them [including the hit "Feudin' and Fightin' "] to many I have heard in this season's pretentious and arty musicals.

ROBERT GARLAND, *Journal-American*

Even if the Shuberts, Lee and J.J., had sent me six bottles of scotch for Christmas, instead of the three bottles they did send me, I'm afraid I'd still find little to say in praise of *Laffing Room Only*. Looking at it with the most Christmassy which is to say the most charitable eyes, it remains a tactless, tasteless, and tiresome burlesque show. Nevertheless, many liked it. If you find the old Minsky act about the drooping rifles being revived at the sight of a practically naked woman laughable, you'll roar your head off. I don't mind dirt, but I do mind dullness. *Laffing Room Only* is dull. Departing from the Winter Garden with a headache, a heartache, and a free can of Esso lubricating oil, I yearned for the bad old days when hell really was apoppin'. Nevertheless, I'll not be surprised if next Christmas finds *Laffing Room Only* still at the Winter Garden. And thanks for the Scotch and the motor oil.

BURTON RASCOE, *World-Telegram*

It is no secret that Thornton Wilder got the inspiration for his history of civilization, *The Skin of Our Teeth* [1942], from *Hellzapopin'* [1938] or that his indebtedness to Olsen and Johnson is much more patent that his indebtedness to James Joyce's *Finnegan's Wake* [1939]. But a second serving of *The Skin of Our Teeth* would be more than some stomachs could take; and so the critics said, in effect, about the second O & J show, *Sons o' Fun* [1941], which ran for 742 performances. It is 17th on the long-run list; *Hellzapoppin'* is 5th. If this ratio or arithmetical retrogression is a reliable indicator, *Laffing Room Only* should enjoy a run of 396 performances, or slightly under a year, and gross well over $2,000,000. But not with any encouragement from me. . . . I am not amused by seeing the President's wife being made the butt of shamelessly vulgar ridicule by a performer wearing a caricature mask of Mrs. Roosevelt. I am uncomfortable at the sight of a man's popping up every few minutes, holding aloft four or five poor squirming rabbits by the ears and yelling, "Harvey!" I fail to respond to the risibility of a man in uniform, with many service stripes, struggling to get into a brassiere, a girdle, and stepins, of a midget, dressed as a baby, being tossed into a playgoer's lap, or to being hit over the head with a paper club by a chorus girl.

	BROADWAY SCORECARD / perfs: 233 / $: +				
rave	favorable	mixed	unfavorable	pan
	2	1	3	2

LAUGH TIME

a vaudeville revue, with material by various writers

produced by Paul Small and Fred Finklehoffe
with Frank Fay, Ethel Waters, and Bert Wheeler

opened September 8, 1943   Shubert Theatre

WILELLA WALDORF, *Post*

A notice handed out with the program read: "Our scenery, in case anyone cares, was last heard of somewhere between Las Vegas, N.M., and Laporte, Ind. En route from Los Angeles we fear it has met with foul play. Want to hear more about our scenery? No? Well, you're going to. It was and is, for all we know, a fusion of the best features of the Taj Mahal, the late Joseph Urban, the Grand Canyon, and early Loew's State. At a later date we may give a special showing of it to satisfy non-believers."

An example of the handiwork of legendary press agent Richard Maney. While this sort of thing didn't sell any tickets, it at least kept the critics amused. (Often more than the show being plugged!) *Laugh Time* was moderately entertaining, and its minimal costs enabled it to run through the fall.

```
BROADWAY SCORECARD / perfs: 126 / $: +

rave     favorable     mixed     unfavorable     pan

 3           4            1
```

LEND AN EAR

an intimate revue, with music, lyrics, and sketches by Charles Gaynor; additional sketches by Joseph Stein and Will Glickman

staged and choreographed by Gower Champion; sketches directed by Hal Gerson

produced by William R. Katzell, Franklin Gilbert, and William Eythe
with William Eythe, Carol Channing, Yvonne Adair, Gene Nelson, and Bob Scheerer

opened December 16, 1948   National Theatre

HERRICK BROWN, *Sun*

Miss Channing adds greatly to the evening's hilarity as she wanders in and out. Whether she's portraying a diva trying to give an operatic performance with the music eliminated or stolidly carrying out her steps in a gunfire-filled ballet in Santo Domingo, she displays a fine talent for comedy.

JOHN CHAPMAN, *Daily News*

I had such a good time at *Lend an Ear* last evening that I forgot to look at the program. This West Coast revue is as friendly as a pup and as smart as a cat, and you'll never have to worry about what is coming next or who will be in it. Everything and everybody will be just perfect for a light-hearted evening. *Lend an Ear* is a frisky and funny song-and-sketch entertainment performed by 21 extraordinarily engaging young people. It is so good it does not need any names to carry it—but it should make some.

ROBERT COLEMAN, *Daily Mirror*

It proceeded to send the friendly first-night audience into something resembling hysterics. The customers howled over the application of svelte slapsticks to such topics as psychiatrists, romantic bosses, columnists, Santo Domingo, opera companies too strapped to hire an orchestra, and a "Gladiola Girl" road company that got lost in the sticks back in the 1920s. The "Gladiola Girl" burlesque is one of the funniest items you are likely to see on a Broadway stage in a host of semesters. Idea, cast, and backgrounds have been blended into a super-duper laugh provoker, immensely funny because it contains so many grains of truth. A huge posy should go to Raoul Pène du Bois for the sets and costumes. It is easy to lend an ear, and even easier to lend an eye to the new arrival. The gifted young cast knocks itself out to please you. It's like attending a party where talented guests work themselves into a tizzy to entertain each other.

ROBERT GARLAND, *Journal-American*

An attabuoyant young song-and-dance show. Charles Gaynor has been pulling his show together for lo these seven years. Pittsburgh was the first to see it. Then it began popping up in unexpected places. Cohasset, say. And Los Angeles. Last night's first New York audience welcomed its opening enthusiastically.

WILLIAM HAWKINS, *World-Telegram*

There is never a jarring note. The show blows along like a breeze from start to finish, gay, exuberant, and endearing. It is hard to distinguish among the players because frankly the show is loaded with talent, and the big kick lies in the fact that you never heard of most of it before. Special gratitude is due for the establishment of a remarkable personality in Carol Channing, who with her timing and range is for our money one of the funniest people extant. A buxom blonde with enormous eyes, she can be ecstatically idiotic or viciously sophisticated in a twinkling. She is an efficient, bored opera singer, garbed suspiciously like Lily Pons's Lucia, a worldly British movie-goer, and one of the most crazily untalented chorus girls ever seen. Gower Champion's rarely [highly] original choreography makes fresh young windmills of the dancers.

RICHARD WATTS JR., *Post*

On the whole, it is about the closest thing to the fabulous *Garrick Gaieties* [1925, 1926] that has yet been offered. To see Yvonne Adair burlesque a soubrette of the Twenties or to hear Carol Channing cry "Horror! Horror! Horror!" in her best Shakespearean tones is worth any playgoer's while.

A fresh, intimate revue best remembered for the "Gladiola Girl," an extended spoof of musical comedies of the 1920s. This clearly inspired Carol Channing's gold-digging performance in *Gentlemen Prefer Blondes* (1949)—in which Yvonne Adair also recreated her "Gladiola" roll—as well as the trans-Atlantic *pastiche* hit *The Boy Friend* (1954). The "Gladiola Girl" itself was a throwback to Rodgers, Hart, and Herb Fields's "Rose of Arizona," from the Second Edition of *The Garrick Gaieties* (1926).

A Tony Award was won by Gower Champion (choreographer). Donaldson Awards were won by Gower Champion (choreographer) and Yvonne Adair (female debut).

BROADWAY SCORECARD / perfs: 460 / $: +

rave	favorable	mixed	unfavorable	pan
6	2			1

LET IT RIDE!

a musical farce, with music by Jay Livingston; lyrics by Jay Livingston and Ray Evans; book by Abram S. Ginnes, additional book material by Ronny Graham, from the 1935 farce *Three Men on a Horse* by John Cecil Holm and George Abbott

directed by Stanley Prager; choreographed by Onna White
produced by Joel Spector
with George Gobel, Sam Levene, and Barbara Nichols

opened October 12, 1961   Eugene O'Neill Theatre

ROBERT COLEMAN, *Mirror*

Let it Ride! figures as an also-ran on our scratch sheet. Gobel and Levene are expert jockeys but we doubt they'll be able to boot this baby home in the money. It has hilarious highspots, but not enough to cross the finish line ahead of the competition. It's just not in a class with its sire, *Three Men on a Horse*.

WALTER KERR, *Herald Tribune*

Is Sam Levene no help in making things louder, faster, livelier? Of course he is. But Mr. Levene, than whom New York boasts no better company, is not in danger of being pursued by a panting Rudolph Bing, and his contributions consist mostly in repairing the holes in the dialogue by plugging them up with his eyebrows. Mr. Levene's eyebrows could sweep streets, and the fact that he always seems to be peering desperately into a burning building (stable, more likely) makes for some wonderfully winning improvisa-

HIS OWN LITTLE ISLAND

Music and Lyrics by JAY LIVINGSTON and RAY EVANS

JOEL SPECTOR
presents

GEORGE GOBEL ✶ SAM LEVENE
BARBARA NICHOLS
in

A New Musical Comedy

with PAULA STEWART

STANLEY GROVER · LARRY ALPERT · TED THURSTON

Book by
ABRAM S. GINNES

Music & Lyrics by
JAY LIVINGSTON & RAY EVANS

Based on the play "Three Men On A Horse" by John Cecil Holm & George Abbott

Directed by STANLEY PRAGER

Dances & Musical Numbers Staged by ONNA WHITE

Settings & Lighting by WILLIAM & JEAN ECKART

60¢

Costumes by
GUY KENT

Musical Director
JAY BLACKTON

Vocal Direction
JERRY PACKER

Production Associate
BUFF COBB

LIVINGSTON and EVANS, Inc.
Sole Selling Agent
G. SCHIRMER, Inc.
New York

Three Men on a Horse, *although I seem to count a fourth body (and what a body!). That's George Gobel, Barbara Nichols, Sam Levene, and jockey aboard Flutterby, who smiles knowingly. That's a good way to lose your money, Sam.* (drawing by Shelley)

384

tion. . . . But even with all this assistance *Let it Ride!* just won't do. Dance director Onna White cooks up some splendid palm-weaving in a burst of harmony performed by sixteen patrolmen ("Just an Honest Mistake"), and its very success calls attention to two truths: (a) it has nothing to do with the show at hand, and (b) the show at hand hasn't had anything like it, musically speaking, in an act and a half.

NORMAN NADEL, *World-Telegram & Sun*

Put a 300-pound jockey on the fastest horse in the world and both will eat a great deal of dust (or mud, depending on the condition of the track) between the starting gate and the wire. The 300-pound jockey is *Let it Ride!*, a pallid musical that opened last night. It adds nothing but dead weight to a fleet farce, and for my money the combination hasn't gotten around the first turn. Not only does *Three Men on a Horse* deserve better treatment, but whipping it into a musical isn't that tough a job. A few phone calls could round up a writing-composing-directing-acting team that could make at last an entertaining musical out of it in four weeks' time. George Gobel is ill-prepared for the legitimate stage—if a role in *Let it Ride!* qualifies as legitimate. He cannot project his voice, and a battery of mikes in the footlights doesn't entirely correct that fault. He appears even more uncertain than the part requires, as when he beats time to stay with the orchestra.

They tried it before as *Banjo Eyes* (1941), with Eddie Cantor on the nag for 126 performances; the title character was not Eddie but a two-man "horse," who did the rhumba. (No, I'm not making this up.) This time around the track, *Three Men on a Horse* fared even worse. George Abbott, that intelligent man of the theatre and coauthor of the original, knew enough to stay far away from both misguided musicalizations.

BROADWAY SCORECARD / perfs: 68 / $: −

rave	favorable	mixed	unfavorable	pan
	1		5	1

LET'S MAKE AN OPERA

a British audience-participation musical, with music by Benjamin Britten; book and lyrics by Eric Crozier

directed by Marc Blitzstein
produced by Peter Lawrence and the Show-of-the-Month Club

opened December 13, 1950   John Golden Theatre

BROOKS ATKINSON, *Times*

It is conductor Normal Del Mar's job to rouse the audience's love for community singing, and this may be regarded as a mistake. To one playgoer whose talents do not go beyond "O, Little Town of Bethlehem," most of Mr. Britten's songs are too difficult to be learned so rapidly and are pitched for people whose voices are changing. The songs are too Britten-esque for Gotham's guys and dolls.

HOWARD BARNES, *Herald Tribune*

Let's not!

ROBERT COLEMAN, *Daily Mirror*

The audience is asked to sing along with the principals and it is even divided into sections which imitate various kinds of birds. And we're not kidding, either.

RICHARD WATTS JR., *Post*

Of the youthful singers, only the pretty Jo Sullivan seemed of professional calibre.

BROADWAY SCORECARD / perfs: 5 / $: −

rave	favorable	mixed	unfavorable	pan
		2	3	2

THE LIAR

a musical comedy, with music by John Mundy; lyrics by Edward Eager; book by Edward Eager and Alfred Drake, from the 1750 Italian comedy *Il Bugiardo* by Carlo Goldoni

directed by Alfred Drake (replacing Norris Houghton); choreographed by Hanya Holm
produced by Dorothy Willard and Thomas Hammond
with William Eythe (replacing Dennis Harrison), Melville Cooper, Paula Laurence, and Barbara Ashley
opened May 18, 1950   Broadhurst Theatre

JOHN CHAPMAN, *Daily News*

Fashion note: The locale is 17th Century Venice, and as any student of painting knows the dames then had high, rounded bust lines. In her first-act costume, which had a V-shaped bodice, Miss Laurence was quite interesting because she looked like an ingeniously arranged double-scoop ice cream cone (Vanilla).

WILLIAM HAWKINS, *World-Telegram & Sun*

It is no surprise that the role was conceived by an actor, or that the actor was Alfred Drake, for whom the part would be a natural. In a little more time, William Eythe [a last-minute replacement] would have conquered it entirely, for he has the flourish, the stamina and the charm, and can talk a song better than most people sing one. Here, toward the end, both he and his material suffer from sheer exhaustion. Eythe's cocky banter is keyed in a zany range that inevitably suggests Carol Channing doing an impersonation of Ronald Colman. . . . The physical production is confectionary in shades of peach ice cream and tomato soup, with costumes by Motley and settings that cleverly shift location in plain sight, by Donald Oenslager.

BROADWAY SCORECARD / perfs: 12 / $: −

rave	unfavorable	mixed	unfavorable	pan
			5	2

LI'L ABNER

a musical comedy, with music by Gene de Paul, lyrics by Johnny Mercer; book by Norman Panama and Melvin Frank, from the comic strip by Al Capp

directed and choreographed by Michael Kidd
produced by Norman Panama, Melvin Frank, and Michael Kidd
with Edith (Edie) Adams, Peter Palmer, Howard St. John, Stubby Kaye, and Charlotte Rae

opened November 15, 1956   St. James Theatre

BROOKS ATKINSON, *Times*

If everyone in *Li'l Abner* were as talented as Michael Kidd, everything would be as brilliant as the ballets, and probably the world would be gayer, too. But it is difficult to make a fluent musical romance out of some characters who may have hearts of gold but are not very bright in the upper story.

JOHN CHAPMAN, *Daily News*

I decided I was going to like it all very much soon after the curtain rose and this fetching little Edith Adams sidled up to this big hunk, Peter Palmer, and said, shyly, "Abner, I brought you some worms." There is a cast which is as remarkable for its ability to entertain as for it picturesqueness, with Edith Adams and Peter Palmer heading the troupe. These two have 35 or 40 playmates, including a whole herd of lightfooted and happy dancers—and not including various geese, donkeys, pigs, and hounds which play their parts better than Sirs Laurence Olivier and Ralph Richardson could play them. . . . Johnny Mercer's lyrics bring to mind the salty and saucy days of Lorenz Hart and Ira Gershwin [as they] jab at our personal and national foibles.

TOM DONNELLY, *World-Telegram & Sun*

Al Capp's two-dimensional cartoon world has not been given a magical third dimension. You could go so far as to say that a dimension has been taken away. Those aren't real Dogpatch people stompin' and whompin' and cavortin' across that stage. Those are (sob!) Broadway actors done up in funny looking costumes. Maybe

Abner (Peter Palmer) and Marryin' Sam (Stubby Kaye) return from the Nation's Capitol to assure Dogpatch denizens that "The Country's in the Very Best of Hands." (set by William and Jean Eckart, costumes by Alvin Colt, photo by Freidman-Abeles)

the task of recreating Dogpatch in persuasive footlights terms was (gulp!) an impossible one. Librettists Norman Panama and Melvin Frank have been unwilling to assume that everybody knows what Dogpatch is all about, and instead they have felt obliged to explain what they are talking about as they go along. It would have been a terrible drag on *Guys and Dolls* [1950] if its creations had assumed the burden of informing the customers that there were gamblers on Broadway, and that these gentlemen were interested in a social and professional pastime known as "betting on the bangtails," and that these chaps associate with "chorus girls" who sometimes work in "night spots". . . . P.S. The ladies who have been assigned the historic and anatomically demanding roles of Moonbeam McSwine [Carmen Alvarez], Stupefyin' Jones [Julie Newmar], and Appassionata Von Climax [Tina Louise] acquit themselves nobly.

WALTER KERR, *Herald Tribune*

Michael Kidd, director and choreographer, knows how to set fists and feet pounding against the floor like a thousand rifles going off at once. Every time he does it the air sizzles and crackles. Every time a friend or enemy takes a snort of Kickapoo Joy Juice or Yokumberry Tonic you can count on the lights to flash, the bare-legged girls to scream, and the muscular males to go spinning through space. Every time—or nearly every time—the orchestra strikes up for one of Johnny Mercer's and Gene de Paul's salutes to comic-strip fury, the beat is driving, the voices are clamoring, and the scenery sways in the wind. It's all done with zip and zingo, and I guess you could say the show was a rip-snorting, ring-tailed roarer, all right.

JOHN McCLAIN, *Journal-American*

If there is one person in the world who is not familiar with Al Capp's strange retinue and ideology, as expressed in his daily comic strip, he would have been frequently baffled and occasionally re-volted last night. For those who don't know about Capp's rustic world, the philosophy of the evening strikes a sour note. At the risk of being called a cornball I think it's poor timing to feature a song about "The Country's in the Very Best of Hands," which attempts to show it isn't, and to haul out and shove all over the stage that dreary caricature of a relentless millionaire. I was not even trans-ported by the joke about the State Department. The man says to the government guy, "How did you get your job?" and the obvious imbecile answers, "Just because I was terribly loyal." No longer very funny. But all this is by way of saying that while I think *Li'l Abner* is often guilty of questionable taste, it is sure to be a great big hit. *Li'l Abner* is bountiful, lively, and tuneful. We won't all agree with its taste or its tenets, but it is a cinch to be with us for many a Dogpatch moon.

Kidd, Mercer, and de Paul came to folksy Dogpatch from their flavorful film musical *Seven Brides for Seven Brothers* (1954). *Li'l Abner* offered more of the same, with an emphasis on movement and dance. Johnny Mercer provided his finest set of Broadway lyrics, and they are simply stunning.

A Tony Award was won by Edith Adams (supporting actress).

```
BROADWAY SCORECARD / perfs: 693 / $: +

  rave     favorable    mixed    unfavorable    pan

   3           1           2           1
```

LITTLE ME

a musical satire, with music by Cy Coleman; lyrics by Carolyn Leigh; book by Neil Simon, from the 1961 fictional memoirs by Patrick Dennis

directed by Cy Feuer and Bob Fosse; choreographed by Bob Fosse
produced by Cy Feuer and Ernest H. Martin
with Sid Caesar, Virginia Martin, Nancy Andrews, and Swen Swenson

opened November 17, 1962   Lunt-Fontanne Theatre

WALTER KERR, *Herald Tribune*

Little Me is a show for people who always did think Sid Caesar ought to be twins. They can promptly get three-and-one-half times their money's worth at the Lunt-Fontanne, for at the Lunt-Fontanne there are seven Sid Caesars on view—sometimes several of them seem to be on stage at once—and of course seven is a lucky number, if you need luck. Mr. Caesar is not a man who needs it. He has poise, elevation, pace, hauteur, winsomeness, guile, the ability to look well in short pants, and bravery. In short, all the things that are Caesar's. He also has a show, a happy holiday of a show, if I'm not rushing the season. The one thing he does need at the moment is a throat-spray and perhaps four or five hours' bed-rest, without having to change a costume, change an accent, slaughter a table with a walking stick, or throw up his right hand with the intensity of an umpire who knows he is going to get killed. But that will come, his throat will clear up, and we can all look forward to laughing as much at the lyrics as we now do at the dialogue. . . . *Little Me* is made of bits and pieces of parody from all over, and it needs fresh invention every minute to keep it so amiably airborne; it gets the necessary invention from all hands. Sum total: a blockbuster so genial it looks like a breeze.

JOHN MCCLAIN, *Journal-American*

If the press agents for *Little Me* are looking for a quote from me they can help themselves to any of the following: "Smash Musical," "Sumptuous Success" or maybe just "Hail, Caesar!"

NORMAN NADEL, *World-Telegram & Sun*

If Caesar, Miss Martin, and Miss Andrews keep *Little Me* moving briskly, it is Swen Swenson, in a mating cakewalk to the tune of "I've Got Your Number," who stops the show. The ovation he earned Saturday isn't likely to be matched this season. A number called "Rich Kid's Rag" is the choreographic coup of the season so far, wherefore the Legion of Merit with palms to Bob Fosse, who staged all the brilliantly satirical musical numbers and dances. . . . Neil Simon,who adapted Dennis's novel, has incorporated three shows worth of outrageously funny gags, which could be his, or Dennis's, or Caesar's, or the total of three men and more. Cy Coleman's music is solid and driving, and Carolyn Leigh's lyrics measure up.

HOWARD TAUBMAN, *Times*

In a nonvintage year ordinary wine must do. *Little Me* looks good because it arrives after a poor crop of musicals. The new musical comedy achieves its comparative rating because it gleams with show-business savvy. Thanks to its speed, pacing, and sheen, it creates the illusion of being fresher and brighter than it is. Neil Simon's book based on a Patrick Dennis novel is a flimsy contrivance. If this tale of a lavishly appointed girl from the wrong side of the tracks in search of wealth, culture, and social position is meant to be satire, it is as innocuous as a bedtime story. If meant as no more than a lighthearted spoof, it plods as much as it romps. Cy Feuer and Mr. Fosse have staged *Little Me* with all the gloss and swiftness in the command of shrewd showmen. But like other experienced technicians, they have been victimized by a law of musical comedies in difficulty: when in doubt stir up motion and step up decibels. They have whipped up a sinking in which the show's distress exceeds the ship's. Knowing Broadway hands have left their imprint on *Little Me*. All it lacks is the glow of enchantment that should warm you after a freshly individual musical.

Like *Do Re Mi* (1960), *Little Me* was an hysterically funny clown show with a popular TV comedian, generally enthusiastic revues—and a disappointing run. Maybe people were too used to seeing Phil and Sid on TV for free; maybe the shows, whose satire included pokes at wide-eyed romantics, were too hard-hearted for the times. (That certainly didn't hurt *How to Succeed in Business Without Really Trying* [1961], the previous Feuer and Martin and Fosse show, but that show was different—it was *perfect*). Anyway, *Little Me* failed, and librettist Neil Simon—whose only play, *Come Blow Your Horn* (1961), had been decidedly uneven—retaliated by writing *Barefoot in the Park* (1963).

A Tony Award was won by Bob Fosse (choreographer).

BROADWAY SCORECARD / perfs: 275 / $: −

rave	favorable	mixed	unfavorable	pan
4	2		1	

THE LITTLEST REVUE

an intimate musical revue, with music mostly by Vernon Duke, lyrics mostly by Ogden Nash, sketches by Nat Hiken, Billy Friedberg, and others; "conceived, cast, and assembled" by Ben Bagley

directed by Paul Lammers; choreographed by Charles Weidman produced by the Phoenix Theatre (T. Edward Hambleton and Norris Houghton) by arrangement with Ben Bagley
with Charlotte Rae, Tammy Grimes, Joel Grey, and Larry Storch

opened May 22, 1956   Phoenix Theatre

JOHN CHAPMAN, *Daily News*

I've read in the papers that there is more than somewhat of measles in town lately. It may be that *The Littlest Revue*, a youthful show at the Phoenix Theatre, has them. At last evening's premiere, anyhow, it came out in spots. Many of these spots are undeniably charming or funny or witty. But about half of the show could be thrown away. . . . The show continues with Joel Grey spoofing Harry Belafonte in a song which begins, "I was born in the Bronx," with that Belafonte squawk emphasizing "Bronx." Then it offers Charlotte Rae, a very funny girl, in a number called "The Shape of Things" [music and lyric by Sheldon Harnick]. After this, my attention began to wander from the stage, and I noticed that the drummer in the orchestra was the spit and image of Estes Kefauver [chairman of the televised hearings of the Senate investigation of Organized Crime]. This cheered me up, so whenever something awful like a song called "Madly in Love" turned up, I'd watch the drummer.

WILLIAM HAWKINS, *World-Telegram & Sun*

The Littlest Revue lives up to its name in a manner which none of the participants could possibly have anticipated. It is short, very short, on gaiety, looks, and humor. Most of the tunes have the slightly listless air of having been rejected from other scores. . . . Tammy Grimes has a reputation in the profession, which is hard to judge here, except for her affecting phrases of the song "Madly in Love." Joel Grey is a warm personality, who sings and dances well enough to back up his comedy ideas.

WALTER KERR, *Herald Tribune*

Mr. Bagley does have one trump card in his skimpy hand. Her name is Charlotte Rae. Tagging a bit behind Miss Rae—well, quite a bit behind—are Tammy Grimes, a firm-jawed girl who cannot keep her blonde hair out of her eyes, and Joel Grey, a night-club entertainer who looks like a miniature Al Jolson but hasn't yet made up his mind just what sort of entertaining he wants to do.

BROADWAY SCORECARD / perfs: 32 / $: NA

rave	favorable	mixed	unfavorable	pan
	2	1	3	1

LIVIN' THE LIFE

a musical comedy, with music by Jack Urbont; lyrics by Bruce Geller; book by Dale Wasserman and Bruce Geller, from "Mark Twain's immortal Mississippi River stories"

directed by David Alexander; choreographed by John Butler
produced by the Phoenix Theatre (T. Edward Hambleton and Norris Houghton)
with Stephen Elliott, Alice Ghostley, James Mitchell, Timmy Everett, and Lee Becker

opened April 27, 1957   Phoenix Theatre

TOM DONNELLY, *World-Telegram & Sun*

There's a Tom Sawyer with a big marshmallow smile and a habit of mugging in a manner that is pretty familiar around Broadway and Hollywood, but I'll bet you my bottom dollar was unknown in the Hannibal, Mo. of 1850. There's a Huckleberry Finn carved out of greasepaint. I can't believe either of these boys would have the least notion which end of a fishing pole to put the worm on. There's the scene where Muff Potter is about to go to trial. Well, it's apparently minstrel day in Hannibal, because smack in the middle of the proceeding a minstrel troupe comes out and does a big number. I haven't seen anything like it since they combined the regular Saturday afternoon hoedown with the trial of Lizzie Borden in *New Faces of 1952*. Except that time they were being satiric. . . . James Mitchell does nicely by Injun Joe's dancing moments, and in the course of the evening Lee Becker makes a peppery and amusing tomboy out of Amy. Alice Ghostley is a great favorite of mine, but I certainly wish she had never tackled the role of Aunt Polly. Miss Ghostley is licked from the moment the curtain goes up.

WALTER KERR, *Herald Tribune*

When Becky Thatcher walks out on Tom Sawyer toward the end of the first act, Tom strides forward to the footlights, clenches his fists, screws up his eyes, and shouts out his very first "Damn!" It seemed to me that the word was a long time coming out of him. It had been on my lips for a good hour before that. Timmy Everett is, so far as I could see, a good dancer; certainly he earned my admiration during a little hop, skip, and jump with Becky before the curtain. But he is not a singer, as he is often asked to be. And he is not—I'll write it in blood—Tom Sawyer.

BROADWAY SCORECARD / perfs: 25 / $: NA

rave	favorable	mixed	unfavorable	pan
			4	2

LOOK, MA, I'M DANCIN'!

a musical comedy, with music and lyrics by Hugh Martin; book by Jerome Lawrence and Robert E. Lee, "conceived" by Jerome Robbins

directed by George Abbott and Jerome Robbins; choreographed by Jerome Robbins
produced by George Abbott
with Nancy Walker, Harold Lang, Janet Reed, Loren Welch, and Alice Pearce

opened January 29, 1948   Adelphi Theatre

ROBERT COLEMAN, *Daily Mirror*

Rack up another hit for George Abbott. If you want to laugh, rush to the Adelphi immediately and buy your tickets. A fast, funny, zippy musical. Nancy Walker is terrific, a one-woman show all by herself. Dead-panned, cynical, big-hearted, Nancy's Lily Malloy is a hilarious satiric gem. To revert to the parlance of the good old days of the Palace, Nancy rocks 'em. Robbins's choreography burlesques dancing of every variety: soft-shoe, buck and wing, steps-and-snappy-cracks, folk, and long-hair.

ROBERT GARLAND, *Journal-American*

There's almost more choreography than Pembroke Davenport, director of the orchestra, can shake his stick at. All sorts, all conditions of choreography; some so-so brilliant; some so-so lackluster; and some just so-so. The most brilliant is "Gotta Dance."

LOUIS KRONENBERGER, *PM*

The most I can say—to be school-masterish about *Look, Ma*—is that it's one of the brightest children I've ever flunked. It's a fine might-have-been; possibly even a fine should-have-been. It has good things in it, good people all about it, a good idea behind it. But it's not a good show. Nor is it that other, *High Button Shoes* [1947] kind of show—an upsy-downsy musical that's up at just the right moment and never down for long. *Look, Ma*, I'm afraid, is never up for long. The trouble is that the music's not good enough and the book's not good at all. The book flubs all its chances. Mr. Martin's music and lyrics represent less than my idea of Mr. Martin's talent: except for Miss Walker's first number [I'm the First Girl"], they're pretty routine, without much lilt or stylishness or wit.

ROBERT SYLVESTER, *Daily News*

There was a funny little kid who used to hang around backstage at the Winter Garden when her pop [Dewey Barto] had his act in the Olsen and Johnson shows [*Hellzapoppin'* (1938)] and daytimes she would answer the casting calls. Any casting calls. She wasn't particular. George Abbott had a casting call for *Best Foot Forward* [1941] and she answered that one. She sluffed across the stage, did a double take at the work light, and Abbott fell out of his chair. There was no role in *Forward* for her but he wrote one in. The kid was a

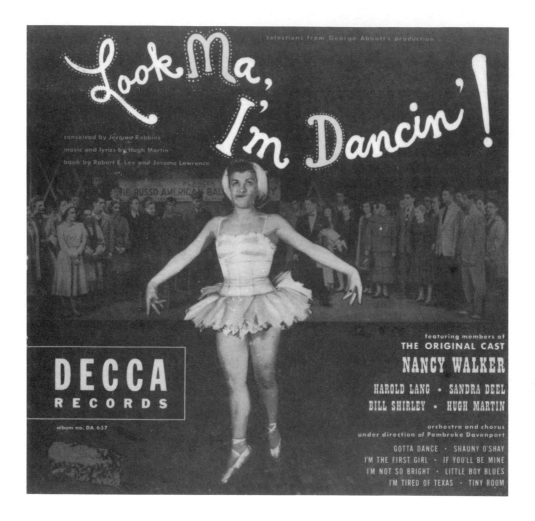

Nancy Walker as "the first girl in the second row in the third scene of the fourth number in fifth position at ten o'clock on the nose." A one-joke show, maybe, but what a joke!

riot. Last night the same Mr. Abbott offered her as the star—name in lights and everything—of his new musical. Her name is Nancy Walker and she took hold of *Look, Ma* and batted it around as if she owned it. This comical brat is simply loaded with talent. She looks a little like Ace Hudkins, the old welter-weight fighter, but when she sings a ballad she is somehow real pretty. She can throw lines away with all the confidence of Bobby Clark or Frank Fay and if anybody will just give her a rhythm song she can rock every note and syllable out of it. . . . By the time the show opened last night the book seemed to have been written (or maybe torn apart) somewhere between here and Philadelphia. The book is by Jerome Lawrence and Robert E. Lee and this reporter sternly resists the temptation to speculate on whether or not Mr. Lee is the original.

RICHARD WATTS JR., *Post*

I am still of the conviction that Jerome Robbins is one of the most talented and imaginative men in the American Theatre, [but] I must go on to add that the show which he and Mr. Abbott ran up struck me as almost steadily disappointing. There are good things in it, three of which represent Mr. Robbins's commendable refusal to be stuffy about his pirouettes. At the end of the first act there is another burlesque ballet in the "Mack Sennett" manner, which, if not as magnificently hilarious as his incomparable "Keystone Kops" number [from *High Button Shoes*] is still very funny. Then there are an engagingly delightful sleep-walking dance and a pleasantly romantic use of the *Swan Lake* thing, just to show what a tasteful and creative choreographer Mr. Robbins is even in his most casual mood. . . . Honesty forces me to confess my belief that the player who did the most to give *Ma* some much-needed attractiveness was the chorus girl who wore a narrow red ribbon in her hair and had a line which went "I had a lovely time at your party."

It might have been a one-joke show, but the joke—Nancy Walker as a brewer's daughter who bankrolls the ballet in order to get "on her toes"—seems like it was worth a whole lot of laughs. Big Hollywood Plans for a Betty Hutton screen version fell through, and *Ma* slipped into oblivion.

A Donaldson Award was won by Harold Lang (male dancer).

LOST IN THE STARS

a musical tragedy, with music by Kurt Weill; book and lyrics by Maxwell Anderson, from the 1948 novel *Cry, the Beloved Country* by Alan Paton

directed by Rouben Mamoulian
produced by the Playwrights' Company (including Anderson and Weill)
with Todd Duncan, Leslie Banks, Warren Coleman, and Inez Matthews

opened October 30, 1949   Music Box Theatre

BROOKS ATKINSON, *Times*

Although the novel had more detail than Mr. Anderson has space for in the theatre, the novel did not have Mr. Weill's music. And here the theatre has come bearing its most memorable gifts. In the past Mr. Weill has given the theatre some fine scores. But at the moment, which is forty minutes after the final curtain, it is difficult to remember anything out of his portfolio as eloquent as this richly orchestrated singing music. Some of it is as artless as a Broadway song. But most of it is overflowing with the same compassion that Mr. Paton brought to his novel. Written with theatrical virtuosity, the score serves as a classical chorus, picking up and projecting the significance of the various scenes. It carries throughout the theatre the fears and hatreds, the wildness, the anguish, and the heavy spiritual burdens of a big story.

HOWARD BARNES, *Herald Tribune*

A soaring musical tragedy. *Lost in the Stars* has excitement, flavor, heart, and a stern authority. Maxwell Anderson has adapted *Cry, the Beloved Country* with immense skill and fidelity. Kurt

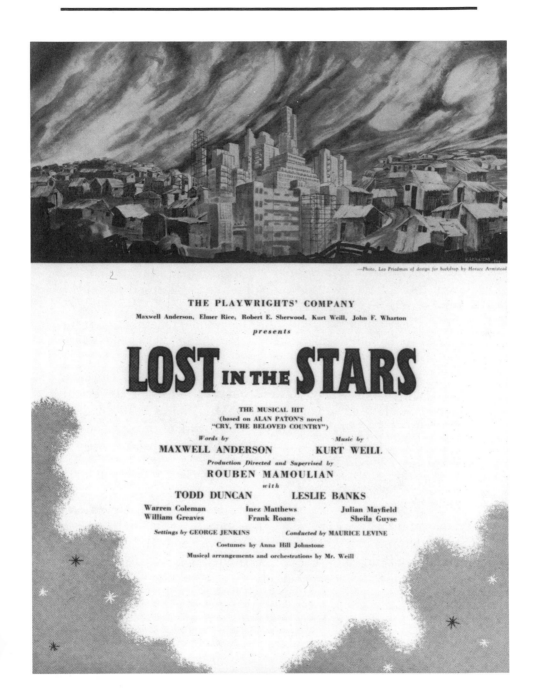

—Photo, Leo Friedman of design for backdrop by Horace Armistead

THE PLAYWRIGHTS' COMPANY

Maxwell Anderson, Elmer Rice, Robert E. Sherwood, Kurt Weill, John F. Wharton

presents

LOST IN THE STARS

THE MUSICAL HIT
(based on ALAN PATON'S novel
"CRY, THE BELOVED COUNTRY")

Words by   *Music by*

MAXWELL ANDERSON   **KURT WEILL**

Production Directed and Supervised by

ROUBEN MAMOULIAN

with

TODD DUNCAN   **LESLIE BANKS**

Warren Coleman   Inez Matthews   Julian Mayfield
William Greaves   Frank Roane   Sheila Guyse

Settings by GEORGE JENKINS   Conducted by MAURICE LEVINE

Costumes by Anna Hill Johnstone

Musical arrangements and orchestrations by Mr. Weill

Horace Armistead's backdrop of Johannesburg, the evil big city, rising from the broken hills of the Veld. (drawing by Horace Armistead)

Weill has composed a beautifully integrated score, which makes dynamic use of both solo and ensemble numbers, while Rouben Mamoulian has staged the offering superbly. Since Todd Duncan, Leslie Banks, and their colleagues give every inflection to a work of true dimensions, there is virtually nothing wanting in *Lost in the Stars*. It is a harrowing theatrical experience, but one of deep satisfaction.

JOHN CHAPMAN, *Daily News*

The Playwrights' Company has been understandably puzzled as to what to call *Lost in the Stars*, for this is a piece which does not fit into an ordinary category. In the program it is called "a Musical Tragedy." After having swallowed the lump in my throat and shaken the last tingle out of my spine, and composed myself for careful statement, I'd call *Lost in the Stars* a work of art. Players, singers, story, songs, sets, and lights have come together under the direction of Rouben Mamoulian—the Mamoulian who staged *Porgy* [1927] and *Porgy and Bess* [1935] [which starred Todd Duncan; Mamoulian also directed *Oklahoma!* (1943) and *Carousel* (1945)]. Finally, with an excellent band of musicians under the direction of Maurice Levine handling Mr. Weill's beats, plaints, and melodies, *Lost in the Stars* becomes a work of theatrical art. It has unity; it seems right—and it has emotional impact.

ROBERT COLEMAN, *Daily Mirror*

In an effort to achieve simplicity, Anderson often achieves pretentious simplicity—which isn't the same thing at all. Let's call *Lost in the Stars* an artistic, rather than a commercial, achievement. There is much to praise in it, though not, we suspect, quite sufficient to give it wide popularity.

ROBERT GARLAND, *Journal-American*

Alan Paton's simple novel became *Lost in the Stars*, an ornate and complicated "musical tragedy" by Maxwell Anderson and Kurt Weill. It is the mislaid simplicity the new arrival is most hurtfully in need of. There is too much of words and music, production and direction, scenery and costume. And group singing! Most of it is good, some of it is excellent. But the beauty and simplicity of *Cry, the Beloved Country* infrequently comes through. Only Todd Duncan, as Stephen Kumalo, seems to sense the novel's artful artlessness.

RICHARD WATTS JR., *Post*

It is not that Mr. Anderson has fallen into that air of pretentiousness which sometimes tends to overwhelm him. It is merely that when he does try for simplicity, it has a rather unpersuasive quality, and the [necessary] eloquence is but rarely forthcoming. There is, indeed, very little lacking in *Lost in the Stars* save inspiration.

Lost in the Stars was greeted with a widely divergent set of reviews, a clear indication that here was an important show which—just as clearly—was certain to meet with audience resistance in some quarters. Profound? Pretentious? Besides being artistically controversial, the strong social message of *Lost in the Stars* no doubt offended a large section of the theatregoing public. (Washington's National Theatre voluntarily closed in 1948 rather than obey an edict to lift their "no coloreds downstairs" seating policy. "America's First Theatre" remained dark until 1952.) The project was instigated by Dorothy (Mrs. Oscar) Hammerstein, who read the novel prior to publication and suggested it to Maxwell Anderson. *Lost in the Stars* was to be Kurt Weill's last experiment in combining music and drama: he died of a heart attack on April 3, 1950, at the age of fifty.

A Donaldson Award was won by Todd Duncan (actor).

BROADWAY SCORECARD / perfs: 28 / $: −

rave	favorable	mixed	unfavorable	pan
3	1	1	2	1

LOUISIANA LADY

a musical comedy, with music by Alma Sanders; lyrics by Monte Carlo; book by Issac Green, Jr. and Eugene Berton, from the 1927 comedy *Creoles* by Samuel Shipman and Kenneth Perkins

directed by Edgar MacGregor; choreographed by Felicia Sorel
produced by Hall Shelton
with Edith Fellows, Monica Moore (replacing Irene Bordoni), and
Charles Judels

opened June 2, 1947   Century Theatre

JOHN CHAPMAN, *Daily News*

It is so undistinguished in music, lyrics, plot, dances, and acting
that it must have been done on purpose. *Louisiana Lady* is being
offered at $3.60 top, which is very low for a musical show these
days—but not low enough. . . . The lyrics, by Monte Carlo (that's
what it says in the program: Monte Carlo), have such themes as
"Gold, Women, and Laughter." Mr. Shelton, the producer, may
be the man who broke his bank on Monte Carlo.

ROBERT GARLAND, *Journal-American*

A mild mixture of muck, music, and magnolias.

LOUIS KRONENBERGER, *PM*

The sets and costumes of *Louisiana Lady* are said to be inherited
from a musical that closed out of town last winter [*In Gay New
Orleans*, sets by Watson Barratt; costumes by Frank Thompson].
Inherited or not, they are palpably the newest things in the show,
the rest of which seems straight out of the era of the buffalo nickel
and the spangled shawl. The music is based on all the pre-Sarajevo
operetta composers in turn; the dancing is based on the rather
outmoded theory that with enough energy you can dispense with
style, and even with skill. And the humor would seem to be based
on the old gag about the lecture bureau that couldn't send a wit as
an afterdinner speaker, so sent two half-wits instead.

BROADWAY SCORECARD / perfs: 4 / $: –

rave	favorable	mixed	unfavorable	pan
				9

LOVE LIFE

a musical "vaudeville," with music by Kurt Weill; book and lyrics by Alan Jay Lerner

directed by Elia Kazan; choreographed by Michael Kidd
produced by Cheryl Crawford
with Nanette Fabray and Ray Middleton

opened October 7, 1948   46th Street Theatre

BROOKS ATKINSON, *Times*

Although billed as "a vaudeville," *Love Life* is cute, complex, and joyless—a general gripe masquerading as entertainment. *Love Life* is an intellectual idea about showmanship gone wrong. Vaudeville has nothing to do with the bitter ideas Mr. Lerner has to express about marriage. Although he is trying to be a philosopher, unhappiness keeps creeping in. He looks jocose on the surface, but he is full of anguish. Most of the pleasures come out of Mr. Weill's music-box. He has never composed a more versatile score with agreeable music in so many moods—hot, comic, blue, satiric, and romantic. But these pleasant interludes are the result of deliberate effort to find something amusing in the lugubrious train of the story. The vaudeville sequences are generally inferior, and contribute nothing at all to the theme. *Love Life* is a pleasant-looking show that represents a lot of hard work by able theatre people who have made an effort to produce something distinguished and original. But Mr. Lerner's heart is not in enjoyment. After a glowing beginning, *Love Life* gets lost in some strange, cerebral labyrinth, and the pretense that it is vaudeville is a pose. Vaudeville is not pale and wan but hearty.

ROBERT COLEMAN, *Daily Mirror*

Cheryl Crawford established a new high standard for Broadway musicals last evening. Author Alan Jay Lerner and composer Kurt Weill have fashioned a superlative entertainment—a song and dance show with great heart, soaring imagination, welcome novelty, and keen observation. *Love Life*, via an adroit blend of story line and vaudeville, depicts the changes in values on American family life since the founding of our nation. It traces the romantic, economic, and cultural thread of an American family from Revo-

Born in 1920, "Baby Nanette" went into vaudeville at the age of 3 and in 1927 graduated to the "Our Gang" film shorts (silent and sound). Arriving on Broadway in 1940, Fabray sparked a half-dozen musicals before finally achieving full stardom with Love Life; but this and the two other mediocre musicals which quickly followed sent her to yet another medium—television. (costume by Lucinda Ballard, photo by Vandamm)

lutionary days to the present. It is an exciting study of the rise, demise, and rebirth of standards. But don't let this brief synopsis of its import scare you away, for *Love Life* is wonderful theatre. You'll love every minute of it. And it is a great achievement because it manages to be constantly entertaining while making its points. Incidentally, we wish to commend Miss Crawford for starting the evening with "The Star Spangled Banner." Praise be, she realizes that our national anthem is not something to be taken for granted, to be put in moth balls and exhumed only in emergencies. And it was appropriate that "The Star Spangled Banner" should raise the curtain on a star-spangled musical.

WILLIAM HAWKINS, *World-Telegram*

The author has a simple solid thing to say, which is so tricked up here with dissimilar elements, that the show's purpose is not clarified until the final scene. There husband and wife reconcile as they teeter toward each other across a tight rope. Before that the show is like a game which keeps the audience fighting for its own assimilation of purposes. *Love Life* may well prove the subject of the most argumentative dinner conversations of the year. It would be wicked to discourage novelty in the theatre, but *Love Life* tries too hard for comfort to be different. It suggests that theatrical conventions like unities of time, place, and subject, were developed over the years for pretty good reasons. There is plenty of entertainment in *Love Life*. The enormous scope of the work and its scrutiny of so specific a subject has led to arbitrary arrangement and selection of material, until the net result is a sample book of show business. It is a harvest from a meadow sown with packs of assorted seeds.

JOHN LARDNER, *Star*

Such is the influence and charm of drama critics in this day and age that I know for sure that the people responsible for *Love Life* will be glad to consider my suggestion that they cancel their second act, which is just as much to them as a hole in the chest, and end the piece with the first act curtain. I also know, however, that having considered the idea, they will drop it into the nearest spittoon and keep right on doing what they're doing. It's the Eightieth Congress all over again. This leaves me with no alternative but the painful one of going straight to the voters and advising those who patronize *Love Life* to file gently but firmly out of the shooting-gallery when the first act is over. Even at its best, *Love Life* glows with a kind of flat, artificial light, like a gas-log fire in a modern bijou apartment. At its worst, when the fire goes out and the smell of gas lingers on, your best bet is to get out into the country air of 46th Street. . . . Roughly speaking, the plot is *The Skin of Our Teeth* [1942], the Thornton Wilder play of a few years ago [directed by Kazan], set to music.

A controversial but unsuccessful attempt, *Love Life* was ultimately strangled by its concept. Weill and Lerner—keen experimenters in the evolving music/drama form—might have become perfectly complementary collaborators, but Weill was to die within two years. An illuminating sidebar on Broadway's most-married songwriter: three of Lerner's first four librettos dealt with divorce (*The Day Before Spring* [1945]), marital discord (*Love Life*), and polygamy (*Paint Your Wagon* [1951]). And his maiden effort (*What's Up* [1943]) took place in a girls' finishing school mistaken for a bordello! What's that Lerner song Richard Burton used to sing in *Camelot* (1960)? Oh, yes: "How to Handle a Woman."

A Tony Award was won by Nanette Fabray (actress).

BROADWAY SCORECARD / perfs: 252 / $: −

rave	favorable	mixed	unfavorable	pan
3	1	3	1	1

LUTE SONG

a play with songs, with music by Raymond Scott; lyrics by Bernard Hanighen; play by Sidney Howard and Will Irwin, from the fifteenth-century Chinese play *Pi-Pa-Ki* by Kao-Tsi-ch'ing;

directed by John Houseman; choreographed by Yeichi Nimura
produced by Michael Myerberg
with Mary Martin, Yul Brynner, Helen Craig, Clarence Derwent, Augustin Duncan, and Mildred Dunnock
opened February 6, 1946   Plymouth Theatre

Mary Martin strums her lute and sings, backed by Robert Edmond Jones's remarkable physical production. (sets and costumes by Robert Edmond Jones, Miss Martin's gown by Valentina, photo by George Karger)

JOHN CHAPMAN, *Daily News*

Visually, *Lute Song* is one of the most exquisite and exciting things I have ever seen upon a stage, and once again Robert Edmond Jones shows he is the first-ranking artist of the contemporary American theatre. But as a piece for the theatre—a story to grip mind and heart—it is a pose. Most earnest and admirably done, yes; but a pose. What life it has throbs in Mr. Jones's magnificent decors and costumes and in snatches of Raymond Scott's interesting score. Life is not in the telling of its story, however. Its story is a selfconscious attitude which doubtless is arty as hell but which reminded this oaf of the annual June play at a girls' school. . . . The great man is Robert Edmond Jones. Whether he is dealing with simple curtains, temple scenes, visions of heaven, or earthly pageants, he is a master, and his costumes are no less than superb.

LOUIS KRONENBERGER, *PM*

Mary Martin has much of her personal attractiveness, and a certain delicacy. I do not think the part best suits her talents, but she sustains it. As the husband, Yul Brynner has looks and grace, but he is not much of an actor, and is not up to the frantic demands of the play's most important role.

BURTON RASCOE, *World-Telegram*

Meanwhile there was a famine in this native village. Her husband's parents died of starvation and Mary Martin was reduced to beggary in a gorgeous while silk gown designed by Valentina [who did the star's clothes while the rest of the costumes were designed by Jones]. In another number by Valentina she had to sell her hair to give her husband's parents a proper burial. Then, in still another Valentina special (all others in rags), she tramped hundreds of miles to the capital, arriving there without a speck of dust and pretty as a picture.

VERNON RICE, *Post*

Charm can be a damaging word. That is the only word, however, applicable to *Lute Song*, starring the Texas nightingale Mary Martin. The musical play is full of charm; it is teeming over with it, and if the use of the word damns this Chinese love story with faint praise, that is how it is intended. . . . Unquestionably, it has been given one of the finest productions of any play done recently. Robert Edmond Jones created costumes that are spectacular in their beauty and sets that are breathtaking in their simplicity. Good taste abounds. Pageantry, mood, and atmosphere are there, too. But over it all is the shroud of dullness.

A visually stunning but obviously non-commercial project, from an unfinished play by Sidney Howard. The Pulitzer Prize–winning dramatist was killed in a freak accident—crushed by a farm tractor—on August 23, 1939, shortly before the release of *Gone With the Wind*, for which he received a posthumous Best Screenplay Oscar.

Donaldson Awards were won by Robert Edmond Jones (scenic designer; costume designer).

BROADWAY SCORECARD / perfs: 142 / $: −

rave	favorable	mixed	unfavorable	pan
1	1	4	2	

MAGDALENA

a costume operetta, with music by Heitor Villa-Lobos; lyrics and "pattern" by Robert Wright and George Forrest; book by Frederick Hazlitt Brown and Homer Curran

directed by Jules Dassin; choreographed by Jack Cole
produced by Edwin Lester, presented by Homer Curran
with Irra Petina, John Raitt, Dorothy Sarnoff, and Hugo Haas

opened September 20, 1948   Ziegfeld Theatre

BROOKS ATKINSON, *Times*

Although Villa-Lobos has been certified as authentic by qualified musicologists, it is impossible to have much of an idea about the score for a very unfortunate reason. *Magdalena* is one

"A Romance of the Magdalena River Jungle." The musical might have been new, but the book and "pattern" (?) were turn-of-the-century balderdash.

of the most overpoweringly dull musical dramas of all time.
Watching the slow process of the plot and production is like being hit over the head with a sledge hammer repeatedly all
evening. It hurts. Even bad musical plays do not need to be so
profoundly dull as this one. Rummaging around among the old
hats in the garret, the entrepreneurs of *Magdalena* have set the
art of music drama back several generations, as though nothing
had been accomplished since *The Prince of Pilsen* [1903]. The
men of letters and ideas who acknowledge authorship of
Magdalena have insisted on hitching a contemporary Brazilian
score to a threadbare show-shop formula with some egregious
Continental flourishes. Not only is the form of the libretto with
stock characters archaic, but the story is unintelligible. The
production is elaborately old-fashioned and the direction is ponderous.

JOHN LARDNER, *Star*

If you can manage, with or without surgery, to take your eyes
and ears to the Ziegfeld Theatre and leave your cerebrum at
home on the hat-rack, it's conceivable that you will enjoy
Magdalena, a lush operetta or "musical adventure" which opened
Monday night in a blaze of lights, color, melody, and dramatic
torpor. The assets of *Magdalena* are a carload of gorgeous
costumes [designed by Irene Sharaff] and the music of Heitor
Villa-Lobos,who is a better composer than you or I or Hoagy
Carmichael. Under the heading of asset 2, there are several talented singers who can spread the news loudly and on key. Under
the heading of humor, there is, somewhere near the beginning of
the second act, a joke. . . . The show purports to be South American through and through. Its players speak their lines in a subtle
and profound form of "foreign" English which you have doubtless
run across before and which consists largely of saying "I do not
care" instead of "I don't care." However, they won't fool you.
They are mostly local folks. As for the story, though it is alleged
to take place in the republic of Colombia, it follows the pure
and classic line of musical comedy as practiced in Culver City,
Calif. and western Manhattan—except, as I said before, it omits
comedy.

☆

One of Edwin Lester's West Coast "great composer" series, this time by a living composer, with an apparently intriguing score devastated by the Broadway professionals.

BROADWAY SCORECARD / perfs: 88 / $: −

rave	favorable	mixed	unfavorable	pan
2	1	1	2	3

MAGGIE

a musical play, with music and lyrics by William Roy; book by Hugh Thomas, from the 1908 comedy *What Every Woman Knows* by J. M. Barrie

directed by Michael Gordon; choreographed by June Graham
produced by Franklin Gilbert and John Fearnley
with Betty Paul, Keith Andes, and Odette Myrtil (replacing Irene Bordoni)

opened February 18, 1953   National Theatre

WILLIAM HAWKINS, *World-Telegram & Sun*

If the show sometimes seems weighty from a physical point of view, it certainly proved too much for its backstage technicians last night, who shifted and lit it as if they had never before attended a performance.

WALTER KERR, *Herald Tribune*

The so-called "comedy" numbers, allotted to Odette Myrtil as a worldly-wise enchantress of thirty years' experience, are as out of place in the gentle humors of Barrie as they are, in themselves, lyrically lame. ("We were on the Bosporous in a rowboat, and suddenly there was no boat.") Miss Myrtil gives them the full treatment—arched eyebrows, industrious innuendo, and all—but they persist in dropping *Maggie* a couple of notches below its best level of inspiration.

JOHN McCLAIN, *Journal-American*

We all know and love Odette Myrtil, but what can you do with such material? It is always difficult in these instances to determine where the deficiency of the author ends and that of the producer and director begins. In this case it is doubly doubtful, because it seems to me that none of them has complemented the other. The show lacks plausibility and humor, and nothing in the way of timing and excitement has been substituted.

RICHARD WATTS JR., *Post*

Odette Myrtil, who has never been a particular heroine of mine, still isn't.

Odette Myrtil was a violin-playing *coquette Parisienne* from the old days. She had been featured in operettas like Emmerich Kalman's *Countess Maritza* (1926) and the Shuberts' Chopin-etta *White Lilacs* (1928), in which she played George Sand. (Chopin lost.) Myrtil's son was one of Broadway's top dance arrangers, Roger Adams of *The Pajama Game* (1954), *Damn Yankees* (1955), et al.

BROADWAY SCORECARD / perfs: 5 / $: −

rave	favorable	mixed	unfavorable	pan
	1	4	1	1

MAKE A WISH

a musical comedy, with music and lyrics by Hugh Martin; book by Preston Sturges (replaced by Anita Loos, who was then replaced by Abe Burrows), from the 1931 comedy *The Good Fairy* by Ferenc Molnár

directed by John C. Wilson; choreographed by Gower Champion
produced by Harry Rigby and Jule Styne in association with Alexander H. Cohen
with Nanette Fabray, Melville Cooper, Harold Lang, Stephen

Innocent Nanette Fabray peers out at bohemian Paris through the orphanage window. Pre-Broadway credits. (drawing by Clemens)

Douglass, Helen Gallagher, Phil Leeds and Le Roi Operti (replacing Franklin Pangborn)

opened April 18, 1951   Winter Garden Theatre

BROOKS ATKINSON, *Times*

Since Raoul Pène du Bois has Gallic blood flowing through his veins, you may expect some gay Parisian scenery, done with the true flair of an artist, and costumes, particularly for the ballets, that are bold and imaginative. For some reason or other, there does seem to be more scenery than show. The performers have to be on their toes to find a way through it. Mr. Champion is the only one who really makes use of the production. At the end of the first act, he has composed a spinning *beaux arts* ball that serves the purpose creditably. But toward the end of the show, he contributes a little gem of ballet cartooning about a department store sale. Now that he and his dancers have accomplished it, this seems to be one of the most inevitable subjects for satiric dancing. Everyone knows the theme—the frantic search for bargains, the nervous attempts to try on hats, the voracious picking over of the merchandise and the unctuous skill of shop-lifting. Apart from these wry details, which are sketched in with acid mimicry, Mr. Champion has developed the cartoon into a whirling low-comedy conclusion.

OTIS L. GUERNSEY JR., `Herald Tribune`

The book credited to Preston Sturges, with revisions attributed to Abe Burrows, seems to be about almost anything that occurred to mind.

JOHN McCLAIN, *Journal-American*

Make a Wish is just about the most insipid and pedestrian story ever told, but it is done with such verve and enthusiasm, the music is so sprightly, the ballets so exciting, the setting so gay, that pretty soon you don't care what it's about. You just like it. The ballet "The Students' Ball," in the first act, is one of the truly exciting interludes in this season's theatre. But it is topped half an hour later by another one called "The Sale." I will say without qualification that this is alone worth the price of admission.

RICHARD WATTS JR., *Post*

The ballet is nothing short of wonderful. It is an enchantingly ferocious number, all about a sale in a Paris department store that turns into a devastating riot, and it succeeds in being at the same time funny and fresh. Although I do not claim to be an expert on the art of the ballet, it seems to me by all odds the most hilarious one I have seen since the "Keystone Kops" number in *High Button Shoes* [1947] and the most imaginative since "The Small House of Uncle Thomas" in *The King and I* [1951, both choreographed by Jerome Robbins]. Helen Gallagher, an attractive young dancer who has brightened every musical comedy or revue in which I have seen her, is of particular help as the heroine's friend. One of the best male dancers in the theatre, as everyone knows by now, is Harold Lang, and he, too, is of great assistance to the proceedings.

Given the overwhelmingly enthusiastic reaction to the choreography, it's surprising that Gower Champion didn't try another full-scale musical until *Bye Bye Birdie* (1960). "The Sale," unflinchingly compared to the best of Jerome Robbins, sounds like one of the greatest show ballets we'll never see. Producer Jule Styne, meanwhile, took Lang and Gallagher on to (brief) stardom as, respectively, *Pal Joey* (1952 revival) and *Hazel Flagg* (1953). Scenic note: the opening scene was revealed through a gigantic Venetian blind.

A Donaldson Award was won by Harold Lang (male dancer).

BROADWAY SCORECARD / perfs: 102 / $: −				
rave	favorable	mixed	unfavorable	pan
	5	2		

MAKE MINE MANHATTAN

a musical revue, with music by Richard Lewine; sketches and lyrics by Arnold B. Horwitt, with "suggestions" from Moss Hart

directed by Hassard Short; sketches directed by Max Liebman;
choreographed by Lee Sherman
produced by Joseph M. Hyman
with Sid Caesar, David Burns, Sheila Bond, Danny Daniels, and
Joshua Shelley

opened January 15, 1948   Broadhurst Theatre

JOHN CHAPMAN, *Daily News*

If you missed the *Music Box Revues* [1921–1924] and the first
and second *Little Shows* [1929, 1930] back in the "good old days,"
no matter: this one is just as good and sometimes—in the dancing,
for instance—it is better. *Manhattan* is everything a revue should
be—which is considerably more than being mere dressed-up
vaudeville. It is young and full of high spirits; it is as topical as this
copy of today's paper; it is wonderfully funny, and witty, too; its
tunes have bounce and so do its dancers; its pace is the pace of New
York—quick and busy every minute. Hassard Short [director of the
Music Box Revues] has driven the show from the opening to the
closing like Ben Hur winning the big chariot race. . . . Sid Caesar
can out-talk Danny Kaye and is much more amusing. At various
times he impersonates, single-handed, a United Nations assembly;
a penny gum machine; a dial telephone; a headwaiter; and an
Italian restaurateur who mixes salad-dressing. He is an entertainer
of great talent.

WILLIAM HAWKINS, *World-Telegram*

Sid Caesar appears so many times that he might as well have
been starred. No great show comic—Willie Howard, Bert Lahr,
even Ed Wynn—would let himself be spotted so often. He would
know it would kill him, artistically if not physically. It nearly does
both to Caesar. In his last number, his voice is not nearly as courageous as he is. Caesar has pace and vigor and plenty of comedy
sense. He assumes the manner of a long line of night club MCs,
and is guilty of lamentable taste. He is certainly not untalented,
but misguided.

LOUIS KRONENBERGER, *PM*

The show offers the best reason I can think of for seeing *Allegro*
[1947]—the ability to appreciate *Make Mine Manhattan*'s often
very funny parody of it [with Sid Caesar as a frustrated dentist].

JOSEPH M. HYMAN presents

BERT LAHR
IN
MAKE MINE MANHATTAN

A New Musical Revue
STAGED BY
HASSARD SHORT
SKETCHES & LYRICS BY ARNOLD B. HORWITT
MUSIC BY RICHARD LEWINE
Sketches Directed by MAX LIEBMAN
with
DAVID BURNS
JACK ALBERTSON · JEAN JONES · LOU WILLS, Jr.
MARY ANN NILES · BOB FOSSE · EARL WILLIAM

Settings by FREDERICK FOX
Choreography by LEE SHERMAN
Costumes by MORTON HAACK
Musical Director JERRY ARLEN

SHUBERT THEATRE
BOSTON
Limited Engagement Beg. Monday, January 10
MATINEES WEDNESDAY and SATURDAY

A revue celebrating the City. For the National Tour, Bert Lahr—a box office star—came in to replace Sid Caesar. Also featured on the road were the husband/wife dance team of Fosse & Niles. Post-Broadway credits. (drawing by Benjamin J. Harris)

420

WARD MOREHOUSE, *Sun*

In a sketch David Burns wears a fur-collared coat that was surely borrowed yesterday afternoon from George Jean Nathan and he drags on a half-wit named Jukes as his successor as dramatic critic of the *Daily Gazette*. The publisher wants to know if Jukes has the qualifications. Why, certainly. Jukes is deaf and blind and he loathes the theatre. He gets the job.

RICHARD WATTS JR., *Post*

The criticism can be biting. For example, none of the reviewers who had hard words for *Allegro* were as devastating in pointing to the one grave weakness of that distinguished musical play as the witty parody on its synthetic distaste for city life, which is one of the brilliant achievements of *Make Mine Manhattan*.

A Donaldson Award was won by Sid Caesar (male debut).

```
BROADWAY SCORECARD / perfs: 429 / $: +

  rave     favorable    mixed    unfavorable    pan

   5           2                       2
```

MAN IN THE MOON

a puppet show, with music by Jerry Bock; lyrics by Sheldon Harnick; book by Arthur Burns

directed by Gerald Freedman
produced by Arthur Cantor and Joseph Harris
with Bil and Cora Baird's Marionette Theatre and Emil Maurer

opened April 11, 1963   Biltmore Theatre

JUDITH CRIST, *Herald-Tribune*

The Bairds' new production brims with inventiveness, imagination and eye-filling artistry and boasts a musical score that might well be the envy of any Broadway show. And why not? Jerry Bock and Sheldon Harnick, the *Fiorello!* [1959] boys, have provided a bagful of delightful songs that set not only a high standard for children's entertainments but also, let us hope, a precedent for skilled professional participations in ventures of this sort.

FRANCES HERRIDGE, *Post*

The lyrics are often more clever than the dialogue. Take for instance the gangster's song—"I like to reap what other people sow, and cook with other people's dough. When night-time comes stealing in, so do I."

When Bock and Harnick came to town with the puppets they had already completed not only *She Loves Me,* which opened two weeks later, but most of *Tevye and His Daughters*—which was having money-raising troubles prior to the involvement of Jerome Robbins and Harold Prince.

```
BROADWAY SCORECARD / perfs: 7 / $: NA

   rave     favorable     mixed     unfavorable     pan

                            4
```

MARIA GOLOVIN

an opera by Gian-Carlo Menotti

directed by Gian-Carlo Menotti
produced by David Merrick and the National Broadcasting Company in association with Byron Goldman
with Franca Duval, Richard Cross, Patricia Neway, and William Chapman

opened November 5, 1958   Martin Beck Theatre

JOHN CHAPMAN, *Daily News*

Gian-Carlo Menotti's *Maria Golovin* is the least effective of his mature works, a tearjerker without the power to exact tears.

Menotti's heart just wasn't in it. . . . The maid gets off a duzy at one point, "Even the lake is as dead as a frying pan."

ROBERT COLEMAN, *Daily Mirror*

Menotti's most compelling work, a distinguished work, a candidate for prizes in this or any season. It is exciting. It is deeply moving. It races the pulses. It stirred the first-nighters to spontaneous outbursts of applause. It's Menotti's best, and that spells terrific.

WALTER KERR, *Herald Tribune*

The hero of *Maria Golovin* owns a gun, and he keeps it hidden in his piano. So, I imagine, does composer Gian-Carlo Menotti. The Menotti flair for shoot-'em-up melodrama has been remarked upon before. I am not sure that it has been sufficiently respected. Consider the boldness—brazenness, even—of the dozens of visual images Mr. Menotti hurls at us in a single, never well-tempered evening while a stir in the pit keeps each of them constant and crackling company. While his principals lift their voices in urgent emotional demand, an escaped prisoner is getting ready to burst in upon them, a child in party costume is being faced with a revolver, fireworks are being set off in the wings to cast a red-and-green glow over the despair on the stage, and an amateur jazz band is beginning to whine its tinny, faraway bravura, nerve-wracked solo in a darkened room. Mr. Menotti is vigorously concerned that each of his successive scenes shall be a *scene*—a particular, cross-handed arrangement of ironies, outrages, and unexpected effects. The concern, together with the surprisingly plausible management of so many colorful devices, is surely a virtue. Do all of the devices work? No, of course not: the composer's musical blood pressure would have to race even higher than it does to embrace and make legitimate so much calculated spectacle. Still, this is adventurous musical theatre, with a stubborn bravado about it that is sometimes foolish but more often stimulating, and I'd go to see it.

JOHN McCLAIN, *Journal-American*

It seems slightly sneaky to me that David Merrick and the National Broadcasting Co. should bill Gian-Carlo Menotti's latest effort as a "new musical drama" and thus trap the drama critics into covering it. I think *Maria Golovin* is quite dreary, if it is to be judged as a Broadway musical. I bow to no man in my admiration of Mr. Menotti's talent, but in this instance I think it is a lot of screaming about pretty trivial stuff. It may have a certain appeal to dedicated opera fans, but regarded on the basis of a Broadway musical (their term, not mine) it is very slow going.

RICHARD WATTS JR., *Post*

A thoroughgoing triumph. The sheer melodramatic forcefulness of the narrative has a power that by no means depends entirely on its musical merits. *Maria Golovin* is a combination of music and drama that is impressive in both fields. The remarkable theatrical sense of Gian-Carlo Menotti gives *Maria Golovin* a stunning quality of dramatic, or, rather, melodramatic excitement.

For ten years Gian-Carlo Menotti was America's musical/operatic darling, with *The Medium and the Telephone* (1947), *The Consul* (1947), and *The Saint of Bleecker Street* (1954)—the latter two winning Pulitzers and Drama Critics Awards—as well as the celebrated television opera "Amahl and the Night Visitors" (1951). Then came *Maria Golovin*, which premiered August 20, 1958, at the American Pavilion of the Brussels World's Fair. Menotti's Broadway fortune was suddenly reversed, and American opera hasn't been heard hereabouts since.

BROADWAY SCORECARD / perfs: 5 / $: −

rave	favorable	mixed	unfavorable	pan
2	2	1	1	1

MARINKA

a romantic operetta suggested by the 1888 Mayerling tragedy, with music by Emmerich Kalman; book and lyrics by George Marion, Jr.; book by George Marion, Jr. and Karl Farkas

directed by Hassard Short; book directed by George Marion, Jr. and Karl Farkas; choreographed by Albertina Rasch
produced by Jules J. Leventhal and Harry Howard
with Joan Roberts, Harry Stockwell, Romo Vincent, and Luba Malina

opened July 18, 1945   Winter Garden Theatre

LOUIS KRONENBERGER, *PM*

It's neither yesterday in Vienna nor today on Broadway. It's simply yesterday on Broadway, and not even the best of that. Many of the tunes are pretty and melodious in a familiar way; but one song sounds much like another, and all the songs could have come out of any operetta written since McKinley was in the White House. I guess there is nothing spectacularly gruesome about the book; there's just a terrible lot of it, mostly in the form of terrible jokes. . . . Mary Grant's peasant costumes at the end of Act One are, indeed, superb. The girls who wear them, however, are another of *Marinka*'s many unexciting features.

BURTON RASCOE, *World-Telegram*

Who wants to hear about the love affairs of Crown Prince Rudolph of Austria-Hungary nowadays? We have just ended a war with an Austrian named Hitler. . . . The cast includes Ethel Levey, first wife of George M. Cohan (she makes an entrance and an exit, smoking a cigar).

BROADWAY SCORECARD / perfs: 165 / $: −

rave	favorable	mixed	unfavorable	pan
	1	1	5	1

MASK AND GOWN

an intimate revue, with music and lyrics by Ronny Graham, June (Sillman) Carroll, Arthur Siegel, and Dorothea Freitag; "continuity" by Ronny Graham and Sidney Carroll

conceived and directed by Leonard Sillman; choreographed by Jim Russell
produced by Leonard Sillman and Bryant Haliday
with T. C. Jones

opened September 10, 1957   John Golden Theatre

WALTER KERR, *Herald Tribune*

Mr. Leonard Sillman teed off the new Broadway season by presenting Mr. T. C. Jones in a series of female impersonations called *Mask and Gown.* The engagement is limited. So is Mr. Jones.

BROADWAY SCORECARD / perfs: 39 / $: −

rave	favorable	mixed	unfavorable	pan
	2		4	1

ME AND JULIET

a musical comedy, with music by Richard Rodgers; book and lyrics by Oscar Hammerstein 2nd

directed by George Abbott; choreographed by Robert Alton
produced by Richard Rodgers and Oscar Hammerstein 2nd
with Isabel Bigley, Bill Hayes, Joan McCracken, and Ray Walston

opened May 28, 1953   Majestic Theatre

BROOKS ATKINSON, *Times*

All the captivating things everyone loves in a Rodgers and Hammerstein show struggle with a book that has no velocity. To tell the truth, *Me and Juliet* looks a little like a rehearsal—beautiful, talented, full of good things, but still disorganized. As the tired sages of show business invariably remark as though one phrase could solve everything: "It needs work."

Backstage scene at Rodgers and Hammerstein's backstage musical.
(drawing by Don Freeman)

JOHN CHAPMAN, *Daily News*

It is at its most interesting when Jo Mielziner's scenery is in motion, ranging from front to back and top to bottom of a big theatre. There is a first-act chorus dance number, "Keep It Gay," which is sheer wizardry—an instantaneous change from a performance in costume as a paying audience would see it to a backstage rehearsal of this same number with the boys and girls in their practice clothes. Light bridges, "pipes," black walls, and a smoking lounge interchange effortlessly with the glamorous curtains and settings a theatre audience sees from its chairs.

ROBERT COLEMAN, *Daily Mirror*

Having set new high standards for musicals throughout the world, Rodgers and Hammerstein dipped into the lower drawer of their desk for *Me and Juliet*. It proved a big disappointment for this dyed-in-the-wool R. & H. fan. Had it been penned and composed by a couple of tyros named Joe Smith and Harold Jones, we would probably write this morning that it was a fair start, showing promise of sorts. But coming from the atelier of the masters it was, to put it kindly, incredible. We kept saying over and over to ourselves: "Dick Rodgers and Oc Hammerstein didn't do it. They couldn't have done it. They'd have taken this one off in Boston for revamping."

WALTER KERR, *Herald Tribune*

Like a lot of lovers bent on declaring their passion, the authors strike a point at which they become tongue-tied. They want to say so much, they want to say it so burstingly, they want to be so sure that no heartfelt endearment is omitted anywhere, that they wind up gasping for breath and making slightly disconnected sounds. *Me and Juliet* is a dizzying collection of independently attractive fragments, so eager to embrace everything that half its treasures slip through its outstretched arms. The love stories begin winningly, and then, in the scurry, lose individuality and warmth. The show-within-a-show begins in what seems a satirical vein, and then blurs and goes limp in the restless and overly ingenious evening. (This last is quite a serious loss; by failing to whip real gayety, humor, and a constant point of view, Rodgers and Hammerstein have come perilously close to writing a show-without-a-show.)

Me and Juliet was not nearly as bad as it sounds; it just followed *South Pacific* (1949) and *The King and I* (1951), that's all. Historical note: during the run of *Juliet*, Abbott stage managers Griffith and Prince went looking for a choreographer for their first production (to be coauthored and directed by Abbott, naturally). Joan McCracken—*Juliet's* Juliet and a top dancing comedienne from *Oklahoma!* (1943), *Bloomer Girl* (1944), and *Billion Dollar Baby* (1945)—offered her husband, a hoofer with virtually no credentials named Fosse. The show: *The Pajama Game* (1954)—and the "Joan McCracken role" was given to Carol Haney, Fosse's dancing partner in the 1953 movie version of *Kiss Me, Kate* (1948).

BROADWAY SCORECARD / perfs: 358 / $: +

rave	favorable	mixed	unfavorable	pan
	1	1	4	1

THE MEDIUM AND THE TELEPHONE
(*L'amour à trois*)

a transfer of the Ballet Society's production of two chamber operas, with music, book, and lyrics by Gian-Carlo Menotti

directed by Gian-Carlo Menotti
produced by Chandler Cowles and Efrem Zimbalist, Jr. in association with Edith Luytens
with Marie Powers, Evelyn Keller, Leo Coleman, and Marilyn Cotlow

opened May 1, 1947   Ethel Barrymore Theatre

BROOKS ATKINSON, *Times*

Between opera and the dramatic stage there is a difference in emphasis that keeps the two mediums fundamentally separate. In relating this tale of the bogus medium who succumbs to her own charlatanism, Mr. Menotti has packed the drama into the music. He is not much interested in the libretto, which is undistinguished in literary style. As a story it is hardly more than a basic idea. All the development, as well as the characterizations, lie in the music. In *Street Scene* [1947] the music illustrates the drama. In *The Medium* the drama is the music. As music it has, of course, the variety and flexibility of a primary art. Some of it is narrative, like the story of the seance; some of it is lyrical, like the daughter's love sequence with the mute Toby; and some of it is diabolically introspective, like the medium's ominous description of her obsession. But if it is true that the producers want *The Medium* judged as theatre fare, there is this very considerable distinction between opera and drama. In opera the music stands between the theatregoer and the actor, which makes for heavy and torpid expression of human emotion. Music and drama are not interchangeable arts. Less distinguished music than Mr. Menotti's frequently strikes brighter sparks on Broadway. For Broadway's native music is the song as in *Porgy and Bess* [1935]. In the current *Street Scene* Kurt Weill has gone about as far as a theatre musician can in extending the song in the direction of opera.

Robert Garland, *Journal-American*

A taut and tingling killer-diller. Writing his own book, his own lyrics, and his own music, the author-lyricist-composer must have cooked them up with Charles Addams behind him, prompting. A good, hair-raising show.

William Hawkins, *World-Telegram*

It is a courageous and laudable thing, this bringing to Broadway Menotti's *The Telephone* and *The Medium*. They are short operas, and their music is modern. If this does not sound like an obviously commercial or popular proposition, let us enlarge on that description immediately. Both works are sung in English by a cast that scarcely lets you miss a word. The former has the charm and wit of a first-rate musical comedy number, but its music is fresher and richer. The latter has the eerie fascination of the most macabre thriller. In fact it is the only successful horror play of this year's theatre.

Louis Kronenberger, *PM*

What is special about Mr. Menotti's talent is that it is an amalgam. One may doubt his ability to write distinctive words or compose really distinguished music; what is beyond dispute is his ability to write words and music that fit like a glove and that notably reinforce each other. Beyond that, Mr. Menotti has a real sense of theatre, in the Broadway rather than just the operatic sense; so that if he is a good deal less than a true playwright, he is a good deal more than a mere librettist. There is genuine melodramatic power in *The Medium*, bred of Mr. Menotti's ability to tell an exciting story, and to communicate—by words in combination with music—the minds and emotions of its characters. The music has very frantic climaxes and some genuinely lyrical episodes, but what seemed to me peculiarly effective about it was what might be called a narrative quality, something that held the story together while keeping it steadily moving.

It has never been easy to sell opera on Broadway. But *The Medium*, explained the critics, was pure melodrama in the best sense of the word. A thrillingly chilling piece of theatre, it still works. But if they did it today, would anybody go?

A Tony Award was won by Horace Armistead (scenic designer).

BROADWAY SCORECARD / perfs: 211 / $: −				
rave	*favorable*	*mixed*	*unfavorable*	*pan*
4	1	1	3	

MEMPHIS BOUND

a musical comedy incorporating the 1878 British comic opera *H.M.S. Pinafore*, with musical adaptaion and new music by Don Walker; new lyrics by Don Walker and Clay Warnick; book by Albert Barker and Sally Benson; "with gratitude to W. S. Gilbert and Sir Arthur Sullivan"

directed by Robert Ross, "assisted" by Eva Jessye; choreographed
by Al White, Jr.
produced by Vinton Freedley, presented by John Wildberg
with Bill ("Bojangles") Robinson, Avon ("Sportin' Life") Long,
Billy Daniels, Ada Brown, and Sheila Guys

opened May 24, 1945   Broadway Theatre

John Chapman, *Daily News*

It has been too many years since I have seen a musical with the
zip, the stomp, and the whoosh of *Memphis Bound.* Musicals of
late have been serious about themselves—sometimes depressingly
so. They go in for solemn quaintness, or "book," or ballets that are
as artistic as all hell. They have slipped away from the days of *Hit
the Deck* [1927] and *Flying High* [1930] and have become works of
dignity. The lacking element might be called breeze. *Memphis
Bound* has breeze. It's as good-natured as a puppy, and frequently
very smart. . . . His [Robinson's] skin is as darkly glistening as
ever, his teeth as white, his smile as comprehensive, and his eyes
as roguish. His feet still fashion those inimitably clear patterns of
taps, and the old, old stair dance has lost none of its capacity to
astonish.

Lewis Nichols, *Times*

Probably Gilbert and Sullivan were thinking of Bill when they
wrote down the original in the first place. Toward the end of the
evening, Mr. Robinson let out a vital statistic: today is his birthday
and he is 67 years old. By the way he goes at *Memphis Bound* he
must have been the reverse victim of that Gilbert and Sullivan trick
having to do with leap year; he is obviously only a fourth of 67. In
his new show he is the "monarch of the sea" in the *Pinafore* part,
a jailed river man in the remainder. His dancing is the same as
always, he still taps up and down the stairs with an agility that
would dizzy a grandchild. Easy and light, he wanders casually
through *Memphis Bound,* singing, talking, tapping.

Wilella Waldorf, *Post*

Memphis Bound endeavors to develop some sort of plot involving the Negroes of Calliboga, Tennessee, who have been presenting *Pinafore* aboard their showboat. Mr. Robinson plays Admiral

Porter, K.C.B. in the *Pinafore* excerpt and his famous dance on the steps is as fascinating as ever. Perhaps he really is 67 years old, but it's hard to believe after watching him cavort through *Memphis Bound*. The modernized *Pinafore* is interesting musically and often very funny as presented by the showboaters. Ralph Rackstraw, the lovelorn sailor, is done fairly straight by Billy Daniels, who has a pleasant tenor. Avon Long, playing Captain Corcoran in a lavender uniform, does a mild swish around the deck while his crew waves handkerchiefs, and there are three Josephines. It seems three girls have been promised the part and since they were practicing in the Andrews Sisters tradition, they do it as a sister act. Unfortunately no uniform pattern seems to have been set for the travesty, which wavers between a Tennessee Negro troupe's *Pinafore* and a sophisticated Broadway exercise in modern rhythms.

March of 1939—and the rush of customers to New York's World's Fair—brought forth not one but two paraphrases of Gilbert and Sullivan: the Federal Theatre's *Swing Mikado* and Mike Todd's *Hot Mikado*, the latter starring Bill Robinson as the Lord High Executioner. In May of 1945, Bojangles tapped back to town as the Monarch of the Sea, only to find George S. Kaufman's *Hollywood Pinafore* breathing down his neck. While all four were flawed, Robinson managed to look better than great as he terped up and down those steps. (The four updaptations made the Gilbert and Sullivan originals look pretty good, too.)

BROADWAY SCORECARD / perfs: 36 / $: −

rave	favorable	mixed	unfavorable	pan
2	3	1	1	1

THE MERRY WIDOW

a revival of the 1907 Viennese operetta, with music by Franz Lehár, adapted by Robert Stolz; lyrics by Adrian Ross; new book by Sidney Sheldon and Ben Roberts, from the original by Victor Leon and Leo Stein

directed by Felix Brentano; choreographed by George Balanchine
produced by Yolanda Mero-Irion for the New Opera Company
with Jan Kiepura, Marta Eggerth (Kiepura), and Melville Cooper

opened August 4, 1943   Majestic Theatre

LOUIS KRONENBERGER, *PM*

Jan Kiepura is as romantic as a carpet-sweeper and as stiff as a
broom—though for my money a stick is no worse than a ham. The
score remains a classic. (The one unpleasant thing about the music
is that its composer, from all reports, has played ball with the
Nazis. But he won't get any royalties from 44th St.) The music, last
night, found its equal in the dancing, which is probably the finest
thing that Balanchine has done on Broadway. The cancan at Max-
im's not only became a thing of great skill and allure, but unlike any
other cancan I've ever seen, completely evoked its own period—a
period that had never heard of jazz. But Balanchine's finest job is
a waltz ballet that is a miracle of lightness and loveliness, while the
pas de deux of Milada Mladova and Chris Volkoff called forth, and
deserved, an ovation.

BURTON RASCOE, *World-Telegram*

This is not the old *Merry Widow*—not by a long shot. The trouble boils down to the unhappy fact that Marta Eggerth and Jan
Kiepura aren't romantic, and neither one of them last night, least
of all Miss Eggerth, was merry. What's more, Mr. Kiepura has not
even learned to waltz. So Sonia and Danilo don't waltz in this
version of *The Merry Widow*. That, of course, is like *Hamlet* without Hamlet. . . . The Nish of David Wayne I liked very much,
although I didn't care particularly for the other comic characters.

WILELLA WALDORF, *Post*

It is probably true that Messrs. Sheldon and Roberts worked
themselves into a frenzy writing a new book, but we are regrettably
obliged to state that it seemed just as bad as all of the old ones.
They had to get on with the plot, after all, and while Melville
Cooper is one of our favorite funny men, we found very little to
laugh at last night until he ate a banana for no particular reason.
Unfortunately it is doubtful if the banana eating will be a regular

feature, the banana market being very black at the moment. . . .
Mr. Kiepura's Polish accent is so intense we thought he was singing
his Polish number in English until a kind friend enlightened us.

BROADWAY SCORECARD / perfs: 322 / $: +

rave	favorable	mixed	unfavorable	pan
2	3		1	2

MEXICAN HAYRIDE

a musical comedy, with music and lyrics by Cole Porter; book by
Herbert and Dorothy Fields

directed by Hassard Short; book directed by John Kennedy; choreographed by Paul Haakon
produced by Michael Todd
with Bobby Clark, June Havoc, Wilbur Evans, and Paul Haakon

opened January 28, 1944   Winter Garden Theatre

JOHN CHAPMAN, *Daily News*

From now on Gypsy Rose Lee can for my money be known as
June Havoc's sister. This lady has a facade which is nothing like a
Greek temple, but noble all the same; a pair of legs Mistinguett
could have envied; and the most remarkable observation platform
since Henry Dreyfuss designed the Twentieth Century Limited.
. . . *Mexican Hayride* is the first $5.50 musical in a dozen years.

ROBERT GARLAND, *Journal-American*

Yes! Yes! Yes, indeed! Which is to report that Broadway in general, and the drama critics in particular, can continue their custom
of writing the word "fabulous" in front of the name of Mike Todd.
For the truth is that last night the fabulous Todd produced a musical
comedy so funny, so tuneful, so beautiful, that you could hardly believe your ears and eyes. This musical-comedy-in-a-thousand is a

A Mexican toreadorable—and how!—ogled by Bobby Clark, who seems to have poked his head through the canvas for a closer look.
(drawing by Alberto Vargas)

436

rich, rowdy, and resplendent extravaganza. An earful, an eyeful, and an uproarious rowdy-dow. And all at the same time!

BURTON RASCOE, *World-Telegram*

Aladdin Todd rubbed his wonderful lamp and lifted us into a dream-world of splendor, mirth, melody, and enchantment.

WILELLA WALDORF, *Post*

Caught running an illegal lottery in competition with the government, Bobby [Clark] escaped the authorities and turned up in a series of hilarious disguises. Joining a band of itinerant musicians, he operated on the flute with impetuous virtuosity and all was going well until he lost his wig, whereupon it became necessary for him to disappear once more and turn up again as an Indian squaw with as fine a set of false teeth as ever graced a pawn shop window. Since Bobby still wears his painted-on spectacles, smokes a cigar, and howls like a coyote or yowls like a tom-cat when aroused, he was an immense success as the mother of a papoose who, oddly enough, also wore painted-on spectacles. As far as we are concerned, this was the high point of the evening, especially since it suddenly occurred to us while Bobby was toothily peddling his tortillas and tamales that he bore a haunting resemblance to Katharine Hepburn. If you go to see *Mexican Hayride* and begin to wonder after a while what on earth you came for, take a firm grip on yourself and stick it out until after the intermission. The second act is worth any amount of torture.

A wartime hit, thanks to favorite comic Bobby Clark and one Porter song hit, the syrupy "I Love You."

Donaldson Awards were won by Bobby Clark (actor); June Havoc (supporting actress); and Paul Haakon (male dancer).

BROADWAY SCORECARD / perfs: 481 / $: +

rave	favorable	mixed	unfavorable	pan
4	3	1		

MICHAEL TODD'S PEEP SHOW

a burlesque revue, with music and lyrics by various writers; sketches mostly by Bobby Clark, H. I. Phillips, William Roos, and Billy K. Wells

directed by Hassard Short; sketches directed by "Mr. Robert Edwin Clark, Esquire;" choreographed by James Starbuck
produced by Michael Todd
with Lina Romay

opened June 28, 1950   Winter Garden Theatre

BROOKS ATKINSON, *Times*

Some years ago our city fathers in their wisdom banned burlesque from this chaste community. Now they will have to decide whether burlesque at $7.20 is more lawful than burlesque at popular prices. For Mr. Todd has exuberantly thrown in all the old hokum—the grinds, bumps, and strip-teases which used to put the license commissioner on his mettle. Mr. Todd's young ladies are beautifully designed and they wear well-ventilated costumes. But Mr. Todd never gets them very far from the midway. Despite its splendor, *Peep Show* is pretty pure corn and runs into some heavy-going. The formula is an old one and gets stupefying before it is worked out. Maybe sex has blown over.

JOHN CHAPMAN, *Daily News*

Peep Show presented by Michael Todd, the Rajah of Razzmatazz, is a gaudy, bawdy stag smoker. Dames, Prince Mike has been heard to say—people want dames. The dames are so numerous I couldn't count them even when I counted their legs and divided by two, and every one of them has more appeal than a charity campaign letter. Mr. Todd seems to think the entire public is sex starved, and being an amiable fellow he wants to help out his fellow man. But as I watched *Peep Show* I got a weird and macabre feeling that Mr. Todd himself doesn't *like* dames. He just likes parts of them. If he ever goes to market to buy the home dinner, I am sure he would go to one of those parts stores and lay in a supply of second joints and breasts. And he seems so fond of navels that he would go quite off his rocker in an orange grove. . . . Lilly Christine seems to be able to revolve in all sections at the same time. I

Mike Todd's final Broadway effort included songs by the King of Thailand, sketch direction by baggy-pants comedian turned director Mr. Robert Edwin Clark, Esq., and "a number of comely young ladies"—all to little avail. (drawing by Nick)

439

did not find her very entertaining but thought she might be handy in the kitchen as an all-purpose mixing machine whose adjustable speeds and movements could whip up anything from mayonnaise and hot-cake batter to ice cream. The first act finale is built around a song, "Blue Night," written by the King of Siam [Bhumibol, H. M. the King of Thailand]. Pretty good song, too. The dames were in Siamese costumes—Babes in Thailand, of course.

ROBERT COLEMAN, *Daily Mirror*

There are short girls, tall girls, middle-sized girls, blonde, brunette, and red-headed girls. Lovelies, all. A real package of eye tonic. And you see plenty of them in their revealing Irene Sharaff costumes. Of course, the Howard Bay sets are nice, too, but the average customer is going to be more interested in what fills those Sharaff designs. Hassard Short staged and lighted the revue for Mahatma Todd, and your old pal, Bobby Clark, directed the sketches. A word of advice: when you see *Michael Todd's Peep Show*, leave the children at home. It boasts too many bare facts for the small fry to appreciate fully.

ROBERT GARLAND, *Journal-American*

Hand-picked by the master of the revels, they are beautiful girls straight from the untired business man's imagination. They can speak when required. Sometimes they can sing in small distant voices. In costumes fashioned after the costume of Gunga Din, they can also move slowly and sexuously about the stage. Whenever there is little else to do, *Peep Show* brings on the girls. They, in turn, in earnest and in numbers, give out generously with gender.

RICHARD WATTS JR., *Post*

Michael Todd's Peep Show arrived at the Winter Garden last night, where the assembled first-nighters temporarily put away thoughts of a possible war in the East and concentrated on such other basic topics as beautiful, bare showgirls and low, rowdy comedians. The songs have been contributed by various notable composers ranging from Jule Styne, who wrote *Gentlemen Prefer Blondes* (1949), to His Majesty, the King of Siam. Mr. Styne's contribution, "Stay with the Happy People," is one of the better numbers, but, as for the Oriental potentate's "Blue Night," on the basis of it I would not advise him to give up his throne in Bangkok for a career in Tin Pan Alley.

○○
○   ○
○   BROADWAY SCORECARD / perfs: 278 / $: –   ○
○   ○
○   *rave*   *favorable*   *mixed*   *unfavorable*   *pan*   ○
○   ○
○   1   2   2   1   ○
○○

MILK AND HONEY

a musical comedy, with music and lyrics by Jerry Herman; book by Don Appell

directed by Albert Marre; choreographed by Donald Saddler
produced by Gerard Oestreicher
with Robert Weede, Mimi Benzell, Molly Picon, and Tommy Rall

opened October 10, 1961   *Martin Beck Theatre*

JOHN CHAPMAN, *Daily News*

It is at its most charming when Molly Picon sings, dances, and mugs her way through the role of a widow who has booked herself on a cruise in the hope of capturing a new man. Miss Picon captured me, too; in her first performance in a Broadway musical, she exhibits all the skills and charms she has learned in something like a half century on Yiddish and vaudeville stages. *Milk and Honey* is at its most exciting when Tommy Rall sings a lovely ballad, "I Will Follow You," and then caps it with an extraordinary solo dance. It is at its most exciting, too, when the boys and girls of the company perform the really original dances devised by choreographer Donald Saddler. . . . I do wish that the Martin Beck Theatre were not so elaborately "bugged" as it is. Miss Benzell, Weede, Rall, and the chorus are well-trained as singers and should be able to make themselves heard without the annoyingly artificial aid of mikes and speakers. The only time I enjoyed this sound amplification last evening was when Weede milked an Israeli goat. He really milked the beast, and I could hear the stuff squirting into the pail.

WALTER KERR, *Herald Tribune*

Milk and Honey has the sunniness of a travel poster and, when it is singing, the bursting energy of a whole town meeting the boat. But its libretto seems to have been written by that stiff and self-conscious fellow who composes tourist guide books. When the singing chorus has calmed down, and the dancers are not at the work they so obviously enjoy, the language and the langours of a pageant set in. "Tomorrow is Israel's Independence Day, and there'll be dancing in the streets," someone informs us, by way of preparing for the very next number. "Such excitement! It's like the Fourth of July!" insists a visitor, once the jubilee has sounded its first note. "For them it *is* the Fourth of July!" comes the announcer's comment, for all the world like a television soundtrack added to illustrative film. The air of deliberate illustration persists: a goat must be milked to show us how it is done, the fact that "Tel Aviv is a small New York" must be explained to us, and brochure rhetoric seems to invade dialogue and lyrics as well. Lyric: "For when my hair was up, my morale was down," which is surely a prosy thought for a light-minded song. Let us say that the evening has, in its best things, the making of a gala holiday show at the Music Hall. But between the big numbers it is not only home-spun; it is too home-movie.

NORMAN NADEL, *World-Telegram & Sun*

Little of this, however, rises much above competent showmanship. Mr. Weede's singing, as might be expected, is resonant, strong, and well-phrased. Miss Benzell's charm and loveliness are as welcome as her singing voice, and it's too bad she doesn't have better opportunity to employ the latter. Composer Jerry Herman is not at his best with ballads, though his derivative music (drawn from Israeli folk and dance forms) is tremendous. Molly Picon's distinctive comedy might better be held in check early in the show, and given free rein later. A talent such as hers should be used most effectively. For all the excellence of these three stars in their respective areas, *Milk and Honey* achieves its periodic triumphs when the secondary players, and the men and women of the company, are in command. Lana Saunders [as Weede's daughter] achieves the sole consistent, inviolate dramatic characterization of the evening. Tommy Rall, as her husband, dances an exquisite and poignant lament ["I Will Follow You"] after he has decided to abandon the land for love of his wife. There isn't a more noble moment all evening.

A theatre party special. *Milk and Honey* became the first Broadway musical to run over 500 performances and *still* lose money. (That record has since been surpassed, and how!)

```
BROADWAY SCORECARD / perfs: 543 / $: —

rave    favorable    mixed    unfavorable    pan

              5          2
```

MISS LIBERTY

a musical comedy, with music and lyrics by Irving Berlin; book by Robert E. Sherwood

directed by Moss Hart; choreographed by Jerome Robbins
produced by Irving Berlin, Robert E. Sherwood, and Moss Hart
starring Eddie Albert, Allyn McLerie, Mary McCarty, and Ethel Griffies

opened July 15, 1949   Imperial Theatre

BROOKS ATKINSON, *Times*

To come right out and say so in public, *Miss Liberty* is a disappointing musical comedy. It is built on an old-fashioned model and it is put together without sparkle or originality. This is the Statue of Liberty antic with songs and lyrics by Irving Berlin, the best-loved songwriter in America, and a book by Robert E. Sherwood, the loftiest playwright in the country who has won the Pulitzer Prize so many times that now he can keep it.

ROBERT COLEMAN, *Daily Mirror*

By curtain time there was an advance sale of nearly half a million dollars for the new click. *Miss Liberty* is unique in that it was

Parisian model Allyn McLerie winks slyly—those foolish New Yorkers think she posed for the new Statue! *Miss Liberty* is best described by the title of one of the cut songs, "Mr. Monotony."

financed by Berlin, Sherwood, and Hart. They are reported to have backed it to the tune of $175,000.

WARD MOREHOUSE, *Sun*

A sharp disappointment. Not the wonder work you'd expect from such a high-powered combination as Berlin, Sherwood, & Hart. Jerome Robbins, in working out lively and imaginative dance routines, has been somewhat more successful in his department than Mr. Berlin has been as composer-lyricist, and he has far exceeded the achievements of Robert Sherwood as the librettist.

ROBERT SYLVESTER, *Daily News*

After letting the freshman team carry the ball for almost the entire first act, *Miss Liberty* handed it over to a 72-year-old pro named Ethel Griffies just before intermission. Things picked up immediately and stayed picked up as long as Miss Griffies was in charge. . . . Motley fashioned costumes which range from the spectacular to the just plain ugly. Miss McCarty changes costume so often that for a while you thought she must be trying to find a dress that looked good.

RICHARD WATTS JR., *Post*

Whatever must be said against it, *Miss Liberty* is neither a botch nor a bore. It is pleasant, good-looking, tuneful, and surprisingly commonplace. It is no doubt unfair to expect more from its authors than from the average writers of girl-and-music entertainment, merely because their reputations are so great. There is no escaping the fact, though, that more is expected.

One of those "enormous advance" musicals, with a trio of top names assembled around a hot "idea." Tickets sell like hotcakes. When the creators finally realize the idea is *not* so hot, what can they do? Give back the money?

A Tony Award was won by Joe Lynn (stage technician).

BROADWAY SCORECARD / perfs: 308 / $: −

rave	favorable	mixed	unfavorable	pan
2	1		2	3

MR. PRESIDENT

a musical comedy, with music and lyrics by Irving Berlin; book by Howard Lindsay and Russel Crouse

directed by Joshua Logan; choreographed by Peter Gennaro
produced by Leland Hayward
with Robert Ryan, Nanette Fabray, and Anita Gillette

opened October 20, 1962   St. James Theatre

WALTER KERR, *Herald Tribune*

Mr. Berlin's songs were heard—clearly, forcefully, and several times each—but they are curious. The old insistent rhythm, and the unembarrassed assertion of melody, are there. "Is He the Only Man in the World?" falls easy as eiderdown across the pit and all over our laps. "They Love Me" makes Miss Fabray get up and go. "Pigtails and Freckles" is perkily plucked out. But because there is nothing in the people or in the root inspiration to lighten anyone's heart, Mr. Berlin's hand seems to rise and fall thoughtlessly, as though he weren't looking at the keys, much of the time. More seriously, the words—which always were simple, but simply evocative—are prosaic, mere wooden soldiers keeping up with the beat. "Take me back to the past, when the world wasn't turning so fast" or "It gets lonely in the White House when you're being attacked, and the loyal opposition gets into the act" isn't good Berlin, it is just weak editorial writing. Strangely, the number of harsh, consonant line-endings which are turned into rhymes increase wildly, and against all the old-fashioned rules for songwriting. Mr. Berlin is not being old-fashioned; he is possibly trying too hard not to be, and the strain makes him self-conscious without actually pushing him.

JOHN McCLAIN, *Journal-American*

There is just no way to be charitable about *Mr. President.* The top talent in our town conceived it yet this new musical is quite simply an old-fashioned dud. None of Mr. Berlin's tunes is poor, and none is great; the Lindsay-Crouse book is mediocre, woefully devoid of inventiveness and wit, and whatever became of the unerring hand of Mr. Logan? For this one he must have used his erring, or left hand. And Mr. Hayward must have been hypnotized by the reputations rather than the product delivered by his artisans. It has been said in defense of the proceedings that good old-fashioned corn is not to be scorned, but here I believe they give corn a bad name. Their assault on The Establishment is, I believe, unfunny and dubiously credible. Of course, the show has an advance sale of more than $2,000,000 and will probably run for several years. But it is far below the potential of its creators and equally below the standard which should be required of a present-day $9.60 attraction.

HOWARD TAUBMAN, *Times*

Has there ever been as dull a President as the man occupying the White House in *Mr. President?* If so, the Nation, praise be, has survived. But where can a musical turn if its Chief is so virtuously homespun and so relentlessly colorless that his Administration is covered with a pious pall? To the First Lady, bless her. In their book for the musical, Howard Lindsay and Russel Crouse offer merely a facile sketch of the President's wife. Irving Berlin, however, gives her several lively songs, and Nanette Fabray does the rest. If it weren't for her effervescent charm as a song-and-dance First Lady, *Mr. President* would be as diverting as a budget message.

RICHARD WATTS JR., *Post*

Its hero is a kind of collective President, done in a non-partisan spirit, although the young good looks of Stephen Henderson and his wife and the attractiveness of their daughter and son suggest a definite identification. But, on the other hand, the show's vintage quality might make you suspect that the authors really had William Howard Taft in mind.

Fact is, everyone was pretty tired. Berlin, Lindsay, and Crouse were all in their 70s. The librettists' last first-rate work was the

Pulitzer Prize–winning *State of the Union* (1945); their *Call Me Madam* (1950) and *The Sound of Music* (1959) were hits *despite* the books. Logan's final satisfying musicals were *Annie Get Your Gun* (1946) and *South Pacific* (1949); from *Wish You Were Here* (1952) on, they got progressively worse, ending with the grisly *Look to the Lilies* (1970) and Bette Davis's *Miss Moffat* (1974).

A Tony Award was won by Solly Pernick (stage technician). Curiously enough, *Miss Liberty's* [1949] only Tony was also won by a stagehand. *Call Me Madam* also received a stagehand Tony, all of which must mean something. Irving Berlin, meanwhile, received a special Tony Award for his final Broadway attempt, but this didn't fool anyone.

BROADWAY SCORECARD / perfs: 265 / $: —

rave	favorable	mixed	unfavorable	pan
		1	1	5

MR. STRAUSS GOES TO BOSTON

a musical comedy suggested by Johann Strauss, Jr.'s visit to the 1872 World Peace Jubilee, with musical adaptation (from Strauss) and original music by Robert Stolz; lyrics by Robert Sour; book by Leonard L. Levinson, from an original story by Alfred Gruenwald and Geza Herczeg

directed by Felix Brentano; choreographed by George Balanchine
produced by Felix Brentano
with George Rigaud, Virginia MacWatters, Ralph Dumke, Ruth Matteson, and Harold Lang

opened September 6, 1945   Century Theatre

HOWARD BARNES, *Herald Tribune*

The book is so bad that it is reasonably certain that embarrassment was felt behind the footlights as well as in front of them. It has something to do with a pin-up boy of his day who became mixed up with a Beacon Hill heriess until his wife arrived from Vienna and President Grant blew in from somewhere or other and got him back on his esthetic beam. Since Felix Brentano, the producer-director of the show, has staged it in a random and ponderous fashion, it falls to pieces with a frightening acceleration.

JOHN CHAPMAN, *Daily News*

The girls shriek and swoon [over Johann Strauss] just as they do today over F. Sinatra—only instead of wearing bobby socks they are clad in bustles which make them look like ostriches in an air-raid shelter. The costumes are by Walter Florell, the Hollywood hatter, and I think that Mr. Florell, in addition to mixing his colors rather unattractively, thought it would be fetching to design a hat for every girl's behind. This is the wrong place for hats.

WARD MOREHOUSE, *Sun*

There is some good dancing from Harold Lang and Helen Gallagher.

BURTON RASCOE, *World-Telegram*

The best thing about *Mr. Strauss Goes to Boston* is that the agony is over before 11 o'clock, and the show lasts less than two hours of playing time. It would be much better if it lasted only thirty minutes. Even the Johann Strauss music takes an awful beating. The lyrics by Robert Sour are witless; but the book by Leonard L. Levinson is simply atrocious, vulgar, cheap, and smutty. George Balanchine did the choreography, which was saved by young Lang, who is good but not as good as the noisy claque last night would leave one to believe.

BROADWAY SCORECARD / perfs: 12 / $: −

rave	favorable	mixed	unfavorable	pan
				8

MR. WONDERFUL

a musical comedy, with music and lyrics by Jerry Bock, Larry Holofcener, and George Weiss; book by Joseph Stein and Will Glickman; "production conceived" by Jule Styne

directed and choreographed by Jack Donohue
produced by Jule Styne and George Gilbert in association with Lester Osterman, Jr.
with Sammy Davis Jr., Jack Carter, Pat Marshall, Olga James, and Chita Rivera

opened March 22, 1956   Broadway Theatre

JOHN CHAPMAN, *Daily News*

A brassy hymn to all the brassy people of Union City, N.J., Broadway, N.Y., and Miami Beach, Fla.—and it was vastly appreciated by an audience whose likes I have not encountered at premieres since the Monday matinees at the Palace Theatre in 1928 and 1929 [customarily attended by vaudeville performers]. It was also quite considerably appreciated by me when I could hear it. Without question, *Mr. Wonderful* is the loudest show ever to be presented in a New York playhouse. The management has got the theatre's stage miked up to within a fraction of an inch of chaos. If your hearing is normal, the best way to attend *Mr. Wonderful* would be to bring two hearing aids, plug one in each ear and turn everything off. . . . The plot of this show needn't bother anybody now, because it couldn't have bothered its authors.

ROBERT COLEMAN, *Daily Mirror*

It's difficult to believe that Joseph Stein and Will Glickman, who gave us the libretto of the captivating *Plain and Fancy* [1954], should have come up with such a shoddy and tasteless book as this one. *Mr. Wonderful* kept reminding us of how really wonderful even *Ankles Aweigh* [1955] was by comparison. . . . Chita Rivera, a real cute chick, clicks with her rolling eyes and sinuous hips.

WALTER KERR, *Herald Tribune*

Whatever this slight, lithe, sleek, and everlasting restless member of the Will Mastin Trio does is dynamically done. He [Davis]

A young Sammy Davis Jr.—"the most electric talent to light up the entertainment world since Al Jolson was going down to the foot-lights and stretching out his hands and picking up audiences as if they were pebbles"—tries to carry a mediocre show on his shoul-ders. Star billing actually went to the Will Mastin Trio, Sammy's nightclub act with his father and uncle (lower right).

451

juts his lower lip clear across the orchestra pit, closes his eyes in a passionate wail, flashes a gigantic ring on his very flexible fingers, and struts, leaps, taps, shuffles, and howls with mercurial abandon. When he stops singing, he blasts into a trumpet. When he throws the trumpet away, he joins his father and his uncle in doing spectacular damage to the Broadway stage floor. When his feet give out, he does impersonations—very good impersonations—of Nat King Cole, Vaughan Monroe, Jimmy Cagney, Jerry Lewis, and quite a few other café movie familiars. But, allowing for the skill that goes into a ten-thirty jamboree in a night-club floor, *Mr. Wonderful* is itself only an impersonation—an impersonation of a musical comedy. . . . Jack Donohue's staging zips along at a professional clip, but you keep feeling it yearning for some place to go. Chita Rivera is hopelessly stranded with some baby-doll mannerisms that are merely alarming.

John McClain, *Journal-American*

Davis dances as well as Bill Robinson, he can sing like a lark, he plays a perfectly adequate trumpet or traps, and he can flatten you with his impressions. It is a remarkable and rewarding turn, but it's still a [nightclub] act. . . . The plot devised by Joseph Stein and Will Glickman has all the subtlety and surprise of a Sanitation Department truck.

Richard Watts Jr., *Post*

The intention was to demonstrate that Mr. Davis is an expert performer, and I think the new musical comedy proves its point. He unquestionably is. But a book show, even a disappearing one, demands a bit of acting, too, and in this he is less happy.

BROADWAY SCORECARD / perfs: 383 / $: −

rave	favorable	mixed	unfavorable	pan
	1	1	4	1

THE MOST HAPPY FELLA

a musical, with book, music, and lyrics by Frank Loesser, from the 1924 Pulitzer Prize–winning play *They Knew What They Wanted* by Sidney Howard

directed by Joseph Anthony, choreographed by Dania Krupska
produced by Kermit Bloomgarden and Lynn Loesser
with Robert Weede, Jo Sullivan, Art Lund (replacing Morley Meredith), Susan Johnson, Shorty Long, and Mona Paulee

opened May 3, 1956   Imperial Theatre

BROOKS ATKINSON, *Times*

As a composer, Mr. Loesser has range and depth enough to give it an overwhelming musical statement. The fiery and passionate arias he has written for the husband and the wife manage to concentrate the emotions in simple, direct, powerful, musical sound, and give *The Most Happy Fella* great dramatic stature. Without severing his connections with Broadway, Mr. Loesser has given Broadway some musical magnificence. . . . Here and there it seems to be overproduced and overacted; some of the sequences are too facile, too slick, and overblown, in the Broadway style that always tries to top everything in town. But in everything that is vital to the theme, the work is first-rate. For the pathetic story of the mail-order bride and the man who loves her is a piece of dramatic literature. Mr. Loesser has caught the anguish and the love in some exalting music. Broadway is used to heart. It is not accustomed to evocations of the soul.

JOHN CHAPMAN, *Daily News*

"Warm All Over." There is no more felicitous description than this of Frank Loesser's new musical. The composer-librettist shows no pretension of grandeur in his work; he isn't trying to write an opera in the heroic style. What he has sought to do is to make a musical play which will tell most of its story in song and recitative and yet stay within the popular idiom of the Broadway show. What he has accomplished is as distinguished as it is delightful. Right now, still savoring my pleasures at the Imperial Theatre, I am the most happy fella.

Newlyweds Tony Esposito (Robert Weede) and Rosabella (Jo Sullivan) float blissfully on a cloud—which does not reflect the plot at all! The logo was quickly changed to a beaming Weede (with no co-star, thank you very much). Pre-Broadway credits. (*drawing by W. Hogarth*)

ROBERT COLEMAN, *Daily Mirror*

Frank Loesser has taken an aging play and turned it into a timeless musical. It is a masterpiece of our era. With rare magic touch, Loesser has blended comedy and feeling. His people sing their thoughts, their joys and heartbreaks, instead of talking about them. Sing them superbly, through one of the most gorgeous scores we have ever heard on a stage. . . . It is Susan Johnson, as a knowing hash-slinger, who proves the surprise of the evening. Her wonderful sense of comedy stopped the proceedings frequently.

WILLIAM HAWKINS, *World-Telegram & Sun*

An overwhelmingly inventive new musical, a rich show drenched in song. It has so much music, so much going on, that you feel Verdi must have rewritten *Oklahoma!*. . . . *The Most Happy Fella* suffers from tension, volume, and a refusal to let anything happen simply. Its novelty entertains, but then exhausts. It should relax, slow down and whisper on occasion—because it has so much that is charming and powerful in it.

WALTER KERR, *Herald Tribune*

Mr. Loesser loves the rich, rolling exhilarating cadences that can spill out into an auditorium whenever a musical show approaches the freedom and the melodic fury of opera, or at least operetta. And at the same time, he refuses to turn his back on the girl who has long since returned his passion, the impish and skipping and crackling straight musical comedy. Mr. Loesser has simply opened his treasure chest and hurled his bountiful prizes in both directions. The ambitious tunes swell mightily, and the torrid ones explode. Still, there's a little something wrong with *Most Happy Fella:* it is heavy with its own inventiveness, weighted down with the variety and fulsomeness of a genuinely creative appetite. It's as though Mr. Loesser had written two complete musicals—the operetta and the haymaker—on the same simple play and then crammed them both into a single structure. I keep wishing that Mr. Loesser had written six shows in the six years since *Guys and Dolls* [1950] instead of packing the energy of all six into one.

JOHN McCLAIN, *Journal-American*

Merely a great, great musical by a guy who likes to write a lot of music and would rather have people sing the story than talk it.

Sure, there are operatic overtones—there are trios and quartets, there are many duets, and in the last act he uses to enormous effect a melodious soliloquy. But in the meantime there is a large assortment of pop numbers, a fair share of earthbound humor, and the all-around punch and polish of a good, old-time song and dancer. For this would seem to be a true wish-fulfillment for the same Loesser who has written so much juke-fodder and such memorable scores as *Guys and Dolls*. It's as if he said, "Look, fellas, this one is for keeps." And it may be. *The Most Happy Fella* is a great tribute to the talents of Frank Loesser. It should also be a stupendous success.

Frank Loesser's foray into the world of Rodgers and Hammerstein revealed a warm, remarkably romantic musical heart. Unexpected, coming from an exceedingly clever wordsmith who only started tinkering with tunes out of necessity. (PFC Loesser couldn't always find a composer, so he started to "write his own"—beginning with the wartime hits "Rodger Young" and "Praise the Lord and Pass the Ammunition.") *Guys and Dolls* unquestionably demonstrated that Loesser could write show tunes as well as anyone, but *The Most Happy Fella* proved him a dramatic composer on the level of Rodgers and Loewe. Loesser also got the girl, divorcing coproducer Lynn Loesser to marry leading lady Jo Sullivan.

Winner of the New York Drama Critics' Circle Award.

BROADWAY SCORECARD / perfs: 676 / $: +

rave	favorable	mixed	unfavorable	pan
4	3			

MUSIC IN MY HEART

a costume operetta, with melodies by Tchaikovsky, adapted by Franz Steininger; lyrics by Forman Brown; book by Patsy Ruth Miller (replacing Frederick Jackson)

directed by Hassard Short; choreographed by Ruth Page

produced by Henry Duffy (replacing Theodore Bachenheimer and James A. Doolittle, whose version—entitled *Song Without Words*—closed out-of-town)

with Charles Fredericks, Martha Wright (replacing Marguerite Piazza), Vivienne Segal, Jan Murray, and Robert Carroll

opened October 2, 1947   Adelphi Theatre

John Chapman, *Daily News*

I got an idea. All we have to do is dig up some money some place, which should be easy, and we do an operetta. It will be about how Harry S. Truman wins the Democratic nomination at the convention next June, and all we need to do is hire us a lyric writer and set it to the music of the late Stephen Foster. It will be as good as *Music in My Heart*. Maybe better. *Music in My Heart* was presented last evening as a belated tribute to the late Peter I. Tchaikovsky, a snowbound Russian who managed to write some of the loveliest and most tropical melodies in the catalogues of G. Schirmer, I. Witmark, G. Ricordi, and I. Berlin. The plot is about how P. I. Tchaikovsky meets a girl from France who can sing, so he sits down at the piano and knocks off a lifetime's work for her in an hour or two. Hassard Short has staged the enterprise as though he had been engaged by the late Mme. Tussaud.

Robert Coleman, *Daily Mirror*

They sprouted enough corn on the stage of the Adelphi Theatre last evening to relieve the European food shortage. The book has the Russian music master falling in love with a glamorous diva, who jilts him for a handsome officer from Imperial Court. Tchaikovsky probably wished that he had been jilted by the singer, for she actually snared him into marriage and then made his life miserable. He wasn't cut out for romance and matrimony anyway. . . . Vivienne Segal was one of the two greatest operetta prima donnas of our time. How she must snicker up her sleeve as she listens to present-day incompetents manhandle music. . . . Shows staged by Hassard Short are noted for taste. *Music in My Heart*, however, seems to have gotten him down, as it did us, for Bobby will draw no posies in the drama year books for his labors on this crude and tasteless sample of Indian maize on the cob.

WILLIAM HAWKINS, *World-Telegram*

Music in My Heart represents one of the greatest research jobs in the history of the theatre. There is not an original idea in it. . . . Vivienne Segal must be thinking during the performance that she has done this show about 12,000 times before, but she continues to be bright, alert, and sure of style.

LOUIS KRONENBERGER, *PM*

Tchaikovsky's [music] has been rolled downhill in a spiked barrel; has been hurled over the precipice; and then been picked up, bleeding and broken, and shoved down the cistern. The doings at the Adelphi Theatre were too sheerly idiotic to be regarded as obscene; but they made it impossible for Broadway to cast a single stone at Hollywood for any cinematic sacrilege whatever; or to refer to a soap opera except in terms of the very highest respect. One reason why this is the most stupefying of the Lives-of-Great-Composers operettas is that it is the most sumptuous; and thus has the most chances to go wrong on the biggest scale. And so far as I can see, it hasn't muffed a single chance. Given the choice of two or more ways of being trite, it unerringly picks the tritest. Given the choice of two or more ways of being trashy, it unfailingly plumps for the trashiest.

BROADWAY SCORECARD / perfs: 124 / $: −

rave	favorable	mixed	unfavorable	pan
			1	8

MUSIC IN THE AIR

a revival of the 1932 musical play, with music by Jerome Kern; book and lyrics by Oscar Hammerstein 2nd

directed by Oscar Hammerstein 2nd
produced by Reginald Hammerstein (for Billy Rose)

with Dennis King, Jane Pickens, Charles Winninger, Conrad Nagel, and Lillian Murphy

opened October 8, 1951   Ziegfeld Theatre

BROOKS ATKINSON, *Times*

Nothing has happened to those Jerome Kern melodies. Now that Mr. Kern has gone, no one else will write the rich, leisurely melodies that recapture a *gemütlichkeit* world which has not existed for a long time and perhaps lived only in a great composer's mind. Although ours is a graceless world, the lovely Kern score is still full of friendship, patience, cheerfulness, and pleasure. These things must be real, because Mr. Kern found them in his heart and wrote the notes that put them into the hearts of music-lovers everywhere. . . . Queer what tricks the memory plays. *Music in the Air* does not consist exclusively of the rapturuous charms of the people of Edendorf, nor of happy village people singing of the glories of being alive. For Oscar Hammerstein had to write a plot to keep them moving across the stage; and it is a shock to discover that half of the first act is wasted on some silly mumbo-jumbo about wicked city people and the composition of an operetta. The plot of *Music in the Air* has a lot of hackneyed playwriting in it.

ROBERT GARLAND, *Journal-American*

While the music is out of Jerome Kern's topmost drawer, the play isn't out of Oscar Hammerstein's. Not by any means. And Mr. Hammerstein is here to fix it by what he has learned since 1932. But I don't see that he has fixed it. It's awkward, it's long-drawn, it's not too interesting. To tell the truth, it seldom comes alive save when it lifts its voice in song.

BERT McCORD, *Herald Tribune*

One of the ironies of this revival is that Mr. Hammerstein, the co-author who staged it for his brother Reginald, is perhaps more responsible than any one else for the fact that the show can't finish in the running today. Just as in the first act scene of *Music in the Air* he satirized the musicals of the twenties, so by his work with Richard Rodgers he has been instrumental in educating audiences to more developed musical theatre. *Music in the Air* is an agreeable revival giving audiences a chance to dream back to the days when they hummed "I've Told Ev'ry Little Star" or "The Song is You," but one suspects that had it been written today by John Doe or Richard Roe, it would receive short shrift.

BROADWAY SCORECARD / perfs: 56 / $: −

rave	favorable	mixed	unfavorable	pan
1		1	5	

THE MUSIC MAN

a musical comedy, with book, music, and lyrics by Meredith Willson; "story" by Meredith Willson and Franklin Lacey, suggested by Willson's 1948 memoir *And There I Stood With My Piccolo*

directed by Morton Da Costa; choreographed by Onna White
produced by Kermit Bloomgarden with Herbert Greene, in association with Frank (Loesser) Productions, Inc.
with Robert Preston, Barbara Cook, David Burns, Pert Kelton, and Iggie Wolfington

opened December 19, 1957   Majestic Theatre

FRANK ASTON, *World-Telegram & Sun*

A knockout, right from the first blare in the Majestic's orchestra pit. It deserves to run at least a decade. . . . If all our stack-tenders looked, sang, danced, and acted like Miss Barbara, this nation's book learning would be overwhelming.

BROOKS ATKINSON, *Times*

Dollars to doughnuts, Meredith Willson dotes on brass bands. In *The Music Man*, he has translated the thump and razzle-dazzle of brass-band lore into a warm and genial cartoon of gaudy American life. Since the style is gaudy and since David Burns plays a small town mayor with low-comedy flourishes, *The Music Man* is a cartoon and not a valentine. But. Mr. Willson's sophistication is skin-

Professor Harold Hill—playing a trumpet, rather than one of those "Seventy-Six Trombones"—with Marian the Librarian, walking on air. (drawing by David Klein)

deep. His heart is in the wonderful simplicities of provincial life in Iowa in 1912, and his musical show glows with enjoyment. Willson's music is innocent; the beat is rousing and the tunes are full of gusto. He has given it the uniformity of a well-designed crazy-quilt in which every patch blends with its neighbor. By some sort of miracle, his associates have caught his point of view exactly. Morton Da Costa's droll, strutting direction; Don Walker's blaring orchestrations; Howard Bay's jovial scenery, including a racing locomotive that drowns the orchestra players in steam when the curtain goes up—these aspects of the production have Willson's own kind of gaiety.

JOHN CHAPMAN, *Daily News*

One of the few great musical comedies of the last 26 years. It was 26 years ago that *Of Thee I Sing* [1931] appeared and set a standard for fun and invention which has seldom been reached. Its equal arrived in 1950—*Guys and Dolls*—and I would say that *The Music Man* ranks with these two. This musical is put together so expertly and acted and sung and danced by so many enchanting people that it should be either twice as long or performed twice at each performance.

ROBERT COLEMAN, *Daily Mirror*

Kermit Bloomgarden has found the right people to make it as vivid as a Turner sky. He's made a 10-strike in landing Robert Preston for the title role. We don't have to tell you that we've been beating the drums for Bob over the years. But it took his current vehicle to bring home to us just how versatile our boy really is. He paces the piece dynamically, acts ingratiatingly, sings as if he'd been doing it all his life, and offers steps that would score on the cards of dance judges. A triumphant performance in a triumphant musical! What a show! What a hit! What a solid hit!

WALTER KERR, *Herald Tribune*

It's the beat that does it. The overture of *The Music Man* drives off with a couple of good, shrill whistles and a heave-ho blast from half the brass in the pit, with the heartier trombonists lurching to their feet in a blare of enthusiasm. The curtain sails up to disclose the most energetic engine on the Rock Island Railroad (circa 1912) hurtling across the proscenium with real smoke pouring out of its smokestack and real steam rolling along the rails. The itch is upon us. Meredith Willson has whipped out an entire first choral scene without a note of music. The words, the hands, the knees, and the insane Rock Island roadbed do all the work: grunts, roars, gossip, and a form of St. Vitus Dance all merge into a syncopated conversation that is irresistible. . . . Mr. Preston is impatient with dialogue. Let a couple of people talk, and he fidgets. Let a split-second gap in chatter turn up, and his feet start working. A fairly fierce light turns up in his eyes, an urgent whisper begins to conspire with the underscoring, and the first thing you know designer Howard Bay's attractively pastel Main St. is beginning to sway in the breeze. Mr. Preston is also indefatigable: he's got zest and gusto and a great big grin for another slam-bang march tune ("Seventy-Six Trombones") and for a wonderfully impish soft-shoe in the Public Library (it seems that "Marian, the Librarian" is so hard-hearted she'd let his corpse lie on the floor till it turned to carrion). Mr. Preston, to pin the matter down, is jim-dandy.

JOHN MCCLAIN, *Journal-American*

A whopping hit. This salute by Meredith Willson to his native Iowa will make even Oklahoma look to its laurels.

This one got away from Feuer and Martin, who initiated the project in 1951. Nobody thought Willson—a minor music man of the airwaves who had been a flutist for John Philip Sousa in the early 1920s—would come up with much. Except Frank Loesser, who continued to encourage Willson and push the project. Six years later *The Music Man* finally blasted Broadway, with all those trombones. There had never been anything quite like it before, and there never has been since. Loesser kept his hand in, as associate producer, publisher, and licensor of the immensely lucrative stock and amateur rights. It has also been claimed that Frank wrote "My White Knight," a beautiful ballad which does seem to be derived from a *Most Happy Fella* (1956) cutout. ("My White Knight" was bumped out of the 1962 movie version and replaced with a new, second-rate Willson ballad.) Whatever the case may be, *The Music Man* took critics and audiences by storm, totally overwhelming the recently opened *West Side Story*.

Winner of the New York Drama Critics' Circle Award. In addition to winning the Tony Award for Best Musical, Tonys were won by Meredith Willson (composer); Meredith Willson and Franklin Lacey (librettists); Kermit Bloomgarden with Herbert Greene, in association with Frank (Loesser) Productions, Inc. (producers); Robert Preston (actor); Barbara Cook (supporting actress); David Burns (supporting actor); Herbert Greene (musical director); and Sam Knapp (stage technician).

BROADWAY SCORECARD / perfs: 1,375 / $: +

rave	favorable	mixed	unfavorable	pan
7				

MY DARLIN' AIDA

a costume opera, with music by Giuseppe Verdi; book and lyrics by Charles Friedman, from the 1871 opera *Aida*

production supervised by Hassard Short; directed by Charles Friedman; choreographed by Hanya Holm
produced by Robert L. Joseph
with Dorothy Sarnoff, Elaine Malbin, William Olvis, and Howard Jarrett

opened October 27, 1952   Winter Garden Theatre

BROOKS ATKINSON, *Times*

Verdi's music in *My Darlin' Aida* is romantically Italian. Charles Friedman's new libretto is American, with a strong dash of *Uncle Tom's Cabin* seasoning. Despite the beauty of the singing by Dorothy Sarnoff and Elaine Malbin, there is no way of avoiding the fact that the music and the libretto have nothing in common except, perhaps, a certain shoddiness of style.

WALTER KERR, *Herald Tribune*

There may be some questions raised about Mr. Friedman's part in the adventure, but no one is going to ask where they spent the three hundred thousand. As a spectacle, *My Darlin' Aida* is a dazzling show. Lemuel Ayers has devised some gargantuan splendors to fill the vast stage of the Winter Garden. In addition to the conventional columns and chandeliers of the old South, there are any number of inventive and haunting images. There is a tiny skeleton church set against the greens and blacks of a moonlit graveyard. There is a levee in the noonday sun that is alive with reds, oranges, and blues. There is a stunning boudoir—chartreuse, this time—and a drawing room in bronze and coral brocades. For contrast, there are the dark and brooding slave quarters, and, while the show as a whole may be a little long on Spanish moss— the actors were getting snarled in it every once in a while last night—the over-all production plan is bursting with visual excitement. Color is used dramatically, not only in the settings but in Mr. Ayers's sometimes blindingly brilliant costumes and in the lighting with which Hassard Short has bathed this sumptuous charivari. *My Darlin' Aida* is almost never a moving experience, but the brocade, the silver, and the crystal—not to mention the music— may make it up to you.

JOHN MCCLAIN, *Journal-American*

It is gargantuan, gorgeous, and extremely grotesque. One can't help wondering why it was done. It didn't seem to me that the job of transplanting Verdi from the Nile to the Confederacy served any purpose. In making the switch Friedman had to dream up a story that feebly attempted to keep the elements of the opera, but certainly added nothing to it. While I do not pretend to be an authority on Verdi's original Italian lyrics, I think it is safe to say that Friedman's new ones do not appreciably enhance the music, either. In straight opera you know the plot and through the years you have gained a fair knowledge of what the familiar arias are about, even though you don't understand them. But in *Darlin'* you have a whole new problem: trying to cope with a nonsensical story and at the same time attempting to figure out just what the tenors and sopranos are saying when they're straining for that high note.

Charles Friedman had directed the book of *Carmen Jones* (1943), so this one seemed (?) a natural. Staging wizard Hassard Short (also of *Carmen Jones*) and Lemuel Ayers assembled an evening of overwhelming visual splendor, but that was all. No Oscar Hammerstein in sight.

A Donaldson Award was won by Lemuel Ayers (costume designer).

BROADWAY SCORECARD / perfs: 89 / $: −

rave	favorable	mixed	unfavorable	pan
2		2	1	2

MY DEAR PUBLIC

a "revusical story," with music and lyrics by Irving Caesar, Sam Lerner, and Gerald Marks; book by Irving Caesar and Charles Gottesfeld

directed by Edgar MacGregor (replacing Joseph Pevney); choreographed by Felicia Sorel and Henry Le Tang (replacing Carl Randall)
produced by Irving Caesar
with Willie Howard (replacing Joe Smith), Ethel Shutta, Nanette Fabray (replacing Joe Hodges), David Burns (replacing Karl Malden), and Jesse White (replacing Charles Dale)

opened September 9, 1943   46th Street Theatre

JOHN CHAPMAN, *Daily News*

Thanks to the infinite comfort of a faltering memory, I cannot remember a worse musical comedy. . . . A cheer for Miss Fabray, who has the looks and bounce that musical comedy heroines are made of.

ROBERT GARLAND, *Journal-American*

The piece is presented by Irving Caesar, who, even if you don't ask me, should be ashamed of himself. The book—which is incredible—is by Irving Caesar, too, aided by a guy called Gottesfeld. The songs also have a Caesarian flavor, heaven help them. There's a biblical line about rendering unto Caesar the things which are Caesar's. Well, the thing which is Caesar's is at the 46th Street Theatre. And he's welcome to it.

LOUIS KRONENBERGER, *PM*

One of the most terrific bores I have ever sat through. Aside from half a dozen laughs Willie Howard manages to raise almost in sheer defiance, and some of Georgie Tapps's dancing, last night's show is about as relentlessly undiverting as anything you can think of. A more suspicious man than myself might mutter something about a conspiracy, but I am perfectly willing to believe it was only a mistake. . . . *My Dear Public* is about how Barney Short (the zipper manufacturer) backs a play by an arty young poet from the Village. At least it is for awhile. Later on, it doesn't seem to be about anything.

BURTON RASCOE, *World-Telegram*

Two swallows do not a summer make, even when the birds are Willie Howard and Nanette Fabray.

The *Daily News* review was headlined: "Caesar Is Buried, Not Praised." Irving's claim to fame was as lyricist for Gershwin's "Swanee" (1919) and Youman's "Tea for Two" (1925). The ensemble of the original version of *My Dear Public*—which folded after a four-week tryout in early 1942—included two singing groups, The Martins (including *Best Foot Forward* [1941] songwriters Hugh Martin and Ralph Blane) and The Revuers (including Betty Comden, Adolph Green, and Judith Tuvim). The Revuers performed three of their own numbers, the maiden Comden and Green efforts to be heard (almost) on Broadway. Tuvim finally made her Broadway musical debut in 1956 in Comden and Green's *Bells Are Ringing*, her name anglicized to Holliday.

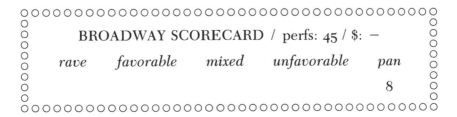

BROADWAY SCORECARD / perfs: 45 / $: —

rave	favorable	mixed	unfavorable	pan
				8

MY FAIR LADY

a musical comedy, with music by Frederick Loewe; book and lyrics by Alan Jay Lerner, from the 1914 comedy *Pygmalion* by George Bernard Shaw

directed by Moss Hart; choreographed by Hanya Holm
produced by Herman Levin
with Rex Harrison, Julie Andrews, Stanley Holloway, Cathleen Nesbitt, and Robert Coote

opened March 15, 1956   Mark Hellinger Theatre

BROOKS ATKINSON, *Times*

Although their contributions have been bountiful, [the creators] will not object if this column makes one basic observation. Shaw's crackling mind is still the genius of *My Fair Lady*. Yet it would not be fair to imply that *My Fair Lady* is only a new look at an old comedy. For the carnival version adds a new dimension: it gives a lift to the gaiety and the romance. Loewe's robust, versatile music is, no doubt, implicit in *Pygmalion*. But Mr. Loewe has given it heartier exuberance. Although the Old Boy had a sense of humor, he never had so much abandon. *Pygmalion* was not such a happy revel. *My Fair Lady* is a wonderful show. To Shaw's agile intelligence it adds the warmth, loveliness, and excitement of a memorable theatre frolic.

JOHN CHAPMAN, *Daily News*

The composer, Frederick Loewe, and the lyrist, Alan Jay Lerner, have written much the way Shaw must have done had he been a musician instead of a music critic. . . . There could be a no more captivating pair of players than Rex Harrison and Julie Andrews— and even dear Gertrude Lawrence was a no more enchanting Eliza Doolittle than Miss Andrews. Physically, *My Fair Lady* is splendid and splendorous, with scene designer Oliver Smith and costumer Cecil Beaton collaborating on the quality-rich atmosphere of the London of 1912. At proper moments, Hanya Holm introduces some light-hearted dances, and the visual high-spot of the evening is a scene at the Ascot race track. With all its extra musical trappings, *My Fair Lady* remains pure Shaw—and the man who has held it all

This one looks like it just might be good; think we should write away for tickets? (This pre-production artwork has been heavily retouched—Rex and Julie's facial features were drawn in!)

together and made it into an uncommonly stylish production is the director, Moss Hart.

ROBERT COLEMAN, *Daily Mirror*

One of the all-time great song-and-dancers. Lerner, with breath-taking skill, has kept the essence of the original, and penned lyrics that beautifully complement the Shavian dialogue. The Lerner-Loewe songs are not only delightful, they advance the action as well. They are ever so much more than interpolations, or inter-ruptions. They are a most important and integrated element in about as perfect an entertainment as the most fastidious playgoer could demand. In case you have the mistaken notion that brains and fun don't mix, perish the thought. For *My Fair Lady* is a felicitous blend of intellect, wit, rhythm, and high spirits. A mas-terpiece of musical comedy legerdemain. A new landmark in the genre fathered by Rodgers and Hammerstein. A terrific show!

WILLIAM HAWKINS, *World-Telegram & Sun*

My Fair Lady prances into that rare class of great musicals. Quite simply, it has everything. The famed *Pygmalion* has been used with such artfulness and taste, such vigorous reverence, that it springs freshly to life all over again. The show is dumbfoundingly beautiful to look at, and it is magnificently performed. The songs are likely to be unforgettable. *My Fair Lady* takes a grip on your heart, then makes you exult with laughter. It is a legendary evening.

WALTER KERR, *Herald Tribune*

Don't bother to finish reading this review now. You'd better sit right down and send for those tickets to *My Fair Lady*. First things first. . . . Mr. Harrison's slouch is a rhythmic slouch. His voice is a showman's voice—twangy, biting, confident beyond question. His leaps over the fashionable furniture are the leaps of a true enthusiast. But most of all Mr. Harrison is an actor, he believes every cranky, snappish, exhilarating syllable of the Alan Jay Lerner lyric he is rattling off, and a fourteen-carat character simply crashes its way onto the stage. Julie Andrews's eyes flash, her jaws turn to cement, and the glorious venom in her heart rips across the foot-lights in a howl labeled "Just You Wait." Miss Andrews is funny, she is pathetic, she is savagely true. Eliza isn't just a doll, she's a demon with a soul you can understand. [In "The Rain in Spain" scene] you listen astonished—astonished because you believe in her so completely that you didn't really suppose she could make it. Suddenly her delight becomes yours. And when Mr. Harrison bounces irresistibly to the center of the stage and begins to kick out a tango rhythm to the sounds she has just made there is no controlling the joy in the theatre. Indeed, very little of the number was heard last night: the audience erupted right along with the characters. After that you couldn't have stopped *My Fair Lady* if you'd invited the authors of *Buttrio Square* [1952], *Hit the Trail* [1954], and *Carnival in Flanders* [1953] to work over the second act.

In their previous shows, Lerner and Loewe had continually tested and prodded the boundaries of musical theatre form. While this worked in *Brigadoon* (1947), their other attempts were exciting-but-flawed near misses like *The Day Before Spring* (1945), *Love Life* (Lerner/Weill, 1948), and *Paint Your Wagon* (1951). In *My Fair Lady* Lerner and Loewe simply (!) tried to write a perfect, well-made musical in the Rodgers and Hammerstein tradition. And they certainly succeeded. At the world premiere in New Haven, the audience eruption following "The Rain in Spain" stopped the show dead, as they say. The hysteria continued unabated, Harrison and Coote sitting in frozen astonishment: nothing like this ever happened in drawing room comedy! Finally Miss Andrews—who at twenty already knew her way around—grabbed her colleagues by the elbows (the number ended with them all collapsed on the couch), dragged them down to the apron, and led them in a bow. And the rest, as they say, is history. (At future performances, Mr. Harrison controlled all bows.)

Winner of the New York Drama Critics' Circle Award. In addition to winning the Tony Award for Best Musical, Tonys were won by Frederick Loewe (composer); Alan Jay Lerner (librettist); Moss Hart (director); Hanya Holm (choreographer); Herman Levin (producer); Rex Harrison (actor); Oliver Smith (scenic designer); Cecil Beaton (costume designer); and Franz Allers (musical director). Julie Andrews lost the Best Actress Award to Judy Holliday (for *Bells Are Ringing*).

```
○○○○○○○○○○○○○○○○○○○○○○○○○○○○○○○○○○○○○○○○○○○○
○                                                            ○
○        BROADWAY SCORECARD / perfs: 2,717 / $: +            ○
○                                                            ○
○      rave    favorable    mixed    unfavorable    pan      ○
○                                                            ○
○        7                                                   ○
○                                                            ○
○○○○○○○○○○○○○○○○○○○○○○○○○○○○○○○○○○○○○○○○○○○○○
```

MY ROMANCE

an operetta, with music by Sigmund Romberg (replacing Denes Agay and Philip Redowski); book and lyrics by Rowland Leigh, from the 1913 drama *Romance* by Edward Sheldon

directed by Rowland Leigh; choreographed by Frederic N. Kelly
produced by the Messrs. Shubert
with Anne Jeffreys, Lawrence Brooks (replacing Charles Fredericks), and Luella Gear (replacing Mary Jane Sloan)

opened October 19, 1948   Shubert Theatre

BROOKS ATKINSON, *Times*

Mr. Romberg is a great fellow for volume. Like Bobby Clark's singing, his composing may not be so good, but it is loud and noticeable.

JOHN CHAPMAN, *Daily News*

The operetta tells about a minister who falls in love with an Italian opera star. She is naughty and he is pure and never the twain shall meet no matter how hot their passion. In an operetta, unfulfilled love makes audiences feel fine. Last evening's audience felt fine and wrung four encores out of Miss Jeffreys and Mr. Brooks in their "In Love with Romance" number. Don't pay any attention to me when I tell you that most of the time the show bored me stiff.

JOHN LARDNER, *Star*

According to statistics over which I have no control, *My Romance* is the fortieth musical of its kind to be made to the order of the Shubert family by the house composer, Sigmund Romberg, the poor man's Strauss. So extensive by weight and volume is *My Romance,* and so fraught with the spirit of haven't-we-met-before, that some of the pew-holders on opening night went home from their devotions with an uneasy feeling that the clan Shubert had called in all the 39 previous Romberg shows, from the turnpikes of South Dakota, the ice-packed trails of the Yukon, and the buffalo wallows of Burma, and put them on the stage together in one big wad to celebrate the occasion. This suspicion was unjust. The production is brand new, in the special sense of the term which means that if it ever happened before, you can't prove it. *My Romance* has a plot, bright lights, a large cast, a lot of costumes, and was caught by the clockers in 2 hours 45 minutes net, exclusive of intermissions. It has a quantity of Romberg songs which, if laid end to end—well, wait a minute. What do I mean *if* laid end to end? That's the way they are laid. In regard to lyrics, you know that Mr. Leigh has got the muse where he wants her when he rhymes "palmist" with "alarmist" and "deportment" with "important."

```
BROADWAY SCORECARD / perfs: 95 / $: −

  rave     favorable     mixed     unfavorable     pan

              1                        1            7
```

NELLIE BLY

a musical comedy, with music by James Van Heusen; lyrics by Johnny Burke; book by Joseph Quillan (replacing Morrie Ryskind and Sig Herzig), suggested by events in the life of Nellie Bly (née Elizabeth Seaman, 1867–1922)

directed by Edgar MacGregor (replacing Charles Friedman); choreographed by Edward Caton and Lee Sherman (replacing Robert Sidney)
produced by Nat Karson and Eddie Cantor

with William Gaxton, Victor Moore, Joy Hodges (replacing Marilyn Maxwell), and Benay Venuta

opened January 21, 1946   Adelphi Theatre

JOHN CHAPMAN, *Daily News*

The only thing I really liked about it was [co-producer] Karson's backdrop representing the public square in Moscow. When a backdrop arouses my attention, it is time for me to go home—which is what I did, with a short detour to the office to write this piece. The head manager, I gather from the radio spot announcements, is Eddie Cantor, who has been reminding people that he once worked for Ziegfeld. Sure he did, and he was pretty good, too. But Ziegfeld is no longer with us and Cantor has been in the movies and on the radio for so long that I have come to believe that he, too, has departed. Nothing that happened last evening leads me to believe otherwise.

ROBERT GARLAND, *Journal-American*

We eternal optimists who go down to our seats on passes told ourselves that William Gaxton possibly could have been mistaken when he told a member of the Drama Critics' Circle that *Nellie Bly* was no show for critics, hastening to add that it was an "audience show." But, as last night's premiere wore on in the showshop Mr. Gaxton refers to as a "dump of dumps," we eternal optimists began to shed our optimism and the Adelphi began to shed its audience. Gaxton said that *Nellie Bly* is not a critic's show. He can say that again! . . . . In the title role is Joy Hodges, pinch-hitting for Marilyn Maxwell, who got out from under after Philadelphia. According to the program, Miss Hodges is the only actress on the current stage who gets up at a quarter to seven in the morning. She should have stood in bed.

LOUIS KRONENBERGER, *PM*

Victor Moore and Billy Gaxton are squatting way out on a limb in *Nellie Bly*. It's a show they have virtually no chance to shine in and none whatever to save. The best thing in the show—which is probably the worst thing you can say about one—is one or two of the bright sets. They might more suitably be hung with crepe.

BURTON RASCOE, *World-Telegram*

The best vehicle Gaxton and Moore have had since *Of Thee I Sing* [1931] even if, on the road, the two original authors took their hats and left the show, refusing to allow their names to be used in any billing. Two directors also walked out on it and three choreographers got temperamental and washed their hands of the whole affair. . . . Do you know what made me an embarrassment to my wife, to my colleagues sitting nearby and to people who have more reserve than I have? It was this:

MR. GAXTON: "You nincompoop!"

MR. MOORE: "Don't speak that way to me; we nincompoops are organized now."

Nellie Bly was a reporter for the *New York World* who, following the lead of Jules Verne's fictional Phileas Fogg (1873), set out around the world in November 1889. She made it in 72 days, cabling dispatches en route and selling lots of papers. Nellie Bly's musical comedy barely made it from Philly to Broadway. It was followed a few months later by the Orson Welles/Cole Porter musicalization of *Around the World*, another fabulous flop at the "dump of dumps."

BROADWAY SCORECARD / perfs: 16 / $: −

rave	favorable	mixed	unfavorable	pan
1			1	6

THE NERVOUS SET

a musical satire, with music by Tommy Wolf; lyrics by Fran Landesman; book by Jay Landesman and Theodore J. Flicker, from the novel by Jay Landesman

directed by Theodore J. Flicker
produced by Robert Lantz
with Richard Hayes, Tani Sietz, Larry Hagman, Del Close, Gerald Hiken, and Thomas Aldredge

opened May 12, 1959   Henry Miller's Theatre

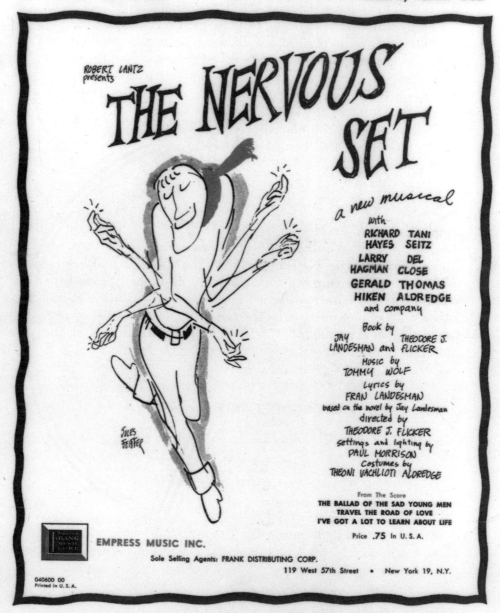

A "beat" hero snaps his fingers, several sets of them. (drawing by Jules Feiffer)

FRANK ASTON, *World-Telegram & Sun*

A weird experience. Something exclusively for the beat, bop, and beret brigade.

ROBERT COLEMAN, *Daily Mirror*

A nerve-wracking musical. It's a song-and-dancer about the beat-niks, and it left us beat to the feet. It was a happy moment when our tootsies started trotting to the Henry Miller's exit last evening. . . . Theoni Vachlioti Aldredge's costumes range mostly from crummy blue jeans to torn cast-offs that a proud hobo would scorn.

WALTER KERR, *Herald Tribune*

A beat-generation musical full of phrases like "get straight," "I'm gonna make it to the end of the green light," and "I'm getting bugged with this creep bit." So when last night's hero finally got around to saying, "We could have a dog!" I quite naturally turned to the glossary the program so considerately provides to see what the term "dog" meant. It meant dog. You know, the kind with four legs and a tail. . . . I can only tell you that the beatnik mind is now within inches of the fifth-rate work of the early 'twenties, and that lyrics on the order of "Shubert's Alley is as chic as Rudy Vallee" will soon be ready for Earl Carroll. I do suppose that another of Fran Landes-man's rhymes dealing with "Rejection, that youthful rejection, like an acne infection" is a bit more contemporary, but I'm less sure it has a future. In short, there is nothing here that Cole Porter couldn't have done twenty times better, while well-dressed.

This one was beat, all right. *The Nervous Set* actually contained one exceptional song, "The Ballad of the Sad Young Men," which is reason enough for a footnote; but it goes in the books as the Broad-way musical debut of Larry Hagman, the twenty-eight-year-old son of what's her name. (You know who I mean, the one from *Peter Pan* [1954].)

○○
○   BROADWAY SCORECARD / perfs: 23 / $: −   ○
○   *rave*   *favorable*   *mixed*   *unfavorable*   *pan*   ○

rave	favorable	mixed	unfavorable	pan
	1	1	2	3

○○

NEW FACES OF 1952

a musical revue, with music and lyrics mostly by Ronny Graham, June (Sillman) Carroll, Arthur Siegel, Sheldon Harnick, and Michael Brown; sketches mostly by Ronny Graham and Melvin (Mel) Brooks

staged by John Murray Anderson; sketches directed by John Beal (replacing Roger Price); choreographed by Richard Barstow
produced by Leonard Sillman
with June Carroll, Robert Clary, Virginia de Luce, Alice Ghostley, Ronny Graham, Eartha Kitt, Carol Lawrence, and Paul Lynde

opened May 16, 1952   *Royale Theatre*

BROOKS ATKINSON, *Times*

Don't look now, but an excellent light revue has come to town. *New Faces of 1952* includes some new talent as well as some new faces, and it has been expertly staged by John Murray Anderson. According to the program, the cast includes seventeen performers, singers and dancers, none of whom has been famous up to now; and the sketches, songs, and lyrics have been written by eight hidden geniuses. But some of them are not going to be obscure for longer than another half hour. For Alice Ghostley, a funny ballad singer and clown, has a voice as well as a sense of humor. Eartha Kitt not only looks incendiary but she can make a song burst into flame. June Carroll can sing and also write lyrics. And Ronny Graham is a grinning droll with authority as well as good nature. Without being precious or snobbish, *New Faces of 1952* has intelligence. Everyone associated with the production works in the same key of pace and skimming good nature. Although it has considerable splendor, nothing weighs heavily on the buoyant spirit of a bright and gay revue. Leonard Sillman, the diligent impresario, has assembled a company of attractive young people who are overflowing with genuine talent. The summer nights may not be so desolate after all.

JOHN CHAPMAN, *Daily News*

Everybody has been saying that the revue form of entertainment is outdated and we won't have the fun we used to have at the *Music Box Revues* [1921–1924] and the *Little Shows* [1929–1931], and now comes *New Faces* to prove that everybody was wrong. This revue, produced by Leonard Sillman at precisely the right intimate theatre, is young and peppy and handsome and funny. As its title promises, its charming principals and supporting players are new or fairly new to the Broadway stage; but its success is due in large measure to an old face—the old, old face of a veteran director, John Murray Anderson. Mr. Anderson, who dates way back, may count *New Faces of 1952* as one of his best pieces of work.

WALTER KERR, *Herald Tribune*

My own nomination for heroine of the evening is Miss Alice Ghostley, a patient, determined comedienne with vast amounts of self-control and a real instinct for satirical mayhem. She stops the first act cold with what is probably the evening's happiest inspiration—a "Boston Beguine" [music and lyrics by Sheldon Harnick]—as she belts out some stentorian rhythms to the accompaniment of wonderfully inhibited gestures. She is funny, too, as the woebegone mother in a sketch [by Melvin Brooks] which turns *Death of a Salesman* [1949] into a family affair among pickpockets, and I even liked her in a Restoration comedy bit which tends to labor a single joke to infinity. Second in command—second only because she has not been given all the material she deserves—is Eartha Kitt, a fetchingly cat-like songstress who does inexplicably pleasant things with a little French lyric, *"Bal Petit Bal"* [music and lyrics by Francis Lemarque], and who drives home a sulky number called "Monotonous" [music by Arthur Siegel; lyrics by June Carroll] to top the second act.

A well-crafted, highly entertaining intimate revue. Unlike most of Leonard Sillman's entertainments (?), *New Faces of 1952* was chock-full of talent, both onstage and at the typewriter/piano. But the format was doomed: the television variety show came along, offering Milton Berle or Sid Caesar in your own living room with new material each week. More topical, easier to get a good seat, and you didn't have to wear shoes.

```
ooooooooooooooooooooooooooooooooooooooooooo
o                                                            o
o       BROADWAY SCORECARD / perfs: 365 / $: +               o
o                                                            o
o    rave      favorable      mixed      unfavorable    pan  o
o                                                            o
o     2            4             1                           o
o                                                            o
ooooooooooooooooooooooooooooooooooooooooooooo
```

NEW FACES OF 1956

a musical revue, with material by various writers including June (Sillman) Carroll, Arthur Siegel, Marshall Barer, Dean Fuller, Matt Dubey, Harold Karr, Paul Nassau, Michael Brown, Paul Lynde, and Louis Botto

conceived and supervised by Leonard Sillman; sketches directed by Paul Lynde; choreography by David Tihmar
produced by Leonard Sillman and John Roberts in association with Yvette Schumer
with Jane Connell, Tiger Haynes, T.C. Jones, Virginia Martin, Bill McCutcheon, John Reardon, Maggie Smith, and Inga Swenson

opened June 14, 1956   Ethel Barrymore Theatre

WILLIAM HAWKINS, *World-Telegram & Sun*

There is a pale and reddish-haired dame, Virginia Martin by name, who does a fabulous and absurd satire on studio acting ["Talent," music and lyrics by Paul Nassau], then turns out to sing both sweet and uproarious as the mood claims her. Jane Connell can similarly turn herself into various assorted moods and people, ancient TV contestant or heroine of African films, all with the greatest of ease. One of the show's great moments, and certainly one of the funniest things in our theatre, is Maggie Smith's descent of a staircase as a Follies Girl draped in thousands of oranges. Miss Smith is chic as the sleek sketch heroines, too. Then there is Inga Swenson, a blonde doll with a sweet voice.

FRANCES HERRIDGE, *Post*

My guess is that you won't see many of them again. The biggest catch in Sillman's collection is a baldheaded man named T.C. Jones, who has a flair for impersonating deep-voiced actresses, especially Tallulah Bankhead. With a blond wig falling over one eye, a whisky voice, and a cynical slouch, he is a genial Tallulah, introducing whatever number has to be introduced. And he is usually much funnier than the number itself. The exception is one hilarious take-off on the *Ziegfeld Follies*—choose your year—where the showgirls are worried by falling headdresses and are all but inundated by their ornamentation.

WALTER KERR, *Herald Tribune*

Quite early in the new *New Faces* there's one of those picture-frame numbers ["One Perfect Moment"], in which a resplendent lady [Maggie Smith] stands at the head of an insanely tilting table surveying the perfect world that is hers. First thing you know, though, things are slipping away on her; the wineglass out of her hand, the food right off the table, the musician at her elbow smack through the floor. On the whole, I felt more or less as the lady did about Leonard Sillman's entry for 1956. The world that surrounds the performers is just about perfect. Designer Peter Larkin has shown his hand—and handsomely—with the first few bars of the overture: instead of patiently looking at a lowered curtain while the orchestra warms up, we are entertained instead by a series of flowing tapestries and flying figurines, with three wonderfully spiraling stairways shooting into the air behind them. Thereafter there is a constant pictorial magic, modest in its dimensions but engagingly tricky as it flows blithely by: blue-crystal doll houses, jungle huts breaking wildly away in the high tropical winds, Paris bars, and Jamaican mansions. Thomas Becher's costumes flash and flare against gliding backgrounds, while Peggy Clark's lighting—managed with the light-battens in full view all evening—is endlessly dazzling.

JOHN McCLAIN, *Journal-American*

The single hero of this Broadway week seems to be Peter Larkin, the scenic designer. Wednesday night he emerged with most of the raves for *Shangri-La;* last night he dominated *New Faces of '56.* For once again, it seemed to me, the auspices far outshone the

*A Ziegfeldian (?) dress parade, with Maggie Smith—the one with
the big oranges—navigating an especially difficult descent. Other
New Faces include future Broadway musical notables Jane* (Mame)
Connell, Inga (110 in the Shade) *Swenson, and an egg-laden Virginia* (Little Me) *Martin.* (set by Peter Larkin, costumes by Thomas Becher, photo
by Freidman-Abeles)

material. It is no news to anybody that the revue is a rough show biz medium; truly hilarious sketches are as hard to come by as a pair for *Fair Lady*. Maybe Sillman would be better advised to forget the faces and just look for "New Writers of '57."

For three seasons Peter Larkin displaced Jo Mielziner and Oliver Smith as Broadway's number one set designer, with *Teahouse of the August Moon* (1953), *Ondine* (1954), *Peter Pan* (1954), *Inherit the Wind* (1955), *No Time for Sergeants* (1955), and—on successive evenings—*Shangri-La* and *New Faces of 1956*. Larkin's imaginative sets were marvels of stage design, but not always mechanically practical; the incredible construction costs (and large number of stagehands required for operation) soon caused Larkin's star to fade. Female impersonator T.C. Jones, as Tallulah, served as mistress of ceremonies; the Tallulah Bankhead–headed *Ziegfeld Follies of 1956*, which was scheduled to compete with *New Faces*, collapsed in May during its pre-Broadway tryout. Jones's critical success as a *New Face* led Sillman to present him in a virtually one-man (?) showcase, *Mask and Gown* (1957).

BROADWAY SCORECARD / perfs: 220 / $: −

rave	favorable	mixed	unfavorable	pan
1	2	2	1	1

NEW FACES OF 1962

a musical revue, with material by various writers

conceived and directed by Leonard Sillman; sketches co-directed by Richard Maury; choreographed mostly by James Moore
produced by Carroll and Harris Masterson
with Patti Karr, Joey Carter, and Marian Mercer

opened February 1, 1962   Alvin Theatre

WALTER KERR, *Herald Tribune*

One of the showier showgirls in the revue at the Alvin is named Sylvia, and Sylvia, according to the program notes, formerly "fought in the Israeli army." Sylvia didn't know when she was well off. To put things as gently as possible, Leonard Sillman's *New Faces of '62* is a disgrace. It is a disgrace because it flatly and emphatically and even defiantly refuses to do the one thing it was created to do: find, and show off, fresh talent. On various occasions before we have been in Mr. Sillman's debt. However casual some of the earlier entertainments in this series may have been, however rickety the materials and/or rasping the tunes, there has almost always been a heartening flash of personality to mark down on the scorecard, a sudden shaft of satirical song to tuck away among one's memories. This one draws an unbelievable blank.

HOWARD TAUBMAN, *Times*

With a warning that machines are taking over everywhere, *New Faces of 1962* introduces itself as possibly the last all-people revue. The prospect may be dire, but don't grieve. The machines couldn't do much worse. A host of authors has produced songs, sketches, and quick blackouts that have a gift for trying to make satiric points not worth making or for failing to make any point at all. Ideas are on desperately short supply; taste is deplorable; style is a matter of chance.

BROADWAY SCORECARD / perfs: 28 / $: −

rave	favorable	mixed	unfavorable	pan
	2		1	4

NEW GIRL IN TOWN

a musical, with music and lyrics by Bob Merrill; book by George Abbott, from the 1921 drama *Anna Christie* by Eugene O'Neill

directed by George Abbott; choreographed by Bob Fosse
produced by Frederick Brisson, Robert E. Griffith, and Harold S. Prince
with Gwen Verdon, Thelma Ritter, George Wallace, and Cameron Prud'homme

opened May 14, 1957   46th Street Theatre

FREDERICK BRISSON, ROBERT E. GRIFFITH AND HAROLD S. PRINCE
PRESENT

Gwen Verdon
Thelma Ritter

in the New Musical

New Girl in Town

WITH

GEORGE WALLACE   CAMERON PRUD'HOMME

BOOK BY GEORGE ABBOTT
MUSIC & LYRICS BY BOB MERRILL
Based on the play "ANNA CHRISTIE" by EUGENE O'NEILL
DANCES & MUSICAL NUMBERS STAGED BY BOB FOSSE
SCENERY & COSTUMES DESIGNED BY REUBEN TER-ARUTUNIAN

MUSICAL DIRECTION BY HAL HASTINGS
ORCHESTRATIONS BY ROBERT RUSSELL BENNETT & PHILIP J. LANG
DANCE MUSIC DEVISED BY ROGER ADAMS

PRODUCTION DIRECTED BY GEORGE ABBOTT

46th STREET THEATRE
220 West 46th Street
Opens Thursday Evening, May 9th
MATINEES WEDNESDAY AND SATURDAY
MAIL ORDERS NOW

Gwen Verdon at the bar, from a different angle. Watered-down O'Neill, but leading ladies Verdon and Thelma Ritter managed to pull it off—and shared a Tony Award for their efforts. (drawing by Oscar Liebman)

485

BROOKS ATKINSON, *Times*

If *New Girl in Town* proves anything, it reminds us that O'Neill's bittersweet drama of the barge captain's daughter is a wonderful bit of American stage literature. Mr. Abbott uses *Anna Christie* as a kind of safe anchorage in a storm of dancing and singing. After making standard whoop-de-doo in waterfront bars, on the piers, or in dance halls, he returns to the solid story of the barge captain's daughter. The showmanship of *New Girl in Town* seems commonplace against the blunt simplicity of *Anna Christie*. Nothing Mr. Abbott can do has the solidity of O'Neill. Since Miss Verdon gives such a moving performance as Anna, this elaborate musical show provokes an impertinent notion: how much better *Anna Christie* would be without so many gaudy trappings.

JOHN CHAPMAN, *Daily News*

Miss Verdon is remarkable. She acts with great honesty and effect, she sings bewitchingly, she dances with boundless skill, and is very beautiful. Miss Ritter is the one, though, who provides practically all the fun of the show. In the role of the temporarily cast-off companion of Anna's father, she is sleazy, raffish, warm-hearted, alcohol-hungry, and a superb comedienne. She has been away from Broadway for a decade, and last night I discovered that this has been much too long a time for a woman so gifted in pantomime, timing, and humor. . . . Bob Fosse's dance numbers—and his dancing company—are extraordinarily good, except for a questionable dream sequence in which the now-purified Miss Verdon imagines that she has returned to her once-sordid life.

TOM DONNELLY, *World-Telegram & Sun*

George Abbott [throws] away just about everything that makes O'Neill O'Neill. It's unfortunate that Mr. Abbott has sought to solve his problems of adaptation by eliminating O'Neill instead of by translating him into musical terms. Perhaps *Anna Christie* is florid and a trifle threadbare. Still, the only scenes in *New Girl in Town* that pack any wallop are those that are reasonably true to the master. If *New Girl in Town* is, at bottom, hollow, it has a bright and lively surface. The approach may be misguided, but the execution is brilliantly professional. The show lacks inner drive, but it has that Abbott pace. It has all the trimmings that usually make for popular success, and I won't be at all surprised if the cash customers are inclined to ignore the fact that there is no tree under all those ornaments.

WALTER KERR, *Herald Tribune*

The songs, and the high kicks Bob Fosse has arranged for them, inhabit only the nooks and corners of the evening; we keep ducking into friendly bars and gaslit alleys for some fun on the sly. The method leaves the O'Neill story looking surprisingly wan. Mr. Abbott, in reworking the tooth-and-nail love story, has minded his business and played the whole thing straight (perhaps too straight—there was some sound, robust comedy in the original that is missing here). But with the secondary figures being handed most of the hi-jinks, Gwen Verdon's Anna becomes a somewhat ghostly, sorrowing, forlorn little chick; you're awfully relieved when she hikes those long skirts and lets rip after nearly an hour and a half. And the turbulent love tangle with Mat never quite bursts into either a musical, or dramatic, blaze. . . . The orchestrations of Robert Russell Bennett and Philip J. Lang keep a schmaltzy confection like "Sunshine Girl" ("The sunshine girl has raindrops in her eyes") lilting delectably. But there are more than raindrops spattering down on *New Girl in Town*. Someone has watered the beer.

JOHN MCCLAIN, *Journal-American*

This has been a great year for discovering or rediscovering Eugene O'Neill: *Long Day's Journey* grabbing most of the season's awards, *Moon for the Misbegotten* brilliantly presented at the Bijou, and *The Iceman Cometh* enjoying a lusty revival at the Circle-in-the-Square downtown. Now comes *New Girl in Town*, a musical based on his *Anna Christie*. Devout O'Neill fans will not find much of the original, but they will be treated to a thoroughly zestful and engaging period piece, a show with style, humor, and a rollicking score.

RICHARD WATTS JR., *Post*

There was a time last evening when the suspense in *New Girl in Town* seemed to consist of wondering how the libretto would manage to get Miss Verdon into her dancing.

☆

Abbott, Fosse, and the producing team of Brisson, Griffith, and Prince followed *The Pajama Game* (1954) and *Damn Yankees* (1955) with the troubled *New Girl in Town*, which barely managed to pull itself together. The combination of O'Neill drama and Broadway musical comedy was ineffectively merged, with the score offering little diversion. *New Girl's* prime asset (and saving grace) was, not surprisingly, Gwen Verdon. A major disagreement over the "sordid" dream sequence caused a permanent split between Fosse and the Abbott/Prince camp. Fosse and Verdon went on to the empty-but-successful *Redhead* (1959), while Abbott, Griffith, and Prince did *Fiorello!* (1959).

Tony Awards were won by Thelma Ritter and Gwen Verdon (actress, tied with each other!).

BROADWAY SCORECARD / perfs: 431 / $: +

rave	favorable	mixed	unfavorable	pan
	4		3	

NO STRINGS

a musical, with music and lyrics by Richard Rodgers; book by Samuel Taylor

directed and choreographed by Joe Layton
produced by Richard Rodgers in association with Samuel Taylor
with Richard Kiley, Diahann Carroll, Polly Rowles, Noelle Adam, Bernice Massi, and Alvin Epstein

opened March 15, 1962   54th Street Theatre

JOHN CHAPMAN, *Daily News*

Rodgers just can't think of any wrong notes, so his melodies are beguiling—and the lyrics he has written for them are pleasant and graceful. Joe Layton has directed *No Strings* as if his life depended upon it, and has staged some odd and twitchy dances for the mannequins and their boy friends. I do wish somebody had thought of some jokes.

WALTER KERR, *Herald Tribune*

The nicest thing to be said about *No Strings* is Diahann Carroll. Miss Carroll is a girl with a sweet smile, brilliant dark eyes, and a profile regal enough to belong on a coin. When she sings, she draws energy from everywhere: from her fingers (you can see it draining out of them and into her quivering roots), from her elegant shoulders, from the floorboards, from the balcony, from the buildings across the street. And when she is finished with a song it takes her a good, long shudder—with eyes closed—to send all that tingling power back where it belongs. Otherwise, the new musical is a show in which the actors never have to go anywhere. Everything comes to them. Everything except an idea. . . . Mr. Rodgers has, for the first time, added his own lyrics to the melodies that so cheerfully flow from him, and the temptation to listen so hard to them that you don't hear the music is almost irresistible. Supposing this unfair focus really to have been resisted, how are they? They are perfectly satisfactory—no less, but no more. Though the words get the work done professionally enough, they do not rise into the shadow of that near-poetry that makes lyrics lyrical. They seem also, unless I am mistaken, to be using up some of Mr. Rodgers's composing energy without quite tapping his composer's inspiration.

JOHN McCLAIN, *Journal-American*

Mr. Rodgers is responsible for several amiable innovations. There is no pit orchestra—the musicians work offstage as a group or occasionally wander about onstage alone or in small combinations, insinuating themselves into the story. The stage is set by the players, and an unconventional assortment of varicolored lights, strips of material, frames on hinges and platforms are moved about, without halting the action, to suggest locales in Paris, Deauville, Honfleur, and the Riviera [sets and lighting designed by David Hays]. Perhaps the happiest departure created by either Mr. Rodgers or perhaps Joe Layton, who choreographed and directed, is the one of having everybody in the cast enunciate properly and sing and speak with enough power to be heard distinctly all over the house.

Richard Kiley and Diahann Carroll stroll through David Hays's innovatively designed impression of haute couture *Paris.* (set and lights *by David Hays, costumes by Fred Voelpel and Donald Brooks, photo by Freidman-Abeles*)

NORMAN NADEL, *World-Telegram & Sun*

By this time, the good people who are responsible for *No Strings* must be starting to suspect that a book, not a dog, is man's best friend. *No Strings* has a book—by the distinguished playwright, Samuel Taylor. It is not, however, a good book. The persistence of its inadequacy undermines what otherwise might have been an impressively original and occasionally striking musical play. The opening of *No Strings* is spectacular. The ingredients are a black stage, on which a circle of blue glows darkly; the sudden intrusion of four cool and compact spotlights; the exquisite definition, in voice, face, and figure, of Diahann Carroll; the pensive obbligato of a solo flute, and "The Sweetest Sounds". . . . While the [plot] is taking place (or, actually, not taking place), Rodgers is pulling off the coup which is bound to set *No Strings* apart from most other musicals of many years past: his orchestra, a jazz chamber ensemble consisting of brass, woodwinds, percussion, and no strings [orchestrated by Ralph Burns]. Instead of depositing them in the pit, he weaves them into the play. Only the singing of Miss Carroll is a brighter thread in the musical texture than the masterful and meticulous work of these gentlemen. Rodgers's weaving of these materials is the sole element of *No Strings* which qualifies unequivocally as art.

HOWARD TAUBMAN, *Times*

Richard Rodgers need not have worried. He is still a magician of the musical theatre. It will surprise no one that his lines have a touch of the wholesome ease of Hammerstein and a *soupçon* of the peppery impertinence of Lorenz Hart. If Mr. Rodgers is not yet as polished as either of his colleagues, he is good enough to walk—and sing—alone.

Sounds like an interesting show, doesn't it? But don't look for a revival, not with *that* book. Too bad. The musical concept—accompanists weaving through the action—seems to have worked extremely well; curiously, nobody has attempted a further development of this idea.

Tony Awards were won by Richard Rodgers (composer); Joe Layton (choreographer, tied with Agnes de Mille for *Kwamina*); and

Diahann Carroll (actress, tied with Anna Maria Alberghetti for *Carnival*). Richard Rodgers also won a special Tony Award.

```
○○○○○○○○○○○○○○○○○○○○○○○○○○○○○○○○○○○○○○○○○○○○○
○                                                             ○
○       BROADWAY SCORECARD / perfs: 580 / $: +                ○
○                                                             ○
○    rave     favorable     mixed     unfavorable     pan     ○
○                                                             ○
○      1          3            2                       1      ○
○                                                             ○
○○○○○○○○○○○○○○○○○○○○○○○○○○○○○○○○○○○○○○○○○○○○○○
```

NOWHERE TO GO BUT UP

a musical comedy, with music by Sol Berkowitz; book and lyrics by James Lipton, suggested by the exploits of Prohibition agents Izzy Einstein and Moe Smith; previously announced as *Izzy and Mae*

directed by Sidney Lumet; choreographed by Ronald (Ron) Field
produced by Kermit Bloomgarden and Herbert Greene in association with Steven H. Scheuer
with Tom Bosley, Martin Balsam, Bruce Gordon, Dorothy Loudon, and Phil Leeds
opened November 10, 1962   Winter Garden Theatre

WALTER KERR, *Herald Tribune*

If Bobby Clark were alive, the new show at the Winter Garden might be. For this sort of antic you don't want actors, you want men who could go into vaudeville if there were no other work around. Tom Bosley grins his pencil-thin grin and wears a Friar Tuck tonsur with animation and some aplomb. Mr. Bosley is a good actor. But he is no fool. Martin Balsam, an even better actor, naturally faces worse. Mostly he is just standing there, nodding his head and wondering from exactly what angle feverish Dorothy Loudon will attack him next. Which, come to think of it, is better than watching him make a ballet-leap entrance with a clutch of posies in his fist. Miss Loudon vibrates intensely through two songs, tending to proclaim by her quiver how "sock" each of them is going to be instead of letting us discover her charms by ourselves.

NORMAN NADEL, *World-Telegram & Sun*

Miss Loudon has the priceless talent of flinging herself in all directions at once while she sings. She can curl a lip in eloquent,

During a production number in a speakeasy, prohibition agent Tom Bosley holds onto juvenile Bert Convy who serenades ingenue Mary Ann Mobley. "Don't let anyone tell you that Nowhere to Go But Up is a little horror," warned Howard Taubman, "because it's a big one."

earthy discontent; show consuming anger with a thrusting, lateral movement of her jaw; employ her baleful blue eyes like a club, or illuminate them for a caress.

HOWARD TAUBMAN, *Times*

Don't let anyone tell you that *Nowhere to Go But Up* is a little horror. Because it's a big one. What happens to the confectioners of ambitious musical sweets? Are they so bedeviled by the rush and responsibility of a formidable enterprise that they forget their taste and sense of proportion? Do they look at their handiwork so long and lovingly that, like a foolish parent with a spoiled child, they fail to see its glaring faults? Squirming before the tumultuous ineptitudes of *Nowhere to Go But Up*, one marvels somberly at the caprices of the musical theatre. Must it remain, even to seasoned professionals, an elusive enigma wrapped in an impenetrable mystery? Why don't they recognize a lack of invention, a failure of imagination, an absence of humor? . . . . Mary Ann Mobley, by the way, was Miss America in 1959, but with the help of ingenious make-up, she manages to resemble every other musical-comedy soubrette.

This from Kermit Bloomgarden, producer of the Pulitzer Prize–winning *Death of a Salesman* (1949), *The Diary of Anne Frank* (1955), and *Look Homeward, Angel* (1957). Bloomgarden entered the musical field with *The Most Happy Fella* (1956) and—from a novice writer—*The Music Man* (1957). So this little number surely must have showed *some* promise. Along with the authors, *Nowhere to Go But Up* marked the Broadway musical debuts of director Sidney Lumet, a one-time *Dead End* (1935) kid, and choreographer Ron Field, one of Liza Elliott's childhood playmates in *Lady in the Dark* (1941). As for Bloomgarden's further musical adventures, already on tap was the absurdist escapade *Side Show*—which ultimately arrived rechristened *Anyone Can Whistle* (1964).

BROADWAY SCORECARD / perfs: 9 / $: −

rave	favorable	mixed	unfavorable	pan
	2		1	4

OF THEE I SING

a revival of the 1931 Pulitzer Prize–winning musical satire, with music by George Gershwin; lyrics by Ira Gershwin; book by George S. Kaufman and Morrie Ryskind

directed by George S. Kaufman; choreographed by Jack Donohue (replacing Helen Tamiris)
produced by Chandler Cowles and Ben Segal
with Jack Carson, Paul Hartman, Jack Whiting, Lenore Lonergan, Betty Oakes, and Florenz Ames

opened May 5, 1952   Ziegfeld Theatre

BROOKS ATKINSON, *Times*

Nothing much having changed since 1931, *Of Thee I Sing* is still a hilarious and pertinent musical burlesque. In 1931 George S. Kaufman and Morrie Ryskind appeared to be applying the bastinado to the Republican party; and everyone, including the Pulitzer trustees, was very happy. In the revival, the Democrats are the victims. But the same whirligig contempt for Government applies and has the same galvanic effect on the audience. For *Of Thee I Sing* is still a marvelous carnival with a subject that is always timely and worth kicking around.

WALTER KERR, *Herald Tribune*

If everything at the Ziegfeld were as good as the overture, this would be a happier report this morning. When the orchestra drives into "Of Thee I Sing," "Because," and "Love Is Sweeping the Country" the audience just cannot help breaking into frequent and exhilarating applause. The fire of Gershwin and all the nostalgic associations we have for the Kaufman–Ryskind *Of Thee I Sing* come crowding back. But somewhere the salt has lost its savor. It is twenty-one years now since *Of Thee I Sing* won a Pulitzer Prize for its ribald invasion of those smoke-filled rooms and that sleepy Senate chamber. It isn't that times have got much better—just that they've changed. *Of Thee I Sing* is satire, but, with the disappearance of so many points of reference, it doesn't seem very satirical any more. It begins, in fact, to take on the quality of a comic opera set in a never-never land as remote as Oz, and the insertion of last-minute gags about Truman, taxes, Dixiecrats, and minks don't help very much. If anything, they call special attention to the dim and distant quality of all that was once so devastating.

```
○○○○○○○○○○○○○○○○○○○○○○○○○○○○○○○○○○○○○○○○○○○○
○                                                    ○
○        BROADWAY SCORECARD / perfs: 72 / $: −        ○
○                                                    ○
○    rave    favorable    mixed    unfavorable    pan ○
○                                                    ○
○      3                    2         2               ○
○                                                    ○
○○○○○○○○○○○○○○○○○○○○○○○○○○○○○○○○○○○○○○○○○○○○○
```

OH CAPTAIN!

a musical comedy, with music by Jay Livingston; lyrics by Jay Livingston and Ray Evans; book by Al Morgan and José Ferrer, from the 1953 screenplay *The Captain's Paradise* by Alec Coppel

directed by José Ferrer; choreographed by James Starbuck
produced by Howard Merrill and Theatre Corporation of America
(Donald H. Coleman)
with Tony Randall, Abbe Lane, Jacquelyn McKeever, Edward Platt, Susan Johnson, and Alexandra Danilova

opened February 4, 1958   Alvin Theatre

FRANK ASTON, *World-Telegram & Sun*

Early in José Ferrer's production, the unassuming, Midwestern (Tulsa) Tony Randall does a lightly once-over *pas de deux* with that immortal of the classic ballet, the supreme, divine Danilova. No reason for it. Some screwball thought of it. There it is. Unbelievably entertaining.

BROOKS ATKINSON, *Times*

In case any of our business men are tired, they can count on José Ferrer. His production of *Oh Captain!* will not strain their minds. For the standards of *Oh Captain!* are common. It has everything except taste. The record shows that Mr. Ferrer has genius for the theatre. But at the moment he is overflowing with sympathy for the tired business man. He is giving untired theatregoers a dull time.

Parisian saucier *Abbe Lane stirs things up. This is the unexpur-gated logo; elsewhere they had to draw in a chemise under the apron!* (drawing by Tom Morrow)

JOHN CHAPMAN, *Daily News*

Tony Randall, who played the cynical H. L. Mencken role in a serious play, *Inherit the Wind* [1955], reveals himself as a musical comedy man of exceptional gifts. He sings well enough and will dance if he has to, but his great gift is the high disdain with which he drops a line or ignores an opponent. This is music-show acting with style. . . . Jo Mielziner, the old master, has spread himself on the settings, using every trick of his trade. For a very funny finale, he has arranged for the captain's ship literally to blow its sack.

ROBERT COLEMAN, *Daily Mirror*

In every successful musical, there's always the take-over guy or doll with the know-how and the vitality to steer it over dangerous shoals. In this instance, it's Randall who dominates the hi-jinks as the skipper who can change from a stodgy family man into a gay Lothario, like a chameleon switching colors. He sings songs as though he's been belting them over all his life. He steps like a member of Ballet Theatre, teaming with Alexandra Danilova in a hilarious show-stopper. And he acts the triple-threat role so persuasively as to make you forget that Alec Guinness did it in the film. Terrific is the word for Tony. Abbe Lane is a bombshell of sultry sex. What looks! What curves! What a gal! What a lucky man is hubby Xavier Cugat!

WALTER KERR, *Herald Tribune*

Perhaps they should try making Broadway musicals out of bad movies. They're still having trouble making them out of good ones. . . . Abbe Lane, who is better constructed than the plot, arranges her sort-of-sorry mouth into an attractive pout and has fun with the lazy, seductive beat of a number called "Femininity." Edward Platt makes a hearty jest of "I've Been There and I'm Back," and Susan Johnson, sporting purple hair and sequins on her eyelids, gives all she has (a very great deal) to "Give It All You've Got." In general, though, the bouncy score sounds curiously as though it belonged to a film called "The Big Broadcast of 1958."

Dorothy Lamour made her Broadway debut on July 16, replacing Abbe Lane. Lamour bid Broadway adieu on July 19, as *Oh Captain!* capsized.

OKLAHOMA!

a musical play, with music by Richard Rodgers; book and lyrics by Oscar Hammerstein 2nd, from the 1931 folk play *Green Grow the Lilacs* by Lynn Riggs; tryout title: *Away We Go!*

directed by Rouben Mamoulian; choreographed by Agnes de Mille produced by the Theatre Guild
with Betty Garde, Alfred Drake, Joseph Buloff, Joan Roberts, Lee Dixon, Howard Da Silva, and Celeste Holm

opened March 31, 1943   St. James Theatre

JOHN ANDERSON, *Journal-American*

A beautiful and delightful show, fresh and imaginative, as enchanting to the eye as Richard Rodgers's music is to the ear. It has, at a rough estimate, practically everything. Even Guild First Nighters, suspected for years of not having hands, applauded.

HOWARD BARNES, *Herald Tribune*

Songs, dances, and a story have been triumphantly blended. *Oklahoma!* is a jubilant and enchanting musical. The Richard Rodgers score is one of his best, and that is saying plenty. Oscar Hammerstein 2nd has written a dramatically imaginative libretto and a string of catchy lyrics; Agnes de Mille has worked small miracles in devising original dances to fit the story and the tunes, while Rouben Mamoulian has directed an excellent company with great taste and craftsmanship.

LOUIS KRONENBERGER, *PM*

Mr. Hammerstein's lyrics have less crispness and wit than Lorenz Hart's at their best, but the songs in *Oklahoma!* call for less sophisticated words, and Mr. Hammerstein has found very likeable

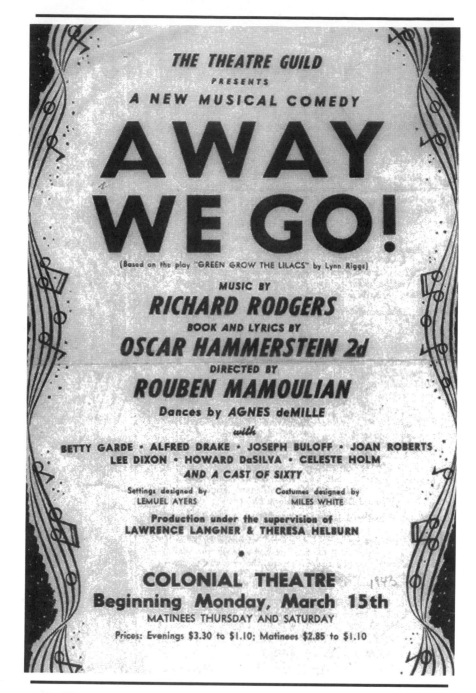

Away We Go! *sounds like a burlesque smoker with leggy girls and baggy-pants comics. They renamed the show before moving on to Broadway, using the title of the big eleven o'clock song (but retaining that exclamation point).*

ones. . . . *Oklahoma!*—for the record—tells of the trouble a couple of nice guys in cowboy boots have in winning a couple of pretty farm girls. A comic peddler and a villainous hired man provide the competition, and dutifully scram at the stroke of 11.

BURNS MANTLE, *Daily News*

Oklahoma! really is different—beautifully different. With the songs that Richard Rodgers has fitted to a collection of unusually atmospheric and intelligible lyrics by Oscar Hammerstein 2nd, *Oklahoma!* seems to me to be the most thoroughly and attractively American musical comedy since Edna Ferber's *Show Boat* [1927] was done by this same Hammerstein and Jerome Kern.

WARD MOREHOUSE, *Sun*

Oklahoma! is charming and leisurely. And tunely. And certainly not topical. It's of an era in American life before anybody ever heard of Gabes or Sfax [sites of recent battles]—and probably only vaguely of Tunisia. It reveals Mr. Rodgers, shorn only for the moment of Larry Hart, in good form indeed. And nobody in last night's audience seemed to have a better time than Mr. Hart himself, who applauded the proceedings from a seat in Row B.

BURTON RASCOE, *World-Telegram*

The Guild has combined some of the best features of the ballet at the Met with some of the best features of the great tradition of Broadway's own indigenous contribution to the theatre—a girl show with lovely tunes, a couple of comics, a heavy, pretty costuming, and an infectious spirit of gayety and good humor. *Oklahoma!* is fresh, lively, colorful, and enormously pleasing. Richard Rodgers has written for the show one of the finest musical scores any musical play ever had. Next to Mr. Rodgers, however, must stand the amazing Agnes de Mille, whose choreography, carried out to perfection by her ballet [corps], is actually the biggest hit of the show. The "Out of My Dreams" and "All 'er Nothin' " dances are such supreme aesthetic delights as to challenge anything the Met can produce this season. They are spinetingling, out of this world.

WILELLA WALDORF, *Post*

Old-fashioned homespun charm is the keynote of the production from the time the curtain goes up, and for a while last night it all seemed just a trifle too cute. For some reason known only to the producers, a flock of Mr. Rodgers's songs that are pleasant enough, but still manage to sound quite a bit alike, are warbled in front of Laurey's farmhouse, one after another, without much variety in the presentation. It was all very picturesque in a studied fashion, reminding us that life on a farm is apt to become a little tiresome.

Critics and audiences alike were overwhelmed by *Oklahoma!*'s innovative blend of song, story, and dance. This was no accident; both Hammerstein (with Kern) and Rodgers (with Hart) had long worked toward integration in such works as *Show Boat* (1927) and *On Your Toes* (1936). They had also done pioneering film musical work: *Love Me Tonight* (1932, Rodgers and Hart) and the less successful *High, Wide, and Handsome* (1936, Kern and Hammerstein). Both movies—not at all coincidentally—were directed by Rouben Mamoulian, whose prior stage work included the Theatre Guild's folk play *Porgy* (1927) and its musicalization *Porgy and Bess* (1935). When the Guild decided to musicalize their 1931 folk play *Green Grow the Lilacs*, Mamoulian was the logical choice. Rodgers went back even further with the Guild: his first important job had been composing (and conducting) the fabled *Garrick Gaieties* (1925). As Larry Hart was not interested in the proposed "cowboy opera," Rodgers enlisted Hammerstein. The pair had previously written a few college songs in 1919. Agnes de Mille came in via her success with Aaron Copland's ballet "Rodeo" (1942); she'd been fired from her previous Broadway assignments. *Oklahoma!* was especially striking in its use of ballet to further action: the plot hinges on a decision—the heroine's choosing to go to the box social with the "wrong" man—which is developed and motivated in "Laurey's Dream Ballet" at the end of the first act. To a generation that grew up on shows like *Carousel* (1945), *South Pacific* (1949), and *West Side Story* (1957), *Oklahoma!* might seem somewhat less than overpowering; but we must remember that Rodgers, Hammerstein, Mamoulian, and de Mille had to first put the horse before the surrey. If *Oklahoma!* looks a little tame in revival, Rodgers and Hammerstein's glorious score remains enchantingly refreshing.

Oklahoma! received a special citation from the Pulitzer committee. (It was ineligible for the regular Prize, being adapted from a play. No Award was given that season.)

BROADWAY SCORECARD / perfs: 2,248 / $: +

rave	favorable	mixed	unfavorable	pan
5	2	1		

OKLAHOMA!

a return engagement of the 1943 musical play

directed by Rouben Mamoulian, restaged by Jerome Whyte; choreographed by Agnes de Mille
produced by the Theatre Guild
with Ridge Bond, Patricia Northrup, Henry Clarke, and Jacqueline Sundt

opened May 29, 1951   Broadway Theatre

ROBERT GARLAND, *Journal-American*

In 1943, no present-day dramatic critic was officially in evidence. From Brooks Atkinson, in Russia, to me, in the doghouse, strangers started the song-and-dancer on its way. They liked it. All but one, and she's dead [Wilella Waldorf].

OTIS GUERNSEY JR., *Herald Tribune*

It is as near to fool-proof entertainment as may be seen in our time. Its only social significance is the musical suggestion that the farmer and the cowpoke ought to be pals. Its single realistic character, Jud Fry, is a terror in this ideal setting, and he is conveniently ditched after he has served his purpose of accenting the rosiness around him. There appears to be nothing here that can age, and the irresistible patterns of love and laughter are no sign of immaturity in the first Rodgers and Hammerstein collaboration. Rather, they represent a sure sense of joyous entertainment in a general and universal form, later honed down into specific themes like realistic emotion, war, or cultural difference. The latter may be more striking, but *Oklahoma!* accomplishes equally well its purpose of pure diversion.

WILLIAM HAWKINS, *World-Telegram & Sun*

No wonder it never closed! One look at *Oklahoma!* and you see why it had to become a classic. It is still so fresh and strong and bright, and the score is so grand, for all the familiarity that tempts you to sing every number aloud. The fact that the show set several styles might have dated it, since its innovations have become requisites. But it remains pristine because it is simple, direct, and strong. It moves like a sunny wind blowing ripples in a field of ripe grain. *Oklahoma!* was not the first show to use ballet, but it was the show which made the dance of narrative and character, as opposed to muscular exhibition, an integral part of nine out of ten musicals. Even more breathtaking was the use of an extremely serious neurotic person, and a realistically ugly situation, in a musical comedy. . . . For all its talk of haystacks and interest in grain, *Oklahoma!* is probably the least corny musical you ever saw.

VERNON RICE, *Post*

Which came first, *Oklahoma!* the show or Oklahoma the State, is now hard to tell, for both have been around so long that it is difficult to separate one from the other. I'm glad that this troupe decided to pause here for the summer at the end of its eight years of traveling [this was the first National Company]. For some reason or other there is a feeling that we Oklahomans don't do anything but strum our "geetars" and sing hillbilly tunes through our noses. There on the stage is proof that we sing only Rodgers and Hammerstein songs. Why, we've been starting the day off for years with "Oh, What a Beautiful Mornin'." Ever since I was a child I've been going to parties in a surrey with the fringe on top, singing the song with the same name as Old Dobbin pulled off into the sun-bleached horizon designed by Lemuel Ayers. People in these parts sort of smirk when I wear my bright blue trousers and my gray suede cowboy boots and a shocking pink scarf tied around my neck. Nobody believes me when I tell them that Miles White only calls these our casual clothes. . . . Soon we'll be admitting we named the State after the show.

This was a visit by the First National Company of the show, which began touring October 15, 1943, and finally closed May 2, 1953!

BROADWAY SCORECARD / perfs: 72 / $: NA

rave	favorable	mixed	unfavorable	pan
2	4	1		

OKLAHOMA!

another return engagement of the 1943 musical play

directed by Jerome Whyte; choreographed by Agnes de Mille, restaged by Betty Gour
produced by Richard Rodgers and Oscar Hammerstein 2nd
with Ridge Bond, Florence Henderson, Alfred Cibelli, Jr., and Barbara Cook

opened August 31, 1953   City Center

WALTER KERR, *Herald Tribune*

One of [the improvements] is a blonde, corn-fed (I mean that in the nicest possible way), apple-cheeked lass named Florence Henderson. Miss Henderson plays Laurey and she is the real thing, right out of a butter-churn somewhere. She torments her man with a wonderfully stubborn and come-and-get-me air, she snarls out 'seches' and 'airs' and 'yows' of the mock-Oklahoma dialect as though she'd been born with corntassel in her mouth, and when she gets around to "Many a New Day" and "People Will Say We're in Love," she sings her heart out. You not only like this Laurey, you believe in her. . . . Is it exactly the show we all saw when we were a lot younger? Well, no. (This is just for the record; I don't want my grandchildren thinking they're seeing the precise inspiration I've been yapping about all these years, and looking at me in pity.) The dances, for instance, don't look as though Agnes de Mille had put a finger, or a metronome, to them in quite a long while. The outlines are still there. With just slightly better dancers, and with just a little tightening of line, it would still lift you out of your seat. But there's always a shade of raggedness, an ounce of slack, to disconcert you and to make you start remembering how it really was.

JOHN McCLAIN, *Journal-American*

Scarcely a man is now alive who has not memorized the score or become related by marriage to some number of the cast. As the orchestra began the overture the audience broke into involuntary applause; it was as though somebody began playing "My Old Kentucky Home" during a French train strike. And when the curtain went up there was that familiar scene of the hot corn country with the old doll churning and the handsome young cowboy (it doesn't matter much who) coming in singing "Oh, What a Beautiful Mornin'." Then the joint rocked. This is not now, and never was, a very stimulating book. There is never the slightest doubt as to how it will all be resolved, it is lacking in ingenuity and laughs; but it is lifted to a high level by the insistent brilliance of the music and the pace of the performance. . . . I was not overwhelmed with the abilities of Barbara Cook in the Ado Annie role (originally played by Celeste Holm), but that may be due to the sort of senility that besets fans who insist nobody could have beaten Jack Dempsey in his prime.

Mayor Impellitteri (who?) proclaimed it "Rodgers and Hammerstein Week." During the limited engagement, there were four Rodgers and Hammerstein musicals playing on the Main Stem, the others being *South Pacific* (1949), *The King and I* (1951), and *Me and Juliet* (1953). Mr. Atkinson commented that there would also be a few other shows on the boards, from writers "who were happy enough to have one play on at a time." This *Oklahoma!* was the first stop of a new National Company being put out by the boys, who had bought the production rights from the Theatre Guild.

BROADWAY SCORECARD / perfs: 40 / $: NA

rave	favorable	mixed	unfavorable	pan
5	2			

This logo—quickly prepared for the newly titled musical during its tryout—heralded Oklahoma! *throughout the country for over ten years. By 1953, Rodgers and Hammerstein had bought out the original producers. (drawing by Witold Gordon)*

OLIVER!

a British musical play, with music, book, and lyrics by Lionel Bart, from the 1838 novel *Oliver Twist* by Charles Dickens

directed by Peter Coe
produced by David Merrick and Donald Albery
with Clive Revill, Georgia Brown, Bruce Prochnik, and David Jones (replacing Michael Goodman)

opened January 6, 1963   Imperial Theatre

JOHN CHAPMAN, *Daily News*

One of the most impressive British products to be imported here since the first Rolls Royce.

WALTER KERR, *Herald Tribune*

In the week-and-a-half since Christmas I've spent a good bit of time watching children put together elaborate mechanical toys with pieces that flap into place and clap together on cue and go up and down and sideways and are very colorful and make splendid noises and don't really hold interest for terribly long. I felt as though I were still watching them at *Oliver!* last night. This importation from England has enormous energy but it is energy of a peculiarly mechanical kind . . . a sense of "keep banging the shutters, boys, a pause or a silence might kill us." This is particularly true of the evening's comedy, which is mostly a matter of throwing water in the wrong face, walloping a lass with a ladle or stamping on someone's foot until someone falls down. The humor is especially peculiar, however, in the case of Fagin, that sly old master of thieves. Clive Revill starts him off rather interestingly with fastidious speed, taking snuff and strutting with a cane in a jaunty cock-of-the-walk rhythm, then quickly deteriorates into pre–Mack Sennett mugging as he springs to his hiding place, clutches his treasures, and measures his pearls like so many yards of muslin, a jeweler's glass in his eye. Between the voice changes and the double takes, he seems like Peter Ustinov telling stories on the Jack Paar show, which is absolutely fine for the Jack Paar show but very confusing here. *Oliver!* is like looking at a comic-book condensation of a Dickens classic with the radio on.

The Annie *of the 1960s, only with better songs, a better book, and genuine charm. Pre-Broadway credits. (drawing by Irene Haas)*

JOHN McCLAIN, *Journal-American*

Simply scrumptious. It represents a breakthrough for the British in a field which has so long been dominated by Americans.

RICHARD WATTS JR., *Post*

The most important quality of *Oliver!* is the frankness and expertness of its showmanship. Its beauty, melodiousness, humor, and occasional pathos are shrewdly combined in a pattern that isn't ashamed to be good fun. The resourceful maintenance of the Dickensian mood, amid the trappings of a musical show, arises to a great extent from the splendid settings created by Sean Kenny. Handsome and imaginative in themselves, the sets designed by the brilliant young Irishman, whose work has put him at the head of his profession in the London theatre, have a functional deftness that enables the performance to move smoothly and rapidly. What is more important, though, is the pictorial excitement with which they capture the dramatic quality of the raffish slums of Victorian London.

David Merrick hedged his bets on this one. Concerns had been raised over how certain anti-Semitic inferences of the 1960 London production would be received by New York's Jewish community. Merrick arranged a fourteen-week West Coast tryout, which would give him plenty of time to iron out any offending material—and guarantee recoupment of the entire investment prior to Broadway! As it turned out, Merrick needn't have worried on either count. *Oliver!*'s New York reviews were delayed by a newspaper strike, but the electronic media jumped into the breach. Radio station WNEW's "guest critic" called *Oliver!* "the greatest musical of all time. A truly great classic of the theatre: transcendent, unique, incomparable, prodigious, stunning." The "guest critic" was, coincidentally enough, David Merrick. He subsequently tried the same guaranteed-profit West Coast approach on three more big-budget musicals, the Dickensian import *Pickwick* (1965), Gower Champion's *The Happy Time* (1968), and the hapless *Baker's Wife* (1976). All were dismal, and nobody asked drama critic Merrick for his opinion. *The Happy Time*, in fact, posted a record $950,000 loss at a (happy?) time when you could still produce a full-scale smash—like Merrick's *Promises, Promises* (1968)—for a mere half-million.

Tony Awards were won by Lionel Bart (composer); Sean Kenny (scenic designer); and Donald Pippin (musical director).

BROADWAY SCORECARD / perfs: 774 / $: +

rave	favorable	mixed	unfavorable	pan
5		1	1	

ON THE TOWN

a musical comedy, with music by Leonard Bernstein; book and lyrics by Betty Comden and Adolph Green (additional lyrics by Leonard Bernstein), based on "an idea" (the 1944 ballet "Fancy Free") by Jerome Robbins

directed by George Abbott; choreographed by Jerome Robbins
produced by Oliver Smith and Paul Feigay
with Sono Osato, Nancy Walker, Betty Comden, Adolph Green, John Battles, Robert Chisholm, and Cris Alexander

opened December 28, 1944   Adelphi Theatre

JOHN CHAPMAN, *Daily News*

Not even the ministrations of able George Abbott as director, nor the presence of such enjoyable players as Sono Osato and Nancy Walker, can make *On the Town* anything but a dullish musical comedy. It is not without its scenic thrills, for one of the producers, Oliver Smith, is a top-flight stage designer. Mr. Smith's effects, even when they verge on the spectacular, are achieved with remarkable economy. I don't mean the economy of money-saving, but of effort. His settings seem to work without any trouble and in no time at all, and this is admirable in a business where your mind's eye often pictures forty $150-a-week stage hands running around like crazy behind a curtain. The next-to-closing-scene, in which a subway train arrives at Coney and the whole wonderland of sky rides is suddenly revealed, is an example of stage designing

NEW YORK'S No. 1 MUSICAL HIT

OLIVER SMITH and PAUL FEIGAY present

ON THE TOWN

Directed by
GEORGE ABBOTT
Book and Lyrics by
BETTY COMDEN & ADOLPH GREEN
Music by LEONARD BERNSTEIN
Dances by JEROME ROBBINS
Production Designed by OLIVER SMITH
Costumes Designed by ALVIN COLT
Musical Direction: MAX GOBERMAN
with
SONO OSATO   NANCY WALKER

ADELPHI · 54th ST. EAST OF B'WAY · MATINEES WED. & SAT.

"New York's No. 1 Musical Hit," ushering in a new-styled blend of music, comedy, and dance. (drawing by Dowden)

at its best. But director, players, and designers cannot alone make a musical. I hate to keep harping on this subject, but a musical needs some music with lyrics to match. Words which make a rhyme and have rhythm do not necessarily make a lyric, nor do thirty-two bars full of notes automatically make a song. The score of *On the Town* by Leonard Bernstein, and the lyrics by Miss Comden, Adolph Green, and Mr. Bernstein, are almost always disappointing. . . . There are ballets, of course. Cripes, what I would give to see a good old hoofing chorus again!

Louis Kronenberger, *PM*

On the Town is not only much the best musical of the year; it is one of the freshest, gayest, liveliest musicals I have ever seen. It has its faults, but even they are engaging, for they are the faults of people trying to do something different, of people willing to take a chance. This show that grew out of Bernstein's and Robbins's smash ballet, "Fancy Free," should put Broadway—the Broadway of tasteless lavishness, of stale gags and stupid smut, of tired formulas and meaningless furbelows—in its place. For *On the Town* pumps energy and excitement and humor into the musical field; it spurns formulas; indeed, it makes fun of them. In its youthfulness and bounce, and in the gaiety of its fooling, it gives you the kind of fun you got in the heyday of the intimate revue. Of particular merit is the Comden–Green book—the best musical comedy book since *Pal Joey* [1940]. It is touched with lively and unexpected humor, with quick satire, with a welcome cutting of musical-comedy corners. The music and dancing have much the same sort of virtues. Bernstein's score is unhackneyed without being highbrow. His ballet music has no particular distinction and is sometimes just thump or pastiche; but it has a strong, lively beat that goes fine with the dancing. Mr. Robbins's choreography is also unhackneyed without being highbrow. It is crisp, humorous, and fast; once or twice it is exciting. There are, finally, Oliver Smith's extraordinarily good sets, which are somehow an integral part of the show.

Lewis Nichols, *Times*

There can be no mistake about it: *On the Town* is the freshest and most engaging musical show to come this way since the golden day of *Oklahoma!* [1943]. Everything about it is right. It is fast and it is gay, it takes neither itself nor the world too seriously, it has wit. Its dances are well paced, its players are a pleasure to see, and its music and backgrounds are both fitting and excellent. *On the Town* even has a literate book, which for once instead of stopping the action dead speeds it merrily on its way. The Adelphi Theatre is the new Utopia. *On the Town* is a perfect example of what a well-knit fusion of the respectable arts can provide for the theatre. The book Comden and Green have fashioned makes cheerful fun; they are serious about nothing, and oftentimes they offer only suggestions of ideas, allowing the audience to fill in the thought. It has been a long time since a musical comedy audience has been allowed to enjoy a musical comedy book. Only last spring, Mr. Bernstein was earning the Music Critic's annual prize for the best new composition of the year; this morning he will start up the ladder of ASCAP. The charm of *On the Town* is not so much in the individual performances as in the whole. The chorus and ballet numbers, many of them done with an edge of satire, are easy and graceful. Mr. Abbott permits no lags in his evening, and down in the pit and up on the stage everything always is in order. It is an adult musical show and a remarkably good one.

Burton Rascoe, *World-Telegram*

As one of the original and most enthusiastic boosters of Sono Osato, I was deeply disappointed in the choreography provided for her by Jerome Robbins; it is plastic rather than rhythmical and completely uninspired. Although a perfectionist in ballet, Miss Osato is essentially (and that is her high value) a pantomimic co-medienne; and she is not only given a sappy romantic role but very sappy dance figures to waste her talents on. The one who carries the show is Miss Walker, as a man-eating taxi driver. Her comedy is cool, bold, direct and, because there is also something wistfully appealing about her and because her eyes are ready to fight at the drop of a remark, she is very, very funny. Betty Comden, who with Adolph Green is the co-author of the book and lyrics, was very nervous last night, and did not show up as well as she probably will later on.

Wilella Waldorf, *Post*

One of the Ballet Theatre's most successful new presentations was "Fancy Free," a rollicking little number about three gobs on shore leave. The Messrs. Robbins, Smith, and Bernstein have now gathered in a few friends and blown up "Fancy Free" into a full-length musical extravaganza, *On the Town*. Expansive gestures of this sort don't always come off, but this one does, notably in the musical and choreographic departments. *On the Town* is an attractive, tremendously good-natured show done in the modern style, with a slap-happy air about it that is often rather juvenile, sometimes downright amateurish, but almost always ingratiating. The friends called in to do the book are Betty Comden and Adolph Green, members of that little band known as The Revuers, given to cruising around the night club belt indulging in what passes for satire in Saloon Society. Mr. Bernstein's music suffers much of the time from the sad fact that hardly anybody in the cast has enough vocal equipment to handle it. However, the boys and girls don't let this bother them in the least. *On the Town* is a modern piece and if you can't do anything else with modern music, you simply open your mouth and yell, hoping that vitality will make up for lack of vocalism. We might add that on Broadway it almost invariably does.

The success of *Oklahoma!* (1943) not only marked the end of the Rodgers and Hart partnership; it also ended the pioneering musical work of Rodgers and Abbott. Abbott's first five musicals were Rodgers and Hart shows; and Rodgers was silent co-producer for the next two, Hugh Martin and Ralph Blane's *Best Foot Forward* (1941) and Johnny Green's *Beat the Band* (1942). Their shows stressed the importance of dance to the "new" musical, especially *On Your Toes* (1936, Balanchine) and *Pal Joey* (1940, Robert Alton). Rodgers, subconsciously (or perhaps consciously) taking up the mantle of Jerome Kern, moved into musical drama and the ballet world of Agnes de Mille; Abbott remained in *Joey's* fast-paced era and, with first-time choreographers like Robbins and Fosse, forged a new musical comedy dance style which soon outpaced the de Mille school. Young Abbott—already 57 when *On the Town* took the town—continued on his youth kick, and over the next twenty years Bernstein, Comden and Green, Styne, Loesser, Adler and Ross, Merrill, Sondheim (as composer), Bock and Harnick, and Kander and Ebb all blossomed under his tutelage. And as Mr. Abbott phased out of producing, he launched the careers of Feuer and Martin, Robert Fryer, and Griffith and Prince. The history of the modern musical rests with Rodgers and Hammerstein and with Lerner and Loewe on the one hand, and with Mr. A. on the other. Not to be overlooked among *On the Town*'s innovations was the streamlined design by coproducer Oliver Smith (from the ballet world), who demonstrated that sets were not merely backgrounds but elements that could and should move to support action and dance. *On the Town* was the first musical to sell the motion picture rights prior to the opening. M-G-M had discovered the profitability of Broadway with a 50 percent share of *Bloomer Girl* (1944); their screen *On the Town* (1949) featured Gene Kelly and Frank Sinatra and a butchered score. *On the Town* was initially announced with John Latouche ("just out of the Seabees") as lyricist. Bernstein and Latouche would later collaborate on *Candide* (1956), although the talented Latouche—of *Cabin in the Sky* (1940) and *The Golden Apple* (1954)—died before the project was completed.

BROADWAY SCORECARD / perfs: 462 / $: +

rave	favorable	mixed	unfavorable	pan
3	3	1		1

ON YOUR TOES

a revival of the 1936 musical comedy, with music by Richard Rodgers; lyrics by Lorenz Hart; book by Rodgers, Hart, and George Abbott

directed by George Abbott; choreographed by George Balanchine
produced by George Abbott
with Vera Zorina, Bobby Van, Elaine Stritch, Ben Astar, Kay Coulter, and Joshua Shelley

opened October 11, 1954   46th St. Theatre

BROOKS ATKINSON, *Times*

All of us remember that *On Your Toes* has a celebrated ballet, called "Slaughter on Tenth Avenue." But most of us had forgotten that it also has a book which goes on at great length in a style that *The Boy Friend* [1954] is currently satirizing. When *Pal Joey* was revived a few seasons ago [1952], the book seemed closer to the mood of the present day than it had been originally. But the book of *On Your Toes* is labored, mechanical, and verbose. The mood of the day has passed beyond it. There is a lot of excellent material in *On Your Toes*, and the performance is flawless. Is a book, then, a matter of crucial importance? After all, it has only a utilitarian function in the making of musical comedies. Alas, there is no escaping the pedestrianism of this old-fashioned book. In due course, it leads to the pagan excitement of "Slaughter on Tenth Avenue." But the course is long and enervating.

Walter Kerr, *Herald Tribune*

It drifts across stage like an autumn ghost, eerie and echoing and cut from the bough. That its once joyous revelry should be so completely stilled is, as a matter of fact, something of a mystery. Every one expects a musical-comedy "book" to turn yellow and crisp to the fingers; what is truly dumbfounding about the present revival is that even the higher things move gloomily under a cloud. You have to keep telling yourself how much you like them, in or out of context—so powerful is that pall that the drowsy evening casts. Some ghoulish genie, enemy of all things theatrical, is at work. . . . Elaine Stritch deserves a paragraph, if not five or six more encores, all to herself. Screwing up her face into a grisly smile, she parts with the jokes on an at least even-steven, "no decision" basis. Given a couple of exuberant Rodgers tunes to lick, she hauls off mightily. Rocking her blonde curls back and forth, she makes hay with "The Heart Is Quicker Than the Eye." Later on, she does a deceptively wistful chorus of "You Took Advantage of Me"—lifted from quite another show [*Present Arms!* (1928)]— before throwing her low-slung lip, her glassy eye, her knee-joints, fingertips, and amiable hips at the tune. At one point she simply lounges on the proscenium and hoots, if that is the precise word for it.

John McClain, *Journal-American*

Funny tricks one's memory plays. I have been going around for 15 years insisting that *On Your Toes* was one of the greatest musicals of all time. But what I either overlooked or didn't pay any attention to, in the crescendo of pleasant tunes and incomparable dancing, was that it had a dull book. Maybe that didn't matter so much in 1936, but last night it seemed whenever the music and hoofing stopped and the people got around to those old lines the whole vehicle wheezed, coughed, and quit. Compared to our latter era of book shows—*Guys and Dolls* [1950], *South Pacific* [1949], and *The Pajama Game* [1954]—there is no contest. Times have changed vastly, or we've gone a long way in comedy and construction. Possibly both.

A second Broadway revival of *On Your Toes* in 1983—with Abbott and Balanchine again recreating their 1936 work—fared considerably better, achieving a 505-performance run. (The weaknesses were still more-than-apparent, but the competition was minimal.) Critic Walter Kerr's enthusiasm for Elaine Stritch's performance led to his casting her as the leading lady of *Goldilocks* (1958).

BROADWAY SCORECARD / perfs: 64 / $: −

rave	favorable	mixed	unfavorable	pan
		1	5	1

ONCE UPON A MATTRESS

a musical fairy tale, with music by Mary Rodgers; lyrics by Marshall Barer; book by Jay Thompson, Marshall Barer, and Dean Fuller, from the fairy tale "The Princess and the Pea"

directed by George Abbott; choreographed by Joe Layton
produced by the Phoenix Theatre (T. Edward Hambleton and Norris Houghton) and William and Jean Eckart
with Carol Burnett, Joe Bova, Jack Gilford, and Jane White

opened May 11, 1959　　　　　　*Phoenix Theatre*
transferred November 25, 1959　　*Alvin Theatre*

BROOKS ATKINSON, *Times*

Two of the ladies enmeshed in the plot have remarkably fresh talent. Mary Rodgers, the composer, has written a highly enjoyable score. For the record, it must be reported that she is a daughter of Richard Rodgers. But nothing she has written sounds like his portfolio. She has a style of her own, an inventive mind, and a fund of cheerful melodies; and *Once Upon a Mattress* is full of good music. Some of it is sung by a breezy comedienne who comes brawling into the story about half way through the first act and gives it a wonderful lift for the rest of the evening. She is Carol Burnett, a lean, earthy young lady with a metallic voice, an ironic gleam, and an unfailing sense of the comic gesture. As a singer, she discharges Miss Rodgers's music as though she were firing a field mortar. . . . Don't be distressed by the title, and don't expect much from the libretto. But be comforted by the fact that the musical theatre has acquired a genuine new composer and a funny new clown.

ROBERT COLEMAN, *Daily Mirror*

Carol Burnett made an auspicious bow as the Princess Winifred. She is as pixyish as Alice Pearce and as hoydenish as Betty Hutton. She can belt out a song like Dolores Gray. She can cash in on comedy like an Ethel Merman. And yet remain Carol Burnett. A personality in her own right. A future star. If you don't see La Burnett's name in Main Stem marquee lights one of these nights, then we don't know talent when we see it burst across the footlights.

A refreshing spoof with cheerfully bright music, *Once Upon a Mattress* successfully transferred from the Phoenix to Broadway, after which it quickly established itself as a profitable perennial in the stock and amateur market. Carol Burnett, a television comedienne somewhat familiar from the "Tonight" show, made an unlikely fairy tale princess—every bit as unlikely as Carol Channing's Lorelei Lee in *Gentlemen Prefer Blondes* (1949). La Burnett soon saw her name in Main Stem marquee lights with Abbott's *Fade Out—Fade In* (1964), a "star comic" musical built around herself. (Things didn't work out quite so well, though.)

110 IN THE SHADE

a musical play, with music by Harvey Schmidt; lyrics by Tom Jones; book by N. Richard Nash, from his 1954 comedy *The Rainmaker;* previously announced as *Rainbow*

directed by Joseph Anthony; choreographed by Agnes de Mille
produced by David Merrick
with Robert Horton (replacing Hal Holbrook), Inga Swenson, Stephen Douglass, and Will Geer

opened October 24, 1963   Broadhurst Theatre

JOHN CHAPMAN, *Daily News*

We've had to wait a long spell for a topnotch new musical, and we got one last evening. *110 in the Shade* has class and originality. Two men named Schmidt and Jones, strangers to this department, have written exhilarating music and lyrics, and there doesn't seem to be a hackneyed phrase in all the many songs. There are 16 songs in *110 in the Shade* and there isn't a commonplace one among them. And a dazzling new musical comedy star took over the stage for keeps. She is Inga Swenson. She is perfect, and she sings like a dream. . . . Broadway's musical comedy drought is over. The rainmaker is good ol' David Merrick.

WALTER KERR, *Herald Tribune*

Inga Swenson plays Lizzie, and if the musical had no other virtues I'd urge you to see it just to watch her explode. Sometimes she is high-and-mighty angry. When her father and brothers try roping the local sheriff to see if they can't make a woman out of her, the blaze in her eyes blows the benches off the stage. With a "hell, hell, hell," with a sideswipe of her feet, and a wipe of her fist across her face, she makes a windmill of the dishonest world Don

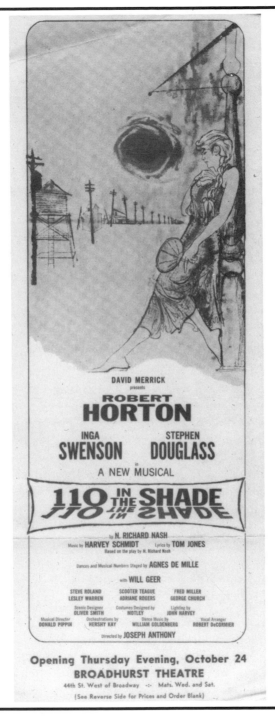

"Gonna Be Another Hot Day" for spinster Lizzie (Inga Swenson)—
unless a rainmaker should happen along. (drawing by Oscar Liebman)

Quixote left behind him. After which her lanky frame folds into portmanteau despair. Miss Swenson remains a person, not simply a performer doing this bit or that. Her appeal—gangling, head-long, subliminally glowing—is constant. And she does have something to glow about, which is the progression of melodic phrases Harvey Schmidt and Tom Jones have bestowed upon her by way of a score. Mr. Horton is giving an applied performance. He applies his arms to the wind, and then stretches his fingers wide, but those outstretched fingers never touch gold dust. Nor does his speaking voice command; it tends to beg. You wind up feeling that Miss Swenson should be converting Mr. Horton; she is clearly the stronger minded of the two. There is a hazy Oliver Smith backdrop with small shadows creeping across the desert that is dazzling as Mr. Horton's spieling con-man is meant to be. On balance? I'd say the question is not whether Mr. Horton falls in love with Miss Swenson, or whether Mr. Douglass does. The question is whether or not you do. I did.

John McClain, *Journal-American*

The Rainmaker was a wonderfully wistful and weepy play which, I thought, never did the business it deserved. But last night it came to the Broadhurst as a musical called *110 in the Shade* and my private guess is that it will more than make up for any loot that may have been overlooked by the original. The strong elements of the story are still there, and they are actually heightened by a haunting and melodious score from Harvey Schmidt and Tom Jones. This is our first top-flight musical of the new season and a distinct credit to this or any other year. . . . Is the New York drought a Merrick publicity stunt?

Howard Taubman, *Times*

Everybody prays for rain, but in *110 in the Shade* there is not much more than tears. Although this new musical play is as dry as the parched land outside the Broadhurst Theatre, there is no danger that even a lightning bolt could ignite it. *The Rainmaker* was a play that had a touch of magic. It has disappeared in this adaptation and been replaced by the surface effects that our musical theatre practices so knowingly. Effect, unfortunately, cannot substitute for warmth, humor, or enchantment. It's cold at *110 in the Shade*— and tearful. Since we're all children of fantasy, we want to believe in Lizzie's plight. But N. Richard Nash, whose play made belief feasible, can blame himself. He has stripped the original into a book that creates about as much illusion as a bare electric light bulb. Somehow the dry bones of the story are more arid than the western landscape in the summer. The feeling for real people is almost nonexistent.

David Merrick snapped up the songwriters from off-Broadway's *The Fantasticks* (1960) for this underappreciated musical. Schmidt and Jones's score is quite splendid, the book is better-than-average, and it all combines to weave a magically atmospheric spell. *110 in the Shade* was a hard sell, due to downbeat subject matter and a not-very-good Rainmaker from the TV Western "Wagon Train" (1957–1962). (Horton became available two weeks before rehearsals started, when *I Picked a Daisy*—the Alan Jay Lerner-Richard Rodgers musical he had chosen over *110*—was cancelled in a shower of creative acrimony. Merrick grabbed Horton, and Hal Holbrook was left in the shade. Lerner's *Daisy* eventually made it to town—unsuccessfully—as *On a Clear Day You Can See Forever* [1966], with music by Burton Lane. The original leading man of that one, Louis Jourdan, didn't make it to Broadway either.) Merrick was able to manage *110* into a moderate hit, and probably would have pushed it further along had he not become preoccupied with his blockbuster across 44th Street, *Hello, Dolly!* (1964).

BROADWAY SCORECARD / perfs: 330 / $: +

rave	favorable	mixed	unfavorable	pan
3	1	1	1	

ONE TOUCH OF VENUS

a musical fantasy, with music by Kurt Weill; lyrics by Ogden Nash; book by S. J. Perelman and Ogden Nash, from the 1885 English novella "The Tinted Venus" by F. Anstey (Thomas Anstey Guthrie)

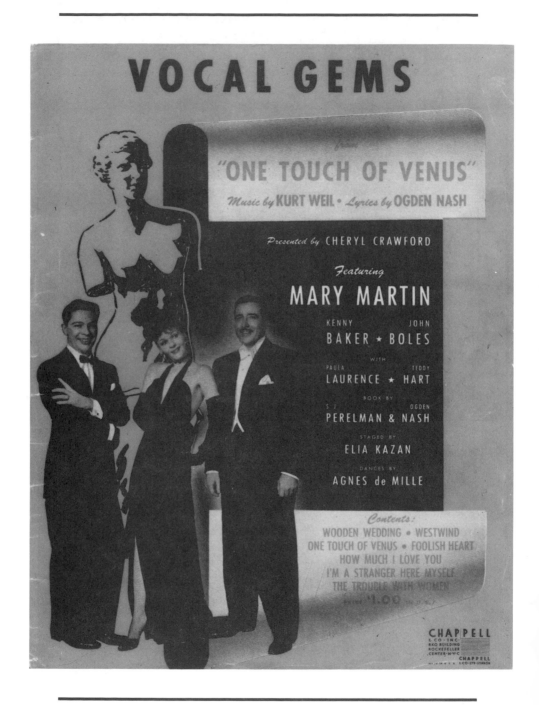

Kenny Baker, Mary Martin (as "Venus"), and John Boles. Kurt Weill's name, incidentally, is misspelled on this music cover. *(gown by Mainbocher)*

directed by Elia Kazan; choreographed by Agnes de Mille
produced by Cheryl Crawford
with Mary Martin, Kenny Baker, John Boles, Paula Laurence,
Teddy Hart, and Sono Osato

opened October 7, 1943   Imperial Theatre

JOHN CHAPMAN, *Daily News*

The Nash lyrics are smartly turned, and I noticed the champion
lyric-turning expert, Cole Porter, cocking an attentive ear from the
second or third row.

ROBERT GARLAND, *Journal-American*

The book and lyrics have a Gilbert and Sullivan flavor peppered
by some cockeyed jingles that even the great W. S. himself
wouldn't have dared asked Sir Arthur to set to music. That one
about the memoirs, for instance: "Oh, boy, what memoirs them
was!" . . . It is one of a reviewer's keener pleasures to be able to
tell the world that Miss Martin has grown into a performer of the
first magnitude; that not only is she lovely, but that she can dance,
act, sing, and project a serious scene—the finale of the piece is
really touching—with the best of them.

LOUIS KRONENBERGER, *PM*

Whatever is wrong with it, *One Touch of Venus* is an unhackneyed and imaginative musical that spurns the easy formulas of
Broadway, that has personality and wit and genuinely high moments of music and dancing. And, it brings Mary Martin back to
prove that she is anything but a one-song girl. *Venus*, like *Oklahoma!* [1943], breaks with musical comedy tradition. But where
Oklahoma! has the smell of new-mown hay, *Venus* is like a trick
perfume. I suppose the simplest way out is to call it sophisticated.
S.J. Perelman and Ogden Nash have dandified the fanciful plot
with their cleverness and wit, and Mr. Nash has worked up some
smart and ingenious lyrics. Kurt Weill has composed all kinds of
songs with all kinds of orchestrations and Agnes de Mille has had
even bolder ideas about dancing than she had in *Oklahoma!* Nobody concerned has been the least bit inhibited. Unfortunately,
nobody has been completely successful.

LEWIS NICHOLS, *Times*

In addition to this there is Mary Martin, the Mary Martin whose heart once belonged to daddy and who shows that Hollywood has done her no harm whatsoever. Her heart this morning will probably be Broadway's, generally. . . . Since music and girls are the soul of musical comedy, *One Touch of Venus* has thought of them also. There is no Rockette chorus kicking from left to right; rather Miss de Mille has gone to work with her sense of humor so that the dancing all seems new and cheerful. Sono Osato likely is to be the toast of the autumn, for she is graceful and alive as well as being beautiful and gives the impression that she, herself, is having a wonderful time. To turn to Mr. Weill: his "Speak Low" is a sure hit unless the musical world has gone mad.

WILELLA WALDORF, *Post*

A new musical comedy that is adult, professional, often comic, and genuinely musical. It's nice to know that Broadway has been given back to the professionals. This is the best score by Mr. Weill that we recall. Since *The Threepenny Opera* [1935] he has disappointed us. *Lady in the Dark* [1941], hit though it was, bored us very thoroughly. It is a long time since we have heard a new and modern score in a musical comedy that struck us as something at once popular and unusually fine. Even the milder songs are orchestrated so beautifully [by Weill] that they make excellent listening. Mr. Nash's lyrics, though sounding at their worst like a rather tired Cole Porter, are often very diverting and even witty. Mary Martin, whose Broadway celebrity rests chiefly upon the fact that she once "sang" something called "My Heart Belongs to Daddy," has developed very nicely in Hollywood, and her performance is graceful, amusing, and well spoken. Miss Martin is still no singer, but she talks her songs cleverly and when she does use her few vocal tones—she has a meagre range—they are pleasant to hear.

Kurt Weill's longest-running Broadway show, enhanced by one of the all-time great show tunes: "Speak Low." Mary Martin, who made a dazzling debut as the gal whose "Heart Belongs To Daddy" in Cole Porter's *Leave It to Me* (1938), finally achieved full Broadway stardom. Prior to *Venus* she headed two out-of-town flops,

Nice Goin' (1939) and Vinton Freedley's *Dancing in the Streets* (1943)—for which she had turned down the female lead in *Away We Go!*, Rodgers and Hammerstein's cowboy song-and-dancer.

Donaldson Awards were won by Agnes de Mille (choreographer); Mary Martin (actress); Kenny Baker (supporting actor); and Sono Osato (female dancer).

BROADWAY SCORECARD / perfs: 567 $: +

rave	favorable	mixed	unfavorable	pan
3	4		1	

OUT OF THIS WORLD

a musical comedy, with music and lyrics by Cole Porter; book by Dwight Taylor and Reginald Lawrence (replaced by F. Hugh Herbert), from the Amphitryon legend

directed by Agnes de Mille (replaced by George Abbott); choreographed by Hanya Holm
produced by Saint Subber and Lemuel Ayers
with Charlotte Greenwood, William Eythe, Priscilla Gillette, William Redfield, David Burns, and George Jongeyans (Gaynes)

opened December 21, 1950   New Century Theatre

BROOKS ATKINSON, *Times*

The enchanting things in *Out of this World* are beside the point. For the authors have in mind one of those sex pranks that used to set the customers to giggling nervously many long years ago before the world got out of knee-britches and when spicy operettas were thought to be hot stuff. Mr. Porter has obligingly fallen into step with some monotonous patter songs and at least one imitation of one of his own classics. *Out of this World* does not get far outside the Broadway library of second-rate operetta routines. On the whole this is a pity. For some of Mr. Porter's songs are among the finest he has written, and he has the singers who can do justice to them. "I Am Loved" is a rapturous lyric as Priscilla Gillette sings it. "Where, Oh, Where?" is beautiful on Barbara Ashley's lips. Everything George Jongeyans [Gaynes] sings is worth a little rejoicing, although Mr. Porter makes pretty parsimonious use of the best voice in the production.

JOHN CHAPMAN, *Daily News*

The top star of *Out of this World* is one of its producers, Lemuel Ayers, who is the set and costume designer. When he co-produced *Kiss Me, Kate* (1948), Mr. Ayers went for artistic inspiration to ancient Italy, and his decor was—and is—splendid. For the investiture of *Out of this World* Mr. Ayers has traveled to ancient Greece and beyond to the summit of Mount Olympus, where the old gods dwelt. You will not see again for some time so many lovely sets, costumes, curtains, and drops.

OTIS L. GUERNSEY JR., *Herald Tribune*

A combination of extravaganza and innuendo. *Out of this World* spins a fable of Olympus, a modern Amphitryon story, with thread unraveled from gold G-strings. The parade of Lemuel Ayers sets and costumes, singers, comedians, and dancers fills the stage and the eye with color and glitter. There is not so much wit, nor as much melody lurking here as the decor and enthusiam would pretend, but production goes a long way toward filling in with a ton of raucous antics. Conveniently for the composer, the word "sex" rhymes with "Jupiter Rex" and "brek-kek-kek-ex," and there you have the outline of this show's book and lyrics.

WILLIAM HAWKINS, *World-Telegram & Sun*

The male dancing chorus is almost as unhampered by godlike raiment as the customers in a steam bath.

JOHN McCLAIN, *Journal-American*

There is a gangling and engaging lady named Charlotte Greenwood, whose legs apparently emerge from her shoulder blades and whose arms hang to her ankles. She made quite a career of these eccentricities as a dancer in various musicals 20-odd years ago [the *Letty* series] and more recently in a series of Hollywood movie extravaganzas, and so last night everybody waited patiently for the nostalgic number to reappear. Well, everybody waited through the entire show and until the spot next-to-closing. And then Miss Greenwood got out and did something called "Nobody's Chasing Me," winding up with the incredible kicks, and of course the balcony buckled and the roof came off the theatre. . . . It would be eminently unfair to give sole direction credit to Miss Agnes de Mille, or George Abbott (who got no billing), any more than it would be to hold Dwight Taylor and Reginald Lawrence entirely responsible for all the lines, since it is no secret that the entire effort underwent drastic changes in the few weeks prior to its opening.

The ill-fated *Out of this World* boasted what is probably Cole Porter's third-best score, after *Kiss Me, Kate* and *Anything Goes* (1934). Porter's final two attempts—*Can-Can* (1953) and *Silk Stockings* (1955)—were long-run hits despite being vastly inferior, which is Just (as the saying goes) One of Those Things.

BROADWAY SCORECARD / perfs: 157 $: −

rave	favorable	mixed	unfavable	pan
1	3	1	1	1

PAINT YOUR WAGON

a musical play, with music by Frederick Loewe; book and lyrics by Alan Jay Lerner

directed by Daniel Mann choreographed by Agnes de Mille
produced by Cheryl Crawford
with James Barton, Olga San Juan, Tony Bavaar, and James Mitchell

opened November 12, 1951   Shubert Theatre

BROOKS ATKINSON, *Times*

By mixing Western gold dust with show vitality, the authors have produced a bountiful and exultant musical jamboree. From

CHERYL CRAWFORD
presents

JAMES BARTON

in

PAINT YOUR WAGON

A New Musical with

OLGA SAN JUAN

TONY BAVAAR   **JAMES MITCHELL**

Book and Lyrics by   *Music by*
ALAN JAY LERNER   FREDERICK LOEWE

Dances and Musical Ensembles by AGNES De MILLE

Scenery Designed by   *Costumes Designed by*
OLIVER SMITH   MOTLEY

Musical Director, FRANZ ALLERS

Lighting by PEGGY CLARK • Orchestrations by TED ROYAL

Production Associate, BEA LAWRENCE

Entire Production Staged by DANIEL MANN

SHUBERT THEATRE
PHILADELPHIA
3 Weeks Only, Beginning Monday, September 17
MATINEES THURSDAY and SATURDAY

1st Subscription Play of The Theatre Guild-American Theatre Society

PRICES: Evenings — Orchestra and Boxes $5.20; Balcony $4.55, $3.90, $3.25; Family Circle $1.95
Matinees: Orchestra and Boxes, $3.90; Balcony $3.25, $2.60, $1.95; Family Circle $1.30
(All Taxes Included)

A wagon train of prospectors follow their "Wandrin' Star," with a couple of Agnes de Mille girls taking up the rear.

530

the technical point of view, *Paint Your Wagon* may not be up to the artistic standard of *Brigadoon* [1947], for it is not quite so meticulously edited and organized. But no complaints on that score are rumbling out of this corner this morning. For the abundance, good humor, and romantic beauty of *Paint Your Wagon* make a very happy evening in the theatre. It's a lot of fun. Everyone associated with the town's newest musical carnival is in good health and humor and has conspired in giving the audience a royal good time.

ROBERT GARLAND, *Journal-American*

It is a lush and lusty score, more lush and lusty than the book and lyrics. But scarcely less monotonous. The last act might be the first act done over. It is not, of course. But it sounds as if it might be. With all its general worthiness, *Paint Your Wagon* remains quite a bit repetitious. It once again proves that you can get enough of the same good thing. You can get too much, really. . . . James Barton is a joy. He can do everything. And does! He walks. He talks. He gets drunk. He gets married. He even sings. And delightfully. James Mitchell repeats his success of former years. Under Miss de Mille's direction, he dances like a gold-rushing dervish. There are some active girls to keep him company. In fact, there is too much dancing, just as there is too much of everything but story and James Barton. Mr. Barton strolls through the musical play with freedom all his own. Daniel Mann, who has, as they say, directed, lets him have his way. It is tactful that he should. Bits of this, of that, and of the other thing make a not unimpressive whole. *Brigadoon* never unwound itself. The same authors' *Paint Your Wagon* never winds itself. That is where the trouble largely lies.

WILLIAM HAWKINS, *World-Telegram & Sun*

It is a show of real distinction, courage, and novelty, and one people will remember. It has gigantic faults, which make it all the more remarkable that it wields the impression it does. The greatest weakness lies in its reproducing emotions literally instead of depicting them theatrically. A case in point is the expansive first act, relating the lonely, restless life of the miners. It is an intermittently interesting, unfunny, almost actionless hour and a half before any real agitation or energy captures the stage. Similarly in a brilliant, exciting dance sequence when the central figure [Gemze de Lappe] is supposed to fling herself about to exhaustion, she really does.

WALTER KERR, *Herald Tribune*

Halfway through the evening James Barton eases into a little of the old soft shoe ["In Between"], and it is a bright and shining moment. Twice in the first act Agnes de Mille catches hold of a striking mood. At the opening of the second act Miss de Mille cuts loose with a roaring dance-hall fandango ["Hand Me Down that Can o' Beans"], and she follows it almost immediately with an exquisitely touching number called "Another Autumn." But the rest of *Paint Your Wagon* is much too earnest a proposition. The authors and director have been determined that their musical shall be down to earth, realistic, honest. They have eschewed the caricature of routine musical comedy. But in their passion for being straightforward, they have forgotten to put in the fun. Writing an "integrated" musical comedy—where the people are believable and the songs are logically introduced—is no excuse for not being funny from time to time. *South Pacific* (1949) is funny. But Mr. Lerner seems more interested in the authenticity of his background than in the joy of his audience. The "musical play" that isn't funny had better be moving. The tipoff on *Paint Your Wagon* is the fact that the most emotionally rewarding moments of the evening come from the dancers. *Paint Your Wagon* is filled with talented people, but a lot of the time they have to get out and push.

RICHARD WATTS JR., *Post*

There are a number of times when the show blazes forth with admirable vitality. I cannot help thinking, though, that there is something just a little flat about it. The brilliant present-day crop of American musical-comedy writers, among whom Mr. Lerner holds high rank, have accustomed us to a lofty standard in the narratives of their work. And *Paint Your Wagon* makes a particular attempt to see to it that its story is something more than a time-lag between songs. Yet Mr. Lerner's tale of the joys and sorrows of a California boom town seldom manages to be very interesting. *Paint Your Wagon* is so lavish with its songs, dances, and colorful atmosphere that I feel more than customarily ungrateful when I say the result is mildly disappointing.

☆

An ambitious, serious musical which suffered from an unrelenting somberness. A rather interesting score was obscured in the process. An admirable attempt but ultimately dreary.

Donaldson Awards were won by Tony Bavaar (supporting actor; male debut); Olga San Juan (female debut); and Gemze de Lappe (female dancer).

BROADWAY SCORECARD / perfs: 289 /$: −

rave	favorable	mixed	unfavorable	pan
1	2	1	3	

THE PAJAMA GAME

a musical comedy, with music and lyrics by Richard Adler and Jerry Ross; book by George Abbott and Richard Bissell, from Bissell's 1953 novel *7½ Cents*

directed by George Abbott and Jerome Robbins; choreographed by Bob Fosse (with Jerome Robbins)
produced by Frederick Brisson, Robert E. Griffith, and Harold S. Prince
with John Raitt (replacing Ralph Meeker), Janis Paige, Eddie Foy, Jr., and Carol Haney

opened May 13, 1954   St. James Theatre

JOHN CHAPMAN, *Daily News*

I mention Abbott and Robbins first because they are the directors of this show, and without their knowhow and their senses of humor *The Pajama Game* might not have come off as well as it did. It is very difficult to take bunches of actors, songs, scenery, and dancers, throw in a spot of plot and come out with a Broadway show that is first class. This is no task for amateurs, and thank goodness Robbins and Abbott are professionals. The directors also have this year's overnight star, Carol Haney. Miss Haney looks like a tall but awkward Audrey Hepburn. She has a froggy voice, slanty

This sounds like one of those shows you can afford to miss. Who was to know that things would work out so well? Note comedienne Charlotte Rae, billed ahead of Carol Haney; her part was cut during rehearsals, with the songs handed over to Janis Paige. Pre-Broadway credits.

534

eyes and an impish grin—and I haven't decided yet whether she is funnier acting or dancing. But I will say that a song-and-dance number titled "Steam Heat," in which Miss Haney is teamed with Buzz Miller and Peter Gennaro, is one of the funniest and most artful turns I ever saw on a stage.

ROBERT COLEMAN, *Daily Mirror*

A sure-fire winner. A deliriously daffy delight! A royal flush and a grand slam rolled into one!

WALTER KERR, *Herald Tribune*

Broadway looks well in pajamas. The bright, brassy, and jubilantly sassy show is not just the best new musical of the season. That would be fairly easy. It's a show that takes a whole barrelful of gleaming new talents, and a handful of stimulating ideas as well, and sends them tumbling in happy profusion over the footlights. *The Pajama Game* has a fresh and winning grin on its face from the outset. The dances by Bob Fosse (new to Broadway, but courtesy of M-G-M) are fast, funny when they ought to be, and neatly dovetailed into a hard-driving book. Mr. Fosse has, furthermore, worked out some amiable comic fantasies for an animated cartoon named Carol Haney. Miss Haney looks like a bow-legged gosling. Her mouth and nose seem to have been designed as partial illustrations for *Huckleberry Finn*. And she makes "Steam Heat" hotter than even its doting composers could have hoped. . . . Of course, behind all the brand-new names and the brightly creative stage business stands a gentleman named George Abbott. As wizard of the enterprise, he has wrought a humdinger.

JOHN McCLAIN, *Journal-American*

Well, here it is, folks, at long last—a superb new musical. *The Pajama Game* is fast, raucous, and rollicking; it is the best book show that's hit the town since *Guys and Dolls* (1950). This is a whale of an evening. . . . When the music might offer merely the opportunity for a pedestrian girl-boy number, the authors and choreographers have combined to endow it with particular styling and speed. The hit number, "Hey There," which must be introduced by John Raitt, in solo, is lifted out of the commonplace by having him sing it into a tape recorder, playing back the second chorus as

a duet with himself. Eddie Foy, Jr. And Reta Shaw take an innocuous number called "I'll Never Be Jealous Again" and stop the
proceedings dead with a soft-shoe routine. Stanley Prager and
Carol Haney make similar history with another bit ["Her Is"] which
could have been lost with less inspired business. "There Once Was
a Man," delivered by Raitt and Janis Paige is not only a striking
example of Richard Adler–Jerry Ross music, but a great tribute to
the inventiveness of the directors and the skill of the principals.
Equal citations should be given Bob Fosse who is, I assume, responsible for such highlights as the "Once a Year Day" ballet,
"Hernando's Hideaway," and the "Jealousy Ballet." They are all
extremely simple and mad and marvelous.

RICHARD WATTS JR., *Post*

On first hearing, which doesn't always provide a verdict for the
ages, the words and music by Richard Adler and Jerry Ross suggest
something of the manner of good road-company Rodgers and Hammerstein, which isn't to be sneered at by anybody. I remember
most pleasantly two numbers called "Hernando's Hideaway" and
"7½ Cents," but all of the songs, if they are not altogether masterpieces, have the commendable quality of gay liveliness, and they
are offered with a gusto and relish that bring out the best that is in
them.

The Pajama Game was actually directed by Abbott, with Robbins
along to oversee first-time choreographer Fosse. Robbins staged
two numbers, "There Once Was a Man" and "7½ Cents." Many
noticed a strong affinity between the work of songwriters Adler and
Ross and their mentor Frank Loesser, who had recommended
them for the job when he turned it down. (Well-supported rumor
has it that Loesser contributed, in whole or part, four items—
including the main musical strain of "Hey There" and "A New
Town Is a Blue Town.") Bissell's satirical chronicle of the making of
The Pajama Game was also musicalized, as *Say, Darling* (1958).

In addition to winning the Tony Award for Best Musical, Tonys
were won by Richard Adler and Jerry Ross (composers); George
Abbott and Richard Bissell (librettists); Bob Fosse (choreographer);

Frederick Brisson, Robert E. Griffith, and Harold S. Prince (producers); and Carol Haney (supporting actress). In addition to winning the Donaldson Award for Best Musical, Donaldsons were won by Richard Adler and Jerry Ross (composers; lyricists); George Abbott and Richard Bissell (librettists); George Abbott and Jerome Robbins (directors); Bob Fosse (choreographer); and Carol Haney (supporting actress; female dancer).

BROADWAY SCORECARD / perfs: 1,063 / $: +

rave	favorable	mixed	unfavorable	pan
6	1			

PAL JOEY

a revival of the 1940 musical comedy, with music by Richard Rodgers; lyrics by Lorenz Hart; book by John O'Hara (with George Abbott) from the 1939 novel by John O'Hara

production supervised and choreographed by Robert Alton; directed by David Alexander
produced by Jule Styne and Leonard Key in association with Anthony B. Farrell
with Vivienne Segal, Harold Lang, Helen Gallagher, Lionel Stander, and Elaine Stritch

opened January 2, 1952   Broadhurst Theatre

BROOKS ATKINSON, *Times*

In 1940 *Pal Joey* was regarded by its satellites as the musical that broke the old formula and brought the musical stage to maturity. There was a minority, including this column, that was not enchanted. But no one is likely now to be impervious to the tight organization of the production, the terseness of the writing, the liveliness and versatility of the score, and the easy perfection of the lyrics. Since the days of *Oklahoma!* (1943) the musical stage has grown in awareness and artistry. On Forty-fourth Street, where *Pal Joey* is now installed, Mr. Rodgers is represented by the scores of *South Pacific* (1949) and *The King and I* (1951), which are musically more ambitious. But it is true that *Pal Joey* was a pioneer in the moving back of musical frontiers, for it tells an integrated story with a knowing point of view. The Rodgers and Hammerstein musicals are moving toward folk operas. *Pal Joey* does not stray outside the bailiwick of commercial musical comedy, and the dance routines, satiric in accent, are pretty much in the old patterns. But there is something refreshing about the return of musical comedy in an unhackneyed rendering. Brimming over with good music and fast on its toes, *Pal Joey* renews confidence in the professionalism of the theatre.

ROBERT COLEMAN, *Daily Mirror*

Like good wine, and unlike most musicals, this wonderful song-and-dancer has grown better with age. To tell the truth, we didn't realize what a masterpiece *Pal Joey* really was until we caught it last night. The gorgeous music by Rodgers, the great lyrics by Hart, and the sophisticated book by O'Hara are a perfect entertainment combination. New York is a breezier and brighter town now that *Pal Joey* has checked in. The champ is back in superlative form.

WILLIAM HAWKINS, *World-Telegram & Sun*

One of the biggest, most enthusiastic premiere audiences in years welcomed *Pal Joey* back to Broadway last night, on a tidal wave of cheers. The musical is as brisk, cutting, funny, and crisp as it was Christmas night of 1940 when it opened the first time. All the people who have been raving about it ever since will now have only to compete with a new crowd of fans. Vivienne Segal, with her infinite economy of style, lush magnetism, and immaculate enunciation, is every inch a star. The audience bellowed just to see her, when she first walked down the steps into the night club. She got a howl with a two-word line, then with a monosyllable, and finally slayed them with a nicely turned glance. This was a night to howl about.

WALTER KERR, *Herald Tribune*

Helen Gallagher blows the roof off with a satiric first-act dance, "That Terrific Rainbow," and between times is the best looking thing on stage. Elaine Stritch winds up for a knockout with her "Zip" number in the second act, and managed her only dialogue scene in a fine jaundiced manner. "I Could Write a Book" is still there, too, and Robert Alton has made the by now overly familiar parody on night-club flower songs seem fresh and very funny. In short, just about everything is in first-rate shape at the Broadhurst except the hard, dry core of character and style that O'Hara wrote into his central figure [as performed by Harold Lang].

RICHARD WATTS JR., *Post*

As one of the original enthusiasts for *Pal Joey*, I am happy to report that the famous musical comedy is every bit as brilliant, fresh, and delightful as it seemed when it set new standards for its field over ten years ago. As presented last night in a handsome, vigorous, and dynamic production, this remarkably believable and fascinating tale of the rise and fall of a night-club insect is so vital and alive that it is impossible to think of it as a revival. Put it down, instead, as the best and most exciting new musical play of the season, and the town's hit. I hate to inflict on it so seemingly serious-minded a label, but *Pal Joey* is very definitely an authentic work of art. But it is also great fun, in its strangely savage and sardonic fashion. John O'Hara's book is biting, real, and filled with its author's celebrated gift for recognizable talk and characters. Mr. Rodgers's score is gayly delightful, and the late Lorenz Hart's lyrics are so sly, witty, inventive, and sparkling that they are a constant joy. When *Pal Joey* was first produced it seemed virtually revolutionary in its toughness and scorn for musical-comedy sentimentality. To tell the truth, it shocked people because it took as its central figures a kept man and the rich woman who kept him, and it didn't molest him with moral disapproval.

A rarity among musicals. *Pal Joey* was one of those not-so-successful shows with a rabid core of fans maintaining it was "before its time." In this case they were right, with some of the critics themselves questioning whether they were perhaps mistaken in 1940. Composer Jule Styne, a Rodgers fan, saw a 1951 summer stock *Joey* in East Hampton (N.Y.) and decided to mount a full-scale Broadway revival. The problem was finding someone who could handle the Gene Kelly role. A "name" star was a necessity; the best they could come up with was Harold Lang, Broadway's top dancer but not much of an actor. (The stock Joey was pretty good but totally unknown, a hoofer called Fosse.) Despite a somewhat weak acting job from Lang, Styne's award-winning production far outran the original's 374 performances. Which is not to say that *Pal Joey* is a well-made musical; the content is "modern" but the book is rough and old-fashioned. But there's nothing wrong with that, is there? And the score was—and remains—sterling.

Winner of the New York Drama Critics' Circle Award. Tony Awards were won by Robert Alton (choreographer, who was restaging his 1940 dances); Helen Gallagher (supporting actress); and Max Meth (musical director.) In addition to winning the Donaldson Award for Best Musical, Donaldsons were won by Richard Rodgers (composer); Lorenz Hart (lyricist); John O'Hara (librettist); David Alexander (director); Robert Alton (choreographer); Vivienne Segal (actress); Helen Gallagher (supporting actress); Harold Lang (male dancer); Oliver Smith (scenic designer); and Miles White (costume designer).

BROADWAY SCORECARD / perfs: 542 / $: +

rave	favorable	mixed	unfavorable	pan
5	2			

PAL JOEY

another revival of the 1940 musical comedy

directed by Gus Schirmer, Jr.; choreographed by Ralph Beaumont
produced by the New York City Center Light Opera Company (Jean Dalrymple)
with Bob Fosse, Carol Bruce, Sheila Bond, and Eileen Heckart

opened May 31, 1961   City Center Theatre

FRANK ASTON, *World-Telegram & Sun*

Nobody could be nastier than Bob Fosse in his new characterization. He makes himself look little, skinny, and dissolute. He thinks he's pretty, the way he slicks back his side hair with a caressing palm. He keeps a cigaret hanging insolently out of his mouth and seems to be chewing gum. When he smiles he grins, when he grins he laughs, and his laugh has a jerky, empty false sound. Bob Fosse makes himself a complete heel, just the kind to sponge off women as he tries to become more than a punk in a nightclub floor show. He is the best lead in *Pal Joey* I've seen. His dancing, and he did lots of it last evening, was one of those incredible mixtures of art and gymnastics. He was marvelous. So was the whole shebang. . . . Although Miss Heckart brought her glass-cracking voice and jaw angles onstage only once, that once was worth waiting for. As the case-hardened Chicago newspaper woman, she worked expertly on her double scotch without ice, choked mildly over Fosse's phonier claims, then sang that number "Zip" that shreds intellectual strippers. We reporters should write exposés half as devastatingly as Miss Heckart sings them. . . . Leaving the theatre, I about burst with enjoyment.

JOHN CHAPMAN, *Daily News*

Anybody who wants to put on a production of *Pal Joey* must first of all find somebody to play Joey, and the City Center has come up with the perfect man—the perfect heel, so to speak. He is Bob Fosse, who has essayed the role of this Chicago night club small-timer before [in the 1951 summer stock production which led to Jule Styne's successful 1952 Broadway revival]. Fosse is still the best of the Joeys, surpassing even the first one, Gene Kelly. Fosse, beside being an admirable and individualistic dancer, is a good actor, and he gives the proper phony slickness to the role.

ROBERT COLEMAN, *Mirror*

A whale of a *Pal Joey*. Though it's selling for a $3.95 top, you couldn't find better entertainment at twice or triple that figure. This is one of those musicals that wears its years well, that doesn't show its song-and-dance wrinkles. *Pal Joey* is a Hit! Hit! Hit! All over again. And why shouldn't it be? It's a tuneful, cleverly worded, flavorsome, satiric lullaby for the stay-up lates who used to make it easy and blow it fast. It's a cutting gem, a classic of its kind.

RICHARD WATTS JR., *Post*

To do no beating about any bushes, there just isn't a more richly entertaining musical comedy than *Pal Joey*. Witty, humorous, sardonic, tough in viewpoint, realistic in characterization, and won-

Joey (Bob Fosse at 23) appraises a passing showgirl, while Vera (Carol Bruce) glowers from the far-left table. This photo is from the 1951 summer stock package which led directly to Pal Joey's *award-winning 1952 revival.* (photo by J. Peter Happel)

derfully tuneful, it is vigorously alive and thoroughly delightful, and the additional good news is that it was splendidly revived in a well-cast production which captured its spirit and quality with the proper zest and vitality. When it was first presented shortly before the war, there were those who were shocked at a musical comedy which had a kept man as its central character and a second act concerned with a blackmailing plot. There is emphatically nothing soft or sentimental in the outspoken narrative of *Pal Joey* but its triumph is that its realistic material is woven into a pattern of song, dance, and story remarkable for being not only bright and humorous but also likeable.

Fosse, recovering from the debacle of *The Conquering Hero* (1961), returned to the stage in his only New York legit appearance other than the short-lived revue *Dance Me a Song* (1950). Within a couple of months he was back in his old choreographic shoes, doctoring *How to Succeed in Business Without Really Trying*. *Pal Joey* was re-revived with Fosse by City Center in 1963 for another 15 performances, with Viveca Lindfors and Kay Medford in support.

BROADWAY SCORECARD / perfs: 31 / $: NA

rave	favorable	mixed	unfavorable	pan
6		1		

PARK AVENUE

a musical comedy, with music by Arthur Schwartz; lyrics by Ira Gershwin; book by Nunnally Johnson and George S. Kaufman

production supervised by Arnold Saint Subber; book directed by George S. Kaufman; choreographed by Helen Tamiris (replacing Eugene Loring)
produced by Max Gordon
with Leonora Corbett, Arthur Margetson, Raymond Walburn, Mary Wickes, and David Wayne (replacing Jed Prouty)
opened November 4, 1946   Shubert Theatre

The creators of Of Thee I Sing, The Band Wagon, *and other classics came up empty on this one. Pre-Broadway credits.*

544

BROOKS ATKINSON, *Times*

Some of the most imposing people in show business are collaborating on a singularly unimposing musical comedy. Since all of these journeymen have panicked the town in the past, it is surprising to find them generously contributing to sobriety now. But the one joke they belabor throughout the evening is the mirthless one of divorce among the gold-plated classes; and they have nothing much to say about it except that they think it is funny. *Park Avenue* is a finger-tips carnival—thin, disdainful, and general. It ain't funny, McGee.

HERRICK BROWN, *Sun*

Ira Gershwin has contributed vastly more to the evening's fun than have the authors of the book. When three of the wives are singing of their troubles in the fields of hair-dos, fur coats, and nail polish in "Don't Be a Woman If You Can"; when the quartet of husbands, to a South American rhythm, is proclaiming that it is a "Land of Opportunitee"; and when Leonora Corbett is burlesquing cowboy songs in "Sweet Nevada," rhyming "horseback" with "divorce back," *Park Avenue* is at its best.

WILLIAM HAWKINS, *World-Telegram*

The sun total is the violent maltreatment of a lonely gag. The dialogue sounds like a single section of a classified joke book.

LOUIS KRONENBERGER, *PM*

I feel fairly grateful to *Park Avenue* for some of the things it isn't; I only wish I could feel half as friendly toward almost all the things it is. It is pleasant, for a change, not to find the book of a musical comedy entrusted to a couple of strictly-from-hunger hacks, and to encounter lines you can respond to rather than writhe at. It is also a relief not to have to chase an elaborately imbecilic plot through 20 to 30 elaborately exotic scenes. And it's something to be glad that the songs have words to them, instead of wishing that they might be hummed. But despite its evident desire to reach farther back in the theatre than Bald Head Row, *Park Avenue* is a pretty flat and tiresome evening. This relative sophistication merely raises your hopes in order to douse them, merely ups the ante without fattening the pot. The trouble is that Mr. Kaufman and Mr.

Johnson's marriage-and-divorce joke is served up hot and cold, creamed and fricasseed, in soup and in salad, and you feel about it at the end of the evening much as you do about turkey the third day after Thanksgiving. All the same, I hope they write some more musicals together, for they're brighter being dull than most librettists being bright.

Despite the assembled talents, this one simply didn't work. Unfortunately for us all, the quick failures of *The Firebrand of Florence* (1945) and *Park Avenue* combined to convince fifty-year-old Ira Gershwin—whose contributions were delightfully well-crafted in both cases—to leave Broadway forever. A society note: the twelve debutantes (i.e., chorines) were named Brenda Stokes, Brenda Follansbee, Brenda Follansbee-Stokes, Brenda Follansbee-Stokes-Follansbee, Brenda Cathcart, Brenda Cathcart-Cartcath, Brenda Wright Jr. Sr. 3rd, Brenda Quincy Adams, etc. Additional note for those of you who are interested in such things: the Messrs. Schwartz and Gershwin provided an exquisitely beautiful ballad, "Goodbye to All That."

BROADWAY SCORECARD / perfs: 72 / $: −

rave	favorable	mixed	unfavorable	pan
	1	1	4	2

A PARTY WITH BETTY COMDEN AND ADOLPH GREEN

an intimate revue of previously-written material, with music mostly by Leonard Bernstein and Jule Styne; lyrics by Betty Comden and Adolph Green

produced by the Theatre Guild
with Betty Comden and Adolph Green

opened December 23, 1958   John Golden Theatre

BROOKS ATKINSON, *Times*

To practice their profession Miss Comden and Mr. Green have to write some of the whipped cream that merchantable musical shows require, and they write it with immaculate skill. If boy must meet girl in the last scene, let Miss Comden and Mr. Green attend to the formalities. But no one else writes satire with quite so much compactness and precision. What Al Hirschfeld is to the satiric line and S. J. Perelman to the satiric word, they are to the satire of song and sketch. Miss Comden, elegant and reserved, Mr. Green, affable and ironic—they compose a perfect combination. Now and then Mr. Green horses around like a wit on a buffoon's holiday, and he is altogether delightful. But they never sacrifice their role as commentators on the contemporary scene from the outside. Two brilliant minds are at work on the follies and vulgarities of the world. They observe but they do not participate. For they have style, taste, and standards. They also have manners.

JOHN CHAPMAN, *Daily News*

According to the rule of the trade, a theatre reviewer must be calm, cool, collected, impersonal, unprejudiced, and a curmudgeon. But can I help it if I'm uncalm, uncool, uncollected, personal, and prejudiced over Betty Comden? All she has to do is give me that Mona Lisa smile and bat her eyes once and I'm a goner. She doesn't even have to sing. But sing she does. And so does her lyric-writing partner, Adolph Green, who looks something like an Idaho potato. This little combo, with the assistance of an unseen but splendid pianist, Peter Howard, put me in the jolliest of holiday moods.

WALTER KERR, *World Tribune*

What I like best about Betty Comden, whose *Party with Adolph Green* is at the Golden Theatre, is her frown. It is a very interesting frown. It doesn't seem to come from anywhere. The effect is enchanting, and it is just right for most of the deadpan parodies and lightly satirical pastiches that the unsteady *diseuse* and her buzzsaw partner, Mr. Adolph Green, are hauling out of the Broadway trunk. With his Fernandel-type face, his several sets of teeth, and his eyes that manage to come together to form a triangle, Adolph Green is almost constantly gnawing at something: his colleague's ear-lobes, J.J. Shubert, art houses that "take a faint pleasure in presenting a badly faded print of 'Madame Curie,' " and Rimsky-Korsakov's "Bumble Bee."

```
BROADWAY SCORECARD / perfs: 82 / $: +

   rave      favorable      mixed      unfavorable      pan

     2            5
```

PETER PAN

a musical fantasy, with music by Mark (Moose) Charlap, additional music by Jule Styne; lyrics by Carolyn Leigh, additional lyrics by Betty Comden and Adolph Green; book uncredited, from the 1904 fantasy by James M. Barrie

directed and choreographed by Jerome Robbins
produced by Edwin Lester, presented by Richard Halliday
with Mary Martin (Halliday), Cyril Ritchard, Kathy Nolan, and Margalo Gillmore

opened October 20, 1954   Winter Garden Theatre

BROOKS ATKINSON, *Times*

If Mary Martin is satisfied, so are the folks out front. A lot of the exuberance of Texas has stolen into the legend now. Peter Pan may have been a proper Victorian original. He is a healthy, fun-loving American now. Among the other stars of the production, put Jerome Robbins's name high on the list. Mr. Robbins began as a choreographer. Without taking leave of that profession, he has directed this phantasmagoria with inventiveness and delight. The adventures of Peter Pan are marvelously enlivened in Never Never Land by any number of comic ballets for children, Indians and pirates—rushing and winning in style, though never alien to the innocent spirit of Barrie. Mr. Robbins has done a wonderful job. There is room for some arguments about this full-gauged show. By the time the third act rolls around, it begins to look over-produced. A Hollywood-like lust of production for production's sake makes

Peter, who has just found his shadow, crows. "I don't know what all the fuss is about," commented Walter Kerr, "I always knew Mary Martin could fly." (costume by Motley)

things look ponderous toward the end. Nor has the music much taste. Most of it sounds as though it had come out of Tin Pan Alley tune factories. It lacks distinction and has no audible fondness for Barrie. Although the taste in showmanship and in music is common, the taste in performers is impeccable.

JOHN CHAPMAN, *Daily News*

Miss Martin's [12-year-old] daughter, Heller Halliday, makes a pleasing debut as Liza, a maidservant, and has a nice little song-and-dance turn with her mother, who somehow manages to look at least as young as Heller.

WILLIAM HAWKINS, *World-Telegram & Sun*

Mary Martin's *Peter Pan* has the unfettered inventiveness of a crowd of kids making up games as they go along. Sometimes the new musical reminds you of a youngster's birthday party. There is all the shouting and racing around, the havoc, the leaping and flying, the rare sob, the endless turbulence, and at last the faintly bittersweet ending. And then the polite goodbye with a twinkle. The entire hullabaloo is rowdy with the surcharged excitement of swimming holes and tree houses, of rival secret societies, and the gay fine wild war of being very young, and thinking it will last forever.

WALTER KERR, *Herald Tribune*

I don't know what all the fuss is about. I always knew Mary Martin could fly. She's always bounced along as though the earth were made of inner-spring mattresses, and that piping, rollicking voice of hers would carry anyone aloft, wires or no wires, any old time. Be that as it may, from the moment Miss Martin zooms in out of the night through gigantic nursery windows—barely bothering to stop at the footlights—until the moment when she bests the scurrilous Captain Hook in a swordfight by scooping right over his scoundrelly head, Miss Martin and her musical-comedy version of *Peter Pan* are sky-high with joy. The flying, before we get past it, is nothing short of miraculous. For the first time in my theatregoing experience, it's been designed rather than limited to a couple of quick exits—in effect, it's been choreographed by director Jerome Robbins. Result: it's not so much a nervous stunt as a rapturous lyrical experience, and you're going to be popeyed with happy disbelief at the first-act curtain: Peter brushing away the heavens at hurricane force while Wendy and family bobble gently behind him, with moon and stars slipping swiftly away beneath their dangling feet. It's the way *Peter Pan* always should have been, and wasn't.

RICHARD WATTS JR., *Post*

As one who feels that the antic whimsies of Barrie can do with a lot of enlivening, I thought it was a considerable improvement. It can hardly be said that the music or the production in general bother much about adhering to the Barrie-esque mood, and, while it didn't seem to me that the assorted talents of the songwriters worked out quite as brightly as might have been expected, my own conviction is that the note of Broadway musical comedy was a pleasant antidote to some of the saccharinity of the original text. There wasn't too much time left for the Barrie archness. The tale of Peter and Wendy, the pirates, the Indians, and Never-Never Land is all there, though perhaps slightly abbreviated, which is all right with me. In addition, the current *Peter Pan* has all sorts of features to offer, from a friendly Kangaroo to a Lost Child with spectacles [Ian Tucker], who looked disturbingly like Truman Capote. But the chief virtue of the production is its air of high spirits that keeps away the curse of excessive sentimentality.

Originally mounted for Edwin Lester's West Coast circuit, Comden, Green, and Styne were brought in (and half the songs thrown out) to revamp the show for Broadway—resulting in a somewhat uneven score. The New York run was cut short for a previously scheduled, live telecast of the production which established Mary as *Peter* to a whole generation.

Tony Awards were won by Mary Martin (actress); Cyril Ritchard (supporting actor); and Richard Rodda (stage technician). Donaldson Awards were won by Mary Martin (actress) and Cyril Ritchard (actor; supporting actor).

PHOENIX '55

a musical revue, with music by David Baker; lyrics by David Craig; sketches by Ira Wallach; idea conceived by Nicholas Benton and Stark Hesseltine

directed by Marc Daniels; choreographed by Boris Runanin
produced by the Phoenix Theatre (T. Edward Hambleton and Norris Houghton)
with Nancy Walker (Craig), Harvey Lembeck, and Gemze de Lappe

opened April 23, 1955   Phoenix Theatre

JOHN CHAPMAN, *Daily News*

Phoenix '55 is a wonderful evening of merriment and wit—and in it Nancy Walker steps into the ranks of such notable lady clowns as Fanny Brice. . . . As a good show must, it saves the best item for last. This is a side-splitting burlesque of Ed Murrow's TV interviews. Kenneth Harvey, with the permanent cigaret and the look of frozen affability, is Murrow, who has sent his cameras to the home of Lembeck and Miss Walker because they are parents of 22 children ranging from ages 2 to 17. This is a perfect sketch and a glorious satire as it discloses the lazy husband and his exhausted slattern of a wife drinking beer in the kitchen. When Murrow asks her to show the audience around, she struggles wearily out of her chair, points to the table and says, "This is the table. It's chipped." Dragging herself a few feet, she says. "This is the corner where I stand when I want to be alone."

WILLIAM HAWKINS, *World-Telegram & Sun*

The laughter that goes on at *Phoenix '55* is just like that lovely thunder you usually hear in a football stadium. It starts deep, thickens and spreads, then blasts. There is no doubt that most of the lightning that precipitates that thunder is the wit and polish of that remarkable performer, Nancy Walker. You can't watch the final sketch of the show and not avow that Nancy Walker is the funniest woman in the hemisphere. Just one more Walker note. Toward the end, Nancy suddenly sidles out of a dance number and delivers a gentle torch song. The delivery is knowing and fearless, and the lyrics are really phrased. What a talent!

WALTER KERR, *Herald Tribune*

The Phoenix starts off its new revue by suggesting, with a sly modesty, that some of its shows this season have been dogs—just plain dogs. It then proceeds to make up for all past sins by tossing at the customers a fresh, beautifully styled, and hilariously funny end-of-the-season offering. Most of the hilarity comes from the brooding, woebegone miseries of Nancy Walker. Miss Walker has had, over the seasons, her ups and downs as a comedienne. In *Phoenix '55* it's practically all ups. . . . Just before intermission, choreographer Boris Runanin hands her a nine-scene modern ballet (of the "Age of Anxiety" school) that is good enough to compete with the masterworks of the late Fanny Brice. Miss Walker symbolically caressing the toe of a young dreamer "in search of a problem to go with his solution." Miss Walker coming down off her toes to find everybody else dead. Miss Walker seeking out a "father" with tree-branch finger tips—these are now images to cherish. Nor does the second act fail her. Thanks to sketch-writer Ira Wallach, there is a thoroughly malicious caricature of one Geraldine Page, in dungarees [satirizing that season's comedy *The Rainmaker*]. And in an 11 o'clock blockbuster called "Upper Birth," this permanently sour, permanently slatternly clown parlays a one-joke sketch into five or six minutes of hysteria. Miss Walker is right back at the head of the class.

BROADWAY SCORECARD / perfs: 97 / $: NA

rave	favorable	mixed	unfavorable	pan
3	2	1	1	

PIPE DREAM

a musical comedy, with music by Richard Rodgers; book and lyrics by Oscar Hammerstein 2nd, from the 1954 novel *Sweet Thursday* by John Steinbeck

directed by Harold Clurman; choreographed by Boris Runanin
produced by Richard Rodgers and Oscar Hammerstein 2nd
with Helen Traubel, William Johnson, Judy Tyler, and Mike Kellin

opened November 30, 1955   Shubert Theatre

JOHN CHAPMAN, *Daily News*

It is a big show—big enough, it appeared last evening, to be unwieldy—and for a surprising amount of the time it is dull. Hammerstein and Rodgers are great gentlemen of the musical theatre and perhaps they are too gentlemanly to be dealing with John Steinbeck's sleazy and raffish denizens of Cannery Row. It has the dubious novelty of presenting the ex-Wagnerian soprano, Helen Traubel, in the role of the madam of an H-house. I felt a little sorry for this lady when she had to sing a paean of praise of her joint called "The Happiest House on the Block." Richard Wagner, of course, got her in a lot of dirty situations—but he wrote in German.

WILLIAM HAWKINS, *World-Telegram & Sun*

A certain homely swaying beauty of the music pervades the show. It is the sort of score you might hope Stephen Foster would write in the modern idiom.

WALTER KERR, *Herald Tribune*

In a forthright song called "The Man I Used To Be," the handsome bearded hero of *Pipe Dream* tells us that he isn't having much fun any more because he's "got a mission now." I wonder if something strangely similar isn't beginning to happen to Rodgers and Hammerstein. All through the thoroughly possible new musical, the authors seem unable to keep their minds on cheerfulness. Philosophy keeps breaking in. . . . Every bit of [the story], it should be quickly said, is accompanied by light, deft, sometimes wonderfully melodic improvisation by Richard Rodgers. And sometimes the music is able to take such firm hold of the proceedings that genuine gayety rears its welcome head. As a trumpet blares out the giddy notes of a "Bum's Opera," a spindly no-good in red suspenders, bandana, blue flannel shirt, and obtrusive long winter underwear manages to set the stage writhing. When the heroine, out on her first 'legitimate' date, gets helpful hints in deportment from the orchestra, the old R & H sparkle is in evidence once more. The spectacle of Helen Traubel as a local madam sitting picturesquely among her girls and wishing everybody a Merry Christmas "from our House" is winning indeed. But the frolicsome moments are rare. The people are capable, the material keeps promising to turn into a party. But someone seems to have forgotten to bring along that gallon jug of good, red wine.

JOHN MCCLAIN, *Journal-American*

This is a far cry from the exalted talents of the team that produced *South Pacific* [1949]. They must be human, after all.

From *Oklahoma!"* (1943) through *The King and I* (1951), Rodgers and Hammerstein had maintained an incredibly successful hit factory—not only as songwriters, but as producers (of *I Remember Mama* [1944], *Annie Get Your Gun* [1946], and *The Happy Time* [1950], as well as of their own musicals). The pair were dissimilar in nature and philosophy, though, and the relationship began to sour. Rodgers seems to have considered Hammerstein primarily responsible for their two failures, *Allegro* (1947) and *Me and Juliet* (1953); both had original librettos, while the hits were all adaptations. Hammerstein, on the other hand, seems to have recoiled from Rodgers's apparent concentration on business. (Sondheim's "Franklin Shepard, Inc." from *Merrily We Roll Along* [1981] might very well refer to R & H, as seen by a member of the Hammerstein camp; he has described Hammerstein as a man of limited talent and infinite soul, and Rodgers as a man of infinite talent and limited soul.) For their next project, Hammerstein wanted to do *Fanny* (1954)—which would have meant going into partnership with the rights owner, a novice producer named David Merrick. This Rodgers absolutely would not do. *Pipe Dream* was also owned by others, but Feuer and Martin agreed to step aside in exchange for a slice of the profits (what profits?). The end result was a muddled musical with—strangely enough—one of Rodgers's most inventive later scores lost in the shuffle. Following Hammerstein's death, Rodgers successfully burst forth with another highly inventive musical, *No Strings* (1962).

A Tony Award was won by Alvin Colt (costume designer).

BROADWAY SCORECARD / perfs: 246 / $: −

rave	favorable	mixed	unfavorable	pan
	1	2	4	

THE PIRATES OF PENZANCE

the 1880 comic operetta, with music by Sir Arthur Sullivan; book and lyrics by W. S. Gilbert

directed by Anne Bethell
produced by the D'Oyly Carte Opera Company
with Martyn Green, Thomas Round, and Helen Roberts

opened January 5, 1948   Century Theatre

ROBERT GARLAND, *Journal-American*

There was an awful lot of Gilbert and Sullivan going on and on and on and on last night at the Century Theatre. A long-drawn operatic evening came finally to an end with the chorus singing "Poor Wandering One." Well, this poor wandering one was glad to wander home where Rodgers and Hart were transcribed on the radio. . . . It couldn't be (could it?) that the new Atomic Age and the old Savoy Tradition aren't completely complementary?

BROADWAY SCOREBOARD / perfs: 16 / $: NA

rave	favorable	mixed	unfavorable	pan
2		1		1

PLAIN AND FANCY

a folk musical, with music by Albert Hague; lyrics by Arnold B. Horwitt; book by Joseph Stein and Will Glickman

directed by Morton Da Costa; choreographed by Helen Tamiris
produced by Richard Kollmar and James W. Gardiner in association with Yvette Schumer
with Richard Derr, Barbara Cook, David Daniels, Shirl Conway, and Nancy Andrews

opened January 27, 1955   Mark Hellinger Theatre

BROOKS ATKINSON, *Times*

By mixing Amish people with regulation showmanship, the producers of *Plain and Fancy* have emerged with an interesting if uneven musical comedy. With such genuine characters as the substance of the show, can't the authors find anything better for a second act than the old staples of Broadway? Showmanship will be the death of show business yet. After the first act, *Plain and Fancy* reverts to type—the standard drunk scene, the tawdry glamour of a carnival where sex and sin create a disturbance. The strange beauty of the Amish life is diluted with more familiar Broadway beverages, and *Plain and Fancy* fritters away the finest folk material of the season. The authors have not sustained the grave beauty of a notable first act. Their hearts belong to Broadway.

WILLIAM HAWKINS, *World-Telegram & Sun*

Plain and Fancy is fresh as new-mown hay, bubbly as hard cider and pretty as a bride's smile. There is practically nobody involved in this breezy, dynamic show who does not deserve a big hand. Outstanding credit goes to Barbara Cook, who flings her own heart over the footlights with whatever she does, and sings and dances her way into the hearts of the audience. . . . *Plain and Fancy* makes you feel as if you had on new shoes and your best hat.

WALTER KERR, *World Tribune*

Barbara Cook, right off a blue and white Dutch plate, is delicious all the time, but especially when she perches on a trunk, savors her first worthwhile kiss and melts into the melody of "This Is All Very

RICHARD KOLLMAR
and JAMES W. GARDINER
In association with YVETTE SCHUMER
Present

PLAIN AND FANCY

A NEW MUSICAL COMEDY

With RICHARD DERR • BARBARA COOK
DAVID DANIELS • SHIRL CONWAY
DANIEL NAGRIN • STEFAN SCHNABEL • GLORIA MARLOWE
NANCY ANDREWS • DOUGLAS FLETCHER RODGERS

Book by JOSEPH STEIN & WILL GLICKMAN
Lyrics by ARNOLD B. HORWITT • Music by ALBERT HAGUE
Production Directed by MORTON DA COSTA
Dances & Musical Numbers Staged by HELEN TAMIRIS
Musical & Choral Director FRANZ ALLERS
Orchestrations by PHILIP J. LANG
Sets & Costumes Designed by RAOUL PENE DuBOIS
Lighting by PEGGY CLARK

WORLD PREMIERE OF NEW MUSICAL!
SHUBERT THEATRE
NEW HAVEN
Sat. Eve., Dec. 11 thru Sat. Eve., Dec. 18
MATINEES WEDNESDAY & SATURDAY

The lovers (Gloria Marlowe and David Daniels) fly off to Amish happiness, while the soubrette (Barbara Cook) dreams of taking a flyer—and a smoke!—in sinful Lancaster.

558

New to Me". . . . *Plain and Fancy* is sweet, attractive, and normal as blueberry pie.

A fairly entertaining fifties-style musical, brim full of folksy charm. *Plain and Fancy* was a moderate hit, unlike the more adventurous/ less "show-biz" folk musical, *Paint Your Wagon* (1951). For a while the Pennsylvania Dutch treat was an amateur-group favorite, but within a decade it seemed hopelessly tame and mighty creaky.

BROADWAY SCOREBOARD / perfs: 461 / $: +

rave	favorable	mixed	unfavorable	pan
2	4		1	

POLONAISE

a biography of Thaddeus Kosciusko (1746–1817) set to the music of Frederic Chopin, with musical adaptation and original music by Bronislaw Kaper; lyrics by John Latouche; book by Gottfried Reinhardt and Anthony Veiller

directed by Stella Adler (replacing Edward Duryea Dowling); choreographed by David Lichine
produced by W. Horace Schmidlapp in association with Harry Bloomfield
with Jan Kiepura, Marta Eggerth (Kiepura), Rose Inghram, and Curt Bois

opened October 6, 1945   Alvin Theatre

JOHN CHAPMAN, *Daily News*

Mr. Kiepura can sing like a man possessed, and I don't know of any other tenor with a first-class voice who would attempt what he is doing, eight performances a week. But he just can't act. He poses. He gets up on wagons so he will be higher than anybody else. He makes entrances; at his first entrance, George Washington and some of the army are awaiting for him at West Point, and at his second, a whole damn Polish revolution has to take place before he can come in. His favorite spot is in the middle of the stage at the edge of the apron, and there must be some kind of mark there for him so he won't fall off.

ROBERT GARLAND, *Journal-American*

Throughout *Polonaise,* Thaddeus Kosciusko is merely a turbulent tenor with grease paint on his face, exhibitionism in his heart and familiar, if anachronistic, melodies on his tongue. . . . By the time "Just For Tonight (Etude in E)" was ultimately reprised, it sounded ominously like the piece's theme song.

LOUIS KRONENBERGER, *PM*

The best I can say for the thing as a whole is that it appalled me enough at times to keep me from being bored. The show has simply spared no expense to gum itself up in every possible way. To be sure, there was at the very outset something faintly odd about harnessing the music of a 19th-century composer to the career of an 18th-century patriot, simply because both of them were Poles.

WARD MOREHOUSE, *Sun*

It's Rose Inghram, however, who was yanked out of *Up in Central Park* [1945] a few days before its opening, who stops the show, singing "The Next Time I Care." And in so doing she provided one of the evening's curious interludes. The audience stormed for an encore. But she hesitated. The demand became more insistent. Miss Inghram flushed, smiled, looked at the audience, looked off-stage, smiled again helplessly, took another look offstage. Apparently flagged from the wings, and quite flustered by now, she disappeared. There was no encore.

BURTON RASCOE, *World-Telegram*

The playbill says that the Alvin Theatre is perfumed with Prince Matchabelli's "Stradivari." There was not enough of it used to overcome the odor of dry-rot and mothballs that emanated from the book, the lyrics, and the production of *Polonaise*. Except when Rose Inghram sang "The Next Time I Care," the audience sat on their hands. Miss Inghram's triumph apparently was so distressing to Jan Kiepura that he sang himself blue in the face in a number following Miss Inghram's. But no soap; the audience still sat on its hands for Mr. Kiepura.

WILELLA WALDORF, *Post*

It is about time somebody started a League for the Defense of Dead Composers. It is disturbing that some of Chopin's finest works, "adapted" for the occasion, should be carelessly flaunted on the Broadway stage in a futile attempt to add luster to a stupid, inept, often embarrassingly ludicrous spectacle. Kosciusko was a Pole and presumably Jan Kiepura, who is also a Pole, means to do him honor by impersonating him. But Mr. Kiepura, endowed by nature with a fine tenor voice which he misuses abominably, is an exhibitionist whose stage deportment sometimes seems almost pathologically *mal à propos*. Definitely no actor, Mr. Kiepura nevertheless exudes a spurious emotion while singing that, combined with a set of puppet-show gestures in the worst operatic tradition, results in a more devastating caricature of a pompous *tenore robusto* than any satiric impressionist could ever hope to achieve. . . . Zadel Skolovsky, the concert pianist hired to play Chopin's Polonaise in A-flat while the ballet stormed the Royal Palace, not only performed with vigor at the pianoforte but spoke his one line of dialogue clearly and as if he knew what it meant. Maybe what *Polonaise* needs is a few more concert pianists in some of the other roles.

```
○○○○○○○○○○○○○○○○○○○○○○○○○○○○○○○○○○○○○○○○○○○○○
○                                                    ○
○      BROADWAY SCORECARD / perfs: 113 / $: −        ○
○                                                    ○
○    rave    favorable    mixed    unflavorable    pan   ○
○                                                    ○
○                                              8     ○
○                                                    ○
○○○○○○○○○○○○○○○○○○○○○○○○○○○○○○○○○○○○○○○○○○○○○
```

PORGY AND BESS

a revival of the 1935 folk opera, with music by George Gershwin; lyrics by DuBose Heyward and Ira Gershwin; libretto by DuBose

The triumphant Breen-Davis revival, which finally established the Gershwin masterwork as a worldwide classic. (drawing by Yurman)

Heyward, from his 1925 novel *Porgy* and the 1927 dramatization by Dorothy and DuBose Heyward

directed by Robert Breen
produced by Blevins Davis and Robert Breen
with Cab Calloway, Leslie Scott, and Leontyne Price

opened March 10, 1953   Ziegfeld Theatre

BROOKS ATKINSON, *Times*

It is the fifth *Porgy and Bess* New York has had since the original opening in 1935. It is by odds the best and it is magnificent. For they have restored a great deal of the music that characterized *Porgy and Bess* as opera when it was first produced and they have added music never used before. George Gershwin, if he were alive today, would feel thoroughly vindicated. As a song show *Porgy and Bess* has been delightful during the intervening years. But as an opera with a brilliantly orchestrated [by Gershwin] score, with recitative and all the operatic mumbo-jumbo, it is a major work of art—a tumultuous evocation of life among some high-spirited, poignant, admirable human beings. It is all Gershwin and it is all gold. The long, intricate score, which Alexander Smallens [Gershwin's 1935 conductor] conducts with great skill, gives *Porgy and Bess* a sustained exultation it has not had in recent productions. This is what a theatre classic ought to be—alive in every fiber, full of passion for a theme.

WILLIAM HAWKINS, *World-Tribune & Sun*

It inspires immediate sensuous response, as nothing else in our theatre literature, and little, if anything, in grand opera. Where most big musical melodrama concerns the rich and powerful, *Porgy and Bess* sings of primitive hearts. Its passions move like arrows. Its transitions are lightning-like. Its scope is free as the wind. . . . Through a hair-raising performance, first honors go to Leontyne Price for a characterization clear in detail to the remotest corners of the Ziegfeld, and for singing that can only be described as heavenly. Cab Calloway's remarkable performance as Sportin' Life makes a vital comment on *Porgy and Bess* as a classic. He easily makes this role with its familiar songs entirely his own. If the serpent of Eden ever walked on two legs, he must have looked and behaved just like Calloway.

WALTER KERR, *Herald Tribune*

The Blevins Davis–Robert Breen revival of *Porgy and Bess* has now come to the Ziegfeld after whirlwind engagements in Berlin, Vienna, Paris, and London, and I am surprised that Berlin, Vienna, Paris, and London are still standing. For this is surely the most restless, urgent, and shatteringly explosive production of the Gershwin masterwork we have yet had. The stage is rarely still. As the lights come up slowly on the splintered stairways and sagging shutters of Catfish Row, and as the first strains of "Summertime" cut across the sultry silence of a South Carolina evening, DuBose Heyward's world of frenzied gayety and passionate violence begins to take on sinuous, insistent life. Hands, bodies, and laughing voices unite in a driving, relentless, and finally irresistible rhythm. The theatre is supercharged with an almost animal fury, and a flaming Bess strides into a Charleston back alley that teems with raw and racy vitality. With every step in the familiar narrative, the savage beat is intensified. In the production which Robert Breen has devised, *Porgy and Bess* is an almost uninterrupted series of musical and choreographic detonations, one following the other with the velocity of that hurricane which brings the second act crashing to its climax.

By 1953, Gershwin's final stage work—a financial failure of the 1935–1936 season—was universally accepted as a brilliant masterwork. This Blevins–Davis production met with immense success on its international tour, the talented performers being treated like distinguished artists everywhere—except in America.

BROADWAY SCORECARD / perfs 312 / $: +

rave	favorable	mixed	unfavorable	pan
6	1			

PORTOFINO

a musical comedy, with music by Louis Bellson and Will Irwin; book and lyrics by Richard Ney, additional lyrics by Sheldon Harnick

directed by Karl Genus (replacing John Larson); choreographed by Charles Weidman and Ray Harrison
produced by Richard Ney
with Georges Guétary, Helen Gallagher, and Robert Strauss
opened February 21, 1958   Adelphi Theatre

WALTER KERR, *Herald Tribune*

Helen Gallagher comes through a couple of French doors onto a noticeably wobbling Italian balcony, rubs her right hip up and down against a corner of the building to indicate what the authors conceive to be sex, blinks her pretty eyes, opens her steam-whistle mouth, and clearly says the line, "When I think of him kissing me, I don't know whether to fall down, sit down, or Miltown." She doesn't cringe, or shudder, or hide her head under her wing. She doesn't hand in her notice, effective at the first-act intermission, she doesn't go home to mother. She stands there—*stands* there—with her happy eyelashes fluttering, her brave little heart beating proudly, and steadies herself for the next idiotic musical number, which will take place in spite of the fact that the spotlight that is supposed to be following her is flickering out, the men who are supposed to be operating it are engaged in loud, heated conversation in the booth, and the dress that is supposed to be dazzling is ripping rapidly up the back. Good girl. . . . I will say nothing about Robert Strauss's performance, because I admired him so much in *Stalag 17* [1951]. Nor will I say that *Portofino* is the worst musical *ever* produced, because I've only been seeing musicals since 1919.

JOHN MCCLAIN, *Journal-American*

There seems to be no point in trying to be cute or clever about the simple fact that *Portofino* is unbelievably bad. It is a catastrophe all around.

RICHARD WATTS JR., *Post*

You can't say that actors lack the courage of heroes. The performers in *Portofino* must have known they were in an epoch-making disaster, and yet they went right ahead, beaming happily, singing and dancing and gallantly speaking some of the most inane dialogue in musical comedy history, just as if they were in *My Fair Lady* [1956]. Drama critics, who are sort of brave, too, can salute their unconquerable valor, even though we are unable to supply them with any other comfort. Richard Ney, who not only produced *Portofino* but wrote what one may stretch a point and call its book, as well as most of its lyrics, is obviously also an indomitable man. Against the advice of less hardy spirits, he insisted on bringing his show into town, and his reward is that he has given us something memorable.

This one ranks high on the "Ghastly Musicals" list. Producer Richard Ney was the Hollywood juvenile who played Greer Garson's son in *Mrs. Miniver* (1942) and then married her. (Miss Garson, not Mrs. Miniver.) *Portofino* might have done better with Mrs. Ney as Gallagher and composer Bellson's wife (Pearl Bailey) as Guétary. At least, it couldn't have done worse.

BROADWAY SCORECARD / perfs: 3 / $: —

rave	favorable	mixed	unfavorable	pan
				7

RAZZLE DAZZLE

a musical revue, with music by various composers; sketches and lyrics by Mike (Michael) Stewart

directed by Edward Reveaux; choreographed by Nelle Fisher
produced by David Heilwell and Derrick Lynn-Thomas in association with Madeline Capp and Greer Johnson
with Dorothy Greener, Jet MacDonald, and Jane White

opened February 19, 1951   Arena

JOHN CHAPMAN, *Daily News*

To quote Vivian Blaine's song in *Guys and Dolls* [1950], it all seemed like a horrible dream.

The Arena, a theatre-in-the-round operation located in the Edison Hotel, lasted for several months. Much of the *Razzle Dazzle* material had been seen earlier that season in the off-Broadway revue *Come What May*, which introduced the clever, 23-year-old Michael Stewart to New York.

```
BROADWAY SCORECARD / perfs: 8 / $:  –

rave    favorable    mixed    unfavorable    pan

                3          1                        3
```

THE RED MILL

a revival of the 1906 operetta, with music by Victor Herbert; book and lyrics by Henry Blossom; additional lyrics by Forman Brown

directed by Billy Gilbert; choreographed by Aida Broadbent
produced by Paula Stone and Hunt Stromberg, Jr.
with Eddie Foy, Jr., Michael O'Shea, Odette Myrtil, Carol Stone (Collins) and Charles Collins

opened October 16, 1945   Ziegfeld Theatre

Louis Kronenberger, *PM*

It is 39 years since *The Red Mill* (starring Montgomery and Stone) first opened on Broadway; and very often, watching it revived last night, it seemed that long. Victor Herbert's talent is clashing now with Father Time.

Lewis Nichols, *Times*

Perhaps this generation, which does not deserve a great deal, is lucky to receive any revival of *The Red Mill* whatsoever; for that, credit the Stepping Stones. Paula Stone, in association with Hunt Stromberg, is the producer. Dorothy, along with her husband Charles Collins, is in the company. Fred (their father), who with Dave Montgomery was in the original production, sat last evening in the third row.

BURTON RASCOE, *World-Telegram*

For the old Dave Montgomery role the young producers have had the extraordinary sense to engage Eddie Foy, Jr. Here, I beg leave to say, is one of the great comedians of our time, much better than his father was (although his father was very, very good), the only man living to dispute Bobby Clark's position as the ace zany of the period. (Where have they been keeping him?) You should see Eddie Junior perform. He has everything. He has limitless and effortless grace; he can tap, soft-shoe and make monkeys out of a lot of lauded ballet dancers; he can say "How do you do" in a way that makes me convulse with laughter, and he has some pantomimic stunts that are among the funniest things I ever saw on the stage. . . . Miss Stone and Mr. Stromberg have given the show a production the like of which would have stricken the late Charles Dillingham, original producer of the musical (who liked to cut his corners closely and watched his pennies), with a nervous break-down. He would (I think) have said that the very idea of spending so much money on a couple of clowns in a music show was downright anarchic, immoral, and contrary to good business practices.

BROADWAY SCORECARD / perfs: 531 / $: +

rave	favorable	mixed	unfavorable	pan
1	4			3

REDHEAD

a mystery musical comedy, with music by Albert Hague; lyrics by Dorothy Fields; book by Herbert and Dorothy Fields, Sidney Sheldon and David Shaw

directed and choreographed by Bob Fosse
produced by Robert Fryer and Lawrence Carr
with Gwen Verdon, Richard Kiley, and Leonard Stone

opened February 5, 1959   46th Street Theatre

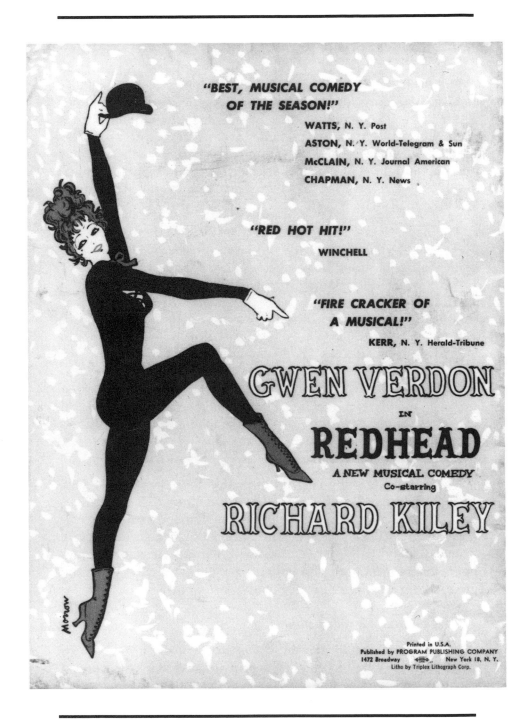

Verdon and Fosse, that's all. And that was more than enough!
(*drawing by Tom Morrow*)

FRANK ASTON, *World-Telegram & Sun*

She is on stage almost every minute, dancing, singing, joking, talking, being tossed, being threatened, getting a skinful, losing her man, regaining him, eluding a strangler—this tiny, lovely demon jams at least a week of hard, inspired labor into about 2½ hours. She is a rocketing, endearing success. Her hair is as pretty and pink as a broiled salmon steak, and lots more appetizing.

BROOKS ATKINSON, *Times*

The book is as complicated as an income-tax return and just about as entertaining. . . . Mr. Fosse has written one of his best comic ballets, a sort of burlesque of *My Fair Lady's* [1956] "Ascot Gavotte," which is a satiric cartoon in its own right. When "The Uncle Sam Rag" is strutting across the stage, *Redhead* seems to promise something original in the way of ironic musical theatre. But the promise is not fulfilled. *Redhead* drifts off at random into anything that may work for the moment. Everything works for Miss Verdon, whose humors and radiance are unique and priceless. But the rest of *Redhead* provokes the awful thought that musical comedy is a lost art. Perhaps in the future all musical comedies should be written by choreographers.

JOHN CHAPMAN, *Daily News*

Now we have four really tip-top musicals in town—*My Fair Lady*, *West Side Story* [1957], *The Music Man* [1957], and *Redhead*. And the new one has something that the other three haven't got; namely, Gwen Verdon. Once again this astonishing young woman lights up a whole big stage with her dancing, her singing, her instinct for comedy. Her unlimited energy and, most of all, the great charm which goes with being a girl named Gwen Verdon.

WALTER KERR, *Herald Tribune*

A sort of pink-champagne-and-black-tights murder mystery, with Gwen Verdon spending the first act finale quivering and popeyed against a darkened backstage wall while an ominous shadow with a swirling cloak looms ever more mightily over her. I went out for an intermission cigarette, though, feeling wonderfully certain that no one would kill her. Not that doll. . . . Choreographer Bob Fosse keeps thinking up fetching postures, parades, chases, and tailspins for her to dive unblinkingly into, and she dives—well, magnificently.

RICHARD WATTS, JR., *Post*

You would have to go back to memories of Gertrude Lawrence to find a kinship in charm, skill, and authentic glamor, and even Miss Lawrence couldn't dance with Miss Verdon's humorous brilliance.

Gwen Verdon and choreographer Bob Fosse sparked this mediocre melomusical. Veteran librettist Herbert Fields—who in the 1920s had forged new musical comedy trails in collaboration with Rodgers and Hart—died on March 24, 1958. Sister Dorothy's disorientation resulted in a negligible book and a set of lyrics far below her norm. Nevertheless, *Redhead* won a bouquet (or should we say bucket?) of Tony Awards and was the hit of the season, competing against such world-beaters as *Flower Drum Song*, *Goldilocks*, and even *Whoop-Up*. Verdon and Fosse, who since 1953 had collected seven Tonys, officially joined hands (or should we say feet?) and got hitched.

In addition to winning the Tony Award for Best Musical, Tonys were won by Albert Hague (composer); Herbert and Dorothy Fields, Sidney Sheldon and David Shaw (librettists); Bob Fosse (choreographer); Robert Fryer and Lawrence Carr (producers); Gwen Verdon (actress); Richard Kiley (actor); Leonard Stone (supporting actor, tied with Russell Nype for *Goldilocks*); and Rouben Ter-Arutunian (costume designer).

BROADWAY SCORECARD / perfs: 455 / $: +

rave	favorable	mixed	unfavorable	pan
4	3			

REGINA

a dramatic opera, with music and words by Marc Blitzstein, from the 1939 drama *The Little Foxes* by Lillian Hellman

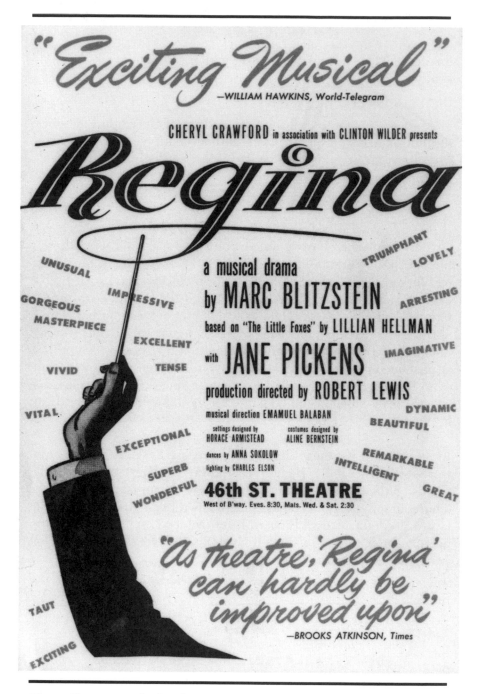

This tells us very little about Regina *except that it was exciting and*
highly musical. The complimentary adjectives were pulled from
critical quotes on the back of the herald. (*Atkinson's "rave" is slightly*
reworded and deceptively taken out of context.)

directed by Robert Lewis; choreographed by Anna Sokolow
produced by Cheryl Crawford in association with Clinton Wilder
with Jane Pickens, Brenda Lewis, Priscilla Gillette, William Wilderman, and Carol Brice

opened October 31, 1949   46th Street Theatre

BROOKS ATKINSON, *Times*

Marc Blitzstein ought to be well satisfied with the treatment the theatre has given him. In *Regina* he has crossed the border-line between popular theatre and modern opera, and the theatre has kept step with him perfectly. As theatre, this production of *Regina* could hardly be improved upon [but] to one theatregoer of long standing *Regina* has softened a hard play. What Mr. Blitzstein has added to it does not compensate for the loss in force, belligerence, and directness. . . . William Wilderman's ailing Horace Giddens is intelligently played and sung more dynamically than his heart condition warrants. There is one point in the drama when Mr. Blitzstein comes nearer knocking him off than Regina does.

JOHN CHAPMAN, *Daily News*

I wish I could ask the printers downstairs to put a "Bravo!" in type for me; but in strictest conscience I can't. Cheryl Crawford, the producer, is a doughty lady who on several occasions has dared to flaunt convention and present musicals which have been different yet delightful. Instead, it becomes necessary to observe that most of the time the music and the singing of *Regina* got in the way of what used to be a good play called *The Little Foxes*. Every time the plot got hot somebody would start an aria and when the song was ended the plot would be as cold as a Birdseye lamb chop. As the evening wore on—that is a good phrase, let me repeat it: as the evening wore on, I developed the conviction that Mr. Blitzstein had written frontground music instead of background music, and this was a mistake. There is no profit in taking a work out of one medium and putting it into another unless the change is for the better, or unless the change reveals something new and admirable. Maxwell Anderson and Kurt Weill took a novel and made it into a magical musical, *Lost in the Stars* [which opened the previous night]. They succeeded in translating one artist's creation into another and equally interesting kind of work. Mr. Blitzstein has not made Miss Hellman's play into a valid semi-opera. The only strength of *Regina* is the original strength which was put into *The Little Foxes*.

ROBERT GARLAND, *Journal-American*

Before *Regina* opened I could not imagine why, in the first place, Marc Blitzstein thought it would be worth while to set *The Little Foxes* to music. Ten years ago, with Tallulah Bankhead as the Dixie Devil of the present title, it was no singing matter. Now, it is!, a real achievement for Mr. Blitzstein (book, score, and orchestration) and Lillian Hellman who, writing *The Little Foxes*, wrote more lastingly than she knew. When words are too melodramatic to be spoken, they are better sung. Thus it is with *The Little Foxes*. Without the composer's complementary setting, the nasty Alabama Hubbards are no more than talky pre-Tennessee Williams samples of Southern Comfort at its most discomforting. Only Regina has character. Marc Blitzstein now gives character to all the Hubbard kinfolk, rounding out each member of the hate-filled household. When singing or speaking against the orchestra, his score provides their third dimension, making their machine-made machinations dramatically musical and musically dramatic; as dramatically arresting as any theatre thing on Broadway. More so than many, believe me! During many a year of first-nighting, few first-nights have provided the unlooked-for excitement and satisfaction of last night's first night. Marc Blitzstein's music makes on-stage mountains out of molehills.

WILLIAM HAWKINS, *World-Telegram*

About *Regina* it is impossible to be objective and professional. I can only say personally that it is the most exciting musical theatre I know since *Rosenkavalier* [1911]. This new lyric drama headily defies classification. If opera even suggests awkward people, florid vocalizing, and clumsy acting, then *Regina* is certainly not opera. But it is a tense taut story, already familiar as Lillian Hellman's *The Little Foxes*, released into musical terms in a splendidly rich fabric of sound. The aural intention of Marc Blitzstein is complex and subtle. Infallibly realized, it is as if he had never heard of a formula.

☆

An intriguing combination of music and drama, with one of the musical theatre's outstanding scores. Blitzstein accomplished the Broadway music/drama that his colleague Kurt Weill theorized but never quite achieved. Weill's final attempts at this were restricted by the limitations of his collaborators, Langston Hughes and Elmer Rice on *Street Scene* (1947), and Maxwell Anderson on *Lost in the Stars* (1949). Blitzstein, as his own lyricist/librettist, was able to weave a musical texture throughout the piece in a way that only the most talented and complementary collaborators could do. Those of you so inclined can look at "Lionnet (Birdie's Aria)," for example, or the final scene in which Regina virtually murders her husband, battles her brothers for the spoils, and is defeated by her daughter. These are not mere songs; they are *dramatic scenes* told in words and music! If *Regina* was "caviar to the general," it remains a glorious treasure to the discriminating.

Tony Awards were won by Aline Bernstein (costume designer) and Maurice Abravanel (musical director).

BROADWAY SCORECARD / perfs: 56 / $: —

rave	favorable	mixed	unfavorable	pan
2	1	2	2	1

RHAPSODY

a Viennese-style operetta, with music by Fritz Kreisler, adapted by (Robert) Russell Bennett; lyrics by John Latouche, additional lyrics by Blevins Davis and Russell Bennett; book by Leonard Louis Levinson and Arnold Sundegaard, from an original story by A. N. Nagler

directed and choreographed by David Lichine
produced by Blevins Davis in association with Lorraine Manville Dresselhuys
with Annamary Dickey, George Young, and Eddie Mayehoff

opened November 22, 1944   Century Theatre

ROBERT GARLAND, *Journal-American*

As an example of what money can't do, it's a masterpiece. Although this may sound impossible, it manages to live down to the rumors which preceded its exposure. I forget how many hundred thousand dollars were spent on *Rhapsody*. Did I say "spent?" Well, squandered would be a better word. Everything that could be wrong is wrong about it. Not in all my on-the-aisle-seated days has a big time theatrical production been so misbegotten, so flat-footed, so pretentious. If I could have my way, *Rhapsody* and almost everybody connected with it would go around to Cain's Storehouse and stand in a corner for the next hundred years.

LOUIS KRONENBERGER, *PM*

Its book would curdle the millennium.

BURTON RASCOE, *World-Telegram*

The audience response was ghastly. The walkers out were legion.

BROADWAY SCORECARD / perfs: 13 / $: —

rave	favorable	mixed	unfavorable	pan
				8

RUGANTINO

an imported "Roman musical spectacle," with music by Armando Trovaioli; book and lyrics by Pietro Garinei and Sandro Giovaninni; English subtitles by Alfred Drake

directed by Pietro Garinei and Sandro Giovaninni; choreographed by Dania Krupska
produced by Alexander H. Cohen and Jack Hylton
with Nino Manfredi, Ornella Vanoni, and Aldo Fabrizi

opened February 6, 1964   Mark Hellinger Theatre

WALTER KERR, *Herald Tribune*

The choreography that has been arranged for the girls in nineteenth-century riding hats, for the girls with lanterns, and for the girls in pom-pom masquerade (together with the clowns on stilts) is entirely conventional. You have only to see the costumes to know the steps. And the score by Armando Trovaioli is sweet enough, in its semi-pop way, to remind you of Puccini's younger brother, Victor Romberg.

RICHARD WATTS JR., *Post*

It is filled with sex, dagger-thrusts, some humor of an earthy sort, and a public beheading of its hero. Unfortunately, there is also a catch amid its lavish display of action and song. It has the bad luck of being resolutely and resoundingly dull.

Everybody was singing in Italian, fortunately; it might have been even worse in English. Must have seemed like a sure fire World's Fair money-maker to Mr. Cohen.

BROADWAY SCORECARD / perfs: 28 / $: −

rave	favorable	mixed	unfavorable	pan
	2		2	2

RUMPLE

a musical comedy, with music by Ernest G. Schweikert; lyrics by Frank Reardon; book by Irving Phillips

directed by Jack Donohue; choreographed by Bob Hamilton
produced by Paula Stone (Sloane) and Michael Sloane
with Eddie Foy (Jr.), Gretchen Wyler, Stephen Douglass, and Barbara Perry

opened November 6, 1957   Alvin Theatre

BROOKS ATKINSON, *Times*

A short India rubber-man with the strut of a braggart and a vagrant grin, Foy [as a cartoonist's character who jumps off the page] dances amiably around the stage, carrying a gaudy umbrella that beats both the rhythm and the humor. He was trained in the old school of theatrical jesting. Perhaps that accounts for an innocence of style that is so timeless and winning. And perhaps it also accounts for the impression he gives of being detached from the main business of the show. His eyes are always wandering in the direction of the wings or the balcony after the manner of the old vaudevillian; he acknowledges the presence of an audience but he does not woo it. It is as if he would perform just as amusingly if there were no one in the house. Speaking in a small voice, he tosses his jokes away absent-mindedly as though he did not have much confidence in them. He is right in this instance. *Rumple* is an elaborately dull show.

WALTER KERR, *Herald Tribune*

In despair he throws himself headlong onto the nearest couch and cries "Maybe I'm getting old. Maybe I'm not funny. Maybe nobody loves me any more." Nonsense. You're in the prime of life, Eddie. The best is yet to come. Funny? Who else could draw a chalk line across the stage, forget he has drawn it, and twenty minutes later stumble over it? Who else could unravel a girl's knitted red dress with such delicate dispatch, dance on his knees like a talented grasshopper, steal a drink by hooking an umbrella into another fellow's glass? We love you, Eddie. Now, about that show you're in. It isn't very good, Eddie. It's rather long on idle fantasy and rather short on working jokes.

BROADWAY SCORECARD / perfs: 45 / $: −				
rave	*favorable*	*mixed*	*unfavorable*	*pan*
1	2		3	1

SADIE THOMPSON

a musical play, with music by Vernon Duke; lyrics by Howard Dietz; book by Howard Dietz and Rouben Mamoulian, from John Colton and Clemence Randolph's 1922 drama *Rain*, adapted from the story "Miss Thompson" by W. Somerset Maugham

directed by Rouben Mamoulian; choreographed by Edward Caton
produced by A. P. Waxman
with June Havoc (replacing Ethel Merman), Lansing Hatfield, and Ralph Dumke

opened November 16, 1944   Alvin Theatre

John Chapman, *Daily News*

When Ethel Merman bowed out of the cast and Miss Havoc took over it was reported that Miss Merman left because she wasn't satisfied with Howard Dietz's lyrics. If this is true Miss Merman made a mistake, for the lyrics are all right. But Vernon Duke's score is heavy and dull and of scant variety. What George Gershwin could have done with the *Sadie Thompson* setup! Or Vincent Youmans! The earthiness which could have been put into Sadie's songs, and the revivalist life which would have been put into the Reverend Davidson's. But what one heard last night was just music by the yard. *Sadie Thompson* has all of the elements of a superb musical show except one—it doesn't have any music. It's unfortunate that so ambitious, expensive, intelligently planned, and accurately cast a show should lack the score to make it come alive.

Louis Kronenberger, *PM*

In any artistic sense it was in the cards for *Sadie Thompson* to fail, for it has been tortured into a form that simply does not fit it. But the things that might have redeemed it as entertainment, the music and dancing that might have given it their own kind of lift and drama, are not there either; so that, despite some scattered virtues, *Sadie Thompson* really fails twice. The fundamental trouble, of course, is that you can't take a dramatic story, whose power lies in its tensions, and constantly interrupt its action with here a song and there a dance and somewhere else a stage procession. Frantically the thing becomes all starts and stops, and hence a mess. *Rain* was, among other things, a play of mood, in which the

June Havoc as Sadie Thompson, ready to go out in the Rain. (*costume design by Azadia Newman [Mrs. Rouben Mamoulian]*)

steady downpour performed a dramatic function. In *Sadie Thompson* it rains real water every so often, but in an absent-minded sort of way, just so you won't forget it is supposed to be raining continuously; and the play is no more atmospheric than it is tense. *Sadie Thompson* is a musical that you have to sit through in something like a serious frame of mind, for from beginning to end it is absolutely lacking in comedy. You could, I think, make a successful opera of *Rain*, by really translating its drama and its mood into completely musical terms; but you can't make a musical play. *Sadie Thompson*, having killed off its own innate drama, can find nothing much to substitute but a kind of lavish dullness.

BURTON RASCOE, *World-Telegram*

Believe it or not, it has happened! A musical in a class with *Oklahoma!* [1943] has come to town! In fact, this new operetta is one of the most beautifully integrated shows of its kind I have ever seen or heard. I am still all atremor over the sheer, exciting beauty of this thing. But I must confess I was never more surprised in my life. Why was I surprised? Because Vernon Duke had never before given me any indication that he could write a melodious tune, and although I have carefully listened to and studied his more serious compositions (played by the highbrow orchestras and signed Vladimir Dukelsky, which is his real name) I have never before been convinced that he wasn't addicted to writing notes down on a sheet of musical composition paper without any reference to what the notes would sound like. Yet, in *Sadie Thompson* Mr. Duke has written a musical score that is not only full of heavenly sounds, pulse-quickening and ear-caressing but, in every instance, designed to interpret the text, elucidate character, further the action, and contribute to the harmonic unity of the production.

WILELLA WALDORF, *Post*

The idea of making a musical show out of *Rain* never appealed to this department, partly because the play has always seemed too good a show on its own to require any fancy trimmings, partly because we have never been quite able to accept anybody in the role of Sadie Thompson but the late Jeanne Eagels. Let us report, therefore, that *Sadie Thompson* proved uncommonly enjoyable. The success of the evening—for it was distinctly a success as far as this reporter is concerned—was due in part to the beautiful production accorded the work under Rouben Mamoulian's astute direction. But more than anything else it was due to the surprisingly effective performance of June Havoc as Sadie. We say surprisingly because Miss Havoc's talents have hitherto escaped us. In *Mexican Hayride* [1944], for instance, she struck us as a mere fanny wriggler. Yet last night she came out on the Alvin stage and acted Sadie well enough to become a worthy successor to Jeanne Eagels. This is the highest compliment anybody could ever possibly pay Miss Havoc, and we shall leave it at that. . . . *Sadie Thompson* is a good show. It always was and it still is, music, ballet, clever Boris Aronson scenery, and all. Over it hovers the spirit of Mr. Mamoulian, a director who knows how to create striking stage effects and at the same time make actors out of, well out of Miss Havoc, for instance.

Rouben Mamoulian was instrumental in creating the emotionally effective texture of *Porgy and Bess* (1935), *Oklahoma!* (1943), and *Carousel* (1945). But here he had no Hammerstein to write the libretto, and things fell short—as would be the case on his other "just miss" musical dramas, *St. Louis Woman* (1946) and *Lost in the Stars* (1949). *Sadie's* weaknesses could have been glossed over had Ethel Merman not walked out after a week of rehearsals: she didn't like the lyrics. (The star had her husband "fix" the rhymes, to Howard Dietz's loud displeasure. Dietz had similar problems with Mary Martin on *Jennie* [1963], which arguments Dietz did *not* win as *Jennie* was coproduced by Mary's husband.) And so, another promising musical down the *Rain*. Composer Duke tried a *Sadie* satire for Bette Davis in *Two's Company* (1952), which didn't work out too well either. And Ethel Merman went on to play her replacement June Havoc's real-life Mama in *Gypsy* (1959).

BROADWAY SCORECARD / perfs: 60 / $: −

rave	favorable	mixed	unfavorable	pan
3			4	1

SAIL AWAY

a musical comedy, with book, music, and lyrics by Noël Coward; choreographed by Joe Layton

produced by Bonard Productions (Helen Bonfils, Haila Stoddard) in association with Charles Russell
with Elaine Stritch, James Hurst, Margalo Gillmore, Alice Pearce, and Grover Dale

opened October 3, 1961   Broadhurst Theatre

WALTER KERR, *Herald Tribune*

The librettist-composer never does get around to introducing all of his amiable people to one another, let alone welding them together into a cheerful "party-mix." He begins a standoffish romance between pretty Patricia Harty and a slightly coy dancer named Grover Dale. He begins another, so standoffish as to suggest neurosis or at the very least bad breath, between a fine singer, James Hurst, and our Miss Stritch. Thereafter, between the bounce of beach balls, the sightseeing of bikinis, and the click of Rolliflexes, he alternates scenes in which passion gets nowhere and the precise temperature-readings are hard to remember. When Miss Harty confesses, late in the adventure, that she cannot quite recall whether her swain is an architect or an agriculturist, you understand her problem. You'd almost forgotten he was in the show.

JOHN McCLAIN, *Journal-American*

It struck me that the power was missing from the revered Coward dialogue. Where is his way with a word? Small scenes that might have been gay and inventive became sodden and serious. Who had the hero say to the heroine in his darkest moment: "If that's the way you feel, there's really nothing more to be said, is there?" Not the Noël Coward I used to know. *Sail Away*, in spite of all the rooting and the shouting, doesn't really go anywhere.

NORMAN NADEL, *World-Telegram & Sun*

Noël Coward's *Sail Away* easily could have qualified as the musical of the year if it had opened in 1936.

HOWARD TAUBMAN, *Times*

There are bound to be unexpected moments even in a well-rehearsed cruise. It was a delightful idea of Mr. Coward's to have Mimi Paragon [Stritch], his cruise hostess, air a leash of dogs on the deck. It was a poodle's own idea to forget that he was a performer. No sooner had an actor responded with the resourcefulness his role as a steward required when the young man in Mimi's life entered and murmured romantically that there was something unusual in the air tonight.

RICHARD WATTS JR., *Post*

Coward's humorous scorn is too entertaining to have a serious love story get in its way. It does get in the way, too. It was reported when *Sail Away* was having its pre-Broadway tryout that an entire sub-plot dealing with a romance [between Jean Fenn—who was co-starred with Stritch—and William Hutt] was cut out, and, after enduring the two romantic love affairs that still comprise the serious part of the narrative, the imagination reels from the thought of sitting through three of them.

```
BROADWAY SCORECARD / perfs: 167 / $: −

  rave     favorable     mixed     unfavorable     pan

              5             1                         1
```

ST. LOUIS WOMAN

a musical play, with music by Harold Arlen; lyrics by Johnny Mercer; book by Arna Bontemps and Countee Cullen, from their 1933 dramatization of Bontemps's 1931 novel *God Sends Sunday*

directed by Rouben Mamoulian (replacing Lemuel Ayers); choreographed by Charles Walters (replacing Anthony Tudor)
produced by Edward Gross
with Harold Nicholas, Ruby Hill (replacing Muriel Rahn), Pearl Bailey, Fayard Nicholas, Rex Ingram, and June Hawkins
opened March 30, 1946   Martin Beck Theatre

JOHN CHAPMAN, *Daily News*

The best Negro musical in many seasons, and the best new musical of this season up to this late date. Mr. Arlen is one of the dwindling number of songsmiths who still believe that a man should turn out a tune, even if he has to steal if from himself, and Mr. Mercer is a lyricist who can work up a mess of words which is neither arty nor smarty, but just right. In the main *St. Louis Woman* is a pleasure—I think, because every number is a number. Each scene, each song, has been presented as though it was designed to be the best of the evening. I suppose much of the credit for this must go to Rouben Mamoulian, the director. Mr. Mamoulian is at his best when he is handling the movement of groups, and in *St. Louis Woman* he has three chances for spacious effects. The first is the first-act finale—a cakewalk contest in a ballroom, in which various Negro couples compete by dancing for the huge prize cake. Mamoulian's second chance comes with the second-act curtain, a funeral scene, in which some of his old *Porgy and Bess* [1935] technique is useful. And the third is the third-act curtain, an exciting and intricate spectacle of a crowd watching a race from outside the fence.

ROBERT GARLAND, *Journal-American*

St. Louis Woman would be better if it got a move on. And everything would be lovely—lovelier than it was, at any rate—if the story didn't keep getting in the way. It's a foolish story at best. And when, along about the middle of the second act, Biglow Brown [Rex Ingram] gets shot and dies, *St. Louis Woman* gets shot and dies along with him. The book is its own worst opponent, a graceless tripper-upper. *St. Louis Woman* is all dressed up and rarin' to go. Only it goes down hill all evening. . . . Pearl Bailey, who came up from the Village Vanguard to dance and sing in the USO, will be remembered after *St. Louis Woman* is gone. Hers were the opening night ovations. *St. Louis Woman*'s woman is Pearl.

LOUIS KRONENBERGER, *PM*

It runs quite sadly downhill, and doesn't as a whole come off. It is not a musical comedy; it has very little dancing, no chorus lines, no regulation production numbers. The burden of the evening rests on the story, as told in words and music; and the story cannot

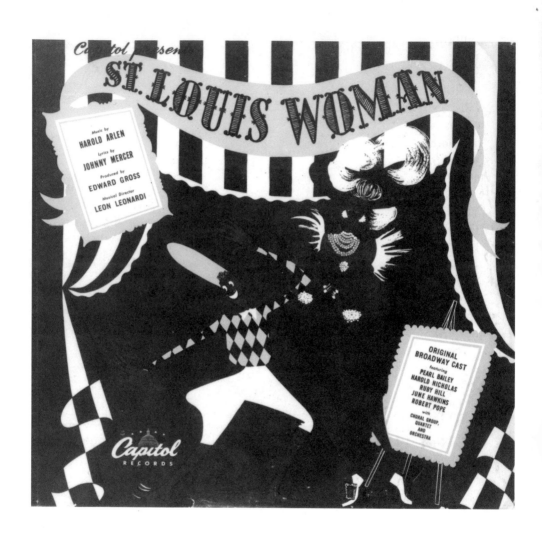

Pint-sized jockey Li'l Augie (Harold Nicholas) taps while his St. Louis Woman *(Ruby Hill) keeps him in tow.*

586

stand up under it. For the story is obvious and commonplace, with a certain folk-operatic flavor, but without the proper operatic sell and excitement. It is an all-Negro period piece, in spots a "blues" piece, and it is made tedious from being spun out to excessive length, and made trivial from being glazed with musical-comedy icing. A real musical play would have made fewer compromises. And though the book is the work of two very reputable Negro writers, one questions whether the kind of glib characterization it falls back on, the kind of stock humor and melodrama, is in the Negro's best interest. Whether so or not, the triteness and long-windedness of the story prove dramatically disastrous. It is really when *St. Louis Woman* takes time out from its more serious pursuits that it comes to life. It lets itself bust out dancing only once, but then it breaks into a fine, happy cakewalk contest ["Cakewalk Your Lady"] that has that blend of humor and style which makes the cakewalk one of the really great folk dances. The show rations its fun very skimpily, but when it lets Pearl Bailey sing a couple of sexy songs in her lusty, half-innocent, half-insinuating way, gaiety sweeps onto the stage. The finale of the show, too—though a descent into pure musical comedy—has real humor and freshness. But the show has bounce only at intervals—and then only by snubbing its more serious intentions.

LEWIS NICHOLS, *Times*

There are some nice things in *St. Louis Woman*, but unfortunately there are not enough of them. Like Little Augie, its leading gentleman, the new musical play is troubled by a curse, in this case the plot. With a Negro company which quite probably could dance its way to heaven, and with costumes and the outward air of a carnival, *St. Louis Woman* prefers to remain conversational. No doubt the basic trouble is that it never fully decides what it wishes to be. Presumably the original design was to make a folk play of it, something on the order of *Porgy and Bess*. When Augie's friends are dancing and singing, it is at times good musical comedy—but then it remembers its more serious purpose, and returns to the plot. It is a hybrid affair, and unfortunate. . . . A young lady named Pearl Bailey can sing a song so that it stays sung; although she is not imitating, her style is roughly on the order of Ethel Waters's. No one expects Mr. Arlen to write a "Stormy Weather" every time he goes to the piano, but in truth his score is not his best. An occasional air is catchy, but there are no great novelties. The blending of composer, lyricist, and singer is reached completely only twice, when Miss Bailey cries down "Legalize My Name" and "A Woman's Prerogative."

BURTON RASCOE, *World-Telegram*

I enjoyed *St. Louis Woman* so much that, when the final curtain descended I felt I should have liked to see the whole thing all over again. *St. Louis Woman* is not to be compared to *Carousel* [1945] any more than *The Clouds* is to be compared to *Medea*; but if comparisons are in order, *St. Louis Woman* is much better than *Carmen Jones* [1943] or *Porgy and Bess*, both all-Negro musicals and both, in their separate ways, very good.

VERNON RICE, *Post*

Producers have nightmares about the kind of misfortunes that have dogged *St. Louis Woman* since it first went into rehearsal. That it did open at all was probably as much of a surprise to producer Edward Gross as to anybody else, and the news that the musical is entertaining, and at times exciting stuff, will cheer him but little at this point. Among the happenings was a change in the directors after the show went on the road for its pre-Broadway tour. Then a new choreographer was called in as well as a change in the leading lady, with a last minute switch to Ruby Hill, who had the role in the first place. It was probably impossible to keep track of the number of times the book was rewritten. . . . It is at this point Rouben Mamoulian, famed director of the two current hits, *Oklahoma!* [1943] and *Carousel* [1945] enters the scene and becomes the actual hero of the play. From all appearances, he has whittled away the book as much as possible and what is left is very little but a frame upon which he can hang some of his directorial feats. He has given the show such speed that one has hardly time enough to think whether the book is any good or not, nor care. He fills his stage as much as possible and then goes to town with his use of rhythm and picturizations. After one climax is passed, you think it can never be topped by the next one, but it always is. Each scene becomes a challenge, and Mamoulian wins.

Born with a silver spoon in her mouth, this *St. Louis Woman* led an amazingly tortured life. M-G-M's Sam Katz and Arthur Freed provided the entire backing *and* M-G-M star Lena Horne. (The studio had done very well with its 50 percent share of Arlen's *Bloomer Girl* [1944].) Problems arose even before rehearsals started, when N.A.A.C.P. Executive Secretary Walter White denounced the show for "offering roles that detract from the dignity of our race." (*Variety* noted with raised eyebrows that White didn't complain about the Deep South melodrama *Strange Fruit* [1946], which featured miscegenation, lynchings—and White's daughter Jane in the lead.) The uproar caused Horne to withdraw from the project, telling the world that *St. Louis Woman* "sets the Negro back one hundred years, is full of gamblers, no-goods, etc., and I'll never play a part like that." And this was just the beginning. Two days before rehearsals began, librettist Countee Cullen—a noted Harlem poet—died. Lem Ayers, designer of *Oklahoma!* and *Bloomer Girl*, wasn't much of a director and was fired on the road. (He soon turned producer, with *Kiss Me, Kate* [1948].) Rouben Mamoulian might have been able to make some sense of *St. Louis Woman*, but he came in too late and faced insurmountable odds. Finally, at the end of the tryout, star Ruby Hill was fired and replaced by the more experienced Muriel Rahn, of *Carmen Jones*. After three previews in New York, the cast *en masse*—P. Bailey, spokeswoman—refused to perform opening night unless Rahn was fired and Hill reinstated. (What's a producer to do? She was, and she was.) What with one thing and another, some superb Arlen music got lost in the shuffle. The composer later transformed the piece into the "blues opera" *Free and Easy* (1959), which was presented in Amsterdam by the International touring company of *Porgy and Bess*. The dramaturgical problems of 1946 were, unfortunately, augmented rather than solved in the process, and the inclusion of early Arlen blues hits served to weaken the score. *St. Louis Woman* remains a fascinating failure.

A Donaldson Award was won by Pearl Bailey (female debut).

THE SAINT OF BLEECKER STREET

an opera, with words and music by Gian-Carlo Menotti

directed by Gian-Carlo Menotti
produced by Chandler Cowles
with David Poleri, Virginia Copeland, Davis Cunningham, and Gloria Lane

opened December 27, 1954   Broadway Theatre

BROOKS ATKINSON, *Times*

A magnificent theatrical experience, the most powerful drama of the season. Menotti's medium of expression is music, which has passion and glory enough for this simple fable of ordinary people caught up in matters of spirit they can hardly understand. His sense of the theatre has purged the formalities of opera out of his drama and left us with its humanity. The music is Mr. Menotti's tool of expression. But *The Saint of Bleecker Street* is all theatre, too. In a worn corner of this city, Mr. Menotti has found the people and the faith for a superb drama. . . . As in many European theatres, the stage has been raised on an incline that gives Mr. Menotti's stage pictures a completeness that is new to Broadway. Robert Randolph's settings [after paintings by George Tooker], which have been expressively lighted by Jean Rosenthal, are like the backgrounds to old religious paintings, and they serve to set off the figures of the actors like sculpture.

JOHN CHAPMAN, *Daily News*

There can be no doubt now concerning Gian-Carlo Menotti's genius. His three-act opera, *The Saint of Bleecker Street*, is a work of bold and stunning theatrical effectiveness, both as a musical work and as a drama. Chandler Cowles gave it a superb production last evening, a production which does great honor to the American stage. Menotti did it all—he wrote the libretto and the music, did the casting, and directed it. His score is a thing of thrills and surprises—sombre, gentle, gay, and explosive in turn, and imaginatively orchestrated. It is a far richer work than any of the one-act operas Menotti has done, and is wonderful musical theatre. It is the full expression of Menotti's gift for drama.

Winner of the Pulitzer Prize for Music. Winner of the New York Drama Critics' Circle Award. A Tony Award was won by Thomas Schippers (conductor).

BROADWAY SCORECARD / perfs: 92 / $: —

rave	favorable	mixed	unfavorable	pan
3	3		1	

SALLY

a revival of the 1920 musical comedy, with music by Jerome Kern; lyrics mostly by P. G. Wodehouse and Clifford Grey; book by Guy Bolton

directed by Billy Gilbert; choreographed by Richard Barstow
produced by Hunt Stromberg, Jr. and William Berney
with Willie Howard, Bambi Linn, and Bob Shackleton
opened May 6, 1948   Martin Beck Theatre

BROOKS ATKINSON, *Times*

Willie Howard is willing, but the show is weak. He has never had less to do, even during the years when he was not working. Instead of turning the pages of the book, Willie should have tossed it out of the window. He has always had jokes enough for a festive evening in the back of his head.

JOHN CHAPMAN, *Daily News*

Distance has not lent enchantment to Jerome Kern's *Sally*. The space of nearly 27 years in time and three blocks in the city has done regrettable damage to a once-delightful musical. Not even Willie Howard, who is indestructibly and immortally funny, could keep last evening's presentation from being rather dull. If I weren't such a confoundedly old poop, and if I hadn't seen Miss Miller at the New Amsterdam in 1921, I might have had a better time last evening. But I doubt it.

WILLIAM HAWKINS, *World-Telegram*

Sally is a show that was written in a period when musicals were designed to be done with great glamour. They were produced opulently, filled with sensational looking show girls, and starred extraordinarily versatile personalities like Marilyn Miller and Mary Eaton. When you revive one of those shows with none of that glamour, it is pretty thin entertainment.

One of many attempts to revive favorite musicals from the pre-*Oklahoma!* (1943) era. Most were outright failures, excepting the 1945 production of Victor Herbert's *The Red Mill* (1906), which was surprisingly popular with wartime audiences, and the 1946 remounting of *Show Boat* (1927).

BROADWAY SCORECARD / perfs: 36 / $: —

rave	favorable	mixed	unfavorable	pan
	3		4	1

SARATOGA

a musical, with music by Harold Arlen (with Johnny Mercer); lyrics by Johnny Mercer; book by Morton Da Costa, from the 1941 novel *Saratoga Trunk* by Edna Ferber

directed by Morton Da Costa; choreographed by Ralph Beaumont
produced by Robert Fryer
with Howard Keel, Carol Lawrence, Odette Myrtil, Edith King (replacing Jane Darwell), and Carol Brice

opened December 7, 1959   Winder Garden Theatre

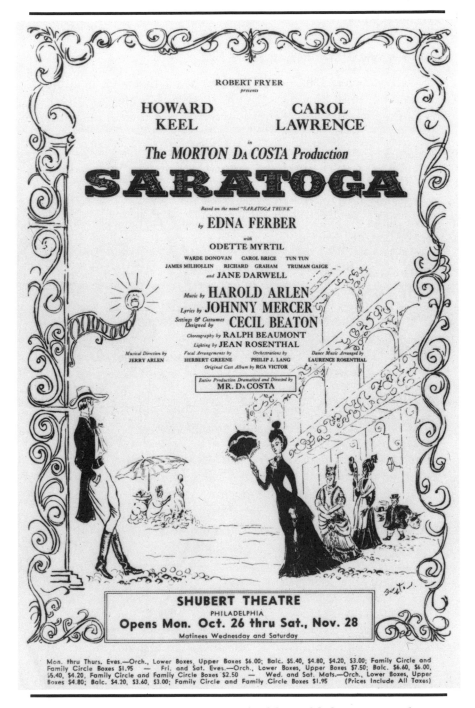

ROBERT FRYER

presents

HOWARD KEEL   CAROL LAWRENCE

in

The MORTON DA COSTA Production

SARATOGA

Based on the novel "SARATOGA TRUNK"

by EDNA FERBER

with

ODETTE MYRTIL

WARDE DONOVAN   CAROL BRICE   TUN TUN
JAMES MILHOLLIN   RICHARD GRAHAM   TRUMAN GAIGE
and JANE DARWELL

Music by HAROLD ARLEN
Lyrics by JOHNNY MERCER
Settings & Costumes Designed by CECIL BEATON
Choreography by RALPH BEAUMONT
Lighting by JEAN ROSENTHAL

| *Musical Direction by*
JERRY ARLEN | *Vocal Arrangements by*
HERBERT GREENE | *Orchestrations by*
PHILIP J. LANG | *Dance Music Arranged by*
LAURENCE ROSENTHAL |

Original Cast Album by RCA VICTOR

Entire Production Dramatized and Directed by
MR. DA COSTA

SHUBERT THEATRE
PHILADELPHIA
Opens Mon. Oct. 26 thru Sat., Nov. 28
Matinees Wednesday and Saturday

Mon. thru Thurs. Eves.—Orch., Lower Boxes, Upper Boxes $6.00; Balc. $5.40, $4.80, $4.20, $3.00; Family Circle and Family Circle Boxes $1.95 — Fri. and Sat. Eves.—Orch., Lower Boxes, Upper Boxes $7.50; Balc. $6.60, $6.00, $5.40, $4.20, Family Circle and Family Circle Boxes $2.50 — Wed. and Sat. Mats.—Orch., Lower Boxes, Upper Boxes $4.80; Balc. $4.20, $3.60, $3.00; Family Circle and Family Circle Boxes $1.95   (Prices Include All Taxes)

Gambler Howard Keel is approached by gold-digging Carol Lawrence and her entourage (Jane Darwell, Carol Brice, and the dwarf Tun Tun). Pre-Broadway credits. (set and costume design by Cecil Beaton)

JOHN CHAPMAN, *Daily News*

Saratoga belongs to Cecil Beaton, being the most beautifully costumed musical I have ever seen. It has a charming cast, including a new and glamorous Carol Lawrence, and several fine-singing songs by Harold Arlen and Johnny Mercer. It also has the most complicated music-show plot since Richard Wagner wrote *Siegfried* (1876). . . . The best of *Saratoga* is in the men's and women's costumes Beaton has designed in the fashion of 1880. If my wife will start wearing bustles and bows and trains all in such wonderful fabrics and colors, I'll go along by wearing top hats, weskits, and toothpick pants. But my wife probably can't afford Beaton as a dressmaker.

WALTER KERR, *Herald Tribune*

I'm sure all hearts lifted at the sound of Harold Arlen's overture at the Winter Garden last evening. I know mine did. The really distressing thing about *Saratoga* is that it might all have been good. The evening is constantly slipping in and out of focus like a tired print of an attractive old film, but whenever the image leaps forward with any clarity you get a strong inkling of the period fun that was possible. . . . No doubt most of the perspiration stems from Mr. Da Costa's book. Mr. Da Costa is an exceedingly efficient and inventive director who seems here to have stumbled onto terrain that is just not his own: as a writer, he has jumbled his exposition, trailed his own plotting, and permitted himself to fall back on patently unconfident jokes. But the gap that counts most comes near the beginning: we are never given time to get near the people we must care about.

RICHARD WATTS JR., *Post*

Saratoga is a large and elaborate musical drama loaded with beauty and talent. The only trouble is it is also weighed down with something less helpful, a very dull and cumbersome libretto. It is a great misfortune, because there is so much to be said for *Saratoga*. For the first half hour or so, everything is wonderful. The general pace and high spirits seemed to promise an evening of joyful contentment. It was only when the beautiful Clio met the handsome Clint Maroon and they started singing about love being like poker that I worried.

Harold Arlen's final musical was a lifeless affair, ill-conceived by a director/librettist without a concept. But there was some mighty special music from Mr. Arlen.

A Tony Award was won by Cecil Beaton (costume designer).

BROADWAY SCORECARD / perfs: 80 / $: —

rave	favorable	mixed	unfavorable	pan
	1		6	

SAY, DARLING

a play with songs, with music by Jule Styne; lyrics by Betty Comden and Adolph Green; book by Richard Bissell, Abe Burrows, and Marian Bissell, from the 1957 satirical novel by Richard Bissell

directed by Abe Burrows; choreographed by Matt Mattox
produced by Jule Styne and Lester Osterman
with David Wayne, Vivian Blaine, Johnny Desmond, Robert Morse, and Matt Mattox

opened April 3, 1958   ANTA Theatre

FRANK ASTON, *World-Telegram & Sun*

Here's one theatregoer who votes major triumphs of the proceedings to Robert Morse. He is amazingly droll as an ineffectual, limp-wristed, over-mannered big shot of the theatre world.

BROOKS ATKINSON, *Times*

How much better it was when it was called *The Pajama Game* [1954]! For *Say, Darling*, billed as "a comedy about a musical," is the end of a cycle. First came Richard Bissell's novel about a middle western pajama factory, entitled *7½ Cents* [1953]. Second, the musical comedy that Mr. Bissell and George Abbott mined out of the novel and called *The Pajama Game*. Third, a novel, called

Say, Darling, which Mr. Bissell wrote about his experiences during the gestation of *The Pajama Game*. Now Mr. Bissell has headed into the last round-up. . . . Bring in George Abbott and they might have ended up with something as uproarious as the show they started with.

ROBERT COLEMAN, *Daily Mirror*

Say, Darling, which zoomed into the ANTA Theatre last evening, is a rib-tickler about inside show business [with] a lot of pertinent and impertinent things to say about the business of which there's no business like. If it's lusty laughs you're looking for, you'll find plenty of them at the ANTA. Here's jet-propelled japery from a sophisticated tap.

WALTER KERR, *Herald Tribune*

The new romp is smart, sassy, and wonderfully funny. What makes the splashily decorated and winningly performed nonsense so steadily entertaining, I think, is the fact that Mr. Bissell is essentially a fraud. With the hay coming up from under his collar, and a yearning for Iowa nights painted all over his face, he likes to pretend that Broadway is an impossible area populated with idiot backers, producers who slide all over grand pianos, song writers with egos higher than their ASCAP ratings, female stars with neither minks on their backs nor morals on their minds, and directors who abhor all the decent things like drinking and smoking but like to play squash. . . . The determined satirists introduce us to a glossy young nincompoop who wears white shoes, paws everybody in the chummiest possible manner, flickers his indolent eyelids as he drops knowing phrases like "I don't like that kind of negative thinking," and generally behaves himself like a land-crab on roller-skates. They call this fellow a producer, and they encourage a brilliantly comic young actor named Robert Morse to shiver his jello shoulders, flip his feet out in front of him as though he had just kicked them off, and look as though he had recently eaten a very distressing blintz every time anybody is rude to him.

JOHN McCLAIN, *Journal-American*

The story of a story that became a musical that became a story that became a musical. A rose is a rose is a rose, and I believe this is a hit is a hit is a hit. I would call *Say, Darling* a big, fat smash.

A satirical show business cartoon. Robert Morse's caricature of the boy producer was amazingly successful, even though Harold Prince was relatively unknown at the time. Johnny Desmond was also properly overbearingly obnoxious, as a thinly veiled Richard Adler. The songs in the not-so-good show-within-the-show were supposed to sound like rather awful pastiches of vulgar pop music, and they did; which, unfortunately, counted against *Say, Darling* as satisfying entertainment. Better you should read the novel. You'll love it, darling.

BROADWAY SCORECARD / perfs: 332 / $: −

rave	favorable	mixed	unfavorable	pan
2	2	2	1	

THE SEVEN LIVELY ARTS

a musical extravaganza, with music and lyrics by Cole Porter; ballet music by Igor Stravinsky; sketches by Moss Hart, George S. Kaufman, Ben Hecht, and others

directed by Hassard Short; sketches directed by Philip Loeb; choreographed by Jack Donohue; ballets choreographed by Anton Dolin
produced by Billy Rose
with Beatrice Lillie, Bert Lahr, Benny Goodman, Alicia Markova, Anton Dolin, and Doc Rockwell

opened December 7, 1944   Ziegfeld Theatre

JOHN CHAPMAN, *Daily News*

Well, thank goodness, THAT'S over with! Now we can all relax. Billy Rose opened *The Seven Lively Arts* at the Ziegfeld Theatre last night. For more than one reason this will be a news report rather than a notice—if there's a difference—for the $24 tickets, the colossal buildup, the free champagne served in the basement, and the presence of the dressiest, pushingest, celebrated-est, damnedest audience in many years made the premiere a news event rather than a show. Billy Rose is on his own, and there will be no mention here but this of the late Florenz Ziegfeld, and no comparisons. Billy bought the theatre, made it clean and beautiful again. He engaged talent ranging from Salvador Dali to Igor Stravinsky, with a detour to [monologist] Doc Rockwell. He spent money like a Persian prince on Bel Geddes sets, Mary Grant costumes, girls who can sing, girls who look beautiful, writers who can write, and ushers who can ush. There is so much in Mr. Rose's show that it can hardly be catalogued and the wonder is that it can be played. It skips from a jam session by Benny Goodman and his crew to a rigidly classical dance by two of the top ballet artists, Markova and Dolin; it runs from glittering production numbers to simple blackouts, and Cole Porter takes the music from love songs to blazing jungle numbers.

ROBERT GARLAND, *Journal-American*

Last night at Sixth Ave. and 54th St., Billy Rose passed a miracle. He turned back the cloth and, abracadabra, there was no World War II. If seeing were believing, there never would be! Once again, as in the good old days, the Ziegfeld was the most beautiful theatre on Manhattan, an audience was all dressed up for the evening, a long line of limousines was waiting at the curb, a star-studded service was a prop for comedy, and champagne flowed like water. Seats for last night's first performance were $24 each, when you could get them. Champagne was free, and you could get all of that you wanted. And, as if wine for everybody were not enough, there were also paintings by Salvador Dali, depicting the seven lively arts and what he would do with them. Along with the entertainment, of which they were an offspring, last night's high hat, low neck congregation found them vastly entertaining. The lack is doubtless mine. . . . Somewhere in this *Seven Lively Arts* a show of shows is buried. Last night it didn't happen to be forthcoming. There's even more gold in them there ills up at the Ziegfeld. Now that the current conflict has been pushed miraculously into the future, dig down and get it, Billy.

BURTON RASCOE, *World-Telegram*

The lavishness of the production is simply breath-taking. You never saw such a dream-world as the one Norman Bel Geddes (sets) and Mary Grant (costumes) have provided as the background for this revue. Fragonard pastorals and Guerin visions of ancient Balbec are reproduced in heroic size on the stage, peopled by exquisitely beautiful girls wearing such fabrics as you can only associate with Marco Polo's tales of the pleasure dome of Kublai Khan. . . . Musically (though not lyrically) Cole Porter seems to have lost his inspiration. The score is serviceable without being distinguished or memorable, only one song—["Is It the Girl (or Is It the Gown?)"]—having a catchy melody. But this musical deficiency is hardly noticeable in a show otherwise so opulent in all other respects—so enormously funny and voluptuous to the eye. For the reopening of the Ziegfeld under his aegis, Billy Rose has shot the works—about $2,000,000 for the theatre and production—and it looks as though he were going to live up to his slogan, "The public be served."

WILELLA WALDORF, *Post*

It is something like one of those all-star benefit performances where excerpts from *Charlot's Revue* (1924) are sandwiched in between the stage show from the Paramount Theatre and an extravaganza in which a lot of old-fashioned girls dressed in pink swing out over the audiences on strands of roses decorated with colored lights, while a low comedian indulges in a monologue about the female form divine and somebody presents gems from *Aida*, with elephants. In case this this sounds a trifle confused, it is a fair example of how we felt on leaving the Ziegfeld Theatre at ten minutes before midnight last night. . . . Miss Lillie's sketches were written for her by Moss Hart and most of them are content to give her a chance to show how funny she can be without much help from an author. The Porter score in general is undistinguished and reminiscent of so many earlier hits by the same composer that he seems at times to be plagiarizing his own collected works.

Billy Rose, in battle with Mike Todd for the mantle of Showman of the Day, bought the Ziegfeld and overproduced this extravaganza.

(Music from Porter, Stravinsky, and Benny Goodman?) The staggering array of talents seemed staggered by it all—except Lillie and Lahr, of course. Walter Kerr, who had not yet become a critic, offered me a couple of his favorite moments so I pass them on: Lillie vigorously swinging the key to her hotel room—an *enormous* key tied to the end of a chiffon handkerchief—at the gents in the audience throughout a number "in one"; and Bert Lahr, as a member of the stagehands union, asking plaintively if he's expected to carry a very small chair *alone?* ("That man was appreciated in his time," comments Mr. Kerr, "but not enough.")

A Donaldson Award was won by Beatrice Lillie (actress).

BROADWAY SCORECARD / perfs: 183 / $: −

rave	favorable	mixed	unfavoráble	pan
2	2	2	1	1

SEVENTEEN

a musical comedy, with music by Walter Kent; lyrics by Kim Gannon; book by Sally Benson, from the 1916 novel by Booth Tarkington

directed by Hassard Short; book directed by Richard Whorf; choreographed by Dania Krupska
produced by Milton Berle, Sammy Lambert, and Bernie Foyer
with Kenneth Nelson, Anne Crowley, Helen Wood, Ellen Mc-Cown, and Dick Kallman

opened June 21, 1951   Broadhurst Theatre

JOHN CHAPMAN, *Daily News*

The musical comedy business is getting so elaborate with its settings by artists, direction by artists, lighting by artists, and acting by more artists—not to mention financial backing by those greatest of all artists, the people who have a little money left over— that mere tunes are of small importance. And lyrics just don't count at all. So it is with *Seventeen*. Why go to the enormous trouble and expense of presenting a musical comedy if the music isn't the best part of the show? No hit in the history of this curious business ever succeeded on anything other than its songs, and I failed to hear any last evening. The composer and lyrist turned up one number out of their total batch of 13 that interested me—and it sounded so much like Disney's "Zip-A-Dee-Doo-Dah" [by Allie Wrubel and Ray Gilbert, from the 1946 *Song of the South*] that I felt embarrassed for the authors. I guess it must be hard to write songs. Hardly anybody is doing it these days, except a precious handful of old men like Porter, Berlin, Hammerstein, and Rodgers and one comparatively young fellow, Loesser.

A low-keyed, moderately pleasant summer show coproduced by Milton Berle, of all people. *Hello, Lola*, a 1926 musicalization of the Tarkington novel, was greeted by critic Alan Dale of the *New York American* with: "*Hello, Lola*. Goodbye, Lola." Strangely enough, and totally off the subject, Alan Jay Lerner admits that he was named after this very same Alan Dale (née Alfred J. Cohen). A drama critic, imagine!

BROADWAY SCORECARD / perfs: 189 / $: −

rave	favorable	mixed	unfavorable	pan
	2	1	2	2

SEVENTH HEAVEN

a musical comedy, with music by Victor Young; lyrics by Stella Unger; book by Victor Wolfson and Stella Unger, from the 1922 melodrama by Austin Strong

directed by John C. Wilson; choreographed by Peter Gennaro
produced by Gant Gaither and William Bacher
with Gloria DeHaven, Ricardo Montalban, Kurt Kasznar (replacing Paul Hartman), Robert Clary, Chita Rivera, and Beatrice Arthur (replacing Fifi D'Orsay)

opened May 26, 1955   ANTA Theatre

JOHN CHAPMAN, *Daily News*

A musical version of *Seventh Heaven* has been talked about for many years, and now we have it. Now that we have it, there isn't much to do about it. . . . I don't think Miss DeHaven or Mr. Montalban has a song that anybody could remember but themselves.

WALTER KERR, *Herald Tribune*

Evelyn Waugh once remarked of a certain film company that it employed a group of experts to study each new property bought by the studio, isolate the precise quality that made it successful, and kill it. I'm terribly afraid that something like that has happened to *Seventh Heaven*. The one thing that *Seventh Heaven* has had all the years—in memory, anyway—is a fond, schmaltzy innocence, an honest and wistful and appealing grade of corn. This is the quality that librettists Victor Wolfson and Stella Unger have apparently been afraid of, and they have pared it away to make room for a commodity often referred to as "sex." For all its determination to seem new-hat and reasonably red-hot, *Seventh Heaven* does not really capture the sort of sizzle that has been known to drive good family men to fatal distraction. Its zing is a little too calculated, and a little too mechanical, for that. What it does do is smear just enough mascara on its simple little face to keep you from believing in stars, garrets, a hero who wants to be a street-cleaner, and a girl who meets him in dreamland every night at eleven o'clock. . . . Chita Rivera is wonderfully explosive in a series of much too similar high-kicking routines.

FRANK QUINN, *Daily Mirror*

Chita Rivera is a gal of flashy, bold personality. This long-stemmed miss is a thrilling dancer who struts and slinks like a panther. She does a howl of a routine with her calypso can-can. She is magnetic and catches the eye with her every movement.

Related note: Peter Gennaro, the ex-"Steam Heat" dancer making his choreographic bow, discovered two dancing ladies whom he took along for important spots in *West Side Story* (1957): Chita Rivera, who had already made a small splash in *Mr. Wonderful*

(1956), and her *Seventh Heaven* understudy Lee Becker. Gennaro and Becker were two of four dancers from Harold Prince musicals who went on to choreograph future Prince shows. Gennaro, from *The Pajama Game* (1954), did *West Side* and *Fiorello!* (1959); Carol Haney, also from *Pajama Game*, did *She Loves Me* (1963); Lee Becker Theodore did *Baker Street* (1965) and *Flora, the Red Menace* (1965); and Becker's *West Side* replacement, Patricia Birch, did *A Little Night Music* (1973), *Candide* (1974), and *Pacific Overtures* (1976).

BROADWAY SCORECARD / perfs: 44 / $: −

rave	favorable	mixed	unfavorable	pan
1	1	2	2	1

SHANGRI-LA

a musical comedy, with music by Harry Warren; lyrics by Jerome Lawrence and Robert E. Lee, additional lyrics by Sheldon Harnick; book by James Hilton, Jerome Lawrence, and Robert E. Lee (with Luther Davis, unbilled), from Hilton's 1933 novel *Lost Horizon*

directed by Albert Marre (replacing Marshall Jamison); choreographed by Donald Saddler
produced by Robert Fryer and Lawrence Carr
with Dennis King (replacing Lew Ayres), Shirley Yamaguchi (replacing Susan Cabot), Martyn Green, Harold Lang, Jack Cassidy, Alice Ghostley, and Carol Lawrence

opened June 13, 1956   Winter Garden Theatre

JOHN CHAPMAN, *Daily News*

Lost Horizon was a charming and imaginative piece of work. Most of the people in charge of converting this fantasy into a musical called *Shangri-La* have gone to extraordinary lengths to de-imagine it. Except for the sorcery of Peter Larkin's lovely setting, *Shangri-La* is earthbound. Instead of transporting an audience to an idyllic Never-Never Land in Tibet, it dumps the audience on a hot curbstone in Tin Pan Alley. It is difficult for me to make an offhand decision as to which is the more ordinary—the music by Harry Warren or the lyrics by Jerome Lawrence and Robert E. Lee. *Shangri-La* left me as cold as a penguin's toes. . . . Alice Ghostley is a good comedienne, but her material is ghastly.

WALTER KERR, *Herald Tribune*

If you'd been having a bad time of it in our modern civilization and you were suddenly dumped into an exceedingly peaceful valley filled with attractive girls, quite a few art treasures, and no immediate prospect of either death or taxation, what would you do? I imagine you'd yawn, stretch, relax, get your feet off the ground, and gently twiddle your thumbs. Well, that's what everybody in *Shangri-La* did Wednesday night, and it's rather deadly. "I had the strangest feeling," remarks Dennis King shortly after his arrival, "that the world had stopped turning on its axis." And so, as the evening wore on, did I.

JOHN McCLAIN, *Journal-American*

For a show dealing with a delightful Never-Never Land, *Shangri-La* has had something less than a Utopian history: Several important members of the cast left after the opening in Boston; the director was replaced, and the authors finally stopped the proceedings and did an almost entire re-write. Yesterday afternoon, just before its Winter Garden opening, a scenic mountain weighing something in the neighborhood of a ton fell over backstage.

James Hilton was, perhaps, the most fortunate of the *Shangri-La* group—he died in 1954. Historical note: at the opening night party, juvenile Jack Cassidy introduced his pal Jerry Bock to *Shangri-La* ghost-lyricist Sheldon Harnick.

BROADWAY SCORECARD / perfs: 21 / $: −

rave	favorable	mixed	unfavorable	pan
	2		3	2

SHE LOVES ME

a musical comedy, with music by Jerry Bock; lyrics by Sheldon Harnick; book by Joe Masteroff, from the 1937 Hungarian comedy *Parfumerie* by Miklos Laszlo

directed by Harold Prince; choreographed by Carol Haney
produced by Harold Prince in association with Lawrence N. Kasha and Philip C. McKenna
with Barbara Cook, Daniel Massey, Barbara Baxley, Jack Cassidy, Nathaniel Frey (replacing Sig Arno), and Ludwig Donath

opened April 23, 1963   Eugene O'Neill Theatre

JOHN CHAPMAN, *Daily News*

So charming, so deft, so light, and so right that it makes all the other music-shows in the big Broadway shops look like clodhoppers. This was an evening in which everything came together—click!—except for a few moments when a pesky traveler scrim got stuck and stopped the show in its tracks. By now the audience was so solidly with *She Loves Me* that it took the mishap as a merry interlude and applauded the unseen stagehand who finally wrenched the curtain loose and moved it offstage. Jerry Bock and Sheldon Harnick have written music and lyrics for the season's gayest, smartest score. The songs keep dancing and swirling out as if Harold Hasting's intimate, almost all-string orchestra were blowing shimmering soap bubbles up from the pit. The orchestrations are among the best ever written by Don Walker.

WALTER KERR, *Herald Tribune*

The real trouble isn't that the plot is pin-sized. It's that librettist Joe Masteroff hasn't told it very well. He sets up the love letters, but rather vaguely and in part rather late. He sets up the fact that both come to work in the same shop and almost instantly begin to quarrel, but the things that prod them into tiffs and spats and crosspatch scratching are pretty glancing and uncertain, too. Masteroff doesn't so much spin out his fable, as sieve it with odd lumps turning up whenever he doesn't dare move it one whit faster. As it happens, some of the lumps are interesting, if irrelevant. . . . Mention of "Try Me" brings up the matter of the kind of lyrics, and the scattered musical line, that Jerry Bock and Sheldon Harnick are

HAROLD PRINCE
in association with
LAWRENCE N. KASHA & PHILIP C. McKENNA
presents

BARBARA COOK   DANIEL MASSEY
BARBARA BAXLEY in

SHE LOVES ME
The Happiest New Musical

with
JACK CASSIDY · SIG ARNO · RALPH WILLIAMS
JO WILDER · WOOD ROMOFF · GINO CONFORTI
also starring
LUDWIG DONATH

Book by   Music by   Lyrics by
JOE MASTEROFF   JERRY BOCK   SHELDON HARNICK
(Based on a Play by **MIKLOS LASZLO**)

Musical Numbers Staged by   Settings and Lighting by   Costumes by
CAROL HANEY   WILLIAM & JEAN ECKART   PATRICIA ZIPPRODT

Musical Direction   Orchestrations by   Incidental Music Arranged by
HAROLD HASTINGS   DON WALKER   JACK ELLIOTT

Production Directed by
HAROLD PRINCE

OPENS TUESDAY, APRIL 23
EUGENE O'NEILL THEATRE
230 WEST 49th STREET, NEW YORK CITY   -:-   CIrcle 6-8870
Matinees Wednesday and Saturday
PRICES: Every Eve.—Orch. $9.60; Mezz. $7.50; Balc. $6.90, $5.75, $4.60
Wed. Mat.—Orch. $5.75; Mezz. $4.80; Balc. $4.30, $3.00
Sat. Mat.—Orch. $6.25; Mezz. $5.75; Balc. $4.80, $3.60

Yet another great logo from Morrow, for Broadway's "Happiest New Musical." Pre-Broadway credits. (drawing by Tom Morrow)

pursuing with perhaps too much stubborness. The show is not without attractive melodies; but it is heavily laden with the sort of number that goes out of its way to peddle plot information. The result often seems less a snatch of lyrical feeling than a blackboard diagram, with odd clauses shooting off everywhere and defying a man's ear to reassemble them into a pleasing pattern. Prose, that's what these things are—and as they creep into the love songs, they don't make the love songs more winning. *She Loves Me* has, at the very least, the courage to cling to its small story and to pursue its methods resolutely. No doubt it should be respected for that. But the clinging itself is clumsily managed, making things seem a little shopworn around the corner. [*The Shop Around the Corner* was a 1940 Hollywood adaptation of the Laszlo play.]

NORMAN NADEL, *World-Telegram & Sun*

A musical play with which everyone can fall in love. *She Loves Me* (aptly named) is that rare theatrical jewel, an intimate musical that affectionately enfolds an audience instead of shouting it down. It is dear, charming, and wholeheartedly romantic. The music does not thrust itself forward. Instead, it gracefully embellishes the action, accents the speech, adds sparkle to the humor, and transcends the power of words when the mood is romantic. It is, most of the way, an integral part of the play—which is a musical excellence in itself. . . . The expression "sings her heart out" certainly applies to Miss Cook, who has both the heart and voice to do it. Her clear soprano is not only one of the finest vocal instruments in the contemporary musical theatre, but it conveys all the vitality, brightness, and strength of her feminine young personality, which is plenty. Daniel Massey is not in Miss Cook's league musically. He is, however, easily her match as a performer, adding skill to what she seems to achieve by instinct. As Georg, he fills out a character with exceptional thoroughness for any play, and notably for a musical. These two, along with everyone else in the company, owe a great deal to lyricist Sheldon Harnick. He has put their love affair into lyric words, just as Bock has put it into music. "Ice Cream," sung by Miss Cook, is the crowning glory of this music-lyric combination.

HOWARD TAUBMAN, *Times*

A bonbon of a musical has been put on display, and it should delight who knows how many a sweet tooth. *She Loves Me* has been assembled by confectioners who know and respect their metier. They have found the right ingredients of sugar and raisins and nuts to add to their fluffy dough and have created a taste surprise, like an inspired *dobos torta* one would encounter in a romantic Budapest of long ago. The humors of *She Loves Me* are gentle rather than robust. The characters are the familiar figures of happily bittersweet fairy tales; yet they have individuality and charm. You keep thinking that you cannot digest an array of desserts, no matter how attractive and tasty they are, but you find yourself relishing nearly all of them. The secret is this: Everyone concerned with *She Loves Me* has played fair with the basic ingredients. The songs not only capture the gay, light spirit of the story but also add an extra dimension of magic to it. For this musical has not been put together with tape and glue and memories of bygone successes. The songs have not been added awkwardly to provide a star with a turn or the show with a production number. Who besides the songwriters should be credited with the appealing manner in which they have been integrated in the production? Certainly Don Walker, for the brightness of his arrangements, particularly if he is the man responsible for the clever part writing. To Harold Prince, who staged *She Loves Me* with so much inventive gaiety, belongs some of the credit here, too.

A bejewelled music box—or should we say candy box?—of a show, with the best score of the sixties. The commercial failure of *She Loves Me* was partially due, as producer/director Prince has suggested, to managerial miscalculation: the "perfect" theatre for the piece was too small to support it financially. But it was also too quiet, too romantic, "too good for the average man" of its day. That doesn't make it any less superb, with major credit due the Messrs. Bock and Harnick. Incidental matrimonial note: during the preparation of *She Loves Me*, Harnick himself was briefly a newlywed (briefly new and briefly wed). His better half: Elaine May, and the two must have made an even more eloquently loquacious couple than dear Amalia and Georg.

A Tony Award was won by Jack Cassidy (supporting actor).

BROADWAY SCORECARD / perfs: 320 / $: −

rave	favorable	mixed	unfavorable	pan
4	2	1		

SHINBONE ALLEY

a musical fantasy, with music by George Kleinsinger; lyrics by Joe Darion; book by Joe Darion and Mel Brooks, based on Kleinsinger and Darion's 1954 opera *archy and mehitabel*, from the stories by Don Marquis

director unbilled (Norman Lloyd, replaced by Sawyer Falk); choreographed by Rod Alexander (with Arthur Mitchell)
produced by Peter Lawrence
with Eartha Kitt, Eddie Bracken, Erik Rhodes, George S. Irving, Jacques D'Amboise, and Allegra Kent

opened April 13, 1957   Broadway Theatre

BROOKS ATKINSON, *Times*

After wading in musical banality for quite a long time, it is pleasant to meet a show that at least aims at something fresh. *Shinbone Alley* falls short of the target; but George Kleinsinger, who composed the music, and Joe Darion and Mel Brooks, who wrote the libretto, have tried to use the theatre to create a world of sardonic fantasy. If you are wondering how a coherent show could be made out of the "archy and mehitabel" verses, you are on the right track. Although the authors have arranged some odd and interesting episodes, they have not been able to pull the work together. Mr. Kleinsinger is the man who has had most fun and been most successful. He has improvised an animal and insect world out of music with humor, drollery, street tunes, and jukebox pandemonium. The world of cats is ideal for ballet. In Jacques D'Amboise, *Shinbone Alley* has a brilliant dancer, who leads a ferocious cat-and-dog scramble. With Allegra Kent, another gifted dancer, he puts a foundation under the vagrant second act with a beautifully designed number labeled "Vacant Lot Ballet." Rod Al-

Eartha, as mehitabel the cat, looks Kittenish as Eddie Bracken's cockroach archie takes notes. (drawing by Al Hirschfeld)

exander has staged the ballets admirably. Too bad *Shinbone Alley* does not really come alive as a stage composition. For the point of view is sly and original, and a good deal of the stage work is subtle, agile, and imaginative.

JOHN CHAPMAN, *Daily News*

It brightens the musical comedy scene like a lightning bug. It is original, it is witty, and it bubbles over with the happiest score in town. *Shinbone Alley* is as unstereotyped as a show can get.

WALTER KERR, *Herald Tribune*

I haven't the faintest idea of how you could turn the enchanting "archy and mehitabel" stories of Don Marquis into a Broadway musical comedy—and neither does anyone at the Broadway. This must be said in sorrow, because the often talented folk of *Shinbone Alley* have gone about their work with such sincere and wistful good will. They have even hit a live image here and there. If, for instance, the whole mock-sorrowful saga could somehow have been given the sharp black-and-white lines of a mountainous fireplace [designed by Eldon Elder] before which Eartha Kitt briefly sits sipping milk through a straw, the miracle might conceivably have happened. For a moment, as the lights go up on a mournfully housebroken "mehitabel" listening with positive revulsion to decent people calling her "kitty," the blend of a curled-up figure and a universe scrawled in crayon is just right. Or, taking quite a different tack, the authors and designers summon up a kind of wild Disney raffishness for the time it takes to sing a Shinbone lullaby ("mother dear will be hustling") to a basket of highly illegitimate pussy-cats nesting in an ash-can. Once again the possible form of a possible show hovers suggestively, and fleetingly, over the stage. Miss Kitt, as the feline who was known to walk out on a tomcat just once (he was dead), strolls away from her unwelcome litter of kittens with a surly and discouraged "I see them" that summarizes in a bored sentence the immemorial way of all flesh (female or feline).

archy and mehitabel, a so-called "back alley opera," was successfully recorded in 1954 by Carol Channing, Eddie Bracken, and

David Wayne. This led to an expanded, live version; but how do you do a stage musical in which the main characters are cats?

○○
○   BROADWAY SCORECARD / perfs: 49 / $: −   ○

rave	favorable	mixed	favorable	pan
	2		4	1

SHOW BOAT

a revival of the 1927 musical, with music by Jerome Kern; book and lyrics by Oscar Hammerstein 2nd, from the novel by Edna Ferber

staged by Hassard Short; book directed by Oscar Hammerstein 2nd; choreographed by Helen Tamiris
produced by Jerome Kern and Oscar Hammerstein 2nd (for M-G-M)
with Jan Clayton, Ralph Dumke, Carol Bruce, Charles Fredericks, Kenneth Spencer, and Buddy Ebsen

opened January 5, 1946   Ziegfeld Theatre

JOHN CHAPMAN, *Daily News*

It is what every musical should be—and no other has ever been. *Show Boat* deserves about every superlative that can be found on a typewriter keyboard. It is a musical play in the grand manner, housed in the perfect theatre for it. As a production, it is beautiful. As an evening of music it is thrilling. You who have seen *Show Boat* before—go see it again; see it and live again. You lucky others who have not seen it, and who know it only as a dance set or a radio program—go see it, and discover what it is like to attend a musical play in the grand manner.

ROBERT GARLAND, *Journal-American*

Author-producer-director Hammerstein requests that the "presentation" be referred to as a "new production" rather than as a "revival." It seems that the word revival carries with it uncalled-for connotations of "warmed-over theatrical fare." Very well, then. In this new production, *Show Boat* continues to suffer from its old "last-act trouble," as its first producer, Florenz Ziegfeld, used to call it. The operetta still starts a story it never really finishes. From the moment Magnolia and Gaylord are married at the conclusion of the opening stanza, the Mississippi River saga hides behind its music and sings its plot around in all directions. A midway, a music hall, a convent, a boarding house, and, at long last, back to the levee again. . . . The immortal Jerome Kern score maintains its magical appeal. It was, it is, it always will be *Show Boat*'s crowning glory.

LOUIS KRONENBERGER, *PM*

No, our memories didn't lie. *Show Boat* is great stuff. The years have done very little to it; only here and there, in fact, have they caught up with it. As musicals go, it is full-bodied and full-flavored. The story may be all schmaltz and corn and hokum, full of romantic trappings and sentimental gestures and melodramatic flourishes. But it is all of a piece, and it holds your interest.

WARD MOREHOUSE, *Sun*

Show Boat is still magnificent. It was in 1927 and it was in 1932 [when revived], and it always will be. Here's a musical play with beauty, pathos, nostalgia, panoramic pattern, and a Jerome Kern score that will endure for as long as the theatre exists. If the story now runs down and runs somewhat to patness in its final phases, if portions of the narrative now seem a bit labored and if a few of the present players are not up to the form of their predecessors, these faults are but minor. The Kern music is still overpoweringly beautiful. The production is stunning. Jan Clayton is a fragile and lovely Magnolia, and Carol Bruce, in a role forever to be associated with the melancholy and legendary Helen Morgan, comes through wonderfully. Saturday evening was Kern's, as it should have been and as Oscar Hammerstein wanted it to be. It is indeed ironic that the late composer was denied the privilege of being present as his music held a brilliant premiere audience in its spell. The town is in the debt of Oscar Hammerstein for bringing *Show Boat* back.

BURTON RASCOE, *World-Telegram*

I didn't think that anyone could ever take Helen Morgan's place as Julie. I was wrong about that. Carol Bruce carries the torch with splendor. As she takes her encore, standing forlorn against the cornice of the white proscenium, white lights blazing upon her, she is glorified, sublimely plastered. Patience itself, poignantly smiling at grief. Nor shall I ever forget a little touch—her exit after she has painfully climbed down from the piano, drunk and disorganized, having finished singing "Bill." The droop of her shoulders is death in life; her sag is all we ever need to know of defeat. . . . Hitherto I have loved Lucinda Ballard (as a costume designer) this side of idolatry. I think I may be excused if I not only dissemble my love but seem, this morning, to kick her downstairs. For I have never seen such garish, preposterous, inappropriate costumes in a musical since *Memphis Bound* [1945].

WILELLA WALDORF, *Post*

Nothing is easier, of course, than harking back to the original performance with a tear in the eye and a sob in the throat, and pronouncing the new version a disappointment. This we have no intention of doing, partly because we were never among those starry-eyed theatregoers of the twenties who insisted that the old *Show Boat* was the greatest musical show of this century and the last. *Show Boat* has always seemed to us a decorative, somewhat overdone extravaganza, distinguished by a really superior Jerome Kern score. The story which Mr. Hammerstein dug out of Edna Ferber's novel had the virtue of being somewhat less hackneyed twenty years ago than it is now, and so had the music, but even back in 1927 we found some of the goings-on at the Ziegfeld rather on the ponderous side, a bit oversentimental and even rather foolish at times in their down-to-the-depths, up-to-the-heights leaping from success to failure, failure to success, etc., with the old folks done up in the end in a bevy of white wigs. . . . *Show Boat* has always been noted more for sentiment than humor and Ralph Dumke's Cap'n Andy is very 1946 musical comedy indeed, meaning that it is not very funny.

This revival was posthumously coproduced by composer Jerome Kern, who died on November 11, 1945, prior to the start of rehearsals. The *Show Boat* libretto was already beginning to look old-fashioned in 1946; a couple of the critics tell us that it was a bit creaky in 1927. The score, though, was still golden, and so it remains! Critic Wilella Waldorf collapsed after turning in her bad notice—she'd been suffering from a heart ailment—and died on March 12, 1946. She didn't like *Oklahoma!* (1943), *Carmen Jones* (1943), or *Carousel* (1945) either.

In addition to winning the Donaldson Award for Best Musical, Donaldsons were won by Jerome Kern (composer); Oscar Hammerstein 2nd (lyricist; librettist); and Carol Bruce (supporting actress).

BROADWAY SCORECARD / perfs: 417 / $: +

rave	favorable	mixed	unfavorable	pan
4	2	1	1	

SHOW GIRL

an intimate revue, with music and lyrics by Charles Gaynor; sketches by Charles Gaynor and Ernest Chambers

production supervised by Oliver Smith; sketches directed by Charles Gaynor; choreographed by Richard D'Arcy
produced by Oliver Smith, James A. Doolittle, and Charles Lowe
with Carol Channing (Lowe) and Jules Munshin

opened January 12, 1961   Eugene O'Neill Theatre

FRANK ASTON, *World-Telegram & Sun*

Lost in admiration for Carol Channing all through her *Show Girl* last evening, I kept thinking of one word—shaggy. I was fascinated by the lady's oyster-sized eyes, facile mouth, iceberg teeth, and that break-away face which kept hanging out expressions of frightened pleasure over the storms of applause. "Shaggy" probably has a subconscious hookup with the bleached brush serving as the Channing golden tresses. The hair has to be short. She shakes her head so violently that the whip of long locks would break her neck. I hope Miss Channing understands "shaggy" suddenly means talented, hilarious, irresistible, huggable, and other words we fellows

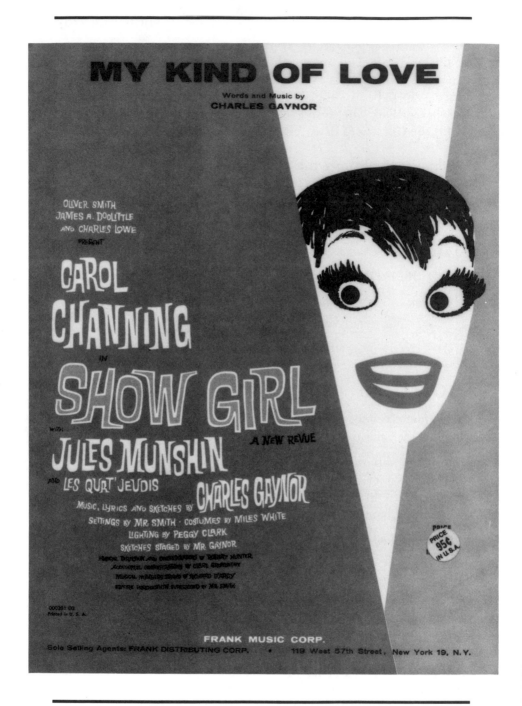

"The girl in the show must be me," discovers a startled Show Girl.
Little did Carol know that Dolly! *was just around the corner.*
(*drawing by David Klein*)

616

will be writing soon on lacy valentines. Miss Channing slyly kids the critics on their use of such tired adjectives as "moving, meaty, trenchant." All right, Miss Channing is moving, meaty, trenchant. And lots more. She has a whangdoodle of a show.

WALTER KERR, *Herald Tribune*

I've missed Carol Channing. I hadn't even realized I was missing her until she came on at the Eugene O'Neill last night, a towering cornstalk in a husk of slinky red. Then, there she was, bowing and beaming, looking shy and fussed and fearsome, and I knew why it was life had seemed empty lately. There's some sort of embarrassed innocence—an air of being caught where she shouldn't by the high-school principal—about this girl, in spite of all that effusive energy. Even as she's warming you up with "The Girl in the Show" her two turned-in feet are edging nervously against one another, and abashedly away from the footlights. Whenever she gets a great big laugh in "Calypso Pete," she whips around at you in delighted misbelief, breaking into a surprised smile you could drive a truck right through. And because she is so quick with that disarming grimace that asks "What did I say?" she can be twice as lethal when it's lethal-time. Late in Act Two, Marlene Dietrich is hauled kicking to the block. I didn't exactly catch the moment in which Miss Channing turned into Miss Dietrich—it was all very mysterious, and the devil clearly had something to do with it—but in no time at all savage Germanic phrases were being silently mouthed at the careless man in the spotlight booth and I can't begin to describe the messy things that were happening to the filmy, feathery thing she was wearing. An honest heart makes for the sauciest satire, I guess.

JIM O'CONNOR, *Journal-American*

The lights were dimmed, and the curtain went up last night at the Eugene O'Neill Theatre. And there on a bare stage (there was practically no scenery) stood a tall, thin, blonde girl with wide eyes, wide mouth, long arms, long legs—and a frightened look. She advanced to the footlights and started to sing. From all parts of the house came loud, enthusiastic applause before she could voice a note. She waved a hand of greeting. The handclapping continued. She tried again to sing and finally managed to make herself heard above the acclaim. The lone girl on the big stage was Carol

Channing. The number she was doing—amid tears of joy at the warm reception she was receiving—was "The Girl in the Show." What a woman! What a show! What a talent!

○○○
○   ○
○   BROADWAY SCORECARD / perfs: 100 / $: +   ○
○   ○
○   rave   favorable   mixed   unfavorable   pan   ○
○   ○
○   4   2   1   ○
○○○

SILK STOCKINGS

a musical comedy, with music and lyrics by Cole Porter; book by George S. Kaufman, Leueen MacGrath (Kaufman), and Abe Burrows (actually by Burrows, replacing Kaufman and MacGrath), from the 1939 satire *Ninotchka* by Melchior Lengyel

directed by Cy Feuer (replacing George S. Kaufman); choreographed by Eugene Loring (replaced by Jerome Robbins)
produced by Cy Feuer and Ernest H. Martin
with Hildegarde Neff, Don Ameche, Gretchen Wyler (replacing Yvonne Adair, Sherry O'Neil, and Marilyn Ross), and George Tobias

opened February 24, 1955   Imperial Theatre

BROOKS ATKINSON, *Times*

We can all afford to relax now. Everything about *Silk Stockings* represents the best goods in the American musical comedy emporium. People who remember the Garbo *Ninotchka* may miss its subtlety. In place of subtlety, it offers the wittiest dialogue of recent years, Cole Porter's best work, and enormous gusto and skill in performance. This is one of Gotham's memorable shows, on a level with *Guys and Dolls* [1950]. As in the most expert musical comedies, everything contributes to the vitality of everything else. The topic of Soviet dialectical earnestness has put Mr. Porter back in his best form, His music, with some clever burlesques of the Russian folk chorus, is bold, ironic, and melodious with great variety in form. And his intricately worded lyrics rank with those earlier rhymes of his that have become part of the popular American culture.

ROBERT COLEMAN, *Daily Mirror*

A saucy, sexy, satiric saturnalia. It kids the pants off Communism. George S. Kaufman, Leueen MacGrath, and Abe Burrows, who did the book, have used their slapstick with devastating effect on the Comrades. It would even make Bulganin laugh, if he had a sense of humor. It's brash, tuneful, and immensely funny. It moves like a rocket bent on reaching the moon in a hurry, and is calculated to make you roar with laughter and bring pain to the Comrades where it will hurt most.

WILLIAM HAWKINS, *World-Telegram & Sun*

Most of the time it behaves like a horse that does not know which way to run.

WALTER KERR, *Herald Tribune*

After threatening to come into town during the Thanksgiving season, the Christmas season, and the New Year's season, *Silk Stockings* finally decided to give itself up for Lent. It opened Thursday, the end-product of a fabulous out-of-town sortie in which the authors were changed, the directors were changed, the choreographers were changed, and the changes were changed. Of the gallant little band that sailed into rehearsal last October, many brave hearts are now asleep in the deep. What has been wrought in all this travail? Well, not a miracle, certainly. But not precisely a clambake, either. If *Can-Can* (1953) can, I rather imagine *Silk Stockings* will.

JOHN McCLAIN, *Journal-American*

Don Ameche is a big new star all over again; at long last here is a leading man who can sing without posing and flinging his arms about, who can read a line in an entirely natural manner, whose performance is unostentatious and charming. . . . *Silk Stockings* has the old professional polish of timing—it always moves. People were saying the show was in terrible trouble on the road, where it made nothing but money. Well, it may not be perfection in its present form, but my prediction is that it will only make more money.

Silk Stockings was initially announced as a Frank Loesser–George S. Kaufman—Jerome Robbins project; but Loesser bowed out to concentrate on his folk opera *The Most Happy Fella* (1956), and Robbins became unavailable when his Broadway-bound *Peter Pan* (1954) needed extensive revisions. The *Silk Stockings* tryout revealed major maladies, so show-doctor Abe Burrows—from *Guys and Dolls* (1950) and *Can-Can* (1953)—was brought in to fix the book. Feuer—who had taken over *The Boy Friend* (1954) by literally locking director and author out of the theatre—did the same here, causing Kaufman to proclaim loudly and publicly that he'd been fired. Third-billed Yvonne Adair—of *Gentlemen Prefer Blondes* (1949)—did not play the out-of-town premiere and soon departed, never having performed her role. Two cities and two replacements later she was rehired, played the Boston opening, and was then re-replaced. By this time Robbins had re-entered the picture, putting the show in presentable shape for Broadway. The record shows that Feuer and Martin fired the directors of *The Boy Friend, Silk Stockings,* and *The Act* (1977); the choreographers of the latter two musicals and *How to Succeed in Business Without Really Trying* (1961); and the librettists of *Guys and Dolls, Silk Stockings,* and *How to Succeed.* All of these shows were maneuvered past their early troubles, but working with Feuer and Martin—described by Kaufman as "Jed Harris rolled into one"—couldn't have been pleasant. And if *Silk Stockings* was their fourth consecutive hit since *Where's Charley?* (1948), they went 1-for-6 over the rest of their Broadway careers, including the especially lousy *Whoop-Up* (1958) and *Skyscraper* (1965).

	BROADWAY SCORECARD / perfs: 478 / $: +			
rave	*favorable*	*mixed*	*unfavorable*	*pan*
3	2	1	1	

SING OUT, SWEET LAND!

an American folk-music pageant, with music edited and arranged by Elie Siegmeister; book by Walter Kerr

directed by Leon Leonidoff; book directed by Walter Kerr; choreographed by Doris Humphrey and Charles Weidman
produced by the Theatre Guild
with Alfred Drake, Burl Ives, Bibi Osterwald, and Alma Kaye

opened December 27, 1944   International Theatre

JOHN CHAPMAN, *Daily News*

Sing Out, Sweet Land! is, to put it simply and directly, just wonderful. A cavalcade of American song from Colonial times down to just about now, it is the newest delight in a generous season. It is smartly staged, amusingly set, craftily orchestrated, and sung by a completely engaging group of people. It brings to the theatre a new personality—so far as the theatre is concerned—in Burl Ives, a round and friendly fellow who is a captivating ballad singer. Boy, did I have a time! You will, too. Just sit there and relax and let it come to you, and then say thanks for something new in the way of a musical show.

ROBERT GARLAND, *Journal-American*

Again the Guild has done it! Something new and fresh and fascinating, something to cheer about and cherish. For this is the happy fusion of drama, dance, and music to which Rouben Mamoulian has been referring. This, my friends, is IT! *Sing Out, Sweet Land!* is as tuneful as *Oklahoma!* [1943], as colorful as *Mexican Hayride* [1944], as earthy as *Follow the Girls* [1944] and as American as a rodeo. I never expect to get enough of it!

WARD MOREHOUSE, *Sun*

The idea of *Sing Out, Sweet Land!* is a good one, that of depicting the pageantry of America in song and story, and when the folk music is being rendered the production is enchanting. But between the songs there are stretches of talk, talk that is neither stirring nor nostalgic and that does not serve to bring the periods to life. . . . *Sing Out, Sweet Land!* is expensive, pictorial, and melodious. When it is being sung it has charm and distinction and it is exciting theatre, but it is greatly handicapped by inept and plodding narration. . . . Alfred Drake, who came into Broadway's consciousness as the hero of *Oklahoma!*, does extraordinarily well. It is Burl Ives, however, who stops and steals the show. When Mr. Ives is downstage singing such ballads as "Blue Tail Fly" and "Rock Candy Mountain," the Guild's folk revue is something superb.

LEWIS NICHOLS, *Times*

In staging the production, Leon Leonidoff has permitted a good deal of burlesque to come in; if history is being written in *Sing Out, Sweet Land!*" there is no need for a 1944 beer-hall version of "Bicycle Built for Two," The show had its choice of burlesque or, by playing it straight, to offer nostalgia, and the choice was wrong.

WILELLA WALDORF, *Post*

At its best, *Sing Out, Sweet Land!*" is tuneful and gently amusing. At its worst, it is monotonous and corny. We can recommend a whole evening of it only to people who simply dote on American folk music and don't care much what happens as long as one of the old tunes bobs up every so often.

An expanded amateur show from Catholic University in Washington, D.C. Walter Kerr first came to Broadway with an earlier Catholic U. transfer, *Count Me In* (1942). Kerr continued teaching drama at Catholic until George Abbott brought him back to New York for good with *Touch and Go* (1949).

A Donaldson Award was won by Burl Ives (supporting actor).

BROADWAY SCORECARD / perfs: 102 / $: —

rave	favorable	mixed	unfavorable	pan
4			3	1

SLEEPY HOLLOW

a musical comedy, with music by George Lessner; book and lyrics by Russell Maloney and Miriam Battista (Maloney), suggested by Nicholas Bela, "with the assistance of Marc Connelly," from the 1819 story "The Legend of Sleepy Hollow" by Washington Irving

directed by John O'Shaughnessy; choreographed by Anna Sokolow
produced by Lorraine Lester
with Gil Lamb, Betty Jane Watson, Hayes Gordon, and Mary McCarty

opened June 3, 1948   St. James Theatre

ROBERT COLEMAN, *Daily Mirror*

After setting a long-run record for musicals, *Oklahoma!* [1943], one of the greatest of song-and-dance shows, vacated the St. James Theatre to make way for one of the worst. Titled *Sleepy Hollow*, the new arrival is based on Washington Irving's "Legend of Sleepy Hollow." That noise you heard last night was Irving spinning giddily in his grave.

WILLIAM HAWKINS, *World-Telegram*

A tedious, dragged out production with no visible distinction. It had the air of having been written and restaged yesterday afternoon. In the last analysis, *Sleepy Hollow* is both.

A Tony Award won by Jo Mielziner (scenic designer, for his entire season of work which also included *South Pacific* and *Death of a Salesman*).

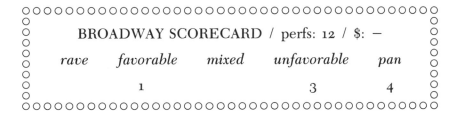

BROADWAY SCORECARD / perfs: 12 / $: —

rave	favorable	mixed	unfavorable	pan
	1		3	4

SMALL WONDER

a musical revue, with music by Baldwin Bergersen and Albert Selden; lyrics by Phyllis McGinley and Billings Brown (Burt Shevelove); sketches by Charles Spaulding, Max Wilk, George Axelrod, and Louis Laun

directed by Burt Shevelove; choreographed by Gower Champion
produced by George Nichols 3rd
with Tom Ewell, Alice Pearce, Mary McCarty, and Joan Diener

opened September 15, 1948   Coronet Theatre

JOHN CHAPMAN, *Daily News*

I'd say the only department in which *Small Wonder* falls short is the tune department, but this is nothing new in the musical comedy business of these times. The melodies of Baldwin Bergersen and Albert Selden are at best pleasant, but scarcely deserving of the lyrics provided by Phyllis McGinley and Billings Brown [Burt Shevelove]. The dance numbers (and practically everybody in the company dances) are a credit to Gower Champion. The sketches, along with the lyrics, are intelligent and amusing.

ROBERT COLEMAN, *Daily Mirror*

We might be willing to recommend *Small Wonder* to you if the tariff were $4.80 or under, but we cannot honestly do so when there's a six-buck top. The customer is entitled to more when he lays out that kind of dough.

RICHARD WATTS JR., *Post*

The best sketches [are successful] in great part due to a pretty and engaging girl comic named Mary McCarty. It is clear that she is decidedly a performer to be watched. When she mocks the uncomfortable histrionics common to such Duses of the screen as the Misses Turner, Bacall, Scott, and Lamour, Miss McCarty proves herself a satirical comedienne of talent and intelligence. . . . The dances seemed to come in for especial admiration, although they struck me as strenuously commonplace.

☆

Small Wonder marked Gower Champion's Broadway debut as a choreographer, although he attracted much more attention (and his first Tony Award) two months later with *Lend an Ear*. Director Burt Shevelove modestly chose to use a pseudonym for his modest lyrics, hence "Billings Brown." Composer Albert Selden went on to become a producer, with credits including *Man of La Mancha* (1965) and Shevelove's *Hallelujah, Baby!* (1967).

BROADWAY SCORECARD / perfs: 134 / $: −

rave	favorable	mixed	unfavorable	pan
	3	2	3	

SOMETHING FOR THE BOYS

a musical comedy, with music and lyrics by Cole Porter; book by Herbert and Dorothy Fields

staged by Hassard Short; book directed by Herbert Fields; choreographed by Jack Cole
produced by Mike Todd
with Ethel Merman, Paula Laurence, Bill Johnson, and Allen Jenkins

opened January 7, 1943   Alvin Theatre

LOUIS KRONENBERGER, *PM*

Mr. Porter has lost his old "Begin-the-Beguine" and "I-Get-a-Kick-Out-of-You" magic, and has apparently abandoned his old "You're-the-Top" nimble smartness with words. If *Something for the Boys* doesn't come close to *Anything Goes* [1934], it's because Mr. Porter isn't the composer he once was. For Miss Merman is no less of a wow.

BURNS MANTLE, *Daily News*

My best advice to you this morning is that you had better run, not walk, to the nearest agency, if you can't get to the theatre, and

Something FROM the Boys!

A quote ad, with Hirschfeld caricatures of the critics! (drawings by Al Hirschfeld)

626

reserve seats for the near future. For here we have another one of those happy overnight hits that will run out the season and be greatly in demand. It doesn't matter much what you personally may think about it. It is a perfect sample of the sort of musical comedy entertainment that 98 per cent of the playgoing populace revels in. And as a plus quality it has Ethel Merman in fine health and buoyant spirits, riding the air waves with abandon. Abandon and shouting melody as well. She is the star of the show. No Gaxton. No Moore. No anybody with whom she has to share her billing. Unless it be Cole Porter. He wrote all the songs, and no one can write Merman songs as well as he, just as no one can sing Porter songs better than she. The Merman has gained confidence; with the confidence has come an improved stage presence and a better sense of comedy. She didn't work with the best comedians [Willie Howard, Victor Moore, Jimmy Durante, Bert Lahr] for nothing. She can clown now without suggesting an irresponsible talent turned loose in the backroom of a hot spot. She has abandoned the torch, but nursed the flame of a genius for the art known as putting over a song.

LEWIS NICHOLS, *Times*

Ethel Merman gives a performance that suggests all Merman performances before last night were simply practice. Merman in good voice is a raucous overtone to the trumpets of a band; it is a soft trill for a torch song, it is tinny for a parody and fast for one of Mr. Porter's complicated lyrics. Accompanying the voice are all the necessary gestures, the role of the eye or the wave of the hand to suggest friendly ribaldries or separations forever and more. . . . Bill Johnson is present to sing the male part of such songs as can't be done entirely by Miss Merman.

BURTON RASCOE, *World-Telegram*

Michael Todd went to town with *Something for the Boys* at the Alvin last night. What he brought was Ethel Merman. And his packaging of that Koh-i-noor-in-the-rough was super de luxe, first priorities, ration A, topside—in a word, the coffee. Men growing old ungracefully wept to see what they never hoped to see again— the staging of a musical show as glamorous, kinetic, balanced, and seductive as the still lamented Ziegfeld in his hey-day used to stage them. Miss Merman is a darling who seems to grow darlinger by the minute; for it seems to me I can remember back in a not-too-distant past when I thought she was only a second-rate younger-generation Blanche Ring who would never have any rings on her fingers and bells on her toes. [Ring was a famous "shouter" of the pre-World War I period, one of her trademarks being the 1909 "I've Got Rings on My Fingers (and Bells on My Toes").] But last night I said here's a gal with the comic genius of Fanny Brice (or nearly) in the days when Miss Brice was playing in the Ziegfeld shows, and what she can do with a song, if it is a Cole Porter song and not the caterwauling of jive, is a stirring delight.

The sixth of seven Cole Porter/Herbert Fields collaborations (1928–1944)—all of which were successful! This one didn't have a single song hit, but with Merman on hand the wartime pleasure seekers didn't care.

```
BROADWAY SCORECARD / perfs: 422 / $: +

rave      favorable     mixed     unfavorable     pan

 6            2
```

SOMETHING MORE!

a musical comedy, with music by Sammy Fain; lyrics by Marilyn and Alan Bergman; book by Nate Monaster, from the 1962 novel *Portofino P.T.A.* by Gerald Green

directed by Jule Styne; choreographed by Bob Herget
produced by Lester Osterman (and Jule Styne, with ABC-Paramount)
with Arthur Hill, Barbara Cook, Joan Copeland (replacing Viveca Lindfors), Ronny Graham, and Peg Murray

opened November 10, 1964   Eugene O'Neill Theatre

WALTER KERR, *Herald Tribune*

Why can't it all be as simple as Barbara Cook makes it? Twice in *Something More!* Miss Cook just turns front and lets the simple

LESTER OSTERMAN

presents

ARTHUR   BARBARA
HILL   **COOK**

in a

New Musical Comedy

SOMETHING MORE!

Book by   Music by   Lyrics by
NATE   SAMMY   MARILYN & ALAN
MONASTER   **FAIN**   **BERGMAN**

Based on "Portofino P.T.A." by GERALD GREEN

Also Starring

VIVECA   RONNY
LINDFORS   **GRAHAM**

with

MICHAEL   PEG   VICTOR R.   RICO   JO JO
KERMOYAN   MURRAY   HELOU   FROEHLICH   SMITH

Scenery & Lighting by   Costumes by
ROBERT RANDOLPH   **ALVIN COLT**

Musical Direction   Orchestrations   Vocal Arrangements
by   by   & Direction by
OSCAR   RALPH   ROBERT   BUSTER
KOSARIN   **BURNS** & **PRINCE**   **DAVIS**

Dances & Musical Numbers Staged by
BOB HERGET

Directed by
JULE STYNE

Original Cast Album on ABC-Paramount Records
An ABC-Paramount — On Stage Recording

Whitney Darrow, Jr.

S H U B E R T   T H E A T R E   PHILADELPHIA
Monday, Sept. 28 thru Saturday, Oct. 24
Opening Night 7:30   Other Eves. 8:30   Mats. Wed. and Sat. at 2:00
PUBLIC PREVIEW SATURDAY, SEPTEMBER 26 AT 8:30

A suburban novelist moves his family from Mineola to Portofino (Italy) in search of fulfillment, but comes up empty. "If you're tired of clogged sinks, car pools, and crab grass, you need Something More!" *the herald promises enticingly. (drawing by Whitney Darrow, Jr.)*

phrases of a simple Sammy Fain tune float toward us without fuss, without selling, without winking or blinking or having to stamp her pretty foot. The sweetness is direct, personal, and should be packaged as a substitute for honey, no matter how many bees are thereby put out of business. Miss Cook is one of the true treasures of our musical-comedy theatre. . . . Mr. Fain's simpler tunes are attractive, but the more extended ones tend to wander about in search of a resolution and I thought I heard a bit too much Cole Porter now and again. As for Mr. Monaster's book and the lyrics provided by Alan and Marilyn Bergman, let's say no more than that they are unmistakably continental. "Take off that coat, I want to fight you *al fresco*" is surely continental, and I know that when a woman sings "Tortoni, spumoni, and oh my minestrone" that I'm in Italy. I can't be fooled about a thing like that. How pleasant it would have been to have scrapped everything else and just made it a Cook's tour.

NORMAN NADEL, *World-Telegram & Sun*

Dances, though energetic, are often inappropriate—as the Russian routine by Italian moving men in Mineola.

DOUGLAS WATT, *Daily News*

Sammy Fain's music is at least rhythmic and on the move most of the time, but the lyrics Marilyn and Alan Bergman have set to it, with glue, all but smother Fain's talents. Jule Styne, who is best known as a songwriter and who should never have let these songwriters out of his sight, carries off his first directorial job with skill.

Surely it was unwise even to whisper the name "Portofino." Couldn't they have just said "based on a novel by Gerald Green"? *Something More!* wasn't quite as bad as *Portofino* (1958); however, they don't give prizes for that. Perky ingenue Barbara Cook bid farewell to the Broadway musical following three successive failures, *The Gay Life* (1961), *She Loves Me* (1963), and this little number. She turned up again in *The Grass Harp* (1971), but not as a perky ingenue.

SONG OF NORWAY

a costume operetta, with music from themes by Edvard Grieg; musical adaptation and lyrics by Robert Wright and George Forrest; book by Milton Lazarus, from a play by Homer Curran

directed by Charles K. Freeman; choreographed by George Balanchine
produced by Edwin Lester
with Irra Petina, Helena Bliss, Lawrence Brooks, Robert Shafer, Sig Arno, Alexandra Danilova, Frederic Franklin, and the Ballets Russe de Monte Carlo

opened August 21, 1944   Imperial Theatre

Louis Kronenberger, *PM*

Presumably there are only two popular plots into which a composer can be fitted—either he must be the victim of unrequited love and, after composing deathless music to his fair one, pine away and die; or he must be enmeshed for a time with an amorous and capricious opera singer. Of the two plots, I confess I find the latter less painful, and since in the present case the diva is Irra Petina, it even has its advantages. For Miss Petina, besides having a good voice, has a likeable personality and a nice comedy manner. She, indeed, manages to keep the proceedings fairly light, though she cannot prevent their becoming too long. Like almost all operettas, *Song of Norway* has more book than is good for it—and no better book than most. One can accept the popular style of *Song of Norway* and yet feel disappointed that so fine a choreographer as George Balanchine, and such fine dancers as Danilova, Franklin, and others of the Ballet Russe de Monte Carlo have left so little imprint on it. *Song of Norway* has all the choreographic staples of operetta, from peasants dancing in the marketplace to fashionable folk waltzing in a ballroom. But the effects, for the most part, are no more than agreeably commonplace. Balanchine has not done his usual job by a long shot.

BURTON RASCOE, *World-Telegram*

The cheers, bravos, bravas, and handclapping were a long time dying out at the Imperial last night; for gratified music lovers had just been presented with a thrilling production of a new operetta which is destined to become a classic in the field, along with *Blossom Time* (1921), *Rosalinda* (1942), *Rose-Marie* (1924), *Sally* (1920), and *The Student Prince* (1924).

WILELLA WALDORF, *Post*

A huge, elaborate, densely populated production that is often genuinely melodious—though not, surprisingly enough, as often as you would suppose, lavishly embellished with ballet and even reasonably well equipped with comedy. Looking back, we can't imagine how the producers restrained themselves sufficiently to omit animals. Even without animals, however, we found it all pretty overwhelming. It was George Balanchine and the Ballet Russe de Monte Carlo, headed by Alexandra Danilova and Frederic Franklin, who have the biggest share of the evening, however, with one whole session given over, of course, to the "Peer Gynt" suite. Mr. Balanchine's choreography struck us as routine throughout, even with the Ballet Russe dancing, but it was good old-style ballet the customers apparently love. The musical numbers and the ballet seemed to be clinging to the old tried and true operetta formula with choruses finishing numbers all waving hands in the air, lights suddenly going off on everybody in the room but one singer who stood in a spot and warbled while everybody else stood as in a trance, etc. . . . There's enough in *Song of Norway* to please almost any taste much of the time. It is probably destined to take up the torch when *Blossom Time* finally drops from sheer exhaustion, if it ever does.

The last of the old-fashioned costume operettas. The form had virtually died on Broadway by 1929, although the old chestnuts kept trouping the hinterlands into the 1950s. *Song of Norway* was an immense hit, helped by public sympathy for the country of Grieg (then under Nazi occupation).

BROADWAY SCORECARD / perfs: 860 / $: +

rave	favorable	mixed	unfavorable	pan
3	4		1	

SOPHIE

a musical biography of Sophie Tucker (1884–1966), with music and lyrics by Steve Allen; book by Phillip Pruneau

directed by Jack Sydow (replacing Gene Frankel); choreographed by Donald Saddler
produced by Len Bedsow and Hal Grossman in association with Michael Pollack and Max Fialkov
with Libi Staiger, Art Lund, Rosetta LeNoire, and Phil Leeds

opened April 15, 1963   Winter Garden Theatre

ROBERT COLEMAN, *Daily Mirror*

Only Sophie Tucker herself could have carried this one off. Soph, we're sorry. We had hoped to ring bells and dance in the street this morning, but it just wasn't to be. *Sophie* is no Sophie. Unlike you, darling, it's no champ. We kept hoping that you would step on in the second half, light up the stage, and send us all home happy.

WALTER KERR, *Herald Tribune*

There were ghosts at the Winter Garden Monday night, but not one of them was Sophie Tucker's. Ghost of old movies. Ghosts of ancient backstage plays. Ghosts of every line of dialogue ever spoken by a palpitating hoofer as he dashed in from the dressing-rooms to say that the headliner had just come down with frostbite and they'd better get somebody to take her place quick. And do you know who's out front tonight? William Morris! In point of fact, there was no need to look about for Miss Tucker's ghost, for Miss Tucker was there—in the auditorium. Before the show started, the

Sophie Tucker (Libi Staiger) sure looks like a Red Hot Mama on paper, but on stage she was a cold fish. Good logo, anyway. Pre-Broadway credits. (drawing by Barnell)

634

great beaming lady got up to take a bow, proving that her sense of timing was as immaculate as ever. Before the show started was the time to do it. NOTHING happens, really, except that Miss Staiger meets people on trains: on the steps of trains, in the coaches of trains, on the back platforms of trains. Between trains Steve Allen's tunes come galloping along, at a very steady trot, and they are the square root of all typical tunes. Richard Rodgers is famous for his "wrong note." Mr. Allen may become famous for always arriving at the right note, and you have no idea how monotonous that can be. Let's allow for the infectious presence of Rosetta LeNoire who [sounds] rather more like Miss Tucker than Miss Staiger does. . . . Fred Voelpel's costumes are, I regret to say, ghastly (Mr. Voelpel has designed some of the least interesting feminine undergarments ever to make the Winter Garden seem truly wintry).

HOWARD TAUBMAN, *Times*

For being subjected to double jeopardy, Sophie Tucker is entitled to relief, legal or otherwise. Not only did Miss Tucker have her story turned into a musical of shattering dullness, but she also had to sit through it. Didn't Miss Tucker have any fun? Didn't she give audiences excitement and pleasure? Shouldn't a musical, however worshipful it may be to its heroine, make one feel that it was worth the trouble of leaving home and television set?. . . . William Morris's heirs have a cause for complaint, not so much for defamation of character as for utter lack of it.

```
BROADWAY SCORECARD / perfs: 8 / $: −

   rave    favorable    mixed    unfavorable    pan
                           1           3           3
```

THE SOUND OF MUSIC

a musical play, with music by Richard Rodgers; lyrics by Oscar Hammerstein 2nd; book by Howard Lindsay and Russel Crouse,

LELAND HAYWARD · RICHARD HALLIDAY
RICHARD RODGERS · OSCAR HAMMERSTEIN 2nd
present

MARY MARTIN
In A New Musical Play
THE SOUND OF MUSIC

Music by
RICHARD RODGERS
Lyrics by
OSCAR HAMMERSTEIN 2nd

Book by
HOWARD LINDSAY and **RUSSEL CROUSE**
Suggested by "The Trapp Family Singers" by Maria Augusta Trapp

THEODORE BIKEL
with
PATRICIA NEWAY   KURT KASZNAR   MARION MARLOWE
JOHN RANDOLPH   NAN McFARLAND   LAURI PETERS   BRIAN DAVIES
MARILYN ROGERS   MURIEL O'MALLEY   ELIZABETH HOWELL   KAREN SHEPARD

Entire Production Directed by
VINCENT J. DONEHUE

Musical Numbers Staged by **JOE LAYTON**
Scenic Production by **OLIVER SMITH**
Costumes by **LUCINDA BALLARD**
Mary Martin's clothes by **MAINBOCHER**
Lighting by **JEAN ROSENTHAL**

Musical Director   Orchestrations by   Choral Arrangements by
FREDERICK DVONCH   **ROBERT RUSSELL BENNETT**   **TRUDE RITTMAN**

Mary, with guitar, teaches the Trapp kids to sing "Do-Re-Mi."
(costumes by Lucinda Ballard, photo by Friedman-Abeles)

636

from the 1949 autobiography *The Trapp Family Singers* by Maria Augusta Trapp

directed by Vincent J. Donehue; choreographed by Joe Layton
produced by Leland Hayward, Richard Halliday, Richard Rodgers, and Oscar Hammerstein 2nd
with Mary Martin (Halliday), Theodore Bikel, Patricia Neway, Kurt Kasznar, and Marion Marlowe

opened November 16, 1959   Lunt-Fontanne Theatre

FRANK ASTON, *World-Telegram & Sun*

The loveliest musical imaginable. It places Rodgers and Hammerstein back in top form as melodist and lyricist. The Lindsay–Crouse dialogue is vibrant and amusing in a plot that rises to genuine excitement. Oliver Smith's delicately lavish sets are peopled with figures of taste, talent, and looks. Everyone in front of the opening audience was burdened with that estimable quality called charm.

BROOKS ATKINSON, *Times*

Although Miss Martin, now playing an Austrian maiden, has longer hair than she had in *South Pacific* [1949], she still has the same common touch that wins friends and influences people, the same sharp features, goodwill, and glowing personality that makes music sound intimate and familiar. . . . The best of *The Sound of Music* is Rodgers and Hammerstein in good form. Mr. Rodgers has not written with such freshness of style since *The King and I* [1951]. Mr. Hammerstein has contributed lyrics that also have the sentiment and dexterity of his best work. But the scenario of *The Sound of Music* has the hackneyed look of the musical theatre [they] replaced with *Oklahoma!* in 1943. It is disappointing to see the American musical stage succumbing to the clichés of operetta. The revolution of the Forties and Fifties has lost its fire. But *The Sound of Music* retains some of the treasures of those golden days—melodies, rapturous singing, and Miss Martin. The sound of music is always moving. Occasionally it is also glorious.

WALTER KERR, *Herald Tribune*

I can only wish that some one had not been moved to abandon the snowflakes and substitute cornflakes. Before *The Sound of Mu-*

sic is halfway through its promising chores it becomes not only too sweet for words but almost too sweet for music. Is it director Vincent J. Donehue who has made the evening suffer from little children? There are seven tots necessary to the narrative, and I am not against tots. But must they bounce into bed in their nightgowns so often, and so armingly? Must they wear so many different picture-book skirts, and fluff them so mightily, and smile to relentlessly, and give such precocious advice to their elders? The cascade of sugar is not confined to the youngsters. Miss Martin, too, must fall to her knees and fold her hands in prayer, while the breezes blow the kiddies through the window. She must always enter as though the dessert were here, now. The pitch is too strong; the taste of vanilla overwhelms the solid chocolate; the people on stage have all melted long before our hearts do.

JOHN McCLAIN, *Journal-American*

The most mature product of the team. It has style, distinction, grace, and persuasion; it may not have the popular appeal of *Oklahoma!* or *South Pacific*, but it has more importance. It seemed to me to be the full ripening of these two extraordinary talents.

RICHARD WATTS JR., *Post*

The new Rodgers and Hammerstein show has a warm-hearted, unashamedly sentimental, and strangely gentle charm that is wonderfully endearing. *The Sound of Music* strives for nothing in the way of smash effects, substituting instead a kind of gracious and unpretentious simplicity. Aided by Richard Rodgers's most beguiling recent score, a pleasant book, a tasteful and attractive production, and a fine cast headed by Mary Martin at her best, the result is a most winning musical. This is the report of one who had the unhappiness to find *Flower Drum Song* [1958] gravely disappointing, to a degree that made him fear the Masters had lost the fresh imagination of their touch. I think my unjustified suspicion is worth noting because both the score and the lyrics of *The Sound of Music* are particularly rich in freshness and imagination. The new offering is filled with charming songs, and one of their most attractive features is that they seem so modest and unhackneyed.

☆

A coyly old-fashioned operetta or a warm, lovely musical, take your pick. It certainly was a crowd pleaser, though. *The Sound of Music* was Oscar Hammerstein's final work: he died on August 23, 1960.

In addition to winning the Tony Award for Best Musical (tied with *Fiorello!*), Tonys were won by Richard Rodgers (composer, tied with Jerry Bock); Howard Lindsay and Russel Crouse (librettists, tied with Jerome Weidman and George Abbott); Leland Hayward, Richard Halliday, Richard Rodgers, and Oscar Hammerstein 2nd (producers, tied with Robert E. Griffith and Harold S. Prince); Mary Martin (actress); Patricia Neway (supporting actress); Oliver Smith (scenic designer, tied with Howard Bay for *Toys in the Attic*); and Frederick Dvonch (musical director).

BROADWAY SCORECARD / perfs: 1,433 / $: +

rave	favorable	mixed	unfavorable	pan
3	3		1	

SOUTH PACIFIC

a musical play, with music by Richard Rodgers; lyrics by Oscar Hammerstein 2nd; book by Oscar Hammerstein 2nd and Joshua Logan, from James A. Michener's 1948 Pulitzer Prize–winning *Tales of the South Pacific*

directed and "musical staging" by Joshua Logan
produced by Richard Rodgers and Oscar Hammerstein 2nd in association with Leland Heyward and Joshua Logan
with Mary Martin, Ezio Pinza, Myron McCormick, Juanita Hall, William Tabbert, and Betta St. John (Striegler)

opened April 7, 1949   Majestic Theatre

BROOKS ATKINSON, *Times*

Although Mr. Rodgers and Mr. Hammerstein are extraordinarily gifted men, they have not forgotten how to apply the seat of

Mary Martin tells us about her little "Honey-Bun." (costume by Motley)

the pants to the seat of the chair. One thing that makes *South Pacific* so rhapsodically enjoyable is the hard work and organization that have gone into it under Mr. Logan's spontaneous direction. The authors and producers have a high regard for professional skill, and everything they have put their hands to is perfectly wrought. Fortunately, Mr. Rodgers and Mr. Hammerstein are also the most gifted men in the business. . . . If the country still has the taste to appreciate a masterly love song, "Some Enchanted Evening" ought to become reasonably immortal. For Mr. Rodgers's music is a romantic incantation; and, as usual, Mr. Hammerstein's verses are both fervent and simple. Mr. Pinza's bass voice is the most beautiful that has been heard on a Broadway stage for an eon or two. He sings this song with infinite delicacy of feeling and loveliness of tone. As a matter of fact, Mr. Pinza is also a fine actor; and his first appearance on the one and only legitimate stage is an occasion worth celebrating.

HOWARD BARNES, *Herald Tribune*

A show of rare enchantment. It is novel in texture and treatment, rich in dramatic substance, and eloquent in song, a musical play to be cherished. Under Logan's superb direction, the action shifts with constant fluency. Borrowing the lap dissolve from the screen, he has kept the book cumulatively arresting and tremendously satisfying. The occasional dances appear to be magical improvisations. It is a long and prodigal entertainment, but it seems all too short. The Rodgers music is not his finest, but it fits the mood and pace of *South Pacific* so felicitously that one does not miss a series of hit tunes. In the same way the lyrics are part and parcel of a captivating musical unity.

ROBERT COLEMAN, *Daily Mirror*

Programmed as a musical play, *South Pacific* is just that. It boasts no ballets and no hot hoofing. It has no chorus in the conventional sense. Every one in it plays a part. It is likely to establish a new trend in musicals. Rodgers and Hammerstein have fashioned a score to rival the one they did for *Oklahoma!* [1943]. There isn't a bit of filler in it. Every number is so outstanding that it is difficult to decide which will be the most popular.

WILLIAM HAWKINS, *World-Telegram*

Having more than justified some of the most terrifyingly enthusiastic advance reports ever circulated, *South Pacific* soared exquisitely over the Majestic stage last night and made it quite clear that the theatre is going to be blessedly enchanted for many months to come. This is the ultimate modern blending of music and popular theatre to date, with the finest kind of balance between story and song, and hilarity and heartbreak. Mary Martin, whose star has been riding high for a number of shows, achieves a new heaven for herself with an authoritative versatility nobody in the theatre can equal.

RICHARD WATTS JR., *Post*

An utterly captivating work of theatrical art. I do not think it is first-night excess which causes me to hail it as one of the finest musical plays in the history of the American theatre. . . . For a long time everyone has known that Mary Martin was exceedingly expert and charming in the ways of musical comedy. But nothing I have ever seen her do prepared me for the loveliness, humor, gift for joyous characterization, and sheer lovableness of her portrayal of Nellie Forbush, the gay high-spirited nurse from Little Rock, who is so shocked to find her early racial prejudices cropping up. Hers is a completely irresistible performance.

The critics pretty much said it all. While *Carousel* (1945) was superior in material, *South Pacific*—the first of the Rodgers and Hammerstein musicals produced by Rodgers and Hammerstein themselves—exuded showmanship, and more than doubled the earlier show's run. *South Pacific* also had a more universal appeal—the country was filled with ex-G.I.'s and their families—and, unlike the team's three earlier shows, was built around two ticket-selling stars.

Winner of the Pulitzer Prize for Drama, only the second musical to be so honored, following *Of Thee I Sing* (1931). Winner of the New York Drama Critics' Circle Award. In addition to winning the Tony Award for Best Musical, Tonys were won by Richard Rodgers (composer); Oscar Hammerstein 2nd and Joshua Logan (librettists);

Joshua Logan (director); Rodgers and Hammerstein in association with Leland Heyward and Joshua Logan (producers); Mary Martin (actress); Ezio Pinza (actor); Juanita Hall (supporting actress); Myron McCormick (supporting actor). A Tony Award was won by Jo Mielziner (scenic designer) for his entire season of work, which also included *Death of a Salesman* and *Sleepy Hollow*. In addition to winning the Donaldson Award for Best Musical, Donaldsons were won by Richard Rodgers (composer); Oscar Hammerstein 2nd (lyricist); Oscar Hammerstein 2nd and Joshua Logan (librettists); Joshua Logan (director); Mary Martin (actress); Juanita Hall (supporting actress); Myron McCormick (supporting actor); and Ezio Pinza (male debut).

BROADWAY SCORECARD / perfs: 1,925 / $: +

rave	favorable	mixed	unfavorable	pan
8				

STOP THE WORLD—I WANT TO GET OFF

a British "new-style musical," with book, music, and lyrics by Leslie Bricusse and Anthony Newley

directed by Anthony Newley; choreography by John Broome, restaged by Virginia Mason
produced by David Merrick in association with Bernard Delfont
with Anthony Newley and Anna Quayle

opened October 3, 1962   Shubert Theatre

JOHN CHAPMAN, *Daily News*

To paraphrase any of Anthony Newley's several "seldoms," seldom has so much anticipation been built up over so little a show as *Stop the World—I Want to Get Off*. From what I'd read and been told, this English revue was going to be the last word in style and wit. What I saw was an overly precious little affair with a couple of good songs and a couple of good sketches, a few timid jokes, and an overdose of pantomime in imitation of Marcel Marceau. Newley wanders through numbers which are, I suppose, gentle remonstrances over the shortcomings of mankind. Occasionally, for no particular reason, he cries "Stop the world!"—and then he walks around a bit mewling like a famished kitten.

ROBERT COLEMAN, *Mirror*

Stop the World—I Want to Get Off is the kind of show you are likely to love to loathe. Frankly, we can take it or leave it, mostly leave it. It would be fascinating to watch the faces of tired business men when they take it.

NORMAN NADEL, *World-Telegram & Sun*

Let's say you've been painting. Not still lifes, abstracts or figures, but walls, ceiling and woodwork. You are so full of the smell of paint that you're no longer aware of it. Then you open a window, and suddenly the incoming fresh air smells spiced, strange, foreign. It's wonderfully invigorating, but it takes getting used to. Anthony Newley opened a window for the musical theatre last night, providing the wholesome vigor it's been needing. Like clean air in a painty room, *Stop the World—I Want to Get Off* also takes some getting used to—not just because it's foreign (English) but because it is so unexpectedly fresh.

HOWARD TAUBMAN, *Times*

Starting as a brave attempt to be fantasy with satirical overtones, *Stop the World—I Want to Get Off* ends by being commonplace and repetitious. A good deal of imagination and invention sugarcoat the work. Billed as "a new-style musical," it has an assortment of theatrical devices from mime to jive, which give the appearance of novelty. But the substance is banal. What begins as gallantly and brightly as a shiny new balloon that promises to stay airborne all evening turns droopy and finishes by collapsing. The basic sentimentality in this "new-style musical," neatly masked in the early stages by the vivacity of the production finally stands revealed. Not that *Stop the World* is ashamed of the corn; it rejoices in the stuff. . . . In fairness it should be recorded that it has had a long and prosperous career in London. Many who have seen it there swear by its originality, as many will here. But its freshness is no more than skin-deep, and its satire, apart from several spirited thrusts at the Russians and Germans, is not even that deep.

☆

David Merrick imported this curious conversation piece featuring "new-style" entertainer Anthony Newley and his enormously popular song hit "What Kind of Fool Am I?," and cannily spun it into a top money-maker. Due to its minimal production expense—$75,000, compared to $250,000 for *Carnival* (1961) and $350,000 for *Gypsy* (1959)—and relatively minuscule operating costs, *Stop the World* boasts Merrick's third highest profit/investment ratio (after *Hello Dolly!* [1964] and *42nd Street* [1980]).

A Tony Award was won by Anna Quayle (supporting actress).

BROADWAY SCORECARD / perfs: 556 / $: +

rave	favorable	mixed	unfavorable	pan
1	2		2	2

STREET SCENE

a "dramatic musical" with music by Kurt Weill; lyrics by Langston Hughes (with Elmer Rice); book by Elmer Rice, from his 1929 Pulitzer Prize–winning drama

directed by Charles Friedman; choreographed by Anna Sokolow
produced by Dwight Deere Wiman and The Playwrights' Company (including Elmer Rice)
with Norman Cordon, Anne Jeffreys, Polyna Stoska, Brian Sullivan (replacing Richard Manning), and Hope Emerson

opened January 9, 1947   Adelphi Theatre

BROOKS ATKINSON, *Times*

Add to the text of Elmer Rice's *Street Scene* a fresh and eloquent score by Kurt Weill and you have a musical play of magnificence and glory. Eighteen years ago Rice's ballad of a dingy side of New York rose high above the horizon of the theatre, and it has always remained there as a cherished masterpiece. For nothing else has recaptured so much of the anguish, romance, and beauty of cos-

Hell's Kitchen slice of life, illustrating Kurt Weill's tenement opera.
(drawing by Siebel)

mopolis. Now Mr. Weill, the foremost music maker in the American theatre, has found notes to express the myriad impulses of Mr. Rice's poem and transmuted it into a sidewalk opera. Mr. Weill's record includes some notable scores for *Johnny Johnson* [1936], *Knickerbocker Holiday* [1938], and *Lady in the Dark* [1941]. But obviously this is the theme he has been waiting for to make full use of his maturity as a composer. For he has listened to the main street cries of Mr. Rice's garish fable—the hopes, anxieties, and grief of people trying to beat a humane existence out of a callous city. The main theme he has conveyed in the rueful wonder of the song Mrs. Maurrant sings in the summer moonlight ("Somehow I Never Could Believe"); in her daughter's romantic lament ("What Good Would the Moon Be?"); in the janitor's brooding song ("Marble and a Star") and in the horror-stricken chorale entitled "The Woman Who Lived Up There." In these songs, and in the ominous orchestrations [by Weill] that accent the basic moods of the drama, Mr. Weill is writing serious music enkindled by the excitement of New York.

JOHN CHAPMAN, *Daily News*

From Elmer Rice's bitter and compassionate drama, Mr. Rice, Langston Hughes, and Kurt Weill have made a moving, remarkable opera—a work of great individuality which makes no compromise with Broadway formula. The authors call their work a dramatic musical, but it may well be called a metropolitan opera—a work that catches in both score and story the feel of tenement house life. As was the play, it is set before a shabby warren into which are crowded the races, the lovers, the haters, and the big and little events of city life. It is a grim Knickerbocker holiday. *Street Scene* is a far from ordinary event in the theatre, and I salute the courage, imagination, and skill of those who have made it.

LOUIS KRONENBERGER, *PM*

Whatever may be wrong with the musical version of *Street Scene*, there is one thing overwhelmingly right: it thoroughly interests you. Whether the pulse that beats through it is quite that of the original play, or even that of New York's harsh, hectic, humane tenement life, there is a pulse of some kind. It manages to key you up; and even when there are things to carp at, the critic in you keeps deferring to the playgoer. In the Broadway sense, *Street*

Scene is not, to be sure, a musical at all. It is captioned "a dramatic musical" and on just such lines has it been composed. Kurt Weill has sought to achieve in music the atmosphere, the tensions, the theatrical values of the play—to express rather than merely embellish Elmer Rice's scenario. Curiously enough, though the evening is in general a success, Mr. Weill's music, judged by its precise intentions, is partly a failure. Mr. Weill is a very accomplished musician; but the strictly operatic side of *Street Scene* is *musically* not very rewarding. Some of it is rather pretentious, and some of it as facilely florid as movie music. Moreover, Mr. Weill has given musical expression to a good deal of fairly casual dialogue; nor has this taken the form of low-pitched recitative. It is pitched much higher, and the palpitant music sometimes collides with the prosaic words to the point of bathos. Going by results, *Street Scene* would have been better off had some things that are sung been spoken.

RICHARD WATTS JR., *Post*

Elmer Rice's famous play, *Street Scene,* represented a kind of historic peak in the drama of sheer, meticulous realism. There can certainly be no question of the musical version's fidelity. It may, as a matter of fact, be too faithful for its own good. At least, the current *Street Scene* is certainly at its best when it forgets about its loftier ambitions and gets around to being a good Broadway musical show, proud and unashamed. Its lighter numbers, the song of the apartment-house gossips, the dance of the house trollop and her young man, the gay song of the girl graduates, the games of the children, are delightful. Indeed, all the dances staged by Anna Sokolow are fresh, amusing, and winning. In the dramatic scenes, though, the whole thing falters, and to a great extent that is a tribute to the continuing theatrical power of Mr. Rice's play. I cannot help thinking, for example, that the emotional effect is hampered, rather than heightened, when the realistic narrative goes into song. For me all the effect that the dramatist has achieved when the maddened stagehand, who has just killed his wife and her lover, is being dragged away by the police is hastily dissipated as the stricken daughter rushes up to him and starts singing: "Why did you do it?"

☆

Kurt Weill didn't quite achieve what he was aiming at. *Street Scene* certainly had lots of especially good music and plenty of drama. What was missing, though, was gripping entertainment. Outside of one standout boogie-woogie ("Moon-faced, Starry-eyed," performed by Sheila Bond and future Tony Award–winning choreographer Danny Daniels), *Street Scene* simply didn't involve audiences the way Rice's 1929 play had. Weill was joined in his quest to create a place for modern opera on Broadway by Marc Blitzstein (with *Regina* [1949]) and Gian-Carlo Menotti, who created immense excitement with *The Medium and The Telephone* (1947) and two Pulitzer Prize–winners, *The Consul* (1950) and *The Saint of Bleecker Street* (1954).

A Tony Award was won by Lucinda Ballard (costume designer, for her entire season of work). Kurt Weill received a special Tony Award. A Donaldson Award was won by Polyna Stoska (supporting actress).

BROADWAY SCORECARD / perfs: 148 / $: −

rave	favorable	mixed	unfavorable	pan
2	5		1	

SUBWAYS ARE FOR SLEEPING

a musical comedy, with music by Jule Styne; book and lyrics by Betty Comden and Adolph Green, from the 1957 novel by Edmund G. Love

directed and choreographed by Michael Kidd
produced by David Merrick
with Sydney Chaplin, Carol Lawrence, Orson Bean, and Phyllis Newman (Green)

opened December 27, 1961   St. James Theatre

WALTER KERR, *Herald Tribune*

There are at least eighteen dancing Santa Clauses in *Subways Are for Sleeping* and only one is missing—the real one. The old boy with the bag of presents seems to have skipped Adolph Green, Betty Comden, and Jule Styne this year. . . . Perhaps it all comes down to this: Betty Comden and Adolph Green are sophisticates, alive and alert when they are free to be wry, knowing, engagingly impertinent. But their materials here virtually rule out their instincts: they are "hep" creatures jabbing vaguely at something fey, sentimental, two blocks from the Christmas show at the Music Hall. The discrepancy shows, and the show moves as fitfully as the holiday traffic outside.

JOHN McCLAIN, *Journal-American*

Subways Are for Sleeping is a disappointing musical and this is due, I believe, to the fact that it is based on a feeble idea. Despite the talents of Betty Comden and Adolph Green, the fact remains that there is nothing highly hilarious or entertaining or remotely believable in this hoked-up kingdom of vagrants who infest the city. They are a dreary and rancid lot, and it didn't strike me that there was enough ingenuity in the story, or the dance numbers by Michael Kidd, to lift the proceedings out of the trash basket and imbue it with the sort of magical fairy-tale quality from which great musicals emerge. All this is the more deplorable because the music by Jule Styne towers over the evening like a kiosk: gay, haunting, slick, and singable. Deplorable, too, because of some truly funny moments involving Orson Bean and a fantastically comic girl named Phyllis Newman, in a situation which has very little bearing on anything else in the show. This Southern-type doll, working entirely in a bath towel, halts everything with her delivery of "I Was a Shoo-In" and Mr. Bean comes back later to a similar triumph with "I Just Can't Wait," the plaint of a swain who can't wait to see his girl with some clothes on.

HOWARD TAUBMAN, *Times*

If it weren't for disturbances on the stage and in the pit, *Subways Are for Sleeping* would be. The new musical stumbles as if suffering from somnambulism. Its book is dull and vapid, and its characters barely breathe. Occasionally it gives off a burst of energy, like a man struggling to stay awake, but the effort is not sustained. Someone must have slipped it barbiturates instead of Benzedrine. Hardly anyone seems to believe in the musical's main thesis that

David Merrick's famous quote ad. You can fool some of the people some of the time. . . . (Notice "Mail orders filled through Jan. 1963"—a full year in advance!)

it's fun to sleep in a subway or museum or to walk a poodle once a day (well-trained dog, Lancelot) to earn $1.50 for a meal.

This one was so obviously mediocre that Merrick was ready with one of his greatest ploys, the legendary *Subways* Quote Ad. Pulling namesakes of the critics from the phonebook—Brooks Atkinson had, fortunately, just retired—he invited them to the show and (with plenty of wine-and-dine) "helped" them prepare quotes. "The musical of the century!" exclaimed the *other* John Chapman, while Richard Watts—whose photo in the ad revealed him as Broadway's first and only black theatre critic—opined "It deserves to run for a decade." The papers refused the ad—except the *Herald Tribune*, which was fooled and ran it in an early edition. But that was enough: the ensuing publicity was monumental, helping the *Subways* run for six months.

A Tony Award was won by Phyllis Newman (supporting actress).

BROADWAY SCORECARD / perfs: 205 / $: −

rave	favorable	mixed	unfavorable	pan
	2	2	2	1

SWEETHEARTS

a revival of the 1913 operetta, with music by Victor Herbert; lyrics by Robert B. Smith; book by Harry B. Smith and Fred de Gresac, revised by John Cecil Holm

directed by John Kennedy; choreographed by Catherine Littlefield and Theodore Adolphus
produced by Paula Stone (Sloane) and Michael Sloane
with Bobby Clark, Marjorie Gateson, and June Knight

opened January 21, 1947   Shubert Theatre

BROOKS ATKINSON, *Times*

Since Herbert's sweethearts are pretty languid for a cold night in 1947, it is a fortunate thing that Mr. Clark, the illustrious clown,

Bobby Clark with his trademarks: painted-on glasses, stubby cigar and cane. The full-stage photo shows June Knight (upper left) waving to Bobby (upper right), while comedienne Marjorie Gateson and lovers Gloria Story & Mark Dawson stand center. (scenery by *Peter Wolf, costumes by Michael Lucyk, photos by Vandamn*)

has decided to pay as little attention as possible to the music, the plot, and the scenery. Everything in it goes to him by default, including the audience, which was more exhausted than he appeared to be at the final curtain. Early in the first act he bounces on, wearing again that old cloth coat and flat hat, brandishing the walking stick and playing sleight-of-hand with a live cigar. To all honest Americans, that has long since become the prologue to an exuberant evening of abdominal laughter. There is no use in trying to describe it here. It conveys nothing to report that he wears about ten changes of costume, including the gingham wrapper of a lyrical laundry woman and the dusty campaign uniform of a pre-historical hussar. Shut your eyes for a moment, and Bobby pops out in something fresh and outlandish, looking like teacher's pet— smug and simpering. Bobby's genius is his fantastic vitality. There's hardly a moment in his performance when he has not thought of some gag to start guffawing. He dances happily around the ironing board like an inspired imp. He keeps up a running conversation of jokes and puns that fortunately have nothing to do with the play— ogling and leering with boyish mischief. [In "Pilgrims of Love"] he is by turns grave, startled, coy, bravura, and condescending; and as far as the audience is concerned, he might go on singing until two tomorrow morning.

JOHN CHAPMAN, *Daily News*

Bobby Clark is the funniest man of his age and weight in show business—and perhaps the strongest. On those buckling knees, on that low-hung backside, he can carry a show farther than a Pennsylvania freightcar can. He almost carries the revision of Victor Herbert's *Sweethearts* which was presented last evening. Atlas and the entire Santini family could do no more. . . . Once on a slight pretext he appears hauling a cart and, looking into the audience, queries, "Pardon me, but did anyone see a horse going up the aisle?"

LOUIS KRONENBERGER, *PM*

As everyone has been saying for years, Bobby Clark is a very funny fellow; and at the Shubert Tuesday night he was almost funny enough to save a very feeble show. He loped and he leered, he harrumphed and puffed his cigar, he laundered underwear and heaved it onto far-distant clothes lines, he got rigged up as everything but Millard Fillmore and Whistler's Mother, he languidly dangled a lace handkerchief and lustily trod a measure, he sang right notes and wrong ones, he spat on the plot, he fell against the performers, he crept into the fireplace and slid off a sofa. He displayed energy, ingenuity, and versatility. He once more proved himself a notable comic. But to overcome all he was up against, he would have had to be a magician as well.

BROADWAY SCORECARD / perfs: 288 / $: +

rave	favorable	mixed	unfavorable	pan
	4		4	

TAKE A BOW

a vaudeville revue

directed by Wally Wanger; choreographed by Marjery Fielding produced by Lou Walters
with Jay C. Flippen, Chico Marx, Gene Sheldon, and Pat Rooney

opened June 15, 1944   Broadhurst Theatre

John Chapman, *Daily News*

Chico Marx played the old poker game from *The Cocoanuts* [1925] with Gene Sheldon and discovered that Sheldon was funnier than he was.

BROADWAY SCORECARD / perfs: 12 / $: −

rave	favorable	mixed	unfavorable	pan
	2	1	2	3

TAKE ME ALONG

a musical comedy, music and lyrics by Bob Merrill; book by Joseph Stein and Robert Russell, from the 1933 comedy *Ah, Wilderness!* by Eugene O'Neill; previously announced as *Connecticut Summer*

directed by Peter Glenville; choreographed by Onna White (with Herbert Ross)
produced by David Merrick
with Jackie Gleason, Walter Pidgeon, Eileen Herlie, Una Merkel (replacing Ruth Warrick), and Robert Morse

opened October 22, 1959   Shubert Theatre

BROOKS ATKINSON, *Times*

In the first act *Take Me Along* is more like *Destry Rides Again* [1959] than *Ah, Wilderness!* The music blares, the dancers prance, and Broadway goes through its regular routine—substituting energy for gaiety. Everyone is in motion, but nothing moves inside the libretto. If the producers of *Take Me Along* decide to play the second act twice, they will have this department's full endorsement. . . . Mr. Gleason has so many friends that everything he did all through the show brought down the house. But this department was a little island of discontent during Mr. Gleason's first act, when his practiced clowning and his portly bravado made a cheap-jack out of the half-tragic figure of Uncle Sid.

JOHN CHAPMAN, *Daily News*

When a dream ballet turns up in the middle of a show I often shut my eyes and wait until they get the damn thing over with. There is a dream ballet here in which Morse, in his first fit of intoxication, gets all mixed up about Salome, Camille, and other characters he has read about. Staged by Onna White [actually by Herbert Ross], danced by a fine company and costumed in Aubrey Beardsley style by Miles White, this is the best and most imaginative music-show ballet I can recall.

ROBERT COLEMAN, *Daily Mirror*

Frankly, we wondered why they bothered to run a line in the program saying it's based on *Ah, Wilderness!*

WALTER KERR, *Herald Tribune*

As Mr. Gleason hints that, once they are married, there will be some reason for slipping upstairs nights, the spinsterish lady [Eileen Herlie] leaps to her feet and soars shrilly into a Menotti-like declaration of shock. Since Mr. Gleason remains unabashed, Miss Herlie is forced into further tremors, each more delectable than the one that has preceded it. You can not only see her spine tingle, you can hear it. With fluttering fingers, the flute-like tones of a ravaged nightingale, and a profound interior determination to keep the conversation going until she is one solid blush, Miss Herlie sings "I Get Embarrassed" with the skill of a slightly deranged Duse. . . . But the hum of the mosquitos can be heard before long, and the hum is drowsy.

JOHN McCLAIN, *Journal-American*

This latest winner in the Merrick stable burst into the Shubert Theatre last night like a berserk brewery truck, and will probably remain there as long as Pidgeon's legs and Gleason's bay window can hold out.

The second of Bob Merrill's Eugene O'Neill adaptations, with a somewhat better score than *New Girl in Town* (1957). Jackie Gleason's highly publicized feud with Merrick—he even had golf balls emblazoned with the producer's mustachioed countenance, to "inspire" his fairway drives—helped take them along for a year. Once Gleason trundled off, the show quickly faded, despite critical acclaim for replacement William Bendix.

A Tony Award was won by Jackie Gleason (actor).

BROADWAY SCORECARD / perfs: 448 / $: +

rave	favorable	mixed	unfavorable	pan
2	3	1	1	

TENDERLOIN

a musical comedy, with music by Jerry Bock; lyrics by Sheldon
Harnick; book by George Abbott and Jerome Weidman, from the
1959 novel by Samuel Hopkins Adams

directed by George Abbott; choreographed by Joe Layton
produced by Robert E. Griffith and Harold S. Prince
with Maurice Evans, Ron Husmann, Wynne Miller, and Eileen
Rodgers

opened October 17, 1960   46th Street Theatre

FRANK ASTON, *World-Telegram & Sun*

George Abbott has whomped another whopper of a musical. I
was completely Abbottized in song, dance, and merriment.

ROBERT COLEMAN, *Daily Mirror*

Robert Griffith and Harold Prince have been leading the song-
and-dance circuit with five straight hits [*The Pajama Game* (1954),
Damn Yankees (1955), *New Girl in Town* (1957), *West Side Story*
(1957), and *Fiorello!* (1959)], but they finally struck out.

WALTER KERR, *Herald Tribune*

Tenderloin is a musical which takes place in the days when New
York was young and sinful, and Maurice Evans has an extremely
unsympathetic part in it. He plays a crusading minister who wants
to eliminate the production numbers. In case you are wondering
what an actor who has long and valiantly served the serious drama
is doing in the unfamiliar world of musical comedy, don't give it a
second thought. Mr. Evans is perfectly at home. *Tenderloin* is the
most serious comedy I ever saw. It begins with a hymn in a Park
Avenue church, and thereafter gets soberer and soberer and soberer. Mastermind George Abbott has let someone talk him into
applying his magic to an unaccountably dour documentary. Hurrah
and everything for good, clean fun, but where is it?

JOHN MCCLAIN, *Journal-American*

Sad to say, I believe *Tenderloin* is a clinker. The hero, so-called,
is a certain Reverend Brock, who is obviously a facsimile of the Dr.

Parkhurst who tried ineffectually to clean up the police and the underworld just before the turn of the century. The trouble with the play is that it is very difficult to have so much fun with vice and corruption and debauchery and then make a monument of the guy who is going to break it all up. In a world concerned with so many major matters it seems trivial to harken back to this dreary minister who put a few policemen and prostitutes out of business.

As had happened before and would happen again, the writers and producers of a major hit—the distinctively original, Pulitzer Prize–winning *Fiorello!*—rushed to create a second, similarly flavored hit. As had happened before, it just didn't work. Curiously enough, *Tenderloin* shared some of the dichotomic problems of Abbott's other turn-of-the-century metropolitan musical, *A Tree Grows in Brooklyn* (1951). And, like *Brooklyn*, *Tenderloin* boasts one of the better scores of the decade.

BROADWAY SCORECARD / perfs: 216 / $: −

rave	favorable	mixed	unfavorable	pan
	2		5	

13 DAUGHTERS

a Hawaiian musical, with book, music, and lyrics by Eaton Magoon, Jr.; additional book material by Leon Tokatyan

directed by Billy Matthews; choreographed by Rod Alexander
produced by Jack H. Silverman
with Don Ameche, Monica Boyer, Ed Kenney, and Sylvia Syms

opened March 2, 1961   54th Street Theatre

WALTER KERR, *Herald Tribune*

It is written somewhere that all lines of Oriental-type dialogue beginning "it is written somewhere" ought not to have been (written somewhere). How brave Don Ameche is, and how incorruptible. He doesn't wince as he hobbles to the center of the 54th St. stage to enunciate, all too distinctly, "It is written somewhere that a bird in the hand is worth twice the one in the bushel." He just grins his friendly grin, blinks pleasantly beneath his taped-down eyebrows, shrugs his Confucius-burdened shoulders, and pads gently away, his honor intact. He Plays the Game as well as the show, with the result that it is up to you to divorce the man from his material. If the material is at once cast into outer darkness, the man himself remains in a state of theatrical grace, performing with the self-control of a craftsman and the conscience of a king. *13 Daughters* is a show about Hawaii that originated in Hawaii before it was a state and before I was in one, and it has been given musical translation by composer Eaton Magoon, Jr. into approximately the period of "Button Up Your Overcoat" (at least the first two lines of a song called "Puka Puka Pants" sound like "Button Up Your Overcoat," and I suspect the next two lines would be better if they did.)

Hawaii, which entered the Union in 1959, arrived on Broadway in 1961 and bid Times Square a quick "Aloha." Jane Austen's *Pride and Prejudice*–family from *First Impressions* (1959) had five daughters, as did that milkman from Anatevka. Thirteen is at least eight too many, what with all those grass skirts (not to mention "Puka Puka Pants"). And think of all those stage mothers! Broadway got a second dose of Mr. Magoon's Hawaii—for one night, anyway—with *Heathen!* (1972). That exclamation point is theirs, folks, not mine.

BROADWAY SCORECARD / perfs: 28 / $: −				
rave	favorable	mixed	unfavorable	pan
	3		2	2

THREE FOR TONIGHT

a "Diversion in Song and Dance," with special material by Robert Wells

directed and choreographed by Gower Champion
produced by Paul Gregory

with Marge and Gower Champion, Harry Belafonte, and Hiram Sherman

April 6, 1955   Plymouth Theatre

BROOKS ATKINSON, *Times*

Why is Harry Belafonte so magnificent in *Three for Tonight*? Probably because he is a dedicated man. Nothing interests him except the singing of a song. He represents the fanatacism of the dedicated artist. Eliminating himself, he concentrates on the songs with fiery intensity. Although his manners are simple, his singing personality is vibrant and magnetic. Mr. Belafonte never makes a mistake in taste or musicianship, for he is all artist, and a rousing performer in any show. When Mr. Belafonte is not singing, Marge and Gower Champion are usually dancing, and this is something to celebrate, also. They come bearing dances in many moods, all of them attractive. As everyone knows, Mr. and Mrs. Champion are effortless dancers. But they are also people of intelligence who hate the hackneyed and despise the pretentious. *Three for Tonight* is ideal for them, and vice versa.

JOHN CHAPMAN, *Daily News*

Marge Champion who, with her husband Gower, is not unknown to TViewers, made her Broadway debut last evening and she captured what is left of my stony old heart. She is a pixy, a doll, and a darling. Last evening, when she and Gower were circling the stage in a lovely soft-shoe number, my memory took me back to the impish gaiety and stylish grace of Fred and Adele Astaire.

ROBERT COLEMAN, *Daily Mirror*

Paul Gregory has become a one-man Feuer and Martin, socking homers every time at the plate. *Don Juan in Hell* [1951], *John Brown's Body* [1953], *The Caine Mutiny Court Martial* [1954], and now *Three for Tonight*. The latter immediately captured the affections of the first-nighters. The remarkable thing about the Gregory creations is that they rely primarily on imagination, taste, and talent. They use only such props and decor as are necessary to dress a stage. They never permit backgrounds to get in the way of, or overpower, the stellar performers. Gregory has proved again

Gower and Marge high-step it. (photo by Leo Friedman)

662

that lavish expenditures are not necessary for decorative externals, that such things only hamper genius. He is an Elizabethan or a Renaissance Italian at heart, for he realizes that the show is the thing, not the trappings. So, he has brought us another terrific hit.

WILLIAM HAWKINS, *World-Telegram & Sun*

Three for Tonight is like drinking pink champagne in a big florist's on Easter. It makes you feel like a peppermint stick. Best of all it looks so gay and effervescent and easy, you think you can do it all yourself. This is more of a party than a show. This *Three for Tonight* is one of those rare shows that is in a class by itself. The Champions grow remarkably as entertainers, in all the right ways. Gower has directed the show most inventively. In high style prancing, he is the nearest thing to Astaire since Astaire. Marge is very pretty and feminine and in bloom-looking. She has a remarkable gift for wrenching your heart or making you feel bubbly, with just a glance. They are both so deft and swift and light. Yet they never do anything for a physical reason alone. Every movement is rife with story or emotion. The Champions dance out with the chorus a miniature musical comedy, with all the good points, and none of the bad, of most Broadway counterparts. Champion has made gala parades of the chorus exits and entrances.

WALTER KERR, *Herald Tribune*

Producer Paul Gregory doesn't need three for tonight so long as he's got Harry Belafonte for tonight. The singer makes it clear that he is more than a night-club fad. With the varied, moving, in every way brilliant performance he offers us in *Three for Tonight*, Mr. Belafonte indicates that he is ready to join company with the great entertainers. This young man is an artist.

Despite Gower Champion's third consecutive set of raves for his staging—following *Lend an Ear* (1948) and *Make a Wish* (1951)—it was another five years before he finally got a shot at a full-scale musical, with immediately dazzling results: *Bye Bye Birdie* (1960), *Carnival* (1961), and *Hello, Dolly!* (1964).

BROADWAY SCORECARD / perfs: 85 / $: +

rave	favorable	mixed	unfavorable	pan
4	3			

THREE TO MAKE READY

a musical revue, with music by Morgan Lewis; sketches and lyrics by Nancy Hamilton

"devised and staged" by John Murray Anderson; sketches directed by Margaret Webster; choreographed by Robert Sidney
produced by Stanley Gilkey and Barbara Payne
with Ray Bolger, Brenda Forbes, Gordon MacRae, Harold Lang, Bibi Osterwald, and Arthur Godfrey

opened March 7, 1946   Broadhurst Theatre

BURTON RASCOE, *World-Telegram*

When Mr. Bolger sang and danced "The Old Soft Shoe," we all went crazy. Mr. Bolger gave us everything he had—and that is a kind of generosity that leaves you quivering with gratitude. There will be many tender palms today, my own among them. An ermined dowager near me gave vent to an ear-piercing whistle and there were animal-like shrieks of delight mingled with other rackets delicious to a performer's ears. If this is what is called ovation, Mr. Bolger got one that will be the talk of Shubert Alley for months to come. . . . Sketches, lyrics, music, and production are all a pretty sorry mess for Mr. Bolger to be the star of. But what a thrill he is as a dancer, a comedian, a satirist, and an artist, not only with his feet but with every nerve of his body and every muscle of his face.

Ray Bolger made the third and final edition of Nancy Hamilton's intimate revue series a hit. The less successful earlier editions were entitled, logically enough, *One for the Money* (1939) and *Two for the Show* (1940).

THREE WISHES FOR JAMIE

a musical play, with music and lyrics by Ralph Blane; book by Charles O'Neal and Abe Burrows (Burrows replacing Charles Lederer), from O'Neal's 1949 novel *The Three Wishes of Jamie McRuin*

directed by Abe Burrows (replacing Albert Lewis); choreographed by Ted Cappy, with Herbert Ross (replacing Eugene Loring)
produced by Albert Lewis and Arthur Lewis
with Anne Jeffreys (replacing Marion Bell), John Raitt, Bert Wheeler (replacing Cecil Kellaway), and Charlotte Rae

opened March 21, 1952   Mark Hellinger Theatre

BROOKS ATKINSON, *Times*

Mr. O'Neal is the author of an Irish novel that won the Christopher Award and provided the basic material. Mr. Burrows is, among other things, part author of *Guys and Dolls* [1950]. To judge by the placidity of what they have written, Mr. O'Neal and Mr. Burrows have battled to a draw. The Irish legend Mr. O'Neal and Mr. Burrows have evoked has a more immediate Broadway than Irish ancestry. *Three Wishes for Jamie* descends from Broadway operetta of the second decade of this century, which expired because it became a bundle of clichés.

JOHN MCCLAIN, *Journal-American*

Maybe we've all been carried away by *Oklahoma!* [1943], *Brigadoon* [1947], and *Finian's Rainbow* [1947]. Certainly somebody will someday write a musical in which everybody is not dressed in kilts or chaps or does not speak with a brogue or a drawl, and I will rejoice. But this isn't it.

RICHARD WATTS JR., *Post*

It strikes me that a woman's barrenness is perhaps not the happiest subject conceivable for romantic fantasy, whether it is Irish or not, but I must say that *Three Wishes For Jamie* at least handles it painlessly. Nevertheless, it is my impression that the revelation by a jealous rejected suitor of the girl's physical condition does not make for a particularly effective first-act curtain, even in a musical play of serious aims. This, however, is not the end of Jamie's misfortunes. He and his wife finally decide to adopt a boy, but it turns out that the child is dumb. I can report, though, that he regains his speech.

Author O'Neal named his dancing juvenile character O'Ryan, after his ten-year-old son (Ryan O'Neal).

BROADWAY SCORECARD / perfs: 94 / $: −

rave	favorable	mixed	unfavorable	pan
	4		3	

TOP BANANA

a musical comedy, with music and lyrics by Johnny Mercer; book by Hy Kraft

directed by Jack Donohue; choreographed by Ron Fletcher
produced by Paula Stone (Sloane) and Mike Sloane
with Phil Silvers, Rose Marie, Jack Albertson, Bob Scheerer, and Joey Faye

opened November 1, 1951   Winter Garden Theatre

BROOKS ATKINSON, *Times*

Phil Silvers will have to look after his health this winter. He is king-pin in a very funny musical show that ought to last as long as he can. Unless he is also Superman he will be a physical wreck

Phil Silvers in the Berle-esque dream sequence. Nice tie! (set by Jo Mielziner, costume by Alvin Colt, photo by John Bennewitz)

667

before *Top Banana* is a decade old and he will lose what voice he has left at the moment. But this column hopes that he will husband his strength as frugally as possible. For this is a very funny show; and things being as they are at the moment, the country needs it sorely. *Top Banana* looks a little like an illiterate *Guys and Dolls* [1950]. Strictly speaking, it is the lampoon of some television comic who is a colossal egotist and also has talent. No one can imagine who that can be.

JOHN CHAPMAN, *Daily News*

Top Banana is a good, old-fashioned musical. If these words look like faint praise, they are not meant so, for I had an old-fashioned good time. I am not ashamed to say that it never occurred to me to think of the art of the modern musical, and I lost track of the play about an hour and a half before Hy Kraft, the author, did. All the book seems to want is for things to get going as soon as the curtain goes up and keep on going until the curtain comes down—a simple and honest ambition that some of our modern musical theatre might wish it had. At the Winter Garden last evening I felt just like a tired business man—and it felt good.

ROBERT COLEMAN, *Daily Mirror*

That uproar you heard in the neighborhood of Broadway and 51st Street last night wasn't blasting for the foundation of a new building, but a smart audience splitting its sides laughing at *Top Banana*. We haven't heard yaks like those that vibrated the Winter Garden's rafters for many a season. It has the wallop of a heavy-weight and the pace of a fast express. If you want to howl and have a high old time of it, you'd better rush to the box-office immediately. We think you'll love it, unless you hate to laugh.

WILLIAM HAWKINS, *World-Telegram & Sun*

Broadway became Broadway again last night with a rip and a roar. *Top Banana* zooms through the evening with a laughing swoosh that leaves your hair mussed, your ears ringing, and your stomach muscles limp. Silvers is the frantic, bossy, jealous, talented roadhog of a television show. It is no coincidence that Milton Berle was sitting down front last night, laughing his head off. It would seem he co-operated to the extent of being sued by his ghost-writer this week.

WALTER KERR, *Herald Tribune*

It's all right this morning—you can start going to the theatre again. *Top Banana* isn't the kind of show that is ever going to the Berlin Festival, but it's a hearty, cheerful, fast, and funny rough-house which has dipped deep into the ragbag of old burlesque tricks and come up with the cream. It is a field day for Phil Silvers, who has grown into a happy and confident comedian in the past few years. Cast as a onetime burlesque comedian going through the agonies of holding onto his television rating, Silvers clowns through the evening looking remarkably like an enraged rabbit. He spends most of his time casting a jaundiced eye at his fellow performer and, even allowing for those glasses, he seems to have an extraordinary assortment of jaundiced eyes. His voice runs the gamut from a high treble squeal to a thin, resonant rasp, his timing is perfect, and his manner—even when he is at his most aggressive—is wonderfully innocent.

RICHARD WATTS JR., *Post*

The one man among the newer stage comics who seems worthy of the company of such surviving masters as Bobby Clark and Bert Lahr is Phil Silvers, and he has never been in better form than he is in *Top Banana*. He has the authentic and zestful skill of the true comedian, and he is just about as funny a man as the theatre has offered us in a long while. *Top Banana* suffers greatly from split personality. Its star is a constant joy and its book and music are anything else. A young woman calling herself Rose Marie depressed me considerably by singing what seemed to me one of the longest songs in history ["*Sans Souci*"].

A clown show built around Phil Silvers—old-fashioned, brash, and irresistible. Phil even got to sing a duet with a dog, dedicated to his "quinine" friends. *Top Banana* was already in the profit column when Silvers went on a much-needed vacation. Rather than take a summer hiatus, the producers opted to replace their Top Banana with Jack Carter—and quickly lost so much money that they were forced to fold.

Tony and Donaldson Awards were won by Phil Silvers (actor).

TOUCH AND GO

an intimate revue, with music by Jay Gorney; sketches and lyrics by Jean and Walter Kerr

directed by Walter Kerr; choreographed by Helen Tamiris
produced by George Abbott
with Kyle MacDonnell, Nancy Andrews, Peggy Cass, Jonathan Lucas, and Helen Gallagher

opened October 13, 1949   Broadhurst Theatre

BROOKS ATKINSON, *Times*

By throwing a few brains around where they are not too conspicuous, Jean and Walter Kerr have written a capital light revue, put on with skill and wit last evening. Being literate people who can read as well as sit down in the theatre, the Kerrs know what is going on in the manners of our time, and they say so with charm and impishness. *Touch and Go* is good-humored, bright, original, and intelligent—an excellent antidote to a long winter. The Kerrs have accomplished that almost impossible feat of bringing good minds into the squalid mart of Broadway and satirizing intelligent topics with swift dexterity and without feeling condescending about it. In speed, looks, and style, *Touch and Go* is in the best professional taste, and mighty pleasant company for a friendly evening.

JOHN CHAPMAN, *Daily News*

Having had some laughs—including an unexpected whoop when Cinderella flushed the toilet—I came away from the Broadhurst Theatre last evening with the pleasant feeling that I had had a good time. The most successful topical satire is the *Hamlet* number, in which the company, aware that such lugubrious plots as *Carousel* [1945], *Allegro* [1947], and *Street Scene* [1947] have become musical comedy hits, decides to put on a bouncing wow titled *Great Dane a-Comin'*. It is set to snatches of Rodgers, Weill, Porter, and others, and it is grand fun to hear the King, the Queen, and their courtiers sing "This is a Real Nice Castle," or to hear Hamlet intone to Ophelia that she's a queer one. The lugubrious in the drama is nicely needled in a sketch in which *Cinderella* is performed as though Elia Kazan had directed it. The old Cinderella plot is there, but somewhat mixed up with *A Streetcar Named Desire* [1947] and *Death of a Salesman* [1949]. When the Prince comes hunting for Cinderella she is in the w.c. The wicked stepmother and the wicked sisters pretend that nobody else is home, but just then Cinderella pulls the chain and the Prince realizes she is home after all.

ROBERT COLEMAN, *Daily Mirror*

George Abbott paid a visit to Catholic University in Washington, D.C. last season, and discovered an intimate revue by Jean and Walter Kerr and Jay Gorney that caught his fancy. So last evening it arrived at the Broadhurst Theatre, titled *Touch and Go*. That title, incidentally, may prove a prophetic one.

A Tony Award was won by Helen Tamiris (choreographer).

BROADWAY SCORECARD / perfs: 176 / $: −

rave	favorable	mixed	unfavorable	pan
4	1	2	1	

TOVARICH

a musical comedy, with music by Lee Pockriss; lyrics by Anne Croswell; book by David Shaw, from Robert E. Sherwood's 1936 adaptation of the comedy by Jacques Deval

directed by Peter Glenville (replacing Delbert Mann); choreographed by Herbert Ross

Grand Duchess Vivien Leigh Charlestons her way to a Tony Award, toasted by Prince Jean Pierre Aumont. (costumes by Motley, photos by Friedman-Abeles)

672

produced by Abel Farbman and Sylvia Harris in association with Joseph Harris
with Vivien Leigh, Jean Pierre Aumont, Alexander Scourby, Louise Troy, and George S. Irving

opened March 18, 1963   *Broadway Theatre*

WALTER KERR, *Herald Tribune*

The lady's [Leigh's] singing voice is a light baritone, something on the order of Marlene Dietrich with a head cold, but that's suitable enough, remind us as she does of the Snow Queen out of a lost fairy-tale: why shouldn't something husky and northern cling to her, along with all that glitters and glistens? Jean Pierre Aumont plays her husband, and his voice might possibly be considered even less musical than hers, but he is French and, as is well known, the French have only to speak—laughing a little in the middle of each sentence—to seem to be singing. In any case, M. Aumont is the sort of performer who gives his full battlefield attention to a lyric—thinking it, believing it, swearing by it—and he brings so much surprised directness to everything he is doing that you keep on noticing him even when he is off at the sides merely clapping his hands to urge the real dancers on. It's a plain joy to watch two such professionals taming a musical with as much ardor as they would normally bring to a straight play. . . . The tunes edge up against Kurt Weill and Richard Rodgers much too much, neither lyrics nor book are exactly drowned in comedy, director Peter Glenville throws a brother-and-sister comedy team at us so stridently that we want to bite back.

NORMAN NADEL, *World-Telegram & Sun*

Miss Leigh was greeted by a thunderous ovation at her first appearance, and small wonder. The lady is lovely—slender, poised, gracious in manner, articulate in her speech. People were quite ready to forgive an initial, nervous excess of gesture, and some trouble with her pseudo-Russian accent. I was not as ready to forgive when she began to sing. Miss Leigh has a coarse, untrained voice of almost no real control. It is deficient in femininity, warmth, piquancy, and sparkle—which is too bad, in that Miss Leigh's personality has an abundance of these very qualities.

RICHARD WATTS JR., *Post*

Time and music haven't done much to enhance the romantic spell of *Tovarich*, but Vivien Leigh has. It is the charm of Miss Leigh rather than of the story that must keep things going. Miss Leigh atones for many a lapse. Her beauty and air of personal distinction equip her perfectly for the role of the imperious but human Grand Duchess, and her gift for comedy and drama is always present. If she hasn't a phenomenal singing voice, she is a joy when dancing gaily with an American boy [Byron Mitchell] to a pleasant air called "Wilkes-Barre, Pa." and being carried aloft in a chorus number by the Russian nobility. It is fine to have her around again.

A Tony Award was won by Vivien Leigh (actress).

BROADWAY SCORECARD / perfs: 264 / $: —

rave	favorable	mixed	unfavorable	pan
	4	2	1	

A TREE GROWS IN BROOKLYN

a musical play, with music by Arthur Schwartz; lyrics by Dorothy Fields; book by Betty Smith and George Abbott, from the 1943 novel by Betty Smith

directed by George Abbott; choreographed by Herbert Ross
produced by George Abbott in association with Robert Fryer
with Shirley Booth, Johnny Johnston, Marcia Van Dyke, and Nathaniel Frey

Opened April 19, 1951   Alvin Theatre

BROOKS ATKINSON, *Times*

Everything being exactly in order, *A Tree Grows in Brooklyn* turns out to be one of those happy inspirations that the theatre

George Abbott with Robert Fryer Presents

Shirley Booth
Johnny Johnston

A Tree Grows in Brooklyn

A New Musical Comedy

(Based on BETTY SMITH'S Novel)

Book by	Music by	Lyrics by
BETTY SMITH & GEORGE ABBOTT	ARTHUR SCHWARTZ	DOROTHY FIELDS

with

MARCIA VAN DYKE · NATHANIEL FREY · NOMI MITTY · LOU WILLS, Jr.

Scenery and Lighting by JO MIELZINER   Costumes by IRENE SHARAFF
Choreography by HERBERT ROSS   Musical Supervision by JAY BLACKTON
PRODUCTION DIRECTED BY GEORGE ABBOTT

MAIL ORDERS NOW ★ OPENS THURS APR 19

Please enclose stamped, self-addressed envelope with
check or money orders and specify several alternate dates.

PRICES(Tax Included): Opening Night sold out; Evenings: Orchestra $7.20;
Mezzanine $6.00; Balcony $4.80, 4.20, 3.60, 3., 2.40, 1.80. Matinees
WED. & SAT.: Orchestra $4.20; Mezzanine $3.60; Balcony $3., 2.40, 1.80.

ALVIN THEATRE
250 West 52nd St., N. Y. 19, N. Y.

Brooklyn lass Katie Nolan looks forward to wedded bliss, but husband Johnny's a ne'er-do-well headed for tragedy. (drawing by George George)

675

dotes on. With the richest score Arthur Schwartz has written in years, it opened last evening to begin a long and affectionate career. It makes all the performers look their best and makes the audience feel thoroughly contented. Certainly Shirley Booth does. She has never had a part so ideally suited to her style of warm, magnetic comedy; and she has never given a more glowing performance, an endearing folk characterization which is funny and lovable at the same time. To hear Miss Booth singing "Love Is the Reason" in a sort of comic fugue arrangement is to enjoy musical comedy at its best. Mr. Schwartz has a basic theme which he has developed with gusto and devotion, and Dorothy Fields has found idiomatic lyrics to express the comedy and the pensiveness of the music. Some of the songs are in the tradition of the old romantic melodies of the period—good-hearted and expansive in easy rhythms. But Mr. Schwartz has many moods this time; and he and Miss Fields have written everything from a Brooklyn jubilee like "That's How It Goes" to the rhapsodic "I'll Buy You a Star." In short, it is a darlin' show. People in Brooklyn ought to be proud.

JOHN CHAPMAN, *Daily News*

A Tree Grows in Brooklyn is a splendid musical—or two musicals. The first act is marvelously funny, with Shirley Booth giving the performance of her or almost any other comedienne's life. The second act is a very touching one as it completes the story of a Brooklyn Liliom who is a wonderful fellow even if he is a rumpot and a failure. There has been nothing on the music-show stage which tugs so strongly at the heartstrings as this act does since Noel Coward's *Bittersweet* [1929]. Shirley Booth is truly something. I suspect she can do anything in the theatre and do it better than anybody else can. It wouldn't surprise me if she signed up at the Met for the female lead in *Tristan and Isolde.* Her business in *A Tree Grows in Brooklyn* is to be funny, and she had me weeping with laughter. I had quite a bit of eye trouble last evening. If it wasn't from laughing it was from being deeply moved.

OTIS L. GUERNSEY JR., *Herald Tribune*

There are two shows within the stage version of *A Tree Grows in Brooklyn,* and by far the better one is Shirley Booth singing and carrying on as a somewhat faded good-time girl. The other, a watery hymn of failure with musical hope shining through the musical tears, has been plucked by Betty Smith and George Abbott from Miss Smith's successful novel about a Brooklyn childhood. Set to catchy, sentimental music by Arthur Schwartz and street-corner lyrics by Dorothy Fields, there is nothing outstanding in either direction about this half of the act. It is simply a monotonous exposition of a mildly pathetic story, shaded off the stage by the spreading foliage of Miss Booth's grand performance. Speaking in a thin nasal voice in the accent heard east of the Bridge, Miss Booth combines earthy expressions with the gestures of emphatic refinement in a delightful comedy turn. She is right in there pitching when the orchestra tunes up, too. In tune or in fine sarcastic fettle, Miss Booth gives light and contour to a gloomy, flat piece of work.

WILLIAM HAWKINS, *World-Telegram & Sun*

Had a lovely, lovely time at the Alvin last night. Wish you were there. *A Tree Grows in Brooklyn* is unique in what it can do to an audience. Practically all the time, you stifle pleasant, sentimental tears, yet you are constantly laughing. It is a terribly rare combination of heart and craftsmanship and exquisite taste that makes you love being the target of its emotions. I have rarely had more fun laughing, and never had more fun crying. This is an experience of real honesty, taste, and ingenuity. . . . The jewel of the evening is Shirley Booth. If you think she reached the top of her form in *Come Back, Little Sheba* (1950), just wait till you see this. Her songs and dances are captivating, her jokes are gems. The star could have a dozen encores on "Love Is the Reason."

RICHARD WATTS JR., *Post*

It is not exactly a secret these days that Miss Booth is one of the wonders of the American stage, a superb actress, a magnificent comedienne, and an all-around performer of seemingly endless versatility. In a pinch, I suppose she could even play Juliet. For some reason or other, I had never suspected that, among Miss Booth's talents, was the ability to put over a song and even go into a dance when necessary. She is a delight to all beholders. Furthermore, she can take a line of dialogue that is only passably funny and make it seem like a true masterpiece of hilarity. Combining humorous brilliance with a kind of rich humanity, her performance is a complete joy.

☆

Shirley Booth dazzled the critics, the audiences, and the somewhat uneven *Tree Grows in Brooklyn* by turning to musical comedy after her mesmerizing dramatic performance in *Come Back, Little Sheba* (1950). For the record, Miss Booth received a Best Actress Tony and Oscar for *Sheba*, as well as Tonys for *Goodbye, My Fancy* (1948) (supporting actress) and *The Time of the Cuckoo* (1952) (actress). Not to mention a couple of Emmys (1962, 1963) for starring in the TV series "Hazel."

A Donaldson Award was won by Shirley Booth (actress).

BROADWAY SCOREBOARD / perfs: 267 / $: —

rave	favorable	mixed	unfavorable	pan
4	1		2	

TWO ON THE AISLE

a musical revue, with music by Jule Styne; sketches (mostly) and lyrics by Betty Comden and Adolph Green

directed by Abe Burrows; choreographed by Ted Cappy
produced by Arthur Lesser
with Bert Lahr, Dolores Gray, Elliott Reid, and Colette Marchand

opened July 19, 1951   Mark Hellinger Theatre

BROOKS ATKINSON, *Times*

Genuine entertainment, full of brains, talent, wit, humor, and splendor. Betty Comden and Adolph Green have written the pithiest material any revue has had in these parts for a long time; and Jule Styne's music is all right, too. Miss Comden and Mr. Green are the right *litterateurs* for Mr. Lahr's comic antics. He wraps that creased mug and those startled eyes around their impish sketches and lets loose that madman's ululation that has delighted America for years. . . . For the past two or three decades, or at any rate it seems so, Miss Gray has been stunning British audiences with her

The immortal Bert Lahr goes "Gotterdammerung," with show girls. (set by Howard Bay, costumes by Joan Personette, photo by Graphic House)

performing in *Annie Get Your Gun* [1,304 performances]. Now that she is back in America, the State Department should refuse her any more visas. Miss Gray has a voice that can be heard over an orchestra pit, and she has style. She has a fresh approach to everything that comes her way.

JOHN CHAPMAN, *Daily News*

Miss Gray is something rare as a singer—you can hear her. She is a well-constructed female baritone, and when she sings she sings right out loud. I guess she, Ethel Merman, and Mary Martin are the only ones like her left. . . . Memo to Santa Claus: Can't you fix it next Christmas for Bert Lahr to get material that is as funny as he is?

ROBERT GARLAND, *Journal-American*

Even if her type is smaller than Mr. Lahr's, Miss Gray is wonderful. She has everything but subtlety and I am tired of most of that. Dolores Gray is the truest talent to arrive on Broadway since, say, Ethel Merman or Mary Martin. But, when you come to think of it, she is not like anybody but herself. . . . As for Jule Styne's music, that is good and loud.

RICHARD WATTS JR., *Post*

Give me Bert Lahr darting about the stage in a lot of funny costumes and I am almost certain to have a good time. If only because *Two on the Aisle* gives the great clown a beautiful chance to frolic, there should be reason to cheer for it. Since, in addition, it offers a stunning new star to Broadway in the person of a brilliant young singing comedienne named Dolores Gray, is filled with good comic ideas, and has pace, tunefulness and vigor, this is the time to reintroduce the old critical practice of dancing in the streets. It has been a long time since Mr. Lahr has had so many opportunities to do the things that he manages to perfection. I recommend to you Bert Lahr pretending that he is Valentino and Helen Hayes as Queen Victoria, impersonating a veteran baseball player on a television show, emerging as Captain Universe set down on the planet Venus, doing Siegfried at the Metropolitan, and offering a primitive burlesque sketch as T. S. Eliot or Cole Porter might have written it. This is what we have been waiting for, a Bert Lahr field day.

BROADWAY SCOREBOARD / perfs: 276 / S: +

rave	favorable	mixed	unfavorable	pan
5		2		

TWO'S COMPANY

a musical revue, with music mostly by Vernon Duke; lyrics mostly by Ogden Nash, additional lyrics by Sammy Cahn; sketches mostly by Charles Sherman and Peter De Vries

production supervised by John Murray Anderson (replacing Charles Sherman and Jerome Robbins); sketches directed by Jules Dassin; choreographed by Jerome Robbins
produced by James Russo and Michael Ellis
with Bette Davis, Hiram Sherman, David Burns (replacing Nathaniel Frey), and Nora Kaye

opened December 15, 1952   Alvin Theatre

JOHN CHAPMAN, *Daily News*

A man named Eisenhower got all the way to Korea and out of there without anybody knowing about it because the newspapers helped keep the secret. It's been different with BETTE DAVIS. Everybody must know about her, so I'm not blabbing when I report that BETTE DAVIS appeared last evening in a revue, *Two's Company*. I never did find out who the other one of the two mentioned in the title was, but BETTE DAVIS (that's the way they spell her nine times in the program) does have with her a few upper and lower case entertainers. She also has with her a number of songs and sketches which are mostly lower case. The show seems to be a triumph of matter over mind. . . . The dancing, by Nora Kaye, Bill Callahan, and Maria Karnilova is very good, and Miss Kaye can be funny as well as classical.

WILLIAM HAWKINS, *World-Telegram & Sun*

Her dancing is likely to consist of hip rolls, marching, and none too steady lifts by a whole corps of male partners. Her singing is

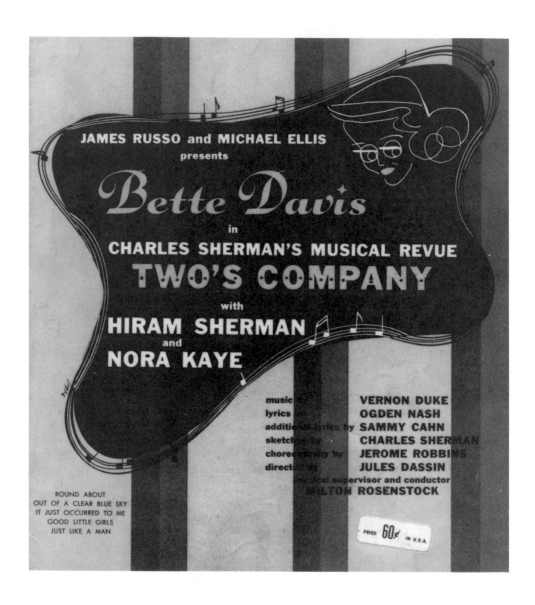

Bette Davis seems rather sedated; not surprising, under the cir-cumstances. Pre-Broadway credits. (drawing by Sybil)

deep, husky, very articulate and rhythmic, but not very musical. In sketches she can do almost anything better than whoop off a laugh line. But *Two's Company* is a triumph of personality and will power. Miss Davis is electric, as she has always been on the screen. Now, more than ever, she is not only anxious that you like her. She is grimly determined that you shall, and you will. Her goal is to give you a memorable evening. She will try on all the funny hats and shoes, black out her teeth, tell bathroom jokes, and stand on her head if asked. Somewhere along the line you are dazzled and in the end awed. You may suspect that it has never crossed Bette Davis's mind that Mary Martin, Ethel Merman, Marilyn Miller, or Gertrude Lawrence ever did anything she cannot do as well. This naive and humorless faith is both endearing and awesome.

WALTER KERR, *Herald Tribune*

It's always fun to see a distinguished actress unbend, and in *Two's Company* Bette Davis unbends all over the place. She trucks right out and lets herself be tossed into the air by four or five chorus boys. She ties an old bandana around her hair, drapes herself in a moth-eaten sweater, and slouches in sneakers through a sketch about tenement passion. She blacks out her teeth, jams a corncob pipe in her mouth, and lets loose with the yowls of a hillbilly ballad. Indeed, Miss Davis unbends so much that there's some doubt in my mind whether she'll ever be able to straighten up again. The trouble with this business of encouraging a serious performer to let her hair down, climb off that Hollywood pedestal, and rough it up with the lowbrow comics is that it all adds up to a single joke, and the same one. Unless the performer has hitherto unsuspected and thoroughly genuine talents of the music-hall sort—which Miss Davis would not seem to possess—the descent from Parnassus thins out into a stunt, eminently suitable for parties alongside the family swimming pool but hardly the stuff with which to sustain an entire theatrical evening. It's a lot like listening to Beethoven's Fifth played on a pocket comb. You marvel that it can be done at all. And five minutes is just about enough of it.

JOHN McCLAIN, *Journal-American*

The unveiling of any big musical is always a glamorous and exciting event in our town and *Two's Company* promised even more. It had Bette Davis as star; it had suffered a series of misadventures which provoked daily publicity throughout the land; it had been re-written and re-directed by everybody from John Greenleaf Whittier to John Murray Anderson, and until curtain time you could get odds of 5-to-2 that it might never open in New York.

A legendary fiasco, with Bette Davis—fleeing a hostile Hollywood—running into all sorts of problems on the legitimate stage. After a couple of months she got "sick," and that was that.

A Tony Award was won by Hiram Sherman (supporting actor). Donaldson Awards were won by Jerome Robbins (choreographer) and Nora Kaye (female dancer).

BROADWAY SCORECARD / perfs: 90 / $: −

rave	favorable	mixed	unfavorable	pan
1		2	2	2

THE UNSINKABLE MOLLY BROWN

a musical biography of Molly Tobin Brown (1860–1924), with music and lyrics by Meredith Willson; book by Richard Morris; previously announced as *The Unsinkable Mrs. Brown*

directed by Dore Schary (replacing Vincent J. Donehue); choreographed by Peter Gennaro
produced by the Theatre Guild and Dore Schary
with Tammy Grimes, Harve Presnell, and Cameron Prud'homme

opened November 3, 1960   Winter Garden Theatre

FRANK ASTON, *World-Telegram & Sun*

I'll hate myself clear through today's Final for saying this. Although Harve Presnell sings like the dickens, the dancers are exciting, and the performers burst with talent, the show doesn't meet its own possibilities or the standards of the old *Music Man* [1957] master. Comedy is lusty—yowling miners, "royal guests" in mock processional "with crowns," and Miss Grimes herself with her croaks, chin angle, shoulder pushing, sturdy legs, funny tummy line, cuss words, and general adorability. She is practically the whole show—awfully little to carry the whole burden.

JOHN CHAPMAN, *Daily News*

Tammy Grimes herself is unsinkable, being a buoyant sprite, and I wish that *The Unsinkable Molly Brown* were as consistently ebullient as she is. But, even with music and lyrics by Meredith (*The Music Man*) Willson, there are lapses in this big offering. Lapses of momentum, mainly, as people come out and do an "in one" scene and seem to be waiting for the stage hands to bring up another setting.

ROBERT COLEMAN, *Daily Mirror*

Molly is a boorish egomaniac, always seeking to buy the respect that she never earns. The real Molly may have had a heart of gold, but it doesn't shine through in the Morris script. We kept wanting to give her the back of our hand. . . . Miss Grimes, who's become something of a cult, is a perfect fright in the early passages. She has distorted her mouth into an Eddie Foy grin, done weird makeup tricks to her eyes and has to wear a dress for a spell that looks like a gunny-sack. But as things move along, she assumes a goodly measure of tawdry glamor. And she's immensely dynamic.

WALTER KERR, *Herald Tribune*

One haughty hoot from her train-whistle voice and you feel the Sante Fe is coming, and you'd just better duck. It has—I don't believe it, but I was there—an eerie delicacy beneath all its bravura, a kind of mountain-stream ripple that wavers and whispers between every two notes. I have it. Helen Morgan has been crossed with Rosetta Duncan. That isn't a person up there on the stage at all. It's Raggedy Ann out of the Cabinet of Doctor Caligari. . . . Richard Morris has honed-out some fine corn fed dialogue; but his left hand is all thumbs, and the plotting and planning and untidy segueing from one scene to another might easily have been left in an alley in Boston. The structure gasps often, waiting for Miss Grimes. Meredith Willson's music keeps the timpani popping, and all concerned have been exceedingly wise in retaining

Harve Presnell to sing the principal love songs. It's a pleasure, Mr. Presnell, even if you don't know which hand to hook into which side of the belt for the next five minutes or so. But the score is also, let us say, similar to Mr. Willson's *The Music Man* (no doubt a good place to steal from), and it is similar to itself pretty often. That same old rhythm erupts like clockwork. Dore Schary's stage direction seems in as much trouble as the Titanic every now and then.

Molly Brown proved that Meredith Willson—you know, the guy who wrote *The Music Man*—was just another one-show phenom. Keenly disappointing, as the critics (and everyone) seem to have been routing for the man who had come out of nowhere with the sleeper hit of the decade. *Molly* managed to get by nevertheless, on her rambunctiousness and her advance sale.

A Tony Award was won by Tammy Grimes (supporting actress).

BROADWAY SCORECARD / perfs: 532 / $: +

rave	favorable	mixed	unfavorable	pan
	3	2	2	

UP IN CENTRAL PARK

a costume operetta, with music by Sigmund Romberg; lyrics by Dorothy Fields; book by Herbert and Dorothy Fields, suggested by William "Boss" Tweed's Central Park project of 1870–1872

directed by John Kennedy; choreographed by Helen Tamiris
produced by Michael Todd
with Wilbur Evans, Betty Bruce, Noah Beery, Sr., and Maureen Cannon

opened January 27, 1945   Century Theatre

JAMES ARONSON, *Post*

It wasn't quite real, last Saturday night after the opening of Mike Todd's *Up in Central Park*. I mean riding from the theatre in a brougham (courtesy Mr. Todd) through the snow-covered hills and meadows of the Park, to a midnight supper for the company (same courtesy) at the Tavern-on-the-Green. . . . Too much of the humor was of the begorra-begorra, back-of-me-hand-to-ye school, straight off the ancient four-a-day boards. At times the vaudeville brogue was so thick you couldn't smell the flowers in the Park for the corned beef and cabbage. And I like corned beef and cabbage.

Louis Kronenberger, *PM*

Mr. Romberg's music has, to be sure, its agreeable side: if it is too reminiscent and unvaried, at least, it is often melodious enough. Dorothy Fields's lyrics are nothing special, but they are at least brighter than the book. It's too bad that *Up in Central Park* can't shake off dullness, for it's a commendable departure from formula musicals. The trouble is, it departed with only the haziest idea of its destination.

Lewis Nichols, *Times*

Up in Central Park is as big as its namesake, and it is just as pretty to look at. There, however, the favorable comparison must end. The Park teems with life and zest and gaiety, the show does not. *Up in Central Park* plods along where it should dance, it talks where it should laugh; it is long and, to be frank about it, is pretty dull. The Park should form a wonderful setting for a musical show, but this one needs someone like Commisioner [Robert] Moses to do a bit of landscaping or doctoring.

An old-fashioned operetta hit, benefitting from wartime nostalgia and Mike Todd huckstering.

A Donaldson Award was won by Howard Bay (scenic designer).

BROADWAY SCORECARD / perfs: 504 / $: +				
rave	favorable	mixed	unfavorable	pan
2	4			2

THE VAGABOND KING

a revival of the 1925 operetta, with music by Rudolph Friml; lyrics by Brian Hooker; book by Brian Hooker and W. H. Post, revised by Russell Janney, from the 1901 play *If I Were King* by Justin Huntly McCarthy

directed by George Ermoloff; choreographed by Igor Schwezoff
produced by Russell Janncy
with John Brownlee, Frances McCann, and José Ruben

opened June 29, 1943   Shubert Theatre

JOHN ANDERSON, *Journal-American*

It is, I know, a losing fight that is put up against the writers of librettos, but there is no harm in pointing out again the essential foolishness of the idea that a man may be so completely changed in appearance by taking a bath and putting on a costume that his closest friends can't recognize him. Since this is the cornerstone of the plot of *The Vagabond King*, I am obliged to view it with the customary skepticism. But this is obviously beside the point. *The Vagabond King* has proved that it survives such monstrous trifles, and for all I know it will prove it again. The customers last night gave resounding evidence that it was their dish, and they are welcome to any points of mine to get it.

LOUIS KRONENBERGER, *PM*

When I first heard *The Vagabond King* back in 1925, I lost my wallet at some point in the proceedings, and came away muttering "To Hell with Burgundy!" in a sense not intended by the lyric-writers. . . . Though it lacks style, the present production has schmaltz enough. If you liked it once, you'll like it again.

THE VAMP

a musical satire, with music by James Mundy; lyrics by John La-touche; book by John Latouche and Sam Locke, from a story by Latouche; tryout title: *Delilah*

directed by David Alexander; production supervised and choreo-graphed by Robert Alton
produced by Oscar S. Lerman, Martin B. Cohen, and Alexander F. Carson
with Carol Channing, David Atkinson, Bibi Osterwald, and Matt Mattox

opened November 10, 1955   Winter Garden Theatre

BROOKS ATKINSON, *Times*

Offering Miss Channing in almost any role verges on inspiration. For she is a likable comic with a rangy style and a pair of large, innocent eyes. As the seasons go by she looks less and less like flesh and blood and more and more like an animated cartoon. Now she has also learned how to make her singing voice sound like a jew's harp—all twangy, deep, and mellow. No one knows where her broad accent comes from. It's like a bad dream of the Middle West, and very funny. . . . Noise and fury are the things most character-istic of *The Vamp*. One cannot help recalling how easily Jerome Robbins said everything that it is trying to say in a crisp ballet about the Mack Sennett comedies a few seasons ago [in *High But-ton Shoes* (1947)]. Miss Channing's big, baby eyes stare through the follies of this huge show as if she could not believe what she is seeing. What she is seeing is all too true.

JOHN CHAPMAN, *Daily News*

In the first scene of *The Vamp*, Carol Channing is a healthy Bronx farm girl who cleans up all the chores—like feeding the chickens, pitching hay, and hauling water from the well—in no time at all—and she sings bass besides. In all the loud and lusty scenes which follow she does most of the other chores, too, and no set of theatrical managers ever had a better hired girl. Miss Chan-ning is, to state the case briefly, superb and unique. Miss Chan-ning is no less than wonderful, and she really has learned how to sing bass. If you want to see a movie siren drive men mad, don't

Carol Channing, as the deadliest of the species, shows off her Theda Bara pose. During the tryout they changed the title from Delilah *to* The Vamp.

bother with those old flickers at the Modern Museum. Go see our Carol at the Winter Garden.

WILLIAM HAWKINS, *World-Telegram & Sun*

If ever a girl gave her all to make a show a hit, Carol Channing does, with the best will in the world and her fine talent, to *The Vamp*. But the big, noisy musical at the Winter Garden is like a floppy mantle thrown around her neck, out of style and charmless. Every once in a while there are real silent pictures shown, some taken of the cast, some actually old. This is a dangerous stunt, because they have a way of looking better than what is on the stage, and make *The Vamp* look aggressively unoriginal.

WALTER KERR, *Herald Tribune*

Some shows are born dull, some have dullness thrust upon them. *The Vamp*, which hobble-skirted its way into the Winter Garden, must once—long ago, in those first story conferences—have been a beautiful baby. Casting wide-eyed, bullfrog-throated Carol Channing as a slinky siren of the silver screen was clearly a captivating idea. Unfortunately, no one seems to have had a single idea since. . . . Miss Channing has been trotted out at every turn. She is, as everyone knows, a glorious zany. With long platinum braids bouncing over her shoulder and a quaver in her voice that makes every final syllable sound as though it had been played on a vibra-harp, the star plunges into the business with rugged fortitude. By dropping her voice to the Winter Garden basement or pronouncing "human" as though it obviously ought to be spelled "hew-min," she teases laughs from a desert-dry script. . . . [Channing] has been turned, all too transparently, into a work-horse for the authors. Song after song is hurled at her—songs that might have been suitable for a second-rate ingénue, songs that make almost no use of all of her singing talents—and she is simply ordered to bring them alive. The task is an impossible one and the procedure has a further penalty: when Bibi Osterwald, cast as a gossip columnist, is finally given a single ragtime rhythm ["Ragtime Romeo"] to belt out she is able—out of her own winning slyness, and out of sheer relief—to stop the show cold. Miss Channing is valiant, but she is being victimized.

☆

Carol Channing had been absent from the musical stage since her spectacular emergence as Lorelei Lee in *Gentlemen Prefer Blondes* (1949). (She briefly followed Rosalind Russell in *Wonderful Town* [1953], prior to taking the show on tour.) *The Vamp* was custommade to fit the specialized Channing talents, but things didn't quite work out. And she didn't get another chance until 1964, when that *Dolly!* musical came along.

BROADWAY SCORECARD / perfs: 60/$: −

rave	favorable	mixed	unfavorable	pan
	1		4	2

VINTAGE '60

a satirical revue, with songs and sketches by Jack Wilson, Alan Jeffreys, Maxwell Grant, and others (including Fred Ebb and Sheldon Harnick)

entire production supervised and "comedy direction" by Michael Ross; "staged" and choreographed by Jonathan Lucas
produced by David Merrick in association with Zev Bufman, George Skaff, and Max Perkins
with Barbara Heller, Fay De Witt, Dick Patterson, Mickey Deems, Bert Convy, Bonnie Scott, and Michele Lee

opened September 12, 1960   Brooks Atkinson Theatre

WALTER KERR, *Herald Tribune*

If *Vintage '60* proves anything at all, it proves that fresh, inexperienced young people can come to New York and goof just exactly like talented, middle-aged professionals sometimes do. The kids who are cavorting at the radiantly refurbished and newly-named Brooks Atkinson Theatre (Brooks Atkinson himself, sitting in aisle-seats especially numbered for him, looked just as radiant last night, possibly because he doesn't have to be mean this morning) all come from California. Breezy as the people are, the ideas too often have circles under their eyes.

JIM O'CONNOR, *Journal-American*

A jarring note was the lampooning of Vice-President Nixon in a travesty on the Republican Presidential Convention. Since no digs were taken at the Democrats or Senator Kennedy, this ill-advised burlesque may cost *Vintage '60* some Republican support.

The "lack of Republican support" didn't make much of a difference to *Vintage '60*. Merrick's decision to bring the show in—at minimal personal financial risk—seems to have stemmed from his desire to have seven shows running on Broadway at once.

BROADWAY SCORECARD / perfs: 8 / $: −

rave	favorable	mixed	unfavorable	pan
1	1	2	3	

WEST SIDE STORY

a musical drama, with music by Leonard Bernstein; lyrics by Stephen Sondheim (and Leonard Bernstein, billing removed); book by Arthur Laurents, from a "conception of Jerome Robbins," suggested by Shakespeare's tragedy *Romeo and Juliet*; previously announced as *East Side Story*

directed by Jerome Robbins; choreographed by Jerome Robbins and Peter Gennaro
produced by Robert E. Griffith and Harold S. Prince by arrangement with Roger L. Stevens
with Carol Lawrence, Larry Kert, Chita Rivera, Art Smith, Mickey Calin (Michael Callan), Ken LeRoy, and Lee Becker

opened September 26, 1957   Winter Garden Theatre

FRANK ASTON, *World-Telegram & Sun*

West Side Story is more than a Romeo meowing to a Juliet on a fire escape. It is a marvel peculiar to this country. Here we breed

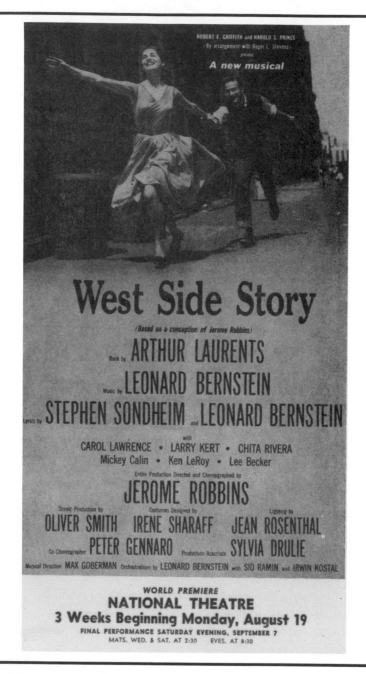

Carol Lawrence and Larry Kert fly down the street, shot on location at 418 West 56th St. "West Side Story is a musical with all kinds of glowing auspices," boasted the hype on the back of the herald. Pre-Broadway credits, including co-lyricist Leonard Bernstein. (photo by Friedman-Abeles)

evil in our cities, but here we also parade a Bernstein and a Robbins so that a big part of this tortured world may say, "America
must be proud of boys like those." And theatre-going Americans
may reply, "You're darn tootin' we are."

BROOKS ATKINSON, *Times*

Although the material is horrifying, the workmanship is admirable. Gang warfare is the material of *West Side Story*, and very
little of the hideousness has been left out. But the author, composer, and ballet designer are creative artists. Pooling imagination
and virtuosity, they have written a profoundly moving show that is
as ugly as the city jungles and also pathetic, tender, and forgiving.
West Side Story is an incandescent piece of work that finds odd bits
of beauty amid the rubbish of the streets. Everything is of a piece.
Everything contributes to the total impression of wildness, ecstasy,
and anguish. The astringent score has moments of tranquility and
rapture, and occasionally a touch of sardonic humor. And the ballets convey the things that Mr. Laurents is inhibited from saying
because the characters are so inarticulate. The hostility and suspicion between the gangs, the glory of the nuptials, the terror of the
rumble, the devastating climax—Mr. Robbins has found the patterns of movement that express these parts of the story. This is one
of those occasions when theatre people, engrossed in an original
project, are all in top form. The subject is not beautiful. But what
West Side Story draws out of it is beautiful.

JOHN CHAPMAN, *Daily News*

The American theatre took a venturesome forward step last
evening. This is a bold new kind of musical theatre—a juke-box
Manhattan opera. The various fine skills of show business are put
to new tests, and as a result a different kind of musical has emerged.
The manner of telling the story is a provocative and artful blend of
music, dance, and plot. The music is by Leonard Bernstein, and it
is superb. In it there is the drive, the bounce, the restlessness, and
the sweetness of our town. It takes up the American musical idiom
where it was left when George Gershwin died. It is fascinatingly
tricky and melodically beguiling.

WALTER KERR, *Herald Tribune*

The radioactive fallout from *West Side Story* must still be descending on Broadway this morning. Jerome Robbins has put to-

gether, and then blasted apart, the most savage, restless, electrifying dance patterns we've been exposed to in a dozen seasons. He never runs out of his original explosive life-force. Though the essential images are always the same—two spitting groups of people advancing with bared teeth and clawed fists upon one another—there is fresh excitement [in each number]. When the knives come out, and bodies begin to fly wildly through space under buttermilk clouds, the sheer visual excitement is breathtaking. He has been almost sacrificially assisted in this macabre onslaught of movement by Leonard Bernstein, who for the most part has served the needs of the onstage threshing-machine, dramatizing the footwork rather than lifting emotions into song. Which brings us to the fact that there is another side to *West Side Story*. This show is, in general, not well sung. It is rushingly acted. And it is, apart from the spinetingling velocity of the dances, almost never emotionally affecting. The evening hurtles headlong past whatever endearing simplicities may be hidden in Arthur Laurent's text or Stephen Sondheim's lyrics. This is the show that could have danced all night, and nearly did. But the dancing is it. Don't look for laughter or—for that matter—tears.

JOHN McCLAIN, *Journal-American*

The most exciting thing that has come to town since *My Fair Lady* [1956]. Here is one of the rare blends of talent that obviously struck no snags. Together [they] devised book, music, lyrics, and choreography which should remain for many seasons as the most fortunate union in the history of money. Young Mr. Sondheim has gone all the way with the mood of his lyrics. His ballads are the lament of the sincere, and he can come up with the most hilarious travesty of our times in "Gee, Officer Krupke"—a plaint which should settle the problem of juvenile delinquency forever. This brings us to [scenic designer] Oliver Smith. Without stopping the action he lowers fire escapes from the sky, changes a Bronx backyard to a Never-Never Land, and without pretension creates the atmosphere of our sinister streets and playgrounds. *West Side Story* is something quite new in the theatre, and it is just great.

RICHARD WATTS JR., *Post*

To say that he turns the two rival gangs into companies of ballet dancers might indicate a softening process that would weaken the starkness of his dramatic narrative, but, surprisingly, this is far from altogether true. The idea did bother me at the start, but the choreography has been fused with the story so effectively that the ugliness and horror of the war to the death between the boys is never lost. As for Bernstein's music, I should say that its mood lies somewhere between the sardonic bite of his score for *Candide* [1956] and his considerably more popular songs from *Wonderful Town* [1953]. If it leans more in the direction of the former, it is because of what seemed to me a certain chilliness that didn't altogether capture the hot-bloodedness of grimly embattled youth.

While the 1950s had seen a couple of exceptionally written superhits (like *Guys and Dolls* [1950] and *My Fair Lady*), *West Side Story* was the first musical blockbuster to shatter new ground since *South Pacific* (1949). *West Side* was a little too advanced for its audiences, who seem to have been uncomfortable with the subject matter: the initial run was considerably shorter than the runs of lesser musicals like *Fanny* (1954), *Damn Yankees* (1955), and *Bells Are Ringing* (1956). It wasn't until the 1961 movie version that the *West Side* score entered the public consciousness: since then the show has been properly recognized as a classic blend of music, words, and dance. In terms of the score: it has been rumored that while Bernstein was off trying to fix *Candide*, lyricist Sondheim wrote some of the music himself. Bernstein's co-lyricist billing mysteriously disappeared from the credits during the tryout, presumably as a trade-off. (The composer was careful to take full public credit for the few lyrics he contributed to *On the Town* [1944] and *Candide*; it seems highly unlikely that he'd disclaim his *West Side* work without a pretty good reason.) Whatever the case may be, the score is all of a piece—and it is all superb!

Tony Awards were won by Jerome Robbins (choreographer) and Oliver Smith (scenic designer). The season's major awards were swept by *The Music Man*. Robbins also received an Oscar for co-directing the 1961 motion picture version, as well as a special Oscar for recreating his choreography.

WHAT MAKES SAMMY RUN?

a musical comedy, with music and lyrics by Ervin Drake; book by Budd and Stuart Schulberg, from the 1941 novel by Budd Schulberg

directed by Abe Burrows (replacing Arthur Storch); choreographed by Matt Mattox
produced by Joseph Cates
with Steve Lawrence, Sally Ann Howes, Robert Alda, and Bernice Massi

opened February 27, 1964   54th Street Theatre

JOHN CHAPMAN, *Daily News*

Abe Burrows has directed *What Makes Sammy Run?* and has kept it moving. But moving backward, maybe.

NORMAL NADEL, *World-Telegram & Sun*

The most zestfully evil musical of the year. Steve Lawrence's Sammy is the ultimate rat-fink, with palms, battle stars, and oak-leaf cluster. Blue-eyed Lawrence begins by running like an urchin and winds up walking like a tin Caesar. He looks better snarling than ordinary men do smiling. He can belt a song to the far wall, break down a girl's resistance as if he were splitting pistachios with his teeth, and utter black betrayals as piously as prayer. Invisible as colored fireworks in this saga of the insatiable Sammy is the deft hand of director Abe Burrows, who didn't start with the show but brought it to Broadway. Burrows, as any school child knows, could doctor McGuffey's First Reader into the laugh hit of the season. In this case, he diverts your attention from situations which are perhaps too familiar on the musical stage, and from a few sags in the script. He does this, with the help of the talent which producer

What Makes Sammy Run? *Steve Lawrence, that's what. Sammy goes Hollywood, with a statuesque lovely statuing over him (despite his elevator shoes).* (drawing by Oscar Liebman)

Cates has collared, by trying every technique that has ever worked in a show. So *Sammy* sometimes looks like an encyclopedia of the American musical, but it's entertainment.

RICHARD WATTS JR., *Post*

The deplorable Sammy Glick is even more unpleasant than he was in the novel. Where the book found a certain sympathy for him by its glimpse into his impoverished boyhood background on the East Side, the musical play reveals him at his worst. Nor is he granted the alleviating circumstance of being, as was the eminent Joey [of *Pal Joey* (1940)], something of a boob, because Sammy is a very shrewd and knowing operator, indeed. . . . The unattractiveness of its central figure offers quite a problem to the lovely Sally Ann Howes. Miss Howes is playing a screen writer who temporarily falls for Sammy and, granting the unaccountability of feminine taste in such matters, it requires all her skill as an actress to make one believe that an intelligent girl could have fallen even a moment for the wiles of such a fellow. It is a notable tribute to her that she surmounts the obstacle and gives a charming and remarkably credible performance.

A trouble-ridden, long-running flop, complete with front page "star" troubles. Steve Lawrence added lines at will, publicly "bad-mouthed" the show, and called in sick for 32 performances—including the big Christmas/New Year's holiday week! On his next excursion through stormy Broadway seas, Lawrence made sure to run things himself. *Golden Rainbow* (1968) it was called, from the 1957 comedy *A Hole in the Head*. A *real* stinker.

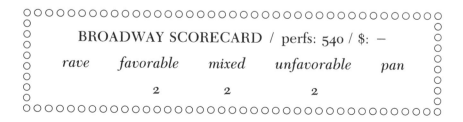

BROADWAY SCORECARD / perfs: 540 / $: −

rave	favorable	mixed	unfavorable	pan
	2	2	2	

WHAT'S UP

a musical comedy, with music by Frederick Loewe; lyrics by Alan Jay Lerner; book by Arthur Pierson and Alan Jay Lerner

staged and choreographed by George Balanchine; book directed by Robert II. Gordon
produced by Mark Warnow
with Gloria Warren, Jimmy Savo, Johnny Morgan, and Patricia Marshall

opened November 11, 1943   National Theatre

JOHN CHAPMAN, *Daily News*

The high spot is when Jimmy Savo follows the current Broadway musical fashion by having his own dream ballet with just one girl, Phyllis Hill. The girl is the usual will-o-the-wisp in a ballet skirt, and Jimmy is forever pursuing her. But she's a big girl, and Jimmy, a little guy, has to keep lugging a chair around so he can stand on it and clutch at his dream. It is a really funny number. Balanchine has cooked up a second dream ballet in which the army, in pajamas, dances with the schoolgirls, in their nighties. It's all right, in a gentle sort of way. The men dance and sing all right and manage to look like soldiers, which is an achievement in view of the manpower shortage in Broadway musicals. . . . The songs, by Alan Jay Lerner and Frederick Loewe, seem fresh and sometimes tuneful.

LOUIS KRONENBERGER, *PM*

About most shows this season one's only wish is that they had never occurred to their authors. Last night's show at least reached the level of making one wish that something could have been done about it. A pint-sized musical comedy consisting of a dozen nice girls and boys plus Jimmy Savo, *What's Up* has plenty of youth and friendliness to offer. Unfortunately, it knows it and—having very little else in its kit—plays them up for ten times what they're worth. The result is so painfully, so epically cute, that by the end of the evening I would have welcomed a hatchet-faced old maid or a besotted old man.

LEWIS NICHOLS, *Times*

No one expects a musical comedy book to rank as high literature—although one or two have—but something a little this side of embarrassing does no harm. *What's Up* is all right when it is tap dancing or singing, but when it settles down to conversations the entire course of the world seems to slow down until it has finished. If somebody only had bothered to do something about the book which concerns the crew of an airplane, plus an Indian potentate, being quarantined in a girls' school because of measles— and one girl, in love, calling the President to see what he could do. . . . Frederick Loewe wrote the music, the tunes being agreeable rather than outstanding. Mr. Lerner has attached lyrics that are not particularly outstanding.

WILELLA WALDORF, *Post*

As pretty and sweet and self-consciously cute as a movie starlet, and just as vapid. Early in the evening a determined, if somewhat coy, effort was made to introduce some dirt into the proceedings, but the off-color motif faded out as rapidly as some of the voices, and from then on it was up to George Balanchine to think up some new twirls to garnish Frederick Loewe's tunes, which are pretty and sweet and, like the ingénues, a little hard to tell apart.

This pedestrian wartime musical marked the Broadway debut of the team of Lerner and Loewe. (Loewe had been around briefly, with the 1938 flop operetta, *Great Lady*.) The new team made remarkable progress with their next two efforts, the unconventional *Day Before Spring* (1945) and the exceptional *Brigadoon* (1947).

BROADWAY SCORECARD / perfs: 63 / $: —

rave	favorable	mixed	unfavorable	pan
1	1	2	4	

WHERE'S CHARLEY?

a musical comedy, with music and lyrics by Frank Loesser; book by George Abbott, from the 1892 farce *Charley's Aunt* by Brandon Thomas

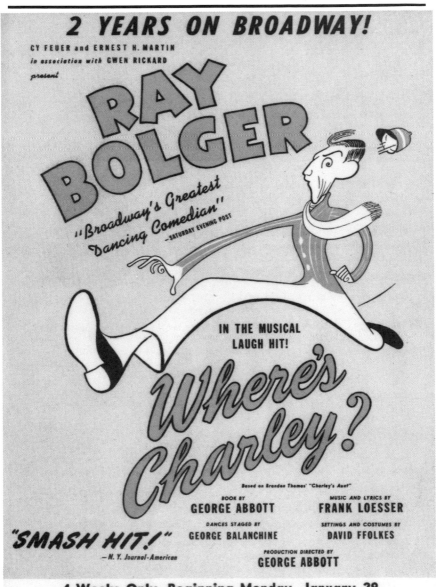

Oxford undergrad Ray Bolger dashing to change into his dress. This was actually Hirschfeld's caricature from Three to Make Ready *(1946), with suitable collegiate garb drawn on for the occasion. Return engagement, 1951.* (drawing by Al Hirschfeld)

directed by George Abbott; choreographed by George Balanchine
produced by Cy Feuer and Ernest H. Martin in association with
Gwen Rickard (Bolger)
with Ray Bolger, Allyn McLerie, Byron Palmer, and Doretta Morrow

opened October 11, 1948   St. James Theatre

BROOKS ATKINSON, *Times*

Ray Bolger is not the greatest man in the world. But why quib-
ble? In *Where's Charley?*, he is great enough to make a mediocre
musical show seem thoroughly enjoyable. An eminent hoofer of the
bucolic breed, he pushes the show aside now and then to spin
rhapsodically through his mocking dances, grinning like a country
gawk and translating love into leaps, whirls, and comic staggers.
Mr. Bolger skips impishly through like a rustic caricature with
winged feet. Sometimes he bounces clear across that rusty plot.
Where's Charley? is a rhetorical question. Where's Bolger? is more
to the point. Fortunately, he is all here at the moment, and in fine
fettle, too. As the music master, *Where's Charley?* offers Frank
Loesser, who is a very interesting composer. Mr. Loesser is a
song-writer celebrated for "Rodger Young" [1945], the most stirring war ballad, and "Jingle, Jangle, Jingle" [1942, music by Joseph
Lilley] which jongled across the juke-boxes across the world a few
years ago. For *Where's Charley?* he has scribbled off a lively score
in a number of entertaining styles—Gilbert and Sullivan pastiche
for the beginning, a marching song complete with umph-umph out
of a French horn, a comic chorale for some female gossips, and
standard romances in a pleasantly sentimental vein. Mr. Loesser
combines song-writing with composing, which is a most acceptable
notion.

JOHN CHAPMAN, *Daily News*

Except when he is leering confidingly at an audience or laughing
at himself in a mirror, Ray Bolger's face has the look of someone
who has just sucked a lemon for the first time in his life. He is tall
and stooped and narrow. His limbs are not very well riveted to his
frame, like those of a cardboard Hallowe'en skeleton. He is therefore perfectly endowed by nature to be the best dancing comedian
in our theatre—and he is just that. Lucky he is, for *Where's*

Charley? would not be as engaging as it is without him. High spot for me is Bolger's solo number, "Once in Love with Amy," in which his dancing ranges from the finest of soft-shoe work to the most exuberant high-stepping. Those limbs, which seem so preciously attached, are like watch-spring steel—tireless. Another moment of real comedy is when he is in the aunt's masquerade, spending time with some partially clad lovelies in the ladies' dressing room. Noting that the girls are always regarding themselves in the pier glass, he figures he should, too—and busts out laughing.

WILLIAM HAWKINS, *World-Telegram*

A sublimely satisfactory evening. With its taste, its beauty, and its vigor, it is the sort of show you fall in love with, and go back to see over and over again. Last night the audience was ready and willing to stop the show after nearly every number, and often the cast was left frozen in tableaux while the onlookers beat the skin off their hands. If they continue to be one third as good in the future, they can wind the town around their little fingers.

WARD MOREHOUSE, *Sun*

Where's Charley? is an old-style book show, and George Abbott's book is humorless. There is a routine score from Frank Loesser, with only a bright spot here and there. Actually, *Where's Charley?* has Ray Bolger and very little else. Bolger is a lanky, wide-eyed buffoon who dances with his legs, arms, eyes, and hands. He does a bit of tap and he holds you completely in his spell when he goes into his enchanting soft-shoe routine. A superior dancer and comedian, this man Bolger. He needs better songs, a better book, a better show. *Where's Charley?* is a lackadaisical musical comedy. *Charley's Aunt* was better straight.

RICHARD WATTS JR., *Post*

The odd thing is that *Charley's Aunt* is, in its primitive sort of way, a lively and entertaining farce, when it is acted and directed with the required imagination. When Jose Ferrer played it in 1940, under Joshua Logan's direction, every one was astonished to discover that this presumably doddering old play still had a lot of fun in it, and it turned out to be one of the hits of the season. Last night, with music, dancing, and chorus girls added, all the humor seemed to have been drained from it. For most of the time, every-body sat around and waited for Mr. Bolger to go into his dance.

Bolger—and Frank Loesser's "Once in Love with Amy"—carried *Where's Charley?* to immense success despite a critical drubbing (except for Bolger personally). This was the third consecutive poorly reviewed show that Bolger built into a hit, following *By Jupiter* (1942) and *Three to Make Ready* (1946). His two future musicals, *All American* (1962) and *Come Summer* (1969), received similar critical (but not financial) receptions. And if *Charley* didn't mark a particularly auspicious artistic debut for first-timers Loesser, Feuer, and Martin, their next attempt—opening just as *Charley* ended his two-year run—was the perfectly crafted *Guys and Dolls* [1950].

A Tony Award was won by Ray Bolger (actor), who also won a Donaldson Award (male dancer).

BROADWAY SCORECARD / perfs: 792/$: +

rave	favorable	mixed	unfavorable	pan
	4		5	

WHOOP-UP

a musical comedy, with music by Moose Charlap; lyrics by Norman Gimbel; book by Cy Feuer, Ernest H. Martin, and Dan Cushman, from Cushman's 1953 novel *Stay Away, Joe*

directed by Cy Feuer; choreographed by Onna White
produced by Cy Feuer and Ernest H. Martin
with Susan Johnson, Paul Ford, Ralph Young, Romo Vincent, and Sylvia Syms

opened December 22, 1958   Shubert Theatre

BROOKS ATKINSON, *Times*

In *Whoop-Up*, the American Indian has a hearty sense of humor, laughs very loud, and can pick up a song cue with speed and gusto.

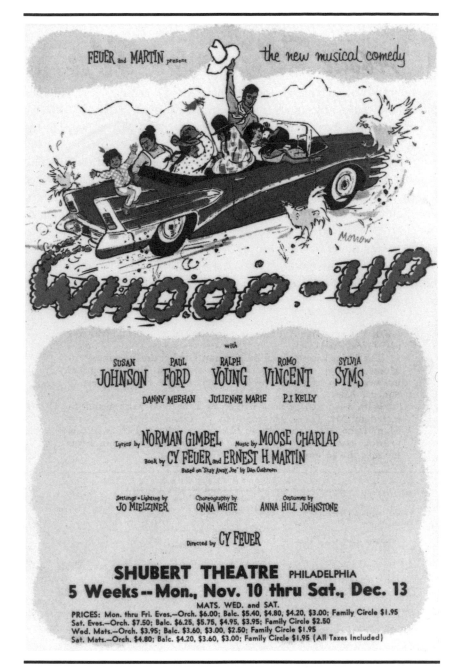

The hero's red Cadillac sputters onto the Reservation, sorely in need of a new muffler. According to the herald, Whoop-Up—Montana's word for a wild party—"does for the wild and wooly Indian country of Montana what Guys and Dolls did for Broadway." Sure. (drawing by Tom Morrow)

He can also dance with the acrobatic abandon of the old-time
vaudeville trooper. *Whoop-Up* is set on an Indian reservation in
northern Montana (which looks a little like Broadway) and shows a
parcel of white folks and Indians quarreling to music by Moose
Charlap. Since it is neither funny nor romantic, Mr. Feuer, in his
capacity as director, has stepped up the decibel count by way of
compensation to the customers. The overture shakes the roof. The
singing rattles the windows. . . . Jo Mielziner, a scene designer of
terrifying eminence, has filled the stage with mobile Montana scenery, and Onna White has choreographed some furious Indian dancing. But it seemed to one observer last evening that *Whoop-Up*
really has its heart in the silent movies, when the piano player used
to bang out the war dance. The Indians are really only extras—Fort
Lee, Hollywood, or Broadway as the case may be. Heap hokum at
top speed.

ROBERT COLEMAN, *Daily Mirror*

Over the past few seasons, Cy Feuer and Ernest Martin have
batted 1.000, socking out five straight homers. With *Whoop-Up*,
Feuer and Martin get wood on the ball, but, in the parlance of the
trade, it doesn't have eyes to go for a hit.

WALTER KERR, *Herald Tribune*

Whoop-Up is full of Indians, or at least it is full of actors who
have smeared such vast quantities of a rather muddy makeup over
themselves as to seem to need our gratitude somewhat less than
they do a good, hot bath. . . . *Whoop-Up*, like the shiny red Cadillac in which its leering hero lives, has no motor to send it scooting
across those Jo Mielziner plains. The book coughs desperately, the
lyrics spin and spin without generating any friction, and there's
nothing for the pretty girls to do but get out and walk. They walk
nicely, to be sure, but it must be tiring.

Feuer and Martin had given Broadway "five straight musical homers": *Where's Charley?* (1948), *Guys and Dolls* (1950), *Can-Can*
(1953), *The Boy Friend* (1954), and *Silk Stockings* (1955)—although
Charley and the two Cole Porter shows were, perhaps, unearned

runs. *Whoop-Up* proved a costly error, and sputtered off as soon as its advance sale whooped out.

BROADWAY SCORECARD / perfs: 56 / $: —

rave	favorable	mixed	unfavorable	pan
	2	1	3	1

WIENER BLUT (VIENNA LIFE)

an Austrian revival of the 1900 Viennese operetta, with music by Johann Strauss; book and lyrics by Victor Leon and Leo Stein

directed and adapted by Tony Niessner; choreographed by Fred Meister
produced by the Greek Theatre Association/James A. Doolittle and Felix G. Gerstman
with Erwin Von Gross and Maria Kowa

opened September 11, 1964   Lunt-Fontanne Theatre

JOHN CHAPMAN, *Daily News*

If you don't like the plot which the mistress of ceremonies seeks to divulge to you in English, you can invent your own plot as the show goes along. It will be at least as good.

NORMAN NADEL, *World-Telegram & Sun*

Last night's music was marred only by a lack of accord among orchestra, conductor, and singers. Some of the instrumentalists played the lilting Viennese music as if they were wearing concrete cuff links.

ALAN RICH, *Herald Tribune*

The Viennese know how to whip their cream, and they also know how to flog it to a pulp. If that was the authentic Johann Strauss style at the Lunt-Fontanne Theatre last night, my name is Peter Rabbit. . . . The scenery, flown over from Vienna (economy class, I presume), is rickety and otherwise awful.

HOWARD TAUBMAN, *Times*

One of the nice things about a Viennese operetta in the original language is that you miss most of the jokes. *Wiener Blut* takes place in Vienna of 1915, the year of the famous Congress that danced, and some of the comic routines look as if they were well along even then.

```
BROADWAY SCORECARD / perfs: 27 / $: NA

  rave     favorable     mixed     unfavorable     pan

            2              1            2             1
```

WILDCAT

a musical comedy, with music by Cy Coleman; lyrics by Carolyn Leigh; book by N. Richard Nash

directed and choreographed by Michael Kidd
produced by Michael Kidd and N. Richard Nash (for Desilu Productions, Inc.)
with Lucille Ball, Keith Andes, Edith King, and Paula Stewart

opened December 16, 1960   Alvin Theatre

WALTER KERR, *Herald Tribune*

She wrestles a man to the floor in a handshake, she does one of those Rockette choo-choo-train steps as she trundles another fellow away in a stand-up wheelbarrow, and she spread-eagles her arms every livin' moment as though every livin' moment were one more finale. It's all done with gusto and skill and, I am sure, perfect honesty. But, somehow, it's a ritual, a posture she's dived into for a demanding photographer, a stance and a shoulder-toss and a double-double-take which all seem to have been dictated by the tick of an efficient clock. Miss Ball is pouring her whole heart into a stencil. Mostly the numbers find two fellows lifting Miss Ball into the air at center stage and then down again, without having ac-

"Hey, Look Me Over" calls out Wildcat Lucy, who's determined to be rolling in oil by the final curtain. (*drawing by Tom Morrow*)

complished anything much. . . . Mr. Nash has taken the characters
and the atmosphere and even the whimsy of his attractive play, *The
Rainmaker* (1954), and transformed them lock, stock, and ranch-
hands to musical-comedy territory, except that his magic hero now
summons oil from the earth instead of balm from the heavens.
These aren't very comfortable in the broader, bolder humors of the
song-and-dance stage. Designer Peter Larkin provides an arresting
sky the color of tomato juice, and another one the color of orange
juice, before everyone runs out of juice.

ROBERT COLEMAN, *Daily Mirror*

Don Tomkins, who teamed with Zelma O'Neal to steal the show
via "The Varsity Drag" in *Good News* [1927] 30 years ago, did it
again last evening with Lucy in "What Takes My Fancy."

JOHN McCLAIN, *Journal-American*

The rich get richer, and a redhaired millionairess named Lucille
Ball figures to make another bundle with a new musical, *Wildcat*, in
which she is the star and solo backer. While it falls woefully short of
expectations, it still exhibits enough of Miss Ball, blares forth moderately rousing music, and provides sufficient hoopla and boffola to
satisfy the millions who love Lucy. It should have been so much
better, I think, but what I think will matter little. It is an increasing
bore to be faced once more with a musical with no book, yet this one
by N. Richard Nash is a new champion in the nothing sweepstakes.

HOWARD TAUBMAN, *Times*

The most stirring event of the evening was a feat of stage engineering, for which Peter Larkin, the designer, and the backstage
crew deserve the credit. As Joe and the company sing "Corduroy
Road," a wood hut was dismantled. Part of it was used to make a
road, and another part went into the construction of a grand-looking
derrick with drilling apparatus in action.

RICHARD WATTS JR., *Post*

A tremendous disappointment. *Wildcat* has a bright and pleasant
score by Cy Coleman, and its production is at least colorful, but,
weighed down by N. Richard Nash's cumbersome and amazingly
uninteresting and unhumorous libretto, and staged with a surpris-

ing lack of imagination, it merely serves to handicap its star. Miss Ball is entangled in as undramatic a narrative as ever put a musical comedy to sleep. Since *Wildcat* was directed by Michael Kidd, it had seemed certain that the evening would be filled with exciting dance numbers. One has only to recall *Destry Rides Again* [1959] to realize what Mr. Kidd can do when he turns the boys and girls loose in mining camp. Apparently his magic doesn't work among the oil drillers.

If Bette Davis could do it (remember *Two's Company* [1952]?), why not Lucy? Reeling from the divorce which broke up her twenty-year partnership with Desi, Lucy came to Broadway— totally backed by the Arnaz/Ball production company. "If this venture isn't all I hope and pray it will be, I don't want my pals to get clobbered with me," she explained. (And if it *was* a smash hit, who would get all those profits?) So the show got clobbered, the hearty redhead got a "respiratory infection complicated by exhaustion" (remember *Two's Company*?), and everybody else got back on the unemployment line.

BROADWAY SCORECARD / perfs: 171 / $: —

rave	favorable	mixed	unfavorable	pan
	3		4	

WISH YOU WERE HERE

a musical comedy, with music and lyrics by Harold Rome; book by Arthur Kober and Joshua Logan, based on the 1937 comedy *Having Wonderful Time* by Arthur Kober

"direction and dances" by Joshua Logan (with Jerome Robbins); swimmers trained by Eleanor Holm Rose
produced by Leland Hayward
with Sheila Bond, Jack Cassidy, Patricia Marand, Sidney Armus, and Paul Valentine

opened June 25, 1952   Imperial Theatre

BROOKS ATKINSON, *Times*

A humorous, tender, romantic comedy has been flattened out into a one-dimensional, repetitious Broadway show. There is no tenderness under the panoply of this expertly organized musical. It lacks variety and subtlety. For all its friskiness, it is joyless; and it gives the impression of saying the same thing over and over again. The dancing is tight and routine. The pace of the performance is hard and tiring. Nearly everything is overacted as though Mr. Logan and his associates were afraid that the audience would not know how satirical it is. What was warm and disarming fifteen years ago has become cold and mechanical. It goes through the motions with professional authority, but it represents the triumph of showmanship over sympathy for some obscure but lovable human beings.

ROBERT COLEMAN, *Daily Mirror*

Jo Mielziner has designed fascinating trick settings, featuring railings that rise from the stage floor, a basketball court and a swimming pool. Reams have already been written about that swimming pool, but we should like to add that director Logan made too many sacrifices for the three or four minutes in which he uses it to excellent advantage.

WILLIAM HAWKINS, *World-Telegram & Sun*

Wish You Were Here has most of the innocence and simplicity you should expect from a musical of 1937's *Having Wonderful Time*. As an outsize, heavily produced tuner, though, it lacks dazzle and never really explodes. It is pertinent to note that the evening's biggest laugh comes from Paul Valentine [the "wolf"] being pushed into the pool with his clothes on.

JOHN McCLAIN, *Journal-American*

The trick of introducing an actual swimming pool into the proceedings merely made last night's sweltering audience wish they could jump in with the cast.

VERNON RICE, *Post*

It seemed odd, surrounded by such "old" pros [Hayward, Logan, Mielziner, Rome, and Kober], to keep hoping for professionalism. The boys and girls of dear, old Camp Karefree were always whooping it up, but the spirit of Amateur Night around the campfire constantly prevailed. It's been no secret since June 2, when the musical comedy began playing a series of previews in town, because the size of the production and a built-in swimming pool prevented the show from going on the usual pre-Broadway tour, that there was trouble. Hourly bulletins were generally forthcoming from those who seemed to have made a career on keeping up with the events around the Imperial. The patient was languishing. A crisis was near. A crisis had passed. Old Doc Logan was operating. Old Doc Logan had decided not to operate. And so it went. Well, folks, things are not that bad. They aren't good, but the hysteria of the patient's interested parties clouded the reports from its bedside. . . . Going to Camp Karefree in *Wish You Were Here* is not any more fun than going to it would be in real life.

A surprise hit despite the overall air of mediocrity. Harold Rome's popular title song helped, no doubt; but it seems to be what the people wanted, escapist entertainment (we were, it seems, at war again). For the record, this was *not* musical comedy's first swimming pool: *Viva O'Brien* (1941) built one into the Majestic for its three-week run. Predating *Oklahoma!* (1943), *Viva O'Brien* was set in the New Mexican desert and featured a diving exhibition by Olympic gold medalist Pete Desjardins (why not?).

Tony Awards were won by Sheila Bond (supporting actress) and Abe Kurnit (stage technician).

BROADWAY SCORECARD / perfs: 598 / $: +				
rave	*favorable*	*mixed*	*unfavorable*	*pan*
	1	1	5	

WONDERFUL TOWN

a musical comedy, with music by Leonard Bernstein (replacing Leroy Anderson); lyrics by Betty Comden and Adolph Green (replacing Arnold B. Horwitt); book by Joseph Fields and Jerome

Chodorov, from their 1940 comedy *My Sister Eileen*, dramatized from stories by Ruth McKenney

directed by George Abbott; choreographed by Donald Saddler (with Jerome Robbins)
produced by Robert Fryer
with Rosalind Russell, George Gaynes, Edith Adams, and Henry Lascoe

opened February 25, 1953   Winter Garden Theatre

BROOKS ATKINSON, *Times*

According to the Constitution, Rosalind Russell cannot run for President until 1956. But it would be wise to start preparing for her campaign at once. For she can dance and sing better than any President we have had. She is also better looking and has a more infectious sense of humor. In *Wonderful Town* she makes the whole city wonderful; and she will make the whole country wonderful when she is elected President in 1956. Everyone is more inspired than usual in the administration of *Wonderful Town*. Dispensing with hurdy-gurdy techniques, Leonard Bernstein has written a bright and witty score in a variety of modern styles without forgetting to endow it with at least one tender melody and a good romantic number. The score carries forward the crack-brained comedy of the book with gaiety and excitement. Comden and Green have written some extraordinarily inventive lyrics in a style as unhackneyed as the music. And Donald Saddler has directed the most exuberant dances of the season. Sometimes gifted people never quite get attuned to each other in the composition of a musical circus. But in *Wonderful Town* everyone seems to have settled down joyfully to the creation of a beautifully organized fandango—the book, the score, and the ballets helping each other enthusiastically.

JOHN CHAPMAN, *Daily News*

This new musical moved into my sentimental heart close alongside *Guys and Dolls* (1950) as one of the gayest, smartest shows of recent times. Everybody has done admirable work, and it seems to me that the star of the whole delightful lot is Leonard Bernstein, the composer of the music. There hasn't been much music in our musicals lately, and Bernstein has come to the rescue. With the

Roz Russell forsakes her native Ohio to embrace New York, that Wonderful Town. (*drawing by Heilbron*)

fine assistance of Don Walker, the arranger, and a splendid orchestra led by Lehman Engel, Bernstein has achieved a Broadway score of remarkable quality. Many times last evening I felt there hasn't been anyone around like him since George Gershwin for jauntiness, tricky and intriguing modulations, and graceful swoops into simple and pleasant melody.

ROBERT COLEMAN, *Daily Mirror*

A great musical roared into the Winter Garden last evening like a hurricane, and left a brilliant first-night audience limp from applauding and hoarse from cheering. And the new toast of the town is its wonderful star, Rosalind Russell, who proves that she's as magnetic on stage as in the movies. She had the premierites rolling in the aisles and blistering their palms. Blonde Edith Adams also won *bravas* as Eileen, of the baby face and the innocent eyes, who has an irresistible way with men. She can sing, act, dance, and soothe the eyes. She's got everything.

WILLIAM HAWKINS, *World-Telegram & Sun*

Wonderful Town, wonderful show, wonderful Rosalind Russell! The town's newest musical was greeted by such frequent roars of approval last night that the performers looked stunned at the wall of sound. As for the star, she not only vindicated Hollywood as a prep school for personal appearances, but proved herself a great entertainer in any competition you care to name. Miss Russell scales about eight gamuts in the course of the evening. She sings harmony like a Duncan Sister, puts away a delightful gagged-up lyric about losing her men, pantomimes some wildly bad fiction, and practices a conga that would ground the Flying Condonas. As if that were not enough, she adds a fantastic parody of swing, performed in a shrewd daze, and sings a wildly paced ragtime affair. She is backed up, surrounded, and supported, but never inundated, by full-blooming talent on every side. The George Abbott touch is a grip of iron on the wonderful evening that is *Wonderful Town*.

WALTER KERR, *Herald Tribune*

It's never been any secret that Miss Russell could rear back, hoist her chin, look down her nose, and curl a wisecrack off her lower lip with withering magnificence. What she's been keeping from us is the open-armed abandon, the sheer animal spirits with which she can set a whole stage to rocking around her. In *Wonderful Town*, she finds no fewer than four joyous opportunities for stopping the show in its well oiled tracks. Miss Russell may never be quite able to sing a song; but she certainly knows how to animate one. As the evening scurries along, this exuberant and apparently inexhaustible performer tears into an explosive conga, the while she is manhandled by half the Brazilian Navy. (When Hollywood visitors are hoisted into the air by a detachment of chorus boys, there is usually a certain grim panic about the operation; Miss Russell looks as though she could get up there any time she wanted to, and all by herself if necessary.) In the second act, she sets the beat for an exercise in rhythmic mayhem known as "Swing"—proving herself a past mistress of glassy-eyed jive—and, together with Edith Adams, she brings the final frenzied curtain down on a rollicking duet labeled "Wrong Note Rag."

A typical "Abbott" musical, in the very best sense. What looked fairly simple and worked like a dream was actually the result of a nightmare of a production period. ("More hysterical debate, more acrimony, more tension, and more screaming than with any other show I was ever involved with," says Mr. A.) Social note: Allyn McLerie—an *On the Town* (1944) chorine who eventually moved up into Sono Osato's top-billed role, followed by leads in *Where's Charley?* (1948) and *Miss Liberty* (1949)—divorced lyricist Adolph Green after the *Wonderful Town* opening to marry leading man George Gaynes. No hard feelings, apparently, as Mr. and Mrs. Gaynes did the 1957 London production of Green's *Bells Are Ringing* (1956). Political note: Once *Two's Company* (1952) was safely (?) open, Jerry Robbins went up to Boston to help out his former colleagues. Once *Wonderful Town* was safely open, Robbins went down to the House Un-American Activities Committee to turn in his former colleagues—including *Wonderful Town* librettist Jerome Chodorov. Also named as Communists by Robbins were Chodorov's brother Edward, actress Madeline Lee (Mrs. Jack) Gilford and a half-dozen others. All were blacklisted except J.R., who testified that he quit the Party in 1947 because they treated him like "a puppet."

Winner of the New York Drama Critics Award. In addition to winning the Tony Award for Best Musical, Tonys were won by Leonard Bernstein (composer); Joseph Fields and Jerome Chodorov (librettists); Donald Saddler (choreographer); Robert Fryer (producer); Rosalind Russell (actress); Raoul Pène du Bois (scenic designer); and Lehman Engel (musical director, for *Wonderful Town* and the Gilbert and Sullivan season). In addition to winning the Donaldson Award for Best Musical, Donaldsons were won by Leonard Bernstein (composer); Betty Comden and Adolph Green (lyricists); Joseph Fields and Jerome Chodorov (librettists); Rosalind Russell (actress); Edith Adams (supporting actress; female debut); George Abbott (director); and Raoul Pène du Bois (costume designer).

BROADWAY SCORECARD / perfs: 559 / $: +

rave	favorable	mixed	unfavorable	pan
7				

ZIEGFELD FOLLIES OF 1943

a musical revue, with music mostly by Ray Henderson; lyrics mostly by Jack Yellen; sketches by various writers

directed by John Murray Anderson; choreographed by Robert Alton

produced by the Messrs. Shubert in association with Alfred Bloomingdale and Lou Walters (by arrangement with Billie Burke Ziegfeld)

with Milton Berle, Ilona Massey, Arthur Treacher, and Jack Cole

opened April 1, 1943   Winter Garden Theatre

JOHN ANDERSON, *Journal-American*

Anyone with reasonably good eyesight is bound to get his money's worth and a customer with a touch of deafness, suitably intermittent, may find it so much velvet.

LOUIS KRONENBERGER, *PM*

"Who'd have thought," said Moss Hart to Lillian Hellman and me before last night's show, "that we'd see another *Follies*? "What

"We are moving to the
IMPERIAL THEATRE
Tuesday Evening, January 25th"

Milton Berle

ZIEGFELD FOLLIES

Would you follow this man? (costume by Miles White)

makes you think," said Miss H., "that we will?" . . . Milton Berle is on hand in large amounts, which is not the best way to enjoy him. While he can raise a laugh, he also re-raises and re-raises it until everyone drops out.

WARD MOREHOUSE, *Sun*

As one veteran first-nighter remarked last evening, it's something for which the tired welder has been waiting.

BURTON RASCOE, *World-Telegram*

The program says they have an "arrangement" with Mrs. Billie Burke Ziegfeld, the impresario's widow. The "arrangement" with Mrs. Ziegfeld must have been that she was never to see it. . . . By facial expressions and gestures, Berle can make things as flat and crude as "That was Lee Shubert's teeth falling out" (when a slight crash inadvertently occurs behind the backdrop) seem very laughable to some.

A Shubert-produced *Ziegfeld Follies* mounted without any taste, class, or elegance. Needless to say, it was the longest-running edition of the *Follies*, a real crowd-pleaser for undiscriminating wartime audiences.

BROADWAY SCORECARD / perfs: 553 / $: +

rave	favorable	mixed	unfavorable	pan
	1	2	2	3

ZIEGFELD FOLLIES OF 1957

a musical revue by various writers; sketches edited by Arnold Auerbach

directed by John Kennedy; choreographed by Frank Wagner
produced by Mark Kroll and Charles Conaway

with Beatrice Lillie, Billy De Wolfe, Harold Lang, Jane Morgan, and Carol Lawrence

opened March 1, 1957   Winter Garden Theatre

Tom Donnelly, *World-Telegram & Sun*

A great big clambake minus the clams. The real tragedy of the occasion is that the brilliant, the magnetic, the droll, the incomparable, the superlative Beatrice Lillie is stranded without any material. The show has bushels of pink feathers and beads and gew-gaws, but no material. . . . Everybody will be wondering what that [1956] edition with Tallulah, which was considered too deficient for exposure on Broadway, could possibly have been like.

Walter Kerr, *Herald Tribune*

Miss Beatrice Lillie makes her first entrance in the new *Ziegfeld Follies* out of the snow. Two enormous doors open wide to silhouette the lady against falling flakes, a great black muff held demurely in her arms, a wide black hat made of dried pampas grass billowing over her eyes. She sidles into what turns out to be a rather ravishing restaurant. She studies the menu—at pole-vault length. She savors the wine (she mistrusts it), she engages in delicate battle with some exceptionally limp celery (or was it asparagus in Hollandaise sauce?), and she almost catches a large ear of buttered corn as it frolics right off the table. Turning her attention to an impetuous lobster, she tidily trims its claws with a pair of garden shears, pausing only to dip her handsomely gloved hands into the finger bowl. Sated after her four-minute joust with a magnificent cuisine, she rises to go—a figure of sad, savage, baffling splendor. For those four wild minutes I laughed as though I might never laugh again. And I damn near didn't. . . . A trio composed of Jane Morgan, Micki Marlo, and Carol Lawrence (watch that girl) finally succeeded in stopping the show, a rather dangerous thing to do considering how slowly it was moving.

John McClain, *Journal-American*

There are really only a couple of kind words which come to mind in connection with the *Ziegfeld Follies* which opened at the Winter Garden last night: Beatrice Lillie. For if it were not for her incredible antics and mad merriment it is doubtful that the show would have come to town. What is lacking are the elements that went into the great *Follies* of the past, the taste and talent, the sense of style and elegance. If it does nothing else this production will be a reminder and a tribute to Ziegfeld's memory; it proves that size and affluence are not enough. . . . Maybe the whole trouble is being stuck with the name *Ziegfeld Follies*. Why don't they just call it *An Evening with Beatrice Lillie?*"

The last edition of the *Ziegfeld Follies* to date, although the series really died with Flo in 1932. "That edition with Tallulah" collapsed after four weeks on the road in the spring of 1956. Miss Bankhead was supported by Carol Haney, Joan Diener, and David Burns, with choreography by Jack Cole.

BROADWAY SCORECARD / perfs: 123 / $: —

rave	favorable	mixed	unfavorable	pan
	2		2	3

Broadway Scorecard Summary

Rating shows by their critical reception does not reflect their true quality, any more than rating them by the length of run would. It does lead to some interesting observations, though. (Note: The scorecards can't be compared on a strict numerical basis because the number of critics varied from time to time.)

The following shows received unanimous raves. No surprises here, except for the omission of some of our most innovative classics (usually because they were *too* innovative for one or two critics):

Brigadoon
An Evening with Beatrice Lillie
Guys and Dolls
How to Succeed in Business Without Really Trying
The Music Man
My Fair Lady
South Pacific
Wonderful Town

The following shows belong in the same company, receiving all-but-unanimous raves (with one holdout):

The Boy Friend
Bye Bye Birdie

Carmen Jones
Carousel
Gentlemen Prefer Blondes
Kiss Me, Kate
The Pajama Game
Pal Joey (1961 revival)
Porgy and Bess (1953 revival)

The non-raves were favorable except for *Bye Bye Birdie* and *Carousel* (mixed), and *Carmen Jones* and *Gentlemen Prefer Blondes* (unfavorable). It should be noted that the otherwise discerning Wilella Waldorf seems to have had a distinct aversion to Mr. Hammerstein—she disliked *Show Boat, Oklahoma!, Carmen Jones*, and *Carousel*. "All right," she told her readers at the end of her nit-picking review of the latter, "go ahead and shoot."

The following shows received raves from all but two critics, and clearly belong in the proverbial winner's circle. Most of them, anyway:

Call Me Madam
Call Me Mister
Carnival
Damn Yankees
Do Re Mi
Finian's Rainbow
Fiorello!
The Golden Apple
Gypsy
Hello, Dolly!
La Plume de Ma Tante
Oklahoma! (1951 return engagement)
Oliver!
Pal Joey (1952 revival)
Something for the Boys
Top Banana
Two on the Aisle
West Side Story

Three of these shows lost money: the commercial transfer of the Phoenix Theatre's highly innovative *Golden Apple*, and the two

Phil Silvers musicals. *Top Banana* had already recovered its costs when the star took a much needed eight-week vacation; the producers decided to replace him (rather than shut down for the long, hot summer) and took a bath. Why the ecstatically hailed *Do Re Mi* failed is less explainable. Maybe the critics simply liked it more than the audiences did?

The following shows round out the list of musicals which opened to unanimously positive reviews, although closer to favorable than rave:

> *Annie Get Your Gun*
> *The Consul*
> *Fiddler on the Roof*
> *High Spirits*
> *Inside U.S.A.*
> *Irma La Douce*
> *The King and I*
> *The Most Happy Fella*
> *A Party with Comden and Green*
> *Peter Pan*
> *Redhead*
> *Three for Tonight*

Readers with a statistical state of mind will appreciate the fact that some 38 of 275 productions received unanimously favorable reviews. (The original production of *Oklahoma!* was knocked off the list by Wilella.) Only two of these lost money: *High Spirits*, with personal raves for critics' darling Bea Lillie unable to compensate for an otherwise mediocre evening; and the aforementioned *Do Re Mi*.

Quite a few other shows maintained a better-than-favorable average despite some mixed or unfavorable reviews:

> *Angel in the Wings*
> *Ballet Ballads*
> *Bells Are Ringing*
> *Flower Drum Song*
> *A Funny Thing Happened on the Way to the Forum*
> *Laugh Time*

Lend an Ear
Little Me
Make Mine Manhattan
Mexican Hayride
New Faces of 1952
Oklahoma!
One Touch of Venus
The Saint of Bleecker Street
She Loves Me
Show Boat (1946 revival)
Show Girl
Song of Norway
The Sound of Music

The only financially unsuccessful entries on the above list: *Little Me, The Saint of Bleecker Street,* and the cherished *She Loves Me.*

The reception of the following financial "hits" fell somewhere between mixed and favorable. All are flawed, perhaps, but there was usually at least one spectacular element that more than made up for it; and the list includes a few genuine ground-breakers:

Billion Dollar Baby
Bloomer Girl
Can-Can
A Connecticut Yankee (1943 revival)
Fanny
Follow the Girls
Funny Girl
High Button Shoes
Jamaica
Kismet
Li'l Abner
New Girl in Town
No Strings
On the Town
Once Upon a Mattress
110 in the Shade
Plain and Fancy
Silk Stockings
Take Me Along

The Unsinkable Molly Brown
Up in Central Park

Then there are the hits which received mixed-to-negative receptions—usually including some downright pans. The great American theatregoing public bought tickets nevertheless, and presumably enjoyed themselves:

Camelot
Early to Bed
Laffing Room Only
Look Ma, I'm Dancin'
Me and Juliet
The Red Mill (1945 revival)
Stop the World—I Want to Get Off
Sweethearts (1947 revival)
Three to Make Ready
Where's Charley?
Wish You Were Here

The hit with the poorest reviews—I know you were about to ask—was *Me and Juliet*, which proves that it is possible to make your show virtually review-proof if you first write *Oklahoma!, Carousel, South Pacific,* and *The King and I.* Actually, *Me and Juliet* was a better show than the reviews indicated; the critics, expecting something exceptional, reacted in disappointment. Which goes to show what can happen if you first write *Oklahoma!, Carousel, South Pacific,* and *The King and I.* Running a close second (from the bottom) was *Wish You Were Here*, the show built around a swimming pool. Not incidentally, both came during a three-and-a-half-year dry spell with only one blockbuster hit, *Wonderful Town.*

Finally, let's look at some shows *below* the unfavorable level. Which include, I regret to say, Kurt Weill and Ira Gershwin's *Firebrand of Florence* and—even more regretfully—Frank Loesser's *Greenwillow.* Both shows simply and unquestionably didn't work, despite better-than-pretty-good scores (and heaven knows we need all the good songs we can get). Also way down on the list are three theatre party specials borne of stellar names and little more: Mary Martin's troubled *Jennie*, Judy Holliday's double-trouble *Hot Spot*, and—with five pans (out of seven)—*Mr. Presi-*

dent from the Messrs. Berlin, Logan, Lindsay, and Crouse. These last three shows, incidentally, opened within a twelve-month period and left thousands upon thousands of advance-sale ticket buyers bemoaning their investment. What a waste of $9.60!

For the sake of posterity, and because these titles have undoubtedly never appeared on *any* list *anywhere*, let us name the shows which received unanimous drubbings. As with the hats-in-the-air rave garnerers at the head of this summary, there's no question here:

> *Allah Be Praised!*
> *Buttrio Square*
> *The Duchess Misbehaves*
> *The Girl From Nantucket*
> *Hairpin Harmony*
> *Happy Town*
> *Hit the Trail*
> *If the Shoe Fits*
> *A Lady Says Yes*
> *Louisiana Lady*
> *Mr. Strauss Goes to Boston*
> *My Dear Public*
> *Polonaise*
> *Portofino*
> *Rhapsody*

The good news is that most of these stunners are from the long-ago 1940s. (The bad news is that our post-Golden Era modern-day musical theatre keeps coming up with more names to add to the list!)

Chronological List of the Broadway Musicals of the Golden Era

———————◆———————

*T*HE productions discussed in this book are listed below, ordered by the date of opening. This gives us an at-a-glance look at what was playing on the night that such-and-such came to town—and what was to come next.

YEAR	OPENING DATE	TITLE
1943	January 7	*Something for the Boys*
	March 31	*Oklahoma!*
	April 1	*Ziegfeld Follies of 1943*
	June 17	*Early to Bed*
	June 29	*The Vagabond King* (revival)
	August 4	*The Merry Widow* (revival)
	August 12	*Chauve-Souris 1943*
	September 4	*Blossom Time* (revival)
	September 8	*Laugh Time*
	September 9	*My Dear Public*
	September 16	*Bright Lights of 1944*
	October 1	*Hairpin Harmony*

Year	Opening Date	Title
	October 7	*One Touch of Venus*
	November 11	*What's Up?*
	November 17	*A Connecticut Yankee* (revival)
	December 2	*Carmen Jones*
1944	January 13	*Jackpot*
	January 28	*Mexican Hayride*
	April 8	*Follow the Girls*
	April 20	*Allah Be Praised!*
	May 18	*Dream with Music*
	June 15	*Take a Bow*
	August 21	*Song of Norway*
	October 5	*Bloomer Girl*
	November 16	*Sadie Thompson*
	November 22	*Rhapsody*
	December 7	*The Seven Lively Arts*
	December 23	*Laffing Room Only*
	December 27	*Sing Out, Sweet Land!*
	December 28	*On the Town*
1945	January 10	*A Lady Says Yes*
	January 27	*Up in Central Park*
	March 22	*The Firebrand of Florence*
	April 19	*Carousel*
	May 21	*Blue Holiday*
	May 24	*Memphis Bound*
	May 31	*Hollywood Pinafore*
	June 1	*Concert Varieties*
	July 18	*Marinka*
	September 6	*Mr. Strauss Goes to Boston*
	October 6	*Polonaise*
	October 16	*The Red Mill* (revival)
	November 8	*The Girl from Nantucket*
	November 22	*The Day Before Spring*
	December 21	*Billion Dollar Baby*
1946	January 5	*Show Boat* (revival)
	January 21	*Nellie Bly*
	February 6	*Lute Song*
	February 13	*The Duchess Misbehaves*
	March 7	*Three to Make Ready*

YEAR	OPENING DATE	TITLE
	March 30	*St. Louis Woman*
	April 18	*Call Me Mister*
	May 16	*Annie Get Your Gun*
	May 31	*Around the World (in Eighty Days)*
	September 17	*Gypsy Lady*
	November 4	*Park Avenue*
	December 5	*If the Shoe Fits*
	December 26	*Beggar's Holiday*
1947	January 9	*Street Scene*
	January 10	*Finian's Rainbow*
	January 21	*Sweethearts* (revival)
	March 13	*Brigadoon*
	April 3	*Barefoot Boy with Cheek*
	May 1	*The Medium* and *The Telephone (L'Amour à Trois)*
	June 2	*Louisiana Lady*
	October 2	*Music in My Heart*
	October 9	*High Button Shoes*
	October 10	*Allegro*
	December 5	*Caribbean Carnival*
	December 11	*Angel in the Wings*
	December 26	*The Cradle Will Rock* (revival)
1948	January 5	*The Pirates of Penzance* (revival)
	January 15	*Make Mine Manhattan*
	January 29	*Look, Ma, I'm Dancin'*
	April 30	*Inside U.S.A.*
	May 5	*Hold It!*
	May 6	*Sally* (revival)
	May 9	*Ballet Ballads*
	June 3	*Sleepy Hollow*
	September 15	*Small Wonder*
	September 16	*Heaven on Earth*
	September 20	*Magdalena*
	October 7	*Love Life*
	October 11	*Where's Charley?*
	October 19	*My Romance*

YEAR	OPENING DATE	TITLE
	November 13	*As the Girls Go*
	December 16	*Lend an Ear*
	December 30	*Kiss Me, Kate*
1949	January 13	*Along Fifth Avenue*
	January 22	*All for Love*
	April 7	*South Pacific*
	July 15	*Miss Liberty*
	October 13	*Touch and Go*
	October 30	*Lost in the Stars*
	October 31	*Regina*
	December 8	*Gentlemen Prefer Blondes*
1950	January 6	*Happy As Larry*
	January 17	*Alive and Kicking*
	January 20	*Dance Me a Song*
	February 2	*Arms and the Girl*
	March 15	*The Consul*
	May 18	*The Liar*
	June 28	*Michael Todd's Peep Show*
	October 12	*Call Me Madam*
	November 2	*The Barrier*
	November 24	*Guys and Dolls*
	December 13	*Let's Make an Opera*
	December 14	*Bless You All*
	December 21	*Out of This World*
1951	February 19	*Razzle Dazzle*
	March 29	*The King and I*
	April 18	*Make a Wish*
	April 19	*A Tree Grows in Brooklyn*
	May 14	*Flahooley*
	May 29	*Oklahoma!* (return engagement)
	June 21	*Seventeen*
	July 19	*Two on the Aisle*
	October 8	*Music in the Air* (revival)
	November 1	*Top Banana*
	November 12	*Paint Your Wagon*
1952	January 2	*Pal Joey* (revival)
	March 21	*Three Wishes for Jamie*

Year	Opening Date	Title
	April 16	*Four Saints in Three Acts* (revival)
	May 5	*Of Thee I Sing* (revival)
	May 15	*New Faces of 1952*
	June 25	*Wish You Were Here*
	October 2	*An Evening with Beatrice Lillie*
	October 14	*Buttrio Square*
	October 27	*My Darlin' Aida*
	December 15	*Two's Company*
1953	February 11	*Hazel Flagg*
	February 18	*Maggie*
	February 25	*Wonderful Town*
	March 10	*Porgy and Bess* (revival)
	May 7	*Can-Can*
	May 28	*Me and Juliet*
	August 31	*Oklahoma!* (return engagement)
	September 8	*Carnival in Flanders*
	December 3	*Kismet*
	December 10	*John Murray Anderson's Almanac*
1954	March 5	*The Girl in Pink Tights*
	March 11	*The Golden Apple*
	April 8	*By the Beautiful Sea*
	May 13	*The Pajama Game*
	September 13	*Hayride*
	September 30	*The Boy Friend*
	October 11	*On Your Toes* (revival)
	October 20	*Peter Pan*
	November 4	*Fanny*
	December 2	*Hit the Trail*
	December 27	*The Saint of Bleecker Street*
	December 30	*House of Flowers*
1955	January 27	*Plain and Fancy*
	February 24	*Silk Stockings*
	April 6	*Three for Tonight*
	April 18	*Ankles Aweigh*
	April 23	*Phoenix '55*

YEAR	OPENING DATE	TITLE
	May 5	*Damn Yankees*
	May 26	*Seventh Heaven*
	September 6	*Catch a Star*
	September 27	*Iolanthe* (revival)
	November 10	*The Vamp*
	November 30	*Pipe Dream*
1956	March 15	*My Fair Lady*
	March 22	*Mr. Wonderful*
	May 3	*The Most Happy Fella*
	May 22	*The Littlest Revue*
	June 13	*Shangri-La*
	June 14	*New Faces of 1956*
	November 15	*Li'l Abner*
	November 26	*Cranks*
	November 29	*Bells Are Ringing*
	December 1	*Candide*
	December 6	*Happy Hunting*
1957	March 1	*Ziegfeld Follies of 1957*
	April 13	*Shinbone Alley*
	April 27	*Livin' the Life*
	May 14	*New Girl in Town*
	September 10	*Mask and Gown*
	September 26	*West Side Story*
	October 17	*Copper and Brass*
	October 31	*Jamaica*
	November 6	*Rumple*
	December 19	*The Music Man*
1958	January 23	*The Body Beautiful*
	February 4	*Oh Captain!*
	February 21	*Portofino*
	April 3	*Say, Darling*
	October 11	*Goldilocks*
	November 5	*Maria Golovin*
	November 11	*La Plume De Ma Tante*
	December 1	*Flower Drum Song*
	December 22	*Whoop-Up*
	December 23	*A Party with Comden and Green*

Year	Opening Date	Title
1959	February 5	*Redhead*
	March 9	*Juno*
	March 19	*First Impressions*
	April 23	*Destry Rides Again*
	May 11	*Once Upon a Mattress*
	May 12	*The Nervous Set*
	May 21	*Gypsy*
	October 7	*Happy Town*
	October 8	*At the Drop of a Hat*
	October 22	*Take Me Along*
	November 2	*The Girls Against the Boys*
	November 16	*The Sound of Music*
	November 23	*Fiorello!*
	December 7	*Saratoga*
1960	February 10	*Beg, Borrow or Steal*
	March 8	*Greenwillow*
	April 14	*Bye Bye Birdie*
	April 20	*From A to Z*
	April 28	*Christine*
	May 11	*The King and I* (revival)
	September 12	*Vintage '60*
	September 29	*Irma La Douce*
	October 17	*Tenderloin*
	November 3	*The Unsinkable Molly Brown*
	December 3	*Camelot*
	December 16	*Wildcat*
	December 26	*Do Re Mi*
1961	January 12	*Show Girl*
	January 16	*The Conquering Hero*
	March 2	*13 Daughters*
	April 3	*The Happiest Girl in the World*
	April 13	*Carnival*
	May 18	*Donnybrook*
	May 31	*Pal Joey* (revival)
	June 13	*The Billy Barnes People*
	October 10	*Milk and Honey*
	October 12	*Let It Ride*

YEAR	OPENING DATE	TITLE
	October 14	How to Succeed in Business Without Really Trying
	October 23	Kwamina
	November 2	Kean
	November 18	The Gay Life
	December 27	Subways Are for Sleeping
1962	January 27	A Family Affair
	February 1	New Faces of 1962
	March 15	No Strings
	March 19	All American
	March 22	I Can Get It for You Wholesale
	May 8	A Funny Thing Happened on the Way to the Forum
	May 19	Bravo Giovanni
	October 2	Eddie Fisher at the Winter Garden
	October 3	Stop the World—I Want to Get Off
	October 20	Mr. President
	November 10	Nowhere to Go but Up
	November 17	Little Me
1963	January 6	Oliver!
	March 18	Tovarich
	April 11	Man in the Moon
	April 15	Sophie
	April 19	Hot Spot
	April 23	She Loves Me
	October 3	Here's Love
	October 17	Jennie
	October 24	110 in the Shade
	December 8	The Girl Who Came to Supper
1964	January 16	Hello, Dolly!
	February 6	Rugantino
	February 16	Foxy
	February 27	What Makes Sammy Run?
	March 26	Funny Girl
	April 4	Anyone Can Whistle
	April 7	High Spirits

Year	Opening Date	Title
	April 15	*Cafe Crown*
	May 26	*Fade Out–Fade In*
	September 11	*Wiener Blut (Vienna Life)*
	September 22	*Fiddler on the Roof*
	October 20	*Golden Boy*
	October 27	*Ben Franklin in Paris*
	November 10	*Something More!*
	December 15	*I Had a Ball*

Notable Careers in the
Musical Theatre

THIS section will help the reader follow the careers of specific writers, directors, choreographers, producers, designers, and performers. More than fifty notable musical theatre folk have been selected listing productions with which they were associated (in chronological order). In some cases, they did not officially receive credit. In other cases, they might have been associated in an unlikely capacity (e.g., someone we know as a choreographer appearing as a dancer). For details, see the show entry. There are, of course, many passing references to these people in discussion of shows with which they weren't associated; these are noted in the general index.

GEORGE ABBOTT   *director; librettist; producer*

BORN: *June 25, 1887, Forrestville, N.Y.*

Abbott came to Broadway in 1913 as an actor. He wrote his first play in 1925, the hit comedy *The Fall Guy*. He directed his first play in 1926, the ground-breaking *Broadway* (which he also co-authored). He began producing plays in 1932. His first musical, for which he staged the book, was *Jumbo* (1935). This began an important collaboration with Rodgers and Hart, including the pioneering *On Your Toes* (1936) and *Pal Joey* (1940). He began producing musicals with *The Boys from Syracuse* (1938).

On the Town	December 28, 1944
Billion Dollar Baby	December 21, 1945

Beggar's Holiday	December 26, 1946
Barefoot Boy with Cheek	April 3, 1947
High Button Shoes	October 9, 1947
Look, Ma, I'm Dancin'	January 29, 1948
Where's Charley?	October 11, 1948
Touch and Go	October 13, 1949
Call Me Madam	October 12, 1950
Out of This World	December 21, 1950
A Tree Grows in Brooklyn	April 19, 1951
Pal Joey (revival)	January 2, 1952
Wonderful Town	February 25, 1953
Me and Juliet	May 28, 1953
The Pajama Game	May 13, 1954
On Your Toes (revival)	October 11, 1954
Damn Yankees	May 5, 1955
New Girl in Town	May 14, 1957
Once Upon a Mattress	May 11, 1959
Fiorello!	November 23, 1959
Tenderloin	October 17, 1960
Pal Joey (revival)	May 31, 1961
A Funny Thing Happened On the Way to the Forum	May 8, 1962
Fade Out—Fade In	May 26, 1964

Abbott has remained active in the theatre, although his last notable success was the long-running farce *Never Too Late* (1962). Later Broadway credits include *Flora, the Red Menace* (1965), *The Education of H*Y*M*A*N K*A*P*L*A*N* (1968), *The Fig Leaves are Falling* (1969), a 1973 revival of *The Pajama Game*, *Music Is* (1976), a 1982 revival of *On Your Toes*, and a revival of *Broadway* which opened on the evening of his 100th birthday.

LEMUEL AYERS   *scenic designer; costume designer; producer*

BORN: *January 22, 1915, New York, N.Y.*
DIED: *August 14, 1955, New York, N.Y.*

Ayers came to Broadway as a set designer in 1939. His first hits were the thriller *Angel Street* (1941) and the Theatre Guild's *The Pirate* (1942)—which led to his first musical assignment on the Guild's *Oklahoma!*

Oklahoma!	March 31, 1943
Song of Norway	August 21, 1944
Bloomer Girl	October 5, 1944
St. Louis Woman	March 30, 1946
Inside U.S.A.	April 30, 1948
Kiss Me, Kate	December 30, 1948
Out of This World	December 21, 1950
Oklahoma! (return engagement)	May 29, 1951
Music in the Air (revival)	October 8, 1951
My Darlin' Aida	October 27, 1952
Oklahoma! (return engagement)	August 31, 1953
Kismet	December 3, 1953
The Pajama Game	May 13, 1954

GEORGE BALANCHINE   *choreographer*

BORN: *January 9, 1904, St.Petersburg, Russia*
DIED: *April 30, 1983, New York, N.Y.*

After ten years with the Ballets Russe, Balachine was brought to Broadway by ballet-turned-Broadway composer Vernon Duke to choreograph the ballets in *Ziegfeld Follies of 1936*. Balanchine then went to work with Rodgers and Hart (and Abbott) on *On Your Toes* (1936) and other important early musicals.

The Merry Widow (revival)	August 4, 1943
What's Up	November 11, 1943
Dream with Music	May 18, 1944
Song of Norway	August 21, 1944
Mr. Strauss Goes to Boston	September 6, 1945
Where's Charley?	October 11, 1948
On Your Toes (revival)	October 11, 1954
House of Flowers	December 30, 1954

Balanchine became artistic director of Ballet Society (New York City Ballet) in 1946, and gradually left Broadway to concentrate on dance.

IRVING BERLIN   *composer; lyricist; producer*

BORN: *May 11, 1888, Temun, Russia*
DIED: *September 22, 1989, New York, N.Y.*

Pop songs by Berlin were interpolated into Broadway musicals as early as 1908. His first important shows were the dance revues *Watch Your Step* (1914) and *Stop! Look! Listen!* (1915). In 1921, Berlin and producer Sam H. Harris built the Music Box Theatre to house their *Music Box Revues* (1921–1924). Berlin spent most of the next twenty years writing pop songs and film scores, visiting Broadway with the influential revue *As Thousands Cheer* (1933) and the rousing Army relief show, *This Is the Army* (1942).

Annie Get Your Gun	May 16, 1946
Miss Liberty	July 15, 1949
Call Me Madam	October 12, 1950
Mr. President	October 20, 1962

Berlin called it quits following the stony critical reception accorded *Mr. President.* He provided one last show tune for the 1966 revival of *Annie Get Your Gun.*

LEONARD BERNSTEIN *composer*

BORN: *August 25, 1918, Lawrence, Mass.*

Bernstein attracted the media spotlight in 1943 when he led the New York Philharmonic as a last-minute replacement. (In the days of Koussevitsky and Stokowski and Rodzinski, 26-year-old American Jews simply did not lead symphony orchestras.) A second jolt came with the 1944 premiere of the Bernstein/Robbins ballet "Fancy Free," which provided the source material for *On the Town.*

On the Town	December 28, 1944
The Cradle Will Rock (revival)	December 26, 1947
Wonderful Town	February 25, 1953
Candide	December 1, 1956
West Side Story	September 26, 1957

Theatre always took a back seat to Bernstein's classical music career. Although he has developed several projects since *West Side Story*, only one has reached Broadway: the ill-fated *1600 Pennsylvania Avenue* (1976), with book and lyrics by Alan Jay Lerner.

JERRY BOCK *composer*

BORN: *November 23, 1928, New Haven, Conn.*

Catch a Star	September 6, 1955
Mr. Wonderful	March 22, 1956
Ziegfeld Follies of 1957	March 1, 1957
The Body Beautiful	January 23, 1958
Fiorello!	November 23, 1959
Tenderloin	October 17, 1960
Man in the Moon	April 11, 1963
She Loves Me	April 23, 1963
Fiddler on the Roof	September 22, 1964

Bock's two post-*Fiddler* musicals were both interesting but disappointing failures, *The Apple Tree* (1966) and *The Rothschilds* (1970). Since then he has chosen to remain silent.

ABE BURROWS *director; librettist*

BORN: *December 18, 1910, New York, N.Y.*
DIED: *May 17, 1985, New York, N.Y.*

Burrows came to Broadway from a successful career as a radio scriptwriter.

Guys and Dolls	November 14, 1950
Make a Wish	April 18, 1951
Two on the Aisle	July 19, 1951
Three Wishes for Jamie	March 21, 1952
Can-Can	May 7, 1953
Silk Stockings	February 24, 1955
Happy Hunting	December 6, 1956
Say, Darling	April 3, 1958
First Impressions	March 19, 1959
How to Succeed in Business Without Really Trying	October 14, 1961
What Makes Sammy Run?	February 27, 1964

Burrows—who had replaced other writers on his biggest hits, *Guys and Dolls* and *How to Succeed*—was himself replaced on his last two musicals, *Breakfast at Tiffany's* (1966) and the 1974 revival of *Good News*. His final hit was the comedy *Forty Carats* (1968), which he directed.

GOWER CHAMPION   *director; choreographer*

BORN: *June 22, 1920, Geneva, Ill.*
DIED: *August 25, 1980, New York, N.Y.*

Champion came to Broadway when his supper-club dance act "Gower and Jeanne (Tyler)" was featured in the revue *The Streets of Paris* (1939). He made his choreographic debut with the Vernon Duke/Howard Dietz Coast Guard show *Tars and Spars* (1944).

Small Wonder	September 15, 1948
Lend an Ear	December 16, 1948
Make a Wish	April 18, 1951
Three for Tonight	April 6, 1955
Bye Bye Birdie	April 14, 1960
Carnival	April 13, 1961
Hello, Dolly!	January 16, 1964
High Spirits	April 7, 1964

Following *I Do! I Do!* (1966), Champion embarked on a long string of poor shows: *The Happy Time* (1968), *Prettybelle* (1971), *Sugar* (1972), *Mack and Mabel* (1974), *Rockabye Hamlet* (1976), and *A Broadway Musical* (1978). Success returned at the final minute—with *42nd Street* (1980), which opened on Broadway within hours of Champion's untimely death.

CAROL CHANNING   *actress*

BORN: *January 31, 1921, Seattle, Wash.*

Bennington girl Channing made her New York debut in Marc Blitzstein's controversial song-play *No for an Answer* (1941) at the Mecca Temple (City Center). She quickly moved to Broadway as Eve Arden's understudy in Cole Porter's *Let's Face It* (1941).

Lend an Ear	December 16, 1948
Gentlemen Prefer Blondes	December 8, 1949
The Vamp	November 10, 1955
Show Girl	January 12, 1961
Hello, Dolly!	January 16, 1964

After touring extensively with *Dolly!*, Channing returned to Broadway in the Abe Burrows farce *Four on a Garden* (1971), the *Gentlemen Prefer Blondes* revision *Lorelei* (1974), and the 1978 revival of *Hello, Dolly!* Later road appearances include the British farce *The Bed Before Yesterday* (1976), the pre-Broadway edition of *Jerry's Girls* (1984), and *Legends* (1986).

JACK COLE *choreographer*

BORN: *April 27, 1914, New Brunswick, N.J.*
DIED: *February 16, 1974, Los Angeles, Cal.*

Cole danced with the Denishawn and Humphrey-Weidman Groups before forming his own dance company in 1937. He appeared in a half-dozen Broadway shows before choreographing his first musical, *Something for the Boys*.

Something for the Boys	January 7, 1943
Ziegfeld Follies of 1943	April 1, 1943
Allah Be Praised!	April 20, 1944
Magdalena	September 20, 1948
Alive and Kicking	January 17, 1950
Carnival in Flanders	September 8, 1953
Kismet	December 3, 1953
Jamaica	October 31, 1957
Donnybrook!	May 18, 1961
Kean	November 2, 1961
A Funny Thing Happened on the Way to the Forum	May 8, 1962
Foxy	February 16, 1964

Following *Man of La Mancha* (1965), Cole choreographed two out-of-town failures: *Chu-Chem* (1966)—in which he also appeared—and *Mata-Hari* (1967).

BETTY COMDEN *lyricists; librettists; entertainers*
ADOLPH GREEN

(*Comden*) BORN: *May 3, 1915, New York, N.Y.*
(*Green*) BORN: *December 2, 1915, New York, N.Y.*

Comden and Green began their careers in 1939 writing and performing satiric material as members of "The Revuers." The group appeared in the pre-Broadway tryout of *My Dear Public* (1943).

They reached Broadway—as writers and performers—when Green's roommate, Leonard Bernstein, was commissioned to turn his ballet "Fancy Free" into a musical comedy.

On the Town	December 28, 1944
Billion Dollar Baby	December 21, 1945
Two on the Aisle	July 19, 1951
Wonderful Town	February 25, 1953
Peter Pan	October 20, 1954
Bells Are Ringing	November 29, 1956
Say, Darling	April 3, 1958
A Party with Comden and Green	December 23, 2958
Do Re Mi	December 26, 1960
Subways Are for Sleeping	December 27, 1961
Fade Out—Fade In	May 26, 1964

As the well-made comedy musical went into a decline, so did Comden and Green. Their later credits include *Hallelujah, Baby!* (1967), *Applause* (1970), *Lorelei* (1974), *On the Twentieth Century* (1978), *A Doll's Life* (1982), and *Singin' in the Rain* (1985).

BARBARA COOK   *actress*

BORN: *October 25, 1927, Atlanta, Ga.*

Flahooley	May 14, 1951
Oklahoma! (return engagement)	August 31, 1953
Plain and Fancy	January 27, 1955
Candide	December 1, 1956
The Music Man	December 19, 1957
The King and I (revival)	May 11, 1960
The Gay Life	November 18, 1961
She Loves Me	April 23, 1963
Something More!	November 10, 1964

Since ending her career as Broadway's favorite ingénue, Cook has appeared in only one musical, *The Grass Harp* (1971). She has successfully toured her nightclub/concert act, which played Broadway as *A Concert for the Theatre* (1986). She also appeared in the British (but not American) production of *Carrie* (1988).

CHERYL CRAWFORD   *producer*

BORN: *September 24, 1902, Akron, Ohio*
DIED: *October 7, 1986, New York, N.Y.*

Crawford began her Broadway career in 1928 as casting director for the Theatre Guild. In 1930 she co-founded the Group Theatre. Her first musicals were Kurt Weill's *Johnny Johnson* (1936) and the successful 1942 revival of *Porgy and Bess.*

One Touch of Venus	October 7, 1943
Brigadoon	March 13, 1947
Love Life	October 7, 1948
Regina	October 31, 1949
Flahooley	May 14, 1951
Paint Your Wagon	November 12, 1951
Jennie	October 17, 1963

Crawford followed *Jennie* with two more failures, *Chu-Chem* (1966) and *Celebration* (1969). Her final production was the Mary Martin/ Carol Channing starrer *Legends* (1986), which closed on the road.

AGNES DE MILLE   *choreographer*

BORN: *1905, New York, N.Y.*

De Mille's first Broadway assignment was the Dietz and Schwartz revue *Flying Colors* (1932), from which she was fired. Other 1930s work included Cole Porter's London musical *Nymph Errant* (1933) and Harold Arlen's *Hooray for What!* (1937). Her choreography for Aaron Copland's ballet "Rodeo" (1942) brought her to *Oklahoma!*

Oklahoma!	March 31, 1943
One Touch of Venus	October 7, 1943
Bloomer Girl	October 5, 1944
Carousel	April 19, 1945
Brigadoon	March 13, 1947
Allegro	October 10, 1947
Gentlemen Prefer Blondes	December 8, 1949
Out of this World	December 21, 1950
Oklahoma! (return engagement)	May 29, 1951
Paint Your Wagon	November 12, 1951
Oklahoma! (return engagement)	August 31, 1953
The Girl in Pink Tights	March 5, 1954

Goldilocks	October 11, 1958
Juno	March 9, 1959
Kwamina	October 23, 1961
110 in the Shade	October 24, 1963

De Mille's final Broadway assignment (other than revivals of *Oklahoma!* and *Brigadoon*) was the unsuccessful Ray Bolger musical *Come Summer* (1969).

ALFRED DRAKE   *actor; director; librettist*

BORN: *October 7, 1914, New York, N.Y.*

Drake began singing as a choir boy in Brooklyn. He came to Broadway in the chorus of a stock production of *The Mikado* (1935). After serving as William Gaxton's understudy in *White Horse Inn* (1936), he moved to his first principal role in Rodgers and Hart's *Babes in Arms* (1937).

Oklahoma!	March 31, 1943
Sing Out, Sweet Land!	December 27, 1944
Beggar's Holiday	December 26, 1946
The Cradle Will Rock (revival)	December 26, 1947
Kiss Me, Kate	December 30, 1948
The Liar	May 18, 1950
Kismet	December 3, 1953
Kean	November 2, 1961
Rugantino	February 6, 1964

Since *Kean*, Drake has appeared in two musicals: Vernon Duke's out-of-town failure *Zenda* (1963) and the 1973 stage version of *Gigi*.

NANETTE FABRAY   *actress*

BORN: *October 27, 1922, San Diego, Cal.*

Fabray began in vaudeville at the age of three. After arriving on Broadway with *Meet the People* (1940), she played a small role in Porter's *Let's Face It* (1943) and soon replaced the female lead in Rodgers and Hart's *By Jupiter* (1942).

My Dear Public	September 9, 1943
Jackpot	January 13, 1944
High Button Shoes	October 9, 1947

Love Life	October 7, 1948
Arms and the Girl	February 2, 1950
Make a Wish	April 18, 1951
Mr. President	October 20, 1962

Mr. President is Fabray's final Broadway musical to date.

CY FEUER *producer; director*
ERNEST H. MARTIN *producer*

(Feuer) BORN: *January 15, 1911, New York, N.Y.*
(Martin) BORN: *August 28, 1919, Pittsburgh, Pa.*

Feuer and Martin came to Broadway from Hollywood; Feuer was head of the music department at Republic Pictures, while Martin was programming chief for the local CBS radio affiliate.

Where's Charley?	October 11, 1948
Guys and Dolls	November 24, 1950
Can-Can	May 7, 1953
The Boy Friend	September 30, 1954
Silk Stockings	February 24, 1955
Whoop-Up	December 22, 1958
How to Succeed in BusinessWithout Really Trying	October 14, 1961
Little Me	November 17, 1962

Feuer and Martin's future musicals were far less auspicious, including *Skyscraper (1965)*, *Walking Happy* (1966), and *The Act* (1977). Feuer was replacement director of the final Rodgers musical, *I Remember Mama* (1979).

DOROTHY FIELDS *lyricist; librettist*

BORN: *July 15, 1905, Allenhurst, N.J.*
DIED: *March 28, 1974, New York, N.Y.*

Fields began her career as lyricist to composer Jimmy McHugh with the hit revue *Blackbirds of 1928*. During the Depression she went to Hollywood, where she became a favorite collaborator of Jerome Kern. Fields returned to Broadway with composer Arthur Schwartz for the Merman musical *Stars in Your Eyes* (1939), which was followed by a series of librettos co-authored with her brother Herbert.

Something for the Boys	January 7, 1943
Mexican Hayride	January 28, 1944
Up in Central Park	January 27, 1945
Annie Get Your Gun	May 16, 1946
Arms and the Girl	February 2, 1950
A Tree Grows in Brooklyn	April 19, 1951
Carnival in Flanders	September 8, 1953
By the Beautiful Sea	April 8, 1954
Redhead	February 5, 1959

Fields's final two shows, for which she wrote lyrics to Cy Coleman's music, were *Sweet Charity* (1966) and *Seesaw* (1973).

HERBERT FIELDS   *librettist*

BORN: *July 26, 1897, New York, N.Y.*
DIED: *March 24, 1958, New York, N.Y.*

Fields began his career as librettist to Rodgers and Hart, with a series of hits including *Dearest Enemy* (1925) and *A Connecticut Yankee* (1927). He moved into a seven-show collaboration with Cole Porter—all hits!—including *Fifty Million Frenchmen* (1929) and *DuBarry Was a Lady* (1939).

Something for the Boys	January 7, 1943
A Connecticut Yankee (revival)	November 17, 1943
Mexican Hayride	January 28, 1944
Up in Central Park	January 27, 1945
Annie Get Your Gun	May 16, 1946
Arms and the Girl	February 2, 1950
Carnival in Flanders	September 8, 1953
By the Beautiful Sea	April 8, 1954
Redhead	February 5, 1959

BOB FOSSE   *director; choreographer*

BORN: *June 23, 1927, Chicago, Ill.*
DIED: *September 23, 1987, Washington, D.C.*

A nightclub hoofer, Fosse appeared in national tours of *Call Me Mister* (1946) and *Make Mine Manhattan* (1948) before coming to Broadway.

Dance Me a Song	January 20, 1950
The Pajama Game	May 13, 1954
Damn Yankees	May 5, 1955
Bells Are Ringing	November 29, 1956
New Girl in Town	May 14, 1957
Copper and Brass	October 17, 1957
Redhead	February 5, 1959
The Conquering Hero	January 16, 1961
Pal Joey (revival)	May 31, 1961
How to Succeed in Business Without Really Trying	October 14, 1961
Little Me	November 17, 1962

Fosse's next show was Frank Loesser's out-of-town failure *Pleasures and Palaces* (1965), which was followed by the hits *Sweet Charity* (1966), *Pippin* (1972), *Chicago* (1975), and *Dancin'* (1978). His final musical was the ill-conceived *Big Deal* (1987).

ROBERT FRYER *producer*

BORN: *November 18, 1920, Washington D.C.*

Fryer began his producing career as an associate to George Abbott.

A Tree Grows in Brooklyn	April 19, 1951
Wonderful Town	February 25, 1953
By the Beautiful Sea	April 8, 1954
Shangri-La	June 13, 1956
Redhead	February 5, 1959
Saratoga	December 7, 1959
Hot Spot	April 19, 1963

In 1966 Fryer produced two hit musicals, *Sweet Charity* and *Mame.* Later shows include *Chicago* (1975), *On the Twentieth Century* (1978), *Sweeney Todd* (1979), and *Merrily We Roll Along* (1981).

OSCAR HAMMERSTEIN 2ND *lyricist; librettist; producer*

BORN: *July 12, 1895, New York, N.Y.*
DIED: *August 23, 1960, Doyleston, Pa.*

Hammerstein began his career stage-managing for his operetta-producing Uncle Arthur, who soon teamed him with veteran lyricist-librettist Otto Harbach (of *The Firefly* [1912] and many others). Harbach and Hammerstein collaborated on smash operettas like Friml's *Rose-Marie* (1924) and Romberg's *The Desert Song* (1926). Hammerstein turned to musical drama with Jerome Kern, pioneering the form with *Show Boat* (1927) and *Music in the Air* (1932). Then came a long, fallow period, that finally ended when Hammerstein started work with his final collaborator, Richard Rodgers.

Oklahoma!	March 31, 1943
Carmen Jones	December 2, 1943
Carousel	April 19, 1945
Show Boat (revival)	January 5, 1946
Annie Get Your Gun	May 16, 1946
Allegro	October 10, 1947
South Pacific	April 7, 1949
The King and I	March 29, 1951
Oklahoma! (return engagement)	May 29, 1951
Music in the Air (revival)	October 8, 1951
Me and Juliet	May 28, 1953
Oklahoma! (return engagement)	August 31, 1953
Pipe Dream	November 30, 1955
Flower Drum Song	December 1, 1958
The Sound of Music	November 16, 1959
The King and I (revival)	May 11, 1960

SHELDON HARNICK *lyricist*

BORN: *December 27, 1924, Chicago, Ill.*

New Faces of 1952	May 15, 1952
Two's Company	December 15, 1952
John Murray Anderson's Almanac	December 10, 1953
The Littlest Revue	May 22, 1956
Shangri-La	June 13, 1956
The Body Beautiful	January 23, 1958
Portofino	February 21, 1958
Fiorello!	November 23, 1959
Vintage '60	September 12, 1960
Tenderloin	October 17, 1960

Man in the Moon	April 11, 1963
She Loves Me	April 23, 1963
Fiddler on the Roof	September 22, 1964

Harnick and Bock collaborated on two more musicals, *The Apple Tree* (1966) and *The Rothschilds* (1970), as well as ghost writing songs for *Baker Street* (1965) and *Her First Roman* (1968). Harnick also collaborated with Richard Rodgers on the short-lived *Rex* (1976).

MICHAEL KIDD *director; choreographer*

BORN: *August 12, 1919, New York, N.Y.*

Kidd was a former copy boy for the Daily Mirror. A solo dancer with Ballet Theatre, he danced one of the leads in the premiere of Bernstein and Robbins's "Fancy Free" (1944).

Concert Varieties	June 1, 1945
Finian's Rainbow	January 10, 1947
Hold It!	May 5, 1948
Love Life	October 7, 1948
Arms and the Girl	February 2, 1950
Guys and Dolls	November 24, 1950
Can-Can	May 7, 1953
Li'l Abner	November 15, 1956
Destry Rides Again	April 23, 1959
Wildcat	December 16, 1960
Subways Are for Sleeping	December 27, 1961
Here's Love	October 3, 1963
Ben Franklin in Paris	October 27, 1964

Kidd's musicals since *Li'l Abner* have all been failures, including *Skyscraper* (1965), *Breakfast at Tiffany's* (1966), *The Rothschilds* (1970), *Cyrano* (1973), and the 1974 revival of *Good News*.

ALAN JAY LERNER *lyricist; librettist*

BORN: *August 31, 1918, New York, N.Y.*
DIED: *June 14, 1986, New York, N.Y.*

Lerner was a radio scriptwriter just out of Harvard when he met Frederick Loewe. The pair collaborated on the rewrite of *Patricia*

(1941), an out-of-town flop; their version, *Life of the Party* (1942), also closed out of town.

What's Up	November 11, 1943
The Day Before Spring	November 22, 1945
Brigadoon	March 13, 1947
Love Life	October 7, 1948
Paint Your Wagon	November 12, 1951
My Fair Lady	March 15, 1956
Camelot	December 3, 1960

All of Lerner's musicals following Loewe's retirement failed: *On a Clear Day You Can See Forever* (1966, Burton Lane), *Coco* (1969, André Previn), a musicalization of his 1958 film *Gigi* (1973, Loewe), *1600 Pennsylvania Avenue* (1976, Leonard Bernstein), *Carmelina* (1979, Lane), and *Dance a Little Closer* (1983, Charles Strouse).

BEATRICE LILLIE   *actress*

BORN: *May 29, 1894, Toronto, Canada*
DIED: *January 20, 1989, Henley-on-Thames, England*

Lillie made her stage debut in 1914. After establishing herself as a top revue comedienne, she was imported to Broadway with Jack Buchanan and Gertrude Lawrence in *Charlot's Revue of 1924*. Lillie and Lawrence remained trans-Atlantic stars for the rest of their careers. Lillie specialized in revues, including Noël Coward's *This Year of Grace* (1928) and Dietz and Schwartz's *At Home Abroad* (1935).

The Seven Lively Arts	December 7, 1944
Inside U.S.A.	April 30, 1948
An Evening with Beatrice Lillie	October 2, 1952
Ziegfeld Follies of 1957	March 1, 1957
High Spirits	April 7, 1964

Lillie was forced into retirement in 1967 by a stroke.

FRANK LOESSER   *composer; lyricist; producer*

BORN: *June 29, 1910, New York, N.Y.*
DIED: *July 28, 1969, New York, N.Y.*

A few songs interpolated in the flop revue *The Illustrators' Show* (1936) won lyricist Loesser a Hollywood contract. He wrote film scores with composers Hoagy Carmichael, Burton Lane, Jule Styne, and Arthur Schwartz. While serving in the Army, he began writing music as well as lyrics. When Hollywood music men Feuer and Martin decided to storm Broadway as producers, they invited Loesser along to write their first show.

Where's Charley?	October 11, 1948
Guys and Dolls	November 24, 1950
The Most Happy Fella	May 3, 1956
The Music Man	December 19, 1957
Greenwillow	March 8, 1960
How to Succeed in Business without Really Trying	October 14, 1961

Loesser's final musical was the costume operetta *Pleasures and Palaces* (1965), which closed out of town.

FREDERICK LOEWE *composer*

BORN: *June 10, 1901, Vienna, Austria*
DIED: *February 14, 1988, Palm Springs, Cal.*

Loewe was the son of the Viennese tenor Edmund Loewe, star of the original production of *The Merry Widow* (1905). Young Loewe came to America and drifted around, working as a cowpoke and a prizefighter. His first Broadway show was the flop costume operetta *Great Lady* (1938). He began working with Alan Jay Lerner in 1942 on *Life of the Party*.

What's Up	November 11, 1943
The Day Before Spring	November 22, 1945
Brigadoon	March 13, 1947
Paint Your Wagon	November 12, 1951
My Fair Lady	March 15, 1956
Camelot	December 3, 1960

Loewe retired following the troubled production period of *Camelot*. He briefly returned to work with Lerner on a few new songs for the 1973 stage production of their 1958 movie *Gigi*.

JOSHUA LOGAN   *director; librettist*

BORN: *October 5, 1908, Texarkana, Tex.*
DIED: *July 12, 1988, New York, N.Y.*

Logan arrived on Broadway as a director in 1935. His first musical was Rodgers and Hart's *I Married an Angel* (1938). Other early musicals included Kurt Weill's *Knickerbocker Holiday* (1938) and Irving Berlin's soldier show *This Is the Army* (1942).

Annie Get Your Gun	May 16, 1946
South Pacific	April 7, 1949
Wish You Were Here	June 25, 1952
Fanny	November 4, 1954
All American	March 19, 1962
Mr. President	October 20, 1962

All of Logan's musicals after *Fanny* failed. Post-1964 efforts included *Hot September* (1965), a musicalization of *Picnic* (1953) that closed out of town; *Look to the Lilies* (1970); and *Miss Moffat* (1974), a musicalization of *The Corn Is Green* (1940) that starred Bette Davis and also closed out of town.

ROUBEN MAMOULIAN   *director*

BORN: *October 8, 1889, Tiflis, Russia*
DIED: *December 4, 1987, Woodland Hills, Cal.*

From 1927–1930, Mamoulian directed a number of plays for the Theatre Guild beginning with *Porgy*. He then went to Hollywood, where he directed a series of innovative films including *Applause* (1929), *Dr. Jekyll and Mr. Hyde* (1931), the Rodgers and Hart *Love Me Tonight* (1932), and *Queen Christina* (1933). The Guild brought him back for his first stage musical in 1935, Gershwin's *Porgy and Bess*. Mamoulian's next Broadway call came in 1943, when the Guild decided to try another musical.

Oklahoma!	March 31, 1943
Sadie Thompson	November 16, 1944
Carousel	April 19, 1945
St. Louis Woman	March 30, 1946
Lost in the Stars	October 30, 1949
Arms and the Girl	February 2, 1950
Oklahoma! (return engagement)	May 29, 1951

Mamoulian's reputation for being impossible to handle eventually made him unhirable in New York, Hollywood, or elsewhere. His last major assignment was as initial director of the Richard Burton–Elizabeth Taylor–Rex Harrison megadisaster *Cleopatra* (1963).

MARY MARTIN *actress*

BORN: *December 1, 1913, Weatherford, Tex.*

Following her auspicious debut as the "My Heart Belongs to Daddy" girl in Cole Porter's *Leave It to Me* (1938), Martin went to Hollywood for four years. Her first two attempts at a Broadway comeback closed on the road, but the third—*One Touch of Venus*—established her as a full-fledged Broadway star.

One Touch of Venus	October 7, 1943
Lute Song	February 6, 1946
South Pacific	April 7, 1949
Peter Pan	October 20, 1954
The Sound of Music	November 16, 1959
Jennie	October 17, 1963

In 1965, Martin headed the first touring company of *Hello, Dolly!*, which included engagements in London and Vietnam. Martin's final Broadway musical (to date) has been *I Do! I Do!* (1966). She has since appeared in a couple of plays, including the ill-fated *Legends* (1986) opposite Carol Channing.

ETHEL MERMAN *actress*

BORN: *January 16, 1909, Astoria, N.Y.*
DIED: *February 15, 1984, New York, N.Y.*

Twenty-one-year-old Merman took Broadway by storm singing three Gershwin songs (including "I Got Rhythm) in *Girl Crazy* (1930). She co-starred in *Anything Goes* (1934), the first of her five Cole Porter musicals, and was soon Broadway's number one musical comedy star.

Something for the Boys	January 7, 1943
Sadie Thompson	November 16, 1944
Annie Get Your Gun	May 16, 1946
Call Me Madam	October 12, 1950
Happy Hunting	December 6, 1956
Gypsy	May 21, 1959

Merman's final Broadway appearances were in the 1966 revival of *Annie Get Your Gun* (produced, as before, by Richard Rodgers) and in 1970 as *Dolly!* for the final months of its record-breaking Broadway run.

DAVID MERRICK *producer*

BORN: *November 27, 1911, St. Louis, Mo.*

St. Louis lawyer Merrick came to Broadway to "learn the business" in 1939. Over the next fifteen years he co- or associate produced four plays, including the moderately successful *Clutterbuck* (1949). In 1951 he secured the musical rights to Marcel Pagnol's *Fanny* and, despite many obstacles, finally got the show on.

Fanny	November 4, 1954
Jamaica	October 31, 1957
Maria Golovin	November 5, 1958
La Plume de Ma Tante	November 11, 1958
Destry Rides Again	April 23, 1959
Gypsy	May 21, 1959
Take Me Along	October 22, 1959
Vintage '60	September 12, 1960
Irma La Douce	September 29, 1960
Do Re Mi	December 26, 1960
Carnival	April 13, 1961
Subways Are for Sleeping	December 27, 1961
I Can Get It for You Wholesale	March 22, 1962
Stop the World—I Want to Get Off	October 3, 1962
Oliver!	January 6, 1963
110 in the Shade	October 24, 1963
Hello, Dolly!	January 16, 1964
Foxy	February 16, 1964
Funny Girl	March 26, 1964

Post-1964 Merrick musicals include *The Roar of the Greasepaint—The Smell of the Crowd* (1965), *Pickwick* (1965), *I Do! I Do!* (1966), *Breakfast at Tiffany's* (1966), *Mata Hari* (1967), *How Now, Dow Jones* (1967), *The Happy Time* (1968), *Promises, Promises* (1968), *Sugar* (1972), *Mack and Mabel* (1974), *The Baker's Wife* (1976), and *42nd Street* (1980).

JO MIELZINER *scenic designer*

BORN: *March 19, 1901, Paris, France*
DIED: *March 15, 1976, New York, N.Y.*

Mielziner came to Broadway in 1923 as a stage manager for the Theatre Guild. His first setting was for the Guild's *The Guardsman* (1925). His first book musical was *Of Thee I Sing* (1931), and he began a fifteen-show relationship with Richard Rodgers with *On Your Toes* (1936).

The Firebrand of Florence	March 22, 1945
Carousel	April 19, 1945
Hollywood Pinafore	May 31, 1945
Annie Get Your Gun	May 16, 1946
Street Scene	January 9, 1947
Finian's Rainbow	January 10, 1947
Barefoot Boy with Cheek	April 3, 1947
Allegro	October 10, 1947
Sleepy Hollow	June 3, 1948
South Pacific	April 7, 1949
Dance Me a Song	January 20, 1950
Guys and Dolls	November 24, 1950
The King and I	March 29, 1951
A Tree Grows in Brooklyn	April 19, 1951
Top Banana	November 1, 1951
Wish You Were Here	June 25, 1952
Can-Can	May 7, 1953
Me and Juliet	May 28, 1953
By the Beautiful Sea	April 8, 1954
Fanny	November 4, 1954
Silk Stockings	February 24, 1955
Pipe Dream	November 30, 1955
The Most Happy Fella	May 3, 1956
Happy Hunting	December 6, 1956
Oh Captain!	February 4, 1958
Whoop-Up	December 22, 1958
Gypsy	May 21, 1959
Christine	April 28, 1960
The King and I (revival)	May 11, 1960
All American	March 19, 1962
Mr. President	October 20, 1962

Mielziner's post-1964 musicals include David Merrick's *Mata Hari* (1967), *1776* (1969), *Look to the Lilies* (1970), Merrick's *Sugar* (1972—the set was thrown out in Washington and Mielziner fired!), *Miss Moffat* (1974), and Merrick's *The Baker's Wife* (1976).

COLE PORTER   *composer; lyricist*

BORN: *June 9, 1891, Peru, Ind.*
DIED: *October 15, 1964, Santa Monica, Cal.*

Porter was first represented on Broadway with the revue *See America First* (1916). After a decade in Europe during which he interpolated songs in numerous revues (mostly British), Porter returned to Broadway as the 1920s ended with songs like "Let's Do It" and "What Is This Thing Called Love?" *Fifty Million Frenchmen* (1929), with librettist Herbert Fields and star William Gaxton, began a hit-filled fifteen-year stretch which included *Anything Goes* (1934) and *DuBarry Was a Lady* (1939).

Something for the Boys	January 7, 1943
Mexican Hayride	January 28, 1944
The Seven Lively Arts	December 7, 1944
Around the World (in Eighty Days)	May 31, 1946
Kiss Me, Kate	December 30, 1948
Out of This World	December 21, 1950
Can-Can	May 7, 1953
Silk Stockings	February 24, 1955

Ill health cut down Porter's activities in the early 1950s. His three final musicals went through incredibly stormy production periods, with two of them managing to come out as hits. But *Silk Stockings* was enough to send Porter into retirement.

HAROLD S. PRINCE   *producer; director*

BORN: *January 30, 1928, New York, N.Y.*

"H. Smith Prince" came to Broadway as an assistant to George Abbott's #1 stage manager, Robert E. Griffith, on Walter Kerr's *Touch and Go* (1947). After several years in the Abbott organization, Griffith and Prince determined to produce musicals of their own—under the guidance of Mr. Abbott, naturally!

The Pajama Game	May 13, 1954
Damn Yankees	May 5, 1955
New Girl in Town	May 14, 1957
West Side Story	September 26, 1957
Fiorello!	November 23, 1959
Tenderloin	October 17, 1960
A Family Affair	January 27, 1962
A Funny Thing Happened on the Way to the Forum	May 8, 1962
She Loves Me	April 23, 1963
Fiddler on the Roof	September 22, 1964

Prince firmly established himself in the late 1960s as Broadway's premier director of musicals, eventually phasing out of producing. Credits include *Baker Street* (1965), *Flora, the Red Menace* (1965, his final Abbott show), *Cabaret* (1966), *Zorba* (1968), *Company* (1970), *Follies* (1971), *A Little Night Music* (1973), *Candide* (1974), *Pacific Overtures* (1976), *On the Twentieth Century* (1978), *Sweeney Todd* (1979), *Evita* (1979), *Merrily We Roll Along* (1981), *A Doll's Life* (1982), *Grind* (1985), *Roza* (1987), and *Phantom of the Opera* (1988).

JEROME ROBBINS *director; choreographer*

BORN: *October 1, 1918, New York, N.Y.*

Robbins came to Broadway as a teenager, debuting in the chorus of Frederick Loewe's first musical *Great Lady* (1938). He joined Ballet Theatre in 1940 as a soloist, making his choreographic debut on April 18, 1944 with Leonard Bernstein's ballet "Fancy Free."

On the Town	December 28, 1944
Concert Varieties	June 1, 1945
Billion Dollar Baby	December 21, 1945
High Button Shoes	October 9, 1947
Look, Ma, I'm Dancin'	January 29, 1948
Miss Liberty	July 15, 1949
Call Me Madam	October 12, 1950
The King and I	March 29, 1951
Wish You Were Here	June 25, 1952
Two's Company	December 15, 1952
Wonderful Town	February 25, 1953
The Pajama Game	May 13, 1954

Peter Pan	October 20, 1954
Silk Stockings	February 24, 1955
Bells Are Ringing	November 29, 1956
West Side Story	September 26, 1957
Gypsy	May 21, 1959
The King and I (revival)	May 1, 1960
A Funny Thing Happened on the Way to the Forum	May 8, 1962
Funny Girl	March 26, 1964
Fiddler on the Roof	September 22, 1964

Robbins joined the New York City Ballet as Associate Artistic Director (with George Balanchine) in 1949. Since the late 1950s he has dedicated most of his energies to the ballet. His only Broadway musical visit since *Fiddler on the Roof* has been the anthology revue *Jerome Robbins' Broadway* (1989).

RICHARD RODGERS   *composer; producer*

BORN: *June 28, 1902, New York, N.Y.*
DIED: *December 30, 1979, New York, N.Y.*

Richard Rodgers and lyricist Lorenz Hart were launched on Broadway in 1919 by producer Lew Fields, father of their librettist Herbert Fields. Success came with the Theatre Guild's *Garrick Gaieties* (1925). After a string of late 1920s hits including *The Girl Friend* (1926) and *A Connecticut Yankee* (1927), the pair went to Hollywood. Innovative film musicals included *Love Me Tonight* (1932) (with director Rouben Mamoulian) and *Hallelujah, I'm a Bum* (1933). They returned to Broadway in 1935 for a series of influential musicals with George Abbott, including *On Your Toes* (1936) and *Pal Joey* (1940). When Rodgers and Hart ended their twenty-five-year collaboration in 1942, Rodgers turned to Oscar Hammerstein.

Oklahoma!	March 31, 1943
A Connecticut Yankee (revival)	November 17, 1943
Carousel	April 19, 1945
Annie Get Your Gun	May 16, 1946
Allegro	October 10, 1947
South Pacific	April 7, 1949
The King and I	March 29, 1951

Oklahoma! (return engagement)	May 29, 1951
Pal Joey (revival)	January 2, 1952
Me and Juliet	May 28, 1953
Oklahoma! (return engagement)	August 31, 1953
On Your Toes (revival)	October 11, 1954
Pipe Dream	November 30, 1955
Flower Drum Song	December 1, 1958
The Sound of Music	November 16, 1959
The King and I (revival)	May 11, 1960
Pal Joey (revival)	May 31, 1961
No Strings	March 15, 1962

Rodgers wrote his own lyrics for *No Strings*, his first musical after Hammerstein's death. Following an abortive collaboration with Alan Jay Lerner, Rodgers turned to Hammerstein's protégé Stephen Sondheim for the unsuccessful *Do I Hear a Waltz?* (1965). Rodgers's final three musicals were ill-advised and below calibre: *Two by Two* (1970, with Martin Charnin), *Rex* (1976, with Sheldon Harnick), and *I Remember Mama* (1970, with Charnin).

HAROLD ROME   *composer; lyricist*

BORN: *May 27, 1908, Hartford, Conn.*

Rome slipped into prominence when an amateur show he wrote for the ILGWU, *Pins and Needles* (1937), became Broadway's longest-running musical (with 1,108 performances surpassing the 441 mark set by the 1931 *Of Thee I Sing*). This was followed by the Music Box revue *Sing Out the News* (1938), sponsored by Sam Harris, George S. Kaufman, and Moss Hart. He returned to Broadway in 1946 after three years in the Army.

Call Me Mister	April 18, 1946
Alive and Kicking	January 17, 1950
Michael Todd's Peep Show	June 28, 1950
Bless You All	December 14, 1950
Wish You Were Here	June 25, 1952
Fanny	November 4, 1954
Destry Rides Again	April 23, 1959
I Can Get It for You Wholesale	March 22, 1962

Rome's final Broadway show was the Yiddish/African musical *The Zulu and the Zayda* (1965). *Scarlett* (1970), his musicalization of

Gone with the Wind, premiered in Tokyo. It was successfully mounted in London as *Gone with the Wind* (1972), but the American version (1973) closed out of town.

ARTHUR SCHWARTZ   *composer*

BORN: *November 25, 1900, Brooklyn, N.Y.*
DIED: *September 3, 1984, Kintnersville, Pa.*

Schwartz and lyricist Howard Dietz set the standard for sophisticated Broadway revues with *The Little Show* (1929) and *The Band Wagon* (1931). After splitting with Dietz in 1937, Schwartz's lyricists (in New York and Hollywood) included Dorothy Fields, Oscar Hammerstein 2nd, Frank Loesser, Ira Gershwin, and—occasionally—Dietz.

Park Avenue	November 4, 1946
Inside U.S.A.	April 30,1948
A Tree Grows in Brooklyn	April 19,1951
By the Beautiful Sea	April 8, 1954
The Gay Life	November 18, 1961
Jennie	October 7, 1963

The unsuccessful-but-lovely *Gay Life* and ill-starred *Jennie* put an end to the career of one of our prime melodists.

HASSARD SHORT   *director; lighting designer*

BORN: *October 15, 1877, Edlington, Lincs, England*
DIED: *October 9, 1956, Nice, France*

Short came to America as an actor in 1901, turning to directing in 1919. Early musicals included Irving Berlin's *Music Box Revue* (1921–1923), Kern and Hammerstein's *Sunny* (1925), Dietz and Schwartz's *The Band Wagon* (1931), Berlin and Moss Hart's *As Thousands Cheer* (1933), and Weill, Gershwin, and Hart's *Lady in the Dark* (1941). Short brought many "modern" stage and lighting effects to the musical theatre.

Something for the Boys	January 7, 1943
Carmen Jones	December 2, 1943
Mexican Hayride	January 28, 1943
The Seven Lively Arts	December 7, 1944
Marinka	July 18,1945

Show Boat (revival)	January 5, 1946
Music in my Heart	October 2,1947
Make Mine Manhattan	January 15, 1948
Michael Todd's Peep Show	June 28, 1950
Seventeen	June 21,1951
My Darlin' Aida	October 27, 1952

OLIVER SMITH   *scenic designer; producer*

BORN: *February 13, 1918, Wawpawn, Wisc.*

Smith's first Broadway show was the hit operetta *Rosalinda* (1942). For Ballet Theatre, he designed the Bernstein/Robbins "Fancy Free" (1944). This became the source material for *On the Town*, which Smith co-produced as well as designed. He became co-director of (American) Ballet Theatre in 1947.

Rhapsody	November 22, 1944
On the Town	December 28,1944
Billion Dollar Baby	December 21, 1945
Beggar's Holiday	December 26, 1946
Brigadoon	March 13, 1947
High Button Shoes	October 9, 1947
Look, Ma, I'm Dancin'	January 29, 1948
Along Fifth Avenue	January 13, 1949
Miss Liberty	July 15, 1949
Gentlemen Prefer Blondes	December 8, 1949
Bless You All	December 14, 1950
Paint Your Wagon	November 12, 1951
Pal Joey (revival)	January 2, 1952
Carnival in Flanders	September 8, 1953
My Fair Lady	March 15, 1956
Mr. Wonderful	March 22, 1956
Candide	December 1, 1956
West Side Story	September 26, 1957
Jamaica	October 31, 1957
Say, Darling	April 3, 1958
Flower Drum Song	December 1, 1958
Juno	March 9, 1959
Destry Rides Again	April 23, 1959
Take Me Along	October 22, 1959
The Sound of Music	November 16, 1959

The Unsinkable Molly Brown	November 3, 1960
Camelot	December 3, 1960
Show Girl	January 12, 1961
Sail Away	October 3, 1961
The Gay Life	November 18, 1961
Eddie Fisher at the Winter Garden	October 2, 1962
110 in the Shade	October 24, 1963
The Girl Who Came to Supper	December 8, 1963
Hello, Dolly!	January 16, 1964
Ben Franklin in Paris	October 27, 1964

Smith's post-1964 musicals include *Kelly* (1965), *Baker Street* (1965), *On a Clear Day You Can See Forever* (1965), *I Do!, I Do!* (1966), *Prettybelle* (1971), *Mass* (1971), *Gigi* (1973), and *Carmelina* (1979).

STEPHEN SONDHEIM   *composer; lyricist*

BORN: *March 22, 1930, New York, N.Y.*

West Side Story	September 26, 1957
Gypsy	May 21, 1959
A Funny Thing Happened on the Way to the Forum	May 8, 1962
Hot Spot	April 19, 1963
Anyone Can Whistle	April 4, 1964

Sondheim followed *Anyone Can Whistle* with his third lyrics-only job, opposite Richard Rodgers on *Do I Hear a Waltz?* (1965). Broadway finally began to appreciate Sondheim with *Company* (1970), which has been followed by *Follies* (1971), *A Little Night Music* (1973), *Pacific Overtures* (1976), *Sweeney Todd* (1979), *Merrily We Roll Along* (1981), *Sunday in the Park with George* (1984), and *Into the Woods* (1987). Despite his continually excellent work, only three of the musicals Sondheim has composed have been commercially successful: *Forum, Company,* and *A Little Night Music.*

JULE STYNE   *composer; producer*

BORN: *December 31, 1905, London, England*

Pop-songwriter Styne came to Broadway from Hollywood, where he specialized in Sinatra songs. His first musical, *Glad to See You!* (1944, with Sammy Cahn), closed out of town.

High Button Shoes	October 9, 1947
Gentlemen Prefer Blondes	December 8, 1949
Michael Todd's peep Show	June 28, 1950
Make a Wish	April 18, 1951
Two on the Aisle	July 19, 1951
Pal Joey (revival)	January 2, 1952
Hazel Flagg	February 11, 1953
Peter Pan	October 20, 1953
Mr. Wonderful	March 22, 1956
Bells are Ringing	November 29, 1956
Say, Darling	April 3, 1958
First Impressions	March 19, 1959
Gypsy	May 21, 1959
Do Re Mi	December 26, 1960
Subways Are for Sleeping	December 27, 1961
Funny Girl	March 26, 1964
High Spirits	April 7, 1964
Fade Out–Fade In	May 26, 1964
Something More!	November 10,1964

Since 1964 Styne has turned out a string of unsuccessful (and in some cases unjustly underappreciated) scores, including *Hallelujah, Baby!* (1967), *Darling of the Day* (1968), *Look to the Lilies* (1970), *Prettybelle* (1971, closed out of town), *Sugar* (1972), *Lorelei* (1974), *Bar Mitzvah Boy* (1978, London), and *One Night Stand* (1980).

THE THEATRE GUILD   *producers*

LAWRENCE LANGNER
THERESA HELBURN

(*Langner*) BORN: *May 30, 1890 Swansea, Wales*
          DIED: *December 26, 1962, New York, N.Y.*

(*Helburn*) BORN: *January 12, 1887, New York, N.Y.*
    DIED: *August 18, 1959, Norwalk, Conn.*

The Theatre Guild, hallowed home of Shaw and O'Neill (and Lunt & Fontanne), first experimented in the musical field in 1925 when they let a bunch of understudies stage a two-performance benefit. With songs by Rodgers and Hart, *The Garrick Gaieties* transferred to a long, successful run. In 1935, the Guild unsuccessfully tried a musical version of their 1927 folk play *Porgy*. In 1943 they tried again, musicalizing another Guild folk play, *Green Grow the Lilacs* (1931).

Oklahoma!	March 31, 1943
Sing Out, Sweet Land!	December 27, 1944
Carousel	April 19, 1945
Allegro	October 10, 1947
Arms and the Girl	February 2, 1950
Oklahoma! (revival)	May 29, 1951
Bells are Ringing	November 29, 1956
A Party with Comden and Green	December 23, 1958
The Unsinkable Molly Brown	November 3, 1960

GWEN VERDON   *actress*

BORN: *January 13, 1926, Culver City, Cal.*

Verdon first appeared in the pre-Broadway tryout of *Bonanza Bound* (1947), a Comden and Green/Jack Cole show. She served as Cole's assistant on *Magdalena* (1948) and *Alive and Kicking* (1950), in which she made her Broadway debut.

Alive and Kicking	January 17, 1950
Can-Can	May 7, 1953
Damn Yankees	May 5, 1955
New Girl in Town	May 14, 1957
Redhead	February 5, 1959

Verdon's all-too-infrequent Broadway appearances since *Redhead* have been in *Sweet Charity* (1966), the non-musical thriller *Children! Children!* (1972), and *Chicago* (1975).

NANCY WALKER   *actress*

BORN: *May 10,1921, Philadelphia, Pa.*

Walker walked into an audition for *Best Foot Forward* (1941) and convulsed director/producer George Abbott, who brought her to full stardom over the course of four 1940s musicals.

On the Town	December 28, 1944
Barefoot Boy with Cheek	April 3, 1947
Look, Ma, I'm Dancin'	January 29, 1948
Along Fifth Avenue	January 13, 1949
Phoenix '55	April 23, 1949
Cooper and Brass	October 17, 1957
The Girls Against the Boys	November 2, 1959
Do Re Mi	December 26, 1960

After years of indifferent material, Walker left Broadway following *Do Re Mi* and has yet to return.

KURT WEILL   *composer*

BORN: *March 2, 1900, Dessau, Germany*
DIED: *April 3, 1950, New York, N.Y.*

Weill fled Nazi Germany in 1933, settling in America in 1935. (His 1928 *Threepenny Opera* was a quick failure when produced on Broadway—without his involvement—in 1933.) His first two American musicals, *Johnny Johnson* (1936) and *Knickerbocker Holiday* (1938), were too political for comfort (or success) despite fascinating scores. The Gertrude Lawrence–starrer *Lady in the Dark* (1941), which brought lyricist Ira Gershwin out of retirement after his brother's death in 1937, was a first-rate show and a solid hit.

One Touch of Venus	October 7, 1943
The Firebrand of Florence	March 22, 1945
Street Scene	January 9, 1947
Love Life	October 7, 1948
Lost in the Stars	October 30, 1949

MILES WHITE   *costume designer*

BORN: *July 27, 1920, Oakland, Cal.*

White designed his first show, *Right This Way* (1938), at the age of 18. His next two productions, *Best Foot Forward* (1941, co-produced by Richard Rodgers) and the Theatre Guild's *The Pirate* (1942), led to the assignment on *Oklahoma!* (1943).

Oklahoma!	March 31, 1943
Ziegfeld Follies of 1943	April 1, 1943
Early to Bed	June 17, 1943
Allah Be Praised!	April 20, 1944
Dream with Music	May 18, 1944
Bloomer Girl	October 5, 1944
Carousel	April 19, 1945
The Day Before Spring	November 22, 1945
Gypsy Lady	September 17, 1946
High Button Shoes	October 9, 1947
Gentlemen Prefer Blondes	December 8, 1949
Bless You All	December 14, 1950
Oklahoma! (return engagement)	May 29, 1951
Pal Joey (revival)	January 2, 1952
Three Wishes for Jamie	March 21, 1952
Two's Company	December 15, 1952
Hazel Flagg	February 11, 1953
Oklahoma! (return engagement)	August 31, 1953
The Girl in Pink Tights	March 5, 1954
Ankles Aweigh	April 18, 1955
Jamaica	October 31, 1957
Oh Captain!	February 4, 1958
Take Me Along	October 22, 1959
Bye Bye Birdie	April 14, 1960
The Unsinkable Molly Brown	November 3, 1960
Show Girl	January 12, 1961
Milk and Honey	October 10, 1961

White's final musicals were *Zenda* (1963), which closed out of town, and *Tricks* (1973). Over the years he designed many editions of the Ringling Bros., Barnum & Bailey Circus and the *Ice Capades*.

The Critics

THIS section offers biographical data on the major critics of the era, followed by a newspaper-by-newspaper rundown of the first string critics from 1943–1964. All newspapers referred to were based in New York unless otherwise indicated.

JOHN ANDERSON   *Journal-American, 1927–1943*

BORN: *October 18, 1896, Pensacola, Fla.*
DIED: *July 16, 1943, New York, N.Y.*

Drama critic for the *Post*, 1924–1927. Became critic for the *Journal-American* in 1927. Author of *Box Office* (1929), a highly informative book about business aspects of the Broadway theatre, and *The American Theatre* (1938). He wrote the plays *The Inspector General* (1930, adapted from Gogol); *The Fatal Alibi* (1932); and *Collision* (1932).

BROOKS ATKINSON   *Times, 1925–1942, 1946–1960*

BORN: *November 28, 1894, Melrose, Mass.*
DIED: *January 13, 1984, Huntsville, Ala.*

Leaving a job as English teacher at Dartmouth College (Hanover, N.H.), Atkinson joined the Springfield (Mass.) *Daily News* as a reporter in 1917. After serving overseas in the Army, he joined the Boston *Evening Transcript* as a police reporter and assistant drama critic in 1919. Moved to the New York *Times* in 1922 as editor of the book review section. Became drama critic in 1925. During leave of absence, served as a *Times* war correspondent in China (1942–1944) and Moscow (1945–1946), winning the 1947 Pulitzer

Prize for Journalism for his reports from Russia. Returned as drama critic in 1946 until reaching the *Times*'s mandatory retirement age in 1960, when he became Critic at Large (1960–1971). Upon leaving his post as daily critic, the Mansfield Theatre was renamed for him. Recipient of a special Tony Award in 1962. Wrote or edited over a dozen books, including *Skyline Promenades* (1925); *Henry Thoreau: The Cosmic Yankee* (1927); *East of the Hudson* (1931); *The Cingalese Prince* (1934); *Cleo for Short* (about his car) (1940); *Broadway Scrapbook* (1947); *Once Around the Sun* (1951); *Tuesdays and Fridays* (1963); *Brief Chronicles* (1966); *Broadway* (1970); and *The Lively Years* (1973), with Al Hirschfeld).

HOWARD BARNES   *Herald Tribune*, 1942–1950

BORN: *November 26, 1904, London, England*
DIED: *March 12, 1968, New York, N.Y.*

Joined the *World* as drama reporter and assistant film critic in 1928. Moved to drama desk of the *Herald Tribune* in 1936. Became critic in 1942 when Richard Watts left for overseas.

JOHN CHAPMAN   *Daily News*, 1943–1971

BORN: *June 25, 1900, Denver, Colo.*
DIED: *January 19, 1972, Westport, Conn.*

Jointed the Denver *Times* as a reporter in 1917. Joined the *Daily News* in 1920, working as a police reporter, a photographer (in Paris), etc. Became drama editor 1929, Hollywood columnist in 1940. Replaced Burns Mantle as critic in 1943. Upon Mantle's death, took over as editor of the *Best Plays* series (1947–1952). Edited his own anthology series. *Theatre* (1953–1956) and *Broadway's* Best (1957–1960). Author of *Tell It To Sweeney: A History of the New York Daily News* (1961).

ROBERT COLEMAN   *Daily Mirror*, 1924–1963

BORN: *August 6, 1900, Bainbridge, Ga.*
DIED: *November 27, 1974, New York, N.Y.*

Began his entertainment career at the age of ten, passing out flyers for a traveling minstrel show; as a teenager, he worked in the box office. Joined the *Morning Telegraph* as a sports reporter in 1924.

Became critic for the *Mirror* in 1924, remaining until the paper ceased publication in 1963.

ROBERT GARLAND   *Journal-American, 1943–1951*

BORN: *April 29, 1895, Baltimore Md.*
DIED: *December 27, 1955, New York, N.Y.*

Served as a Lieutenant during World War I (on the Siberian Front). Joined the Baltimore *News* as a reporter in 1920. Became critic for the Baltimore *Daily Post* in 1922, moving to the Baltimore *American* in 1924. Became theatre columnist for the New York *Telegram* in 1926. Became critic when the *World* and *Telegram* merged in 1928 (through 1936). Press agent for Federal Theatre in 1937. Became critic for the *Journal-American* in 1943. Wrote several plays, none of which were produced in New York, and appeared as an actor in summer stock. During the 1930s he was married to musical comedy star Queenie Smith, best known as heroine of the Gershwins' *Tip-Toes* (1925) and Vincent Youmans's *Hit the Deck* (1927).

WILLIAM HAWKINS, JR.   *World-Telegram, 1946–1956*

BORN: *1912*

Son of the chairman of the board of Scripps–Howard newspapers, he became critic of the *World-Telegram* (a Scripps–Howard paper) in 1946. Hawkins, Sr. died in 1953, leaving a million dollar estate. Hawkins, Jr. resigned in 1956, moved to Italy, and became a novelist. His books include *The Big Red Pocketbook* (1963) and *Tell the Mischief* (1964).

WALTER KERR   *Herald Tribune, 1951–1966*

BORN: *July 8, 1913, Evanston, Ill.*

While a teacher of drama at Catholic University, Washington, D.C. (1938–1949), he wrote books for three school musicals which were remounted on Broadway: *Count Me In* (1942), *Sing Out, Sweet Land* (1944), and *Touch and Go* (1947). His collaborator on the sketches and lyrics for the latter was his wife, Jean, with whom he also wrote the 1946 stage adaptation of Franz Werfel's novel *The Song of Bernadette*. He directed all of the above except *Count Me*

In. He became critic for *Commonweal* magazine in 1950, moving to the *Herald Tribune* in 1951. While on the *Tribune*, he directed Jean Kerr and Eleanor Brooke's comedy *King of Hearts* (1954) and the musical *Goldilocks* (1958), for which he coauthored the book and lyrics. When the *Tribune* ceased publication, he moved to the *Times* as daily critic in 1966. He became Sunday critic in 1967. Winner of the Pulitzer Prize in 1978 for his drama criticism. In 1990, the Ritz Theatre was renamed in his honor. Author of *How Not to Write a Play* (1955); *Criticism and Censorship* (1957); *Pieces at Eight* (1958); *The Decline of Pleasure* (1962); *The Theater in Spite of Itself* (1963) *Tragedy and Comedy* (1966); *Thirty Plays Hath November* (1969); *God on the Gymnasium Floor* (1971); *The Silent Clowns* (1975), and *Journey to the Center of the Theater* (1979).

LOUIS KRONENBERGER   *PM*, 1940–1948

BORN: *December 9, 1904, Cincinnati, Ohio*
DIED: *April 30, 1980, Brookline, Mass.*

Editor for book publishers Boni & Liveright and Alfred A. Knopf (1926–1935). Became an editor at *Fortune* magazine in 1935. Became critic for *Time* magazine in 1938, remaining until 1961. He was simultaneously critic for the newspaper *PM*. Became professor of theatre arts at Brandeis University (Waltham, Mass.) in 1953 and Librarian of the University in 1963. He wrote the Broadway version of Jean Anouilh's *Mademoiselle Colombe* (1954). Author or editor of many books, including the *Best Plays* series (1952–1961).

JOHN LARDNER   *Star*, 1948–1949

BORN: *May 4, 1912, Chicago, Ill.*
DIED: *March 24, 1960, New York, N.Y.*

Son of writer/sportswriter/songwriter Ring Lardner. Joined the *Herald Tribune* as a reporter in 1931, became a syndicated sports columnist in 1933. Became sports columnist for *Newsweek* in 1939. War correspondent in Australia and Asia for *Newsweek* and *The New Yorker* (1942–1945). Became critic for the brief-lived *Star* in 1948. Covered sports, theatre, TV for various magazines through the 1950s. His brother, Ring Lardner, Jr.—one of the "Hollywood Ten"—is the Oscar-winning screenwriter of *Woman of the Year*

(1942) and M*A*S*H (1970), and co-librettist of the musical *Foxy* (1964).

BURNS MANTLE   *Daily News*, 1922–1943

BORN: *December 23, 1873, Watertown, N.Y.*
DIED: *February 9, 1948, Forest Hills, N.Y.*

Began as a printer at the Denver *Post*. Became drama editor of the Denver *Times* in 1898. Moved to Chicago *Inter-Ocean* in 1901. Became Sunday editor of the Chicago *Tribune* in 1908. Moved to New York as critic for the *Evening Mail* in 1911. Became critic for the *Daily News* in 1922 until retirement in 1943. Editor of *Best Plays* series (1919–1947); coeditor of *The Best Plays of 1909–1919* (1933); *A Treasury of the Theatre* (1935); and *The Best Plays of 1899–1909* (1944). Author of *American Playwrights of Today* (1929) and *Contemporary American Playwrights* (1938).

JOHN McCLAIN   *Journal-American*, 1951–1966

BORN: *August 7, 1904, Marion, Ohio*
DIED: *May 3, 1967, London, England*

Joined the New York *Sun* as a reporter in 1929. Moved to the *Journal-American* in 1936 (through 1938). Became a writer at M-G-M, with screenplays including *Lady Be Good* (1941) and *Cairo* (1942). Served as a Navy Commander 1942–1945, winning a bronze star at Iwo Jima. Returned to the *Sun* as columnist in 1945. When the *Sun* ceased publication, became critic for the *Journal-American* in 1951. When the *Journal-American* merged with the *World-Telegram & Sun* and the *Herald Tribune* in 1966, he became travel editor of the *World Journal Tribune*—which ceased publication two days after his death.

WARD MOREHOUSE   *Sun*, 1942–1950

BORN: *November 24, 1906, Savannah, Ga.*
DIED: *December 7, 1966, New York, N.Y.*

Joined the Atlanta *Journal* as a reporter in 1918. Moved to the New York *Tribune* in 1919. Moved to the *Sun* as theatre columnist in 1926, became critic in 1942. When the *Sun* merged with the *World-Telegram* in 1950, he continued as a columnist. Author of the plays *Gentlemen of the Press* (1928); *Miss Quis* (1937); and *U.S.*

90 (1941). Screenplays include *Central Park* (1932) and *It Happened in New York* (1935). Books include the semiautobiographical *Forty-Five Minutes Past Eight* (1939); *George M. Cohan—Prince of the American Theatre* (1943), and *Matinee Tomorrow: 50 Years of Our Theatre* (1949).

NORMAN NADEL   *World-Telegram & Sun*, 1961–1966

BORN: *June 19, 1915, Newark, N.J.*

Joined the Columbus (Ohio) *Citizen* as an editor in 1939, becoming drama critic in 1947. Became critic for the *World-Telegram & Sun* in 1961. Remained as critic when the paper briefly merged with the *Journal-American* and *Herald Tribune* into the *World Journal Tribune* in 1966. One of the few drama critics with musical training, he was a trombonist with the Columbus Symphony (which he helped establish in 1940). Author of *A Pictorial History of the Theatre Guild* (1970).

LEWIS NICHOLS   *Times*, 1942–1946

BORN: *September 1, 1903, Lock Haven, Pa.*
DIED: *April 29, 1982, Greenfield, Mass.*

Joined the *Times* with a summer job in 1926 and stayed, eventually becoming drama editor. When Brooks Atkinson took a leave of absence to cover the War in 1942, he became interim critic. He retired from the *Times* in 1946, but continued as a contributor and rejoined the paper in 1957 as an assistant book reviewer (through 1969).

BURTON RASCOE   *World-Telegram*, 1942–1946

BORN: *October 22, 1892, Fulton, Ky.*
DIED: *March 19, 1957, New York, N.Y.*

In 1902 he moved to Oklahoma Territory, making him one of the few Broadwayites who was actually there in the days when it was a "brand new state" (as they sing in the song). Joined the Shawnee (Oklahoma) *Herald* as a teen-aged reporter in 1906. Joined the Chicago *Tribune* as literary critic in 1917, became drama critic in 1919 (through 1920). Spent the next two decades as literary critic and editor for the *American Mercury* and other magazines, and as editor in chief of the Literary Guild. Became drama critic for the

World-Telegram in 1942. Author and editor of many books, including *Theodore Dreiser* (1925); *Titans of Literature* (1932); *Belle Starr: The Bandit Queen* (1941); and two autobiographies, *Before I Forget* (1936) and *We Were Interrupted* (1947).

HOWARD TAUBMAN   *Times*, 1960–1965

BORN: *July 4, 1907, New York, N.Y.*

Joined the *Times* in 1929. Became music editor in 1935 and music critic in 1955. Replaced Brooks Atkinson as drama critic in 1960. Became Critic at Large for the *Times* in 1965. Author of several books, including *Music on My Beat* (1943); *The Maestro: The Life of Arturo Toscanini* (1951); *How to Build a Record Library* (1953); and *The Making of the American Theatre* (1965).

WILELLA WALDORF   *Post*, 1941–1946

BORN: *1900, South Bend, Ind.*
DIED: *March 12, 1946, New York, N.Y.*

After a brief career as a private detective, joined the *Public-Ledger/ N.Y. Post* syndicate in 1925. Became movie critic for the *Post* in 1926. She claimed to have reviewed over 1,200 films (including shorts and two-reelers), often at the rate of four a day. Became drama editor in 1928, succeeding John Mason Brown as drama critic in 1941. She died on the job, collapsing after turning in her review for the 1946 revival of *Show Boat.*

RICHARD WATTS JR.   *Post*, 1946–1974

BORN: *January 12, 1898, Parkersburg, W.Va.*
DIED: *January 2, 1981, New York, N.Y.*

Joined the Brooklyn *Times* as a reporter in 1922. Moved to the *Herald Tribune* as film critic (1924–1936) and drama critic (1936–1942). Covered the Spanish Civil War for the *Tribune* (1937)–1938). During the War served as press attaché of the U.S. Legation in Dublin (1942) and editor in chief of the U.S. Office of War Information in Chungking, China (1943–1944). Became drama critic for the *Post* in 1946, until his retirement in 1974.

THE FIRST STRING CRITICS, 1943–1964

Daily News
1943	Burns Mantle
1943–1964	John Chapman

Herald Tribune
1943–1950	Howard Barnes
1951–1964	Walter Kerr

Journal-American
1943	John Anderson
1943–1951	Robert Garland
1951–1964	John McClain

Mirror
1943–1963	Robert Coleman
	(paper ceased publication)

PM
1943–1948	Louis Kronenberger
	(paper reorganized as the *Star*)

Post
1943–1946	Wilella Waldorf
1946–1964	Richard Watts Jr.

Star
1948–1949	John Lardner
	(paper ceased publication)

Sun
1943–1950	Ward Morehouse
	(paper merged with *World-Telegram*)

Times
1943–1946	Lewis Nichols
1946–1960	Brooks Atkinson
1960–1964	Howard Taubman

World-Telegram (& Sun)

1943–1946	Burton Rascoe
1946–1956	William Hawkins
1956–1957	Tom Donnelly
1957–1961	Frank Aston
1961–1964	Norman Nadel

the World, I Want to Get Off, Street Scene, Subways Are for Sleeping, Sweethearts, Take Me Along, Three for Tonight, Three Wishes for Jamie, Top Banana, Touch and Go, A Tree Grows in Brooklyn, Two on the Aisle, Up in Central Park, The Vamp, West Side Story, What's Up, Where's Charley?, Whoop-Up, Wiener Blut, Wildcat, Wish You Were Here and *Wonderful Town.*

The following photographs are from the Billy Rose Theatre Collection of the Performing Arts Research Center, The New York Public Library at Lincoln Center, Astor, Lenox and Tilden Foundations: *Beggar's Holiday, Camelot, Can-Can, Carnival, Flahooley, A Funny Thing Happened on the Way to the Forum, Hollywood Pinafore, Inside U.S.A., Li'l Abner, Love Life, Lute Song, New Faces of '56, Pal Joey, South Pacific, Three for Tonight, Top Banana,* and *Two on the Aisle.*

The author thanks the following people for graciously providing illustrative artwork reproduced in this book:

Courtesy of William C. Appleton: *One Touch of Venus.*

Courtesy of Richard Kidwell: *Do Re Mi.*

Courtesy of Charles Lowe: *Gentlemen Prefer Blondes* (photo).

Courtesy of Paul Newman, Esq.: *Anyone Can Whistle, Bloomer Girl, Carmen Jones, Carnival in Flanders, Carousel, The Day Before Spring, Hazel Flagg, Jennie, The King and I, Kismet,* and *Lost in the Stars.*

Courtesy of Kim Sellon: *Look, Ma, I'm Dancin'.*

Courtesy of Don Stubblebine: *Hot Spot* and *Peter Pan.*

Courtesy of Max Woodward: *Alive and Kicking, Allegro, Ankles Aweigh, Annie Get Your Gun, Call Me Madam, Copper and Brass, Fanny, Fiorello!, The Girl in Pink Tights, The Happiest Girl in the World, Happy Town, House of Flowers, Irma la Douce, Juno, Magdalena, Make a Wish, Me and Juliet, Mr. Wonderful, The Most Happy Fella, My Fair Lady, Oklahoma!* (1953), *Oliver!, 110 in the Shade, Paint Your Wagon, Park Avenue, Plain and Fancy, Porgy and Bess, Regina, Saratoga, She Loves Me, A Tree Grows in Brooklyn, West Side Story,* and *Whoop-Up.*

Index

Page numbers in *italics* denote primary discussion of indexed subject.

A *Nous La Liberté*, 102
Aarons, Alex A., 28, 343
Abbott, George, 8, 10, 17, 28, 71–72, 75, 81–82, 84–86, 112, 114–115, 117, 169, 172–173, 183, 197–200, 215–218, 239, 241–243, 303, 306, 312, 383–385, 396–397, 399, 426, 429, 484–488, 511, 514–516, 518–519, 527–529, 533–537, 595–596, 622, 639, 658–659, 670–671, 674–677, 702–705, 716–720, *741–742*
ABC-Paramount, 193, 307, 309, 628
Abel, Walter, 140
Abeles, Joseph, 26. *See also* Friedman-Abeles Studio
Abravanel, Maurice, 220, 575
Act, The, 620
Adair, Tom, 47
Adair, Yvonne, 246, 249, 381–383, 618, 620
Adam, Noelle, 488
Adams, Edith (Edie), 388, 391, 716, 718–720
Adams, Lee, 36, 113–114, 262–265, 297, 300
Adams, Roger, 415
Adams, Samuel Hopkins, 658
Adams, Stanley, 376
Adamson, Harold, 65
Addams, Charles, 430
Addison, John, 168
Adler, Richard, 169, 172–173, 352, 371, 373, 515, 533, 536–537, 597
Adler, Stella, 559
Adolphus, Theodore, 652
Adrian, 124–126
Adrian, Henry, 249–252
Adrian, Louis, 367
Adrian, Max, 130
Agay, Denes, 472
"Age of Anxiety," 553
Ah, Wilderness!, 295, 656
Aida, 464
Alberghetti, Anna Maria, 137–138, 140, 492
Albert, Eddie, 443
Albertson, Jack, 666
Albery, Donald, 338, 508
Alda, Alan, 115–116
Alda, Robert, 116, 272, 275–276, 698
Aldredge, Theoni Vachlioti, 328, 477
Aldredge, Thomas, 475
Aleichem, Sholom, 207
Alexander, Cris, 511
Alexander, David, 292, 395, 537, 540, 689
Alexander, Rod, 609, 659
Alive and Kicking, *33–36*, 128
All American, *36–38*, 706
All for Love, 16, *38–40*, 53
"All or Nothin'," 501

Allah Be Praised!, *40–42*
Allegro, *42–47*, 419, 421, 555, 670
Allen, Steve, 633–635
Allen, Woody, 235
Allers, Franz, 126, 471
Allyson, June, 110
Along Fifth Avenue, *47–48*
Altman, Ruth, 98
Alton, Robert, 82, 191, 292–294, 378, 426, 515, 537, 539–540, 689, 720
Alvarez, Anita, 210, 214, 246, 249
"Always True to You in My Fashion," 369
"Amahl and the Night Visitors," 424
Ameche, Don, 266, 618–619, 659–660
"American Concertette," 153
American National Theatre & Academy, 28, 67–68, 70, 157, 160, 231
Ames, Florenz, 495
Amundsen, Monte, 355
Anatol, 243
And There I Stood with My Piccolo, 460
Anderson, John, 16, 18, 499, 688, 720, 773
Anderson, John Murray, 219, 295, 352–353, 378, 478–479, 664, 681, 684, 720
Anderson, Judith, 352
Anderson, Leroy, 266–268, 715
Anderson, Maxwell, 400–403, 573, 575
Anderson, Robert, 174
Andes, Keith, 414, 710
Andrews, Julie, 98–100, 122, 124–125, 468–472, 639
Andrews, Nancy, 151, 391, 392, 557, 670
Angel in the Wings, *48–50*
Angelus, Muriel, 192
Ankles Aweigh, *50–53*, 230, 450
Anna and the King of Siam, 358
Anna Christie, 484–487
Anna Lucasta, 346
Annie, 13, 509
Annie Get Your Gun, 3, 9–10, 12, 28, *53–57*, 77, 118, 122, 214, 448, 555
"Another Autumn," 532
Anouilh, Jean, 19
Anstey, F., 523
Anthony, Joseph, 453, 520
Anthony, Norman, 107
Anyone Can Whistle, *58–60*, 494
Anything Goes, 55, 143, 343, 529
"Apache," 128
Appell, Don, 441
Archer, John, 175–176
Archibald, William, 153
archy and mehitabel, 609–611
Arden, Eve, 110

Aristophanes, 283, 285
Arlen, Harold, 11, 89–93, 319–322, 343–344, 584–587, 589, 592–595
Armistead, Horace, 401, 431
Arms and the Girl, 61–62
Armstrong, Will Steven, 137–140
Armus, Sidney, 713
Arno, Peter, 25, 118, 277
Arno, Sig, 605, 631
Aronson, Boris, 184, 207, 210, 582
Aronson, Jim, 20, 686
Around the World (in Eighty Days), 62–64, 371, 475
Arthur, Art, 311–312
Arthur, Beatrice, 207, 601
Arthur, Jean, 88
"Arty," 149
As the Girls Go, 12, 65–66
As Thousands Cheer, 91
"Ascot Gavotte," 570
Ashley, Barbara, 67, 387, 528
Ashley, Clayton, 376–377
Astaire, Adele, 343, 661
Astaire, Fred, 84, 343, 661, 663
Astar, Ben, 516
Aston, Frank, 20, 74, 113, 152, 179, 215, 226, 234, 266, 269, 278, 283, 338, 344, 362, 375, 460, 477, 496, 540, 570, 595, 615, 637, 658, 684, 693
At Home Abroad, 337
At the Drop of Another Hat, 66–67
Atkinson, Brooks, 9, 17–21, 23, 29, 33, 43, 47, 48, 50, 65, 74, 75, 80, 88, 96, 98, 103, 109, 113, 115, 117, 131, 142, 164, 167, 174, 195, 203, 210, 215, 222, 226, 246, 254, 266, 269, 279, 286, 287, 295, 311, 332, 335, 344, 352, 355, 358, 363, 364, 367, 369, 386, 388, 400, 405, 411, 417, 426, 429, 438, 443, 453, 459, 460, 464, 468, 472, 478, 486, 495, 496, 503, 506, 516, 519, 527, 529, 537, 545, 547, 548, 557, 563, 570, 572, 573, 578, 590, 591, 595, 609, 618, 637, 639, 645, 652, 656, 661, 665, 666, 670, 674, 678, 689, 692, 704, 706, 714, 716, 773
Atkinson, David, 254–255, 689
Atwater, Edith, 222, 225
Aubuchon, Jacques, 321
Auerbach, Arnold, 88–89, 120–122, 334, 722
Aumont, Jean Pierre, 672–673
Aurthur, Robert Alan, 371–372
Austen, Jane, 221–222, 660
Austin, Lyn, 164
Avedon, Richard, 26, 320
Away We Go!, 499–500, 527
Axelrod, George, 624
Ayers, Lemuel, 243, 336, 366–371, 465–466, 504, 527–528, 584–589, 742–743
Ayres, Christine, 377
Ayres, Lew, 603

Babes in Arms, 296
Babes in Toyland, 224
Bachenheimer, Theodore, 457
Bacher, William, 601
Bagar, Robert, 20, 75
Bagley, Ben, 394–395
Bailey, Pearl, 61–62, 88–89, 321–323, 566, 584–585, 587–589
Bailey, Robin, 347

Baird, Bil, 222–24, 421
Baird, Cora, 222–224, 421
Baker, Benny, 341–342
Baker, David, 164–166, 552
Baker, Kenny, 524–525, 527
Baker, Word, 201, 203
Baker Street, 109, 210, 603
Baker's Wife, The, 510
"Bal Petit Bal," 479
Balanchine, George, 8, 82, 105, 186–189, 319, 322, 434, 448–449, 515–516, 518, 631–632, 701–702, 704, 743
Balieff, Mme. Nikita, 150
Balieff, Nikita, 150
Ball, Lucille, 13, 710–713
"Ballad of the Sad Young Men, The," 476–477
Ballard, Kaye, 138, 259
Ballard, Lucinda, 54, 244–245, 406, 614, 636, 649
Ballet Ballads, 67–70, 261
Ballet Society, 429
Ballet Theatre (American Ballet Theatre), 68
Ballets Russe, 8, 189, 631–632
Balsam, Martin, 492
Bancroft, Anne, 239
Band Wagon, The, 316, 544
Banjo Eyes, 385
Bankhead, Tallulah, 192, 481, 483, 574, 723–724
Banks, Leslie, 400–402
Baranova, Irina, 228
Barclift, Nelson, 62
Barefoot Boy with Cheek, 71–72
Barefoot in the Park, 149, 393
Barer, Marshall, 480, 518
Barker, Albert, 431
Barnell, 634
Barnes, Billy, 86–87
Barnes, Clive, 18, 47, 91, 103, 120, 133, 153, 160, 190, 219, 281, 303, 376, 386, 400, 448, 499, 641, 774
Barnes, Mae, 111
Barnes, Roy, 94
Barratt, Watson, 404
Barrie, J. M., 414, 548–551
Barrier, The, 72–73
Barry, Gene, 285
Barstow, Richard, 71, 478, 591
Bart, Lionel, 508, 511
Barto, Dewey, 397
Barton, Eileen, 48
Barton, James, 250–251, 529–532
Battista, Miriam, 623
Battles, John, 43, 511
Bavaar, Tony, 529, 533
Baxley, Barbara, 605
Bay, Howard, 65, 137, 223–224, 440, 462–463, 639, 687
Bayliss, Gene, 310
Beal, John, 478
Bean, Orson, 352, 649–650
Beat the Band, 515
Beaton, Cecil, 26, 321, 323, 468, 471, 593–595
Beaumont, Ralph, 130, 540, 592
"Because," 495
Becher, Thomas, 481, 482
Becker, Lee, 395–396, 603, 693
Becket, 126, 341
Bedsow, Len, 633
Beery, Noah, Sr., 686
Beethoven, Ludwig van, 116

786

"Before the Parade Passes By," 300
Beg, Borrow or Steal, 73–74
Beggar's Holiday, 74–78
Beggar's Opera, The, 74, 76–78
Behrman, S.N., 203–205, 243
Bela, Nicholas, 623
Belafonte, Harry, 352–353, 394, 661, 663
Belasco, Jacques, 249–250
Bel Geddes, Norman, 598–599
Bell, Marion, 103, 107, 665
Bellaver, Harry, 53
Bells Are Ringing, 74, 78–82, 288, 467, 472, 697, 719
Bellson, Louis, 565–566
Ben Franklin in Paris, 82–84
Bendix, William, 657
Bennett, Michael, 24
Bennett, Robert Russell, 332, 487, 575
Bennewitz, John, 667
Benson, Sally, 431, 600
Benton, Nicholas, 552
Benzell, Mimi, 441–442
Bergen, Polly, 221, 352
Bergersen, Baldwin, 40, 624
Bergman, Alan, 628–630
Bergman, Marilyn, 628–630
Berkowitz, Sol, 492
Berle, Milton, 480, 600–601, 668, 720–722
Berlin, Irving, 11, 53–57, 77, 91, 117–120, 443–448, 457, 601, *743–744*
Berman, Shelley, 201, 258
Berney, William, 591
Bernstein, Aline, 575
Bernstein, Leonard, 10–11, 85–86, 130–132, 166–168, 312, 511–516, 546, 693–697, 715–718, 720, *744*
Berra, Yogi, 171
Berry, Eric, 98
Berry, Ken, 87
Berté, H., 99
Berton, Eugene, 403
Besser, Joe, 332
Best Foot Forward, 48, 397, 467, 515
Bethell, Anne, 556
Bettis, Valerie, 75, 88–89, 334, 337
Bhumibol, King of Thailand, 439–441
"Bicycle Built for Two," 622
Bigelow, Joe, 189
Bigley, Isabel, 272, 275, 426
Bikel, Theodore, 115–116, 637
"Bill," 614
Billion Dollar Baby, 84–86, 153, 306, 429
Billy Barnes People, The, 86–87
Bing, Rudolph, 383
Birch, Patricia, 603
Birch, Peter, 147
Birsky, Socrates, 129
Bissell, Marian, 595
Bissell, Richard, 169, 533, 536–537, 595–596
Bittersweet, 676
Bizet, Georges, 133–135, 137
Black, Dr. Frank, 189
Black Crook, The, 5, 252, 297
Blackstone, Milton, 193
Blackwell, Carlyle, 281
Blaine, Vivian, 272, 276, 595
Blane, Ralph, 467, 515, 665
Bless You All, 88–89
Bliss, Helena, 279, 631
Blithe Spirit, 307

Blitzstein, Marc, 72, 78, 166–168, 353–356, 386, 571–575, 649
Blondell, Joan, 164
Bloomer Girl, 12, 46, *89–93*, 210, 429, 515, 589
Bloomfield, Harry, 559
Bloomgarden, Kermit, 58, 243, 453, 460–462, 464, 492–494
Bloomingdale, Alfred, 40, 42, 191, 720
Blossom, Henry, 567
Blossom Time, *93–94*, 632
Blue Angel, The, 116
Blue Holiday, 94–95
"Blue Night," 439–441
"Blue Tail Fly," 622
Bly, Nellie, 473–475
Blyden, Larry, 226, 231
Bock, Jerry, 11, 95–97, 148, 207, 210, 215, 218, 421–422, 450, 515, 604–608, 639, 658, *745*
Body Beautiful, The, *95–98*
Bois, Curt, 559
Bolender, Todd, 157
Boles, John, 524–525
Bolger, Ray, 8, 35–38, 664, 703–706
Bolin, Shannon, 169
Bolton, Guy, 6, 50, 228, 341, 591
"Bon Vivant," 233
Bonard Productions, 583
Bond, Ridge, 503, 505
Bond, Sheila, 419, 540, 649, 713, 715
Bonfils, Helen, 583
Bontemps, Arna, 584
Booth, Shirley, 111–112, 298, 313–315, 354–355, 674–678
Boothe (Luce), Claire, 19
Borden, Lizzie, 396
Bordoni, Irene, 404, 414
Borodin, Alexander, 52, 364, 366–367
Bosco, Philip, 185
Bosley, Tom, 215–218, 492–493
"Boston Beguine, The," 97, 479
Botto, Louis, 480
Bourne, Hal, 33
Bova, Joe, 318, 518
Boy Friend, The, *98–100*, 310, 382, 517, 620, 708
Boyer, Monica, 659
Boys from Syracuse, The, 296
Bracken, Eddie, 73, 609–611
Brady, Scott, 179
Brand, Max, 179
Brando, Marlon, 149
Brascia, John, 294
Bravo Giovanni, *100–102*, 242
"Breakfast with Dorothy and Dick," 189
Breaux, Marc, 179, 181
Brecht, Bertolt, 78
Breen, Robert, 563–564
Breffort, Alexandre, 338
Brennan, Eileen, 297
Brentano, Felix, 434, 448–449
Brice, Carol, 573, 592–593
Brice, Fanny, 48, 53, 188, 236, 246, 351, 552–553, 628
Bricusse, Leslie, 643
Brigadoon, 3, 10, 46, *103–107*, 186, 214, 471, 531, 665
Bright Lights of 1944, 107–109
Brill, Marty, 115
Brisson, Frederick, 169, 173, 484, 488, 533, 537
Britten, Benjamin, 386

Britton, George, 279
Britton, Pamela, 103, 105 .
Broadbent, Aida, 279, 567
Brook, Peter, 319, 322, 338, 341
Brooks, David, 89, 92, 103, 254
Brooks, Donald, 490
Brooks, Lawrence, 109, 472, 631
Brooks, Matt, 311–312
Brooks, Mel, 36–38, 478–479, 609
Broome, John, 643
Brosset, Colette, 373–374
"Brother, Can You Spare a Dime?," 295
Brotherson, Eric, 246
Brown, Ada, 432
Brown, Anthony, 107
Brown, Billings, 624–625
Brown, Forman, 456, 567
Brown, Frederick Hazlitt, 411
Brown, Georgia, 508
Brown, Herrick, 20, 95, 192, 311, 381, 545
Brown, Kay, 157
Brown, L. Slade, 36, 113
Brown, Max, 179
Brown, Michael, 478, 480
Brown, Molly Tobin, 684, 685
Brown, Russ, 169, 173
Browne, Irene, 256
Brownlee, John, 688
Bruce, Betty, 686
Bruce, Carol, 47, 540, 542, 612, 615
Bryant, Glenn, 133–135
Bryant, Hugh, 168
Bryden, Eugene, 332
Brynner, Yul, 83, 358–362, 408–410
Buchanan, Jack, 361
Buck, Pearl S., 151–152
"Buck and the Bobbie," 174
Buckhantz, Allan A., 289
Bufman, Zev, 692
Bulfinch, 283
Buloff, Joseph, 499
Bunce, Alan, 164
Burke, Billie, 720, 722
Burke, Johnny, 140, 142–143, 185, 473
Burnett, Carol, 197–200, 518–519
Burns, Arthur, 421
Burns, David, 33, 35, 84, 148, 181, 239–243,
    295, 297, 419–421, 460, 464, 466, 527, 681,
    724
Burns, Ralph, 491
Burris, Glenn, 364
Burrows, Abe, 22, 126–128, 221, 272–276, 287,
    323–327, 415, 417, 595, 618–620, 665, 678,
    698, 745
Burton, Richard, 122–126, 408
Butler, John, 160, 201, 395
Butterworth, Charles, 175
"Button Up Your Overcoat," 660
Buttons, "Red," 71, 311
Buttrio Square, 109–111, 310, 471
By Jupiter, 8, 156, 706
By the Beautiful Sea, 111–112
Bye Bye Birdie, 10, 37, 113–115, 139–140, 184,
    374, 418, 663
Byrns, Harold, 177

C'est Moi," 123
Cabaret, 11, 203
Cabin in the Sky, 343, 516

Cabot, Susan, 603
Caesar, Irving, 466–467
Caesar, Sid, 391–393, 419–421, 480
Cafe Crown, 115–117
Cagney, James, 452
Cahn, Sammy, 193–194, 303, 306, 681
Caine Mutiny Court Martial, The, 661
"Cakewalk Your Lady," 587
Calder, Alexander, 42
Calin, Mickey, 693
Call Me Madam, 10, 12, 28, 117–120, 287, 448
Call Me Mister, 89, 120–122
Callahan, Bill, 65, 120, 681
Callan, Mike, 693
Calloway, Cab, 563–564
Calvi, Gerald, 373
Calvin, Henry, 364
"Calypso Pete," 617
Camelot, 70, 115, 122–126, 258, 327, 408
"Camelot," 125
Campanella, Joe, 318
"Can't You Do a Friend a Favor?," 156
Can-Can, 126–130, 171–172, 294, 366, 529,
    619–620, 708
Candide (1956), 130–132, 516, 697
Candide (1974), 603
Cannon, Maureen, 281, 686
Canore, F., 127
Cantor, Arthur, 421
Cantor, Eddie, 385, 473–474
Capote, Truman, 175, 319–322, 551
Capp, Al, 388, 390
Capp, Madeline, 566
Cappy, Ted, 665, 678
Captain's Paradise, The, 496
"Card Song," 136
Caribbean Carnival, 132–133
Carlo, Monte, 403–404
Carlton, Richard, 168
Carmen, 133–136
Carmen Jones, 9, 133–137, 186, 465–466, 588–
    589, 615
Carmichael, Hoagy, 33, 413
Carnival, 12, 37, 137–140, 238, 374, 491, 645
Carnival in Flanders, 140–143, 471
Carnovsky, Morris, 201
Carousel, 3, 7, 9–10, 12, 25, 46, 136, 142, 144–
    147, 209, 214, 230, 359, 363, 402, 502, 582,
    588, 615, 642, 670
Carr, Byrie, 310
Carr, Lawrence, 111, 318, 568, 571, 603
Carradine, John, 239–242
Carroll, Diahann, 140, 321–323, 488–492
Carroll, Earl, 188, 477
Carroll, June, 332, 425, 478–480
Carroll, Pat, 148–149
Carroll, Renee, 108
Carroll, Robert, 457
Carroll, Sidney, 425
Carrot Top, 137
Carson, Alexander F., 689
Carson, Mindy, 96
Carter, Jack, 450, 669
Carter, Joey, 483
Carter, Terry, 371
Carthay, 93
Cass, Peggy, 670
Cassidy, Jack, 197–200, 603–605, 608, 713
Cassini, Oleg, 66
Castillo, 266, 336

Castle, Nick, 295
Cat and the Fiddle, The, 316
Catch a Star!, 148–150
Cates, Joseph, 698, 700
Catherine the Great, 327
Caton, Edward, 473, 579
Cellini, Benvenuto, 220
Cesar, 203
Chagall, Marc, 208
Chambers, Ernest, 615
Champion, Gower, 10–11, 37, 113–115, 137,
    139–140, 143, 297–300, 307, 309, 380, 382–
    383, 415–418, 510, 624–625, 660–663, *746*
Champion, Marge, 143, 661–663
Chaney, Lon, 116
Chaney, Stewart, 188
Channing, Carol, 239, 246–249, 297–300, 381–
    382, 387, 519, 611, 615–618, 689–692, *746–
    747*
Chaplin, Charles, 81, 102
Chaplin, Sydney, 74, 78–82, 236, 649
Chapman, John, 18, 33, 36, 38, 40, 49, 53, 58,
    61, 62, 72, 74, 77, 80, 84, 88, 91, 103, 113,
    117, 122, 126, 131, 133, 135, 137, 144, 148,
    150, 162, 169, 177, 179, 183, 188, 190, 193,
    198, 207, 212, 215, 219, 221, 224, 228, 235,
    244, 246, 252, 254, 259, 272, 278, 280, 281,
    286, 289, 291, 297, 305, 312, 313, 321, 323,
    332, 335, 338, 344, 352, 355, 360, 364, 371,
    377, 378, 381, 387, 388, 394, 402, 404, 410,
    419, 422, 428, 432, 435, 438, 441, 449, 450,
    453, 457, 462, 468, 472, 474, 479, 486, 488,
    498, 508, 511, 520, 525, 528, 533, 541, 547,
    550, 552, 554, 559, 566, 570, 573, 579, 585,
    590, 591, 594, 597, 600, 602, 603, 605, 611,
    612, 621, 624, 643, 647, 654, 655, 656, 661,
    668, 670, 676, 680, 681, 685, 689, 695, 698,
    701, 704, 709, 716, *774*
Chapman, William, 269, 422
Charig, Phil, 148, 228
Charlap, Moose, 157, 548, 706–708
Charley's Aunt, 312, 702, 705
Charlot's Revue of 1924, 361, 599
Charmoli, Tony, 50, 193–194
Charnin, Martin, 316
Chauve-Souris (1922), 150–151
Chauve-Souris (1943), *150–151*
Chayefsky, Paddy, 149
Chiari, Walter, 243
Child, Alan, 61
Chisholm, Robert, 511
Chocolate Soldier, The, 105
Chodorov, Edward, 719
Chodorov, Jerome, 33, 151, 252, 255, 331, 716,
    719–720
Chopin, Frederic, 94, 415, 559–561
Chorus Line, A, 11, 13, 175
Christenberry, Charles W., Jr. 310
Christie, Audrey, 190–191
Christine, *151–152*
Christine, Lilly, 438
Church, Sandra, 276, 279
Chute, B.J., 269
Cibelli, Alfred, Jr., 505
Cinderella, 332, 670–671
"Civil War Ballet," 91
"Civilization," 49
Clair, Rene, 102
Clark, Bobby, 65–66, 399, 435–440, 472, 568,
    652–655, 669

Clark, Buddy, 108
Clark, Peggy, 481
Clark, Robert Edwin, Esq., 438–440
Clarke, Henry, 503
Clary, Robert, 478, 601
Clary, Wilton, 72
Clayton, Jan, 144, 612–613
Clemens, 416
Cline, Edward, 378
Close, Del, 475
Clouds, The, 588
Clurman, Harold, 554
Coca, Imogene, 153
"Cocoa Bean Song, The," 372
Cocoanuts, The, 655
Coe, Fred, 207–208
Coe, Peter, 262, 508
Cohan, George M., 5, 297, 425
Cohen, Alexander H., 20, 66, 107, 109, 415,
    576–577
Cohen, I.W., 270
Cohen, Martin. B., 151, 689
Cole, Cozy, 134
Cole (Abraham), Doris, 94
Cole, Jack, 33–36, 40, 128, 140, 185, 231, 239,
    343, 356, 364–365, 367, 411, 625, 720, 724,
    747
Cole, Nat King, 452
Coleman, Cy, 11, 391–392, 710–713
Coleman, Donald H., 496
Coleman, Leo, 429
Coleman, Robert, 18, 33, 43, 61, 80, 96, 105,
    114, 119, 123, 148, 162, 168, 171, 174, 179,
    183, 185, 194, 195, 217, 224, 235, 239, 248,
    254, 258, 259, 268, 274, 288, 310, 321, 344,
    366, 369, 375, 381, 383, 386, 397, 402, 405,
    423, 428, 440, 443, 450, 455, 457, 462, 470,
    477, 498, 519, 535, 538, 541, 596, 619, 623,
    624, 633, 641, 644, 656, 658, 661, 668, 670,
    685, 708, 712, 714, 718, *774*
Coleman, Warren, 400
Collins, Charles, 567
Colman, Ronald, 387
Colt, Alvin, 63, 180, 274, 389, 556, 667
Colton, John, 579
Comden, Betty, 10, 78–81, 84–86, 181–183,
    197, 467, 511–515, 546–548, 551, 595, 649–
    650, 678, 715–716, 720, *747–748*
"Come and Be My Butterfly," 300
Come Back, Little Sheba, 677–678
Come Blow Your Horn, 149, 393
Come Summer, 46, 706
Come What May, 567
"Comedy Tonight," 239
Conaway, Charles, 722
Concert Varieties, 153–154
Connecticut Summer, 656
Connecticut Yankee, A, 123, *154–157*, 316
Connecticut Yankee in King Arthur's Court, A
    154
Connell, Jane, 480, 482
Connelly, Marc, 107, 623
Conquering Hero, The, 23, *157–160*, 543
Conrad, Eugene, 378
Conried, Hans, 126
Consul, The, 73, *160–163*, 424, 649
Conte, John, 43, 61
Convy, Bert, 493, 692
Conway, Shirl, 557
Cook, Alton, 20, 135

Cook, Barbara, 130–131, 222–223, 225, 243–245, 362–363, 460–464, 505–506, 557, 605–607, 628–630, *748*
Cook, Charles, 286
Cook, Joe, 66
Cook, Roderick, 256
"Cookie Chase, The," 60
Cookson, Peter, 126
Coolidge, Philip, 71
Cooper, Hy, 249
Cooper, Marilyn, 327
Cooper, Melville, 219, 279, 387, 415, 434
Coote, Robert, 122, 468, 471
Copeland, Joan, 628
Copeland, Virginia, 590
Copland, Aaron, 502
Coppel, Alec, 496
Copper and Brass, 164–166
Corbett, Leonora, 543–545
Cordon, Norman, 645
"Corduroy Road," 712
Corey, Irwin, 222, 285, 295
Cotlow, Marilyn, 429
Coudy, Douglas, 313
Coulter, Kay, 516
Count Me In, 622
Countess Maritza, 415
"Country's in the Very Best of Hands, The," 388–389
Courtland, Jerome, 222, 225
Courtney, Marguerite Taylor, 347
Coward, Noël, 256–258, 308, 583–584
Cowles, Chandler, 160, 429, 495, 590
Cox, Wally, 174–175
Cradle Will Rock, The, 166–168
Craig, David, 164–166, 552
Craig, Helen, 408
Cranko, John, 168
Cranks, 168–169
Cranton, Hal, 109
Crawford, Cheryl, 103, 222, 224, 347, 351, 405, 407, 525, 529, 573, *749*
Creoles, 403
Crime of Giovanni Venturi, The, 100
Crist, Judith, 20, 421
Cropper, Roy, 93
Crosby, Bing, 143
Cross, Richard, 422
Croswell, Anne, 671
Crouse, Russel, 117, 218, 287, 446–447, 635–637, 639
Crowley, Anne, 600
Crozier, Eric, 386
Cry, the Beloved Country, 400–402
Cugat, Xavier, 498
Cullen, Countee, 584–589
Cunningham, Davis, 590
Curran, Homer, 411, 631
Cushman, Dan, 706
Cusumano, S., 161
Cutts, Patricia, 356

Daarlin' Man, 353
Da Costa, Morton, 316, 319, 460–462, 464, 557, 592–594
Dagger and the Rose, The, 219
Dale, Alan, 601
Dale, Charles, 108, 466
Dale, Grover, 269, 583

Dali, Salvador, 169, 598
Dalrymple, Jean, 362, 540
D'Amboise, Jacques, 609
Damn Yankees, 12, 66, 82, 130, 149, *169–174,* 415, 488, 658, 697
Damon, Cathryn, 231
Dance Me a Song, 36, *174–175,* 543
"Dance of the Seven Veils," 377
Dancing in the Streets, 343, 527
Dane, Faith, 276
Dangerous Maid, A, 343
Daniels, Billy, 262, 432–433
Daniels, Danny, 36, 307, 419, 649
Daniels, David, 557
Daniels, Marc, 164, 552
Danilova, Alexandra, 496–498, 631–632
Darby, Eileen, 26
D'Arcy, Richard, 615
Darian, Anita, 362
Darion, Joe, 609
Dark of the Moon, 105
Darling, Jean, 144
Darrow, Whitney, Jr., 629
Darwell, Jane, 593
Da Silva, Howard, 166, 215, 499
Dassin, Jules, 411, 681
"Dat Ol' Boy," 136
Davenport, Pembroke, 363, 397
David, Mack, 107, 300
Davidson, John, 231
Davies, Valentine, 301
Davis, Bette, 448, 582, 713
Davis, Blevins, 563–564, 575
Davis, Cherry, 157
Davis, Eddie, 50, 228
Davis, Jack, 26, 284
Davis, Luther, 364, 367, 603
Davis, Meyer, 313, 315–316
Davis, Ossie, 346
Davis, Sammy, Jr., 262–265, 450–452
Davison, Robert, 64, 177
Dawson, Mark, 50, 215, 303, 653
Day Before Spring, The, 10, 106–107, *175–178,* 408, 471, 702
Day Well Spent, A, 297
Dead End, 494
Dear World, 109
Death of a Salesman, 479, 494, 623, 643
Dee, Sylvia, 71
Deems, Mickey, 692
De Falla, Manuel, 190
De Gresac, Fred, 652
DeHaven, Gloria, 601–602
De Havilland, Olivia, 38
De Lappe, Gemze, 531, 533, 552
De Lavallade, Carmen, 318
Delfont, Bernard, 643
De Liagre, Alfred, Jr., 371
Delilah, 689–690
Dell, Gabriel, 50, 58
Dell'Isola, Salvatore, 228
Delmar, Harry, 228
Del Mar, Norman, 386
De Luce, Virginia, 478
De Mille, Agnes, 9–10, 42, 46, 68, 70, 89–92, 103, 105, 107, 144, 147, 214, 246, 249, 252, 255, 266, 312, 342–343, 353–356, 371–373, 491, 499–503, 505, 515, 520, 525–527, 529–532, *749–750*
Dempsey, Jack, 506

Dennis, Patrick, 391–393
De Paul, Gene, 388, 390–391
"Dere's a Cafe on de Corner," 136
Derr, Richard, 557
Derwent, Clarence, 279–280, 408
"Desert Flame, The," 89
Desert Song, The, 18
Desilu Productions, Inc., 710
Desjardins, Pete, 715
Desmond, Florence, 332
Desmond, Johnny, 595, 597
Destry Rides Again, 179–181, 234, 656, 713
Deutsch, Helen, 137, 139
Deval, Jacques, 671
De Vries, Peter, 681
De Witt, Fay, 692
De Wolfe, Billy, 352–353, 723
Dhery, Robert, 373, 375
Diamond, I.A.L., 33
"Diamonds Are a Girl's Best Friend," 246
Diary of Anne Frank, The, 494
Dickens, Charles, 508–510
Dickey, Annamary, 43, 575
Diener, Joan, 364, 366–367, 624, 724
Dietrich, Marlene, 116, 673
Dietz, Howard, 243–244, 316, 334–335, 337, 341–343, 347, 351, 579, 582
Dillingham, Charles, 568
DiLuca, Dino, 321
DiMaggio, Joe, 43, 119, 274
"Dis Flower," 136
"Dis-Donc," 340
"Dites-Moi," 269
Dixon, Lee, 499
Do Re Mi, 130, *181–184,* 238, 393
Dolan, Robert Emmett, 231
Dolin, Anton, 597–598
Dollar, William, 231
Dolly: A Damned Exasperating Woman, 297
"Don Brown's Body," 352
Don Juan in Hell, 661
"Don't Be a Woman If You Can," 545
"Don't Forget 127th Street," 265
Donaldson, W.H., 25
Donath, Ludwig, 605
Donehue, Vincent J., 347, 351, 353, 637–638, 684
Donnelly, Dorothy, 93
Donnelly, Tom, 20, 80, 131, 168, 388, 395, 486, 723
Donnybrook!, 185–186
Donohue, Jack, 450–452, 495, 577, 597, 666
Doolittle, James A., 457, 709
D'Orsay, Fifi, 601
Douglas, Larry, 358
Douglas, Melvyn, 120–122, 354–355
Douglass, Margaret, 89
Douglass, Stephen, 169, 171, 173, 259–260, 417, 520–522, 577
Dove, 176
Dowden, 512
Dowling, Eddie, 295
Dowling, Edward Duryea, 195, 559
Dowling, Robert W., 266
Downs, Johnny, 311
Doyle, David, 73
D'Oyly Carte Opera Company, 337, 556
Drake, Alfred, 75–77, 149, 166, 356–357, 362, 364–369, 371, 387, 499, 576, 621–622, *750*

Drake, Ervin, 698
Dream with Music, 186–189
Dreigroschenoper, Die, 168
Dresselhuys, Lorraine Manville, 575
Dreyfuss, Henry, 435
Drummond-Grant, Ann, 337
DuBarry Was a Lady, 371
Dubey, Matt, 287–288, 480
du Bois, Raoul Pène, 33, 35, 79, 295–296, 381, 417, *720*
Duchess Misbehaves, The, 189–191
Duffy, Gordon, 289
Duffy, Henry, 457
Duke, Robert, 332
Duke, Vernon, 341–343, 394, 579–582, 681
Dulles, John Foster, 344
Dumas, Alexandre, 356–357
Dumke, Ralph, 448, 579, 612, 614
Duncan, Augustin, 408
Duncan, Todd, 400–403
Dunham, Katherine, 94, 153
Dunn, Elaine, 148
Dunn, Patricia, 365
Dunnock, Mildred, 408
Dunphy, Jack, 175
Duquette, Tony, 124–126
Durant, Jack, 250
Durante, Jimmy, 627
Duse, Eleanora, 112, 657
Dussault, Nancy, 181
Duval, Franca, 422
Dvonch, Frederick, 639
Dyer, William, 234

*E*agels, Jeanne, 581–582
Eager, Edward, 186, 387
Early to Bed, 189, *191–193*
East Is West, 152
East Side Story, 693
"Easter Parade," 91
Eaton, Mary, 99, 592
Ebb, Fred, 235, 515, 692
Ebsen, Buddy, 612
Eccentricities of Davey Crockett, 67, 69–70
Eckart, Jean, 58, 96, 170, 173, 215, 261–262, 389, 518
Eckart, William, 58, 96, 170, 173, 215, 261–262, 389, 518
Eckley, Dan, 107
Eddie Fisher at the Winter Garden, 193–195
Eggerth, Marta, 434, 559
Einen Jux Will er Sich Machen, 297
Einstein, Izzy, 492
Eisele, Lou, 251
Eisenhower, Dwight David, 119, 681
Elder, Eldon, 611
"Elegance," 300
Eliot, T.S., 680
Elkins, Hillard, 262–263
Ellen, Vera, 154, 156
Ellington, Edward "Duke," 74–77, 116
Elliott, Stephen, 395
Ellis, Michael, 681
Emerson, Hope, 645
Emperor Jones, The, 133
Engel Lehman, 163, 718, 720
"Entertainers, The," 200
Epstein, Alvin, 234, 488
Ermoloff, George, 688

Ernst, Leila, 332
Errol, Leon, 183
Eskow, Jerome, 115
Essen, Viola, 48
Eula, Joe, 308
Evans, Bonnie, 365
Evans, David, 241
Evans, Joseph, 107
Evans, Maurice, 658
Evans, Ray, 383, 496
Evans, Wilbur, 111, 435, 686
Evening with Beatrice Lillie, An, 195–197, 724
Everett, Timmy, 395–396
"Ev'ry Street's a Boulevard in Old New York,"
    294
"Everybody Ought to Have a Maid," 240–241
Evita, 13
Ewell, Tom, 624
Ewing, Marjorie, 48
Ewing, Sherman, 48
Experimental Theatre, Inc., 67–69
Eythe, William, 381, 387, 527

*F*abray, Nanette, 61–62, 90, 93, 303–304, 306,
    341–342, 405–406, 408, 415, 446–447, 466–
    467, 750–751
Fabrizi, Aldo, 576
Fade Out—Fade In, 197–201, 309, 519
Fagan, Joan, 185
Fain, Sammy, 33, 50, 148, 151–152, 222, 224–
    225, 628–630
Falk, Sawyer, 609
Fall River Legend, 68
"Falling in Love with Love," 331
Family Affair, A, 201–203
"Fancy Free," 312, 513–515
Fanny, 203–206, 278, 341, 347, 697
Fanny (French film), 203
Fantasticks, The, 203, 523
Farbman, Abel, 673
Farkas, Karl, 424–445
Farrell, Anthony B., 38–39, 50–53, 61, 236, 292,
    311, 537
Faust, Frederick, 179
Fay, Frank, 380, 399
Faye, Joey, 40, 42, 190–191, 303–305, 666
Fearnley, John, 193, 362, 414
Fehl, Fred, 26, 54, 170
Feiffer, Jules, 26, 476
Feigay, Paul, 84–85, 511
Feller, Pete, 120
Fellows, Edith, 404
"Femininity," 498
Fenn, Jean, 584
Ferber, Edna, 592, 612, 614
Ferre, Cliff, 174
Ferrer, Jose, 256–257, 353, 496, 705
"Feudin' and Fightin', " 378
Feuer, Cy, 98–100, 126, 272, 275, 323, 326–
    327, 391, 393, 463, 515, 555, 618, 620, 661,
    704, 706–709, 751
Feyder, Jacques, 140
Ffolkes, David, 106–107, 223–224
Fialkov, Max, 633
"Fiddler and the Fighter, The," 199
Fiddler on the Roof, 3, 11–12, 154, 184, 207–210
Field, Ron, 115, 492–494
Fielding, Marjery, 655
Fields, Dorothy, 53, 57, 61, 111–112, 140, 143,
    435, 568, 671, 625, 674–677, 686–687, 751–
    752
Fields, Herbert, 53, 57, 61, 111–112, 140, 143,
    154–156, 382, 435, 568, 571, 625, 628, 686,
    752
Fields, Joseph, 226, 246, 252, 255, 715, 720
Fields, Lew, 5, 29, 57
Finian's Rainbow, 3, 10, 105, 107, 181, 186,
    210–214, 224–225, 286, 665
Finklehoffe, Fred F., 50, 380
Finnegan's Wake, 379
Fiorello!, 3, 10, 97, 215–218, 279, 374, 422, 488,
    603, 658–659
Fioretta, 188
Firebrand, The, 218–220
Firebrand of Florence, The, 218–220, 546
First Impressions, 221–222, 660
Fisher, Eddie, 193–194
Fisher, Nelle, 566
Flahooley, 222–226
Flanders, Michael, 66
Flatt, Ernest, 197
Fledermaus, Die, 8
Fletcher, Robert, 307
Fletcher, Ron, 666
Flicker, Theodore J., 475
"Flickers," 312
Flippen, Jay C., 655
Flora, the Red Menace, 203, 603
Florell, Walter, 76, 449
Flower Drum Song, 226–228, 571, 638
"Flower Song," 136
"Fly Little Heart," 148
Flying High, 432
Foley, Chotzi, 276
Follies, 18, 203
Follow the Girls, 228–230, 621
Fontanne, Lynn, 175, 243
Foran, Dick, 154–156
Forbes, Brenda, 664
Ford, Joan, 266–268
Ford, Paul, 706
Forrest, Edwin, 29
Forrest, George, 279, 281, 356–357, 364, 366,
    411, 631
Forrest, Steve, 96
Fortune Teller, The, 279
Forty-Five Minutes Past Eight, 19
42nd Street, 13, 140, 645
Fosse, Bob, 23, 24, 36, 78, 82, 157–160, 164,
    166, 169, 170–175, 243, 323–325, 327, 391–
    393, 420, 429, 484–488, 515, 533–537, 540–
    543, 568–571, 752–753
Foster, Stephen, 261, 457, 554
Four Saints in Three Acts, 231
1491, 303
Foxy, 159, 231–234
Foy, Eddie, Jr., 185, 304, 533, 536, 567–568,
    577–578
Foyer, Bernie, 600
France, Richard, 111
Frank, Melvin, 388, 390
Frank Productions, Inc., 269, 323, 327, 460, 464
Frankel, Gene, 633
Franklin, Frederic, 631–632
"Franklin Shepard, Inc.," 555
Franzell, Carlotta, 133
Fredericks, Charles, 457, 472, 612
Free and Easy, 589
Freedley, Vinton, 28, 341–343, 432, 525

Freedman, Gerald, 243, 421
Freedman, Bud, 73
Freedman, Charles K., 631
Freeman, Don, 25, 44, 104, 211, 304, 427
Freeman, Stan, 331
Freitag, Dorothea, 425
Frey, Nathaniel, 171, 215, 605, 674, 681
Friedberg, Billy, 394
Friedman, Charles, 47, 133, 464–465, 473, 645
Friedman, Leo, 26, 662
Friedman-Abeles Studio, 26, 79, 124, 138, 180, 277, 328, 345, 349, 389, 482, 490, 636, 672, 694
Friml, Rudolf, 6, 62, 688
From A to Z, 234–236
Fryer, Robert, 111–112, 316–319, 568, 571, 592, 603, 674, 716, 720, 753
Fuller, Dean, 480, 518
Funke, Lewis, 20, 171
Funny Face, 28, 343
Funny Girl, 12, 200, *236–239*, 279
Funny Thing Happened on the Way to the Forum, 3, 60, 154, *239–243*

Gable, Clark, 94
Gage, Faye, 216
Gaither, Gant, 601
Gallagher, Helen, 292–294, 303, 306, 417–418, 449, 537–538, 540, 565–566, 670
Gallico, Paul, 137
"Game, The," 172
Gannon, Kim, 600
Garbo, Greta, 618
Garde, Betty, 499
"Garden of Eden Ballet," 126, 128–129, 171
Gardiner, James W., 557
Gardiner, Reginald, 195
Gardner, Rita, 201
Garinei, Pietro, 576
Garland, Robert, 19, 33, 38, 43, 62, 68, 77, 85, 95, 105, 121, 136, 146, 153, 162, 167, 177, 188, 190, 212, 224, 248, 252, 280, 282, 286, 296, 305, 312, 313, 369, 378, 382, 397, 402, 404, 430, 435, 440, 459, 466, 474, 503, 525, 531, 556, 560, 574, 576, 585, 598, 612, 621, 680, 775
Garrett, Betty, 73–74, 120, 122, 341–342, 378
Garrick Gaieties, 382, 502
Garson, Greer, 566
Gateson, Marjorie, 652–653
Gautier, Dick, 113
Gaxton, William, 28, 140, 143, 313–316, 473–475, 627
Gay, John, 74–75
Gay Life, The, 243–245, 630
Gaynes, George, 527–528, 716, 719
Gaynor, Charles, 380, 382, 615
Gazzara, Ben, 266
Gear, Luella, 190, 472
"Gee, Officer Krupke," 696
Geer, Will, 166, 520
Gelbart, Larry, 157–159, 239, 241, 243
Geller, Bruce, 395
Gennaro, Peter, 82, 215, 446, 535, 601–603, 684, 693
Genovese, Gen, 109
Gentlemen Prefer Blondes, 3, 27, 46, 122, *246–249*, 382, 440, 519, 620, 692
Genus, Karl, 565

George, George, 675
George, George W., 82, 84
Germelshausen, 107
Gershe, Leonard, 179
Gershwin, Arthur, 376–377
Gershwin, George, 6–7, 28, 73, 343, 377, 467, 495, 561–564, 579, 695, 718
Gershwin, Ira, 6–7, 28, 218–220, 343, 377, 388, 495, 543–546, 561
Gerson, Hal, 380
Gerstacker, Friedrich Wilhelm, 107
Gerstman, Felix G., 709
"Gesticulate," 365
"Getting to Know You," 363
Geva, Tamara, 189
Ghostley, Alice, 395–396, 478–479, 603–604
Gibson, Robert, 337
Gibson, Virginia, 287
Gibson, William, 262, 265
"Gigi," 125
Gilbert, Billy, 109–110, 567, 591
Gilbert, Edward, 332
Gilbert, Franklin, 381, 414
Gilbert, George, 221, 450
Gilbert, Ray, 601
Gilbert, W.S., 6–7, 261, 313, 315, 337, 431–433, 525, 556, 704, 720
Gilbert, Willie, 316, 319, 323–325, 327
Giler, Berne, 249
Gilford, Jack, 33, 35, 239–242, 518, 719
Gilkey, Stanley, 352, 664
Gillette, Anita, 36, 446
Gillette, Priscilla, 259, 527, 573
Gillmore, Margalo, 548, 583
Gimbel, Norman, 157, 706
Gingold, Hermione, 221–222, 234–235, 352–353
Ginnes, Abram S., 383
Ginzler, Robert, 113
Giovaninni, Sandro, 576
Giraudoux, Jean, 243
Girl Crazy, 53, 343
Girl from Nantucket, The, *249–252*
Girl in Pink Tights, The, *252–256*
"Girl in the Show, The," 616–618
Girl to Remember, A, 197
Girl Who Came to Supper, The, *256–258*
Girls Against the Boys, The, *258–259*
"Give It All You've Got," 498
"Gladiola Girl," 381–382
Glazer, Benjamin F., 144
Gleason, Jackie, 47–48, 190–191, 228–230, 296, 656–657
Glenville, Peter, 656, 671, 673
Glickman, Will, 33, 95–97, 380, 450–452, 557
"Glitter and Be Gay," 131
Gobel, George," 383–385
God Sends Sunday, 584
Godfrey, Arthur, 664
Godfrey, Isidore, 338
Godkin, Paul, 67–68, 70, 303
Goehr, Rudolph, 286
Gold Diggers of 1932, 301
"Gold, Women, and Laughter," 404
Goldberg, Rube, 84
Golden, Ray, 33, 148
Golden Apple, The, 70, *259–262*, 516
Golden Boy, *262–266*
Golden Rainbow, 130, 700
Goldilocks, 12, 159, *266–269*, 518, 571
Goldman, James, 201–202

Goldman, Robert, 221
Goldman, William, 201–202
Goldner, Charles, 254
Goldoni, Carlo, 387
Goldstone, Nat, 89
Gone with the Wind, 295, 411
Good Fairy, The, 415
Good News, 712
Goodbye, My Fancy, 678
"Goodbye to All That," 546
Goodman, Benny, 13, 597–598, 600
Goodman, David, 508
Goodman, Lee, 174–175
Gordon, Bruce, 492
Gordon, Hayes, 623
Gordon, Max, 219, 313, 315–316, 543
Gordon, Michael, 414
Gordon, Robert H., 33, 40, 47, 334, 701
Gordon, Ruth, 298
Gordon, Witold, 507
Gorney, Jay, 283, 295, 670–671
"Gotta Dance," 397
Gotterdammerung, 679
Gottesfeld, Charles, 466
Gould, Elliott, 327, 329–330
Gould, Morton, 61, 84–86, 153
Goulet, Robert, 122, 124–125
Gour, Betty, 505
Grace, Michael, 352
Graham, June, 414
Graham, Ronald, 186
Graham, Ronny, 100, 102, 383, 425, 628
Granat, Frank, 82
Granger, Farley, 221, 362–363
Grant, Mary, 425, 598–599
Grant, Maxwell, 692
Grant, Ulysses S., 449
Grapes of Wrath, The, 20
Gray, Alexander, 93
Gray, Barbara, 143
Gray, Dolores, 140–143, 179–180, 519, 678, 680
Gray, Gilda, 194
Gray, Oliver, 356
Gray, Timothy, 307
Greanin, Leon, 150–151
Great Dane a-Comin', 671
Great Lady, 702
Great to Be Alive, 343
Greek Theatre Association, 709
Green, Abel, 63
Green, Adolph, 10, 78–81, 84–86, 181–183, 197, 467, 511–515, 546–548, 551, 595, 649–650, 678, 715–716, 719–720, 747–748
Green, Gerald, 628–630
Green, Isaac, Jr., 403
Green, Johnny, 515
Green, Martyn, 556, 603
Green, Mitzi, 84
Green Grow the Lilacs, 499, 502
Greene, Graham, 162
Greene, Herbert, 460, 464, 492
Greener, Dorothy, 566
Greenwillow, 269–272, 327
Greenwood, Charlotte, 527–529
Gregory, Dick, 193–194
Gregory, Paul, 660–661, 663
Grey, Clifford, 591
Grey, Joel, 394–395
Grieg, Edvard, 631, 633
Griffies, Ethel, 443, 445

Griffith, Andy, 179–180
Griffith, Robert E., 169, 173, 215–218, 429, 484, 488, 515, 533, 537, 639, 658, 693
Grimes, Tammy, 307–308, 394–395, 684–686
"Grist for de Mille," 343
Groscup, Marie, 33
Gross, Edward, 584, 588
Gross, Erwin Von, 709
Grosser, Maurice, 231
Grossman, Hal, 633
Gruenwald, Alfred, 448
"Guadalcanal Ballet," 157, 159–160
Guardino, Harry, 58
Guber, Lee, 283
Guernsey, Otis L., Jr., 20, 146, 360, 417, 503, 528, 676
Guetary, Georges, 61–62, 555–556
Guinan, Texas, 248
Guinness, Alec, 498
Gunther, John, 334–335
Guthrie, Tyrone, 130, 132
Guys and Dolls, 3, 10–12, 24, 181, 209, 215, 272–276, 316, 323, 327, 390, 455–456, 462, 518, 535, 566, 618, 620, 665, 697, 706–708, 716
Guys, Sheila, 432
Gwynne, Fred, 301
Gypsy, 3, 10, 12, 28, 202, 209, 238–239, 276–279, 288, 319, 374, 582, 645
Gypsy Lady, 279–281
"Gypsy Love Song," 280

H.M.S. *Pinafore*, 313–315, 431–433
Haakon, Paul, 435, 437
Haas, Hugo, 411
Haas, Irene, 509
Hack, Monroe B., 94
Hackett, Buddy, 331
Haggott, John, 219
Hagman, Larry, 475–477
Hague, Albert, 115, 258, 557, 568, 571
Hahn, Ina, 129
Hair, 11
Hairpin Harmony, 281–282, 310
Haldane, Harry M., 289
Halevy, Ludovic, 133
Haley, Jack, 334–335
Haliday, Bryant, 426
Hall, Adelaide, 346
Hall, Juanita, 226, 321, 323, 639, 643
Hallelujah, Baby!, 625
Halliday, Heller, 550
Halliday, Richard, 218, 347, 351, 548, 637, 639
Hambleton, T. Edward, 70, 259, 394–395, 518, 552
Hamilton, Bob, 577
Hamilton, Kipp, 185
Hamilton, Nancy, 664
Hamilton, Peter, 73
Hammerstein, Arthur, 6
Hammerstein, Dorothy, 403
Hammerstein, Oscar 1st, 6
Hammerstein, Oscar 2nd, 6–11, 21, 24, 42–47, 53–57, 93, 132, 133–137, 144–147, 178, 206, 218, 226–227, 254, 358–363, 426–428, 456, 458–459, 466, 470–471, 499–507, 516, 527, 536, 538, 554–556, 582, 601, 612–615, 635–639, 641–643, 753–754
Hammerstein, Reginald, 50, 458–459

Hammerstein, William, 6
Hammond, Thomas, 387
Hampton, Max, 289
"Hand Me Down that Can o' Beans,"
  532
Haney, Carol, 100, 102, 226, 236, 347, 429,
  533–537, 603, 605, 724
Hanighen, Bernard, 408
Hanley, Ellen, 71, 215
Hansen, William, 105
Happel, J. Peter, 542
Happiest Girl in the World, The, 283–285
"Happiest House on the Block, The," 554
Happy As Larry, 285–287
Happy Hunting, 206, 287–289
Happy Time, The (1950), 555
Happy Time, The (1968), 510
Happy Town, 289–291
Harburg, E.Y., 89, 210, 213–214, 222–226, 283–
  285, 343–344, 346–347
Hargrave, Roy, 341
Harnick, Sheldon, 24, 95–97, 207, 210, 215,
  218, 394, 421–422, 478–479, 515, 565, 603–
  608, 639, 658, 692, 754–755
Harrigan, William H., 5
Harrington, Pat, Sr., 119
Harris, Benjamin, J., 420
Harris, Jed, 94–95, 620
Harris, Joseph, 421, 673
Harris, Leonard, 20, 115
Harris, Sylvia, 673
Harrison, Dennis, 387
Harrison, Ray, 234, 565
Harrison, Rex, 468–471
Hart, Lorenz, 6, 8, 57, 123, 154–156, 189, 193,
  196, 296, 382, 388, 491, 499, 501, 502, 515–
  516, 537–540, 556, 571
Hart, Moss, 122–123, 126, 258, 316, 418, 443–
  445, 468–471, 597, 599, 720
Hart, Teddy, 525
Hart, Tony, 5
Hartman, Grace, 38, 48–50
Hartman, Paul, 38, 48–50, 495, 601
Harvey, Kenneth, 552
Hastings, Hal, 173, 215, 605
Hatfield, Lansing, 579
Having Wonderful Time, 713–714
Havoc, June, 435, 437, 579–582
Hawkins, June, 584
Hawkins, William, 18, 45, 52, 55, 62, 63, 71,
  99, 110, 111, 119, 121, 128, 142, 163, 172,
  205, 212, 225, 248, 254, 274, 286, 292, 321,
  332, 335, 352, 366, 370, 382, 387, 394, 407,
  414, 419, 430, 455, 458, 470, 480, 504, 528,
  531, 538, 545, 550, 552, 554, 557, 563, 574,
  592, 619, 623, 642, 663, 668, 677, 681, 691,
  705, 714, 718, 775
Hayes, Bill, 426
Hayes, Helen, 28, 295, 680
Hayes, Peter Lind, 295
Hayes, Richard, 475
Haynes, Tiger, 480
Hayride, 291–292
Hays, David, 489–490
Hayward, Leland, 117, 218, 276, 446–447, 637,
  639, 643, 713–714
"Hazel," 678
Hazel Flagg, 292–295, 418
Healy, Mary, 62
Hearst, William Randolph, 19

"Heart," 172
"Heart Is Quicker Than the Eye," 517
Heaven Help the Angels, 50
Heaven on Earth, 295–296
Heawood, John, 98
Hebert, Fred, 185
Hecht, Ben, 292–294, 597
Heckart, Eileen, 201, 540–541
"Heidi," 149
Heilbron, 717
Heilwell, David, 566
Helburn, Theresa, 61, 769–770. *See also* Theatre
  Guild
Held, John, Jr., 99, 246
Heller, Barbara, 692
Hellinger, Mark, 16, 38
Hellman, Lillian, 130, 132, 571, 574, 720
Hello, Dolly!, 3, 11–12, 28, 83, 140, 200, 239,
  297–301, 309, 351, 645, 663, 692
"Hello, Dolly!," 299–300
Hello, Lola, 601
"Hello, Young Lovers," 363
Hellzapoppin' (1938), 9, 379, 397
Hellzapoppin' (1967), 109
Hellzapoppin' (1976), 109
Helmore, Tom, 175, 178
Henderson, Florence, 203–205, 256–257, 505
Henderson, Ray, 720
Heneker, David, 338
Henry IV, Part One, 20
Henry VIII, 106
Henry, Horr'ble, 138
Henry, O., 377
Hepburn, Audrey, 533
Hepburn, Katharine, 239, 437
"Her Is," 536
Herbert, F. Hugh, 527
Herbert, Victor, 5, 6, 82, 279–280, 567, 592,
  652, 654
Herczeg, Geza, 448
Here's Love, 130, *301–303*
"Here's That Rainy Day," 143
Herget, Bob, 201, 287, 628
Herlie, Eileen, 36, 656–657
Herman, Jerry, 11, 82–83, 235, 297, 300, 441–
  442
Herman, John, 318
"Hernando's Hideaway," 173, 536
Herridge, Frances, 20, 422, 481
Herzig, Sig, 89, 473
Hesseltine, Stark, 552
Hewer, John, 98
Hewett, Christopher, 221, 234
Hewitt, Alan, 117
"Hey, Look Me Over," 711
"Hey There," 535–536
Heyward, Dorothy, 564
Heyward, DuBose, 7, 561, 564
Higdon, Mary Arlene, 291
High Button Shoes, 70, 294, *303–307*, 312, 397,
  399, 418, 689
High Spirits, 307–309
High, Wide, and Handsome, 502
Hiken, Gerald, 476
Hiken, Nat, 47, 394
Hildegarde, 49
Hill, Arthur, 628
Hill, George Roy, 269
Hill, Phyllis, 701
Hill, Ruby, 584, 586, 589

Hilliard, Bob, 48, 292
Hilton, James, 603–604
Hirschfeld, Al, 25, 165, 182, 199, 247, 260, 365, 547, 610, 626, 703
Hirshman, Col. John J., 133
Hiss, Alger, 163
Hit the Deck, 432
Hit the Trail, 310–311, 471
Hitler, Adolf, 160, 425
Hodges, Joy, 186, 188, 466, 474
Hogarth, W., 293, 454
Holbrook, Hal, 520, 523
Holbrooke, William, 154
Hold It!, 38, 311–312
Hole in the Head, A, 700
Holliday, Judy, 74, 78–82, 317–319, 351, 467, 472
Holloway, Stanley, 468
Hollywood Pinafore, 313–316, 433
Holm, Celeste, 89, 91–93, 499, 506
Holm, Eleanor, 713
Holm, Hanya, 67, 69–70, 122, 151, 259, 369–370, 387, 464, 468, 471, 527
Holm, John Cecil, 383, 652
Holman, Libby, 75
Holofcener, Larry, 148, 450
Homer, 259
Hooker, Brian, 688
Hope, Dolores, 143
Hope, Vida, 98, 100
Hopper, Hedda, 313, 315
Horne, Lena, 343–347, 589
Horner, Harry, 294
Horner, Richard, 307
Horton, Robert, 520–523
Horwitt, Arnold B., 258, 334, 418, 557, 715
Hot Mikado, The, 433
Hot Spot, 316–319
Hotel Paradiso, 60
Houghton, Norris, 259, 387, 394–395, 518, 552
House of Flowers, 319–323
"House of Flowers," 322
Houseman, John, 75, 408
"How to Handle a Woman," 408
How to Succeed in Business Without Really Trying, 3, 23, 102, 275, 319, 323–327, 329, 393, 543, 620
Howard, Barron, 291
Howard, Cy, 42
Howard, Harry, 425
Howard, John, 292
Howard, Peter, 547
Howard, Sidney, 408, 411, 453
Howard, Willie, 47–48, 195, 419, 466–467, 591–592, 627
Howes, Sally Ann, 371–373, 698, 700
Hoysradt, John, 40
Hoyt, Howard, 50
Huckleberry Finn, 395–396
Hughes, Langston, 72–73, 575, 645, 647
Hull, Henry, 290–291
Humphrey, Doris, 72, 621
Hunt, Lois, 109
Hunter, Ian McLellan, 231
Hunter, Mary, 67
Hunter's Moon, 107
Hurst, James, 583
Husmann, Ron, 36, 658
Hutt, William, 584
Hutton, Betty, 399, 519

Hylton, Jack, 373, 576
Hyman, Joseph M., 419

"*I* Am Ashamed That Women Are So Simple," 368
"I Am Loved," 527
I Can Get it For You Wholesale, 239, 327–330
"I Could Be Happy with You," 99
"I Could Hate the Lovable Irish," 186
"I Could Write a Book," 539
"I Did It on Roller Skates," 237
"I Get Embarrassed," 657
"I Got Lost in His Arms," 54
"I Got Rhythm," 55
I Had a Ball, 331
"I Just Can't Wait," 650
"I Love You," 437
I Married an Angel, 189
I Picked a Daisy, 523
I Remember Mama (1944), 555
I Rememer Mama (1980), 109
"I Wanna Get Married," 228, 230
"I Was a Shoo-In," 650
"I Will Follow You," 441, 443
"Ice Cream," 607
Iceman Cometh, The, 487
Idyll of Miss Sarah Brown, The, 272
"If I Loved You," 146
"If I Were a Rich Man," 207
If I Were King, 688
If the Shoe Fits, 332–334
Il Bugiardo, 387
"I'll Buy You a Star," 676
"I'll Never Be Jealous Again," 536
"I'm Called Little Butter-Up," 313
"I'm Calm," 241
"I'm Fascinating," 37
"I'm Goin' Back," 81
"I'm the First Girl," 397–398
Impellitteri, Vincent, 506
"In Between," 532
In Gay New Orleans, 404
"In Love with Romance," 472
Inghram, Rose, 559–561
Ingram, Rex, 584–585
Inherit the Wind, 483, 498
Inside U.S.A., 70, 334–337
"Interplay," 153
Iolanthe, 337–338
Ireland, John, 179
Irma La Douce, 115, 202, 330, 338–341
Irving, George S., 100, 246, 609, 673
Irving, Washington, 623
Irwin, Will, 408, 565
"Is He the Only Man in the World?," 446
"Is It the Girl (or Is It the Gown)?," 599
"I've Been There and I'm Back," 498
"I've Got Rings on My Fingers," 628
"I've Got Your Number," 392
"I've Told Ev'ry Little Star," 460
Ives, Burl, 621–622
Izzy and Moe, 492

*J*ackpot, 93, 341–343
Jackson, Frederick, 456
Jacobi, Lou, 197
Jamaica, 343–347
James, Dan, 89

James, Lilith, 89
James, Olga, 450
Jameson, Joyce, 87
Jamison, Marshall, 111, 603
Janney, Russell, 688
Jarnac, Dorothy, 295
Jarrett, Howard, 464
"Jealousy Ballet," 536
Jeanmaire, Renée Zizi, 253–256
Jefferson, Loretta, 341
Jeffreys, Alan, 692
Jeffreys, Anne, 472, 645
Jenkins, Allen, 625
Jenkins, George, 192–193, 348–350
Jenkins, Gordon, 47
Jennie, 239, 319, *347–351*, 582
Jerome, Helen, 221
Jerome Robbins' Broadway, 13
Jessel, George, 9
Jessye, Eva, 432
Jewison, Norman, 301
"Jingle, Jangle, Jingle," 704
John Brown's Body, 352, 661
John Murray Anderson's Almanac, 352–353
"Johnny," 356
Johnny Johnson, 647
"Johnny One Note," 296
Johnson, Bill (William), 175–176, 554, 625, 627
Johnson, Chic, 9, 119, 378–379, 397
Johnson, Gil, 281
Johnson, Greer, 566
Johnson, Nunnally, 543, 546
Johnson, Susan, 109–110, 185, 453–455, 496–498, 706
Johnston, Johnny, 674
Jolson, Al, 28, 193–194, 395, 451
Jonay, Roberta, 43
Jones, Allan, 341–342
Jones, Arthur, 109
Jones, David, 508
Jones, Robert Edmond, 408–411
Jones, T.C., 426, 480–481, 483
Jones, Tom, 520–523
Jongeyans, George. *See* Gaynes, George
Jonson, Ben, 231
Joseph, Robert L., 464
Jourdan, Louis, 523
Joyce, James, 379
Judels, Charles, 404
"Jug of Wine, A," 177
Jumbo, 62
June Moon, 19
Juno, 130, *353–356*
Juno and the Paycock, 353–355
"Just an Honest Mistake," 385
"Just for Tonight," 560
"Just You Wait," 470

Kallman, Dick, 600
Kalman, Emmerich, 415, 421
Kamarova, Natalie, 376
Kander, John, 11, 201–202, 515
"Kangaroo, The," 101
Kanin, Fay, 243
Kanin, Garson, 181–183, 236, 238
Kanin, Michael, 243
Kao-Tsi-ch'-ing, 408
Kaper, Bronislau, 559
Kapp, David, 185–186

Karger, George, 26, 223, 409
Karnilova, Maria, 100–101, 207, 210, 276, 681
Karr, Harold, 287–288, 480
Karr, Patti, 483
Karson, Nat, 67–68, 156, 473–474
Kasha, Lawrence N., 605
Kasznar, Kurt, 601, 637
"Katinka's Birthday," 151
Katzell, William R., 33, 210, 381
Kauffmann, Stanley, 20–21
Kaufman, George S., 7, 17, 19, 272–276, 313, 315–316, 433, 495, 543–555, 597, 618–620
Kay, Arthur, 279
Kay, Hershy, 116
Kaye, Alma, 621
Kaye, Danny, 8, 419
Kaye, Nora, 681, 684
Kaye, Stubby, 272, 388–389
Kazan, Elia, 405, 408, 525, 671
Kean, 130, *356–358*
Kean, Betty, 50, 52–53
Kean, Jane, 50, 52, 192, 250
Keane, George, 103
Keel, Howard, 592–593
"Keep It Gay," 428
Kefauver, Estes, 394
Kellaway, Cecil, 269, 272, 665
Keller, Evelyn, 429
Kellin, Mike, 50, 554
Kelly, Frederic N., 472
Kelly, Gene, 226, 516, 539, 541
Kelly, Grace, 287
Kelton, Pert, 269, 460
Kennedy, Bob, 250
Kennedy, John, 48, 435, 652, 686, 722
Kennedy, John F., 194, 218, 327, 693
Kenney, Ed, 659
Kenny, Sean, 510–511
Kent, Allegra, 609
Kent, Lennie, 281
Kent, Walter, 600
Keretson, 298
Kern, Jerome, 5–7, 19, 53, 57, 132, 316, 458–459, 501–502, 515, 591, 612–615
Kerr, Jean, 266–268, 352–353, 518, 670–671
Kerr, Walter, 14, 17, 18, 23, 36, 52, 58, 67, 80, 82, 87, 97, 99, 101, 110, 112, 114, 115, 123, 128, 132, 137, 142, 148, 152, 157, 164, 172, 179, 183, 185, 196, 198, 201, 205, 207, 217, 221, 233, 235, 236, 241, 244, 254, 256, 258, 262, 266–268, 271, 278, 283, 288, 289, 292, 294, 297, 301, 307, 310, 318, 322, 325, 329, 331, 337, 340, 346, 350, 352–353, 355, 356, 366, 367, 372, 375, 383, 390, 391, 395, 396, 414, 423, 426, 428, 442, 446, 450, 455, 462, 464, 470, 477, 479, 481, 483, 487, 489, 492, 495, 498, 505, 508, 517, 520, 532, 535, 538, 547, 549, 550, 553, 554, 557, 564, 565, 570, 577, 578, 583, 594, 596, 600, 602, 604, 605, 611, 617, 619, 621–622, 628, 633, 637, 649, 657, 658, 659, 663, 669, 670–671, 673, 683, 685, 691, 692, 695, 708, 710, 718, 723, 775
Kert, Larry, 201, 693–694
Ketchum, Dave, 87
Key, Leonard, 537
Khrushchev, Nikita, 139
Kidd, Michael, 10, 46, 61, 82–83, 107, 126–128, 130, 153, 179–181, 210–212, 214, 272–275, 301, 311–312, 388, 390–391, 405, 649–650, 710, 713, 755

Kiepura, Jan, 434–435, 559–561
Kiley, Richard, 331, 364, 366–367, 488, 490, 568, 571
Kilgallen, Dorothy, 186, 189
King, Edith, 592, 710
King, Dennis, 459, 603–604
King and I, The, 3, 10, 27, 57, 152, 206, *358–363*, 418, 429, 506, 537, 555, 637
King Lear, 116
Kipling, Rudyard, 377
Kipness, Joseph, 107, 303, 331, 373
Kirk, Lisa, 43, 369
Kirkwood, Jimmy (James), 174–175
Kiser, Franklin, 82
Kismet, 52, 205, 254, 281, 362, *364–367*
Kiss Me, Kate, 3, 10, 24, 70, 209, 316, 327, *367–371*, 429, 528–529, 589
Kiss the Girls Goodbye, 19
Kitt, Eartha, 478–479, 609–611
Klein, David, 104, 354, 461, 616
Kleinman, Sy, 148
Kleinsinger, George, 609
Klem, Billy, 35
Klugman, Jack, 276
Knapp, Sam, 464
Knickerbocker Holiday, 193, 647
Knight, June, 186–187, 652–653
Knoblock, Edward, 364
Kobart, Ruth, 239
Kober, Arthur, 713–714
Kollmar, Richard, 95, 186–189, 191–193, 557
Kosciusko, Thaddeus, 559–561
Kostal, Irwin, 371
Kowa, Maria, 709
Krachmalnick, Samuel, 131
Kraft, Hy, 115, 666, 668
Krasny, Diana, 58
Kreisler, Fritz, 575
Krimsky, John, 168
Kroll, Mark, 722
Kronenberger, Louis, 19, 42, 45, 55, 62, 71, 77, 85, 105, 108, 146, 154, 177, 190, 213, 219, 252, 280, 282, 305, 313, 334, 341, 397, 404, 410, 419, 425, 431, 434, 458, 467, 474, 499, 513, 525, 545, 560, 567, 576, 579, 585, 613, 625, 631, 647, 654, 687, 688, 701, 720, 776
Krupska, Dania, 130, 151, 283, 453, 576, 600
Kuhn, Kathryn, 314
Kurnit, Abe, 715
Kurnitz, Harry, 256–257
Kwamina, 173, *371–373*, 491

La Cage Aux Folles, 13
La Kermesse Heroique, 140
La Plume de Ma tante, 341, *373–376*
Lacey, Franklin, 460, 464
Ladd, Hank, 47–49
Lady Be Good, 343
Lady in the Dark, 220, 361, 494, 526, 647
Lady of ?, A, 376–377
Lady Says Yes, A, *376–378*
Laffing Room Only, 378–379
La Guardia, Fiorello H., 215–217
Lahr, Bert, 17, 231–234, 258, 419–420, 597, 600, 627, 669, 678–680
Lamas, Fernando, 287
Lamb, Charles, 357
Lamb, Gil, 623
Lambert, Hugh, 323–325

Lambert, Sammy, 38, 311, 600
Lammers, Paul, 394
Lamour, Dorothy, 498
"Land of Opportunitee," 545
Land of the Living, The, 107
Landesman, Fran, 475–477
Landesman, Jay, 475
Landis, Carole, 376–377
Landon, Margaret, 358
Lane, Abbe, 496–498
Lane, Burton, 210, 214, 378, 523
Lane, Gloria, 163, 590
Lang, Harold, 327, 369, 396, 399, 415, 418, 448–449, 537, 539–540, 603, 664, 723
Lang, Philip J., 487
Langner, Lawrence, 61, 769–770. *See also* Theatre Guild
Lansbury, Angela, 58–60
Lantz, Robert, 356, 475
Lardner, John, 19, 39, 47, 65, 296, 407, 413, 472, 776
Lardner, Ring, 19, 96, 776
Lardner, Ring, Jr., 231, 776
Larkin, Peter, 266, 481–483, 603, 712
Larson, John, 565
Lascoe, Henry, 58, 716
Laszlo, Miklos, 605–607
Latouche, John, 67–70, 74–75, 77–78, 130, 259–262, 516, 559, 575, 689
Laugh Time, 380
Laughton, Charles, 352
Laun, Louis, 624
"Laura de Maupassant," 294
Laurence, Larry, 62
Laurence, Paula, 190, 387, 525, 625
Laurents, Arthur, 58–60, 276–279, 327, 693–696
Laurette, 319, 347, 351
"Laurey's Dream," 502
Lavin, Linda, 202
Lawler, Anderson, 164
Lawrence, Carol, 478, 592–594, 603, 649, 693–694, 723
Lawrence, Eddie, 78
Lawrence, Elliot, 327
Lawrence, Gertrude, 358–362, 468, 683
Lawrence, Jack, 331
Lawrence, Jerome, 396, 399, 603–604
Lawrence, Peter, 386, 609
Lawrence, Reginald, 527, 529
Lawrence, Steve, 698–700
Lawrie, Ted, 67
Layton, Joe, 256–257, 269, 373, 488–489, 491, 518, 583, 637, 658
Lazarus, Milton, 631
Leave It to Me!, 526
"Leave the Atom Alone," 346
Lederer, Charles, 364, 367, 665
Lee, C.Y., 226
Lee, Gypsy Rose, 9, 192, 276, 435
Lee, Kathryn, 65
Lee, Lester, 38
Lee, Lois, 303
Lee (Gilford), Madeline, 719
Lee, Michele, 100–102, 692
Lee, Robert E., 396, 399, 603–604
Lee, Sondra, 297
Lee, Valerie, 301
Leeds, Phil, 151, 417, 492, 633
"Legalize My Name," 588
"Legend of Sleepy Hollow, The," 623

Legs Diamond, 16
Lehar, Franz, 82, 433–434
Leigh, Carolyn, 149, 391–392, 548, 710
Leigh, Rowland, 472–473
Leigh, Vivien, 672–674
Lemarque, Francis, 479
Lembeck, Harvey, 552
Lend an Ear, 114, 248, *380–383*, 663
Lengyel, Melchior, 618
Lenn, Robert, 67–68
Lennart, Isobel, 236
Le Noire, Rosetta, 633–635
Lenya, Lotte, 219–220
Leon, Victor, 433, 709
Leonidoff, Leon, 621–622
Lerman, Oscar, 151, 689
Lerner, Alan Jay, 10–11, 24, 103, 106–107, 122–123, 126, 175, 177–178, 221, 258, 405, 408, 468–471, 516, 523, 529, 532, 601, 701–702, 755–756
Lerner, Sam, 311, 466
LeRoy, Ken, 693
Les Miserables, 13
Lesser, Arthur, 47, 678
Lessner, George, 623
Lester, Edwin, 279–281, 364, 411, 414, 548, 551, 631
Lester, Jerry, 341–342
Lester, Lorraine, 623
Let It Ride!, 383–385
Let's Face It, 8
"Let's Go Steady," 113
Let's Make an Opera, 386
LeTang, Henry, 466
"Letter to the Editor," 292
Levant, Harry, 250
Levene, Sam, 115–116, 272, 383–384
Leventhal, Jules J., 425
Levey, Ethel, 425
Levin, Herman, 88–89, 120–122, 246, 256, 258, 468, 471
Levine, Joseph I., 66
Levine, Maurice, 402
Levinson, Leonard L., 448–449, 575
Lewine, Richard, 258, 418
Lewis, Albert, 665
Lewis, Arthur, 665
Lewis, Brenda, 115, 254, 573
Lewis, Jerry, 109, 452
Lewis, Morgan, 664
Lewis, Robert, 103, 231, 343, 371, 573
Liar, The, 387
Libuse, Frank, 378
Lichine, David, 559, 575
Lieberson, Goddard, 189
Liebman, Max, 419
Liebman, Oscar, 485, 521, 699
Lief, Dr. Nathaniel, 80
"Liffey Waltz," 356
Lili, 137
Liliom, 144–146
Lilley, Edward Clarke, 250
Lilley, Joseph, 704
Lillie, Beatrice, 17, 70, 195–197, 246, 307–309, 334–337, 361, 597, 599–600, 723–724, 756
Lilo, 116, 126, 128, 130
Lindfors, Viveca, 543, 628
Lindsay, Howard, 117, 218, 287, 446–447, 635–637, 639
Linn, Bambi, 147, 327, 591

Lion in Winter, The, 239
"Lionnet," 575
Lippman, Sidney, 71
Lipton, James, 492
Liszt, Franz, 94
Li'l Abner, 19, 181, *388–391*
Little Foxes, The, 571–574
Little Me, 149, *391–393*, 482
Little Night Music, A, 603
Little Show(s), The, 419, 479
"Little Things (Meant So Much to Me)," 88
"Little Tin Box," 215
Little Women, 152
Littlefield, Catherine, 219, 228, 652
Littlest Revue, The, *394–395*
Litwack, Ned C., 295
Litz, Kathleen, 67
Liveright, Horace, 219
Livin' the Life, *395–396*
Livingston, Jay, 383, 496
Livingston, Jerry, 107
Lloyd, Harold, 183
Lloyd, Norman, 609
Lloyd Webber, Andrew, 11
Locke, Sam, 689
Loesser, Frank, 10–11, 24, 96, 215, 269–275, 312, 323–327, 453–456, 460, 463–464, 515, 536, 601, 620, 702–706, 756–757
Loesser, Lynn, 453, 456
Loewe, Frederick, 10–11, 103, 106, 122–123, 126, 175, 177–178, 221, 258, 456, 468–471, 516, 529, 701–702, 757
Logan, Ella, 210, 213
Logan, Joshua, 36–37, 46, 53, 56–57, 189, 203–206, 446–448, 639, 641–643, 705, 713–715, 758
Lollobrigida, Gina, 52
Lonergan, Lenore, 33, 35, 495
Long, Avon, 75, 432–433
Long, Shorty, 453
Long Day's Journey into Night, 487
Longstreet, Stephen, 303
Look Homeward, Angel, 494
Look Ma', I'm Dancin'!, 48, *396–400*
Look to the Lilies, 448
Loos, Anita, 246, 248, 415
Loring, Eugene, 109, 111, 133, 543, 618, 665
Lost Horizon, 603
Lost in the Stars, 7, 249, *400–403*, 573, 575, 582
Louden, Isabelle, 61
Loudon, Dorothy, 492
Louise, Tina, 197, 200, 390
Louisiana Lady, *403–404*
Love, Edmund G., 649
"Love Is a Very Light Thing," 203
"Love Is Sweeping the Country," 495
"Love Is the Reason," 676–677
Love Life, 184, *405–408*, 471
"Love Makes the World Go Round," 138
Love Me Tonight, 502
"Lovely," 241–242
Lowe, Charles, 615
Loy, Myrna, 188
Lucas, Jonathan, 221, 262, 670, 692
Luce, Henry, 19
Luce, Ted, 48
Lucyk, Michael, 653
Lukas, Paul, 117
Luke, Keye, 226
Lumet, Sidney, 492–494
Lund, Art, 185, 453, 633

Lunt, Alfred, 175, 243
Lute Song, 408–411
Luvak, 290
Luytens, Edith, 429
Lynde, Paul, 113, 478, 480
Lynn, Billy, 250
Lynn, Joe, 445
Lynn-Thomas, Derrick, 566
Lysistrata, 193, 283, 285

*M*acArthur, Douglas, 225
McCann, Frances, 688
McCarthy, Justin Huntley, 688
McCarty, Mary, 88, 443, 445, 623–24
McCauley, Jack, 246, 303–304, 306
McClain, John, 19, 58, 81, 83, 87, 89, 99, 125,
  139, 159, 166, 169, 172, 184, 202, 205, 207,
  227, 233, 241, 254, 257, 261, 264, 271, 274,
  288, 294, 299, 302, 318, 325, 329, 331, 340,
  353, 357, 360, 375, 390, 392, 415, 417, 423,
  446, 452, 455, 463, 465, 481, 487, 489, 506,
  510, 517, 522, 528, 535, 555, 565, 583, 596,
  604, 619, 638, 650, 657, 658, 665, 683, 696,
  712, 714, 723, 777
McCord, Bert, 20, 459
McCormick, Myron, 50, 639, 643
McCown, Ellen, 269, 600
McCracken, Joan, 84, 86, 89, 91–93, 174–175,
  426, 429
McCutcheon, Bill, 480
MacDonagh, Donagh, 285–286
McDonald, Jet, 75–76, 311, 566
MacDonald, T.A., 334
MacDonnell, Kyle, 670
McDowell, Roddy, 122
McEnroe, Robert E., 185
McGauley, Hugh, 183
McGinley, Phyllis, 624
MacGowran, Jack, 355
McGrath, Leueen, 618–619
MacGregor, Edgar, 376, 404, 473
McGuire, Biff, 73, 289
McHugh, Jimmy, 65
"Mack Sennett Ballet," 304–306, 312, 399, 418,
  689
McKay, Bruce, 269
McKayle, Donald, 262
McKeever, Jacquelyn, 496
McKenna, Boots, 376
McKenna, Philip C., 605
McKenney, Ruth, 716
MacKenzie, Giselle, 221
McKinley, William, 425
McLerie, Allyn, 443–444, 704, 719
McNair, Barbara, 96
MacRae, Gordon, 664
MacWatters, Virginia, 448
Madden, Donald, 221
Mademoiselle Colombe, 19
"Madly in Love," 394
Madwoman of Chaillot, 243
Magdalena, 142, 411–414
Maggie, 414–415
"Magic Moment," 244
Magoon, Eaton, Jr., 659–660
Mahoney, Will, 301
Mainbocher, 524
Make a Wish, 114, 294, 415–418, 663
Make Mine Manhattan, 418–421
Malbin, Elaine, 464

Malden, Karl, 466
Malina, Luba, 425
Malone, Ray, 111
Maloney, Russell, 623
Maltz, Dr. Maxwell, 376–377
Mame, 11, 482
Mamoulian, Rouben, 7, 9, 46, 61, 93, 144, 147,
  400–402, 499, 502–503, 579, 582, 584–585,
  588–589, 621, 758–759
"Man I Used To Be, The," 554
Man in the Moon, 421–422
Man of La Mancha, 11, 186, 367, 625
"Man Who Broke the Bank at Monte Carlo,"
  404
Man Who Hated People, The, 137
Maney, Richard, 380
Manfredi, Nino, 576
Mann, Daniel, 529–531
Mann, Delbert, 671
Manners, Jayne, 40
Mannes, Marya, 174
Manning, Irene, 175–176
Manning, Richard, 645
Manning, Samuel L., 132–133
Mansfield, Richard, 29
Mantle, Burns, 18, 19, 192, 501, 625,
  777
Manulis, Martin, 189
"Many a New Day," 505
Marand, Patricia, 713
"Marble and a Star, A," 647
Marceau, Marcel, 643
Marchand, Colette, 678
Marchant, Claude, 133
"Marco Polo," 149
Margetson, Arthur, 62, 543
Maria Golovin, 422–424
"Marian, the Librarian," 463
Marie, Julienne, 231–233
Marinka, 424–425
Marion, George, Jr., 40, 191–192, 424–425
Marius, 203
"Mark Twain," 352
Markova, Alicia, 597–598
Marks, Gerald, 311, 466
Marlo, Micki, 723
Marlowe, Marion, 637
Marquis, Don, 609–611
Marre, Albert, 157, 159, 364, 367, 441, 603
Marshall, Patricia (Pat), 175, 177, 450, 701
Martin, Ernest H., 98, 100, 126, 272, 275, 323,
  326–327, 391, 393, 463, 515, 555, 618, 620,
  661, 704, 706–709, 751
Martin, Hugh, 307, 396–397, 415, 467, 515
Martin, Mary, 93, 234, 239, 254, 276, 319, 343,
  347–351, 408–410, 477, 523–527, 548–551,
  582, 636–640, 642–643, 680, 683, 759
Martin, Virginia, 323, 391–392, 480, 482
"Marty," 149
Marx, Chico, 66, 655
Marx, Groucho, 66, 235
Marx, Harpo, 66, 235, 329
Mask and Gown, 425–426, 483
Mason, Jane, 157
Mason, Virginia, 643
Massey, Daniel, 605–607
Massey, Ilona, 720
Massey, Raymond, 352
Massi, Bernice, 488, 698
Masteroff, Joe, 605
Masterson, Carroll, 73, 234, 236, 483

Masterson, Harris, 73, 234, 236, 483
Mastin, Will (Trio), 450–451
Matchmaker, The, 234, 297–298
Matinee Tomorrow, 19
Matteson, Ruth, 448
Matthews, Billy, 73, 659
Matthews, Edward, 231
Matthews, Inez, 231, 400
Mattox, Matt, 347, 595, 689, 698
Mattson, Eric, 144
"Maude, You're Rotten to the Core," 196
Maugham, Dora, 281
Maugham, W. Somerset, 579
Maurer, Emil, 421
Maury, Richard, 483
Maxwell, Marilyn, 474
May, Elaine, 608
May, Marty, 53
May, Mitchell, 289
Mayehoff, Eddie, 153, 575
Mayer, Edwin Justus, 218–219
Mayro, Jacqueline, 82
Me and Juliet, 227, 426–429, 506, 554
Mead, Shepherd, 323
Medea, 325, 588
Medford, Kay, 113, 236, 543
Medium, The, 162, 424, *429–431*, 649
Meehan, Danny, 236, 238
Meeker, Ralph, 533
Megna, John, 269
Meilhac, Henri, 133
Meister, Fred, 709
Memphis Bound, 313, *431–433*, 614
Menotti, Gian-Carlo, 72–73, 160–163, 422–424,
   429–431, 590–591, 649
Mercer, Johnny, 231, 388, 390–391, 584–585,
   592–594, 666
Mercer, Marian, 483
Merchant of Yonkers, The, 297
Mercury Theatre, The, 62–63
Meredith, Burgess, 285–287
Meredith, Morley, 151, 453
Merimee, Prosper, 133
Merkel, Una, 656
Merman, Ethel, 28, 53–57, 93, 102, 117–120,
   198, 219, 276–279, 287–288, 579, 582, 625–
   628, 680, 683, 759–760
Mero-Irion, Yolanda, 434
Merrick, David, 18, 20, 37, 137, 139, 179, 181,
   184, 202–204, 206, 231, 234, 238–239, 243,
   276–278, 297, 300, 327, 338–339, 341, 343,
   346–347, 373, 375, 422–423, 508–511, 520–
   523, 555, 643, 645, 649, 651–652, 692–693,
   760
Merrill, Bob, 137, 139, 236, 238, 297, 300, 484,
   515, 656–657
Merrill, Howard, 496
Merrily We Roll Along, 46, 555
Merry Widow, The, 433–435
Messel, Oliver, 321, 323
Mesta, Perle, 117
Meth, Max, 66, 540
Mexican Hayride, 435–437, 582, 621
Meyerowitz, Jan, 72–73
Michael Todd's Peep Show, 438–441
Michaels, Sidney, 82–83
Michell, Keith, 338
Michener, James, 639
Michiko, 360
Michon, Michel, 150
Middleton, Ray, 53, 405

Miele, Elizabeth, 310
Mielziner, Jo, 45, 56, 112, 126, 129–130, 205–
   206, 212, 274–278, 287, 360, 362–363, 428,
   498, 623, 643, 667, 708, 714, *761–762*
Milhaud, Darius, 342
Milk and Honey, 441–443
Miller, Buzz, 535
Miller, Henry, 29
Miller, Marilyn, 592, 683
Miller, Patsy Ruth, 456
Miller, Warren, 113
Miller, Wynne, 658
Millian, Raphael, 113
Minnelli, Vincente, 174
Minsky Brothers, 9, 378
Miracle on 34th Street, 301
Miss Liberty, 443–446, 488, 719
"Miss Marmelstein," 328–330
Miss Moffat, 448
"Mr. Monotony," 444
Mr. President, 446–448
Mr. Strauss Goes to Boston, 448–449
Mr. Wonderful, 97, 450–452, 602
Mistinguett, 435
Mrs. Miniver, 566
Mitchell, Arthur, 609
Mitchell, Byron, 674
Mitchell, James, 103, 107, 395–396, 529–531
Mitchell, Thomas, 292 295
Mladova, Milada, 40, 434
Mobley, Mary Ann, 493
Modern Times, 102
Molnar, Ferenc, 144–146, 415
Monaster, Nate, 628–630
Monnot, Marguerite, 338, 340
"Monotonous," 479
Monroe, Marilyn, 172
Monroe, Vaughan, 452
Montalban, Ricardo, 343–344, 601–602
Montgomery, Dave, 567–568
Moon for the Misbegotten, 487
"Moon-faced, Starry-eyed," 649
Moore, James, 483
Moore, Monica, 404
Moore, Victor, 313–316, 473–475, 627
More, Julian, 338
Morehouse, Ward, 19, 39, 42, 55, 78, 106, 282,
   296, 369, 421, 445, 449, 501, 560, 613, 621,
   705, 722, 777
Morgan, Al, 496
Morgan, Helen, 613, 685
Morgan, Henry, 33
Morgan, Jane, 723
Morgan, Johnny, 701
Morison, Patricia, 40, 368–369
Moross, Jerome, 67–70, 259–261
Morris, Bobby, 376–377
Morris, Richard, 684–685
Morris, William, 633, 635
Morrow, Doretta, 358, 362, 364, 704
Morrow, Karen, 331
Morrow, Tom, 25, 208, 497, 569, 606, 707, 711
Morse, Robert, 323, 325–326, 329, 595–597, 656
Moses, Robert, 687
Most Happy Fella, The, 3, 13, 102, 130, 151,
   327, *453–456*, 463, 494, 620
Mostel, Zero, 75–77, 153, 207–210, 239–243
Mother's Kisses, A, 173
"Motherhood March," 300
Motley, 126, 129, 387, 445, 549, 640, 672
"Mu-cha-cha," 82

Much Ado About Love, 218
Mulatto, 72
Mundy, James, 689
Mundy, John, 387
Munshin, Jules, 88, 120, 122, 243, 615
Murphy, Lillian, 459
Murray, Jan, 457
Murray, Peg, 628
Murray, Wynn, 295–296
Murrow, Edward, 552
Music Box Revue(s), The, 419, 479
Music in My Heart, 456–458
Music in the Air, 7, 9, 132, 458–460
Music Is, 173
Music Man, The, 3, 10, 12, 269, 303, 319, 460–464, 494, 570, 684–686, 697
"Music of Home, The," 269
"My Baby's Baby," 166
My Darlin' Aida, 464–466
My Dear Public, 93, 466–467
My Fair Lady, 3, 10–12, 24, 57, 70, 107, 122–23, 126, 209, 221, 257, 468–472, 483, 566, 570, 696–697
"My Heart at Thy Sweet Voice," 238
"My Heart Belongs to Daddy," 526
"My Heart Stood Still," 156
My Indian Family, 151
"My Old Kentucky Home," 506
My Romance, 472–473
My Sister Eileen, 716
"My White Knight," 463
Myerberg, Michael, 72, 166, 408
Myers, Henry, 279–280, 283–285
Myrtil, Odette, 414–415, 567, 592

Nadel, Norman, 19, 60, 101, 194, 198, 202, 209, 236, 242, 244, 264, 309, 318, 326, 329, 331, 372, 385, 392, 442, 491, 492, 583, 607, 630, 644, 673, 698, 709, 778
Nagel, Conrad, 459
Nagler, A.N., 575
Naismith, Laurence, 301
Naldi, Nita, 225
Nash, N. Richard, 520, 523, 710–712
Nash, Ogden, 394, 523–526, 681
Nassau, Paul, 289, 480
Nathan, George Jean, 107, 230, 421
National Broadcasting Company, 422–423
Neff, Hildegarde, 618
Nellie Bly, 20, 190, 473–475
Nelson, Gene, 381
Nelson, Kenneth, 600
Nervous Set, The, 475–478
Nesbitt, Cathleen, 468
Nestoy, Johann, 297
New Faces of 1942, 9
New Faces of 1952, 102, 396, 478–480
New Faces of 1956, 480–483
New Faces of 1962, 483–484
New Girl in Town, 12, 130, 484–488, 657–658
"New Town Is a Blue Town, A," 536
Neway, Patricia, 160, 163, 422, 637, 639
Newley, Anthony, 168, 643–645
Newman, Azadia, 580
Newman, Phyllis, 221, 649–650, 652
"Next Time I Care, The," 560
Ney, Richard, 565–566
Nice Goin', 527
Nicholas, Fayard, 584
Nicholas, Harold, 584, 586

Nichols, Barbara, 383–384
Nichols, George, 3rd, 624
Nichols, Lewis, 19, 56, 91, 136, 154, 432, 513, 526, 567, 587, 622, 627, 687, 701, 778
Nick, 439
Niesen, Gertrude, 228–230
Niessner, Tony, 709
Niles, Mary Ann, 36, 174–175, 420
Nimura, Yeichi, 408
Ninotchka, 618
Nixon, Richard M., 693
No Strings, 140, 327, 373, 488–492, 556
No Time for Sergeants, 483
"Nobody's Chasing Me," 529
Nolan, Kathy, 548
Noll, Edward, 48
Norman, Monty, 338
North, Sheree, 327
North, Zeme, 269
Northrup, Patricia, 503
"Not Wanted on the Voyage," 196
Nothing Sacred, 292–294
Nowhere to Go But Up, 492–494
Noyes, Thomas, 164
Nype, Russell, 117, 120, 266–268, 571

"**O** Little Town of Bethlehem," 386
Oakes, Betty, 495
Oakley, Annie, 53, 57
O'Brien, Chet, 189
O'Casey, Sean, 353–355
O'Connor, Jim, 20, 91, 617, 693
Odd Couple, The, 149
Odets, Clifford, 262–265
Odyssey, The, 259
Oenslager, Donald, 282, 387
Oestreicher, Gerard, 441
Of Thee I Sing, 7, 143, 215, 218, 275, 316, 326, 462, 475, 495–496, 544, 642
"Of Thee I Sing," 495
Offenbach, Jacques, 283–285
Oh! Calcutta!, 263
Oh Captain!, 496–499
Oh, Kay!, 343
"Oh, Mein Liebchen," 245
"Oh, What a Beautiful Mornin'," 504, 506
O'Hara, John, 8, 537–540
O'Hara, Maureen, 151–152
O'Keefe, Dennis, 347
Oklahoma!, 3, 5, 9–10, 12, 18, 27, 46, 57, 68, 80, 83, 91–93, 136, 144, 146–147, 156, 186, 214, 230, 358, 362–363, 402, 429, 455, 499–507, 513, 515, 537, 555, 581–582, 588–589, 592, 615, 621, 623, 637–638, 641, 665
Olaf, Pierre, 138, 373, 375
"Old Soft Shoe, The," 664
Old Vic Company, 20
Oliver!, 242, 508–511
Oliver Twist, 508
Olivier, Laurence, 20, 388
Olsen, Ole, 9, 119, 378–379, 397
Olvis, William, 464
On a Clear Day You Can See Forever, 13, 523
"On the Street Where You Live," 125
On the Town, 12, 46, 70, 84–86, 177, 214, 218, 306, 511–516, 697, 719
On with the Show, 310
On Your Toes, 8–10, 89, 189, 502, 516–518
"Once a Year Day," 536
Once and Future King, The, 122

Once in a Lifetime, 316
"Once in Love with Amy," 36, 705–706
Once Upon a Mattress, 319, *518–520*
Ondine, 483
One for the Money, 664
110 in the Shade, 46, 482, *520–523*
"One Perfect Moment," 481
One Touch of Venus, 70, 186, 351, *523–527*
O'Neal, Charles, 665–666
O'Neal, Ryan, 665–666
O'Neal, Zelma, 712
O'Neil, Sherry, 618
O'Neill, Eugene, 29, 484–488, 656–657
O'Neill, Frank, 310
Opatoshu, David, 100
Operti, Le Roi, 417
Oppenheimer, George, 140, 143, 174
Orbach, Jerry, 138
"Ordinary People," 373
Orlob, Harold, 281–282
Osato, Sono, 67–68, 70, 511, 514, 525–527, 719
O'Shaughnessy, John, 623
O'Shea, Michael, 567
O'Shea, Tessie, 198, 256–258
Osterman, Lester, Jr., 130, 197, 200, 307–309,
    450, 595, 628
Osterwald, Bibi, 621, 664, 689, 691
Ostrow, Stuart, 301
Our Gang, 406
Our Town, 43
"Out of My Dreams," 501
Out of this World, *527–529*
Owl and the Pussycat, The, 116
Oxenford, John, 297

*P*acific Overtures, 603
Padula, Edward, 36, 113–115, 175
Page, Geraldine, 553
Page, Ruth, 456
"Page from Old Nantucket, A," 252
Pagnol, Marcel, 203–205
Paige, Janis, 301, 533–534, 536
Paint Your Wagon, 408, 471, *529–533*, 559
Pajama Game, The, 3, 82, 142, 171, 173, 217–
    218, 415, 429, 488, 518, *533–537*, 595, 603,
    658
Pal Joey, 8, 10, 85, 218, 274, 292, 294, 330, 418,
    513, 515, 517, *537–543*, 700
Palmer, Byron, 704
Palmer, Peter, 388–389
Pan, Hermes, 65
Panama, Norman, 388, 390
Pangborn, Franklin, 417
Panko, Tom, 130
"Papa, Won't You Dance with Me," 303, 306
Pardon our French, 119
Parfumerie, 605
Park Avenue, 316, *543–546*
Parker, Dorothy, 130
Parker, Frank, 228
Parker, Lew, 50, 53
Parker, Ross, 373
Parks, Bernice, 75
Parks, Don, 234
Parks, Larry, 73–74
Parsons, Louella, 313, 315
Party with Betty Comden and Adolph Greer, A,
    546–548
"Pas de Deux," 255
Pascal, Milton, 228

Passing Show(s), The, 28
Paton, Alan, 400–402
Patterson, Dick, 87, 197, 692
Paul, Betty, 414
Paulee, Mona, 453
Paxton, Glen, 221
Payne, Barbara, 664
Pearce, Alice, 9, 164, 246, 396, 519, 583, 624
Peck, Charles K., Jr., 151–152
"Peer Gynt Suite," 632
Penn, Arthur, 215, 262
"People," 239
"People Will Say We're in Love," 505
Perelman, S.J., 523–525, 547
Perfect Evening, A, 221
Perkins, Anthony, 269–271
Perkins, Kenneth, 403
Perkins, Max, 692
Pernick, Solly, 448
Perry, Barbara, 285, 577
Perry, Robert E., 311
Personette, Joan, 679
Perutz, Carl S., 129
Peter Pan (1950), 88
Peter Pan (1954), 477, 483, *548–552*, 620
Peters, Brock, 371
Petrillo, James C., 150
Pettina, Irra, 130, 310, 411, 631
Pevney, Joseph, 466
Philanderer, The, 20
Phillips, Eddie, 130, 171, 241
Phillips, H.I., 438
Phillips, Irving, 577
Phoenix '55, *552–553*
Phoenix Theatre, 21, 193, 259, 394–395, 518–
    519, 552
Pi-Pa-Ki, 408
Piazza, Marguerite, 285, 457
Pickens, Jane, 459, 573
Pickwick, 510
Picon, Molly, 441–442
Pidgeon, Walter, 656–657
Pie in the Sky, 282
Pierson, Arthur, 701
"Pigtails and Freckles," 446
Pilbrow, Richard, 265
"Pilgrims of Love," 654
Pinza, Ezio, 102, 203–205, 639, 641, 643
Pipe Dream, 227, *554–556*
Pippin, Donald, 511
Pirates of Penzance, The, 556
Plain and Fancy, 97, 450, *557–559*
Platt, Edward, 496–498
Plautus, 239, 241
Playwrights' Company, The, 353, 400–402, 645
Pleasures and Palaces, 327
Pober, Leon, 73
Pockriss, Lee, 671
Poleri, David, 590
"Politics and Poker," 215
Polk, Gordon, 287
Poll, Martin, 107
Pollack, Michael, 633
Polonaise, *559–561*
"Polonaise in A-flat," 561
Pons, Lily, 382
Pool, John, 86
"Poor Wandering One," 556
Porgy, 402, 502, 563
Porgy and Bess, 7, 9, 73, 402, 430, 502, *561–
    564*, 582, 585, 587–589

Porter, Cole, 8, 11, 24, 62, 64, 100, 126–128, 343, 367–371, 435, 437, 475, 525–529, 597–601, 618, 620, 625–628, 630, 680, 708, 762
Portnoff, Mischa, 285
Portnoff, Wesley, 285
Portofino, 291, 565–566, 630
Portofino P.T.A., 628
Post, W.H., 688
Poston, Tom, 157–159
Pousse-Café, 116
Power, Tyrone, 352
Powers, Marie, 160, 429
Prager, Stanley, 100–102, 383, 536
"Praise the Lord and Pass the Ammunition," 456
Pratt, Peter, 337
Premice, Josephine, 133, 322, 343
Present Arms!, 517
Presnell, Harve, 684–686
Preston, Robert, 4, 82–83, 460–464
Prettybelle, 109
Price, Leontyne, 564
Price, Roger, 478
Pride and Prejudice, 221, 660
Primus, Pearl, 133
Prince of Pilsen, The, 413
Prince, Harold S., 22, 132, 169, 173, 201–203, 207, 210, 215–218, 239, 243, 422, 429, 484, 488, 515, 533, 537, 597, 603, 605, 608, 639, 658, 693, 762–763
Prince, Hughie, 249
Prince, Jack, 179
"Princess and the Pea, The," 518
Prochnik, Bruce, 508
Producers, The, 38
Producers Theatre, 266
Professor Fodorski, 36
Prokofieff, Sergei, 286
Promises, Promises, 11, 511
Proser, Monte, 193, 295, 303
Prouty, Jed, 543
Prowse, Juliet, 193–194
Prud'homme, Cameron, 111, 484, 684
Pruneau, Phillip, 633
Puccini, Giacomo, 369, 577
"Puka Puka Pants," 660
Purlie Victorious, 116
Pursuit of Happiness, The, 61
Pygmalion, 468–470

*Q*uadrille, 323
Quayle, Anna, 643, 645
Quiet Man, The, 185
Quillan, Joseph, 473
Quine, Richard, 316
Quinn, Frank, 20, 602
Quintero, Jose, 116

*R*ack, 196
Rae, Charlotte, 388, 394–395, 534, 665
Rags, 16
"Ragtime Romeo," 691
Rahn, Muriel, 72, 584, 589
Rain, 579–582
"Rain in Spain, The," 4, 471
Rainbow, 520
Rainier, Prince, 287
Rainmaker, The, 520–522, 553, 712
Raitt, John, 140–144, 147, 411, 533–536, 665
Raksin, David, 332

Rall, Tommy, 115, 355–356, 441, 443
Ramin, Sid, 371
Randall, Carl, 466
Randall, Tony, 496–498
Randolph, Clemence, 579
Randolph, Robert, 590
Rasch, Albertina, 425
Rascoe, Burton, 19, 20, 85, 92, 94, 95, 108, 150, 156, 178, 192, 230, 252, 315, 342, 377, 379, 410, 425, 434, 437, 449, 467, 475, 501, 514, 560, 568, 576, 581, 588, 599, 613, 627, 632, 664, 722, 778
Raset, Val, 250
Rattigan, Terence, 256
Ravel, Maurice, 245
Ray, Nicholas, 75
Razzle-Dazzle, 566–567
Rea, Oliver, 353
Reagan, Ronald, 42
Reardon, Frank, 577
Reardon, John, 181, 480
Red, Hot and Blue!, 28, 343
Red Mill, The, 117, 567–568, 592
Redfield, William (Billy), 71, 527
Redhead, 2, 159, 568–571
Redowski, Philip, 472
Reed, Carol, 162
Reed, Janet, 396
Reeder, George, 179, 241
Regina, 571–575, 649
Reid, Elliott, 234, 678
Reilly, Charles Nelson, 297, 323, 326–337
Reiner, Carl, 33, 35
Reiner, Ethel Linder, 130, 231
Reinhardt, Gottfried, 559
Remick, Lee, 58
Renning, 232
Respighi, Ottorino, 372
Reveaux, Edward, 38, 566
Revill, Clive, 338, 508
Revuers, The, 467, 515
Rhapsody, 575–576
Rhodes, Erik, 126, 174, 609
"Rhythm," 196
Rice, Elmer, 645, 647–648
Rice, Vernon, 21, 56, 64, 121, 191, 225, 410, 504, 588, 714
Rich, Alan, 21, 709
Rich, Irene, 65
"Rich Kid's Rag," 392
Richards, Donald, 210
Richards, Lloyd, 331
Richardson, Ralph, 20, 388
Richardson, Tony, 353
Rickard, Gwen, 704
Rigaud, George, 448
Rigby, Harry, 352, 415
Riggs, Lynn, 499
Ring, Blanche, 628
Ritchard, Cyril, 283–284, 352, 548, 551
Ritter, Thelma, 484–486, 488
Rivera, Chita, 113–114, 450–452, 601–602, 693
Robbins, Cindy, 289
Robbins, Jerome, 4, 10–11, 46, 70, 74, 78–82, 84–86, 117, 153, 173, 207, 210, 236, 238–239, 243, 276, 279, 303–306, 312, 319, 358–360, 362, 396–397, 399, 418, 422, 443–445, 511–515, 533, 536–537, 548, 550, 618, 620, 681, 684, 689, 693–697, 716, 719, 763–764
Roberta, 316
Roberts, Allan, 38

Roberts, Ben, 186, 341, 433–434
Roberts, Helen, 556
Roberts, Joan, 425, 499
Roberts, John, 480
Roberts, Roy, 140
Robin, Leo, 246, 252–254
Robinson, Bill, 432–433, 452
"Rock Candy Mountain," 622
Rockwell, Doc, 597–598
Rodda, Richard, 551
"Rodeo," 289, 502
"Rodger Young," 456, 704
Rodgers, Bob, 86–87
Rodgers, Eileen, 658
Rodgers, Mary, 316, 319, 518–519
Rodgers, Richard, 6, 8–11, 18, 21, 29, 42–47,
    53–57, 93, 123, 144–147, 154–156, 178, 189,
    193, 196, 206, 218, 226–227, 254, 296, 319,
    358, 361–363, 382, 426–428, 456, 459, 470–
    471, 488–492, 499–507, 515–517, 519, 523,
    527, 536–540, 554–556, 571, 601, 635–639,
    641–643, 673, 764–765
Rogers, Dick, 249
Rogers, Ginger, 84
Rogers, Jaime, 262
Rogers, Will, 175
"Rollin' in Gold," 232
Roman Comedy, The, 239, 243
Romance, 472
Romanoff, Boris, 150
Romay, Lina, 438
Romberg, Sigmund, 82, 93, 252–256, 472–473,
    686–687
Rome, Harold, 33, 70, 88–89, 120–122, 179,
    203–205, 327, 329–330, 713–715, 765–766
Romeo and Juliet, 693
Romero, Alex, 287
Romoff, Colin, 371
Rooney, Pat, Sr., 272, 655
Roos, William, 65, 438
Roosevelt, Eleanor, 379
Roosevelt, Franklin D., 70
Rosalinda, 8, 632
Rose, Billy, 29, 62, 133–136, 153, 234, 458,
    597–599
Rose, Jane, 355
Rose, Philip, 100, 115–116
"Rose of Arizona," 382
"Rose's Turn," 276
Rose-Marie (actress), 666, 669
Rose-Marie (operetta), 632
Rosenkavalier, Der, 131, 574
Rosenthal, Jean, 181, 590
Ross, Adrian, 433
Ross, Alan, 175
Ross, Annie, 168
Ross, Herbert, 58, 95, 243, 316, 319, 327, 656,
    665, 670, 674
Ross, Jerry, 169, 172–173, 352, 515, 533, 536–
    537
Ross, Marilyn, 618
Ross, Michael, 692
Ross, Robert, 174, 432
Roth, Lillian, 327
"Rotogravure Page," 91
Round, Thomas, 556
Rounseville, Robert, 130
Rowles, Polly, 488
Roy, William, 414
Ruben, Jose, 688
Rubin, Aaron, 258

Rubin, Arthur, 130
Rudolph, Crown Prince, 425
Rugantino, 109, 576–577
Rule, Janice, 283
Rumple, 577–578
Runanin, Boris, 258, 552–554
Runyon, Damon, 96, 272–275
Russell, A.J., 100
Russell, Charles, 583
Russell, Jane, 172
Russell, Jim, 426
Russell, Robert, 656
Russell, Rosalind, 716–720
Russo, James, 681
Ryan, Robert, 446
Ryan, Sue, 376–377
Ryskind, Morrie, 7, 473, 495

"Sad Was the Day," 185
Saddler, Donald, 111, 352, 441, 603, 633, 716,
    720
Sadie Thompson, 184, 579–582
Saidy, Fred, 89, 210, 213–214, 222, 224–225,
    283–285, 343
Sail Away, 583–584
St. Elmo, 282
St. John, Betta, 639
St. John, Howard, 388
St. Louis Woman, 584–590
Saint of Bleecker Street, The, 424, 590–591,
    619
Saint-Saens, Camille, 238
Saint-Subber. See Subber, Arnold Saint
"Sale, The," 417–418
Sales, Soupy, 109
Sallert, Ulla, 82–83
Sally, 591–592, 632
Samson and Delilah, 238
Samuels, Lesser, 269
San Juan, Olga, 529, 533
Sand, George, 94, 415
Sanders, Alma, 403
Sandow, Eugene, 196
Sandrich, Mark, 84
Sandrich, Mark, Jr., 82–84
Sands, Diana, 116
"Sans Souci," 669
Saratoga, 130, 319, 592–595
Saratoga Trunk, 592
Sarnoff, Dorothy, 358, 411, 464
Sartre, Jean-Paul, 356–357
Satie, Erik, 342
Sato, Reiko, 365
Sattin, Lonnie, 96
Saturday Night, 243
Saunders, Lana, 442
Savo, Jimmy, 701
Saxon, Luther, 133, 135
Say, Darling (musical), 330, 536, 595–
    597
Say, Darling (novel), 595–596
Schaefer, George, 95
Schary, Dore, 684, 686
Scheerer, Bob, 98, 174, 381, 666
Schenck, Nicholas, 110
Scheuer, Steven H., 492
Schildkraut, Joseph, 115–116
Schippers, Thomas, 591
Schirmer, Gus, Jr., 540
Schmidlapp, W. Horace, 559

Schmidt, Harvey, 11, 520–523
Schnitzler, Arthur, 243–244
Schorr, William, 89
Schubert, Franz, 93
Schulberg, Budd, 698
Schulberg, Stuart, 698
Schulman, Arnold, 347
Schumer, Yvette, 480
Schwartz, Arthur, 111–112, 243–245, 316, 334, 337, 347, 351, 543, 546, 674–677, 766
Schweikert, Ernest G., 577
Schwezoff, 688
Scott, Bonnie, 323, 692
Scott, Lee, 289
Scott, Leslie, 564
Scott, Raymond, 408, 410
Scourby, Alexander, 673
Scully, Barbara, 93
Seal, Elizabeth, 338, 340–341
Seaman, Elizabeth, 473
Seaton, George, 301
Seesaw, 24
Segal, Ben, 495
Segal, Vivienne, 154–156, 343, 457–478, 537–538, 540
Seiger, Marvin, 73
Seitz, Dran, 282–284
Seitz, Tani, 475
Selden, Albert, 95, 258, 624–625
Sennett, Mack, 61, 305–306, 508
"Sequidilla," 136
Serenade, The, 279
Seven Brides for Seven Brothers, 391
Seven Lively Arts, The, 371, 597–600
"Seven Sheep, Four Red Shirts, and a Bottle of Gin," 372
7½ Cents (novel), 533, 595
"7½ Cents" (song), 536
Seventeen, 600–601
1776, 11
Seventh Heaven (musical), 12, 601–603
Seventh Heaven (play), 601–603
"Seventy-Six Trombones," 461, 463
Shackleton, Bob, 591
Shafer, Milton, 100
Shafer, Robert, 631
Shakespeare, William, 367, 370, 693
"Shall I Tell You What I Think of You?," 363
Shangri-La, 319, 481, 483, 603–604
Shanks, Alec, 373
"Shape of Things, The," 394
Shapiro, Dan, 50, 52, 228
Shapiro, Irvin, 94
Sharaff, Irene, 84, 349, 360, 362, 413, 440
Sharpe, Albert, 210, 214
Shaw, David, 568, 571, 671
Shaw, George Bernard, 107, 125, 468–470
Shaw, Howard, 100
Shaw, Oscar, 99
Shaw, Reta, 536
Shawn, Dick, 200
She Loves Me, 422, 603, 605–609, 630
Sheldon, Edward, 472
Sheldon, Gene, 655
Sheldon, Sidney, 186, 341, 433–434, 568, 571
Shelley, 384
Shelley, Gladys, 189
Shelley, Joshua, 419, 516
Shelton, Hall, 404
Shelton, James, 174
Sheppard, John R., Jr., 75

Sherman, Charles, 47, 107, 681
Sherman, Harold, 249
Sherman, Hiram, 221, 661, 681, 684
Sherman, Lee, 148, 419, 473
Sherwood, Robert E., 443–445, 671
Shevelove, Burt, 239, 241, 243, 624–625
Shinbone Alley, 609–612
Shipman, Samuel, 403
"Shoeless Joe from Hannibal Mo.," 171–172
Shop Around the Corner, The, 607
Short, Hassard, 91, 133–135, 137, 419, 425, 435, 438, 440, 456–457, 464–465, 597, 600, 612, 625, 766–767
Shostakovich, Dmitri, 151
Show Boat, 6, 9, 501–502, 592, 612–615
Show Girl, 615–618
Show Time, 9
Show-of-the-Month-Club, 386
Shubert, J.J., 5, 17, 28–29, 93–94, 118, 279, 376, 378, 415, 472–473, 547, 720, 722
Shubert, Lee, 5, 17, 29, 93–94, 118, 279, 287, 369, 378, 415, 472–473, 720, 722
Shulman, Max, 38–39, 71
Shutta, Ethel, 347, 466
Side Show, 58, 494
Sidney, Robert, 47, 174, 473, 664
Siebel, 646
Siegel, Arthur, 425, 478–480
Siegfried, 594
Siegmeister, Elie, 621
Siepi, Cesare, 100–102
Siff, Andrew, 201
Sigman, Carl, 48
Silk Stockings, 130, 529, 618–620, 708
Sillman, Leonard, 9, 285, 332, 426, 478–481, 483–484
Silverman, Jack H., 659
Silvers, Phil, 181–184, 303–305, 393, 666–669
Simon, Danny, 148–149
Simon, John, 20
Simon, Neil, 28, 148–149, 391–393
Sinatra, Frank, 13, 105, 449, 516
"Sing for Your Supper," 296
"Sing Me Not a Ballard," 219
Sing Out, Sweet Land!, 621–622
Sisters Liked Them Handsome, The, 303
1600 Pennsylvania Avenue, 160
Skaff, George, 692
Skin of Our Teeth, The, 192, 379, 408
Skolovsky, Zadel, 561
Skyscraper, 620
"Slaughter on Tenth Avenue," 89, 516–517
"Sleepin' Bee, A," 322
Sleeping Prince, The, 256
Sleepy Hollow, 623, 643
Slezak, Walter, 203–206
Sloan, Mary Jane, 472
Sloane, Michael, 140, 577, 652, 666
Slocum, Bill, 21, 373
Small, Jack, 40
Small, Mary, 192
Small, Paul, 380
"Small House of Uncle Thomas, The," 360, 418
Small Wonder, 624–625
Smallens, Alexander, 564
Smaxie, 200
Smith, Art, 693
Smith, Betty, 674, 677
Smith, Harry B., 279–280, 652
Smith, Joe, 108, 466
Smith, Loring, 243

Smith, Maggie, 480–482
Smith, Moe, 492
Smith, Muriel, 133–135, 166
Smith, Oliver, 76, 83–85, 88, 107, 124–126, 181, 210, 244–246, 249, 257, 300, 303, 306, 353, 468, 471, 511–514, 522, 540, 615, 637, 639, 696–697, *767–768*
Smith, Queenie, 19
Smith, Robert B., 652
Smith, Rollin, 76
Sokolow, Anna, 130, 164, 285, 573, 623, 645
"Some Enchanted Evening," 641
"Somehow I Never Could Believe," 647
Something for the Boys, 625–628
Something More, 309, *628–631*
Sondheim, Stephen, 11, 46, 58–60, 132, 143, 238–239, 241–243, 276, 288, 316, 319, 515, 693, 696–697, 768
"Song is You, The," 460
Song of Norway, 281, *631–633*
Song Without Words, 457
Sons o' Fun, 9, 379
Sophie, 633–635
Sorel, Felicia, 404, 466
Sound of Music, The, 10, 12, 116, 218, 235, 279, 448, *635–639*
"Sound of Schmaltz, The," 234–235
Sour, Robert, 448–449
Sousa, John Philip, 463
South Pacific, 3, 10–12, 24, 57, 102, 118, 136, 206, 209, 218, 249, 323, 358, 361, 363, 429, 448, 502, 506, 518, 532, 537, 555, 623, 637–638, *639–643*, 697
Spaak, Charles, 140
Spaulding, Charles, 624
"Speak Low," 526
Spearman, Rawn, 231
Specter, Edward, 221
Spector, Joel, 72, 383
Spencer, Kenneth, 612
Spewack, Bella, 367, 371
Spewack, Sam, 327, 367, 371
Spielman, Fred, 376
Spillane, Mickey, 352
Springtime for Hitler, 38
Stagecoach, 295
Stahlhut, 34, 359
Staiger, Libi, 179, 633–635
Stalag 17, 565
Stamer, Fred, 109
Stander, Lionel, 157, 537
Stanford, Paul, 249
Stanley, Pat, 140, 215, 266–268
Stapleton, Jean, 78, 355
Star and Garter, 9, 192
"Star-Spangled Banner, The," 407
Star Spangled Rhythm, 13
Starbuck, James, 203, 438, 496
Stark, Ray, 236, 239
State of the Union, 25, 117, 448
Stay Away, Joe, 706
"Stay with the Happy People," 440
"Steam Heat," 82, 171, 173, 535, 602
Steig, William, 26, 158
Stein, Gertrude, 231
Stein, Joseph, 33, 95–97, 207, 210, 353–355, 380, 450–452, 557, 656
Stein, Leon, 433, 709
Steinbeck, John, 20, 554
Steininger, Franz, 456
Stengel, Casey, 171

Stevens, Craig, 301
Stevens, Marti, 110
Stevens, Roger L., 157–160, 266, 693
Stewart, Michael, 24, 33, 37, 113–115, 137, 139, 297–300, 566–567
Stewart, Paula, 710
Stockwell, Harry, 425
Stoddard, Haila, 583
Stolz, Robert, 433, 448
Stone, Dorothy, 567
Stone, Fred, 567
Stone, Jack, 291
Stone, Leonard, 268, 568, 571
Stone, Paula, 140, 567–568, 577, 652, 666
Stone, Peter, 356–357
Stop the World—I Want to Get Off, 20, *643–645*
Storch, Arthur, 698
Storch, Larry, 226, 394
"Stormy Weather," 587
Story, Gloria, 653
Stoska, Polyna, 645, 649
Strange Fruit, 589
Stratton, Chester, 154
Straus, Oscar, 105
Strauss, Johann, Jr., 8, 448–449, 473, 709
Strauss, Richard, 131
Strauss, Robert, 565
Stravinsky, Igor, 597–598, 600
Street, James, 292
Street Scene, 73, 430, 575, *645–649*, 670
Streetcar Named Desire, A, 671
Streisand, Barbra, 236–239, 327–330
Stritch, Elaine, 48–49, 266, 516–518, 537–538, 583–584
Stromberg, Hunt, Jr., 567–568, 591
Strong, Austin, 601
Strouse, Charles, 11, 36, 113–114, 262–265, 297, 300
Stuarti, Enzo, 62
Student Prince, The, 94, 632
"Students' Ball, The," 417
Sturges, Preston, 140, 142–143, 157–159, 415–517
Styne, Jule, 10, 78, 81, 181–183, 197–198, 221, 236, 238, 246, 276–279, 288, 292–294, 303–307, 309, 415, 418, 440, 450, 515, 537, 539–541, 546, 548, 551, 595, 628–630, 649–650, 678, 680, 769
Subber, Arnold Saint, 22, 313, 316, 319, 322, 369, 371, 453, 527
Subways Are for Sleeping, 649–652
Sullivan, Arthur, 6–7, 261, 313, 337, 431–433, 525, 556, 704, 720
Sullivan, Barry, 266
Sullivan, Brian, 645
Sullivan, Jo, 386, 453–454, 456
Sullivan, Lee, 103
Sumac, Yma, 222, 224–226
"Summertime," 564
"Sunday in Cicero Falls," 91
Sundegaard, Arnold, 575
Sundt, Jacqueline, 503
"Sunflower," 300
"Sunshine Girl, The," 130, 487
Sunshine Sue, 291
"Surprise Party," 235
Susann, Jacqueline, 376–377
Susannah and the Elders, 67
Suzuki, Pat, 226
Swan Lake, 399

"Swanee," 81, 467
Swanlee, 115
Swann, Donald, 66–67
Swanson, Gloria, 305
Sweeney Todd, 13, 136
"Sweet Nevada," 545
Sweet Thursday, 554
"Sweetest Sounds, The," 491
Sweethearts, 652–655
Swenson, Inga, 480, 482, 520–522
Swenson, Swen, 179, 391–392
Swerling, Jo, 272, 275
"Swing," 719
Swing Mikado, The, 433
Swoboda, Vecheslav, 150
Sybil, 682
Sydow, Jack, 633
Sylvester, Robert, 21, 68, 231, 397, 445
Sylvia, 483–484
Syms, Sylvia, 659, 706

*T*abbert, William, 84, 203–205, 639
Taft, William Howard, 447
Take a Bow, 655
"Take It Slow, Joe," 346
Take Me Along, 656–657
"Talent," 480
Tales of the South Pacific, 639
Talva, Galina, 117
Taming of the Shrew, 367
Tamiris, Helen, 53, 56, 88, 111, 140, 203, 222,
    225, 334, 495, 543, 557, 612, 670–671, 686
"Tango," 303
Tapps, George, 189–190, 467
Tarkington, Booth, 600–601
Taste of Honey, A, 60
Taubman, Howard, 20, 37, 83, 102, 125, 159,
    194, 202, 209, 233, 238, 242, 245, 257, 265,
    285, 299, 302, 326, 330, 350, 392, 447, 484,
    491, 493, 494, 522, 584, 607, 635, 644, 650,
    712, 779
Taylor, Albert B., 169, 173
Taylor, Deems, 153
Taylor, Dwight, 527, 529
Taylor, Laurette, 319, 347, 351
Taylor, Robert Lewis, 36
Taylor, Samuel, 488, 491
Tchaikovsky, Peter Ilyich, 456–458
"Tea for Two," 467
Teahouse of the August Moon, 483
Telephone, The, 424, 429–431, 649
Templeton, Fay, 297
Tenderloin, 658–659
Tennent, H.M., Ltd., 338
Ter-Arutunian, Rouben, 317, 571
Terry, Walter, 21, 68
Tevye and His Daughters, 207, 422
Texas Steer, A, 117
"That Dirty Old Man," 241
"That Terrific Rainbow," 538
"That's How It Goes," 676
That's the Ticket!, 70
Theatre Corporation of America, 496
Theatre Guild, The, 17, 42, 61, 78, 144–146,
    499–503, 506, 546, 621, 684, 769–770
Thenstead, Adolph, 132–133
"There are Fairies at the Bottom of My Gar-
    den," 196
"There Once Was a Man," 536
"There's a Hill Beyond a Hill," 132

They Knew What They Wanted, 453
"They Like Ike," 119
"They Love Me," 446
13 Daughters, 659–660
"This Is a Real Nice Castle," 671
"This Is All Very New To Me," 557
This Is the Army, 56
Thomas, Brandon, 312, 702
Thomas, Hugh, 414
Thompson, Frank, 404
Thompson, Fred, 228, 249
Thompson, Sada, 355
Thomson, Virgil, 231
Thoroughly Modern Millie, 309
"Thou Swell," 156
"Thousand Island Song, The," 49
Three for Tonight, 114, 660–664
Three Men on a Horse, 383–385
Three to Make Ready, 664–665, 703, 706
Three Wishes for Jamie, 142, 665–666
Three Wishes of Jamie McRuin, The, 665
Threepenny Opera, The, 78, 168, 526
Thurber, James, 67
Tibbett, Lawrence, 72–73
Tichenor, Tom, 138
Tihmar, David, 480
Time for Singing, A, 109
Time of the Cuckoo, The, 678
Tinted Venus, The, 523
Tittle, Y.A., 299
"To Be Alone with You," 83
"To Keep My Love Alive," 154, 156
"To Life," 209
Tobias, George, 618
Todd, Michael, 9, 57, 64–66, 192, 433, 435–440,
    598, 625–627, 686–687
Tokatyan, Leon, 659
Tom Sawyer, 395–396
Tomkins, Don, 712
Too Many Girls, 193
Tooker, George, 590
Top, Carrot, 138
Top Banana, 666–670
Touch and Go, 622, 670–671
Tovarich, 671–674
Toys in the Attic, 639
Traube, Shepard, 252
Traubel, Helen, 554–555
Treacher, Arthur, 720
Tree Grows in Brooklyn, A, 112, 659, 674–678
Tristan and Isolde, 676
Trivers, Barry, 295
Trovaioli, Armando, 576–577
Troy, Louise, 307, 673
Truex, Ernest, 222, 225
Truman, Harry S., 88, 118, 225, 457, 495
Truman, Margaret, 119
"Try Me," 605
Tucker, Ian, 551
Tucker, Sophie, 633–635
Tudor, Anthony, 175, 313, 584
Tufts, Sonny, 50, 230
Tun Tun, 593
Tussaud, Mme., 457
Tuvim, Judith, 467
Twain, Mark, 154–156
Tweed, William Marcy, 687
"Twelve O'Clock and All Is Well," 228
Two Bouquets, The, 100
Two for the Show, 664
"Two Lost Souls," 171–172

Two on the Aisle, 142, 678–681
Two's Company, 582, 681–684, 713, 719
Twomey, Kay, 249–250
Tyers, John, 279
Tyler, Beverly, 219–220
Tyler, Judy, 554

Umeki, Miyoshi, 226
"Uncle Sam Rag," 570
Uncle Tom's Cabin, 360, 464
Unger, Stella, 601–602
"UNICEF Song, The," 152
Unsinkable Mrs. Brown, The, 684
Unsinkable Molly Brown, The, 115, 303, 684–686
Up in Central Park, 295, 560, 686–687
"Upper Birth," 553
Urban, Joseph, 380
Urbont, Jacques, 395
Ustinov, Peter, 508

"Vacant Lot Ballet," 609
Vagabond King, The, 688
Valentina, 409–410
Valentine, Paul, 310, 713–714
Valentino, Rudolph, 119, 680
Valerio, Frederico, 310
Vallee, Rudy, 323, 477
Vamp, The, 698–692
Van, Bobby, 35, 516
Vance, Vivian, 13, 166
Vandamm, Florence, 26, 76, 314, 406, 653
Van Druten, John, 358
Van Dyke, Dick, 113–115, 258
Van Dyke, Marcia, 674
Van Heusen, James, 140, 142–143, 193–194, 473
Vanoni, Ornella, 576
Vargas, Alberto, 26, 436
"Varsity Drag, The," 712
Veiller, Anthony, 559
Venora, Lee, 289, 356
Venuta, Benay, 164, 292, 474
Verdi, Guiseppe, 455, 464–465
Verdon, Gwen, 33–36, 93, 126–130, 169–173, 294, 341, 484–488, 568–571, 770
Verne, Jules, 62–64, 475
Vernon, Gilbert, 168
Vertes, Marcel, 25, 41, 333
Victor, Eric, 38
Victory Belles, 250
Vienna Life, 709–710
Villa-Lobos, Heitor, 372, 411–413
Vincent, Romo, 425, 706
Vintage '60, 692–693
Violett, Ellen, 164
Viva O'Brien, 715
Vivanco, Moises, 222
Voelpel, Fred, 490, 635
Volkoff, Chris, 434
Voltaire, 130–132
Vye, Murvyn, 144, 359

Wagner, Frank, 722
Wagner, Richard, 594
"Wagon Train," 523
Waiting For Godot, 169
Wake Up and Dream, 100

Walburn, Raymond, 239, 543
Waldorf, Wilella, 20, 92, 94, 108, 147, 153, 156, 178, 188, 192, 220, 230, 252, 282, 315, 342, 380, 432, 434, 437, 501, 503, 514, 526, 561, 581, 599, 614, 622, 632, 702, 779
Walker, Don, 40, 52, 252, 255, 431, 462, 605, 608, 718
Walker, Nancy, 47–48, 71–72, 164–166, 181–183, 258, 396–399, 511, 514, 552–553, 771
Wallace, George, 347, 484
Wallach, Ira, 552
Waller, Thomas "Fats," 189, 191
Wallop, Douglas, 169, 173
Walsh, Mary Jane, 40
Walsh, Maurice, 185
Walston, Ray, 169, 171, 173, 321, 426
Walters, Charles, 111, 584
Walters, Lou, 655, 720
Walton, Tony, 240, 264
Wanger, Wally, 655
War and Peace, 213
Warden, Jack, 96
"Warm All Over," 453
Warnick, Clay, 186, 431
Warnow, Mark, 701
Warren, Gloria, 701
Warren, Harry, 603–604
Warren, Julie, 62, 154
Warrick, Ruth, 656
Wasserman, Dale, 109, 395
Waters, Ethel, 94–95, 380, 587
Watkins, Perry, 75
Watson, Betty Jane, 623
Watson, Susan, 82
Watt, Douglas, 21, 630
Watts, Richard, Jr., 16, 18, 33, 35, 39, 40, 46, 49, 52, 66, 69, 72, 81, 97, 99, 106, 110, 116, 139, 143, 149, 159, 167, 174, 184, 186, 196, 200, 202, 206, 209, 213, 222, 227, 235, 238, 249, 261, 268, 275, 278, 285, 287, 291, 300, 302, 306, 310, 312, 322, 330, 340, 345, 347, 351, 357, 361, 363, 366, 369, 382, 386, 399, 403, 415, 418, 421, 424, 440, 445, 447, 452, 487, 510, 532, 536, 539, 541, 551, 565, 571, 577, 584, 594, 624, 638, 642, 648, 665, 669, 674, 677, 680, 696, 700, 705, 712, 779
Waxman, A.P., 189, 579
Wayne, David, 210, 212, 214, 434, 543, 595, 612
Wayne, Paula, 262–265
Weaver, Fritz, 36
Weber, Joe, 5, 29, 57
Webster, Margaret, 664
Webster, Paul Francis, 33, 148, 151–152
Weede, Robert, 102, 441–442, 453–454
Weidman, Charles, 72, 312, 332, 341, 343, 394, 565, 621
Weidman, Jerome, 116, 215, 218, 327, 639, 658
Weill, Kurt, 11, 73, 78, 168, 193, 218–220, 400–403, 405, 408, 430, 471, 523–526, 573, 575, 645–649, 673, 771–772
Weinstock, Jack, 316, 319, 323–325, 327
Weiss, George (David), 221, 450
Welch, Loren, 396
"Welcome Home" (Fanny), 203
"Welcome Home" (Kwamina), 372
Weldon, Joan, 356
Welles, Orson, 62–64, 475
Wells, Billy K., 438
Wells, Robert, 660
"Were Alive," 355

"Were Thine That Special Face," 370
Wernher, Hilda, 151
West, Bernie, 80
West Side Story, 3, 11–12, 82, 136, 209, 218, 374, 463, 502, 570, 602–603, 658, *693–698*
"What a Blessing to Know There's a Devil," 269, 272
What Every Woman Knows, 414
"What Good Would the Moon Be?," 647
"What Happened to Me Tonight?," 373
"What Is a Friend For?" 321
"What Kind of Fool Am I?," 645
What Makes Sammy Run?, *698–700*
"What Takes My Fancy," 712
"Whatever Lola Wants," 171–172
What's Up, 10, 178, 408, *701–702*
Wheeler, Bert, 38, 380, 665
"When I'm Not Near the Girl I Love," 211
"Where, Oh, Where," 528
Where's Charley?, 36, 312, 327, 620, *702–706*, 708, 719
"While the City Sleeps," 265
White, Al, Jr., 154, 432
White, Jane, 518, 566, 589
White, Jesse, 466
White, Josh, 94
White, Miles, 26, 52, 88–91, 93, 113, 137, 177–178, 188, 249, 294, 303, 306, 345, 504, 540, 656, 721, 772
White, Onna, 316, 331, 338, 383–385, 460, 656, 706–708
White, Pearl, 372
White, T.H., 122
White, Walter, 589
White Lilacs, 94, 415
Whitehead, Robert, 157–160, 231, 234, 243, 266
Whiting, Jack, 259, 292–294, 495
Whittier, John Greenleaf, 684
Whoop-Up, 620, *706–709*
Whorf, Richard, 600
"Who's Got the Pain?," 82, 130, 171–172
"Why Be Afraid to Dance?," 203
"Why Can't You Behave?," 369
Whyte, Jerome, 503, 505
Wickes, Mary, 313, 543
Wiener Blut, *709–710*
Wilbur, Richard, 130
Wildberg, John, 432
Wildcat, *710–713*
Wilder, Clinton, 573
Wilder, Thornton, 297, 379, 408
Wilderman, William, 573
Wilk, Max, 624
"Wilkes-Barre, Pa.," 674
Willard, Dorothy, 387
Willey, Robert A., 269
Williams, Dick, 164
Williams, Frances, 108
Williams, Mary Lou, 94
Williams, Tennessee, 49, 574
Williams, Tom, 289
Willie the Weeper, 67–68
Willman, Noel, 82
Willson, Meredith, 301–303, 460–464, 684–686
Wilson, Dooley, 89
Wilson, Jack, 692
Wilson, John C., 88–89, 154, 175, 177, 246, 369–370, 415, 601
Wilson, Mary Louise, 318
Wilson, Patricia, 215

Wilson, Sandy, 98, 100
Wiman, Dwight Deere, 174, 645
Winchell, Walter, 119
Windust, Bretaigne, 140, 210
Winninger, Charles, 459
Winters, Lawrence, 120
Wish You Were Here, 448, *713–715*
Wittop, Freddy, 137–138, 300
Wittstein, Ed, 357
Witty, Don, 281
Wizard of Oz, The, 224
Wodehouse, P.G., 6, 591
Wolf, Peter, 653
Wolf, Tommy, 475
Wolfington, Iggie, 460
Wolfson, Victor, 601–602
Wolper, Dave, 228
"Woman Who Lived Up There, The," 647
"Woman's Prerogative, A," 588
"Wompom, The," 67
Wonderful Town, 3, 12, 218, 692, 697, *715–720*
Wood, Deedee, 130, 181
Wood, Helen, 600
Woods, Edward, 109
Woodward, Edward, 307
Worley, Jo Anne, 87
Wray, John, 120, 189
Wright, Joyce, 337
Wright, Martha, 457
Wright, Robert (singer), 310
Wright, Robert (songwriter), 279, 281, 356–357, 364, 366, 411, 631
Wrightson, Earl, 219–220
"Wrong Note Rag," 719
Wrubel, Allie, 601
Wyler, Gretchen, 577, 618
Wynn, Ed, 66, 183, 377, 419

Yamaguchi, Shirley, 603
Yarnell, Bruce, 283
Year the Yankees Lost the Pennant, The, 169
Yellen, Jack, 720
"You Took Advantage of Me," 517
Youmans, Vincent, 6, 19, 467, 579
Young, George, 575
Young, Ralph, 706
Young, Victor, 601
"You're Just in Love," 117, 119
"You're Only a Girl That Men Forget," 261
"You've Gotta Get a Gimmick," 276
Yuriko, 360, 362
Yurman, 562

Ziegfeld, Billie Burke, 720, 722
Ziegfeld, Florenz, 6, 27, 29, 248, 364, 474, 598, 613–614, 627–628, 720, 722, 724
Ziegfeld Follies, 481, 720, 722, 724
Ziegfeld Follies of 1943, 720–722
Ziegfeld Follies of 1956, 483, 723–724
Ziegfeld Follies of 1957, 722–724
Zimbalist, Efrem, Jr., 160, 429
Zimmer, Bernard, 140
"Zip," 538, 541
"Zip-A-Dee-Doo-Dah," 601
Zipper, Herbert, 73
Zipprodt, Patricia, 210
Zorba, 13, 203
Zorina, Vera, 186–189, 516

LET THE MAP GUIDE YOU IN LOCATING YOUR THEATRE QUICKLY.

FIND YOUR THEATRE, AND ITS CORRESPONDING NUMBER ON THE MAP WILL GIVE YOU THE EXACT LOCATION

Alvin..........1	Cohan..........20	Globe..........39	Mansfield..........57	Republic..........75
Ambassador..........2	Comedy..........21	Golden..........40	Manhattan Theatre..........58	Ritz..........76
Apollo..........3	Cort..........22	Guild..........41	Masque..........59	Rivoli..........77
Astor..........4	Cosmopolitan..........23	Harris..........42	Mayfair..........60	Roxy..........78
Avon..........5	Craig..........24	Hippodrome..........43	Metropolitan	Royale..........79
Barrymore..........6	Criterion..........25	Hopkins..........44	Opera House..........61	Selwyn..........80
Bayes..........7	Elliott..........26	Hudson..........45	Miller's..........62	Shubert..........81
Beck..........8	Eltinge..........27	Hollywood..........46	Morosco..........63	Strand..........82
Belasco..........9	Embassy..........28	Imperial..........47	Music Box..........64	Times Square..........83
Belmont..........10	Empire..........29	Jolson..........48	National..........65	Town Hall..........84
Bijou..........11	Erlanger's..........30	Liberty..........49	New Amsterdam..........66	Vanderbilt..........85
Biltmore..........12	44th Street..........31	Little..........50	New Yorker..........67	Waldorf..........86
Booth..........13	46th Street..........32	Longacre..........51	Palace..........68	Wallack's..........87
Broadhurst..........14	48th Street..........33	Lyceum..........52	Paramount..........69	Warner..........88
Broadway..........15	49th Street..........34	Lyric..........53	Playhouse..........70	Winter Garden..........89
Capitol..........16	Forrest..........35	Mad. Sq. Garden..........54	President..........71	Ziegfeld..........90
Carnegie Hall..........17	Fulton..........36	Majestic..........55	Plymouth..........72	
Carroll..........18	Gaiety..........37	Manhattan	Princess..........73	
Central..........19	Garrick..........38	Opera House..........56	Rialto..........74	